W9-DFA-716

Signs of Life in the U.S.A.

Sixth Edition

Signs of Life in the U.S.A.

Readings on Popular Culture for Writers

Sonia Maasik
University of California, Los Angeles

Jack Solomon
California State University, Northridge

BEDFORD/ST. MARTIN'S   Boston ◆ New York

For Marlowe and Star

For Bedford/St. Martin's

Senior Editor: John Sullivan III
Editorial Assistant: Alicia Young
Production Supervisor: Jennifer Peterson
Marketing Manager: Molly Parke
Text Design: Anna Palchik
Project Management: Books By Design, Inc.
Cover Design: Donna Lee Dennison
Cover Art: Admission ticket, widescreen television on table, leopard print shoes from the 1960s, and aluminum can: © Royalty-Free/Punchstock. Bag of groceries and SUV: © ThinkStock Images/Jupiter. Popcorn: © Royalty-Free/Masterfile. Nintendo Wii wiimote controller cutout, backpack, and iPod portable digital audio player: © Royalty-Free/Alamy.
Composition: Books By Design, Inc.
Printing and Binding: RR Donnelley & Sons Company

President: Joan E. Feinberg
Editorial Director: Denise B. Wydra
Editor in Chief: Karen S. Henry
Director of Marketing: Karen R. Soeltz
Director of Editing, Design, and Production: Marcia Cohen
Assistant Director of Editing, Design, and Production: Elise S. Kaiser
Manager, Publishing Services: Emily Berleth

Library of Congress Control Number: 2008926833

Preface for Instructors

Each decade of American everyday life tends to bear a certain characteristic stamp, which, while it by no means covers everthing that was important at the time, does identify a certain keynote for future memories. Thus we have the roaring twenties and the sex, drugs, and rock-'n'-roll sixties. Tom Wolfe called the seventies the Me Decade, and the eighties were marked by Wall Street glitter and glitz. As we present the sixth edition of *Signs of Life in the U.S.A.* to the world, it is becoming evident that the "zeroes" too will bear a certain mark, stamped upon it by the explosive rise of interactive technologies. The "You-centered" realms of Web 2.0 combined with the continued dominance of reality TV programming — a genre that brings the audience directly into the show as a participant — have made this the You Decade, and we have accordingly made this the focus of the current edition of our book.

But one thing hasn't changed in the years between the appearance of the first edition of *Signs of Life* in 1994 and the present: the ever-increasing dominance of American life by popular culture. To put this another way, American popular culture is not simply an embellishment on our lives, a superficial ornament that can be put on or taken off at will. Popular culture has virtually *become* our culture, permeating almost everything we do. So if we wish to understand ourselves as a culture, we must learn to think critically about the vast panoply of what was once condescendingly regarded as "mass culture." Indeed, with apologies to a large retail toy chain, "popular culture is us."

Then and Now

This, of course, has not always been apparent to the academic world. When the first edition of *Signs of Life* appeared, the study of popular culture was still embroiled in the "culture wars" of the late 1980s and early 1990s, a struggle for academic legitimacy in which the adherents of popular cultural studies ultimately prevailed. Since then, more and more scholars and teachers have come to recognize the importance of understanding what Michel de Certeau has called "the practice of everyday life" and the value of using popular culture as a thematic ground for educating students in critical thinking and writing. Once excluded from academic study on the basis of a naturalized distinction between "high" and "low" culture, which contemporary cultural analysis has shown to be historically contingent, popular culture has come to be an accepted part of the curriculum, widely studied in freshman composition classrooms, as well as in upper-division undergraduate courses and graduate seminars.

But recognition of the importance that popular culture has assumed in our society has not been restricted to the academy. Increasingly, Americans are realizing that American culture and popular culture are virtually one and the same, and that whether we are looking at our political system, our economy, or simply our national consciousness, the power of popular culture to shape our lives is strikingly apparent. Sometimes this realization has been fraught with controversy, as when after a spate of schoolyard shootings in the late 1990s a host of politicians and pundits pointed their fingers at violent entertainment as the culprit behind the violence. At other times, the growing influence of popular culture has been received more enthusiastically, as in the widespread belief in the Internet as a medium of economic and educational reform and revival. But whether the recognition is tinged with controversy or splashed with enthusiasm, at no time in our history have Americans been more aware of the place of popular culture in their lives.

For this reason, we believe that learning to think and write critically about popular culture is even more important today than it was when we published the first edition of this book. As the boundary between "culture" and popular culture blurs and even disappears, it is all the more essential that our students understand how popular culture works and how it generates meaning. This is why we continue to make semiotics the guiding methodology behind *Signs of Life*, for semiotics leads us, and our students, to take an analytic stance toward popular culture, one that avoids the common pitfalls of uncritical celebration or simple scapegoating.

The reception of the first five editions of this text has demonstrated that the semiotic approach to popular culture has indeed found a place in America's composition classrooms. Composition instructors have seen that students feel a certain sense of ownership toward the products of popular culture and that using popular culture as a focus can help students overcome the sometimes alienating effects of traditional academic subject matter. At the same time, the semiotic method has helped instructors lead their students to analyze critically the popular cultural phenomena that they enjoy writing about and so learn the critical thinking and writing skills that their composition classes are designed to impart.

The Critical Method: Semiotics

Reflecting the broad academic interest in cultural studies, we've assumed an inclusive definition of popular culture. The eight chapters in *Signs of Life in the U.S.A.* embrace everything from the marketing and consumption of the products of mass production to the racial and sexual ideologies that inform the content of our entertainment. Unlike most other popular culture texts, *Signs of Life* adopts an interpretive approach — semiotics — that is explicitly designed to analyze that intersection of ideology and entertainment that we call popular culture. We have chosen semiotics because it has struck us that while students enjoy assignments that ask them to look at popular cultural phenomena, they often have trouble distinguishing between an argued interpretive analysis and the simple expression of an opinion. Some textbooks, for example, suggest assignments that involve analyzing a TV program or film, but they don't always tell a student how to do that. The semiotic method provides that guidance.

As a conceptual framework, semiotics teaches students to formulate cogent, well-supported interpretations. It emphasizes the examination of assumptions and the way language shapes our apprehension of the world. And, because it focuses on how beliefs are formulated within a social and political context (rather than just judging or evaluating those beliefs), it's ideal for discussing sensitive or politically charged issues. As an approach used in literature, media studies, anthropology, art and design coursework, sociology, law, and market research (to name only some of its more prominent field applications), semiotics has a cross-disciplinary appeal that makes it ideal for a writing class of students from a variety of majors and disciplines. We recognize that semiotics has a reputation for being highly technical or theoretical; rest assured that *Signs of Life* does not require students or instructors to have a technical knowledge of semiotics. We've provided clear and accessible introductions that explain what students need to know.

We also recognize that adopting a theoretical approach may be new to some instructors, so we've designed the book to allow instructors to be as semiotic with their students as they wish. The book does not obligate instructors or students to spend a lot of time with semiotics — although we do hope you'll find the approach intriguing and provocative.

The Editorial Apparatus

With its emphasis on popular culture, *Signs of Life* should generate lively class discussion and inspire many kinds of writing and thinking activities. The general introduction provides an overall framework for the book, acquainting students with the semiotic method they can use to interpret the topics raised in each chapter. It is followed by a section on Writing about Popular Culture that not only provides a brief introduction to writing about popular culture but additionally features three sample student essays that demonstrate different approaches to writing critical essays on pop culture topics. Included in that section are two articles that guide students to a critical use of the Internet as a research tool, and a Citing Sources section follows that will help your students document their writing assignments properly.

Each chapter starts with a frontispiece, a provocative visual image related to the chapter's topic, and an introduction that suggests ways to "read" the topic provides model interpretations and links the issues raised by the reading selections. Every chapter introduction contains three types of boxed questions designed to stimulate student thinking on the topic. The Exploring the Signs questions invite students to reflect on an issue in a journal entry or other prewriting activity, whereas the Discussing the Signs questions trigger class activities such as debates, discussions, or small-group work. Reading the Net questions invite students to explore the chapter's topic on the Internet, both for research purposes and for texts to analyze.

The readings themselves are followed by two sorts of assignments. The Reading the Text questions help students comprehend the selections, asking them to identify important concepts and arguments, explain key terms, and relate main ideas to each other and to the evidence presented. The Reading the Signs questions are writing and activity prompts designed to produce clear analytic thinking and strong persuasive writing; they often make connections among reading selections from different chapters. Most assignments call for analytic essays, while some invite journal responses, in-class debates, group work, or other creative activities. Complementing the readings in each chapter are images that serve as visual texts that can be discussed. We've also included a glossary of semiotic terms, which can serve as a ready reference of key terms and concepts used in the chapter introductions. Finally, the instructor's manual (*Editors' Notes to Accompany* SIGNS OF LIFE IN THE U.S.A.) provides suggestions for organizing your syllabus, encouraging student responses to the readings, and using popular culture and semiotics in the writing class.

What's New in the Sixth Edition

Few subjects move so quickly as does the pace of popular culture, and the substantial revision required for the sixth edition of *Signs of Life in the U.S.A.* reflects this essential mutability. First, we have updated our readings, adding twenty-nine new selections that focus on issues and trends that have emerged since the last edition of this book. We have also updated many of the exemplary topics in our introductions, which are used to model the critical assignments that follow, and have adjusted the focus of some chapters to reflect changing conditions. A new chapter, "You-Topian Dreams: MySpace, YourSpace, and the Semiotics of Web 2.0," focuses on the sudden ubiquity of interactive media in our lives. And, because students are increasingly relying on the Internet as a research tool, we've added a selection on evaluating Web sites and one on the problems raised by Wikipedia.

From the beginning, *Signs of Life in the U.S.A.* was predicated on the premise that in a postindustrial, McCluhanesque world, the image has been coming to supplant the printed word in American, and global, culture. That is yet another of the reasons we chose semiotics, which provides a rational basis for the critical analysis of images as the guiding methodology for every edition of our book. Each edition of *Signs of Life* has accordingly included images for critical analysis. In this edition, we have updated our image portfolio (which works as a kind of photo essay on the past three-quarters of a century of American popular culture that asks students to analyze the cultural significance of representative images from *The Wizard of Oz* to *The Evolution of Dance*). We also include new images, many of which are accompanied by discussion and writing questions. The images supplement the readings, offering a visual perspective designed to enhance the critical understanding modeled by the texts, not to replace them. We strongly believe that while the semiotic interpretation of images can help students in the honing of their writing skills, it should not be a substitute for learning critical thinking through the analysis of written texts.

Even as we revise this text to reflect current trends, popular culture continues to evolve. The inevitable gap between the pace of editing and publishing, on the one hand, and the flow of popular culture, on the other, need not affect its use in the classroom, however. The readings in the text, and the semiotic method we propose, are designed to show students how to analyze and write critical essays about any topic they choose. They can choose a topic that appeared before they were born, or they can turn to the latest box office or prime-time hit to appear after the publication of this edition of *Signs of Life in the U.S.A.* To put it another way, the practice of everyday life may itself be filled with evanescent fads and trends, but it is not itself a fad. As the vital texture of our lived experience, popular culture provides a stable background against which students of every generation can test their critical skills.

Acknowledgments

The vastness of the terrain of popular culture has enabled many users of the fifth edition of this text to make valuable suggestions for the sixth edition. We have incorporated many such suggestions and thank all for their comments on our text: Suzanne Arakawa, California State University, San Bernardino; Joy Barta, California State University, San Bernardino; Darcy L. Brandel, Marygrove College; Linsey Cuti, Kankakee Community College; Carol Dillon, University of Nebraska, Omaha; Keith Gumery, Temple University; Andrei Guruianu, Ithaca College; Matthew Horton, Gainesville State College; Jamison Klagmann,

University of Alaska, Fairbanks; Stephen Knadler, Spelman College; Patti J. Kurtz, Minot State University; Christine Lanoie-Newman, El Camino College; Julie Lumpkins, Columbia State Community College; Tim Melnarik, California State University, San Bernardino; Lee Nickoson-Massey, Bowling Green State University; Trina Chance O'Gorman, Montclair State University; Jennifer Plante, Clark University; Preston Rose, Pasadena City College and Los Angeles City College; Miriam Schacht, University of Texas; Elisabeth von Uhl, Montclair State University; Amie L. Whittemore, Kankakee Community College; and Susan D. Wright, Montclair State University.

We are also grateful to those reviewers who examined the book in depth: Eddie Asgill, Bethune-Cookman University; Liz Canfield, Virginia Commonwealth University; Gina Claywell, Murray State University; Chitralekha Duttagupta, Arizona State University; Christine Farris, Indiana University; Denise Tischler Millstein, University of Alabama; Beverly Neiderman, Kent State University; Jean Petrolle, Columbia College; Pauline Uchmanowicz, SUNY, New Paltz; and Kevin Waltman, Univeristy of Alabama. If we have not included something you'd like to work on, you may still direct your students to it, using this text as a guide, not as a set of absolute prescriptions. The practice of everyday life includes the conduct of a classroom, and we want all users of the sixth edition of *Signs of Life in the U.S.A.* to feel free to pursue that practice in whatever way best suits their interests and aims.

We'd like to give special thanks to our colleagues Maja Manojlovic and Steve Steinberg, and a student, Chris Kampe, for their helpful suggestions. And, once again, we wish to thank heartily the people at Bedford/St. Martin's who have enabled us to make this new edition a reality, particularly Joan Feinberg, who has now been at the helm through eight of our textbook projects. We cannot say enough about our editor, John Sullivan, who, having been compared to Maxwell Perkins twice already in our acknowledgments, continues to exhaust all possible superlatives as an editor and friend. He is simply indispensable. Emily Berleth and Nancy Benjamin ably guided our manuscript through the rigors of production, while Alicia Young handled the innumerable questions and details that arose during textbook development. Helane Prottas expertly researched and obtained permission for art, and Sandy Schechter cleared text permissions. In addition, Mary Sanger contributed her intelligence and superb competence to the copyediting of this book. Finally, we wish to dedicate this book to two special friends, Star and Marlowe.

Contents

Preface for Instructors *v*

INTRODUCTION
Popular Signs: *Or, Everything You Always Knew about American Culture (but Nobody Asked)* *1*

Portfolio: Images from the History of Popular Culture 23

Writing about Popular Culture *33*

SCOTT JASCHIK: *A Stand against Wikipedia* *43*

PATTI S. CARAVELLO: *Judging Quality on the Web* *46*

Citing Sources *69*

Chapter 1.
Consuming Passions: *The Culture of American Consumption* *75*

LAURENCE SHAMES: *The More Factor* *86*
  "Frontier; opportunity; more. This has been the American trinity from the very start."

PAIRED READINGS: UNDERSTANDING SHOPPING

MALCOLM GLADWELL: *The Science of Shopping* 93

"Retailers don't just want to know how shoppers behave in their stores. They *have* to know."

ANNE NORTON: *The Signs of Shopping* 101

"Everyone, from the architecture critic at the *New York Times* to kids in the hall of a Montana high school, knows what *Ralph Lauren* means."

Credit Card Barbie [PHOTOGRAPH] 108

A popular play figure for girls makes a purchase.

THOMAS HINE: *What's in a Package* 109

"Packages serve as symbols both of their contents and of a way of life."

JOAN KRON: *The Semiotics of Home Decor* 119

"We use our possessions in the same way we use language — the quintessential symbol — to *communicate* with one another."

ANNE GALLIGAN: *Pottermania: The Marketing behind the Magic* 129

"The Harry Potter series has broken through conventional literary circuitry and become the Sumo wrestler of mass consumption."

ALISON SCHNEIDER: *Frumpy or Chic? Tweed or Kente? Sometimes Clothes Make the Professor* 139

"There was just one problem with the English department's job candidate: his pants."

DAVID GOEWEY: *"Careful, You May Run Out of Planet": SUVs and the Exploitation of the American Myth* 147

"The modern SUV represents a preeminent symbol of American popular culture."

THOMAS L. FRIEDMAN: *Revolution Is U.S.* 157

"Today, globalization often wears Mickey Mouse ears, eats Big Macs, drinks Coke or Pepsi, and does its computing on an IBM PC, using Windows 98, with an Intel Pentium II processor, and a network link from Cisco Systems."

THOMAS FRANK: *Commodify Your Dissent* 163

"We consume not to fit in, but to prove, on the surface at least, that we are rock 'n' roll rebels."

Chapter 2.
Brought to You B(u)y: *The Signs of Advertising*   *171*

ROLAND MARCHAND: *The Parable of the Democracy of Goods*   *182*

"'Body Odor plays no favorites,' warned Lifebuoy Soap. No one, 'banker, baker, or society woman,' could count himself safe from B.O."

When You Come Home [ADVERTISEMENT]   *191*

"The thought of what *might have* happened, is followed by a deep gratitude for what *did* happen."

PAIRED READINGS: CREATING CONSUMERS

JAMES B. TWITCHELL: *What We Are to Advertisers*   *192*

"Mass production means mass marketing, and mass marketing means the creation of mass stereotypes."

SANDRA BLAKESLEE: *If You Have a "Buy Button" in Your Brain, What Pushes It?*   *197*

"'What would happen in this country if corporate marketers and political consultants could literally peer inside our brains and chart the neural activity that leads to our selections in the supermarket and voting booth?'"

STEVE CRAIG: *Men's Men and Women's Women*   *202*

"What might have been a simple commercial about a man ordering and drinking a beer becomes an elaborate sexual fantasy, in many respects constructed like a porn film."

JENNIFER L. POZNER: *Dove's "Real Beauty" Backlash*   *214*

"Even though Dove's 'Real Beauty' ads play to and subtly reinforce the stereotypes they claim to be exposing, it's impossible not to feel inspired by the sight of these attractive, healthy women smiling playfully at us from their places of billboard honor."

WARREN ST. JOHN: *Metrosexuals Come Out*   *217*

"America may be on the verge of a metrosexual moment."

ERIC SCHLOSSER: *Kid Kustomers*   *222*

"The aim of most children's advertising is straightforward: Get kids to nag their parents and nag them well."

GLORIA STEINEM: *Sex, Lies, and Advertising*   *227*

"What could women's magazines be like if they were as editorially free as good books?"

Portfolio of Advertisements

Jeep Compass
Mr. Rooter
American Egg Board
Phoenix Wealth Management
San Diego Convention and Visitors Bureau
Honda Pilot
McCormick Gravy

Chapter 3.
Video Dreams: *Television, Music, and Cultural Forms* *249*

FRANCINE PROSE: *Voting Democracy off the Island: Reality TV and the Republican Ethos* *265*

"The castaways vote, as we do, but it's a democracy that might have been conceived if the spirit of Machiavelli had briefly possessed the mind of Thomas Jefferson."

"You're Fired." [PHOTOGRAPH] *273*

A banner from the Trump Tower promotes the reality TV show *The Apprentice*.

JAMES HAROLD: *A Moral Never-Never Land: Identifying with Tony Soprano* *274*

"Is there anything *morally* wrong with caring about Tony Soprano?"

PAIRED READINGS: ANIMATING ATTITUDE

CARL MATHESON: The Simpsons, *Hyper-Irony, and the Meaning of Life* *283*

"The lifeblood of *The Simpsons*, and its astonishing achievement, is the pace of cruelty and ridicule that it has managed to sustain for over a decade."

DAVID VALLEAU CURTIS and GERALD J. ERION: South Park *and the Open Society* *296*

"At first glance, *South Park* seems to offer little more than crude animation and tasteless jokes expressed with a juvenile and offensive vulgarity."

JAIME J. WEINMAN: *Fox News Attempts to Get Funny* *304*

"Why are the producers of Fox News so desperate to be funny?"

SUSAN DOUGLAS: *Signs of Intelligent Life on TV* *307*

"On the surface, these shows seem good for women. . . . But in too many ways, the women take a backseat to the boys."

ANDRE MAYER: *The New Sexual Stone Age* *312*

"We've returned to an age of rampant chauvinism, where men swagger about in a testosterone rage and women are reduced to sexual ornaments."

MARISA CONNOLLY: *Homosexuality on Television: The Heterosexualization of Will and Grace*   *315*

"Scripts and comic devices have often made it seem that Will and Grace were the perfect heterosexual couple, separated only by sexual orientation."

CYNTHIA TUCKER: *Thug Culture Is a Cancer Destroying Black America*   *326*

"There is now a cottage industry dedicated to defending rap music, a group of enablers who glorify hard-core rap as a legitimate art form reflecting the bitter real-life experiences of ghetto inhabitants."

Chapter 4.
The Hollywood Sign: *The Culture of American Film*   *331*

┌─ **PAIRED READINGS: INVENTING HEROES**

ROBERT B. RAY: *The Thematic Paradigm*   *342*

"To the outlaw hero's insistence on private standards of right and wrong, the official hero offered the admonition, 'You cannot take the law into your own hands.'"

VIRGINIA POSTREL: *Superhero Worship*   *351*

"To the right audience, Halle Berry is more glamorous commanding the elements as Storm in the *X-Men* movies than she is walking the red carpet in a designer gown."

LINDA SEGER: *Creating the Myth*   *356*

"Whatever our culture, there are universal stories that form the basis for all our particular stories. . . . Many of the most successful films are based on these universal stories."

LISA KERNAN: *Trailer Rhetoric*   *365*

"The promotional appeal of genre as a whole rests heavily on familiarity, on the lure and comfort of the known."

TODD BOYD: *So You Wanna Be a Gangsta?*   *375*

"*Boyz N the Hood* demonizes the landscape of Los Angeles while uncritically offering middle-class Atlanta as a metaphoric space where future generations of African Americans can exist free of the obstacles that are depicted in this film."

JESSICA HAGEDORN: *Asian Women in Film: No Joy, No Luck*   *387*

"Because change has been slow, *The Joy Luck Club* carries a lot of cultural baggage."

DAVID DENBY: *High-School Confidential: Notes on Teen Movies*   *396*

"In these movies . . . the senior prom is the equivalent of the shoot-out at the O.K. Corral."

TOM MOORE: *Movie Fantasy vs. Classroom Reality*   *402*

"Films like *Freedom Writers* portray teachers more as missionaries than professionals, eager to give up their lives and comfort for the benefit of others, without need of compensation."

MICHAEL PARENTI: *Class and Virtue*   *406*

"The entertainment media present working people not only as unlettered and uncouth but also as less desirable and less moral than other people."

AEON J. SKOBLE: *Forrest Gump: A Subversive Movie*   *410*

"A Hollywood movie is like a box of chocolates: it tastes good, but it's really bad for you."

VIVIAN C. SOBCHACK: *The Postmorbid Condition*   *414*

"I still can't watch the eyeball being slit in *Un Chien Andalou*. But, as with *Straw Dogs* and *The French Connection*, I could and did watch all the violence in *Pulp Fiction*."

Reservoir Dogs [MOVIE POSTER]   *420*

The poster for the controversial film.

Chapter 5.
You-Topian Dreams: MySpace, YourSpace, and the Semiotics of Web 2.0   *423*

HENRY JENKINS: *Convergence Culture*   *432*

"In the world of media convergence, every important story gets told, every brand gets sold, and every consumer gets courted across multiple media platforms."

PAIRED READINGS: CELEBRATING YOU

STEVEN JOHNSON: *It's All about Us*   *446*

"If Web 1.0 was organized around pages, Web 2.0 is organized around people."

BRIAN WILLIAMS: *Enough about You*   *449*

"It is now possible — even common — to go about your day in America and consume only what you wish to see and hear."

TED FRIEDMAN: *From the Forest to the Trees: The Sims*   *452*

"The Sims . . . is a reflection not only of consumerism, but also of . . . the constant pressure on Americans today, particularly working mothers, to juggle the competing demands of work and home."

ALANA SEMUELS: *Virtual Marketers Have Second Thoughts about Second Life*   *457*

"It turns out that plugging products is as problematic in the virtual world as it is anywhere else."

CLIVE THOMPSON: *Game Theories*   460

"The Gross National Product of EverQuest, measured by how much wealth all the players together created in a single year inside the game . . . turned out to be $2,266 per capita. . . . It was the seventy-seventh richest country in the world. And it didn't even exist."

A. B. HARRIS: *Average Gamers Please Step Forward*   465

"If gaming has evolved to such a great degree, why have the culture surrounding gaming and the mainstream's opinion of that culture remained inert?"

Master Chief Waits in Line [PHOTOGRAPH]   468

A fan becomes the hero of Halo 3.

JOANNE CAVANAUGH SIMPSON: *Multitasking State of Mind*   469

"Call it ADD Nation or IM Generation, but a different batch of students has arrived on college campuses."

DAVID TETEN and SCOTT ALLEN: *Free Speech and Censorship in Online Communities*   473

"You do have the right of free speech, but the owners of a community also have the right to establish and enforce codes of conduct within the community."

Chapter 6.
American Paradox: *Culture and Contradiction in the U.S.A.*   477

DAVID BROOKS: *One Nation, Slightly Divisible*   487

"We sail; they powerboat. We cross-country ski; they snowmobile. We hike; they drive ATVs. We have vineyard tours; they have tractor pulls."

PAIRED READINGS: PROFILING STEREOTYPES

RANDALL KENNEDY: *Blind Spot*   496

"A notable feature of this conflict [over racial profiling] is that champions of each position frequently embrace rhetoric, attitudes, and value systems that are completely at odds with those they adopt when confronting another controversial instance of racial discrimination — namely, affirmative action."

COREY WILLIAMS: *NAACP Symbolically Buries N-Word*   500

"There was no mourning at this funeral."

TIM KASSER: *Mixed Messages*   502

"It is interesting to know that one of the world's wealthiest, most powerful nations appears to be inculcating values not conducive to its citizens' well-being."

"Leave Area Clean" [PHOTOGRAPH] *523*

An image of an unintentionally ironic symbol of disorder.

JACK SOLOMON: *Masters of Desire: The Culture of American Advertising* *524*

"The logic of advertising is entirely semiotic: It substitutes signs for things, framed visions of consumer desire for the thing itself."

SHELLEY FRALIC: *Cheap Chic* *535*

"Best to first deal with the delicious irony of it all — rich, famous, couture-clad celebrities showing up in the local mall."

MARIAH BURTON NELSON: *I Won. I'm Sorry.* *539*

"If you want to be a winner and you're female, you'll feel pressured to play by special, female rules."

ALFRED LUBRANO: *The Shock of Education: How College Corrupts* *546*

"'Every bit of learning takes you further from your parents.'"

RICHARD CORLISS: *The Gospel According to* Spider-Man *553*

"Hollywood doesn't necessarily want to make Christian movies. It wants to make movies Christians think are Christian."

Chapter 7.
We've Come a Long Way, Maybe: *Gender Codes in American Culture* *559*

┌─ **PAIRED READINGS: PERFORMING GENDER**

AARON DEVOR: *Gender Role Behaviors and Attitudes* *567*

"Persons who perform the activities considered appropriate for another gender will be expected to perform them poorly; if they succeed adequately, or even well, at their endeavors, they may be rewarded with ridicule or scorn for blurring the gender dividing line."

DEBORAH BLUM: *The Gender Blur: Where Does Biology End and Society Take Over?* *573*

"How does all this fit together — toys and testosterone, biology and behavior, the development of the child into the adult, the way that men and women relate to one another?"

KEVIN JENNINGS: *American Dreams* *581*

"I pursued what I thought was 'normal' with a vengeance in high school."

SEAN CAHILL: *The Case for Marriage Equality*   586

"Had Mickie and Lois had the right to marry, they would have been able to protect their family and their right to inherit each other's pension in the event of an untimely death."

ANDY MEDHURST: *Batman, Deviance, and Camp*   592

"If I want Batman to be gay, then, for me, he is."

COURTNEY E. MARTIN: *The Famine Mystique*   607

"The famine mystique is killing my generation — sometimes literally, often politically, emotionally, and spiritually."

EMILY PRAGER: *Our Barbies, Ourselves*   613

"I used to look at Barbie and wonder, What's wrong with this picture?"

JOAN MORGAN: *Sex, Lies, and Videos*   616

"'In rap videos, there is no self. Girls become body parts and nothing more.'"

DEBORAH TANNEN: *There Is No Unmarked Woman*   620

"Some days you just want to get dressed and go about your business. But if you're a woman, you can't, because there is no unmarked woman."

JAMES WILLIAM GIBSON: *Warrior Dreams*   625

"Rambo was a worker and a former enlisted man, not a smooth-talking professional."

MICHAEL A. MESSNER: *Power at Play: Sport and Gender Relations*   635

"Sport is a social institution that, in its dominant forms, was created by and for men."

Chapter 8.
Constructing Race: *Readings in Multicultural Semiotics*   647

┌─ **PAIRED READINGS: MEDIATING RACE**

MICHAEL OMI: *In Living Color: Race and American Culture*   655

"Popular culture has been an important realm within which racial ideologies have been created, reproduced, and sustained."

GREG BRAXTON: *Hollywood Loves BBFs 4-Ever*   667

"One African American actress said that she and her actress friends tease one another about forming a support group for characters who had to help out their 'woefully helpless white girls.'"

REBECCA TRAISTER: *Class Act*   672

"*Ugly Betty* is not about being unattractive, or at least not *simply* about being unattractive. It's about class. And ethnicity."

ANGELINE F. PRICE: *Working Class Whites*   678

"Representations of working class whites in the popular media are responsible for the dissemination of 'white trash' as well as 'good country folk' stereotypes in society."

JACK LOPEZ: *Of Cholos and Surfers*   684

"I was lucky; I got the best of both worlds."

JIM WHITMER: *Four Teens* [PHOTOGRAPH]   690

A telling portrait of four midwestern teens.

NELL BERNSTEIN: *Goin' Gangsta, Choosin' Cholita*   691

"White skaters and Mexican would-be gangbangers listen to gangsta rap and call each other 'nigga' as a term of endearment; white girls sometimes affect Spanish accents; blond cheerleaders claim Cherokee ancestors."

MELISSA ALGRANATI: *Being an Other*   697

"I learned at a young age that there are not too many Puerto Rican, Egyptian Jews out there."

FAN SHEN: *The Classroom and the Wider Culture: Identity as a Key to Learning English Composition*   702

"Learning the rules of English composition is, to a certain extent, learning the values of Anglo-American society."

Glossary   713

Index of Authors and Titles   723

Signs of Life in the U.S.A.

POPULAR SIGNS

*Or, Everything You Always
Knew about American Culture
(but Nobody Asked)*

The You Decade

A funny thing happened on the way to the twenty-first century.

America took a You-turn.

Right into what might as well now be called the *You Decade*.

Time made it more or less official, with a lush spread celebrating *You* as Person of the Year for 2006, focusing on such online popular cultural phenomena as YouTube, MySpace, Second Life, the blogosphere, and Wikipedia. But there is more to it than that. For whenever you send in your vote for your favorite contestant on *American Idol*, cast your online ballot for the best Super Bowl advertisement, contribute to Yahoo's "You Witness News" page, organize your own personal TiVo schedule, or create playlists for your MP3s, you are participating in a profound media revolution that is currently turning upside down much of our traditional understanding of the dynamics of the mass media and mass culture.

Traditionally, that dynamic has been of a top-down nature, with corporate elites providing passive consumers with the news, entertainments, and products that they consume, along with the advertisements that promote them. But recently, with the enormous growth of such Web 2.0 phenomena as the whimsically labeled blogosphere, top-down news has turned into a bottom-up conversation in which anyone can become a pundit, while newspapers and online news sites invite input from their readers. Broadband Internet access has turned video creativity over to the masses in such a way that you no longer have to be a famous director or producer to present your own television shows or films to a wide audience, and you don't have to be an authorized critic to respond, with YouTube and related sites offering unlimited opportunity to critique what you find there. Similarly, fans of such popular novels and movies as *Harry Potter* and *The Lord of the Rings* now create their own fantasy story lines on online sites devoted to the extension of the worlds originally created by the likes of J. K. Rowling and J. R. R. Tolkien. In short, what was once a passive and vicarious media experience for the mass of consumers is now becoming active and participatory.

In a related shift, large corporations have begun to ask consumers for their ideas for advertising their products, as General Motors did for a Chevrolet ad that was presented during Super Bowl XLI, and an increasing number of "my this" and "my that" Web pages offer consumers a chance to customize their media experience. Even reality television is part of the "You" phenomenon, enabling ordinary people (you) to become television stars in their own right on numerous reality TV (RTV) programs and to participate in the outcomes of *American Idol*–like shows.

It's All Over Now, Baudrillard

Another way of putting this is that our relationship with the mass media up until now has been more or less a one-way street. Those with the power to control the media (television networks, radio stations, movie studios, newspaper owners, corporate sponsors with advertising dollars to spend) have broadcast their signals to us (TV and radio programs, films, newspapers, and ads), and we have passively received them, without being able to answer back. The late semiologist and sociologist Jean Baudrillard (1929–2007) regarded this situation as being one of the essential conditions of postmodern times and used it as a basis for his analyses of contemporary society. But with so much of the mass media now actively eliciting responses from their audiences, and with consumers of the mass media able to take control of their own media consumption through such technologies as TiVo, the iPod, and the Internet, it appears that something post-postmodern is emerging beyond Baudrillard's perceptions.

Whether the new two-way avenues of mass communication will result in any substantive, post-Baudrillardian changes in American society is a question whose answer remains to be seen, however. On the one hand, the You Decade is definitely opening up channels for democratic communication and expression that have never existed before, and with presidential candidates making use of such popular online social networking sites as MySpace to attract votes and marketers crowding into the user-built worlds of Second Life and related sites, it is clear that the elites are taking notice. Indeed, even you may have felt empowered by the opportunities now being offered to display your own creative work and political opinions to a mass audience thanks to Web 2.0 media technologies. But the very fact that the elites are gobbling up the democratic vistas of the Internet for their own profit-making purposes (Rupert Murdoch purchased MySpace in 2007 and Google swallowed YouTube in 2006) suggests that it all may end up being business as usual, with the "you society" becoming little more than another marketing ploy, an illusion of individualized consumption in what is still a mass consumer society.

We will not attempt to resolve this question here, for the purpose of this book, in part, is not to answer the innumerable questions that arise when we contemplate American popular culture but to enable you to see what the questions are and give you the tools to create answers of your own. Every chapter in *Signs of Life in the U.S.A.* is designed to further that goal, each one focusing on a particular facet of the kaleidoscopic panorama of contemporary American life. But to begin the process, it would be helpful to review the broad history of popular culture itself.

From Folk to Fab

Traditionally, popular or "low" culture constituted the culture of the masses and was opposed to "high" culture, which included such things as classical music and literature, the fine arts and philosophy, and the elite learning that was the province of the ruling classes who had the money and leisure necessary to attain it, and who were often the direct patrons of high art and its artists. Low culture had two main sides to it. One side, most notoriously illustrated by the violent entertainments of the Roman Empire (such as gladiatorial contests, public executions, feeding Christians to lions) continues to be a sure crowd pleaser to this day, as demonstrated by the widespread popularity of violent, erotic, and/or vulgar entertainment (can you spell *Jackass*?). The other side, which we can call "popular" in the etymological sense of being of the people, overlaps with what we now call "folk culture." Quietly existing alongside high culture, folk culture expressed the experience of the masses in the form of ballads, songs, agricultural festivals, fairy tales, feasts, folk art, and so on. Self-produced by amateur performers, folk culture can be best envisioned by thinking of neighbors gathering on a modest Appalachian front porch to play their guitars, dulcimers, zithers, mandolins, fiddles, and whatnot to perform, for their own entertainment, ballads and songs passed down from generation to generation.

Folk culture, of course, still exists. But it has been dwindling, with increasing rapidity, for the past two hundred years, as it becomes overwhelmed by a new kind of popular culture, a commercialized culture that, while still including elements of both the folk and the vulgar traditions, represents the outcome of a certain historical evolution (whose direction the advent of the you society may or may not eventually change). This culture, the popular culture that is most familiar today and that is the topic of this book, is a commercial, for-profit culture aimed at providing entertainment to a mass audience. Corporate

Traditional high culture: Deborah Voigt in performance at the Metropolitan Opera in New York.

rather than communal, it is creative rather than conservative, but its creativity is tied to commodification, turning entertainment into a commodity to be marketed alongside all the other products in a consumer society.

The forces that transformed the low culture of the past into contemporary popular culture arose in the industrial revolution of the late eighteenth century and its accompanying urbanization of European and American society. Along with the rise of corporate capitalism and the advent of electronic technologies, these historical forces shaped the emergence of the mass cultural marketplace of entertainments that we know today. To see how this happened, let's begin with the industrial revolution. Prior to the industrial revolution, most Europeans and Americans lived in scattered agricultural settlements.

While traveling entertainers in theatrical troupes and circuses might come to visit the larger of these settlements, most people, especially those with little money, had to produce their own entertainment. But with the industrial revolution, masses of people who had made their living through agriculture were compelled to leave their rural communities and move to the cities where employment increasingly was to be had. Population began to concentrate in urban centers as the rural countryside emptied, leading to the development of mass societies.

With the emergence of mass society came the development of mass culture. For just as mass societies are governed by centralized systems of governance (consider how the huge expanse of the United States is governed by a federal government concentrated in Washington, D.C.), so too are mass cultures entertained by culture industries concentrated in a few locations (as the film and TV industry is concentrated in Hollywood and its immediate environs). Thanks to the invention of such electronic technologies as the cinema, the phonograph, and the radio at the turn of the nineteenth to the twentieth century, and of television and digital technology in the mid-to-late-twentieth century, the means to disseminate centrally produced mass entertainments to a mass society became possible. Thus, whether you live in Boston or Boise, New York or Nebraska, the entertainment you enjoy is produced in the same few locations and is the same entertainment (TV programs, movies, DVDs, what-have-you) no matter where you consume it. The growth of mass culture has been conditioned as well by the growth of a capitalist economic system in America. That is, it is American-style capitalism that has ensured that mass culture would develop as a for-profit industry.

To get a better idea of how the whole process unfolded, let's go back to that Appalachian front porch. Before electricity and urbanization, folks living in the backwoods of rural America needed to make their music themselves if they wanted music. They had no radios, phonographs, CD players, or iPods, or even electricity, and theaters with live performers were hard to get to and too expensive for poor folk. Under such conditions, the Appalachian region developed a vibrant folk musical culture. But as people began to move to places like Pittsburgh and Detroit, where the steel and auto industries began to offer employment in the late nineteenth and early twentieth centuries, the conditions under which neighbors could produce their own music decayed, for the communal conditions under which folk culture thrives were broken down by the mass migration to the cities. At the same time, the need to produce one's own music declined as folks who once plucked their own guitars and banjos could simply turn on their radios or purchase records to listen to professional musicians perform for them. Those musicians — like Bill Monroe, who invented bluegrass in the 1930s as a commercial synthesis of the folk music traditions he had grown up with — were contracted by recording companies in business to turn a profit, and their music, in turn, could be heard on the radio because corporate sponsors provided the advertising that made (and still makes) commercial radio broadcasting possible.

Traditional folk culture in transition: Bill Monroe is known as the father of bluegrass music.

So what had once been an amateur, do-it-yourself activity (the production of folk music), became a professional, for-profit industry with passive consumers paying for their entertainment either through the direct purchase of a commodity (e.g., a record) or by having to listen to the advertising that encouraged them to purchase the products that sponsored their favorite radio programs. It was and still is possible, of course, to make one's own music (or, more generally, one's own entertainment), but not only is it just easier and perhaps aesthetically more pleasing to listen to a professional recording, in the kind of mass consumer society in which we live, we are, in effect, constantly being trained to be the sort of passive consumers that keep the whole consumer-capitalist system going. If everyone stopped buying DVDs, or stopped watching television or movies, the economy would probably collapse.

This is hardly an exaggeration, for the advent of postindustrial capitalism has made popular culture all the more important with every passing year. With the American economy turning further and further away from industrial production towards the production and consumption of entertainment (including sports), entertainment has been moving away from the margins of our cultural consciousness — as a mere form of play or recreation — to its center as a major buttress of our economy. A constant bombardment of advertising (which, after all, is the driving force behind the financing of the Web 2.0 media — can you spell Google? — just as it was for radio and television a generation or two ago) continually prods us to consume the entertainments that our economy produces. That bombardment has been so successful that our whole cultural consciousness is changing, becoming more childlike, more and more concerned with play rather than with work, even while *at* work (tell the truth now: Are you playing games on your laptop during class, or texting a friend?).

The result of the centuries-long process we have sketched above is the kind of culture we have today: a culture centered on entertainments and entertainers who are worshipped as the gods of precapitalist agricultural production (the corn gods and whatnot) were once worshipped. American culture thus shows signs today of a new evolutionary development in which the high and low cultures of the past are melting into each other in a cultural synthesis that could be called an *entertainment culture* — a culture, that is to say, in which all aspects of society (from politics to the traditional elite arts) are linked by a common imperative to entertain.

Throw another song on the Barbie: Mattel has produced an MP3 player in the shape of the popular girl's toy.

Pop Goes the Culture

Thus, far from being a mere recreational frivolity, a leisure activity that our society could easily dispense with, popular cultural entertainment today constitutes the essential texture of our everyday lives. From the way we entertain ourselves to the goods and services that we produce and consume, we are enveloped in a popular cultural environment that we can neither do without nor escape, even if we wanted to. To see this, just try to imagine a world without the Internet, television, movies, sports, music, shopping malls, advertising, or DVDs, MTV, or MP3s. Still, you might be surprised to find popular culture as the topic for your university composition class, because until recently the study of popular culture was largely excluded from university curricula. As institutions of a high culture that is rapidly dwindling into a sort of "museum" culture that has little to do with ordinary, everyday life, universities have been regarded as havens from, and bastions against, the popular cultural entertainments that have driven high culture from the stage. Not until the advent of "cultural studies," which was first pioneered in English universities and came to America in the late 1980s, did the study of popular culture become a common, and accepted, topic for university study. But as the barrier between high and low culture, privileged and popular, continues to erode in a world where *Romeo and Juliet* is a pop opera and string quartets have been part of the rock scene ever since the Beatles's "Yesterday," where divas like Deborah Voigt feel compelled to undergo gastric bypass surgery in order to maintain their careers in an operatic world that is demanding that its sopranos look more like Britney Spears, the study of pop culture is emerging as a mainstay of contemporary higher education.

This has been especially true in American composition classrooms, which have taken the lead in incorporating popular culture into academic study, both because of the inherent interest value of the subject and because of its profound familiarity to most students. Your own expertise in popular culture means not only that you may know more about a given topic than your instructor but that you may use that knowledge as a basis for learning the critical thinking and writing skills that your composition class is charged to teach you. This book is designed to show you how to do that — how to write about American popular culture as you would write about any other academic subject.

Signs of Life in the U.S.A., then, is designed to let you exploit your knowledge of popular culture so that you may grow into a better writer about any subject. You can interpret the popularity of programs like *CSI: Las Vegas*, for example, in the same manner as you would interpret, say, a short story, because *CSI*, too, constitutes a kind of sign. A sign is something, anything, that carries a meaning. A stop sign, for instance, means exactly what it says, "Stop when you approach this intersection," while carrying the implied message "or risk getting a ticket." Words, too, are signs: You read them to figure out what they mean. You were trained to read such signs, but that training began so long ago that you may well take your ability to read for granted. But all your life you have been encountering, and interpreting, other sorts of signs that you were never formally taught to read, yet you know what they mean anyway. Take the way you wear your hair. When you get your hair cut, you are not simply removing hair: You are making a statement, sending a message about yourself. It's the same for both men and women. For men, think of the different messages you'd send if you got a buzz cut to accompany a goatee, or grew your hair out long, or shaved your head. What does a woman communicate when she chooses beaded braids, or perhaps a Posh Spice look? Why was your hair short last year and long this year? Aren't you saying something with the scissors? In this way, you make your hairstyle into a sign that sends a message about your identity. You are surrounded by such signs. Just look at your classmates.

The world of signs could be called a kind of text, the text of America's popular culture. We want you to think of *Signs of Life in the U.S.A.* as a window onto that text. What you read in this book's essays and introductions should lead you to study and analyze the world around you for yourself. Let the readings guide you to your own interpretations, your own readings, of the text of America.

We have chosen eight "windows" in this edition of *Signs of Life in the U.S.A.*, each of which looks out onto a separate, but often interrelated, segment of the American scene. In some cases, we have put some of the scenery directly into this book, as when we include actual ads in our chapter on advertising or cartoons that can be directly interpreted. In other cases, where it is impossible to put something directly into a textbook, like a TV show or a movie, we have included essays that help you think about specific programs and films, and assignments that invite you to go out and interpret a TV show or movie of your own choosing. Each chapter also includes an introduction written to alert you to the kinds of signs you will find there, along with model analyses and advice on how to go about interpreting the topics that that chapter raises.

We have designed *Signs of Life in the U.S.A.* to reflect the many ways in which culture shapes our sense of reality and of ourselves, from the things that we buy to the way that culture, through such media as television and the movies, constructs our ethnic and gender identities. This text thus introduces you to both the entertainment and the ideological sides of popular culture — and shows how the two sides are mutually interdependent. Indeed, one of the major lessons you can learn from this book is how to find the ideological underpinnings of some of the most apparently innocent entertainments and consumer goods.

Signs of Life in the U.S.A. accordingly begins with a chapter on "Consuming Passions," because America is a consumer culture, and so the environment within which the galaxy of popular signs functions is, more often than not, a consumerist one. This is true not only for obvious consumer products like clothes and sport utility vehicles but for such traditionally nonconsumer items as political candidates as well, who are often marketed like any other consumer product. It is difficult to find anything in contemporary America that is not affected in one way or another by our consumerist ethos or by consumerism's leading promoter, the advertiser. Thus, the second chapter, "Brought to You B(u)y," explores the world of advertising, for advertising provides the grease, so to speak, that lubricates the engine of America's consumer culture. Because television (including MTV) and film are the sources of many of our most significant cultural products, we include a chapter on each. Chapters on Web 2.0, American contradictions, gender, and race round out our survey of everyday life.

Throughout, the book invites you to go out and select your own "texts" for analysis (an advertisement, a film, a fashion fad, a political opinion, and so on). Here's where your own experience is particularly valuable, because it has made you familiar with many different kinds of popular signs and their backgrounds, with the particular popular cultural system or environment to which they belong.

The eight "windows" you will find in *Signs of Life in the U.S.A.* are all intended to reveal the common intersections of entertainment and ideology that can be found in contemporary American life. Often what seems to be simply entertainment, like a TV show, is actually quite political, while what seems political, like health care, can be cast as entertainment as well — as in movies like *Sicko*. The point is to see that little in American life is merely entertainment; indeed, just about everything we do has a meaning, often a profound one.

The Semiotic Method

To find this meaning, to interpret and write effectively about the signs of popular culture, you need a method, and it is part of the purpose of this book to introduce such a method to you. Without a methodology for interpreting signs, writing about them could become little more than descriptive reviews or opinion pieces. There is nothing wrong with writing descriptions and opinions, but one of your tasks in your writing class is to learn how to write academic essays — that is, analytical essays that present theses or arguments that are well supported by evidence. The method we draw upon in this book — a method known as *semiotics* — is especially well suited for analyzing popular culture. Whether or not you're familiar with this word, you are already practicing sophisticated semiotic analyses every day of your life. Reading this page is an act of semiotic decoding (words and letters are signs that must be interpreted), but so is figuring out just what your classmate means by wearing a particular shirt or dress. For a semiotician (one who practices semiotic analysis), a shirt, a haircut, a television image, anything at all, can be taken as a sign, as a message to be decoded and analyzed to discover its meaning. Every cultural activity for the semiotician leaves a trace of meaning, a kind of blip on the semiotic Richter scale, that remains for us to read, just as a geologist "reads" the earth for signs of earthquakes, volcanoes, and other geological phenomena.

Many who hear the word *semiotics* for the first time assume that it is the name of a new, and forbidding, subject. But in truth, the study of signs is neither very new nor forbidding. Its modern form took shape in the late nineteenth and early twentieth centuries through the writings and lectures of two men. Charles Sanders Peirce (1839–1914) was an American philosopher who first coined the word *semiotics*, while Ferdinand de Saussure (1857–1913) was a Swiss linguist whose lectures became the foundation for what he called *semiology*. Without knowing of each other's work, Peirce and Saussure established the fundamental principles that modern semioticians or semiologists — the terms are essentially interchangeable — have developed into the contemporary study of semiotics.

The application of semiotics to the interpretation of popular culture was pioneered in the 1950s by the French semiologist Roland Barthes (1915–1980) in a book entitled *Mythologies* (1957). The basic principles of semiotics had already been explored by linguists and anthropologists, but Barthes took the matter to the heart of his own contemporary France, analyzing the cultural significance of everything from professional wrestling to striptease, toys, and plastics. It was Barthes, too, who established the political dimensions of semiotic analysis. Often, the subject of a semiotic analysis — a movie, say, or a TV program — doesn't look political at all; it simply looks like entertainment. In our society *politics* has become something of a dirty word, and to *politicize* something seems somehow to contaminate it. So you shouldn't feel alarmed if at first it feels a little odd to search for a political meaning in an apparently neutral topic. You may even think that to do so is to read too much into that topic. But Barthes's point — and the point of semiotics in general — is that all social behavior is political in the sense that it reflects some subjective or group interest. Such interests are encoded in what are called *ideologies*, or worldviews that express the values and opinions of those who hold them. Politics, then, is just another name for the clash of ideologies that takes place in any complex society where the interests of all those who belong to it constantly compete with one another.

Take, for example, the way people responded to Michael Moore's *Sicko* in 2007. Those viewers who liked the film shared its anticorporate political values. Conservative viewers, on the other hand, derided *Sicko*, as they loathed *Fahrenheit 9/11* before it. While not all movies are as manifestly political as *Sicko*, careful analysis can usually uncover some set of political values at the heart of a film, although those values may be subtly concealed behind an apparently apolitical facade. Indeed, the political values that guide our social behavior are often concealed behind images that don't look political at all. Consider, for example, the depiction of the "typical" American family in the classic TV sitcoms of the fifties and sixties, particularly all those images of happy, docile housewives. To most contemporary viewers, those images looked "normal" or natural at the time that they were first broadcast — the way families

The popular television show *Leave It to Beaver* (1957–1963) exemplified traditional family values of the 1950s.

and women were supposed to be. The shows didn't seem at all ideological. To the contrary, they seemed a retreat from political rancor to domestic harmony. But to a feminist semiotician, the old sitcoms were in fact highly political, because the happy housewives they presented were really images designed to convince women that their place was in the home, not in the workplace competing with men. Such images — or signs — did not reflect reality; they reflected, rather, the interests of a patriarchal, male-centered society. If you think not, then ask yourself why there were shows called *Father Knows Best*, *Bachelor Father*, and *My Three Sons*, but no *My Three Daughters*. And why did few of the women in the shows have jobs or ever seem to leave the house? Of course, there was *I Love Lucy*, but wasn't Lucy the screwball character whom her husband Ricky had to rescue from one crisis after another?

Such are the kinds of questions that semiotics invites us to ask. They may be put more generally. When analyzing any popular cultural phenomenon, always ask yourself questions like these: Why does this thing look the way it does? Why are they saying this? Why am I doing this? What are they really saying? What am I really doing? In short, take nothing for granted when analyzing any image or activity.

Interpreting Popular Signs

Signs often conceal some interest or other, whether political, or commercial, or whatever. And the proliferation of signs and images in an era of electronic technology has simply made it all the more important that we learn to decode the interests and consciousness behind them. Semiotics, accordingly, is not just about signs and symbols: It is equally about ideology and power. This makes semiotics sound rather serious, and often the seriousness of a semiotic analysis is quite real. But reading the text of modern life can also be fun, for it is a text that is at once popular and accessible, a "book" that is intimately in touch with the pulse of American life. As such, it is constantly changing. The same sign can change meaning if something else comes along to change the environment in which it originally appeared. Take the return of the VW Beetle.

In 1998, after a hiatus of some twenty-five years, the Volkswagen Beetle returned to the American automotive marketplace. But the return of the Beetle was not only a consumer event; it was also a sign, an indicator of a broader trend within American popular culture and consciousness. The question is, of what? To answer that question, we need to look at some history. This is especially important in analyzing the cultural significance of the VW Beetle because of the dramatic changes that have occurred within its history. Originally conceived as a kind of propagandistic challenge to America's ability to provide automotive transport to the common person, the Volkswagen, or "people's wagon," was Adolf Hitler's answer to the Model T. It was expressly designed to connote the superiority of the Third Reich and to be a symbol of Germany's triumphant entry to the center of world power and prosperity.

The defeat of Nazi Germany put a swift end to that significance, and when the VW Beetle first appeared in American showrooms in the 1950s, its meaning changed accordingly. During an era of postwar prosperity when U.S. automobiles, the biggest and gaudiest on earth, were signifiers of American affluence, the humble Beetle was a car for the prudent and the penny pinching. One of the first subcompact "economy cars," the VW Beetle, with its under-one-thousand-dollars price tag, served as a kind of reverse status symbol, identifying its owner as someone who didn't have a lot of money to spend. Realizing this, the advertisers for the Beetle decided to make a virtue

Drive my car: the new VW Beetle.

of necessity, and so used humor to market their product as a homely but sensible alternative in a marketplace of tail-finned extravagance and status sedans.

This humor, and the low cost of the Beetle, contributed to the next stage of VW's semiotic history, which intersected with the rise of the 1960s youth culture. For then the Beetle, along with its wildly popular Microbus cousin, became the car of the counterculture, a cheap set of wheels for freewheeling hippies who disdained the muscle cars, luxury chariots, and ordinary autos of the rest of America. Indeed, original Beetles and Microbuses — preferably plastered with Grateful Dead stickers — retain something of that significance to this day, mixing memory and nostalgia for many an aging baby boomer.

The Beetle disappeared from the American road in the seventies as the hippie scene turned yuppie and a host of more fuel-efficient Japanese subcompacts (in those days they were known simply as Toyotas and Datsuns) provided a more functional alternative in the wake of an exponential increase in gas prices. Volkswagen scrapped the Beetle and turned to the Rabbit, which has never had much cultural significance at all. But, as they say, that was then, and this is now. The question for our semiotic analysis is what does the Beetle signify today? It certainly isn't a sign of Nazi prosperity, nor is it simply a perky economy car (it's a bit too expensive for that). It's no signifier of the counterculture either. But it is a sign, a signifier of current popular cultural preoccupations. To see what it is a signifier of, we need to look at the current system in which the Beetle functions as a sign.

To establish the system in which a sign functions and gets its meaning, we need to look at some things with which the sign can be associated, or related, for from a semiotic perspective, the meaning of a sign largely lies in its relations to other signs, both in its similarities to them and in its differences. In other words, when looking at a popular cultural sign, you want to ask "what is this thing like?" as well as "how is it different from some of the things that it resembles?" By asking such questions, by establishing a set of associations and differences, you can approach the semiotic significance of your topic.

Let's return to the Beetle to see how this works. Ask yourself, with what things can the return of the Beetle be associated? It would be useful to begin with those products that are closest to it: other automobiles. But this association, while essential to our analysis, only takes us so far, because every year witnesses the introduction of new automobile lines as manufacturers seek to stimulate consumption through the introduction of new models and styles. The Beetle's return, in other words, is part of the system of automobile production and consumption, but without any way of distinguishing the Beetle from other cars within the system, its meaning would be limited to a "new car offering in a marketplace that continually offers new models in order to stimulate consumption." This *is* a part of the Beetle's meaning, but there is a lot more to it than that.

Here is where we can consider the role of *difference* in a semiotic analysis. Among the new model car offerings of the new millennium were a host of

SUVs, sedans, pickups, sports cars, subcompacts — in short, the whole array of automotive lines. What made the Beetle different was, in large part, the fact that it was a revival (with some modifications) of a popular, and culturally acclaimed, auto from the golden age of American motoring: the fifties and the sixties. What ended this era was the Arab oil embargo of 1973, which sent gas prices on an irreversible skyrocket and prompted carmakers to search for more functional and fuel-efficient automotive designs (Chrysler's bland K Car might represent the epitome of this chapter in automotive history). The Beetle, which was not as fuel efficient as the new subcompacts from Japan, was a casualty of the gasoline price spike, and it can be argued that the flair of automotive design was as well.

The return of the Beetle, then, marked a return to an earlier era of car design. So, what significance can we find in this? To answer this question, we can look back to the primary system in which the Beetle figures — the system of new car offerings at the turn of the millennium — and look for some more associations or similarities. And what we find are a number of other automobiles that represent the revival of earlier, largely abandoned styles from the golden age of American motoring. These include the return of the sporty two-seater, inaugurated by the Mazda Miata, whose success led to the reintroduction of many such cars, including the two-seated Thunderbird. We also saw the revival of the Mini, the creation of Chrysler's PT Cruiser, which, while a new design, was intended to suggest the styling of a fifties hot-rod jalopy, the Chevrolet HHR, and in 2005 the splashy and eagerly awaited revival of the original Ford Mustang.

So, there has been a pattern of what might be called nostalgic revivals in the automotive marketplace. This pattern already provides a clue to the cultural significance of the return of the Beetle, but before describing that meaning it would be useful to broaden our perspective a bit to see whether the pattern we have found within the system of car production can be found within the broader system of American consumer behavior. And, sure enough, it can. Indeed, the last decade has seen quite a number of revivals from the fifties and sixties. In 2001, for example, S&H Green Stamps, an icon of fifties and sixties consumer culture that disappeared years ago along with such relatives as Blue Chip Stamps and Plaid Stamps, staged a digitalized comeback as S&H greenpoints. In the realm of entertainment, movies such as *Ocean's Eleven* and *The Rat Pack*, along with the emergence of a lounge music scene, represented a revival of the Sinatra/Martin/Davis/Lewis/Bishop era. Then there has been the long-playing revival of retro clothing styles, especially from the 1970s, as well as any number of retro wristwatch designs from the 1920s and 1930s (not to mention the return of the pocket watch and chain).

We could continue searching for related revivals, but the outline of a significant pattern is already emerging. Clearly, the turn of the century witnessed a number of popular cultural retro revivals. Such revivals arguably signify a nostalgia for a bygone era, a desire to return to the products and images of the past. This raises yet another question: Why should Americans desire to return to the past?

Here you need to look at a much broader context in your semiotic analysis: the overall mood and state of American consciousness. By the end of the millennium, that mood was at once jaunty — in the wake of the huge stock market run-up of the nineties — and uncertain, as Americans worried about what Y2K would bring. At times of uncertainty, we tend to cling to what we know, the old verities as it were. In a consumer culture, those things include tried-and-true consumer goods, like, well, VW Beetles or Ford Thunderbirds. The return of such vehicles reflects a calculated gamble on the part of their manufacturers that Americans would embrace them as signifiers of a more certain and comforting past.

But wouldn't you interpret the owner of a Chevrolet HHR differently than the owner of a VW Beetle? Or what about a Thunderbird buyer? Or a Mini Cooper purchaser? All these cars can be associated together and all bear a similar meaning in one context, but there are also their differences to consider. These differences help to establish an even more precise significance for the Beetle, and so, to conclude our analysis, we must turn to them.

What differences can you note between the image of a Beetle owner and, say, a Mini Cooper driver? Though there may be a number of differences to note, gender difference is especially striking here, for the Beetle, with its bright green and yellow color options, as well as its low-octane cuteness, has especially become the choice of female consumers. With its relatively low, but not bargain basement, price tag, the Beetle has become a favorite choice for better-off young people, particularly women early in their careers. While not being nearly as culturally connotative as the Beetle of the sixties, then, the current model has already assumed a certain significance, sending an identifiable signal that is different from that sent by the more "masculine" Mini Cooper.

But after all, aren't these just a couple of small automobiles — motorized transportation with certain technical specifications? At one level, yes, of course. But at another level, they are a lot more than that. For while an object like a VW Beetle or Mini Cooper is indeed what it is — something with an objective, or *denotative*, meaning as a particular kind of automobile — it also has a culturally subjective *connotative* significance that goes well beyond the object itself, an image that it projects. It is the task of a semiotic analysis to find that image, the subtler, yet culturally more profound, connotational significance of things. Of course, you must first be able to recognize what the thing *is*, but you should not stop there. When you interpret people on the basis of the cars they drive — and Americans have always used their automobiles to make statements about themselves — you are moving from denotation to connotation, from the thing itself to the image that it projects *as a sign*. Marketers are well aware of this and are usually as concerned with the connotational significance of their products as they are with their objective substance. Semiotics helps you see those meanings more clearly and how they affect us throughout our everyday lives.

The Classroom Connection

The interpretive analysis of the VW Beetle we have sketched out here is intended to illustrate the kind of thought process that goes into a semiotic analysis. The historical surveying and contextualization, the comparative associations and analytic distinctions, and the drawing of interpretive conclusions that move from denotative to connotative significance are what come first in the writing process. Once you have done that, you will have your thesis, or argument, which will then form the structural backbone of your written analysis. Your paper will present that thesis and defend it with the evidence that your semiotic thinking produced. This process, in essence, is no different from the more conventional interpretive analyses you will be asked to perform in your college writing career. It is in the nature of all critical thinking to make connections and mark differences in order to go beyond the surface of a text or issue toward a meaning. The skills you already have as an interpreter of the popular signs around you — of images, objects, and forms of behavior — are the same skills that you develop as a writer of critical essays that present an argued point of view and the evidence to defend it.

Because most of us tend to identify closely with our favorite popular cultural phenomena and have strong opinions about them, it can be more difficult to adopt the same sort of analytic perspective toward popular culture that we do toward, say, texts assigned in a literature class. Still, that is what you should do in a semiotic interpretation: You need to set your opinions aside in order to pursue an interpretive argument with evidence to support it. Note how in our interpretation of the VW Beetle we didn't say whether or not we like the car: Our concern was what it might mean within a larger cultural context. It is not difficult to express an opinion, but that isn't the goal of analytic writing. Analytic writing requires the martialing of supporting evidence, just as a lawyer needs evidence to argue a case. So by learning to write analyses of our culture, by searching for supporting evidence to underpin your interpretive take on modern life, you are also learning to write critical arguments.

"But how," you (and perhaps your instructor) may ask, "can I know that a semiotic interpretation is right?" Good question — it is commonly asked by those who fear that a semiotic analysis might read too much into a subject. But then, it can also be asked of the writer of any interpretive essay, and the answer in each case is the same: No one can absolutely *prove* the truth of an argument in the human sciences; what you do is *persuade* your audience through the use of pertinent evidence. In writing analyses about popular culture, that evidence comes from your knowledge of the system to which the object you are interpreting belongs. The more you know about the system, the more convincing your interpretations will be. And that is true whether you are writing about popular culture or about more traditional academic subjects.

But often our interpretations of popular culture involve issues that are larger than those involved in music or entertainment. How, for instance, are we to analyze fully the widespread belief — as reflected in the classic sitcoms mentioned earlier — that it is more natural for women to stay at home and take care of the kids than it is for men to do so? Why, in other words, is the concept of housewife so easy to accept, while the idea of a househusband may seem ridiculous? How, in short, can we interpret some of our most basic values semiotically? To see how, we need to take a closer look at those values.

Of Myths and Men

As we have seen, in a semiotic analysis we do not search for the meanings of things in the things themselves. Rather, we find meaning in the way we can relate things together, through association and differentiation, moving from objective denotation to culturally subjective connotation. We've done this with the Volkswagen Beetle, but what about with beliefs? This book asks you to explore the implications of social issues like gender norms that involve a great many personal beliefs and values that we do not always recognize *as* beliefs and values. Rather, we think of them as truths ("Of course it's odd for a man to stay home and take care of the house!"). But from a semiotic perspective, our values too belong to systems from which they take their meaning. Semioticians call these systems of belief *cultural mythologies.*

A cultural mythology, or myth for short, is not some fanciful story from the past; indeed, if the word *myth* seems confusing because of its traditional association with such stories, you may prefer to use the term *value system.* Consider the value system that governs our traditional thinking about gender roles. Have you ever noticed how our society presumes that it is primarily the role of women — adult daughters — to take care of aging and infirm parents? If you want to look at the matter from a physiological perspective, it might seem that men would be better suited to the task: In a state of nature, men are physically stronger and so would seem to be the natural protectors of the aged. And yet, though our cultural mythology holds that men should protect the nuclear family, it tends to assign to women the care of extended families. It is culture that decides here, not nature.

But while cultural myths guide our behavior, they are subject to change. You may have already experienced a transitional phase in the myths surrounding courtship behavior. In the past, the gender myths that formed the rules of the American dating game held that it is the role of the male to initiate proceedings (he calls) and for the female to react (she waits by the phone). Similarly, the rules once held that it is invariably the responsibility of the male to plan the evening and pay the tab. These rules are changing, aren't they? Can you describe the rules that now govern courtship behavior?

A cultural mythology, or value system, then, is a kind of lens that governs the way we view our world. Think of it this way: Say you were born with rose-tinted eyeglasses permanently attached over your eyes, but you didn't know they were there. Because the world would *look* rose-colored to you, you would presume that it *is* rose-colored. You wouldn't wonder whether the world might look otherwise through different lenses. But in the world there are other kinds of eyeglasses with different lenses, and reality does look different to those who wear them. Those lenses are cultural mythologies, and no culture can claim to have the one set of glasses that sees things as they really are.

The profound effect our cultural mythologies have on the way we view reality, on our most basic values, is especially apparent today when the myths of European culture are being challenged by the worldviews of the many other cultures that have taken root in American soil. European American culture, for example, upholds a profoundly individualistic social mythology, valuing individual rights before those of the group, but traditional Chinese culture believes in the primacy of the family and the community over the individual. Maxine Hong Kingston's short story "No Name Woman" poignantly demonstrates how such opposing ideologies can collide with painful results in its tale of a Chinese woman who is more or less sacrificed to preserve the interests of her village. The story, from *The Woman Warrior* (1976), tells of a young woman who gives birth to a baby too many months after her husband's departure to America with most of her village's other young men for it to be her husband's child. The men had left for America in order to earn the money that keeps the impoverished villagers from starving. They may be away for years and so need to be assured that their wives will remain faithful to them in their absence lest they refuse to go at all. The unfortunate heroine of the tale — who, to sharpen the agony, had more likely been the victim of rape than the instigator of adultery — is horribly punished by the entire village as an example to any other wives who might disturb the system.

That Kingston wrote "No Name Woman" as a self-conscious Asian American, as one whose identity fuses both Chinese and Euro-American values, reveals the fault lines between conflicting mythologies. As an Asian, Kingston understands the communal values behind the horrific sacrifice of the No Name Woman, and her story makes sure that her Euro-American readers understand this too. But, as an American and as a feminist, she is outraged by the violation of an individual woman's rights on behalf of the group (or mob, which is as the village behaves in the story). Kingston's own sense of personal conflict in this clash of mythologies — Asian, American, and feminist — offers a striking example of the inevitable conflicts that America itself faces as it changes from a monocultural to a multicultural society.

To put this another way, from the semiotic perspective, how you interpret something is very much a product of who you are, for culture is just another name for the frames that shape our values and perceptions. Traditionally, American education has presumed a monocultural perspective, a melting-pot view that no matter what one's cultural background, truth is culture-blind. Langston Hughes took on this assumption many years ago in his classic poem "Theme for English B," where he observes, "I guess I'm what / I feel and see and hear," and wonders whether "my page will be colored" when he writes. "Being me, it will not be white," the poet suggests, but while he struggles to find what he holds in common with his white instructor, he can't suppress the differences. In essence, that is the challenge of multicultural education itself: to identify the different cultural codes that inform the mythic frameworks of the many cultures that share America while searching for what holds the whole thing together.

That meaning is not culture-blind, that it is conditioned by systems of ideology and belief that are codified differently by different cultures, is a foundational semiotic judgment. Human beings, in other words, construct their own social realities, and so who gets to do the constructing becomes very important. Every contest over a cultural code is, accordingly, a contest for power, but the contest is usually masked because the winner generally defines its mythology as the truth, as what is most natural or reasonable. Losers in the contest become objects of scorn and are quickly marginalized, declared unnatural, or deviant, or even insane. The stakes are high as myth battles myth, with truth itself as the highest prize.

This does not mean that you must abandon your own beliefs when conducting a semiotic analysis, only that you cannot take them for granted and must be prepared to argue for them. We want to assure you that semiotics will not tell you what to think and believe. It *does* assume that what you believe reflects some cultural system or other and that no cultural system can claim absolute validity or superiority. The readings and chapter introductions in this book contain their own values and ideologies, and if you wish to challenge those values you can begin by exposing the myths that they may take for granted.

To put this another way, everything in this book reflects a political point of view, and if you hold a different one it is not enough to simply presuppose the innate superiority of your own point of view — to claim that one writer is being political while you are simply telling the truth. This may sound heretical precisely because human beings operate within value systems whose political invisibility is guaranteed by the system. No mythology, that is to say, begins by saying, "this is just a political construct or interpretation." Every myth begins, "this is the truth." It is very difficult to imagine, from within the myth, any alternatives. Indeed, as you read this book, you may find it upsetting to see that some traditional beliefs — such as the "proper" roles of men and women in society — are socially constructed and not absolute. But the outlines of the myth, the bounding (and binding) frame, best appear when challenged by another myth, and this challenge is probably nowhere more insistent than in America, where so many of us are really "hyphenated" Americans, citizens combining two (or more) cultural traditions in our own persons.

Getting Started

Mythology, like culture, is not static, however, and so the semiotician must always keep his or her eye on the clock, so to speak. History, time itself, is a constant factor in a constantly changing world. Since the earlier editions of this book, American popular culture has moved on. In this edition, we have tried to reflect those changes, but inevitably, further changes will occur in the time it takes for this book to appear on your class syllabus. That such changes occur is part of the excitement of the semiotic enterprise: There is always something new to consider and interpret. What does not change is the nature of semiotic interpretation: Whatever you choose to analyze in the realm of American popular culture, the semiotic approach will help you understand it.

It's your turn now. Start asking questions, pushing, probing. That's what critical thinking and writing is all about, but this time you're part of the question. Arriving at answers, conclusions, is the fun part here, but answers aren't the basis of analytic thinking: questions are. You always begin with a question, a query, a hypothesis, something to explore. If you already knew the answer, there would be no point in conducting the analysis. We leave you to it to explore the almost infinite variety of questions that the readings in this book raise. Many come equipped with their own "answers," but you may (indeed will and should) find such answers raise further questions. To help you ask those questions, keep in mind the three elemental principles of semiotics that we have explored so far:

1. The meaning of a sign can be found not in itself but in its *relationships* (both differences and similarities) with other signs within a *system*. To interpret an individual sign, then, you must determine the general system in which it belongs.
2. Things have both *denotative* (what they *are*) and *connotative* meanings (what they *suggest* as *signs*); semiotics seeks to go beyond the denotative surface to the connotative sign.
3. What we call social "reality" is a human construct, the product of a *cultural mythology* or *value system* that intervenes between our minds and the world we experience. Such cultural myths reflect the values and ideological interests of its builders, not the laws of nature or logic.

Perhaps our first principle could be more succinctly phrased, "everything is connected," our second, "don't stop at the surface," and our third might be simply summarized, "question authority." Think of them that way if it helps. Or just ask yourself whenever you are interpreting something, "what's going on here?" In short, question *everything*. And one more reminder: Signs are like weather vanes; they point in response to invisible historical winds. We invite you now to start looking at the weather.

PORTFOLIO
Images from the History
of Popular Culture

You Tube
Broadcast Yourself™

| Home | Videos | Channels | Community |

| | Videos ▾ | Search | settings / advanced search | | Upload |

Evolution of Dance

Rate: ★★★★☆ 309,341 ratings   **Views:** 83,516,919

| ✉ Share | ♥ Favorite | 📋 Playlists | 🚩 Flag |

🔲 MySpace   📘 Facebook   Digg   (more share options)

Also Watching Now (1)
📺 jaketvee

| Commentary | Statistics & Data |

Video Responses: **20**   Text Comments: **148,786**

▼ **Video Responses (20)**   Post a Video Response

‹
| 00:19 funnyman... | 02:02 gooshay | 00:12 EvilFist | 04:05 TheMaste... |
›

View All - Play All

▼ **Text Comments (148,786)**   Post a Text Comment

Show: average (-5 or better) ▾ Help

ColoradoHero (2 minutes ago)   Reply   0 👎 👍
wow this video has the most views of any video i have seen

ikekll (24 minutes ago)   Reply   0 👎 👍
alanmorri - why ya yawnin' - go do your homework...
say, are you in college?
:>

ninedu (25 minutes ago)   Reply   0 👎 👍
The king of youtube

	From: **judsonlaipply**	
	Joined: 2 years ago	**Subscribe**
	Videos: **2**	

Added: **April 06, 2006**   (More info)
The funniest 6 minutes you will ever see! Remem...

Embed: Customize

`<object width="425" height="355"> <param name="movie" value="h`

▶ **More From: judsonlaipply**

▼ **Related Videos**

	robot dance 01:42 From: swingcheese Views: 16,140,501
	Evolution Of Dance - lol :-) 00:39 From: pigeyedpeas Views: 1,998,749
	OK Go - Here It Goes Again 03:04 From: OkGo Views: 33,650,542
	Evolution of Dance for the rest of us 00:37 From: DCLugi Views: 1,466,029
	Street Dancers 07:35 From: shinzinhu Views: 394,748

Promoted Videos

| Air - Alpha Beta Gaga 04:24 Astralwerks | Tom Cruise 's butt... a... 02:39 valsartdiary | Diff'ren t Strokes Minis... 04:02 MinisodeNet... | Sweeney Todd | Real Guy... 03:13 realguys |

READING THE SIGNS

1. Identify each of the images in the portfolio. To what decade does each belong? Is your class as a whole more familiar with some images than others?

2. In what ways do these images represent American popular culture? What, in your opinion, makes for a lasting mark on popular culture?

3. Does the portfolio of images suggest something about the changing nature of popular culture? Explain your answer.

4. If you were asked to select an image not included in the portfolio that represents some key aspect of popular culture, what image would you choose? Why?

WRITING ABOUT POPULAR CULTURE

Throughout this book, you will find readings on popular culture that you can use as models for your own writing or as subjects to which you may respond, assignments for writing critical essays on popular culture, and semiotic tips to help you analyze a wide variety of cultural phenomena. As you approach these readings and assignments, you may find it helpful to review the following suggestions for writing critical essays — whether on popular culture or on any subject — as well as some examples of student essays written in response to assignments based on *Signs of Life in the U.S.A.* Mastering the skills summarized and exemplified here should prepare you for writing the kinds of papers you will be assigned through the rest of your college career.

As you prepare to write a critical essay on popular culture, remember that you are already an expert in your subject. Being an expert doesn't necessarily mean spending years of study in a library; simply by actively participating in everyday life, you have accumulated a vast store of knowledge about what makes our culture tick. Just think about all you know about movies, or the thousands on thousands of ads you've seen, or even the many unwritten "rules" governing courtship behavior among your circle of friends. All of these help form the fabric of contemporary American culture — and, if you've ever had to explain to a younger sibling why her latest outfit was inappropriate for work or why his comment to a blind date struck the wrong chord, you've already played the role of expert.

Because popular culture is part of everyday life, however, you may take for granted this knowledge: It might not seem that it can "count" as material for a college-level assignment, and you might not think to include it in an essay.

Thus, it can be useful to spend some time, before you start writing, to generate your ideas freely and openly: Your goal at this point is to develop as many ideas as possible, even ones that you might not actually use in your essay. Writing instructors call this process *prewriting*, and it's a step you should take when writing on any subject in any class, not just in your writing class. This textbook includes many suggestions for how you can develop your ideas; even if your instructor doesn't require you to use all of them, you can try them on your own.

Developing Ideas about Popular Culture

The first step in developing your ideas for an essay about any topic is to make sure you understand accurately the reading selections that your instructor has assigned. You want to engage in *active* reading — that is, you want not simply to get the "drift" of a passage but to understand the nuances of how the author constructs his or her argument. With any selection, it can be helpful to read at least twice: first, to gain a general sense of the author's ideas and, second, to study more specifically how those ideas are put together to form an argument. Ask yourself questions, such as the following, that enable you to evaluate the selection:

- What is the **author's primary argument**? Can you identify a **thesis** statement, or is the thesis implied?
- What words or **key terms** are fundamental to that argument? If the fundamental vocabulary of the selection is unfamiliar to you, be sure to check a dictionary or encyclopedia for the word's meaning.
- What **evidence** does the author provide to support the argument?
- What **underlying assumptions** shape the author's position? Does the author consider alternative points of view (counterarguments)?
- What **style** and **tone** does the author adopt?
- What is the **genre** of the piece? You need to take into account what kind of writing you are responding to, for different kinds have different purposes and goals. A personal narrative, for instance, expresses the writer's experiences and beliefs, but you shouldn't expect it to present a fully demonstrated argument.
- Who is the **intended readership** of this selection, and does it affect the author's reasoning or evidence?

As you read, take notes in your book. Doing so will help you both remember and analyze what you read. A pencil or pen is probably the best memory aid ever invented. No one, not even the most experienced and perceptive reader, remembers everything — and let's face it, not everything that you read is worth remembering. Writing annotations as you read will lead you back to important points. And annotating helps you start analyzing a reading — long before you have to start writing an essay — rather than uncritically accepting what's on the page.

Learning to read actively means *interacting* with what you read by responding: You should question, summarize, agree with, refute what the author says. It means that you're having a kind of conversation with the author rather than simply listening to a lecture by an expert. Studies have shown that such interactive learning simply works better than passive learning; if you read actively, you'll gain knowledge at a higher rate and retain it longer.

There's another reason to annotate what you read: You can use the material you've identified as the starting point for your journal notes and essays; and since it doesn't take long to circle a word or jot a note in the margin, you can save a great deal of time in the long run. Note that we suggest using a pencil or pen, not a highlighter. While using a highlighter is better than using nothing — it will at least help you identify key points — writing *words* in your book goes an important step further in helping you analyze what you read. We've seen entire pages bathed in fluorescent yellow highlighter, and that's of doubtful use in finding the important stuff. Of course, if you simply can't bring yourself to mark up your book, you can write on sticky notes instead, and put those in the margins.

So as you read, circle key words, note transitions between ideas, jot definitions of unfamiliar terms (you can likely guess their meaning from the context or look them up later), underline phrases or terms to research on a search engine such as Google, write short summaries of important points, or simply note where you're confused or lost with a question mark or a *huh?!* In fact, figuring out exactly what parts you do and don't understand is one of the best ways to tackle a difficult reading. Frequently, the confusing bits turn out to be the most interesting — and sometimes the most important. We're not suggesting that you cover your pages with notes; often a few words get the job done. Responding to what you read *as* you read will help you become a more active reader — and that will ultimately help you become a stronger writer.

To illustrate what we mean, let's look at the first two paragraphs of an essay that appears in Chapter 7, along with a reader's annotations of it.

Emily Prager

Our Barbies, Ourselves

Our Bodies, Ourselves, very funny

        I read an astounding obituary in the *New York Times* not too long ago. It concerned the death of one *Jack Ryan.*

Who is Zsa Zsa?

A former husband of Zsa Zsa Gabor, it said, Mr. Ryan had been an inventor and designer during his lifetime. A man of eclectic creativity, he designed Sparrow and Hawk missiles when he worked for the Raytheon Company, and, the notice said, when he consulted for Mattel he designed Barbie.

eclectic = widely varied

a guy designed B.

I never wonder who designed B.

If Barbie was designed by a man, *suddenly a lot of things made sense* to me, things I'd wondered about for years. I used to look at Barbie and wonder, What's wrong with this picture? What kind of woman designed this doll? Let's be honest: Barbie looks like someone who got her start at the Playboy Mansion. She could be a regular guest on *The Howard Stern Show*. It is a fact of Barbie's design that her breasts are so out of proportion to the rest of her body that if she were a human woman, she'd fall flat on her face.

Yeah!

Here, the title reminds the reader of a book title he recalls (*Our Bodies, Ourselves*); he knows it addresses women, and he thinks the allusion is funny. Then he wonders who the woman with the funny name is (Zsa Zsa Gabor), defines an unfamiliar word (*eclectic*), and notes an important point (that a man, and not a woman, designed the Barbie doll). These comments are brief and were made quickly, but they can help the reader remember details for class discussion and journal entries.

Signs of Life in the U.S.A. frequently asks you to respond to a reading selection in your journal, sometimes directly and sometimes indirectly, as in suggestions that you write a letter to the author of a selection. In doing so, you're taking an important step in articulating your response to the issues and to the author's presentation of them. In asking you to keep a journal or a reading log, your instructor will probably be less concerned with your writing style than with your comprehension of assigned readings and your thoughtful responses to them. Let's say you're asked to write your response to Emily Prager. You should first think through exactly what Prager is saying — what her point is — by using the questions listed and by reviewing your annotations. Then consider how you feel about it. If you agree with Prager's belief that the Barbie doll perpetuates outmoded ideas about women, why do you feel that way? Can you think of other objects (or even people) that seem to exemplify those same ideas? What alternative ways of designing a doll can you imagine? Note that the purpose of imagining your own doll is not so you'll actually produce one; it's so you think through alternatives and explore the implications of Prager's and your own thoughts. Or say you're irritated by Prager's argument: Again, why do you feel that way? What would you say to her in response? What, perhaps in your own experience as a child, might show that she's wrong? Your aim in jotting all this down is not to produce a draft of an essay. It's to play with your own ideas, see where they lead, and even just help you decide what your ideas are in the first place.

Signs of Life in the U.S.A. includes many visual images, along with accompanying questions for analysis in many cases. The semiotic method lends itself especially well to visual analysis. Here are some questions to consider as you look at images:

- What is the **format of the image**? Is it black and white? Color? Glossy? Consider how the form in which the image is expressed affects its message. If an image is composed of primary colors, does it look fun and lively, for instance?

- What **kind of image** is it? Is it abstract, does it represent an actual person or place, or is it a combination of the two? If there are people represented, who are they?

- Who is the intended **audience** for the image? Is it an artistic photograph or a commercial work, such as an advertisement? If it is an ad, to what kind of person is it directed? Where is the ad placed? If it is in a magazine, consider the audience for the publication.

- What **emotions** does the image convey? Overall, is it serious, sad, funny? Is that expression of emotion, in your opinion, intentional? What emotional associations do you make with the image?

- If the image includes more than one element, what is the most prominent element in the **composition**? A particular section? A logo? A section of writing? A person or group of people? A product? What do each of the parts contribute to the whole?

- How does the **layout** of the image lead your eye? Are you drawn to any specific part? What is the order in which you look at the various parts? Does any particular section immediately jump out?

- Does the image include **text**? If so, how do the image and the text relate to one another?

- Does the image call for a **response**? For instance, does it suggest that you purchase a product? If so, what claims does it make?

Let's look at a sample analysis of an advertisement using the preceding questions (see image on p. 38).

Format: Although this image is reproduced here in black and white, it originally appeared in color. The colors are muted, however, almost sepia-toned, and thus suggest an old-fashioned look.

Kind of image: This is a fairly realistic image, with a patina of rural nostalgia. A solitary woman, probably in her twenties or thirties, but perhaps older, is set against an empty natural expanse. She has a traditional hairstyle evocative of the 1950s or early 1960s and leads an old-fashioned bicycle with a wicker basket attached.

Audience: This image is an advertisement for Lee jeans. The intended audience is likely a woman in her late twenties or older. We see only the model's back, and so she is faceless. That allows the viewer to project herself into the scene, and the nostalgic look suggests that the viewer could imagine herself at a younger time in her life. Note that the product is "stretch" jeans. There's no

suggestion, often made, that the jeans will enhance a woman's sexual appeal; rather, the claim is that the jeans are practical — and will fit a body beyond the teen years. Note the sensible hairstyle and shoes. For an interesting contrast you might compare this ad to one for Guess? jeans.

Emotion: The woman's body language suggests individuality and determination; she's literally "going it alone." She's neither posing for nor aware of the viewer, suggesting that "what you see is what you get." And, perhaps, she doesn't particularly care what you think.

Composition and layout: The layout of the ad is carefully designed to lead your eye: The hill slopes down from top right toward middle left, and the bike draws your eye from bottom right to mid-left, with both lines converging on the product, the jeans. For easy readability, the text is included at the top against the blank sky.

Text: The message, "The things that give a woman substance will never appear on any 'what's in/what's out' list," suggests that Lee Jeans is a product for those women who aren't interested in following trends, but rather want a good, old-fashioned value — "substance," not frivolity.

Response: Lee Jeans would prefer, naturally, that the viewer of the ad buy the product. She would identify with the woman wearing the jeans in the advertisement and be convinced that these practical (if not particulary fashionable) jeans would be a good purchase.

In sum, most fashion ads stress the friends (and often, mates) you will attract if you buy the product, but this ad presents "a road not taken," suggesting the American ideology of marching to the beat of a different drummer, the kind of old-fashioned individualism that brings to mind Robert Frost and Henry David Thoreau. The pastoral surroundings and the "old painting" effect echo artists such as Andrew Wyeth and Norman Rockwell. All of these impressions connote lasting American values (rural, solid, middle American) that are meant to be associated with anti-trendiness and enduring qualities, such as individualism and practicality. And these impressions suggest the advertisers carefully and effectively kept the ad's semiotic messages in mind as they designed it.

These strategies will work when you are asked to respond to a particular reading or image. Sometimes, though, you may be asked to write about a more general subject. Often your instructor may ask you to brainstorm ideas or to freewrite in response to an issue. These are both strategies you can use in your journal or on your own as you start working on an essay. Brainstorming is simply amassing as many relevant (and even some irrelevant) ideas as possible. Let's say your instructor asks you to brainstorm a list of popular toys used by girls and boys in preparation for an essay about the gendered designs of children's toys. Try to list your thoughts freely, jotting down whatever comes to mind. Don't censor yourself at this point. That is, don't worry if something is really a toy or a game, or if it is used by both boys and girls, or if it really is an adult toy. Later on you can throw out ideas that don't fit. What you'll be left with is a rich list of examples that you can then study and analyze. Freewriting works much the same way and is particularly useful when you're not sure of how you feel about an issue. Sit down and just start writing or typing, and don't stop until you've written for at least ten or fifteen minutes. Let your ideas wander around your subject, working associatively, following their own path. As with brainstorming, you may produce some irrelevant ideas, but you may also come to a closer understanding of how you really feel about an issue.

Sometimes your instructor may invite you to create your own topic. Where should you start? Let's say you decide to analyze an aspect of the film industry but can't decide on a focus. Here, the Internet might help. You could explore a search engine such as Yahoo!, specifically its Movies and Films index. There you'll find dozens of subcategories, such as History, Theory and Criticism, Cultures and Groups, and Trivia. Each of these subcategories has many sites to explore: History, for instance, includes the Archives of Early Lindy Hop as well as the Bill Douglas Centre for the History of Cinema and Popular Culture, a wonderful compendium of 25,000 books, posters, and other movie-related memorabilia. With so many sites to choose from, you're bound to find something that interests you. The Net, in effect, allows you to engage in electronic brainstorming and to arrive at your topic.

One cautionary note: In using the Internet to brainstorm, be sure to evaluate the appropriateness of your sources. Many sites are commercial and therefore are intended more to sell a product or image than to provide reliable information. In addition, since anyone with the technological know-how can set up a Web site, some sites (especially personal home pages) amount to little more than personal expression and need to be evaluated for their reliability, accuracy, and authenticity. Scrutinize the sites you use carefully: Is the author an authority in the field? Does the site identify the author, at least by name and e-mail address (be wary of fully anonymous sites)? Does the site contain interesting and relevant links? If you find an advocacy site, one that openly advances a special interest, does the site's bias interfere with the accuracy of its information? Asking such questions can help ensure that your electronic brainstorming is fruitful and productive. If you are not sure of the validity of a Web site, you might want to check with your instructor.

Not all prewriting activities need be solitary, of course. In fact, *Signs of Life* includes lots of suggestions that ask you to work with other students, either in your class or from across campus. We do that because much academic work really is collaborative and collegial. When a scientist is conducting research, for instance, he or she often works with a team, may present preliminary findings to colloquia or conferences, and may call or e-mail a colleague at another school to try out some ideas. There's no reason you can't benefit from the social nature of academic thinking as well. But be aware that such in-class group work is by no means "busy work." The goal, rather, is to help you to develop and shape your understanding of the issues and your attitudes toward them. If you're asked to study how a product is packaged with three classmates, for instance, you're starting to test Thomas Hine's thesis in

"What's in a Package" (Chapter 1), seeing how it applies or doesn't apply and benefiting from your peers' insights.

Let's say you're asked to present to the class a semiotic reading of a childhood toy. By discussing a favorite toy with your class, you are articulating, perhaps for the first time, what it meant (or means) to you and so are taking the first step toward writing a more formal analysis of it in an essay (especially if you receive feedback and comments from your class). Similarly, if you stage an in-class debate over whether Batman is a gay character, you're amassing a wonderful storehouse of arguments, counterarguments, and evidence to consider when you write your own essay that either supports or refutes Andy Medhurst's thesis in "Batman, Deviance, and Camp" (Chapter 7). As with other strategies to develop your ideas, you may not use directly every idea generated in conversation with your classmates, but that's okay. You should find yourself better able to sort through and articulate the ideas that you do find valuable.

Developing Strong Arguments about Popular Culture

We expect that students will write many different sorts of papers in response to the selections in this book. You may write personal experience narratives, opinion pieces, research papers, formal pro-con arguments, and many others. We'd like here to focus on writing analytic essays because the experience of analyzing popular culture may seem different from that of analyzing other subjects. Occasionally we've had students who feel reluctant to analyze popular culture because they think that analysis requires them to trash their subject, and they don't want to write a "negative" essay about what may be their favorite film or TV program. Or a few students may feel uncertain because "it's all subjective." Since most people have opinions about popular culture, they say, how can any one essay be stronger than another?

While these concerns are understandable, they needn't be an obstacle in writing a strong analytic paper — whether on popular culture or any other topic. First, we often suggest that you set aside your own personal tastes when writing an analysis. We do so not because your preferences are not important; recall that we often ask you to explore your beliefs in your journal, and we want you to be aware of your own attitudes and observations about your topic. Rather, we do so because an analysis of, say, *The Aviator* is not the same as a paper that explains "why I like (or dislike) this movie." Instead, an analysis would explain how it works, what cultural beliefs and viewpoints underlie it, what its significance is, and so forth. And such a paper would not necessarily be positive or negative; it would seek to explain how the elements of the film work together to have a particular effect on its audience. If your instructor asks you to write a critical analysis or a critical argument, he or she is requesting neither a hit job nor a celebration of your topic.

As a result, the second concern, about subjectivity, becomes less of a problem. That's because your analysis should center around a clear argument about that movie. You're not simply presenting a personal opinion about it; rather, you're presenting a central insight about how the movie works, and you need to demonstrate it with logical, specific evidence. It's that evidence that will take your essay out of the category of being "merely subjective." You should start with your own opinion, but you want to add to it lots of proof that shows the legitimacy of that opinion. Does that sound familiar? It should, because that's what you need to do in any analytic essay, no matter what your subject matter happens to be.

When writing about popular culture, students sometimes wonder what sort of evidence they can use to support their points. Your instructor will probably give you guidelines for each assignment, but we'll provide some general suggestions here. Start with your subject itself. You'll find it's useful to view your subject — whether it's an ad, a film, or anything else — as a text that you can "read" closely. That's what you would do if you were asked to analyze a poem: You would read it carefully, studying individual words, images, rhythm, and so forth, and those details would support whatever point you wanted to make about the poem. Read your pop culture subject with the same care. Let's say your instructor asks you to analyze a photograph. Look at the details: Who appears in the photo, and what are their expressions? What props are used, and what is the "story" that the photo tells? Is there anything missing from this scene that you would expect to find? Your answers to such questions could form the basis of the evidence that you use in your essay.

If your instructor has asked you to write a semiotic analysis, you can develop evidence as well by locating your subject within a larger system. Recall that a system is the larger network of related signs to which your subject belongs and that identifying it helps to reveal the significance of your subject. This may sound hard to do, but it is through identifying a system that you can draw on your own vast knowledge of popular culture. And that may sound abstract, but it becomes very specific when applied to a particular example. If you were to analyze platform shoes, for instance, it would help to locate them within the larger fashion system — specifically, other choices of footwear. How do the signals sent by wearing a pair of platforms differ from those sent by wearing, say, a pair of Doc Martens? How does the history of platform shoes, specifically their popularity in the 1970s, affect their current appeal? Can you associate the retro look of platforms with any other fashion and popular cultural trends? Teasing out such differences and associations can help you explain the shoes' social and cultural significance.

You can strengthen your argument as well if you know and use the history of your subject. That might sound like you have to do a lot of library research, but often you don't have to: You may already be familiar with the social and cultural history of your subject. If you know, for instance, that the baggy pants so popular among teens in the mid-1990s were a few years before ubiquitous among street-gang members, you know an important historical detail that goes a long way toward explaining their significance. Depending on your assignment, you might want to expand on your own historical knowledge and collect other data about your topic, perhaps through surveys and interviews. If you're analyzing gendered patterns of courtship rituals, for instance, you could interview some people from different age groups, as well as both genders, to get a sense of how such patterns have evolved over time. The material you gather through such an interview will be raw data, and you'll want to do more than just "dump" the information into your essay. See this material instead as an original body of evidence that you'll sort through (you probably won't use every scrap of information), study, and interpret in its own right.

SCOTT JASCHIK
A Stand against Wikipedia

Increasingly, college faculty are concerned about the widespread use of Wikipedia in student research and writing. The problem, as faculty see it, is twofold. First, there is the problem of reliability. Wikipedia does strive to provide reliable information, but given the wide open nature of the site — anyone can contribute — ensuring accuracy is not really possible. This leads to student work that simply disseminates misinformation. Second, even where Wikipedia is accurate (and it can be an accurate source of information), it is, after all, an encyclopedia, and while encyclopedic sources may be suitable for background information, students performing college-level research should seek primary sources and academic-level secondary sources that they find on their own. The following article from insidehighered.com surveys the problems with Wikipedia as a research source as seen by college faculty from a number of universities.

As Wikipedia has become more and more popular with students, some professors have become increasingly concerned about the online, reader-produced encyclopedia.

While plenty of professors have complained about the lack of accuracy or completeness of entries, and some have discouraged or tried to bar students from using it, the history department at Middlebury College is trying to take a stronger, collective stand. It voted this month to bar students from citing the Web site as a source in papers or other academic work. All faculty members will be telling students about the policy and explaining why material on Wikipedia — while convenient — may not be trustworthy. "As educators, we are in the business of reducing the dissemination of misinformation," said Don Wyatt, chair of the department. "Even though Wikipedia may have some value, particularly from the value of leading students to citable sources, it is not itself an appropriate source for citation," he said.

The department made what Wyatt termed a consensus decision on the issue after discussing problems professors were seeing as students cited incorrect information from Wikipedia in papers and on tests. In one instance, Wyatt said, a professor noticed several students offering the same incorrect information, from Wikipedia. There was some discussion in the department of trying to ban students from using Wikipedia, but Wyatt said that didn't seem appropriate. Many Wikipedia entries have good bibliographies, Wyatt said. And any absolute ban would just be ignored. "There's the issue of freedom of access," he said. "And I'm not in the business of promulgating unenforceable edicts."

Wyatt said that the department did not specify punishments for citing Wikipedia, and that the primary purpose of the policy was to educate, not to be punitive. He said he doubted that a paper would be rejected for having a single Wikipedia footnote, but that students would be told that they shouldn't do so, and that multiple violations would result in reduced grades or even a failure. "The important point that we wish to communicate to all students taking courses and submitting work in our department in the future is that they cite Wikipedia at their peril," he said. He stressed that the objection of the department to Wikipedia wasn't its online nature, but its unedited nature, and he said students need to be taught to go for quality information, not just convenience.

The frustrations of Middlebury faculty members are by no means unique. 5 Last year, Alan Liu, a professor of English at the University of California at Santa Barbara, adopted a policy that Wikipedia "is not appropriate as the primary or sole reference for anything that is central to an argument, complex, or controversial." Liu said that it was too early to tell what impact his policy is having. In explaining his rationale — which he shared with an e-mail list — he wrote that he had "just read a paper about the relation between structuralism, deconstruction, and postmodernism in which every reference was to the Wikipedia articles on those topics with no awareness that there was any need to read a primary work or even a critical work."

Wikipedia officials agree — in part — with Middlebury's history department. "That's a sensible policy," Sandra Ordonez, a spokeswoman, said in an e-mail interview. "Wikipedia is the ideal place to start your research and get a global picture of a topic; however, it is not an authoritative source. In fact, we recommend that students check the facts they find in Wikipedia against other sources. Additionally, it is generally good research practice to cite an original source when writing a paper, or completing an exam. It's usually not advisable, particularly at the university level, to cite an encyclopedia." Ordonez acknowledged that, given the collaborative nature of Wikipedia writing and editing, "there is no guarantee an article is 100 percent correct," but she said that the site is shifting its focus from growth to improving quality, and that the site is a great resource for students. "Most articles are continually being edited and improved upon, and most contributors are real lovers of knowledge who have a real desire to improve the quality of a particular article," she said.

Experts on digital media said that the Middlebury history professors' reaction was understandable and reflects growing concern among faculty members about the accuracy of what students find online. But some worry that bans on citing Wikipedia may not deal with the underlying issues.

Roy Rosenzweig, director of the Center for History and New Media at George Mason University, did an analysis of the accuracy of Wikipedia for the *Journal of American History*, and he found that in many entries, Wikipedia was as accurate or more accurate than more traditional encyclopedias. He said that the quality of material was inconsistent, and that biographical entries were generally well done, while more thematic entries were much less so. Like Ordonez, he said the real problem is one of college students using encyclopedias when they should be using more advanced sources. "College students shouldn't be citing encyclopedias in their papers," he said. "That's not what college is about. They either should be using primary sources or serious secondary sources."

In the world of college librarians, a major topic of late has been how to guide students in the right direction for research, when Wikipedia and similar sources are so easy. Some of those who have been involved in these discussions said that the Middlebury history department's action pointed to the need for more outreach to students. Lisa Hinchliffe, head of the undergraduate library and coordinator of information literacy at the University of Illinois at Urbana-Champaign, said that earlier generations of students were in fact taught when it was appropriate (or not) to consult an encyclopedia and why for many a paper they would never even cite a popular magazine or nonscholarly work. "But it was a relatively constrained landscape," and students didn't have easy access to anything equivalent to Wikipedia, she said. "It's not that students are being lazy today. It's a much more complex environment."

When she has taught, and spotted footnotes to sources that aren't appropriate, she's considered that "a teachable moment," Hinchliffe said. She said that she would be interested to see how Middlebury professors react when they get the first violations of their policy, and said she thought there could be positive discussions about why sources are or aren't good ones. That kind of teaching, she said, is important "and can be challenging."

Steven Bell, associate librarian for research and instructional services at Temple University, said of the Middlebury approach: "I applaud the effort for wanting to direct students to good quality resources," but he said he would go about it in a different way. "I understand what their concerns are. There's no question that [on Wikipedia and similar sites] some things are great and some things are questionable. Some of the pages could be by eighth graders," he said. "But to simply say 'don't use that one' might take students in the wrong direction from the perspective of information literacy."

Students face "an ocean of information" today, much of it of poor quality, so a better approach would be to teach students how to "triangulate" a source like Wikipedia, so they could use other sources to tell whether a given entry could be trusted. "I think our goal should be to equip students with the critical thinking skills to judge."

PATTI S. CARAVELLO
Judging Quality on the Web

> *When you conduct research on the Internet, you'll find a dizzying range of sources, from academic journals to government Web sites, from newspapers and popular magazines to blogs, wikis, and social networking and file-sharing sites. Having a plethora of sources at hand with just the click of a mouse has been a boon to researchers in all fields. But the very democratic basis of the Internet that makes all this information so readily available creates a challenge, for it comes with no guarantees of quality control. Indeed, it is incumbent upon you, the researcher, to determine the reliability of the Web sources that you use. The following article from the UCLA Library's Web site, "Judging Quality on the Web," lists criteria that will allow you to evaluate the usefulness and reliability of Internet sources.*

Even after refining a query in a search engine, a researcher often retrieves a huge number of Web sites. It is essential to know how to evaluate Web sites for the same reasons you would evaluate a periodical article or a book: *to ascertain whether you can rely on the information, to identify its inherent biases or limitations, and to see how or whether it fits into your overall research strategy*.

A good (useful, reliable) Web site:

1. Clearly states the author and/or organizational **source** of the information
   Your task:
   - Consider the qualifications, other works, and organizational affiliation of the author
   - Look up the organization which produced the Web site (if it's unfamiliar) to identify its credentials, viewpoint, or agenda
   - If the source is an E-journal, discover whether it is refereed (reviewed by scholars before it is accepted for publication)

2. Clearly states the **date** the material was written and the date the site was last revised
   Your task:
   - If the information is not current enough for your purposes or the date is not given, look elsewhere

3. Provides **accurate** data whose parameters are clearly defined
   Your task:
   - Compare the data found on the Web site with data found in other sources (encyclopedias, reference books, articles, etc.) for accuracy, completeness, recency
   - Ask a librarian about other important sources to check for this information

4. Provides the **type and level** of information you need
   Your task:
   - Decide whether the level of detail and comprehensiveness, the treatment of the topic (e.g., scholarly or popular), and the graphics or other features are acceptable
   - If the site does not provide the depth of coverage you need, look elsewhere

5. Keeps **bias** to a minimum, and clearly indicates point of view
   Your task:
   - Be aware that producing a Web page does not require the checking and review that publishing a scholarly book requires; you might have retrieved nothing but someone's personal opinion on the topic
   - Appealing graphics can distract you from noticing even overt bias, so heighten your skepticism and examine the evidence (source, date, accuracy, level, links)

6. Provides live **links** to related high quality Web sites
   Your task:
   - Click on several of the links provided to see if they are active (or if they give an "error" message indicating the links are not being maintained) and to see if they are useful
   - Check to see if the criteria are stated for selecting the links

7. In the case of **commercial** sites, keeps advertising separate from content, and does not let advertisers determine content
   Your task:
   - Look at the Web address: Sites that are commercial have *.com* in their addresses and might have advertising or offer to sell something. The *.com* suffix is also found in news sites (e.g., newspapers, TV networks) and personal pages (sites created by individuals who have purchased a domain name but who may or may not have a commercial or in-stitutional affiliation)

8. Is clearly organized and **designed** for ease of use
    Your task:
    - Move around the page to see if its organization makes sense and it is easy to return to the top or to the sections you need
    - Decide whether the graphics enhance the content or detract from it

Reading Essays about Popular Culture

In your writing course, it's likely that your instructor will ask you to work in groups with other students, perhaps reviewing each other's rough drafts. You'll find many benefits to this activity. Not only will you receive more feedback on your own in-progress work, but you will see other students' ideas and approaches to an assignment and develop an ability to evaluate academic writing. For the same reasons, we're including three sample student essays that satisfy assignments about popular culture. You may agree or disagree with the authors' views, and you might think you'd respond to the assigned topics differently: That's fine. We've selected these essays because they differ in style, focus, and purpose and thus suggest different approaches to their assignments — approaches that might help you as you write your own essays about popular culture. We've annotated the essays to point out argumentative, organizational, and rhetorical strategies that we found effective. As you read the essays and the annotations, ask why the authors chose these strategies and how you might incorporate some of the same strategies in your own writing.

Essay 1: Personal Experience Essay

Some assignments may allow you to respond to a topic by discussing your own personal experiences and observations. Such assignments enable you to draw on a wealth of details and specific evidence that you have close to hand, and they also enable you to develop your own voice as a writer (because the subject is your own experience, you will want to use the first-person form of address). Dana Mariano, a student at Lehigh University in Bethlehem, Pennsylvania, wrote the following essay, "Patrons of the Arts," about a recent trend that many young people have embraced despite their parents' disapproval: tattooing and body piercing. Mariano was not required to base her discussion on a close reading of the selections. But notice that she combines her own tale of visiting a tattoo parlor with a full and rich consideration of the system into which her visit can be interpreted — thus fulfilling one of the central tenets of the semiotic approach.

Patrons of the Arts

The glow from Tattoo 46's neon sign reflected onto the dashboard of my car and attracted most of the flies from the surrounding area. As I walked into Tattoo 46, I asked myself a very logical question: "What the hell am I doing here?" I was not a biker, a World War II veteran, or a criminal; I was simply an eighteen-year-old girl who wanted a tattoo. Actually, I had wanted a tattoo since I was in the eighth grade, and now I was finally old enough to get one.

I looked around the waiting room of Tattoo 46 and saw plastered on the walls a potpourri of tattoos that ranged from fire-breathing dragons to roses to cartoon characters. I could hear a faint buzz coming from a room in the back that was shut off with a curtain that looked like a bedspread from the sixties. Luckily, I already knew exactly what tattoo I wanted, so I did not have to search for the perfect one from the plethora of tattoos on the walls. I planned to get my tattoo of a Hawaiian flower and get it tattooed onto my lower stomach.

A burly, gray-haired man, who reminded me so much of Jerry Garcia, walked out from another back room and asked, "So, let me guess. You are here to get your belly-button pierced."

"Actually, I would like it if you could do a tattoo of this," I said as I handed him the picture of the tiny narcissus flower my friend Samantha had drawn for me.

"Yeah, I can do this," he said. "Do you have any ID?"

"Sure, here it is," I said triumphantly as I showed him my driver's license.

"Well, well, well. Happy Birthday. So, are you ready to roll?" he asked.

"As ready as I'll ever be," I replied with a voice that lacked any semblance of confidence.

As I walked into the small room, I saw all over the walls pictures of tattooed and pierced people. Most of these people had body piercings in regions where I had only heard people could get them, but I never thought it was truly physically possible. I heard a man scream from the other room, and once again I asked myself, "What the hell am I doing here?" I was a medium-height, blonde, Abercrombie-wearing, sorority type of girl. Why would I get a tattoo or anything other than my ears pierced?

Dana begins with a catchy narrative introduction that establishes her focus on the motivations behind tattooing and body piercing.

Dialogue adds drama to the narrative.

Dana broadens her focus to a general cultural trend.

Looking at society today, one realizes that a variety of people are now getting tattoos and body piercings. These body adornments, which were once an accessory for rebels, punks, bikers, and freaks, are now commonly seen on models, actors, people in the business world, and even teachers. Today, one cannot walk down the street without seeing someone sporting a tattoo, eyebrow ring, tongue ring, or labret (pierced lower lip).

These people are proud to show off their personal artwork. Tattooing and body piercing were once symbols of nonconformity in society; now they almost seem to be a form of conformity. The question is, why have so many decided to pierce their bodies in weird areas and adorn their bodies with tattoos? What exactly has happened to polite society?

She analyzes her subject, drawing on popular culture to describe the semiotic system in which tattoos and body piercing exist.

Celebrities and rock stars have always influenced the way people believe they should look. With many models, rock icons, sports figures, actors, and actresses getting their bodies tattooed and pierced, the public wants to follow in their footsteps. Even the most feminine and revered actresses and models are tattooing themselves with small flowers and butterflies or getting their belly-buttons pierced as a symbol of sexuality. Sports figures such as Dennis Rodman cannot stop with just one tattoo and body piercing. For many, body piercing and tattooing become a strange addiction. Society has always looked at these types of people as role models. If they can pierce and tattoo, why shouldn't the public?

If one looks at the type of people who are piercing themselves, one sees that many are in their thirties and forties, the baby boomers who are in the midlife-crisis age range. Many baby boomers have reached the midlife-crisis age and need something to show a sense of rebellion against society. Also, many baby boomers did not feel that having a tattoo or body piercing was appropriate until now because of its new appeal in polite society and the mainstream.

My mother is one of the people in this category. She got a tattoo five years ago. One could say that she was going through a midlife crisis. She lost one hundred pounds, grew her once-short hair rather long, and bought a very cute red convertible. The last thing on her agenda of making a new woman was to get a tattoo of a butterfly on her lower stomach. Now she is through her midlife crisis, and she feels a sense of youth from her tattoo. She has even said when she dies she wants there to be a hole in her dress where her tattoo is. She wants everyone to be able to see her personal work of art.

Another explanation for this trend is the *National Geographic* syndrome. In other parts of the world, tattooing and piercing have been common practices for thousands of years. In many non-Western cultures and societies, body art is an indicator of nobility and the upper class. In India, when a woman gets married, she is covered with patterns in henna, a type of dye. This body art is considered a sacred symbol of beauty for an Indian woman. Since the world is becoming more and more aware of other cultures, we can see other cultures' ways and are far more accepting of them. The globalization of the world has truly opened up society to be more accepting of one another's cultures, views, and even body adornments.

Dana provides an alternative explanation, which adds depth to her analysis.

A compelling reason for the act seems to be to establish identity. This is why many people my age get body piercings and tattoos. Many teenagers are scared of getting lost in the crowd, and that is why they resort to such measures. It is so hard to stand out in a diverse society; teenagers today go to any measure they can to get more attention. My friend Deanna, who is the valedictorian of my class, recently got her eyebrow pierced. She is one of the people who did this as a form of rebellion and to make a departure from her girly, brainy persona. She did this a few days before graduating high school.

She offers a third explanation and follows it with an extended example.

"So, do you think all the parents will be thrilled to see my beautiful eyebrow ring?" Deanna asked with a sly grin.

"Oh, you know they are going to love it. I am sure that you will make the school so proud sporting your eyebrow ring," I said in one of my more sarcastic tones.

Dialogue dramatizes the point and makes it personal and immediate.

"Do you know that the principal already asked me to take it out for graduation? He said he doesn't want me to give the school a bad look," Deanna said with a hint of pride.

"You aren't going to take it out, are you?" I asked.

"Are you kidding me? Of course not. I refuse to allow people to remember me as perfect little Deanna. I would look like I was the principal's pet, even though I was at one time. I have worked so hard to move away from the old Deanna. This eyebrow ring represents a new, more independent Deanna," she firmly stated.

Whatever the reason, many people have decided to adorn their bodies with tattoos and piercings. Today's diverse society makes it harder and harder for a person to get noticed, so many have changed their appearance so they can stand out in the crowd. The abundance of body piercing and tattooing has also changed the way society looks at beauty. It was once considered ugly and manly for a woman to have a tattoo. Today, it is considered sexy and erotic if a woman has a small, feminine tattoo on her body. The abundance of tattooing and body piercing has certainly changed the way that society views these things that were once considered proper only for freaks.

Dana returns to the intro- duction's dra- matic scene, signaling clo- sure to the narrative.
    As I lay on the cold metal table, I tried to decide whether I truly wanted this tattoo or not. I pulled down my pants and watched my tattoo artist get out a new needle. I was going to do this. I had no idea why, but I was going to get the tattoo I always wanted. There is no rational explanation for why I wanted a tattoo; I just did.

"So why are you getting a tattoo?" my tattoo artist asked.

"I don't know," I said. "I just want one."

Essay 2: Essay Using Outside Sources

Your instructor may assign you an essay topic that requires you to use outside sources, whether it be a full-blown research paper or simply an essay that requires a variety of documented evidence. Such an assignment requires you to think critically about your sources and their reliability. In this essay, Amy Lin of UCLA argues that the Barbie doll, and all its associated products and marketing, essentially is a means for engendering a consumerist ethos in young girls who are the toy's fans. To do so, Amy relies on a range of sources, including articles in *Signs of Life in the U.S.A.*, academic and journalistic sources, and a corporate Web site that presents the panoply of Barbie prod- ucts. Notice that Lin treats toysrus.com not as a source of unbiased informa- tion about the products (that would amount to taking promotional material at face value); rather, she analyzes the Web site as evidence for her larger argu- ment about consumerism. As you read Lin's essay, study how she uses her sources and integrates them into her own discussion.

Barbie: Queen of Dolls and Consumerism

In my closet, a plastic bag contains five Barbie dolls. A cardboard box beside my nightstand holds yet another, and one more box contains a Ken doll. Under my bed we find my Barbies' traveling walk-in closet, equipped with a light-up vanity and fold-out chair and desk. We also find Doctor Barbie along with the baby, sticker band-aids, and sounding stethoscope with which she came. Under my sister's bed are their furniture set, including sofas, loveseats, flower vases, and a coffee table. A Tupperware container holds Ken's pants, dress shirts, and special boots (whose spurs make patterns when rolled in ink) in addition to Barbie's excess clothing that did not fit in the walk-in closet. In a corner of my living room sits the special holiday edition Barbie, outfitted in a gown, fur stole, and holly headband.

These plastic relics prove that, as a young girl, I, like many other females, fell into the waiting arms of the Mattel Corporation. Constantly feeding the public with newer, shinier toys, the Barbie enterprise illustrates America's propensity for consumerism. Upon close examination, Barbie products foster materialism in young females through both their overwhelmingly large selection and their ability to create a financially carefree world for children, sending the message that excessive consumption is acceptable. This consequently perpetuates the misassumption that "the American economy [is] an endlessly fertile continent whose boundaries never need be reached" (Shames 81) among the American youth.

Search the term "Barbie" at toysrus.com, and you will receive 286 items in return — more than enough to create a blur of pinkish-purple as you scroll down the webpage. The Barbie enterprise clearly embraces "the observation that 'no natural boundary seems to be set to the efforts of man'" (Shames 78). In other words, humankind is, in all ways, ambitious; people will keep creating, buying, and selling with the belief that these opportunities will always be available. This perfectly describes the mentality of those behind Barbie products, as new, but unnecessary, Barbie merchandise is put on shelves at an exorbitant rate. At toysrus.com, for example, a variety of four different mermaids, 11 fairies, and two "merfairies" — products from the "Fairytopia-Mermaidia" line — find their place among the search results (toys). Instead of inventing a more original or educational

Amy's introduction is a visual anecdote that illustrates her argument about consumption.

Amy articulates her thesis and refers to Laurence Shames's article as a context.

The corporate Web site is used not as a source of objective information but as evidence to support the thesis.

product, Mattel merges the mermaid world with the fairy world into "Fairytopia-Mermaidia," demonstrating the company's lack of innovation and care for its young consumers' development. Thus the corporation's main motivation reveals itself: profit. Another prime example found among the search results is the "Barbie: 12 Dancing Princesses Horse Carriage" (toys), a more recent product in the Barbie family. The carriage, "in its original form, . . . can seat six princess dolls but . . . can expand to hold all 12 dolls at once" (toys). The dolls, of course, do not come with it, forcing the child to buy at least one for the carriage to even be of any use. But that child will see the glorious picture of the carriage filled with all 12 dolls (which are inevitably on the box), and she will want to buy the remaining 11. In addition, the product description states that the carriage "is inspired by the upcoming DVD release, Barbie in *The 12 Dancing Princesses*" (toys). Essentially, one Mattel creation inspires another, meaning that the DVD's sole purpose is to give Mattel an excuse to create and market more useless merchandise.

Much of this, however, may have to do with branding, a strategy manufacturers utilize that ultimately results in "consumers transfer[ring] a favorable or unfavorable image from one product to others from the same brand" (Neuhaus and Taylor). In accordance with this strategy, all Barbie products must maintain a certain similarity so as not to "'confuse' potential customers . . . and thereby reduce demand for the products" (Sappington and Wernerfelt). This explains the redundancy found in much of Mattel's Barbie merchandise, since the sudden manufacturing of a radically different product could encourage the migration of consumers to another brand. But given that Barbie has become "the alpha doll" (Talbot 74) for girls in today's popular culture, young female consumers clearly associate only good things with Barbie. And who can blame them? Barbie has become a tradition handed down from mother to daughter or a rite of passage that most girls go through. In this way, excessive consumption and the effects of branding are handed down as well, as Barbie dolls are essentially their physical manifestations.

Amy moves to the larger marketing context.

With a company as driven to produce and sell products as Mattel, consumers can expect to find increasingly ridiculous items on toy store shelves. One such product found at toysrus.com is "Barbie and Tanner" (toys), Tanner being Barbie's dog. The doll and dog come with brown pellets that function both as dog food and dog waste, a "special magnetic scooper[,] and trash can" (toys). Upon telling any post-Barbie phase female about this product, she will surely look amazed and ask, "Are you kidding me?" Unfortunately, Tanner's movable "mouth, ears, head and tail" (toys) and "soft[,] . . . fuzzy" coat will most likely blind children to the product's absurdity, instead enchanting them into purchasing the product. Another particularly hilarious item is the "Barbie Collector Platinum Label Pink Grapefruit Obsession" (toys). The doll wears a "pink, charmeuse mermaid gown with deep pink chiffon wedges sewn into the flared skirt and adorned with deep pink bands that end in bows under the bust and at the hip" (toys). And "as a . . . special surprise, [the] doll's head is scented with the striking aroma of pink grapefruit" (toys). Finally, the doll is described as "an ideal tribute to [the] delightful [grapefruit] flavor" (toys). The consumer will find it difficult to keep a straight face as he or she reads through the description, as it essentially describes a doll dedicated to a scent. The doll's randomness shows Mattel's desperation for coming out with new products. Eager to make profit, it seems as though those behind Barbie make dolls according to whatever whim that happens to cross their minds.

In the quest to make profit by spreading the consumerist mindset, Barbie products even manage to commodify culture. Nowadays, Barbie dolls come in a variety of ethnicities. Take, for example, the "Diwali Festival Doll" (toys) from the "Barbie Dolls of the World" (toys) line. Except for the traditional Indian apparel and dark hair, however, the doll could easily be mistaken for Caucasian. And what about Barbie's multiracial doll friends? They are reduced to mere accessories — disposable and only supplementary to Barbie, the truly important figure. Therefore, despite Mattel's attempts at identifying with a larger group of girls, an undeniable "aura of blondness still [clings] to the Mattel doll" (Talbot 82) because its attempts aim more towards creating a larger customer base than anything else.

But enough of dolls. Mattel has grown so large that it can expand its products beyond Barbie's mini-world. Consumers can easily find Barbie brand tennis shoes, rain boots, slippers, bicycles, and helmets. Many of Barbie's non-doll products even reflect the various fads among America's youth, such as video games, skateboards, scooters, guitars, and dance mats (in accordance with the popularity

The paragraph includes a rich array of concrete, specific detail.

Amy develops her argument by considering the cultural and ethnic angle.

A quick, short transition moves the reader to a broader consideration of Mattel's promotion of materialism.

of the game, Dance Dance Revolution). Anne Parducci, Mattel's senior VP of Barbie Marketing claims Mattel does this because it "want[s] to make sure . . . [it] capture[s] girls in the many ways they are spending their time now and in the future" (Edut), that it "want[s] Barbie to represent a lifestyle brand for girls, not just a brand of toys" (Edut). This phenomenon, however, can simply be seen as Mattel trying to "infiltrat[e] girls' lives everywhere they go" (Edut). Either way, Mattel's actions allow materialism to develop at an early age, especially since it makes the latest "it" items more accessible to children. Those behind Barbie figure that if children are going to buy into the latest trends anyway, they might as well buy it from Mattel.

Amy allows for a counter-argument but then refutes it.

Since Barbie products promote the attitude of keeping up with society's crazes, they create a carefree fantasy world for children, obscuring the fact that Mattel's motivation is making money. The company knows that if they enchant children, those children will in turn convince their parents to buy the products for them. The company also knows that commercials are its best opportunities to do this. One recent Mattel commercial advertises the "Let's Dance Genevieve" doll, a doll also inspired by *The 12 Dancing Princesses* DVD that interacts with its owner in three ways: the doll "can dance to music for the girl" (toys), "teach the girl dance moves by demonstrating and using speech prompts" (toys), and "follow along with the girl's dance moves using special bracelets and a shoe accessory" (toys). Girls dressed in ballerina attire give overly joyous reactions to the doll's behaviors, making the doll seem remarkably advanced when, really, the doll can only raise its arms and legs. In addition, computer graphic scenes from the movie run seamlessly into scenes of the girls playing with the doll, and one of these girls is even transposed onto a clip of the movie. This blurs the lines of reality and fantasy, encouraging young viewers to think that if they own the doll, they, too, can feel like "dancing princesses," that somehow the doll can transport its owner into a fairytale world. In actuality, young females will likely tire of the doll within weeks. The commercial even resorts to flattery, describing the doll and its owner as "two beautiful dancers." Finally, the commercial ends with inspirational lyrics, singing, "You can shine." This sort of "vaguely girl-positive" (Edut) advertising only "wrap[s] the Mattel message — buy our products now!" (Edut). Together, all these advertising elements add up to a highly desirable product among young girls.

Barbie undoubtedly increases the materialistic tendencies in children, specifically females, Barbie's target audience. After all, since "Barbie dolls need new clothes and accessories more often than boys' action figures do" (Katz), "young girls learn . . . very early" to "assume consumer roles" (Katz). Interestingly, "Barbie was an early rebel against the domesticity that dominated the lives of baby-boom mothers" (Cross 773), as she shows no "car[e] for babies or children" or "visible ties to parents" (Cross 773). But ironically, instead of "[teaching] girls to shed [such] female stereotypes" (Cross 774), Barbie simply created a new stereotype for females — the shopaholic persona — because "she prompted [young girls] to associate the freedom of being an adult with carefree consumption" (Cross 774). So the overall effect of Barbie's presence on children's lives is a rising in their expectations of material possessions. Or, in other words, Barbie products cause "catalog-induced anxiety" (Easterbrook 404), a condition that can occur "from [viewing] catalogs themselves or from other forms of public exposure of the lives of the rich or celebrated, . . . mak[ing] what a typical person possesses seem paltry, even if the person is one of the many . . . living well by objective standards" (Easterbrook 405). Given that Barbie is a fictitious character, Mattel can make her as beautiful, hip, and rich as it pleases. But what happens when little girls begin comparing their lives to that of Barbie? They think, "If Barbie gets to have such amenities, so should I." And toys like the "Barbie Hot Tub Party Bus" (target) do not help the situation. The product description reads that the bus contains "all the comforts of home like a flat screen TV, dinette table, and beds" (target). Children will inevitably expect these luxuries that, for Barbie, are merely givens in her doll utopia, causing discontent when they discover they cannot have everything they want. It may even reach the point where, "as . . . more material things become available and fail to" satisfy children, "material abundance . . . [can] have the perverse effect of instilling unhappiness — because it will never be possible to have everything that economics can create" (Easterbrook 402).

For my long forgotten Barbie dolls, as for many older females, the dream house has stopped growing. In fact, the house has been

References to Gary Cross's article buttress the essay's argument.

Amy invokes Easterbrook as she explores the long-term implications of Mattel's promotion of consumerism.

Amy signals closure by coming full circle, returning to her opening anecdote.

demolished, leaving my dolls homeless. But this does not mean that women have escaped the effects of years of Barbie-play as they have temporarily escaped the clutches of Mattel. (I say temporarily because even if the female herself has outgrown Barbie, Mattel will suck her back in through her daughters, nieces, goddaughters, and granddaughters.) Since Barbie preaches the admissibility of hyper-consumption to females at a young age, women, unsurprisingly, "engage in an estimated 80% of all consumer spending" (Katz). Women, conditioned from all those trips to the toy store looking for the perfect party dress for Barbie or the perfect convertible to take her to that party, still find themselves doing this — just on a larger scale — in shopping malls. But perhaps men's consumerism is catching up. The recent "proliferation of metrosexuals" (St. John 177) signals a rise in "straight young men whose fashion and grooming tastes have crossed over into areas once reserved for feminine con-

By considering men's consumer habits and male dolls, Amy ends with a refreshing twist.

sumption" (St. John 174). Mattel, too, takes part in this phenomenon through the "reintroduc[tion] [of] the Ken doll" (Talbot 79) which now possesses a "new metrosexual look" (Talbot). Well, one thing is certain: Mattel continues its expansive construction on Barbie's ever-costly dream mansion, and knows that millions of little girls will do the same.

Works Cited

Cross, Gary. "Barbie, G.I. Joe, and Play in the 1960s." Maasik and Solomon 772–78.

Easterbrook, Gregg. "The Progress Paradox." Maasik and Solomon 400–407.

Edut, Ophira. "Barbie Girls Rule?" *Bitch: Feminist Response to Pop Culture* 31 Jan. 1999: 16. Print.

Katz, Phyllis A., and Margaret Katz. "Purchasing Power: Spending for Change." *Iris* 30 Apr. 2000: 36. Print.

Maasik, Sonia, and Jack Solomon, eds. *Signs of Life in the U.S.A.: Readings on Popular Culture for Writers*. 5th ed. Boston: Bedford/St. Martin's, 2006. Print.

Neuhaus, Colin F., and James R. Taylor. "Variables Affecting Sales of
     Family-Branded Products." *Journal of Marketing Research* 9.4
     (1972): 419–22. Print.

Sappington, David E. M., and Birger Wernerfelt. "To Brand or Not to
     Brand? A Theoretical and Empirical Question." *The Journal of
     Business* 58.3 (1985): 279–93. Print.

Shames, Laurence. "The More Factor." Maasik and Solomon 76–82.

St. John, Warren. "Metrosexuals Come Out." Maasik and Solomon
     174–77.

Talbot, Margaret. "Little Hotties: Barbie's New Rivals." *The New
     Yorker.* 4 Dec. 2006: 74+. Print.

Toys "R" Us. Geoffrey LLC, 2006. Web. 14 Nov. 2006.

Essay 3: Open-Ended Analytic Assignment

Your instructor may assign an open-ended topic, one that gives you certain
guidelines but that allows you to pick your own object for analysis. If you
receive such an assignment, first brainstorm possible topics that interest you,
for you'll produce the best writing if you're excited about your subject. And be
sure you understand if your instructor wants you to use specific reading selections as a framework for your analysis, or if you have the latitude to select
your own essays that can buttress your interpretation. The following essay, by
Joshua Keim of California State University, Northridge, is entitled "Nostalgia
Mongering at City Walk"; his intructor asked him to write a semiotic analysis
of the social and cultural values implicit in a retail store of his own choosing.
In this essay, Keim lets his interpretation unfold as he narrates the process of
walking around City Walk.

Nostalgia Mongering at City Walk

*Joshua grabs
the reader's
attention with
a catchy nar-
rative opener.*

I knew I had arrived. I was standing at the west end of City
Walk, in Universal City, California, an avenue of glittering billboards
and myriad neon signs, towering effigies of King Kong, Fender Strato-
casters, and other pop culture icons, each one like a giant animus
floating out of some vast collective unconscious. This was it. From the
Metro Link that dropped me off in Universal City to the tram that conveniently shuttled me up to the top, all signs seemed to point toward
here. This was the virtual mecca of post-industrial consumerism.

City Walk. Is it some evil genius' vision for the future of "retail
therapy" and homage to Manifest Destiny? Or a unique hybrid of
strip mall, expo, and theme park — indeed, since it's adjacent to one
of Los Angeles' most frequented theme parks, Universal Studios?

*He provides
a brief his-
tory of the
creation of
City Walk.*

Designed and built in 1993 by architect Jon Jerde — whose firm the
Jerde Partnership, Inc. is also responsible for that other bastion of
supra-capitalism, the Mall of America in Bloomington, Minnesota —
City Walk was conceived to give the appearance of just that: a virtual "streetscape," a metropolis unto itself, isolated safely atop the
Universal City hillside, and offering, as M. L. Bierman put it, "*risk-
free* consumption in a private dream world" (qtd. in Giaconia,
emphasis added). That's right: "risk-free." In other words, City Walk
was designed to give the appearance of an urban setting without the
influx of certain "undesirable" urban elements, namely street punks,
prostitutes, and bums who might otherwise spoil the illusion (Giaconia). That way you and your family can get down to the business
of buying things.

*Next he asks
a question
that focuses
the essay's
subsequent
discussion.*

Of course, City Walk is not just food courts, gift shops, and
megaplex movie theaters; it's a *fantastic* shopping experience. The
question is, "what is the fantasy?" How are All-Star Collectibles,
Hard Rock Café, and Retro Rad each connected? I needed an
answer — some sign — so I headed east into that pulsing artery of
dreamworks, until I came to it.

You'd almost miss it if weren't for the looming six-foot face of
Sparky the Cat about to knock you over the head or the sixteen-
year-old salesgirl greeting you just outside the door and demonstrating the quantum mechanics of Slinkies with a lollipop in her mouth.
Sparky's Candy and Other Swell Stuff! Located just off the Fountain

Court (or food court) next to a smoothie shop and across from Cama-cho's Mexican restaurant, Sparky's is the perfect post-dining pit stop to grab a little something for the sweet tooth and of course to get a little browsing in — indeed, since the much advertised candy is at the back of the store, you're forced to pass all the merchandise to get to it — while you chomp away on caramels and salt-water taffy at $2.00 per 1/4 lb. since it's part candy store, part *vintage* retailer.

As I gazed in awe at over seven hundred types of Pez dispensers and Wacky Wobblers on display in the store windows, it suddenly occurred to me that Sparky's — along with a number of other City Walk stores — was aggressively selling nostalgia to the masses. As the store's on-line advertisement suggests,

Joshua suggests an initial interpretation of one store.

> Sparky's is a unique fun store that takes you on a joyride through your favorite childhood memories. Whether [the] Fabulous Forties or Generation X, Sparky's uncovers the kid in all of us. Celebrating classic ideas by mixing fun new products with original vintage items, Sparky's is chock full of "Really Swell Stuff." ("Sparky's")

Swell. Even that word smacked of 1950s slang. But before I figured out whose dream they were selling, I wanted to know how they sold it.

In the 1990s, the large proliferation of vintage stores had a lot to do with the Generation Xers who were disenchanted with the American dream — which they believed didn't include them — disillusioned by where they thought the system was heading, and tended to look at the world with a lot of postmodern irony. As a counterculture movement, they were unique in that they were the first generation of American youths who didn't see themselves suc-ceeding more than their parents. As Laurence Shames suggests in "The More Factor," a lot of this skepticism is linked to the fact that Americans, as a result of our frontier myth, have always believed in social mobility and the idea that there would always be "more" of whatever we needed to progress (57). But, as Shames also points out, since 1949 and up through the 1980s, we saw a steady decrease in "income expansion" and thus expectations, and in the early nineties we were still "running out of more" (60, 59). Often, when the future looks dry, people look to the symbols of the past for comfort and

He adds depth to that interpretation by drawing on Shames to explain the cultural mythology underlying the popularity of vintage stores.

guidance, and so vintage fashions (for example, bell-bottoms),
vintage furnishings (lava lamps), and vintage modes of music (the
rockabilly-swing fusion of Brian Setzer) all made a brief return to
the pop culture scene, although each with a slight difference —
hence, compact disc players made-up to look like Victrola record
players for $249.99. Of course, their parents, the baby boomers who
were entering one mass mid-life crisis, were equally frustrated with
their progeny and the glass ceiling, and so they too tried to recap-
ture their innocence by buying it, usually from one of these pop culture appreciation expos. Sparky's is a testament to this cultural
phenomenon and is pandering it to both generations.

But with all the vintage item stores still in full swing, what
sets Sparky's apart?

As I looked at the right window display with all the Wacky
Wobblers — you know, those plastic dolls with bobbing heads you
usually see on car dashboards — I noticed a sign reading "Photo
Spot" and an arrow pointing to a colorful box, which was really a
human-sized replica of the Wacky Wobbler packaging. To take advantage of this photo opportunity, you have to *walk into the store* while
someone photographs you from outside, thereby attracting the
attention of other bystanders — excuse me, consumers. Surely
enough, some tourists were snapping away while one of their friends
was making miming gestures inside the box. As I looked on I
thought, "what an ingenious device to get people to buy these useless baubles." "See yourself in this package, identify with the brand-
name, now see yourself buying the product," it seemed to say. In
fact, each Wacky Wobbler featured the familiar image of some popular cartoon character (Dick Tracy and Jughead) or product mascot
(the Starkist Tuna and the Jolly Green Giant), which implies that
they're selling brand-name identification once more to you.

The dialogue adds drama to the discussion.

"Do you have to pay to take a photo in the box?" I asked the
clerk.

"Nope," she replied, removing the lollipop from her mouth.

"I wish I had a camera. My professor would appreciate this."

"Well, we sell disposable cameras inside," she grinned.

How convenient. It was time I saw the inside of the store.

Just inside the entry, at the center, as the sounds of (yep!)
Brian Setzer oozed out the store, there stood some contraption that
looked like it was straight off the pier at Coney Island called a

"Super Squisher." You've probably seen these things in theme parks before. Basically, you stick a penny in the slot and, through some marvel of science, in less than a minute your penny is transformed into a useless token with the City Walk logo on it. I found this to be a particularly significant form of "behavior modification" (Solomon 161). On the one hand, the machine gets you to take your money out of your pocket to start spending it — and when your kids start clamoring for a penny, you will spend it. On the other hand, it gets you used to the idea of not getting anything of material value for your money, just souvenirs . . . like so many memories. Not having any children, I safely moved on.

By this point I was in what Paco Underhill refers to as the "Decompression Zone," the area in a store that allows consumers to enter a shopping mode, but Sparky's wasn't allowing anyone to decompress (qtd. in Gladwell 404). They were taking the customer right into the time warp. In fact, as I walked in I was suddenly inundated with old-fashioned Coca-Cola machines circa 1955 ($4,800), two racks of Pioneer Roadster go-carts ($399.99), and one of those compact disc Victrolas. These were high-ticket items, and they were just six feet inside the store. Contrary to Underhill's advice, Sparky's didn't seem to be wasting time promoting their most expensive products. Once more, as I looked at the Pioneer Roadster go-carts, I saw not only a reiteration of the frontier myth, but because they were originally conceived as a child's toy, I also imagined neighborhood streets filled with kids racing them and started to associate the go-carts with families and community. So I looked around to see if the store wasn't exploiting this image further.

To the right of the store were the rows of Wacky Wobblers; to the left, the rows of Pez dispensers, each portraying again some cartoon figure and hanging on the rack like a pop culture apotheosis. Over each display was a sign that read "Collect them all!" Why? How many Pez dispensers does one person need? It was obvious that Sparky's was promoting the kind of "pathological buying" that John De Graaff, David Wann, and Thomas H. Naylor warn about in "The Addictive Virus," and that we were stuck in "more mode," or shopping to fill a void (74). In fact, if you check out the Pez Web site (www.pezco.securesites.com), you'll find a whole subculture that's been collecting and auctioning these "interactive cand[ies]" for over fifty years — they've even got a newsletter. So if you buy Homer, you

Joshua makes use of Underhill's terminology as found in Gladwell's essay.

better get Marge, the whole family, and the rest of the population of

Joshua complicates his analysis by articulating another set of social values.

Springfield so your collection will be complete, because you're not just buying Pez now, you're buying the Pez sense of community: social belonging and family values. I could start to see the attraction of these products, not just to children, but to Gen Xers and baby boomers — since as Sparky's ad suggests, they are the collectors. Now I wanted to know what belonging meant.

At the back of the store, G.I. Joes and Barbies stood side by side. These have been two of the largest wardens of gender coding in children's toys for the last forty-plus years, and they were in tandem, on display together at Sparky's. But again, they weren't being sold merely as children's toys but as collector's items. So why would Gen Xers and baby boomers identify with these?

G.I. Joe was first introduced in 1964 as "the first boy's 'Action Figure' in the world," according to Hasbro's Web site ("G.I. Joe").

He locates G.I. Joe in its historical context.

After the Kennedy assassination, the then-dubious new Johnson administration, and the looming conflict in Vietnam, Joe was a paragon of conventional masculinity with his buff, martial posturing, John Wayne swagger, and patriotic self-righteousness. He remained a sort of stronghold against the feminist movement, which threatened to subvert the code. Originally, as Gary Cross argues, the doll "began as a celebration of an *all-male* world of realistic combat" (emphasis added, 774). In fact, G.I. Joe has always reflected politicized gender coding — usually the conservative right's. As a Gen Xer myself, I remember the cartoon series of the 1980s in which Cobra, a fascist dictator, was G.I. Joe's sworn enemy, illustrating Hasbro's attempt to capitalize on the cold war paranoia and anti-Communist sentiment that were still strong during the Reagan administration. As the product box so accurately puts it, Joe's a "real American hero."

However, the collector's edition on display at Sparky's signaled something slightly different. It was the "Pearl Harbor 60th Anniversary series," released in 2001. Joe still represented that John Wayne brand of patriotism like the Joes of old, but the fact that this series

Then he contrasts that context, and the meaning it suggests, with the toy's significance today.

was still being sold had a lot to do with September 11, 2001. Though the toy company might claim the series was released in conjunction with the December 7 anniversary of the attacks on Pearl Harbor of that year, if the series was still bankable it was for another reason. In the first few weeks after the September 11 attacks, every politician and political commentator, including the president himself, was

associating the attack on the World Trade Center with the bombing
of Pearl Harbor, since it was the first strike on American soil since
December 7, 1941 — that "day that [would] live in infamy in the
minds of all Americans," as Roosevelt declared. In this new age of
"terror" and uncertainty, of both dissent and nationalism, Hasbro
promises you that G.I. Joe will be there as a role model of both
"heroic" masculinity and patriotism. And with Operation Iraqi Freedom already begun, it will be interesting to see how these dolls fare.

And then there's Joe's girlfriend. You'd think that after years of
feminist indignation over Barbie's image problems that this doll
would have been boycotted or Mattel would have canceled her by
now. You'd be wrong. Albeit, she's undergone some confusing
wardrobe changes over the last forty-four years, but Barbie is still
the perennial favorite of little girls all over the world. But it's this
year's collector's edition Barbies that should get more than a few
genderologists' trigger-fingers twitching. In the series on display at
Sparky's, "Maria Therese," for example, is the very image of Marian
purity and patriarchal co-dependency in her flowing, starched-white
bridal gown and veil. "Movie Star Barbie," on the other hand, with
her swanky, leopard-print bathing suit, Jackie-O sunglasses, and
Brigitte Bardot feyness harks back to the Hollywood starlets of the
late fifties and early sixties, to signify the American cult of celebrity
worship. And then there's "Fashion Model Barbie," scantily clad in a
pink teddy and negligee, but no sign of "Dr. Barbie" or "Supreme
Court Justice Barbie," if such existed. (Interestingly enough, the
African American version of the same design is in a *black* teddy and
negligee, signifying that colorism is still alive.) The message that
these dolls seem to be sending women is that they are nothing if
not sex objects. Emily Prager remarks in "Our Barbies, Ourselves"
that Barbie "looks like someone who got her start at the Playboy
Mansion" (para. 2). Thus, each Barbie at Sparky's can only recommend women for their breeding ability or their sex appeal. So why is
it that baby boomers are gushing nostalgically over Maria Therese?
"Oh! I used to have one like this," she tells her friend as she picks
up the box. A divorcee, perhaps?

Considering the sexual confusion and evolving gender codes
that Americans have witnessed since the feminist movement and
sexual revolution of the 1960s, it is easy to see why Generation Xers
and baby boomers alike look to Barbie and G.I. Joe for guidance

*Joshua inter-
prets the gen-
der roles
assigned to
Barbie.*

from "simpler times." Barbie has reflected many of these shifts—
from patriarchal to feminist to postfeminist ideals. She has never
failed to represent the promise of empowerment, but only through
sexual fidelity, no matter how many careers she's had. And at the
core, she's always remained the Anglophilic, blond bombshell[1] who
many feminists accuse of inciting such social diseases as domestica-
tion and anorexia, to mention a few. But with Barbie, you will
always know what type of woman she is because the doll beneath
the clothing doesn't change. The same goes for G.I. Joe and masculinity. He will always be a representation of muscular patriotism—
what with his overtly phallic .30 caliber machine gun. And with the
two side by side, the message is even clearer: "In times of war,
ladies, stand by your man." I noticed that "G.I. Jane," released by
Hasbro in 1997, was nowhere to be found—at least not at Sparky's.

He concludes by seeing Kit-Kat clocks as emblematic of Americans' desire for security.

And then I saw the ultimate sign of the times . . . of any time:
the Kit-Kat clock, with its bulging cat eyes and circular clock-face,
was "just like the one in grandma's kitchen," or so the box read.
And it was hanging over the Barbies and G.I. Joes, telling me that
whenever Americans get confused or feel uncertain, they will
inevitably return to those signs representing the mythologies that
the nation was built on for security in their insecure world. Like the
pendulum swing of the Kit-Kat clock's tail, the codes and myths
mentioned—these old standbys—will eventually come back to us
from time to time. And retailers will always count on it because to
them, like the tourist in the Wacky Wobbler box, we are predictable,
prepackaged consumers—predictable because they shape us.

I had to get out of there; I was feeling dizzy. But as I made my
way to the tram stop, I could now connect Sparky's to the other
stores at City Walk. Hard Rock Café: cheeseburgers and fries (comfort
food) and good old rock 'n' roll (comfort music). All-Star Collectibles:
baseballs autographed by Joe DiMaggio in 1956 (when men knew
how to be men, and damn it, that Joltin' Joe was a man's man).

[1]Although in 1968, Mattel did release Christie, Barbie's first African
American friend, and other ethnically representative dolls since, to reflect
changes in multicultural awareness (Zumhagen). However, the point is
that these dolls have never been "Barbie," the central character of the
Barbie storyline, but remained her peripheral counterparts—her *other*
friends.

Retro Rad clothiers: ladies, get your sexy disco platform shoes (the men will love you for it).

As I boarded the tram, I noticed a U.S. marine and his girlfriend a few rows in front of me, holding hands. Her fingers were stroking his neck and sort of sending him off somewhere.

Works Cited

Cross, Gary. "Barbie, G.I. Joe, and Play in the 1960s." Maasik and Solomon 772–78.

De Graaff, John, David Wann, and Thomas H. Naylor. "The Addictive Virus." *Signs of Life in the U.S.A.* 4th ed. Ed. Sonia Maasik and Jack Solomon. Boston: Bedford/St. Martin's, 2003. 71–76. Print.

Giaconia, Paolo. "Universal City Walk: Displacement of Heterotopia." *Arch'It.* DADA Achitetti Associati, 29 Nov. 2002. Web. 1 Dec. 2002.

"G.I. Joe — Authentic Military History." *G. I. Joe Official Site.* Hasbro, 2002. Web. 25 Nov. 2002.

Gladwell, Malcolm. "The Science of Shopping." Maasik and Solomon 642–48.

Maasik, Sonia, and Jack Solomon, eds. *Signs of Life in the U.S.A.: Readings on Popular Culture for Writers.* 5th ed. Boston: Bedford/St. Martin's, 2006. Print.

Prager, Emily. "Our Barbies, Ourselves." Maasik and Solomon 769–71.

Shames, Laurence. "The More Factor." Maasik and Solomon 76–82.

Solomon, Jack. "Masters of Desire: The Culture of American Advertising." Maasik and Solomon 409–19.

"Sparky's." *City Walk Hollywood.* Universal Studios, 2002. Web. 25 Nov. 2002.

"Stuff about Pez." *Pez.com.* Pez Candy, 2002. Web. 25 Nov. 2002.

Zumhagen, Brian. "A Timeline of Barbie's History." *AdiosBarbie.com.* adiosbarbie.com, 2002. Web. 25 Nov. 2002.

CITING SOURCES

When you write an essay and use another author's work — whether you use the author's exact words or his or her ideas — you need to cite that source for your readers. In most humanities courses, writers use the system of documentation developed by the Modern Language Association (MLA). This system indicates a source in two ways: (1) notations that briefly identify the sources in the body of your essay and (2) notations that give fuller bibliographic information about the sources at the end of your essay. The notations for some commonly used types of sources are illustrated in this chapter. For documenting other sources, consult a writing handbook or Joseph Gibaldi's *MLA Handbook for Writers of Research Papers*, Seventh Edition (New York: Modern Language Association of America, 2009).

In-Text Citations

In the body of your essay, you should signal to your reader that you've used a source and indicate, in parentheses, where your reader can find the source in your list of works cited. You don't need to repeat the author's name in both your writing and in the parenthetical note.

SOURCE WITH ONE AUTHOR

Patrick Goldstein asserts that "Talk radio has pumped up the volume of our public discourse and created a whole new political language — perhaps the prevailing political language" (16).

SOURCE WITH TWO OR THREE AUTHORS

Researchers have found it difficult to study biker subcultures because, as one team describes the problem, "it was too dangerous to take issue with outlaws on their own turf" (Hooper and Moore 368).

INDIRECT SOURCE

In discussing the baby mania trend, *Time* claimed that "Career women are opting for pregnancy and they are doing it in style" (qtd. in Faludi 106).

List of Works Cited

At the end of your essay, include a list of all the sources you have cited in parenthetical notations. This list, alphabetized by author, should provide full publication information for each source; you should indicate the date you accessed any online sources.

The first line of each entry should begin flush left. Subsequent lines should be indented half an inch (or five spaces) from the left margin. Double-space the entire list, both between and within entries.

Nonelectronic Sources

BOOK BY ONE AUTHOR

Weisman, Alan. *The World without Us*. New York: Thomas Dunne Books, 2007. Print.

BOOK BY TWO OR MORE AUTHORS

Collins, Ronald K. L., and David M. Skover. *The Death of Discourse*. New York: Westview Press, 1996. Print.

(Note that only the first author's name is reversed.)

WORK IN AN ANTHOLOGY

Prager, Emily. "Our Barbies, Ourselves." *Signs of Life in the U.S.A.: Readings on Popular Culture for Writers*. 6th ed. Ed. Sonia Maasik and Jack Solomon. Boston: Bedford/St. Martin's, 2009. 613–15. Print.

ARTICLE IN A WEEKLY MAGAZINE

Lacayo, Richard. "How Does '80s Art Look Now?" *Time* 28 March 2005: 58+. Print.

(A plus sign is used to indicate that the article is not printed on consecutive pages; otherwise, a page range should be given: *16–25*, for example.)

ARTICLE IN A MONTHLY MAGAZINE

Judd, Elizabeth. "After School." *The Atlantic* June 2005: 118. Print.

ARTICLE IN A JOURNAL

Hooper, Columbus B., and Johnny Moore. "Women in Outlaw Motorcycle Gangs." *Journal of Contemporary Ethnography* 18.4 (1990): 363–87. Print.

PERSONAL INTERVIEW

Chese, Charlie. Personal interview. 28 Sept. 2008.

Electronic Sources

FILM OR VIDEOTAPE

Cinderella Man. Dir. Ron Howard. Perf. Russell Crowe, Renée Zellweger. Miramax, 2005. Film.

TELEVISION PROGRAM

"Collateral Damage." *CSI: Miami*. Perf. David Caruso. KBAK, Bakersfield. 4 May 2009. Television.

COMPACT DISC

Adams, Ryan. *Cold Roses*. Lost Highway, 2005. CD.

E-MAIL

Katt, Susie. "Interpreting the Mall." Message to the author. 29 Sept. 2008. E-mail.

ARTICLE IN AN ONLINE REFERENCE BOOK

"Gender." *Britannica Online*. Encyclopaedia Britannica, 31 July 2004. Web. 30 May 2008.

(Note that the first date indicates when the information was posted; the second indicates the date of access.)

ARTICLE IN AN ONLINE JOURNAL

Schaffer, Scott. "Disney and the Imagineering of History." *Postmodern Culture* 6.3 (1996): n. pag. Web. 12 Aug. 2008.

ARTICLE IN AN ONLINE MAGAZINE

Rosenberg, Scott. "Don't Link or I'll Sue!" *Salon* 12 Aug. 1999. Web. 13 Aug. 2008.

ONLINE BOOK

James, Henry. *The Bostonians*. London and New York, 1886. *The Henry James Scholar's Guide to Web Sites*. Aug. 1999. Web. 13 Aug. 2009.

ONLINE POEM

Frost, Robert. "The Road Not Taken." *Mountain Interval*. New York, 1915. *Project Bartleby Archive*. Ed. Steven van Leeuwen. Mar. 1995. Web. 13 Aug. 2008.

PROFESSIONAL WEB SITE

National Council of Teachers of English. Jan. 2008. Web. 1 May 2008.

PERSONAL HOME PAGE

Stallman, Richard. Home page. Mar. 2008. Web. 4 Mar. 2008.

POSTING TO A DISCUSSION LIST

Diaz, Joanne. "Poetic Expressions." *Conference on College Composition and Communication*. NCTE, 29 Apr. 2006. Web. 4 Jul. 2006.

ONLINE SCHOLARLY PROJECT

Barlow, Michael, ed. *Corpus Linguistics*. Rice U, Apr. 1998. Web. 13 Aug. 2005.

WORK FROM A DATABASE SERVICE

Cullather, Nick. "The Third Race." *Diplomatic History* 33.3 (2009): 507-12. *Academic OneFile*. Web. 1 May 2009.

CONSUMING PASSIONS

*The Culture of
American Consumption*

You Are What You Buy

If you were given a blank check to purchase anything — and everything — you wanted, what would you buy? Try making a list, and then annotate that list with brief explanations for why you want each item. Do your choices say something about yourself that you want others to know? Do they project an image?

Now consider the things you do own. Make another list and annotate it too. Why did you buy this item or that? What compromises did you have to make in choosing one item over another? How often did price or quality affect your decisions? How often did style or image? Which items were presents that reflect someone else's tastes and desires? Do the images sent by your actual possessions differ from the ones sent by your ideal ones? Why? Or why not?

Such questions are a good place to begin a semiotic analysis of American consumer culture, for every choice you make in the products you buy, from clothing to furniture to cars to electronics and beyond, is a sign, a signal you are sending to the world about yourself. Those aren't just a pair of shoes you're wearing: They're a statement about your identity. That's not just an iPod playlist: It's a message about your worldview.

To read the signs of American consumption, it is best to start with yourself, because you've already got an angle on the answers. But be careful and be honest. Remember, a cultural sign gets its meaning from the *system*, or *code*, in which it appears. Its significance does not lie in its usefulness but rather in its symbolism, in the image it projects, and that image is socially constructed. You didn't make it by yourself. To decode your possessions, you've got to ask what you are trying to say with them and what you want other people to think about you. And you've got to remember the difference between fashion and function.

To give you an idea of how to go about analyzing consumer objects and behavior, let's look at a product that on the surface seems completely functional — a tool, not a sign. Let's look at cell phones.

Interpreting the Culture of American Consumption

As you read in the Introduction to this book, an ordinary object, denotatively considered, is just a thing, but connotatively, it can project a meaning or image. In other words, it can be a sign. You also read that the semiotic interpretation of a cultural sign can usefully begin with a historical survey of the object you are interpreting. Such a survey can reveal how the meaning of an object can change depending on the circumstances in which it is found. This is strikingly true in the case of cell phones, which, while practically ubiquitous today, were once rare and expensive. They first appeared for public use in 1982 and were originally hardwired into automobiles (often limousines), which is why some people who recall that era still call them "car phones." In such a context, cell phones were potent status symbols, sending an image of unusual wealth and prestige, the exclusive equipment of VIPs.

But in an era when cell phones can be acquired for free (provided that the consumer also signs up for an activation contract, of course), and when even the latest digitized and video-screened models cost only a fraction of what the original models cost, the cell phone is so common that it doesn't send a status message anymore. Everyone seems to have one. But that doesn't mean that cell phones no longer have a semiotic significance. It simply means that the significance of the cell phone has changed as its history has changed.

To interpret the current significance of the cell phone, we need to situate it in its immediate *system* of related signs and products. One product that is

---

Discussing the Signs of Consumer Culture

On the board, list in categories the fashion styles worn by members of the class. Be sure to note details, such as styles of shoes, jewelry, watches, or sunglasses, as well as broader trends. Then discuss what the clothing choices say about individuals. What messages are people sending about their personal identity? Do individual students agree with the class's interpretations of their clothing choices? Can any distinctions be made by gender, age, or ethnicity? Then discuss what the fashion styles worn by the whole class say: Is a group identity projected by class members?

Apple CEO Steve Jobs demonstrates the
new iPhone during his keynote address
at MacWorld Conference & Expo in
San Francisco, January 9, 2007.

similar to the cell phone, and which thus belongs to the same system, is the
pager. The history of the pager resembles that of the cell phone. Once pagers
were carried almost exclusively by high-status professionals who needed to be
in constant contact with their places of business. This was particularly true for
physicians, who commonly carried pagers when they were "on call" (this was
before the advent of even the earliest cell phones), and so pagers acquired
something of the status of their professional users. The image sent by pagers
changed radically, however, when they came to be the standard equipment of
drug dealers, who used them to set up clandestine drug deals. The former status image declined as a new one emerged: To carry a pager was to send an
image of gangster toughness, and, for many American teens, gangster coolness. Once a signifier of professional prestige and responsibility, the pager
shifted systems and became part of the code of a bad-assed youth culture.

But now pagers might be carried by little children whose parents haven't
gotten them cell phones yet, and so, once again, their significance has changed.
In fact, as cell phones become more and more common, pagers have dwin-
dled in significance and number. Not too long ago, pagers were hot stuff; now,
cell phones enjoy that status.

With almost everyone owning a cell phone these days, one might accordingly expect phones to have a more or less neutral image. After all, they are

genuinely useful and so could well be viewed in solely a functional light as objects, not signs. But that doesn't appear to be the case. Think of those bumper stickers that read HANG UP AND DRIVE, or the fact that some people over forty years of age may apologize for owning one, as in "I own a cell phone, but I only use it for emergencies." People wouldn't make such apologies, or post such messages on their cars, if there weren't a lingering sense that, somehow, something is wrong with cell phones. And what is wrong lies in their cultural connotation, not in the objects themselves.

To see what this significance is, let's look further into the system in which cell phones appear. What often comes to mind when we think of cell phones today is their *association* with a certain kind of consumer, especially people driving SUVs and luxury sedans like the Lexus. There is a functional reason for this: Cell phones have become necessary equipment for the sorts of businesspeople, such as real estate professionals, who must spend a great deal of time in their cars and whose business activities make it important (as well as pleasurable) to drive status automobiles. At the same time, many middle-class parents find that cell phones provide a very good way of keeping track of their children, and SUVs have become the automotive choice of the middle- and upper-middle-class American mom these days. Indeed, all you need to do is utter the words "soccer mom," and immediately an image of a woman driving a Cadillac Escalade while chatting on a cell phone may come to mind.

Another related part of the lingering negativity in the cell phone's connotation has to do with its history, particularly that intermediate era when they were no longer the prerogative of the powerful and wealthy but were still expensive enough to be out of the ordinary consumer's reach. At that time, roughly the late 1980s, cell phones were the common possession of conspicuously consuming yuppies (an image reinforced by a 1980s song called "Car Phone," a parody of the seventies hit "Convoy"), and were widely despised accordingly (as a group, yuppies were quite unpopular in a country with populist traditions). Ironically, even when millions of non-yuppies and anti-yuppies carry cell phones today, the old taint lingers.

But only lingers. For, with the cell phone being so common, its significance is now less a matter of who owns one as how it is used and what model you own. That is, it has become a matter of status to be able to display the latest models, which is one reason so many people rushed out to buy the iPhone when it was first released, even though many expected its price to drop eventually, as it did, sooner rather than later. So, oddly enough, at a time when there are so many phones to choose from, the cell phone is recovering its old status symbol significance, though in a different key and only if you own the right models.

How you use your cell phone is a different matter. For many, of course, the newer phones, like the iPhone, offer an all-in-one multitasking device that enables you to talk, text-message, send and receive e-mail, surf the Web, play games, take pictures, and hang out at such places as MySpace and Friendster. But if you perform any of these tasks in class, or while driving an automobile, or in a movie theater, or restaurant, or any public place, such behavior bears a further cultural significance. To see that, it is again useful to look at a bit of history.

Once upon a time, telephone conversations were conducted in the privacy of one's home or office — or, if in public, with the door to the phone booth shut. Now such conversations, whether for business or for pleasure, take place on the road, in a restaurant or theater, in shops, on the sidewalk, indeed just about everywhere. What was once a private activity is now often a public one, and this privatization of public space is largely responsible for whatever negative connotations remain for the cell phone, though most people are probably not conscious of it.

For to treat publicly shared space as if it were one's private preserve, annoying or endangering others for one's personal pleasure or convenience, is, in essence, antisocial behavior. No one minds when people use their own private space privately, but when public space is treated as if it were private, the sense of a shared, common environment with a set of rules to govern the social interactions that take place within it is lost. And while we may not always be aware of it, this is one reason we may resent cell-phone users, especially in cars and in restaurants and theaters, even when we use cell phones ourselves.

At this point, as is often the case with a semiotic analysis, we can broaden the scope of our investigation to see what other current cultural phenomena can be associated with the cell phone's privatization of public space. We've already considered one such phenomenon: the SUV. Also wildly popular and common, the SUV has something of a negative image as well. In an era of global warming, part of that image is related to what is perceived as the selfishness of its owners, a consumption of too great a share of dwindling oil resources and a contribution of too great a share of greenhouse gases into the atmosphere. That alone is akin to treating public space (the earth) as a private one. But there is another dimension to the matter. Many SUV drivers say that they would have preferred another car but feel safer in an SUV. Whether they put it explicitly or not, what they mean is that if they get into an accident, they want to be in the car that "wins." While this behavior may be perfectly rational, it also can be regarded as being on the selfish side, as an antisocial refusal to share the road in an equal manner, making it, effectively, one's own private preserve.

Similarly, the increasing number of Americans who withdraw behind the literal gates and figurative moats of gated communities that forbid the public to come anywhere near their private streets and sidewalks also can be seen to represent a mode of antisocial behavior (it's no accident that such individuals often drive SUVs). In a dangerous world, this behavior, too, is perfectly rational, but what it signifies is a society that is becoming so mistrustful internally that it is becoming atomized into suspicious individuals whose homes and cars are becoming fortresses against everyone else. The cell phone fits neatly into this system insofar as many of its users own them for safety purposes, and many women carry them because the streets aren't such a safe place for women anymore.

The September 11 attacks augmented this significance in an especially grim way. Stories of final conversations from passengers and crew on doomed airplanes and workers in the World Trade Center lent a new dimension to the image of the cell phone as a safety device. In this sense, it became a signifier within an era of international terrorism, a shift in meaning that undermined, at least for a while, the negative image of the cell phone as the frivolous instrument of inconsiderate people. Once again, we can see from this semiotic adjustment how ordinary objects can be signifiers of changing historical conditions.

The cell phone is such a rich source of semiotic significance that its analysis could go on considerably further, investigating, for instance, the way that it reflects a workaholic world in which people feel the need to conduct their business anywhere and anytime or the way that it has contributed to a new consciousness that demands constant communication (do you flip on your phone for a chat the moment you get out of class?). In both cases, the e-mail and text-messaging revolutions are a part of the same cultural system and reflect a similar cultural significance — something you will have a chance to explore further in Chapter 5, "You-Topian Dreams." But before concluding the current discussion, let's consider a new entrant in the cultural system to which the cell phone belongs: the iPod.

The Invasion of the Music Snatchers

They're everywhere, those sleek little gizmos that enable you to carry an entire personal library of music around with you wherever you go and now enable you to do anything you can do with an iPhone except talk into it. Like cell phones, they enable their users to take what was once a private activity (listening to music) into the public realm. The iPod, of course, was not the first device to make this possible: Its historical system would include the first portable radios, boom boxes, and, perhaps most important, the Sony Walkman, which also featured an earphone-equipped personal concert hall. Indeed, between the iPod and the Walkman there lies a difference more in scale and convenience than in cultural significance, for both devices reflect an entertainment-driven society where people demand, and expect, to be able to take their own personalized entertainment with them everywhere. Throw in TiVo technology, which enables consumers to construct their own private television playlists, as it were, and you have the growing outlines of a culture in which individualized entertainment is introducing a new wrinkle in the history of mass culture. What was once a top-down, one-size-fits-all entertainment system, with top-forty radio play and three major television networks monopolizing the airwaves, is atomizing not only into niche markets constructed by the culture industry but also into one-size-fits-me personal entertainment units that consumers themselves construct. Such customized mass consumption constitutes an American contradiction that we'll explore further in Chapter 6, "American Paradox."

Disposable Decades

When analyzing a consumer sign, you will often find yourself referring to particular decades in which certain popular fads and trends were prominent, because the decade in which a given style appears may be an essential key to the system that explains it. Have you ever wondered why American cultural trends seem to change with every decade, why it is so easy to speak of the sixties or the seventies or the eighties and immediately recognize the popular styles that dominated each decade? Have you ever looked at the style of a friend and thought, "Oh, she's so seventies"? Can you place platform shoes or bell-bottoms at the drop of a hat? A change in the calendar always seems to herald a change in style in a consuming culture. But why?

The decade-to-decade shift in America's pop cultural identity goes back a good number of years. It is still easy, for example, to distinguish F. Scott Fitzgerald's Jazz Age twenties from John Steinbeck's wrathful thirties. The fifties, an especially connotative decade, raise images of ducktail haircuts and poodle skirts, drive-in culture and Elvis, family sitcoms and white-bread innocence, while the sixties are remembered for acid rock, hippies, the student revolution, and back-to-the-land communes. We remember the seventies as a pop cultural era divided among disco, Nashville, and preppiedom, with John Travolta, truckers, and Skippy and Muffy as dominant pop icons. The boom-boom eighties gave us Wall Street glitz and the yuppie invasion. Indeed, each decade since World War I — which, not accidentally, happens to coincide roughly with the rise of modern advertising and mass production — seems to carry its own consumerist style.

Exploring the Signs of Consumer Culture

"You are what you buy." In your journal, freewrite on the importance of consumer products in your life. How do you respond to being told your identity is equivalent to the products you buy? Do you resist the notion? Do you recall any instances when you have felt lost without a favorite object? How do you communicate your sense of self to others through objects, whether clothing, books, food, home decor, electronic goods, or something else?

It's no accident that the decade-to-decade shift in consumer styles coincides with the advent of modern advertising and mass production because it was mass production that created a need for constant consumer turnover in the first place. Mass production, that is, promotes stylistic change because with so many products being produced, a market must be created to consume all of them, and this means constantly consuming *more*. To get consumers to keep buying all the new stuff, you have to convince them that the stuff they already have is passé. Why else do fashion designers completely change their lines each year? Why else do car manufacturers annually change their color schemes and body shapes when the previous year's model seemed good enough? The new designs aren't simply functional improvements (though they are marketed as such); they are inducements to go out and replace what you already have to avoid appearing out of fashion. Just think: If you could afford to buy any car that you want, what would it be? Would your choice a few years ago have been the same?

Mass production, then, creates consumer societies based on the constant production of new products that are intended to be disposed of with the next product year. But something happened along the way to the establishment of our consumer culture: We began to value consumption more than production. Shoppers storm the doors as the Christmas shopping season begins earlier and earlier every year. Listen to the economic news: Consumption, not production, is relied upon to carry America out of its economic downturns. When Americans stop buying, our economy grinds to a halt. Consumption lies at the center of our economic system now, constituting some two-thirds of our economic activity, and the result has been a transformation in the very way we view ourselves.

A Tale of Two Cities

It has not always been thus in America, however. Once, Americans prided themselves on their productivity. In 1914, for example, the poet Carl Sandburg boasted of a Chicago that was "Hog butcher for the world, Tool maker, Stacker of Wheat, Player with Railroads and the Nation's Freight Handler." One wonders what Sandburg would think of the place today. From the south shore east to the industrial suburb of Gary, Indiana, Chicago's once-proud mills and factories rust in the winter wind. At the Chicago Mercantile Exchange, trade today is in commodity futures, not commodities.

Meanwhile, a few hundred miles to the northwest, Bloomington, Minnesota, buzzes with excitement. For there stands the Mall of America, a colossus of consumption so large that it contains within its walls a seven-acre Knott's Berry Farm theme park, with lots of room to spare. You can find almost anything you want in the Mall of America, but most of what you will find won't have been manufactured in America. The proud tag "Made in the USA" is an increasingly rare item.

It's a long way from Sandburg's Chicago to the Mall of America, a trip that traverses America's shift from a producer to a consumer economy. This shift is not simply economic; it is behind a cultural transformation that is shaping a new mythology within which we define ourselves, our hopes, and our desires.

Ask yourself right now what your own goals are in going to college. Do you envision a career in law, or medicine, or banking and finance? Do you want to be a teacher, an advertising executive, or a civil servant? Or maybe you are preparing for a career in an Internet-related field. If you've considered any of these career examples, you are contemplating what are known as service jobs. While essential to a society, none of them actually produces anything. If you've given thought to going into some facet of manufacturing, on the other hand, you are unusual because America offers increasingly fewer opportunities in that area and little prestige. The prestige jobs are in law and medicine and in high-tech operations like Google, a fact that is easy to take for granted. But ask yourself: Does it have to be so?

To ask such questions is to begin to reveal the outline of a cultural mythology based in consumption rather than production. For one thing, while law and medicine require specialized training available to only a few, doctors and lawyers also make a lot of money and so are higher up on the scale of consumption. Quite simply, they can buy more than others can. It is easy to presume that this would be the case anywhere, but in the former Soviet Union physicians — many of whom were women — were relatively low on the social scale. Male engineers, on the other hand, were highly valued for their role in facilitating military production. In what was a producer rather than a consumer culture, it was the producers who roosted high on the social ladder.

To live in a consumer culture is not simply a matter of shopping, however; it is also a matter of being. For in a consumer society, you are what you consume, and the entire social and economic order is maintained by the constant encouragement to buy. The ubiquity of television and advertising in America is a direct result of this system, for these media deliver the constant stimulus to buy through avalanches of consuming images. Consider how difficult it is to escape the arm of the advertiser. You may turn off your TV set, but a screen awaits you at the supermarket checkout counter, displaying incentives to spend your money. If you rush to the restroom to hide, you may find advertisements tacked to the stalls. If you log onto the Internet, ads greet you on your monitor. Resistance is useless. Weren't you planning to do some shopping this weekend anyway?

When the Going Gets Tough, the Tough Go Shopping

In a cultural system where our identities are displayed in the products we buy, it accordingly behooves us to pay close attention to what we consume and why. From the cars we drive to the clothes we wear, we are enmeshed in a web of consuming images. As students, you are probably freer to choose the

---

Reading Consumer Culture on the Net

Log onto one of the many home shopping networks or auction sites. You might try the QVC (www.QVC.com), Shop at Home (www.shopat home.com), or eBay (www.ebay.com). Analyze both the products sold and the way they are marketed. Who is the target audience for the network you're studying, and what images and values are used to attract this market? How does the marketing compare with nonelectronic sales pitches, such as displays in shopping malls and magazines or TV advertising? Does the electronic medium affect your own behavior as a consumer? Does the time pressure of an electronic auction affect your behavior as a consumer? How do you account for any differences in electronic and traditional marketing strategies?

---

particular images you wish to project through the products you consume than most other demographic groups in America. This claim may sound paradoxical: After all, don't working adults have more money than starving students? Yes, generally. But the working world places severe restrictions on the choices employees can make in their clothing and grooming styles, and even automobile choice may be restricted (real estate agents, for example, can't escort their clients around town in VW Beetles). Corporate business wear, for all its variations, still revolves around a central core of necktied and dark-hued sobriety, regardless of the gender of the wearer. On campus, however, you can be pretty much whatever you want to be, which is why your own daily lives provide you with a particularly rich field of consumer signs to read and decode.

So go to it. By the time you finish reading this book, a lot will have changed. Look around. Start reading the signs.

The Readings

As this chapter's lead essay, Laurence Shames's "The More Factor" provides a mythological background for the discussions of America's consuming behavior that follow. Shames takes a historical approach to American consumerism, relating our frontier history to our ever-expanding desire for more goods and services. Next, in a paired set of readings, Malcolm Gladwell reveals the elaborate measures that retail store managers take in order to maximize your consumption when you visit their shops, while Anne Norton offers a semiotic analysis of shopping malls, mail-order catalogues, and the Home Shopping Network, focusing on the ways in which they construct a language of consumption tailored to specific consumer groups. Thomas Hine's interpretation of the packaging that contains America's most commonly consumed products shows how packages constitute complex sign systems intended for consumer "readings." Joan Kron follows with a study of the way we use home furnishings to reflect our sense of personal identity. Anne Galligan then takes on Pottermania, explaining how the boy wizard has taken the world by storm, with a little help from his corporate friends. Alison Schneider dares to go where few dare to tread, into the fashion secrets, and foibles, of college professors, and David Goewey turns to automotive signs in his semiotic analysis of the SUV trend. Finally, Thomas L. Friedman offers prescient insights into the global dimensions of American consumer culture and the cultural conflicts behind the September 11 terrorist attacks, and the chapter concludes with Thomas Frank's musings on how corporate America has turned consumption into a hip signifier of inauthentic counterculturalism.

LAURENCE SHAMES
The More Factor

A bumper sticker popular in the 1980s read, "Whoever dies with the most toys wins." In this selection from The Hunger for More: Searching for Values in an Age of Greed *(1989), Laurence Shames shows how the great American hunger for more—more toys, more land, more opportunities—is an essential part of our history and character, stemming from the frontier era when the horizon alone seemed the only limit to American desire. The author of* The Big Time: The Harvard Business School's Most Successful Class and How It Shaped America *(1986) and the holder of a Harvard M.B.A., Shames is a journalist who has contributed to such publications as* Playboy, Vanity Fair, Manhattan, inc., *and* Esquire. *He currently is working full-time on writing fiction and screen plays, with his most recent publications including* Florida Straits *(1992),* Sunburn *(1995),* Welcome to Paradise *(1999),* The Naked Detective *(2000), and, with Peter Barton,* Not Fade Away *(2003).*

1

Americans have always been optimists, and optimists have always liked to speculate. In Texas in the 1880s, the speculative instrument of choice was towns, and there is no tale more American than this.

What people would do was buy up enormous tracts of parched and vacant land, lay out a Main Street, nail together some wooden sidewalks, and start slapping up buildings. One of these buildings would be called the Grand Hotel and would have a saloon complete with swinging doors. Another might be dubbed the New Academy or the Opera House. The developers would erect a flagpole and name a church, and once the workmen had packed up and moved on, the towns would be as empty as the sky.

But no matter. The speculators, next, would hire people to pass out handbills in the Eastern and Midwestern cities, tracts limning the advantages of relocation to "the Athens of the South" or "the new plains Jerusalem." When persuasion failed, the builders might resort to bribery, paying people's moving costs and giving them houses, in exchange for nothing but a pledge to stay until a certain census was taken or a certain inspection made. Once the nose count was completed, people were free to move on, and there was in fact a contingent of folks who made their living by keeping a cabin on skids and dragging it for pay from one town to another.

The speculators' idea, of course, was to lure the railroad. If one could create a convincing semblance of a town, the railroad might come through it, and a real town would develop, making the speculators staggeringly rich. By these devices a man named Sanborn once owned Amarillo.[1]

But railroad tracks are narrow and the state of Texas is very, very wide. For every Wichita Falls or Lubbock there were a dozen College Mounds or Belchervilles,[2] bleached, unpeopled burgs that receded quietly into the dust, taking with them large amounts of speculators' money.

Still, the speculators kept right on bucking the odds and depositing empty towns in the middle of nowhere. Why did they do it? Two reasons — reasons that might be said to summarize the central fact of American economic history and that go a fair way toward explaining what is perhaps the central strand of the national character.

The first reason was simply that the possible returns were so enormous as to partake of the surreal, to create a climate in which ordinary logic and prudence did not seem to apply. In a boom like that of real estate when the railroad barreled through, long shots that might pay one hundred thousand to one seemed worth a bet.

The second reason, more pertinent here, is that there was a presumption that America would *keep on* booming — if not forever, then at least longer than it made sense to worry about. There would always be another gold rush, another Homestead Act, another oil strike. The next generation would always ferret out opportunities that would be still more lavish than any that had gone before. America *was* those opportunities. This was an article not just of faith, but of strategy. You banked on the next windfall, you staked your hopes and even your self-esteem on it, and this led to a national turn of mind that might usefully be thought of as the habit of more.

A century, maybe two centuries, before anyone had heard the term *baby boomer*, much less *yuppie*, the habit of more had been instilled as the operative truth among the economically ambitious. The habit of more seemed to suggest that there was no such thing as getting wiped out in America. A fortune lost in Texas might be recouped in Colorado. Funds frittered away on grazing land where nothing grew might flood back in as silver. There was always a second chance, or always seemed to be, in this land where growth was destiny and where expansion and purpose were the same.

The key was the frontier, not just as a matter of acreage, but as idea. Vast, varied, rough as rocks, America was the place where one never quite came to the end. Ben Franklin explained it to Europe even before the Revolutionary War had finished: America offered new chances to those "who, in their own

---

[1] For a fuller account of railroad-related land speculation in Texas, see F. Stanley, *Story of the Texas Panhandle Railroads* (Borger, Tex.: Hess Publishing Co., 1976).

[2] T. Lindsay Baker, *Ghost Towns of Texas* (Norman, Okla.: University of Oklahoma Press, 1986).

Countries, where all the Lands [were] fully occupied . . . could never [emerge] from the poor Condition wherein they were born."[3]

So central was this awareness of vacant space and its link to economic promise that Frederick Jackson Turner, the historian who set the tone for much of the twentieth century's understanding of the American past, would write that it was "not the constitution, but free land . . . [that] made the democratic type of society in America."[4] Good laws mattered; an accountable government mattered; ingenuity and hard work mattered. But those things were, so to speak, an overlay on the natural, geographic America that was simply *there*, and whose vast and beckoning possibilities seemed to generate the ambition and the sometimes reckless liberty that would fill it. First and foremost, it was open space that provided "the freedom of the individual to rise under conditions of social mobility."[5]

Open space generated not just ambition, but metaphor. As early as 1835, Tocqueville was extrapolating from the fact of America's emptiness to the observation that "no natural boundary seems to be set to the efforts of man."[6] Nor was any limit placed on what he might accomplish, since, in that heyday of the Protestant ethic, a person's rewards were taken to be quite strictly proportionate to his labors.

Frontier; opportunity; more. This has been the American trinity from the very start. The frontier was the backdrop and also the raw material for the streak of economic booms. The booms became the goad and also the justification for the myriad gambles and for Americans' famous optimism. The optimism, in turn, shaped the schemes and visions that were sometimes noble, sometimes appalling, always bold. The frontier, as reality and as symbol, is what has shaped the American way of doing things and the American sense of what's worth doing.

But there has been one further corollary to the legacy of the frontier, with its promise of ever-expanding opportunities: Given that the goal — a realistic goal for most of our history — was *more*, Americans have been somewhat backward in adopting values, hopes, ambitions that have to do with things *other than* more. In America, a sense of quality has lagged far behind a sense of scale. An ideal of contentment has yet to take root in soil traditionally more hospitable to an ideal of restless striving. The ethic of decency has been upstaged by the ethic of success. The concept of growth has been applied almost exclusively to things that can be measured, counted, weighed. And the hunger for those things that are unmeasurable but fine — the sorts of accomplishment that cannot be undone by circumstance or a shift in social fashion, the kind of

---

[3]Benjamin Franklin, "Information to Those Who Would Remove to America," in *The Autobiography and Other Writings* (New York: Penguin Books, 1986), 242.

[4]Frederick Jackson Turner, *The Frontier in American History* (Melbourne, Fla.: Krieger, 1976 [reprint of 1920 edition]), 293.

[5]Ibid., 266.

[6]Tocqueville, *Democracy in America*.

serenity that cannot be shattered by tomorrow's headline — has gone largely unfulfilled, and even unacknowledged.

2

If the supply of more went on forever, perhaps that wouldn't matter very 15 much. Expansion could remain a goal unto itself, and would continue to generate a value system based on bulk rather than on nuance, on quantities of money rather than on quality of life, on "progress" itself rather than on a sense of what the progress was for. But what if, over time, there was less more to be had?

That is the essential situation of America today.

Let's keep things in proportion: The country is not running out of wealth, drive, savvy, or opportunities. We are not facing imminent ruin, and neither panic nor gloom is called for. But there have been ample indications over the past two decades that we are running out of more.

Consider productivity growth — according to many economists, the single most telling and least distortable gauge of changes in real wealth. From 1947 to 1965, productivity in the private sector (adjusted, as are all the following figures, for inflation) was advancing, on average, by an annual 3.3 percent. This means, simply, that each hour of work performed by a specimen American worker contributed 3.3 cents worth or more to every American dollar every year; whether we saved it or spent it, that increment went into a national kitty of ever-enlarging aggregate wealth. Between 1965 and 1972, however, the "more-factor" decreased to 2.4 percent a year, and from 1972 to 1977 it slipped further, to 1.6 percent. By the early 1980s, productivity growth was at a virtual standstill, crawling along at 0.2 percent for the five years ending in 1982.[7] Through the middle years of the 1980s, the numbers rebounded somewhat — but by then the gains were being neutralized by the gargantuan carrying costs on the national debt.[8]

Inevitably, this decline in the national stockpile of more held consequences for the individual wallet.[9] During the 1950s, Americans' average hourly earnings were humping ahead at a gratifying 2.5 percent each year. By the late seventies, that figure stood just where productivity growth had come to stand, at a dispiriting 0.2 cents on the dollar. By the first half of the

[7]These figures are taken from the Council of Economic Advisers, *Economic Report of the President*, February 1984, 267.

[8]For a lucid and readable account of the meaning and implications of our reservoir of red ink, see Lawrence Malkin, *The National Debt* (New York: Henry Holt and Co., 1987). Through no fault of Malkin's, many of his numbers are already obsolete, but his explanation of who owes what to whom, and what it means, remains sound and even entertaining in a bleak sort of way.

[9]The figures in this paragraph and the next are from "The Average Guy Takes It on the Chin," *New York Times*, 13 July 1986, sec. 3.

eighties, the Reagan "recovery" notwithstanding, real hourly wages were actually moving backwards — declining at an average annual rate of 0.3 percent.

Compounding the shortage of more was an unfortunate but crucial demographic fact. Real wealth was nearly ceasing to expand just at the moment when the members of that unprecedented population bulge known as the baby boom were entering what should have been their peak years of income expansion. A working man or woman who was thirty years old in 1949 could expect to see his or her real earnings burgeon by 63 percent by age forty. In 1959, a thirty-year-old could still look forward to a gain of 49 percent by his or her fortieth birthday.

But what about the person who turned thirty in 1973? By the time that worker turned forty, his or her real earnings had shrunk by a percentage point. For all the blather about yuppies with their beach houses, BMWs, and radicchio salads, and even factoring in those isolated tens of thousands making ludicrous sums in consulting firms or on Wall Street, the fact is that between 1979 and 1983 real earnings of all Americans between the ages of twenty-five and thirty-four actually declined by 14 percent.[10] The *New York Times*, well before the stock market crash put the kibosh on eighties confidence, summed up the implications of this downturn by observing that "for millions of breadwinners, the American dream is becoming the impossible dream."[11]

Now, it is not our main purpose here to detail the ups and downs of the American economy. Our aim, rather, is to consider the effects of those ups and downs on people's goals, values, sense of their place in the world. What happens at that shadowy juncture where economic prospects meld with personal choice? What sorts of insights and adjustments are called for so that economic ups and downs can be dealt with gracefully?

Fact one in this connection is that, if America's supply of more is in fact diminishing, American values will have to shift and broaden to fill the gap where the expectation of almost automatic gains used to be. Something more durable will have to replace the fat but fragile bubble that had been getting frailer these past two decades and that finally popped — a tentative, partial pop — on October 19, 1987. A different sort of growth — ultimately, a growth in responsibility and happiness — will have to fulfill our need to believe that our possibilities are still expanding.

The transition to that new view of progress will take some fancy stepping, because, at least since the end of World War II, simple economic growth has stood, in the American psyche, as the best available substitute for the literal frontier. The economy has *been* the frontier. Instead of more space, we have had more money. Rather than measuring progress in terms of geographical expansion, we have measured it by expansion in our standard of living.

---

[10]See, for example, "The Year of the Yuppie," *Newsweek*, 31 December 1984, 16.
[11]"The Average Guy."

Economics has become the metaphor on which we pin our hopes of open space and second chances.

The poignant part is that the literal frontier did not pass yesterday: it has   25 not existed for a hundred years. But the frontier's promise has become so much a part of us that we have not been willing to let the concept die. We have kept the frontier mythology going by invocation, by allusion, by hype.

It is not a coincidence that John F. Kennedy dubbed his political program the New Frontier. It is not mere linguistic accident that makes us speak of Frontiers of Science or of psychedelic drugs as carrying one to Frontiers of Perception. We glorify fads and fashions by calling them Frontiers of Taste. Nuclear energy has been called the Last Frontier; solar energy has been called the Last Frontier. Outer space has been called the Last Frontier; the oceans have been called the Last Frontier. Even the suburbs, those blandest and least adventurous of places, have been wryly described as the crabgrass frontier.[12]

What made all these usages plausible was their being linked to the image of the American economy as an endlessly fertile continent whose boundaries never need be reached, a domain that could expand in perpetuity, a gigantic playing field that would never run out of room and on which the game would get forever bigger and more filled with action. This was the frontier that would not vanish.

It is worth noting that people in other countries (with the possible exception of that other America, Australia) do not talk about frontier this way. In Europe, and in most of Africa and Asia, "frontier" connotes, at worst, a place of barbed wire and men with rifles, and at best, a neutral junction where one changes currency while passing from one fixed system into another. Frontier, for most of the world's people, does not suggest growth, expanse, or opportunity.

For Americans, it does, and always has. This is one of the things that sets America apart from other places and makes American attitudes different from those of other people. It is why, from *Bonanza* to the Sierra Club, the notion or even the fantasy of empty horizons and untapped resources has always evoked in the American heart both passion and wistfulness. And it is why the fear that the economic frontier — our last, best version of the Wild West — may finally be passing creates in us not only money worries but also a crisis of morale and even of purpose.

3

It might seem strange to call the 1980s an era of nostalgia. The decade, after   30 all, has been more usually described in terms of coolness, pragmatism, and a blithe innocence of history. But the eighties, unawares, were nostalgic for

[12]With the suburbs again taking on a sort of fascination, this phrase was resurrected as the title of a 1985 book — *Crabgrass Frontier: The Suburbanization of America*, by Kenneth T. Jackson (Oxford University Press).

frontiers; and the disappointment of that nostalgia had much to do with the time's greed, narrowness, and strange want of joy. The fear that the world may not be a big enough playground for the full exercise of one's energies and yearnings, and worse, the fear that the playground is being fenced off and will no longer expand — these are real worries and they have had consequences. The eighties were an object lesson in how people play the game when there is an awful and unspoken suspicion that the game is winding down.

It was ironic that the yuppies came to be so reviled for their vaunting ambition and outsized expectations, as if they'd invented the habit of more, when in fact they'd only inherited it the way a fetus picks up an addiction in the womb. The craving was there in the national bloodstream, a remnant of the frontier, and the baby boomers, described in childhood as "the luckiest generation,"[13] found themselves, as young adults, in the melancholy position of wrestling with a two-hundred-year dependency on a drug that was now in short supply.

True, the 1980s raised the clamor for more to new heights of shrillness, insistence, and general obnoxiousness, but this, it can be argued, was in the nature of a final binge, the storm before the calm. America, though fighting the perception every inch of the way, was coming to realize that it was not a preordained part of the natural order that one should be richer every year. If it happened, that was nice. But who had started the flimsy and pernicious rumor that it was normal?

READING THE TEXT

1. Summarize in a paragraph how, according to Shames, the frontier functions as a symbol of American consciousness.

2. What connections does Shames make between America's frontier history and consumer behavior?

3. Why does Shames term the 1980s "an era of nostalgia" (para. 30)?

READING THE SIGNS

1. **CONNECTING TEXTS** Shames asserts that Americans have been influenced by the frontier belief "that America would *keep* on booming" (para. 8). Do you feel that this belief continues to be influential into the twenty-first century? Write an essay arguing for your position. To develop your ideas, consult Tim Kasser's "Mixed Messages" (p. 502).

2. Shames claims that, because of the desire for more, "the ethic of decency has been upstaged by the ethic of success" (para. 14). In class, form teams and debate the validity of Shames's claim.

---

[13]Thomas Hine, *Populuxe* (New York: Alfred A. Knopf, 1986), 15.

3. **CONNECTING TEXTS**   Read or review Joan Kron's "The Semiotics of Home Decor" (p. 119). How is Martin J. Davidson influenced by the frontier myth that Shames describes?

4. **CONNECTING TEXTS**   In an essay, argue for or refute the proposition that the "hunger for more" that Shames describes is a universal human trait, not simply American. To develop your ideas, consult Joan Kron, "The Semiotics of Home Decor" (p. 119), and Thomas L. Friedman, "Revolution Is U.S." (p. 157).

UNDERSTANDING SHOPPING

MALCOLM GLADWELL
The Science of Shopping

Ever wonder why the season's hottest new styles at stores like the Gap are usually displayed on the right at least fifteen paces in from the front entrance? It's because that's where shoppers are most likely to see them as they enter the store, gear down from the walking pace of a mall corridor, and adjust to the shop's spatial environment. Ever wonder how shop managers know this sort of thing? It's because, as Malcolm Gladwell reports here, they hire consultants like Paco Underhill, a "retail anthropologist" and "urban geographer" whose studies (often aided by hidden cameras) of shopping behavior have become valuable guides to store managers looking for the best ways to move the goods. Does this feel just a little Orwellian? Read on. A staff writer for the New Yorker, *in which this selection first appeared, Gladwell has also written* The Tipping Point *(2000) and* Blink: The Power of Thinking without Thinking *(2005).*

Human beings walk the way they drive, which is to say that Americans tend to keep to the right when they stroll down shopping-mall concourses or city sidewalks. This is why in a well-designed airport travellers drifting toward their gate will always find the fast-food restaurants on their left and the gift shops on their right: people will readily cross a lane of pedestrian traffic to satisfy their hunger but rarely to make an impulse buy of a T-shirt or a magazine. This is also why Paco Underhill tells his retail clients to make sure that their window displays are canted, preferably to both sides but especially to the left, so that a potential shopper approaching the store on the inside of the sidewalk — the shopper, that is, with the least impeded view of the store window — can see the display from at least twenty-five feet away.

Of course, a lot depends on how fast the potential shopper is walking. Paco, in his previous life, as an urban geographer in Manhattan, spent a great deal of time thinking about walking speeds as he listened in on the great debates of the nineteen-seventies over whether the traffic lights in midtown should be timed to facilitate the movement of cars or to facilitate the movement of pedestrians and so break up the big platoons that move down Manhattan sidewalks. He knows that the faster you walk the more your peripheral vision narrows, so you become unable to pick up visual cues as quickly as someone who is just ambling along. He knows, too, that people who walk fast take a surprising amount of time to slow down — just as it takes a good stretch of road to change gears with a stick-shift automobile. On the basis of his research, Paco estimates the human downshift period to be anywhere from twelve to twenty-five feet, so if you own a store, he says, you never want to be next door to a bank: potential shoppers speed up when they walk past a bank (since there's nothing to look at), and by the time they slow down they've walked right past your business. The downshift factor also means that when potential shoppers enter a store it's going to take them from five to fifteen paces to adjust to the light and refocus and gear down from walking speed to shopping speed — particularly if they've just had to navigate a treacherous parking lot or hurry to make the light at Fifty-seventh and Fifth.

Paco calls that area inside the door the Decompression Zone, and something he tells clients over and over again is never, *ever* put anything of value in that zone — not shopping baskets or tie racks or big promotional displays — because no one is going to see it. Paco believes that, as a rule of thumb, customer interaction with any product or promotional display in the Decompression Zone will increase at least thirty per cent once it's moved to the back edge of the zone, and even more if it's placed to the right, because another of the fundamental rules of how human beings shop is that upon entering a store — whether it's Nordstrom or K Mart, Tiffany or the Gap — the shopper invariably and reflexively turns to the right. Paco believes in the existence of the Invariant Right because he has actually verified it. He has put cameras in stores trained directly on the doorway, and if you go to his office, just above Union Square, where videocassettes and boxes of Super-eight film from all his work over the years are stacked in plastic Tupperware containers practically up to the ceiling, he can show you reel upon reel of grainy entryway video — customers striding in the door, downshifting, refocusing, and then, again and again, making that little half turn.

Paco Underhill is a tall man in his mid-forties, partly bald, with a neatly trimmed beard and an engaging, almost goofy manner. He wears baggy khakis and shirts open at the collar, and generally looks like the academic he might have been if he hadn't been captivated, twenty years ago, by the ideas of the urban anthropologist William Whyte. It was Whyte who pioneered the use of time-lapse photography as a tool of urban planning, putting cameras in parks and the plazas in front of office buildings in midtown Manhattan, in order to determine what distinguished a public space that worked from one that didn't. As a Columbia undergraduate, in 1974, Paco heard a lecture on Whyte's work and, he recalls, left the room "walking on air." He immediately read everything Whyte had written. He emptied his bank account to buy cameras and film and make his own home movie, about a pedestrian mall in Pough-keepsie. He took his "little exercise" to Whyte's advocacy group, the Project for Public Spaces, and was offered a job. Soon, however, it dawned on Paco that Whyte's ideas could be taken a step further — that the same techniques he used to establish why a plaza worked or didn't work could also be used to determine why a store worked or didn't work. Thus was born the field of retail anthropology, and, not long afterward, Paco founded Envirosell, which in just over fifteen years has counselled some of the most familiar names in American retailing, from Levi Strauss to Kinney, Starbucks, McDonald's, Block-buster, Apple Computer, AT&T, and a number of upscale retailers that Paco would rather not name.

When Paco gets an assignment, he and his staff set up a series of video- 5 cameras throughout the test store and then back the cameras up with Envi-rosell staffers — trackers, as they're known — armed with clipboards. Where the cameras go and how many trackers Paco deploys depends on exactly what the store wants to know about its shoppers. Typically, though, he might use six cameras and two or three trackers, and let the study run for two or three days, so that at the end he would have pages and pages of carefully annotated tracking sheets and anywhere from a hundred to five hundred hours of film. These days, given the expansion of his business, he might tape fifteen thousand hours in a year, and, given that he has been in operation since the late seventies, he now has well over a hundred thousand hours of tape in his library.

Even in the best of times, this would be a valuable archive. But today, with the retail business in crisis, it is a gold mine. The time per visit that the aver-age American spends in a shopping mall was sixty-six minutes last year — down from seventy-two minutes in 1992 — and is the lowest number ever recorded. The amount of selling space per American shopper is now more than double what it was in the mid-seventies, meaning that profit margins have never been narrower, and the costs of starting a retail business — and of failing — have never been higher. In the past few years, countless dazzling new retailing temples have been built along Fifth and Madison Avenues — Barneys, Calvin Klein, Armani, Valentino, Banana Republic, Prada, Chanel, NikeTown, and on and on — but it is an explosion of growth based on no more than a hunch, a hopeful multimillion-dollar gamble that the way to break through is to provide the shopper with spectacle and more spectacle. "The arrogance is gone," Millard Drexler, the president and C.E.O. of the Gap, told me. "Arro-gance makes failure. Once you think you know the answer, it's almost always over." In such a competitive environment, retailers don't just want to know how shoppers behave in their stores. They *have* to know. And who better to ask than Paco Underhill, who in the past decade and a half has analyzed tens of thousands of hours of shopping videotape and, as a result, probably knows more about the strange habits and quirks of the species *Emptor americanus* than anyone else alive?

Paco is considered the originator, for example, of what is known in the trade as the butt-brush theory — or, as Paco calls it, more delicately, *le facteur bousculade* — which holds that the likelihood of a woman's being converted from a browser to a buyer is inversely proportional to the likelihood of her being brushed on her behind while she's examining merchandise. Touch — or brush or bump or jostle — a woman on the behind when she has stopped to look at an item, and she will bolt. Actually, calling this a theory is something of a misnomer, because Paco doesn't offer any explanation for why women react that way, aside from venturing that they are "more sensitive back there." It's really an observation, based on repeated and close analysis of his videotape library, that Paco has transformed into a retailing commandment: a women's product that requires extensive examination should never be placed in a narrow aisle.

Paco approaches the problem of the Invariant Right the same way. Some retail thinkers see this as a subject crying out for interpretation and speculation. The design guru Joseph Weishar, for example, argues, in his magisterial *Design for Effective Selling Space*, that the Invariant Right is a function of the fact that we "absorb and digest information in the left part of the brain" and "assimilate and logically use this information in the right half," the result being that we scan the store from left to right and then fix on an object to the right "essentially at a 45 degree angle from the point that we enter." When I asked Paco about this interpretation, he shrugged, and said he thought the reason was simply that most people are right-handed. Uncovering the fundamentals of "why" is clearly not a pursuit that engages him much. He is not a theoretician but an empiricist, and for him the important thing is that in amassing his huge library of in-store time-lapse photography he has gained enough hard evidence to know how often and under what circumstances the Invariant Right is expressed and how to take advantage of it.

What Paco likes are facts. They come tumbling out when he talks, and, because he speaks with a slight hesitation — lingering over the first syllable in, for example, "re-tail" or "de-sign" — he draws you in, and you find yourself truly hanging on his words. "We have reached a historic point in American history," he told me in our very first conversation. "Men, for the first time, have begun to buy their own underwear." He then paused to let the comment sink in, so that I could absorb its implications, before he elaborated: "Which means that we have to *totally* rethink the way we sell that product." In the parlance of Hollywood scriptwriters, the best endings must be surprising and yet inevitable; and the best of Paco's pronouncements take the same shape. It would never have occurred to me to wonder about the increasingly critical role played by touching — or, as Paco calls it, petting — clothes in the course of making the decision to buy them. But then I went to the Gap and to Banana Republic and saw people touching, and fondling and, one after another, buying shirts

Sports apparel for sale at a NikeTown store in Chicago.

and sweaters laid out on big wooden tables, and what Paco told me — which was no doubt based on what he had seen on his videotapes — made perfect sense: that the reason the Gap and Banana Republic have tables is not merely that sweaters and shirts look better there, or that tables fit into the warm and relaxing residential feeling that the Gap and Banana Republic are trying to create in their stores, but that tables invite — indeed, symbolize — touching. "Where do we eat?" Paco asks. "We eat, we pick up food, on tables."

Paco produces for his clients a series of carefully detailed studies, totalling 10 forty to a hundred and fifty pages, filled with product-by-product breakdowns and bright-colored charts and graphs. In one recent case, he was asked by a major clothing retailer to analyze the first of a new chain of stores that the firm planned to open. One of the things the client wanted to know was how successful the store was in drawing people into its depths, since the chances that shoppers will buy something are directly related to how long they spend shopping, and how long they spend shopping is directly related to how deep they get pulled into the store. For this reason, a supermarket will often put dairy products on one side, meat at the back, and fresh produce on the other side, so that the typical shopper can't just do a drive-by but has to make an entire circuit of the store, and be tempted by everything the supermarket has to offer. In the case of the new clothing store, Paco found that ninety-one percent of all shoppers penetrated as deep as what he called Zone 4, meaning more than three-quarters of the way in, well past the accessories and shirt racks and belts in the front, and little short of the far wall, with the changing rooms and the pants stacked on shelves. Paco regarded this as an extraordinary figure, particularly for a long, narrow store like this one, where it is not unusual for the rate of penetration past, say, Zone 3 to be under fifty percent.

But that didn't mean the store was perfect — far from it. For Paco, all kinds of questions remained.

Purchasers, for example, spent an average of eleven minutes and twenty-seven seconds in the store, nonpurchasers two minutes and thirty-six seconds. It wasn't that the nonpurchasers just cruised in and out: in those two minutes and thirty-six seconds, they went deep into the store and examined an average of 3.42 items. So why didn't they buy? What, exactly, happened to cause some browsers to buy and other browsers to walk out the door?

Then, there was the issue of the number of products examined. The purchasers were looking at an average of 4.81 items but buying only 1.33 items. Paco found this statistic deeply disturbing. As the retail market grows more cutthroat, store owners have come to realize that it's all but impossible to increase the number of customers coming in, and have concentrated instead on getting the customers they do have to buy more. Paco thinks that if you can sell someone a pair of pants you must also be able to sell that person a belt, or a pair of socks, or a pair of underpants, or even do what the Gap does so well: sell a person a complete outfit. To Paco, the figure 1.33 suggested that the store was doing something very wrong, and one day when I visited him in his office he sat me down in front of one of his many VCRs to see how he looked for the 1.33 culprit.

It should be said that sitting next to Paco is a rather strange experience. "My mother says that I'm the best-paid spy in America," he told me. He laughed, but he wasn't entirely joking. As a child, Paco had a nearly debilitating stammer, and, he says, "since I was never that comfortable talking I always relied on my eyes to understand things." That much is obvious from the first moment you meet him: Paco is one of those people who looks right at you, soaking up every nuance and detail. It isn't a hostile gaze, because Paco isn't hostile at all. He has a big smile, and he'll call you "chief" and use your first name a lot and generally act as if he knew you well. But that's the awkward thing: He has looked at you so closely that you're sure he does know you well, and you, meanwhile, hardly know him at all.

This kind of asymmetry is even more pronounced when you watch his shopping videos with him, because every movement or gesture means something to Paco — he has spent his adult life deconstructing the shopping experience — but nothing to the outsider, or, at least, not at first. Paco had to keep stopping the video to get me to see things through his eyes before I began to understand. In one sequence, for example, a camera mounted high on the wall outside the changing rooms documented a man and a woman shopping for a pair of pants for what appeared to be their daughter, a girl in her midteens. The tapes are soundless, but the basic steps of the shopping dance are so familiar to Paco that, once I'd grasped the general idea, he was able to provide a running commentary on what was being said and thought. There is the girl emerging from the changing room wearing her first pair. There she is glancing at her reflection in the mirror, then turning to see herself from the back. There is the mother looking on. There is the father — or, as fathers are known in the trade, the "wallet carrier" — stepping forward and pulling up the jeans. There's the girl trying on another pair. There's the primp again. The twirl. The mother. The wallet carrier. And then again, with another pair. The full sequence lasted twenty minutes, and at the end came the take-home lesson, for which Paco called in one of his colleagues, Tom Moseman, who had supervised the project.

"This is a very critical moment," Tom, a young, intense man wearing little round glasses, said, and he pulled up a chair next to mine. "She's saying, 'I don't know whether I should wear a belt.' Now here's the salesclerk. The girl says to him, 'I need a belt,' and he says, 'Take mine.' Now there he is taking her back to the full-length mirror." 15

A moment later, the girl returns, clearly happy with the purchase. She wants the jeans. The wallet carrier turns to her, and then gestures to the salesclerk. The wallet carrier is telling his daughter to give back the belt. The girl gives back the belt. Tom stops the tape. He's leaning forward now, a finger jabbing at the screen. Beside me, Paco is shaking his head. I don't get it — at least, not at first — and so Tom replays that last segment. The wallet carrier tells the girl to give back the belt. She gives back the belt. And then, finally, it dawns on me why this store has an average purchase number of only 1.33. "Don't you see?" Tom said. "*She wanted the belt*. A great opportunity to make an add-on sale . . . *lost!*"

Should we be afraid of Paco Underhill? One of the fundamental anxieties of the American consumer, after all, has always been that beneath the pleasure and the frivolity of the shopping experience runs an undercurrent of manipulation, and that anxiety has rarely seemed more justified than today. The practice of prying into the minds and habits of American consumers is now a multibillion-dollar business. Every time a product is pulled across a supermarket checkout scanner, information is recorded, assembled, and sold to a market-research firm for analysis. There are companies that put tiny cameras inside frozen-food cases in supermarket aisles; market-research firms that feed census data and behavioral statistics into algorithms and come out with complicated maps of the American consumer; anthropologists who sift through the garbage of carefully targeted households to analyze their true consumption patterns; and endless rounds of highly organized focus groups and questionnaire takers and phone surveyors. That some people are now tracking our every shopping move with video cameras seems in many respects the last straw: Paco's movies are, after all, creepy. They look like the surveillance videos taken during convenience-store holdups — hazy and soundless and slightly warped by the angle of the lens. When you watch them, you find yourself waiting for something bad to happen, for someone to shoplift or pull a gun on a cashier.

The more time you spend with Paco's videos, though, the less scary they seem. After an hour or so, it's no longer clear whether simply by watching people shop — and analyzing their every move — you can learn how to control them. The shopper that emerges from the videos is not pliable or manipulable.

The screen shows people filtering in and out of stores, petting and moving on, abandoning their merchandise because checkout lines are too long, or leaving a store empty-handed because they couldn't fit their stroller into the aisle between two shirt racks. Paco's shoppers are fickle and headstrong, and are quite unwilling to buy anything unless conditions are perfect — unless the belt is presented at *exactly* the right moment. His theories of the butt-brush and petting and the Decompression Zone and the Invariant Right seek not to make shoppers conform to the desires of sellers but to make sellers conform to the desires of shoppers. What Paco is teaching his clients is a kind of slavish devotion to the shopper's every whim. He is teaching them humility.

READING THE TEXT

1. Summarize in your own words the ways that retailers use spatial design to affect the consumer's behavior and buying habits.

2. What is Gladwell's tone in this selection, and what does it reveal about his attitudes toward the retail industry's manipulation of customers?

3. What is the effect on the reader of Gladwell's description of Paco Underhill's appearance and background?

4. Why does Paco Underhill's mother say that he is "the best-paid spy in America" (para. 13)?

READING THE SIGNS

1. **CONNECTING TEXTS**   Visit a local store or supermarket, and study the spatial design. How many of the design strategies that Gladwell describes do you observe, and how do they affect customers' behavior? Use your observations as the basis for an essay interpreting the store's spatial design. To develop your ideas further, consult Anne Norton's "The Signs of Shopping" (p. 101).

2. In class, form teams and debate the proposition that the surveillance of consumers by retail anthropologists is manipulative and unethical.

3. Visit a Web site of a major retailer (such as **www.abercrombieandfitch.com** or **www.gap.com**). How is the online "store" designed to encourage consuming behavior?

4. Write an essay in response to Gladwell's question "Should we be afraid of Paco Underhill?" (para. 17).

ANNE NORTON
The Signs of Shopping

Shopping malls are more than places to shop, just as mail-order cata-
logues are more than simple lists of goods. Both malls and catalogues
are coded systems that not only encourage us to buy but, more pro-
foundly, help us to construct our very sense of identity, as in the J. Peter-
man catalogue that "constructs the reader as a man of rugged outdoor
interests, taste, and money." In this selection from Republic of Signs
(1993), Anne Norton, a professor of political science at the University of
Pennsylvania, analyzes the many ways in which malls, catalogues, and
home shopping networks sell you what they want by telling you who you
are. Norton's other books include Alternative Americas *(1986),* Reflections on Political Identity *(1988),* Ninety-five Theses on Politics, Culture, and Method *(2003), and* Leo Strauss and the Politics of American
Empire *(2004).*

Shopping at the Mall

The mall has been the subject of innumerable debates. Created out of the
modernist impulse for planning and the centralization of public activity, the
mall has become the distinguishing sign of suburban decentralization, spring-
ing up in unplanned profusion. Intended to restore something of the lost unity
of city life to the suburbs, the mall has come to export styles and strategies to
stores at the urban center. Deplored by modernists, it is regarded with affection only by their postmodern foes. Ruled more by their content than by their
creators' avowed intent, the once sleek futurist shells have taken on a certain
aura of postmodern playfulness and popular glitz.

   The mall is a favorite subject for the laments of cultural conservatives and
others critical of the culture of consumption. It is indisputably the cultural
locus of commodity fetishism. It has been noticed, however, by others of a
less condemnatory disposition that the mall has something of the mercado,
or the agora, about it. It is both a place of meeting for the young and one of
the rare places where young and old go together. People of different races and
classes, different occupations, different levels of education meet there. As M.
Pressdee and John Fiske note, however, though the mall appears to be a public place, it is not. Neither freedom of speech nor freedom of assembly is permitted there. Those who own and manage malls restrict what comes within
their confines. Controversial displays, by stores or customers or the plethora
of organizations and agencies that present themselves in the open spaces of

the mall, are not permitted. These seemingly public spaces conceal a pervasive private authority.

The mall exercises its thorough and discreet authority not only in the regulation of behavior but in the constitution of our visible, inaudible, public discourse. It is the source of those commodities through which we speak of our identities, our opinions, our desires. It is a focus for the discussion of style among peripheral consumers. Adolescents, particularly female adolescents, are inclined to spend a good deal of time at the mall. They spend, indeed, more time than money. They acquire not simple commodities (they may come home with many, few, or none) but a well-developed sense of the significance of those commodities. In prowling the mall they embed themselves in a lexicon of American culture. They find themselves walking through a dictionary. Stores hang a variety of identities on their racks and mannequins. Their window displays provide elaborate scenarios conveying not only what the garment is but what the garment means.

A display in the window of Polo provides an embarrassment of semiotic riches. Everyone, from the architecture critic at the *New York Times* to kids in the hall of a Montana high school, knows what *Ralph Lauren* means. The polo mallet and the saddle, horses and dogs, the broad lawns of Newport, Kennebunkport, old photographs in silver frames, the evocation of age, of ancestry and Anglophilia, of indolence and the Ivy League, evoke the upper class. Indian blankets and buffalo plaids, cowboy hats and Western saddles, evoke a past distinct from England but nevertheless determinedly Anglo. The supposedly arcane and suspect arts of deconstruction are deployed easily, effortlessly, by the readers of these cultural texts.

Walking from one window to another, observing one another, shoppers, especially the astute and observant adolescents, acquire a facility with the language of commodities. They learn not only words but a grammar. Shop windows employ elements of sarcasm and irony, strategies of inversion and allusion. They provide models of elegant, economical, florid, and prosaic expression. They teach composition. 5

The practice of shopping is, however, more than instructive. It has long been the occasion for women to escape the confines of their homes and enjoy the companionship of other women. The construction of woman's role as one of provision for the needs of the family legitimated her exit. It provided an occasion for women to spend long stretches of time in the company of their friends, without the presence of their husbands. They could exchange information and reflections, ask advice, and receive support. As their daughters grew, they would be brought increasingly within this circle, included in shopping trips and lunches with their mothers. These would form, reproduce, and restructure communities of taste.

The construction of identity and the enjoyment of friendship outside the presence of men was thus effected through a practice that constructed women as consumers and subjected them to the conventions of the marketplace.

Insofar as they were dependent on their husbands for money, they were dependent on their husbands for the means to the construction of their identities. They could not represent themselves through commodities without the funds men provided, nor could they, without money, participate in the community of women that was realized in "going shopping." Their identities were made contingent not only on the possession of property but on the recognition of dependence.

Insofar as shopping obliges dependent women to recognize their dependence, it also opens up the possibility of subversion.[1] The housewife who shops for pleasure takes time away from her husband, her family, and her house and claims it for herself. Constantly taught that social order and her private happiness depend on intercourse between men and women, she chooses the company of women instead. She engages with women in an activity marked as feminine, and she enjoys it. When she spends money, she exercises an authority over property that law and custom may deny her. If she has no resources independent of her husband, this may be the only authority over property she is able to exercise. When she buys things her husband does not approve — or does not know of — she further subverts an order that leaves control over property in her husband's hands.[2]

Her choice of feminine company and a feminine pursuit may involve additional subversions. As Fiske and Pressdee recognize, shopping without buying and shopping for bargains have a subversive quality. This is revealed, in a form that gives it additional significance, when a saleswoman leans forward and tells a shopper, "Don't buy that today, it will be on sale on Thursday." Here solidarity of gender (and often of class) overcome, however partially and briefly, the imperatives of the economic order.

Shoppers who look, as most shoppers do, for bargains, and salespeople who warn shoppers of impending sales, see choices between commodities as something other than the evidence and the exercise of freedom. They see covert direction and exploitation; they see the withholding of information and the manipulation of knowledge. They recognize that they are on enemy terrain and that their shopping can be, in Michel de Certeau's[3] term, a "guerrilla raid." This recognition in practice of the presence of coercion in choice challenges the liberal conflation of choice and consent.

---

[1] Nuanced and amusing accounts of shopping as subversion are provided in John Fiske's analyses of popular culture, particularly *Reading the Popular* (Boston: Unwin Hyman [now Routledge], 1989), pp. 13–42.

[2] See R. Bowlby, *Just Looking: Consumer Culture in Dreiser, Gissing, and Zola* (London: Methuen, 1985), p. 22, for another discussion and for an example of the recommendation of this strategy by Elizabeth Cady Stanton in the 1850s.

[3] **Michel de Certeau** (1925–1986) French social scientist and semiologist who played an important role in the development of contemporary cultural studies. –EDS.

Shopping at Home

Shopping is an activity that has overcome its geographic limits. One need no longer go to the store to shop. Direct mail catalogues, with their twenty-four-hour phone numbers for ordering, permit people to shop where and when they please. An activity that once obliged one to go out into the public sphere, with its diverse array of semiotic messages, can now be done at home. An activity that once obliged one to be in company, if not in conversation, with one's compatriots can now be conducted in solitude.

The activity of catalogue shopping, and the pursuit of individuality, are not, however, wholly solitary. The catalogues invest their commodities with vivid historical and social references. The J. Peterman catalogue, for example, constructs the reader as a man of rugged outdoor interests, taste, and money.[4] He wears "The Owner's Hat" or "Hemingway's Cap," a leather flight jacket or the classic "Horseman's Duster," and various other garments identified with the military, athletes, and European imperialism. The copy for "The Owner's Hat" naturalizes class distinctions and, covertly, racism:

> Some of us work on the plantation.
> Some of us own the plantation.
> Facts are facts.
> This hat is for those who own the plantation.[5]

Gender roles are strictly delineated. The copy for a skirt captioned "Women's Legs" provides a striking instance of the construction of the gaze as male, of women as the object of the gaze:

> Just when you think you see something, a shape you think you recognize, it's gone and then it begins to return and then it's gone and of course you can't take your eyes off it.
>   Yes, the long slow motion of women's legs. Whatever happened to those things at carnivals that blew air up into girls' skirts and you could spend hours watching.[6]

"You," of course, are male. There is also the lace blouse captioned "Mystery": "lace says yes at the same time it says no."[7] Finally, there are notes of imperi-

---

[4]I have read several of these. I cite *The J. Peterman Company Owner's Manual No. 5*, from the J. Peterman Company, 2444 Palumbo Drive, Lexington, Ky. 40509.

[5]Ibid., p. 5. The hat is also identified with the Canal Zone, "successfully bidding at Beaulieu," intimidation, and LBOs. Quite a hat. It might be argued against my reading that the J. Peterman Company also offers the "Coal Miner's Bag" and a mailbag. However, since the descriptive points of reference on color and texture and experience for these bags are such things as the leather seats of Jaguars, and driving home in a Bentley, I feel fairly confident in my reading.

[6]Ibid., p. 3. See also pp. 15 and 17 for instances of women as the object of the male gaze. The identification of the gaze with male sexuality is unambiguous here as well.

[7]Ibid., p. 17.

alist nostalgia: the Sheapherd's Hotel (Cairo) bathrobe and white pants for "the bush" and "the humid hell-holes of Bombay and Calcutta."[8]

> It may no longer be unforgivable to say that the British left a few good things behind in India and in Kenya, Singapore, Borneo, etc., not the least of which was their Englishness.[9]

As Paul Smith observes, in his reading of their catalogues, the *Banana Republic* has also made capital out of imperial nostalgia.[10]

The communities catalogues create are reinforced by shared mailing lists. The constructed identities are reified and elaborated in an array of semiotically related catalogues. One who orders a spade or a packet of seeds will be constructed as a gardener and receive a deluge of catalogues from plant and garden companies. The companies themselves may expand their commodities to appeal to different manifestations of the identities they respond to and construct. Smith and Hawken, a company that sells gardening supplies with an emphasis on aesthetics and environmental concern, puts out a catalogue in which a group of people diverse in age and in their ethnicity wear the marketed clothes while gardening, painting, or throwing pots. Williams-Sonoma presents its catalogue not as a catalogue of things for cooking but as "A Catalog for Cooks." The catalogue speaks not to need but to the construction of identity.

The Nature Company dedicates its spring 1990 catalogue "to trees," endorses Earth Day, and continues to link itself to the Nature Conservancy through posters and a program in which you buy a tree for a forest restoration project. Here, a not-for-profit agency is itself commodified, adding to the value of the commodities offered in the catalogue.[11] In this catalogue, consumption is not merely a means for the construction and representation of the self, it is also a means for political action. Several commodities are offered as "A Few Things You Can Do" to save the earth: a string shopping bag, a solar battery recharger, a home newspaper recycler. Socially conscious shopping is a liberal practice in every sense. It construes shopping as a form of election, in which one votes for good commodities or refuses one's vote to candidates whose practices are ethically suspect. In this respect, it reveals its adherence to the same ideological presuppositions that structure television's Home Shopping Network and other cable television sales shows.

Both politically informed purchasing and television sales conflate the free market and the electoral process. Dollars are identified with votes, purchases

---

[8]Ibid., pp. 7, 16, 20, 21, 37, and 50.

[9]Ibid., p. 20.

[10]Paul Smith, "Visiting the Banana Republic," in *Universal Abandon?* ed. Andrew Ross for *Social Text* (Minneapolis: University of Minnesota Press, 1988), pp. 128–48.

[11]*The Nature Company Catalog*, The Nature Company, P.O. Box 2310, Berkeley, Calif. 94702, Spring 1990. See pp. 1–2 and order form insert between pp. 18 and 19. Note also the entailed donation to Designs for Conservation on p. 18.

with endorsements. Both offer those who engage in them the possibility to "talk back" to manufacturers. In television sales shows this ability to talk back is both more thoroughly elaborated and more thoroughly exploited. Like the "elections" on MTV that invite viewers to vote for their favorite video by calling a number on their telephones, they permit those who watch to respond, to speak, and to be heard by the television. Their votes, of course, cost money. On MTV, as in the stores, you can buy as much speech as you can afford. On the Home Shopping Network, the purchase of speech becomes complicated by multiple layers and inversions.

Each commodity is introduced. It is invested by the announcer with a number of desirable qualities. The value of these descriptions of the commodities is enhanced by the construction of the announcer as a mediator not only between the commodity and the consumer but between the salespeople and the consumer. The announcer is not, the format suggests, a salesperson (though of course the announcer is). He or she is an announcer, describing goods that others have offered for sale. Television claims to distinguish itself by making objects visible to the eyes, but it is largely through the ears that these commodities are constructed. The consumer, in purchasing the commodity, purchases the commodity, what the commodity signifies, and, as we say, "buys the salesperson's line." The consumer may also acquire the ability to speak on television. Each purchase is recorded and figures as a vote in a rough plebiscite, confirming the desirability of the object. Although the purchase figures are announced as if they were confirming votes, it is, of course, impossible to register one's rejection of the commodity. Certain consumers get a little more (or rather less) for their money. They are invited to explain the virtue of the commodity — and their purchase — to the announcer and the audience. The process of production, of both the consumers and that which they consume, continues in this apology for consumption.

The semiotic identification of consumption as an American activity, indeed, a patriotic one, is made with crude enthusiasm on the Home Shopping Network and other video sales shows. Red, white, and blue figure prominently in set designs and borders framing the television screen. The Home Shopping Network presents its authorities in an office conspicuously adorned with a picture of the Statue of Liberty.[12] Yet the messages that the Home Shopping Network sends its customers — that you can buy as much speech as you can afford, that you are recognized by others in accordance with your capacity to consume — do much to subvert the connection between capitalism and democracy on which this semiotic identification depends.

---

[12]This moment from the Home Shopping Network was generously brought to my attention, on videotape, by Peter Bregman, a student in my American Studies class of fall 1988, at Princeton University.

READING THE TEXT

1. What does Norton mean when she claims that the suburban shopping mall appears to be a public place but in fact is not?
2. What is Norton's interpretation of Ralph Lauren's Polo line?
3. How is shopping a subversive activity for women, according to Norton?
4. How do mail-order catalogues create communities of shoppers, in Norton's view?
5. What are the political messages sent by the Home Shopping Network, as Norton sees them, and how are they communicated?

READING THE SIGNS

1. Visit a local shopping mall, and study the window displays, focusing on stores intended for one group of consumers (teenagers, for example, or children). Then write an essay in which you analyze how the displays convey what the stores' products "mean."
2. Bring a few product catalogues to class, and in small groups compare the kind of consumer "constructed" by the cultural images and allusions in the catalogues. Do you note any patterns associated with gender, ethnicity, or age group? Report your group's interpretations to the whole class.
3. Interview five women of different age groups about their motivations and activities when they shop in a mall. Use your results as evidence in an essay in which you support, refute, or complicate Norton's assertion that shopping constitutes a subversive activity for women.
4. Watch an episode of the Home Shopping Network or similar program, and write a semiotic analysis of the ways in which products are presented to consumers.
5. Select a single mail-order catalogue, and write a detailed semiotic interpretation of the identity it constructs for its market.
6. Visit the Web site for a major chain store (for instance, **www.urbanoutfitters.com**), and study how it "moves" the consumer through it. How does the site induce you to consume?

Credit Card Barbie

READING THE SIGNS

1. Why might girls enjoy playing with a Barbie who shops rather than engaging her in some other kind of activity?
2. Do you think that having Barbie use a credit card to purchase cosmetics has an effect on the girls who play with the doll? If so, what are those effects?

THOMAS HINE
What's in a Package

What's in a package? According to Thomas Hine, a great deal, perhaps even more than what is actually inside the package. From the cereal boxes you find in the supermarket to the perfume bottles sold at Tiffany's, the shape and design of the packages that contain just about every product we consume have been carefully calculated to stimulate consumption. Indeed, as Hine explains in this excerpt from The Total Package: The Evolution and Secret Meanings of Boxes, Bottles, Cans, and Tubes *(1995), "for manufacturers, packaging is the crucial final payoff to a marketing campaign." A former architecture and design critic for the* Philadelphia Inquirer, *Hine has also published* Populuxe *(1986), on American design and culture;* Facing Tomorrow *(1991), on past and current attitudes toward the future;* The Rise and Fall of the American Teenager: A New History of the American Adolescent Experience *(1999);* I Want That! How We All Became Shoppers *(2002); and* The Great Funk: Falling Apart and Coming Together (on a Shag Rug) in the Seventies *(2007).*

When you put yourself behind a shopping cart, the world changes. You become an active consumer, and you are moving through environments — the supermarket, the discount store, the warehouse club, the home center — that have been made for you.

During the thirty minutes you spend on an average trip to the supermarket, about thirty thousand different products vie to win your attention and ultimately to make you believe in their promise. When the door opens, automatically, before you, you enter an arena where your emotions and your appetites are in play, and a walk down the aisle is an exercise in self-definition. Are you a good parent, a good provider? Do you have time to do all you think you should, and would you be interested in a shortcut? Are you worried about your health and that of those you love? Do you care about the environment?

Do you appreciate the finer things in life? Is your life what you would like it to be? Are you enjoying what you've accomplished? Wouldn't you really like something chocolate?

Few experiences in contemporary life offer the visual intensity of a Safeway, a Krogers, a Pathmark, or a Piggly Wiggly. No marketplace in the world — not Marrakesh or Calcutta or Hong Kong — offers so many different goods with such focused salesmanship as your neighborhood supermarket, where you're exposed to a thousand different products a minute. No wonder it's tiring to shop.

There are, however, some major differences between the supermarket and a traditional marketplace. The cacophony of a traditional market has given way to programmed, innocuous music, punctuated by enthusiastically intoned commercials. A stroll through a traditional market offers an array of sensuous aromas; if you are conscious of smelling something in a supermarket, there is a problem. The life and death matter of eating, expressed in traditional markets by the sale of vegetables with stems and roots and by hanging animal carcasses, is purged from the supermarket, where food is processed somewhere else, or at least trimmed out of sight.

But the most fundamental difference between a traditional market and   5 the places through which you push your cart is that in a modern retail setting nearly all the selling is done without people. The product is totally dissociated from the personality of any particular person selling it — with the possible exception of those who appear in its advertising. The supermarket purges sociability, which slows down sales. It allows manufacturers to control the way they present their products to the world. It replaces people with packages.

Packages are an inescapable part of modern life. They are omnipresent and invisible, deplored and ignored. During most of your waking moments, there are one or more packages within your field of vision. Packages are so ubiquitous that they slip beneath conscious notice, though many packages are designed so that people will respond to them even if they're not paying attention.

Once you begin pushing the shopping cart, it matters little whether you are in a supermarket, a discount store, or a warehouse club. The important thing is that you are among packages: expressive packages intended to engage your emotions, ingenious packages that make a product useful, informative packages that help you understand what you want and what you're getting. Historically, packages are what made self-service retailing possible, and in turn such stores increased the number and variety of items people buy. Now a world without packages is unimaginable.

Packages lead multiple lives. They preserve and protect, allowing people to make use of things that were produced far away, or a while ago. And they are potently expressive. They assure that an item arrives unspoiled, and they help those who use the item feel good about it.

We share our homes with hundreds of packages, mostly in the bathroom and kitchen, the most intimate, body-centered rooms of the house. Some packages — a perfume flacon, a ketchup bottle, a candy wrapper, a beer can — serve as permanent landmarks in people's lives that outlast homes, careers, or spouses. But packages embody change, not just in their age-old promise that their contents are new and improved, but in their attempt to respond to changing tastes and achieve new standards of convenience. Packages record changing hairstyles and changing life-styles. Even social policy issues are reflected. Nearly unopenable tamperproof seals and other forms of closures testify to the fragility of the social contract, and the susceptibility of the great mass of people to the destructive acts of a very few. It was a mark of rising environmental consciousness when containers recently began to make a novel promise: "less packaging."

For manufacturers, packaging is the crucial final payoff to a marketing campaign. Sophisticated packaging is one of the chief ways people find the confidence to buy. It can also give a powerful image to products and commodities that are in themselves characterless. In many cases, the shopper has been prepared for the shopping experience by lush, colorful print advertisements, thirty-second television minidramas, radio jingles, and coupon promotions. But the package makes the final sales pitch, seals the commitment, and gets itself placed in the shopping cart. Advertising leads consumers into temptation. Packaging is the temptation. In many cases it is what makes the product possible. 10

But the package is also useful to the shopper. It is a tool for simplifying and speeding decisions. Packages promise, and usually deliver, predictability. One reason you don't think about packages is that you don't need to. The candy bar, the aspirin, the baking powder, or the beer in the old familiar package may, at times, be touted as new and improved, but it will rarely be very different.

You put the package into your cart, or not, usually without really having focused on the particular product or its many alternatives. But sometimes you do examine the package. You read the label carefully, looking at what the product promises, what it contains, what it warns. You might even look at the package itself and judge whether it will, for example, reseal to keep a product fresh. You might consider how a cosmetic container will look on your dressing table, or you might think about whether someone might have tampered with it or whether it can be easily recycled. The possibility of such scrutiny is one of the things that make each detail of the package so important.

The environment through which you push your shopping cart is extraordinary because of the amount of attention that has been paid to the packages that line the shelves. Most contemporary environments are landscapes of inattention. In housing developments, malls, highways, office buildings, even furniture, design ideas are few and spread very thin. At the supermarket, each box and jar, stand-up pouch and squeeze bottle, each can and bag and tube and spray has been very carefully considered. Designers have worked and reworked the design on their computers and tested mock-ups on the store shelves. Refinements are measured in millimeters.

All sorts of retail establishments have been redefined by packaging. Drugs and cosmetics were among the earliest packaged products, and most drugstores now resemble small supermarkets. Liquor makers use packaging to add a veneer of style to the intrinsic allure of intoxication, and some sell their bottle rather than the drink. It is no accident that vodka, the most characterless of spirits, has the highest-profile packages. The local gas station sells sandwiches and soft drinks rather than tires and motor oil, and in turn, automotive products have been attractively repackaged for sales at supermarkets, warehouse clubs, and home centers.

With its thousands of images and messages, the supermarket is as visu- 15 ally dense, if not as beautiful, as a Gothic cathedral. It is as complex and as predatory as a tropical rain forest. It is more than a person can possibly take in during an ordinary half-hour shopping trip. No wonder a significant percentage of people who need to wear eyeglasses don't wear them when they're shopping, and some researchers have spoken of the trancelike state that pushing a cart through this environment induces. The paradox here is that the visual intensity that overwhelms shoppers is precisely the thing that makes the design of packages so crucial. Just because you're not looking at a package doesn't mean you don't see it. Most of the time, you see far more than a container and a label. You see a personality, an attitude toward life, perhaps even a set of beliefs.

The shopper's encounter with the product on the shelf is, however, only the beginning of the emotional life cycle of the package. The package is very important in the moment when the shopper recognizes it either as an old friend or a new temptation. Once the product is brought home, the package seems to disappear, as the quality or usefulness of the product it contains becomes paramount. But in fact, many packages are still selling even at home, enticing those who have bought them to take them out of the cupboard, the closet, or the refrigerator and consume their contents. Then once the product has been used up, and the package is empty, it becomes suddenly visible once more. This time, though, it is trash that must be discarded or recycled. This instant of disposal is the time when people are most aware of packages. It is a negative moment, like the end of a love affair, and what's left seems to be a horrid waste.

The forces driving package design are not primarily aesthetic. Market researchers have conducted surveys of consumer wants and needs, and consultants have studied photographs of families' kitchen cupboards and medicine chests to get a sense of how products are used. Test subjects have been tied into pieces of heavy apparatus that measure their eye movement, their blood pressure or body temperature, when subjected to different packages. Psychologists get people to talk about the packages in order to get a sense of their innermost feelings about what they want. Government regulators and private health and safety advocates worry over package design and try to make it truthful. Stock-market analysts worry about how companies are managing their "brand equity," that combination of perceived value and consumer loyalty that is expressed in advertising but embodied in packaging. The retailer is paying attention to the packages in order to weed out the ones that don't sell or aren't sufficiently profitable. The use of supermarket scanners generates information on the profitability of every cubic inch of the store. Space on the supermarket shelf is some of the most valuable real estate in the world, and there are always plenty of new packaged products vying for display.

Packaging performs a series of disparate tasks. It protects its contents from contamination and spoilage. It makes it easier to transport and store goods. It provides uniform measuring of contents. By allowing brands to be created and standardized, it makes advertising meaningful and large-scale distribution possible. Special kinds of packages, with dispensing caps, sprays, and other convenience features, make products more usable. Packages serve as symbols both of their contents and of a way of life. And just as they can very powerfully communicate the satisfaction a product offers, they are equally potent symbols of wastefulness once the product is gone.

Most people use dozens of packages each day and discard hundreds of them each year. The growth of mandatory recycling programs has made people increasingly aware of packages, which account in the United States for about forty-three million tons, or just under 30 percent of all refuse discarded. While forty-three million tons of stuff is hardly insignificant, repeated surveys have shown that the public perceives that far more than 30 percent — indeed, nearly all — their garbage consists of packaging. This perception creates a political problem for the packaging industry, but it also demonstrates the power of packaging. It is symbolic. It creates an emotional relationship. Bones and wasted food (13 million tons), grass clippings and yard waste (thirty-one million tons), or even magazines and newspapers (fourteen million tons) do not feel as wasteful as empty vessels that once contained so much promise.

Packaging is a cultural phenomenon, which means that it works differently in 20 different cultures. The United States has been a good market for packages since it was first settled and has been an important innovator of packaging technology and culture. Moreover, American packaging is part of an international culture of modernity and consumption. At its deepest level, the culture of American packaging deals with the issue of surviving among strangers in a new world. This is an emotion with which anyone who has been touched by modernity can identify. In lives buffeted by change, people seek the safety and reassurance that packaged products offer. American packaging, which has always sought to appeal to large numbers of diverse people, travels better than that of most other cultures.

But the similar appearance of supermarkets throughout the world should not be interpreted as the evidence of a single, global consumer culture. In fact, most companies that do business internationally redesign their packages for each market. This is done partly to satisfy local regulations and adapt to available products and technologies. But the principal reason is that people in different places have different expectations and make different uses of packaging.

The United States and Japan, the world's two leading industrial powers, have almost opposite approaches to packaging. Japan's is far more elaborate than America's, and it is shaped by rituals of respect and centuries-old traditions of wrapping and presentation. Packaging is explicitly recognized as an expression of culture in Japan and largely ignored in America. Japanese packaging is designed to be appreciated; American packaging is calculated to be unthinkingly accepted.

Foods that only Japanese eat — even relatively humble ones like refrigerated prepared fish cakes — have wrappings that resemble handmade paper or leaves. Even modestly priced refrigerated fish cakes have beautiful wrappings in which traditional design accommodates a scannable bar code. Such products look Japanese and are unambiguously intended to do so. Products that are foreign, such as coffee, look foreign, even to the point of having only Roman lettering and no Japanese lettering on the can. American and European companies are sometimes able to sell their packages in Japan virtually unchanged, because their foreignness is part of their selling power. But Japanese exporters hire designers in each country to repackage their products. Americans — whose culture is defined not by refinements and distinctions but by inclusiveness — want to think about the product itself, not its cultural origins.

We speak glibly about global villages and international markets, but problems with packages reveal some unexpected cultural boundaries. Why are Canadians willing to drink milk out of flexible plastic pouches that fit into reusable plastic holders, while residents of the United States are believed to be so resistant to the idea that they have not even been given the opportunity to do so? Why do Japanese consumers prefer packages that contain two tennis balls and view the standard U.S. pack of three to be cheap and undesirable? Why do Germans insist on highly detailed technical specifications on packages of videotape, while Americans don't? Why do Swedes think that blue is masculine, while the Dutch see the color as feminine? The answers lie in unquestioned habits and deep-seated imagery, a culture of containing, adorning, and understanding that no sharp marketer can change overnight.

There is probably no other field in which designs that are almost a century 25 old — Wrigley's gum, Campbell's soup, Hershey's chocolate bar — remain in production only subtly changed and are understood to be extremely valuable corporate assets. Yet the culture of packaging, defined by what people are buying and selling every day, keeps evolving, and the role nostalgia plays is very small.

For example, the tall, glass Heinz ketchup bottle has helped define the American refrigerator skyline for most of the twentieth century (even though it is generally unnecessary to refrigerate ketchup). Moreover, it provides the tables of diners and coffee shops with a vertical accent and a token of hospitality, the same qualities projected by candles and vases of flowers in more upscale eateries. The bottle has remained a fixture of American life, even though it has always been a nuisance to pour the thick ketchup through the little hole. It seemed not to matter that you have to shake and shake the bottle, impotently, until far too much ketchup comes out in one great scarlet plop. Heinz experimented for years with wide-necked jars and other sorts of bottles, but they never caught on.

Then in 1992 a survey of consumers indicated that more Americans believed that the plastic squeeze bottle is a better package for ketchup than the glass bottle. The survey did not offer any explanations for this change of preference, which has been evolving for many years as older people for whom the tall bottle is an icon became a less important part of the sample. Could it be that the difficulty of using the tall bottle suddenly became evident to those born after 1960? Perhaps the tall bottle holds too little ketchup. There is a clear trend toward buying things in larger containers, in part because lightweight plastics have made them less costly for manufacturers to ship and easier for consumers to use. This has happened even as the number of people in an average American household has been getting smaller. But houses, like packages, have been getting larger. Culture moves in mysterious ways.

The tall ketchup bottle is still preferred by almost half of consumers, so it is not going to disappear anytime soon. And the squeeze bottle does contain visual echoes of the old bottle. It is certainly not a radical departure. In Japan, ketchup and mayonnaise are sold in cellophane-wrapped plastic bladders that would certainly send Americans into severe culture shock. Still, the tall bottle's loss of absolute authority is a significant change. And its ultimate disappearance would represent a larger change in most people's visual environment than would the razing of nearly any landmark building.

But although some package designs are pleasantly evocative of another time, and a few appear to be unchanging icons in a turbulent world, the reason they still exist is because they still work. Inertia has historically played a role in creating commercial icons. Until quite recently, it was time-consuming and expensive to make new printing plates or to vary the shape or material of a container. Now computerized graphics and rapidly developing technology in the package-manufacturing industries make a packaging change easier than in the past, and a lot cheaper to change than advertising, which seems a far more evanescent medium. There is no constituency of curators or preservationists to protect the endangered package. If a gum wrapper manages to survive nearly unchanged for ninety years, it's not because any expert has determined that it is an important cultural expression. Rather, it's because it still helps sell a lot of gum.

So far, we've been discussing packaging in its most literal sense: designed ₃₀ containers that protect and promote products. Such containers have served as the models for larger types of packaging, such as chain restaurants, supermarkets, theme parks, and festival marketplaces. . . . Still, it is impossible to ignore a broader conception of packaging that is one of the preoccupations of our time. This concerns the ways in which people construct and present their personalities, the ways in which ideas are presented and diffused, the ways in which political candidates are selected and public policies formulated. We must all worry about packaging ourselves and everything we do, because we believe that nobody has time to really pay attention.

Packaging strives at once to offer excitement and reassurance. It promises something newer and better, but not necessarily different. When we talk about a tourist destination, or even a presidential contender, being packaged, that's not really a metaphor. The same projection of intensified ordinariness, the same combination of titillation and reassurance, are used for laundry detergents, theme parks, and candidates alike.

The imperative to package is unavoidable in a society in which people have been encouraged to see themselves as consumers not merely of toothpaste and automobiles, but of such imponderables as lifestyle, government, and health. The marketplace of ideas is not an agora, where people haggle, posture, clash, and come to terms with one another. Rather, it has become a supermarket, where values, aspirations, dreams, and predictions are presented with great sophistication. The individual can choose to buy them, or leave them on the shelf.

In such a packaged culture, the consumer seems to be king. But people cannot be consumers all the time. If nothing else, they must do something to earn the money that allows them to consume. This, in turn, pressures people to package themselves in order to survive. The early 1990s brought economic recession and shrinking opportunities to all the countries of the developed world. Like products fighting for their space on the shelf, individuals have had to re-create, or at least represent, themselves in order to seem both desirable and safe. Moreover, many jobs have been reconceived to depersonalize individuals and to make them part of a packaged service experience.

These phenomena have their own history. For decades, people have spoken of writing resumes in order to package themselves for a specific opportunity. Thomas J. Watson Jr., longtime chairman of IBM, justified his company's famously conservative and inflexible dress code — dark suits, white shirts, and rep ties for all male employees — as "self-packaging," analogous to the celebrated product design, corporate imagery, and packaging done for the company by Elliot Noyes and Paul Rand. You can question whether IBM's employees were packaging themselves or forced into a box by their employer. Still, anyone who has ever dressed for success was doing a packaging job.

Since the 1950s, there have been discussions of packaging a candidate 35 to respond to what voters are telling the pollsters who perform the same tasks as market researchers do for soap or shampoo. More recently, such discussions have dominated American political journalism. The packaged candidate, so he and his handlers hope, projects a message that, like a Diet Pepsi, is stimulating without being threatening. Like a Weight Watchers frozen dessert bar, the candidate's contradictions must be glazed over and, ultimately, comforting. Aspects of the candidate that are confusing or viewed as extraneous are removed, just as stems and sinew are removed from packaged foods. The package is intended to protect the candidate; dirt won't stick. The candidate is uncontaminated, though at a slight remove from the consumer-voter.

People profess to be troubled by this sort of packaging. When we say a person or an experience is "packaged," we are complaining of a sense of excessive calculation and a lack of authenticity. Such a fear of unreality is at least a century old; it arose along with industrialization and rapid communication. Now that the world is more competitive, and we all believe we have less time to consider things, the craft of being instantaneously appealing has taken on more and more importance. We might say, cynically, that the person who appears "packaged" simply doesn't have good packaging.

Still, the sense of uneasiness about encountering packaged people in a packaged world is real, and it shouldn't be dismissed. Indeed, it is a theme of contemporary life, equally evident in politics, entertainment, and the supermarket. Moreover, public uneasiness about the phenomenon of packaging is compounded by confusion over a loss of iconic packages and personalities.

Producers of packaged products have probably never been as nervous as they became during the first half of the 1990s. Many of the world's most famous brands were involved in the merger mania of the 1980s, which produced debt-ridden companies that couldn't afford to wait for results either from their managers or their marketing strategies. At the same time, the feeling was that it was far too risky to produce something really new. The characteristic response was the line extension — "dry" beer, "lite" mayonnaise, "ultra" detergent. New packages have been appearing at a rapid pace, only to be changed whenever a manager gets nervous or a retailer loses patience.

The same skittishness is evident in the projection of public personalities as the clear, if synthetic, images of a few decades ago have lost their sharpness and broken into a spectrum of weaker, reflected apparitions. Marilyn Monroe, for example, had an image that was, Jayne Mansfield notwithstanding, unique and well defined. She was luscious as a Hershey's bar, shapely as a Coke bottle. But in a world where Coke can be sugar free, caffeine free, and cherry flavored (and Pepsi can be clear!), just one image isn't enough for a superstar. Madonna is available as Marilyn or as a brunette, a Catholic schoolgirl, or a bondage devotee. Who knows what brand extension will come next? Likewise, John F. Kennedy and Elvis Presley had clear, carefully projected images. But Bill Clinton is defined largely by evoking memories of both. As our commercial civilization seems to have lost the power to amuse or convince us in new and exciting ways, formerly potent packages are recycled and devalued. That has left the door open for such phenomena as generic cigarettes, President's Choice cola, and H. Ross Perot.

This cultural and personal packaging both fascinates and infuriates. There 40 is something liberating in its promise of aggressive self-creation, and something terrifying in its implication that everything must be subject to the ruthless discipline of the marketplace. People are at once passive consumers of their culture and aggressive packagers of themselves, which can be a stressful and lonely combination.

READING THE TEXT

1. How does Hine compare a supermarket with a traditional marketplace?

2. What does Hine mean when he asserts that modern retailing "replaces people with packages" (para. 5)?

3. How does packaging stimulate the desire to buy, according to Hine?

4. How do Americans' attitudes toward packaging compare with those of the Japanese, according to Hine?

READING THE SIGNS

1. Bring one product package to class, preferably with all students bringing items from the same product category (personal hygiene, say, or bottled water). In class, give a brief presentation in which you interpret your package. After all the students have presented, compare the different messages the packages send to consumers.

2. Visit a popular retail store, such as Urban Outfitters or Victoria's Secret, and study the ways the store uses packaging to create, as Hine puts it, "a personality, an attitude toward life" (para. 15). Be thorough in your observations, studying everything from the store's bags to perfume or cologne packages to clothing labels. Use your findings as evidence for an essay in which you analyze the image the store creates for itself and its customers.

3. In your journal, write an entry in which you explore your motives for purchasing a product simply because you liked the package. What did you like about the package, and how did it contribute to your sense of identity?

4. Visit a store with an explicit political theme, such as the Body Shop or Whole Foods, and write a semiotic analysis of the packaging you see in the store.

5. **CONNECTING TEXTS**   Study the packages that are visible to a visitor to your home, and write an analysis of the messages those packages might send to a visitor. To develop your ideas, consult Joan Kron's "The Semiotics of Home Decor" (p. 119).

JOAN KRON
The Semiotics of Home Decor

Just when you thought it was safe to go back into your living room, here comes Joan Kron with a reminder that your home is a signaling system just as much as your clothing is. In Home-Psych: The Social Psychology of Home and Decoration *(1983), from which this selection is taken, Kron takes a broad look at the significance of interior decoration, showing how home design can reflect both an individual and a group identity. Ranging from a New York entrepreneur to Kwakiutl Indian chiefs, Kron further discusses how different cultures use possessions as a rich symbol system. The author of* High Tech: The Industrial Style and Source Book for the Home *(1978) and of some five hundred articles for American magazines, she is particularly interested in fashion, design, and the social psychology of consumption. Currently an editor-at-large at* Allure *magazine, Kron has also published* Lift: Wanting, Fearing, and Having a Face-Lift *(1998).*

On June 7, 1979, Martin J. Davidson entered the materialism hall of fame. That morning the thirty-four-year-old New York graphic design entrepreneur went to his local newsstand and bought fifty copies of the *New York Times* expecting to read an article about himself in the Home section that would portray him as a man of taste and discrimination. Instead, his loft and his life-style, which he shared with singer Dawn Bennett, were given the tongue-in-cheek treatment under the headline: "When Nothing but the Best Will Do."[1]

Davidson, who spent no more money renovating his living quarters than many of the well-to-do folks whose homes are lionized in the *Times*'s Thursday and Sunday design pages — the running ethnographic record of contemporary upper-middle-class life-style — made the unpardonable error of telling reporter Jane Geniesse how much he had paid for his stereo system, among other things. Like many people who have not been on intimate terms with affluence for very long, Davidson is in the habit of price-tagging his possessions. His 69-cent-per-bottle bargain Perrier, his $700 Armani suits from Barney's, his $27,000 cooperative loft and its $150,000 renovation, his sixteen $350-per-section sectionals, and his $11,000 best-of-class stereo. Martin J. Davidson wants the world to know how well he's done. "I live the American dream," he told Mrs. Geniesse, which includes, "being known as one of Barney's best customers."[2]

---

[1]Jane Geniesse, "When Nothing but the Best Will Do," *New York Times*, June 7, 1979, p. C1ff.
    [2]Ibid.

Davidson even wants the U.S. Census Bureau's computer to know how well he has done. He is furious, in fact, that the 1980 census form did not have a box to check for people who live in cooperatives. "If someone looks at my census form they'll think I must be at the poverty level or lower."[3] No one who read the *Times* article about Martin Davidson would surmise that.

It is hard to remember when a "design" story provoked more outrage. Letters to the editor poured in. Andy Warhol once said that in our fast-paced media world no one could count on being a celebrity for more than fifteen minutes. Martin Davidson was notorious for weeks. "All the Martin Davidsons in New York," wrote one irate reader, "will sit home listening to their $11,000 stereos, while downtown, people go to jail because they ate a meal they couldn't pay for."[4] "How can one man embody so many of the ills afflicting our society today?"[5] asked another offended reader. "Thank you for your clever spoof," wrote a third reader. "I was almost convinced that two people as crass as Martin Davidson and Dawn Bennett could exist."[6] Davidson's consumption largesse was even memorialized by Russell Baker, the *Times*'s Pulitzer Prize–winning humorist, who devoted a whole column to him: "While simultaneously consuming yesterday's newspaper," wrote Baker, "I consumed an article about one Martin Davidson, a veritable Ajax of consumption. A man who wants to consume nothing but the best and does."[7] Counting, as usual, Davidson would later tell people, "I was mentioned in the *Times* on three different days."

Davidson, a self-made man whose motto is "I'm not taking it with me and while I'm here I'm going to spend every stinking penny I make," couldn't understand why the *Times* had chosen to make fun of him rather than to glorify his 4,000-square-foot loft complete with bidet, Jacuzzi, professional exercise gear, pool table, pinball machine, sauna, two black-tile bathrooms, circular white Formica cooking island, status-stuffed collections of Steiff animals, pop art (including eleven Warhols), a sound system that could weaken the building's foundations if turned up full blast, and an air-conditioning system that can turn cigarette smoke, which both Davidson and Bennett abhor, into mountain dew — a loft that has everything Martin Davidson ever wanted in a home except a swimming pool and a squash court.

"People were objecting to my life-style," said Davidson. "It's almost as if there were a correlation between the fact that we spend so much on ourselves and other people are starving. No one yells when someone spends $250,000

---

[3]Author's interview with Martin Davidson.

[4]Richard Moseson, "Letters: Crossroads of Decadence and Destitution," *New York Times*, June 14, 1979, p. A28.

[5]Letter to the Editor, *New York Times*, June 14, 1979, p. C9.

[6]Letter to the Editor, ibid.

[7]Russell Baker, "Observer: Incompleat Consumer," *New York Times*, June 9, 1979, p. 25.

for a chest of drawers at an auction," he complained. "I just read in the paper that someone paid $650,000 for a stupid stamp. Now it'll be put away in a vault and no one will ever see it."[8]

But Dawn Bennett understood what made Davidson's consumption different. "It's not very fashionable to be an overt consumer and admit it,"[9] she said.

What Are Things For?

As anyone knows who has seen a house turned inside out at a yard sale, furnishing a home entails the acquisition of more objects than there are in a spring housewares catalog. With all the time, money, and space we devote to the acquisition, arrangement, and maintenance of these household possessions, it is curious that we know so little about our relationships to our possessions.

"It is extraordinary to discover that no one knows why people want goods," wrote British anthropologist Mary Douglas in *The World of Goods*.[10] Although no proven or agreed-upon theory of possessiveness in human beings has been arrived at, social scientists are coming up with new insights on our complicated relationships to things. Whether or not it is human nature to be acquisitive, it appears that our household goods have a more meaningful place in our lives than they have been given credit for. What comes across in a wide variety of research is that things matter enormously.

Our possessions give us a sense of security and stability. They make us feel in control. And the more we control an object, the more it is a part of us. If it's *not mine*, it's *not me*.[11] It would probably make sense for everyone on the block to share a lawn mower, but then no one would have control of it. If people are reluctant to share lawn mowers, it should not surprise us that family members are not willing to share TV sets. They want their own sets so they can watch what they please. Apparently, that was why a Chicago woman, furious with her boyfriend for switching from *The Thorn Birds* to basketball, stabbed him to death with a paring knife.[12]

10

---

[8]Author's interview with Martin Davidson.

[9]Author's interview with Dawn Bennett.

[10]Mary Douglas and Baron Isherwood, *The World of Goods* (New York: Basic Books, 1979), p. 15. A number of other social scientists have mentioned in recent works the lack of attention paid to the human relationship to possessions: See Coleman and Rainwater, *Social Standing*, p. 310. The authors observed that "the role of income in providing a wide range of rewards — consumption — has not received sufficient attention from sociologists." See Carl F. Graumann, "Psychology and the World of Things," *Journal of Phenomenological Psychology*, Vol. 4, 1974–75, pp. 389–404. Graumann accused the field of sociology of being thing-blind.

[11]Lita Furby, "Possessions: Toward a Theory of Their Meaning and Function Throughout the Life Cycle," in Paul B. Baltes (ed.), *Life-Span Development and Behavior*, Vol. 1 (New York: Academic Press, 1978), pp. 297–336.

[12]"'Touch That Dial and You're Dead,'" *New York Post*, March 30, 1983, p. 5.

Besides control, we use things to compete. In the late nineteenth century the Kwakiutl Indian chiefs of the Pacific Northwest made war with possessions.[13] Their culture was built on an extravagant festival called the "potlatch," a word that means, roughly, to flatten with gifts. It was not the possession of riches that brought prestige, it was the distribution and destruction of goods. At winter ceremonials that took years to prepare for, rival chiefs would strive to outdo one another with displays of conspicuous waste, heaping on their guests thousands of spoons and blankets, hundreds of gold and silver bracelets, their precious dance masks and coppers (large shields that were their most valuable medium of exchange), and almost impoverishing themselves in the process.

Today our means of competition is the accumulation and display of symbols of status. Perhaps in Utopia there will be no status, but in this world, every human being is a status seeker on one level or another — and a status reader. "Every member of society," said French anthropologist Claude Lévi-Strauss, "must learn to distinguish his fellow men according to their mutual social status."[14] This discrimination satisfies human needs and has definite survival value. "Status symbols provide the cue that is used in order to discover the status of others, and, from this, the way in which others are to be treated," wrote Erving Goffman in his classic paper, "Symbols of Class Status."[15] Status affects who is invited to share "bed, board, and cult,"[16] said Mary Douglas. Whom we invite to dinner affects who marries whom, which then affects who inherits what, which affects whose children get a head start.

Today what counts is what you eat (gourmet is better than greasy spoon), what you fly (private jet is better than common carrier), what sports you play (sailing is better than bowling), where you matriculate, shop, and vacation, whom you associate with, how you eat (manners count), and most important, where you live. Blue Blood Estates or Hard Scrabble zip codes as one wizard of demographics calls them. He has figured out that "people tend to roost on the same branch as birds of a feather."[17] People also use status symbols to play net worth hide-and-seek. When *Forbes* profiled the 400 richest Americans,[18] its own in-house millionaire Malcolm Forbes refused to disclose his net worth but was delighted to drop clues telling about his status

---

[13]Ruth Benedict, *Patterns of Culture* (Boston: Houghton Mifflin [1934], 1959); Frederick V. Grunfeld, "Homecoming: The Story of Cultural Outrage," *Connoisseur*, February 1983, pp. 100–106; and Lewis Hyde, *The Gift* (New York: Vintage Books, [1979, 1980], 1983), pp. 25–39.

[14]Edmund Leach, *Claude Lévi-Strauss* (New York: Penguin Books, 1980), p. 39.

[15]Erving Goffman, "Symbols of Class Status," *British Journal of Sociology*, Vol. 2, December 1951, pp. 294–304.

[16]Douglas and Isherwood, *World of Goods*, p. 88.

[17]Michael J. Weiss, "By Their Numbers Ye Shall Know Them," *American Way*, February 1983, pp. 102–6 ff. "You tell me someone's zip code," said Jonathan Robbin, "and I can predict what they eat, drink, drive, buy, even think."

[18]"The Forbes 400," *Forbes*, September 13, 1982, pp. 99–186.

entertainments — his ballooning, his Fabergé egg hunts, his châteaux, and his high life-style. It is up to others to translate those obviously costly perks into dollars.

A high price tag isn't the only attribute that endows an object with status. Status can accrue to something because it's scarce — a one-of-a-kind artwork or a limited edition object. The latest hard-to-get item is Steuben's $27,500 bowl etched with tulips that will be produced in an edition of five — one per year for five years. "Only one bowl will bloom this year,"[19] is the headline on the ad for it. Status is also found in objects made from naturally scarce materials: Hawaii's rare koa wood, lapis lazuli, or moon rock. And even if an object is neither expensive nor rare, status can rub off on something if it is favored by the right people, which explains why celebrities are used to promote coffee, cars, casinos, and credit cards.

If you've been associated with an object long enough you don't even have to retain ownership. Its glory will shine on you retroactively. Perhaps that is why a member of Swiss nobility is having two copies made of each of the Old Master paintings in his collection. This way, when he turns his castle into a museum, both his children can still have, so to speak, the complete collection, mnemonics of the pictures that have been in the family for centuries. And the most potent status symbol of all is not the object per se, but the *expertise* that is cultivated over time, such as the appreciation of food, wine, design, or art.

If an object reflects a person *accurately*, it's an index of status. But *symbols* of status are not always good indices of status. They are not official proof of rank in the same way a general's stars are. So clusters of symbols are better than isolated ones. Anyone with $525 to spare can buy one yard of the tiger-patterned silk velvet that Lee Radziwill used to cover her dining chair seats.[20] But one status yard does not a princess make. A taxi driver in Los Angeles gets a superior feeling from owning the same status-initialed luggage that many of her Beverly Hills fares own. "I have the same luggage you have," she tells them. "It blows their minds," she brags. But two status valises do not a glitterati make. Misrepresenting your social status isn't a crime, just "a presumption," said Goffman. Like wearing a $69 copy of a $1,000 watch that the mail-order catalog promises will make you "look like a count or countess on a commoner's salary."[21]

"Signs of status are important ingredients of self. But they do not exhaust all the meanings of objects for people," wrote sociologists Mihaly Csikszentmihalyi and Eugene Rochberg-Halton in *The Meaning of Things: Domestic Symbols*

---

[19] Steuben Glass advertisement, *The New Yorker*, April 4, 1983, p. 3.

[20] Paige Rense, "Lee Radziwill," *Celebrity Homes* (New York: Penguin Books, 1979), pp. 172–81.

[21] *Synchronics* catalogue, Hanover, Pennsylvania, Fall 1982.

of the Self.[22] The study on which the book was based found that people cherished household objects not for their status-giving properties but especially because they were symbols of the self and one's connections to others.

The idea that possessions are symbols of self is not new. Many people have noticed that *having* is intricately tied up with *being*. "It is clear that between what a man calls *me* and what he simply calls *mine*, the line is difficult to draw," wrote William James in 1890.[23] "Every possession is an extension of the self," said Georg Simmel in 1900.[24] "Humans tend to integrate their selves with objects," observed psychologist Ernest Beaglehole some thirty years later.[25] Eskimos used to *lick* new acquisitions to cement the person/object relationship.[26] We stamp our visual taste on our things making the totality resemble us. Indeed, theatrical scenic designers would be out of work if Blanche DuBois's boudoir could be furnished with the same props as Hedda Gabler's.

Csikszentmihalyi and Rochberg-Halton discovered that "things are cherished not because of the material comfort they provide but for the information they convey about the owner and his or her ties to others."[27] People didn't value things for their monetary worth, either. A battered toy, a musical instrument, a homemade quilt, they said, provide more meaning than expensive appliances which the respondents had plenty of. "What's amazing is how few of these things really make a difference when you get to the level of what is important in life,"[28] said Csikszentmihalyi. All those expensive furnishings "are required just to keep up with the neighbors or to keep up with what you expect your standard of living should be."

"How else should one relate to the Joneses if not by keeping up with them," asked Mary Douglas provocatively.[29] The principle of reciprocity requires people to consume at the same level as one's friends.[30] If we accept hospitality, we have to offer it in return. And that takes the right equipment and the right setting. But we need things for more than "keeping level" with our friends. We

---

[22]Mihaly Csikszentmihalyi and Eugene Rochberg-Halton, *The Meaning of Things: Domestic Symbols of the Self* (New York: Cambridge University Press, 1981), p. 18.

[23]William James, *Principles of Psychology*, Vol. 1 (New York: Macmillan, 1890), p. 291.

[24]Georg Simmel, *The Philosophy of Money*, trans. Tom Bottomore and David Frisby (Boston: Routledge & Kegan Paul, 1978), p. 331.

[25]Ernest Beaglehole, *Property: A Study in Social Psychology* (New York: Macmillan, 1932).

[26]Ibid., p. 134.

[27]Csikszentmihalyi and Rochberg-Halton, p. 239.

[28]Author's interview with Mihaly Csikszentmihalyi.

[29]Douglas and Isherwood, *World of Goods*, p. 125. Also see Jean Baudrillard, *For a Critique of the Political Economy of the Sign*, trans. Charles Levin (St. Louis, MO: Telos Press, 1981), p. 81. Said Baudrillard: "No one is free to live on raw roots and fresh water. . . . The vital minimum today . . . is the standard package. Beneath this level, you are an outcast." Two classic novels on consumption are (1) Georges Perec, *Les Choses* (New York: Grove Press, [1965], 1967). (2) J. K. Huysmans, *Against the Grain (A Rebours)* (New York: Dover Publications, [1931], 1969).

[30]Douglas and Isherwood, *World of Goods*, p. 124.

human beings are not only toolmakers but symbol makers as well, and we use our possessions in the same way we use language — the quintessential symbol — to *communicate* with one another. According to Douglas, goods make the universe "more intelligible." They are more than messages to ourselves and others, they are "the hardware and the software . . . of an information system."[31] Possessions speak a language we all understand, and we pay close attention to the inflections, vernacular, and exclamations.

The young husband in the film *Diner* takes his things very seriously. How could his wife be so stupid as to file the Charlie Parker records with his rock 'n' roll records, he wants to know. What's the difference, she wants to know. What's the difference? How will he find them otherwise? Every record is sacred. Different ones remind him of different times in his life. His things *take* him back. Things can also *hold* you back. Perhaps that's why Bing Crosby's widow auctioned off 14,000 of her husband's possessions — including his bed. "'I think my father's belongings have somehow affected her progress in life,'" said one of Bing's sons.[32] And things can tell you where you stand. Different goods are used to rank occasions and our guests. Costly sets of goods, especially china and porcelain, are "pure rank markers. . . . There will always be luxuries because rank must be marked," said Douglas.[33]

One of the pleasures of goods is "sharing names."[34] We size up people by their expertise in names — sports buffs can converse endlessly about hitters' batting averages, and design buffs want to know whether you speak spongeware, Palladio, Dansk, or Poggenpohl. All names are not equal. We use our special knowledge of them to show solidarity and exclude people.

In fact, the social function of possessions is like the social function of food. Variations in the quality of goods define situations as well as different times of day and seasons. We could survive on a minimum daily allotment of powdered protein mix or grains and berries. But we much prefer going marketing, making choices, learning new recipes. "Next to actually eating food, what devout gastronomes seem to enjoy most is talking about it, planning menus, and remembering meals past," observed food critic Mimi Sheraton.[35] But it's not only experts who thrive on variety. Menu monotony recently drove a Carlsbad, New Mexico, man to shoot the woman he was living with. She served him green beans once too often. "Wouldn't you be mad if you had to eat green beans all the time?" he said.[36] If every meal were the same, and if everyone dressed alike and furnished alike, all meanings in the culture would be wiped out.[37]

[31] Ibid., p. 72.
[32] Maria Wilhelm, "Things Aren't Rosy in the Crosby Clan as Kathryn Sells Bing's Things (and not for a Song)," *People*, May 31, 1982, pp. 31–33.
[33] Douglas and Isherwood, *World of Goods*, p. 118.
[34] Ibid., p. 75.
[35] Mimi Sheraton, "More on Joys of Dining Past," *New York Times*, April 9, 1983, p. 48.
[36] "Green Beans Stir Bad Blood," *New York Times*, March 26, 1983, p. 6.
[37] Douglas and Isherwood, *World of Goods*, p. 66.

The furnishings of a home, the style of a house, and its landscape are all part of a system — a system of symbols. And every item in the system has meaning. Some objects have personal meanings, some have social meanings which change over time. People understand this instinctively and they desire things, not from some mindless greed, but because things are necessary to communicate with. They are the vocabulary of a sign language. To be without things is to be left out of the conversation. When we are "listening" to others we may not necessarily agree with what this person or that "says" with his or her decor, or we may misunderstand what is being said; and when we are doing the "talking" we may not be able to express ourselves as eloquently as we would like. But where there are possessions, there is always a discourse.

And what is truly remarkable is that we are able to comprehend and 25 manipulate all the elements in this rich symbol system as well as we do — for surely the language of the home and its decor is one of the most complex languages in the world. But because of that it is also one of the richest and most expressive means of communication.

Decor as Symbol of Self

One aspect of personalization is the big I — Identity. Making distinctions between ourselves and others. "The self can only be known by the signs it gives off in communication," said Eugene Rochberg-Halton.[38] And the language of ornament and decoration communicates particularly well. Perhaps in the future we will be known by our computer communiqués or exotic brainwaves, but until then our rock gardens, tabletop compositions, refrigerator door collages, and other design language will have to do. The Nubian family in Africa with a steamship painted over the front door to indicate that someone in the house works in shipbuilding, and the Shotte family on Long Island who make a visual pun on their name with a rifle for a nameplate, are both decorating their homes to communicate "this is where our territory begins and this is who we are."

Even the most selfless people need a minimum package of identity equipment. One of Pope John Paul I's first acts as pontiff was to send for his own bed. "He didn't like sleeping in strange beds," explained a friend.[39] It hadn't arrived from Venice when he died suddenly.

Without familiar things we feel disoriented. Our identities flicker and fade like ailing light bulbs. "Returning each night to my silent, pictureless apartment, I would look in the bathroom mirror and wonder who I was," wrote D. M. Thomas, author of *The White Hotel*, recalling the sense of detachment he felt while living in a furnished apartment during a stint as author-in-residence at a

---

[38]Eugene Rochberg-Halton, "Where Is the Self: A Semiotic and Pragmatic Theory of Self and the Environment." Paper presented at the 1980 American Sociological Meeting, New York City, 1980, p. 3.

[39]Dora Jane Hamblin, "Brief Record of a Gentle Pope," *Life*, November 1978, p. 103.

Washington, D.C., university. "I missed familiar things, familiar ground that would have confirmed my identity."[40]

Wallpaper dealers wouldn't need fifty or sixty sample books filled with assorted geometrics, supergraphics, and peach clamshells on foil backgrounds if everyone were content to have the same roses climbing their walls. Chintz wouldn't come in forty flavors from strawberry to licorice, and Robert Kennedy Jr.'s bride Emily wouldn't have trotted him around from store to store "for ten hours" looking for a china pattern[41] if the home wasn't an elaborate symbol system — as important for the messages it sends to residents and outsiders as for the functions it serves.

In the five-year-long University of Chicago study[42] into how modern Americans relate to their things, investigators Mihaly Csikszentmihalyi and Rochberg-Halton found that we all use possessions to stand for ourselves. "I learned that things can embody self," said Rochberg-Halton. "We create environments that are extensions of ourselves, that serve to tell us who we are, and act as role models for what we can become."[43] But what we cherish and what we use to stand for ourselves, the researchers admitted, seemed to be "scripted by the culture."[44] Even though the roles of men and women are no longer so tightly circumscribed, "it is remarkable how influential sex-stereotyped goals still remain."[45] Men and women "pay attention to different things in the same environment and value the same things for different reasons," said the authors.[46] Men and children cared for action things and tools; women and grandparents cared for objects of contemplation and things that reminded them of family. It was also found that meaning systems are passed down in families from mothers to daughters — not to sons.

Only children and old people cared for a piece of furniture because it was useful. For adults, a specific piece of furniture embodied experiences and memories, or was a symbol of self or family. Photographs which had the power to arouse emotions and preserve memories meant the most to grandparents and the least to children. Stereos were most important to the younger generation, because they provide for the most human and emotional of our needs — release, escape, and venting of emotion. And since music "seems to act as a modulator of emotions," it is particularly important in adolescence "when daily

[40]D. M. Thomas, "On Literary Celebrity," *The New York Times Magazine*, June 13, 1982, pp. 24–38, citation p. 27.

[41]"Back Home Again in Indiana Emily Black Picks Up a Freighted Name: Mrs. Robert F. Kennedy, Jr.," *People*, April 12, 1982, pp. 121–23, citation p. 123.

[42]Eugene Rochberg-Halton, "Cultural Signs and Urban Adaptation: The Meaning of Cherished Household Possessions." Ph.D. dissertation, Department of Behavioral Science, Committee on Human Development, University of Chicago, August 1979; and Mihaly Csikszentmihalyi and Eugene Rochberg-Halton, *The Meaning of Things: Domestic Symbols of the Self* (New York: Cambridge University Press, 1981).

[43]Author's interview with Eugene Rochberg-Halton.

[44]Csikszentmihalyi and Rochberg-Halton, *Meaning of Things*, p. 105.

[45]Ibid., p. 112.

[46]Ibid., p. 106.

swings of mood are significantly greater than in the middle years and . . . later life."[47] Television sets were cherished more by men than women, more by children than grandparents, more by grandparents than parents. Plants had greater meaning for the lower middle class, and for women, standing for values, especially nurturance and "ecological consciousness."[48] "Plateware," the term used in the study to cover all eating and drinking utensils, was mentioned mostly by women. Of course, "plates" are the tools of the housewife's trade. In many cultures they are the legal possession of the women of the house.

The home is such an important vehicle for the expression of identity that one anthropologist believes "built environments" — houses and settlements — were originally developed to "*identify a group* — rather than to provide shelter."[49] But in contemporary Western society, the house more often identifies a person or a family instead of a group. To put no personal stamp on a home is almost pathological in our culture. Fear of attracting attention to themselves constrains people in crime-ridden areas from personalizing, lack of commitment restrains others, and insecurity about decorating skill inhibits still others. But for most people, painting some sort of self-portrait, decoratively, is doing what comes naturally.

All communications, of course, are transactions. The identity we express is subject to interpretation by others. Will it be positive or negative? David Berkowitz, the "Son of Sam" murderer, didn't win any points when it was discovered he had drawn a circle around a hole in the wall in his apartment and written "This is where I live."[50] A person who fails to keep up appearances is stigmatized.

READING THE TEXT

1. Summarize how, according to Kron, our possessions act as signs of our identity.

2. How do our living spaces work to create group identity?

3. Why did *New York Times* readers object to the consumption habits of Martin J. Davidson?

4. In your own words, explain how possessions give one a sense of "stability" (para. 10).

READING THE SIGNS

1. In a small group, discuss the brand names of possessions that each of you owns. Then interpret the significance of each brand. What do the brands say about each of you and about the group?

---

[47]Ibid., p. 72.

[48]Ibid., p. 79.

[49]Amos Rapoport, "Identity and Environment," in James S. Duncan (ed.), *Housing and Identity: Cross-Cultural Perspectives* (London: Croom Helm, 1981), pp. 6–35, citation p. 18.

[50]Leonard Buder, "Berkowitz Is Described as 'Quiet' and as a Loner," *New York Times*, August 12, 1977, p. 10.

2. With your class, brainstorm factors other than possessions that can communicate a person's identity. Then write an essay in which you compare the relative value of possessions to your own sense of identity with the additional
factors your class brainstormed.

3. Write an essay in which you argue for or against Kron's claim that "to put no
personal stamp on a home is almost pathological in our culture" (para. 32).

4. Analyze semiotically your own apartment or a room in your house, using
Kron's essay as a critical framework. How do your possessions and furnishings act as signs of your identity?

5. **CONNECTING TEXTS**   Compare and contrast Kron's discussion of possessions with
that of Tim Kasser ("Mixed Messages," p. 502). Which author do you find more
persuasive, and why?

ANNE GALLIGAN

Pottermania: The Marketing behind the Magic

*If there ever really was a magic formula, the words "Harry Potter" must
be it, for few people in history have been able to conjure up so much fame
and fortune as J. K. Rowling has by inventing them. But as Anne Galligan
explains in this article that originally appeared just as the fifth cinematic
installment of the boy wizard's saga was about to be released, it wasn't
all magic. With names like AOL-TimeWarner and Coca-Cola invested in
the* Harry Potter *empire, the success of the series has had quite a boost
from some very high-profile marketing strategists. As Galligan observes,
the* Harry Potter *books were "written, produced, and marketed from a
complex and interdependent literary and business infrastructure that is
intently focused on maximizing opportunities in the marketplace." Hey,
even a magician can benefit from the Real Thing. Galligan is a postdoctoral fellow with the Australian Studies Centre, University of Queensland, and is the author, with David Carter, of* Making Books: Studies in
Contemporary Australian Publishing *(2007).*

I must confess to being a seriously reluctant reader of the Harry Potter books.
In fact, I had sworn to ignore the books, movies, press releases, countdowns
and statistics, the interviews with children breathless with admiration for the
young wizard's adventures and the world of Hogwarts. As a reader, this is my
right. As a parent it is probably irresponsible, but as a commentator on books

and publishing it has become virtually impossible. So I wonder, why has this series of books, not even ten years old, become so maddeningly pervasive?

With extraordinary speed the contents of the Harry Potter series escaped the boundaries of its print container and the domain of the literary bestseller. But this escalation did not happen just because a good story and promotable author came online. The reinvention of the media industries over the last twenty-five years has placed the publishing house as a content generator within global entertainment powerhouses. Complex sets of business and creative subsidiaries are now built into the synergetic infrastructure of giant media corporations in order to facilitate the streaming of content across multiple media platforms. This simply means that a book can be turned into a film, cartoon, video, computer game or multiple toy, sleepwear or lolly licenses from within the same group of companies.

The Rowling series was ideally suited to this multi-purposing of content, not because it was written for this, but because both the author and the book — the plots, characters and themes — are so digestible. They fit so many of the traditional stereotypes of the literary worlds. The personal history of this one author revives the romance of the literary hero, one that many British publishers were afraid Jeffery Archer had killed off. The story behind the writing of the first Harry Potter, a book that simply set out to tell a good story for the children's market, has become pivotal to the myth. It is regularly recounted: the struggling single Mum, "pretty, penniless JKR"[1] with "fairytale golden hair," living on welfare and a Scottish Arts Grant in a mouse-infested flat, writing compulsively.[2]

The manuscript was rejected by seven, nine, eleven, or twelve publishers, depending on which version you read.[3] It found a suitably nurturing home at Bloomsbury, a respected, middle-size London publisher, established on the principle of "bringing quality to the mass market."[4] The book was an immediate bestseller with Scholastic paying $100,000 for US publishing rights. The roller-coaster ride began as Rowling crossed over from Muggle to empowered princess. A global following crossing divisions of age, gender, class, and country emerged.

---

[1] J. K. Rowling: The Interview. A special program for BBC2, produced by the Newsnight team. Bloomsbury.com. http://www.bloomsbury.com/harrypotter/wizard/section/news.asp?s=1&pageNo=13. Accessed Aug. 7, 2003.

[2] "Bulletin EdDesk Article." Harry Potter (121/24/Arts and Entertainment/Stories). http://bulletin .ninemsn.com.au/bulletin.eddesk.nsf/0/. p. 5 of 6. Accessed Aug. 19, 2003.

[3] Seven publishers turned it down according to Maurice Chittenden in "The magic returns," *Cairns Post*, June 21, 2003. Jeff McMullen quotes eleven in "Wild about Harry: The boy wizard." Ninemsn. http:// ninemsn.com.au/60/stories/2000_07_23/story_203.asp. Accessed Aug. 7, 2003. Nigel Newton quotes twelve in "CE of Bloomsbury Publishing comments on broad portfolio and electronic distribution." TWST.com. p. 2 of 3. http://www.twst.com/notes/articles/lrs016.html. Accessed Sept. 2, 2003.

[4] "Corporate and Investor Relations," Bloomsbury.com, 2003. http://www.bloomsbury-ir.co.uk/ html/about/a_history.html. Accessed Aug. 8, 2003.

Building the Brandname

The Empire expanded when Rowling signed a one million–pound deal with 5
Warner Bros, a subsidiary of America Online-TimeWarner, for rights to the
first two films and worldwide merchandising rights. AOL-TimeWarner was, by
this time, the world's largest media conglomerate, strategically positioned to
exploit the rising star of Harry Potter across its bank of entertainment subsidiaries. The production and promotion environment that was to direct the
transfiguration had reached a sophisticated level of functionality enabling
what Murray argues is a continuing "cross-promotion of the Harry Potter
brand in an endless web of corporate self-referentiality."[5]

The nature and scope of the book game shifted. AOL-TimeWarner raked
in $1.8 billion in global ticket sales from the first two movies. Coca-Cola paid
$150 million for its food license, Lego $100 million for the construction
license. Mattel became the "worldwide master toy licensee for the literary
characters";[6] games, puzzles, trading cards, and action figures abound. There
is the Harry Potter Robe with built-in fiber optic lights, the Ice Pumpkin Slushie
Maker, Late Night Ride Towel, branded school gear, castles, sorting hats, and
fake forehead scars. Bertie Bott's Jelly Beans are popular with flavors of ear
wax, boogers, grass, and vomit. It seems the vomit beans sell particularly well
at video outlets, giving an entirely new meaning to the interactive experience.[7]
Hornby, an almost forgotten maker of model trains, proudly produced a replica
Hogwarts Express. Profits soared by 45 percent.[8]

The publishing companies associated with "the Harry" are also prosper-
ing. Book sales escalated after the first film release with Barbara Marcus of
Scholastic acknowledging that "Not everyone is a reader first."[9] Nigel Newton,
Bloomsbury CEO, delights that each film is "effectively a two-hour commercial for the book."[10] This strong response is expected to feed into a constantly
regenerating promotions cycle with two Harry Potter books and five films still
to come, and new generations of young readers moving into Harry's orbit.

With the release of HP4, Scholastic USA posted a 37 percent increase in
profits and investors debate whether to "gussy up" their portfolios with a little

[5]Simone Murray. "Harry Potter, Inc.: Content recycling for corporate synergy," M/C, Aug. 2002, p. 2
of 8. http://media-culture.org.au/0208/recycling.html. Accessed Aug. 28, 2003.

[6]"Warner Bros. awards Harry Potter toy license to Mattel," Writenews.com. Feb. 11, 2003. http://
www.writenews.com/2000/021100_mattel_potter.htm. Accessed Aug. 15, 2003.

[7]"Bookstores abuzz with Harry hype," MSNBC News. http://stacks.msnbc.com/news/928864.asp
?0si=-&cpl=1. Accessed Aug. 15, 2003.

[8]Op cit. Chittenden.

[9]David Kirkpatrick. "Merchandisers try to harness Harry Potter's magic," *International Herald
Tribune*, June 16, 2003. http://www.iht.com/cgi-bin/generic.cgi?template=articleprint.tmplh&ArticleId
=99415. Accessed Aug. 15, 2003.

[10]"CE of Bloomsbury Publishing comments on broad portfolio and electronic distribution," TWST
.com. Feb. 16, 2002. http://www.twst.com/notes/articles/lrs016.html. Accessed Sept. 2, 2003.

Scholastic stock.[11] Shares in Bloomsbury Publishing PLC have performed "an act of levitation worthy of Potter himself" according to BusinessWeek online.[12] In a populist gesture, Bloomsbury is splitting seventeen million company shares into four, making them more accessible to parents. At $3.80 each, a few shares might be the next best-ever birthday present for the kids.[13] The synergies created by the Potter brand name are working dynamically to create that extra edge in the marketplace. The consumer can now read the books, watch the movies and videos, play with the toys, master the computer games, and then perhaps, buy into the company.

Through all this, Rowling reigns benignly, generously crafting a few more books about the magic realm for charity, penned under pseudonyms that everyone knows, Kennilworthy Whisp (*Quidditch through the Ages*), and Newt Scamander (*Fantastic Beasts and Where to Find Them*). She has struggled, we are told, to reign in the excesses of the merchandising mega-lords with whom she must continue to do business. Jo "wants to protect her stories from becoming encrusted with marketing pitches and mechandisers' plugs."[14] Twice a year she negotiates with Warner on possible Potter products and claims success in vetoing particularly crass prototypes. The Moaning Myrtle Toilet Seat, for example, did not eventuate.

Word is spread through multiple media outlets that this is a benevolent partnership; no one is out to screw the public. Apparently, TimeWarner is operating on a "less is more" principle — a few hundred instead of the 1000 products for a typical Warner blockbuster.[15] There are unusual acts of restraint and generosity. Coca-Cola agreed that Harry Potter's likeness will not be used on its labels and the characters will not drink Coke in its ads. Coca-Cola is also funding a three-year, eighteen-million-dollar global literacy campaign — Reading Is Fundamental.[16] This has not happened before and sets an extraordinary precedent. 10

But this is not good enough for the SaveHarry.com crusade.[17] Organized by the Centre for Science in the Public Interest, the health-advocacy group plans to stop this use of the world's beloved Harry Potter to market junk food to kids. One nutritionist declares that the partnership between Coca-Cola and

---

[11] Justin Lahart, "When Harry met rally," cnnmoney. http://money.cnn.com/2003/06/19/markets/pottermania. Accessed Sept. 2, 2003. "Scholastic is fund manager's favorite stock," cnnmoney. http://money.cnn.com/2002/02/19/investing/favorite _stock/. Oct. 2001. Accessed Dec. 8, 2003.

[12] Kerry Capell and Heidi Dawley, "Harry Potter and the tower of profits," BusinessWeek online, Jul. 7, 2000. http://www.businessweek.com/bwdaily/dnflash/july2000/ nf00707f.htm. Accessed Sept. 24, 2003.

[13] Op cit. Chittenden.

[14] Op cit. Kirkpatrick.

[15] Anne D'Innocenzio. "Harry Potter working magic for retailers," Live onwisconsin. Oct. 29, 2001. http://www3.jsonline.com/onwisconsin/movies/oct01/ harry30102901.asp. Accessed Aug. 15, 2003.

[16] "Harry Potter's magic millions," money.telegraph, Nov. 11, 2001. http://www.telegraph.co.uk/money/main.jhtml?xml=/money/2001/11/11/ccpott11.xml. Accessed Aug. 15, 2003.

[17] "Global campaign protests Coca-Cola's use of Harry Potter to market junk food," Save Harry! Press Room. http://www.saveharry.com/pressreleaseB.html. Accessed Aug. 15, 2003.

Harry Potter "is a sad example of unconscionable marketing." Rowling might have lured children into developing a reading habit, but "there is no reason for her to help undermine their health." Another supporter protests, "Let's keep kids safe from the liquid-candy hucksters." The group urges JKR to use her royalties to fund nutrition campaigns.[18]

This controversy is a mini-version of the debates surrounding the reception of the series across the adult population. Conservative groups charge that the books/films are anti-Christian, promoting witchcraft and satanism. Left-wing writers rage that they feed the British class system, consumer capitalism, mindless authoritarianism, genetic determinism and escapism. To feminists the characterization is heavily sexist, endorsing male leadership models, while many educationists fret that classroom behavior portrays girls as academically more capable and resourceful than boys. However, the media attention generated by these passionate advocates of various persuasions feeds the increasingly broad marketing loop. In the book trade, any publicity is good publicity. The swelling ranks of the adult audience, the intergenerational factor so essential to the successful multi-streaming of content, is increasingly acknowledged by Potter promoters.[19]

The Plot Thickens

The story continues as Harry Potter crosses into the world of everyday commerce in spin-offs that could not have been predicted. There has been a massive increase in visits to the optometrist in the UK. One article declares that "Harry Potter has had a positive effect on the eye health of children around the world."[20] Kids wearing glasses are no longer the victims of playground banter. Potteresque glasses with extra-thick round frames are cool. The authorized Harry Potter lens "is more attractive," "will stay clear and intact for longer" and is "Super-crafty." When the lens becomes too dirty or is breathed on, the HP symbol appears — magic engraved initials that remind the wearer to clean them.[21] In an unusual breakthrough for optometrists, authorized web sites advertise the Harry Potter movies. This demonstrates a remarkable infiltration of the marketplace, when healthcare web sites, peripheral to the entertainment industry, are inducted into a global branding strategy.

In another take-up, the Harry Potter brand name has been co-opted to drive a tourism campaign, promoting Britain with its historic sites, castles,

[18]Ibid.

[19]"Pure 'Potter' business magic is intergenerational," June 30, 2003. http://www.digerati007.net/planetrockstar/news.htm. Accessed Sept. 24, 2003.

[20]Jas Walia. "Harry Potter, bless that soul!" Indian Newslink. April (1) Edition. http://www.indiannewslink.co.nz/April%20(I)%202003%20Web%20Edition/youth_harryp.htm. Accessed Sept. 24, 2003.

[21]D & J Brewer, Opticians. "The Web Site for Eyesite." http://www.brower.co.uk/opticians/childrensspectacles.html. Accessed Aug. 19, 2003.

ghosts and fabled haunts as a "magical" holiday destination.[22] This "reinvention of England" according to the Harry Potter model,[23] is an appreciative response from the British Tourist Authority (now VisitBritain) for the "sheer Britishness of the film and variety of locations it covers."[24] At Rowling's insistence, all actors in the cast are British and the movies are filmed entirely in England. Harry Potter Theme Tours are organized by tourist agencies across the country while the UK Tourism homepage unabashedly promotes the local film industry, Bollywood in Britain. A J. K. Rowling Biography site is an inextricable promotion of both the Potter Kingdom and the British one, with Jo guiding the viewer through childhood sites and film locations, and Harry (Daniel Radcliffe) presenting a "Guide to Visiting Castles."[25] In a spirit of mutual endorsement, the HP books and films are awarded a tourism Oscar for their Outstanding Contribution to English Tourism, Harry joining the ranks of former recipients, HM The Queen and Manchester United.[26]

Potter is also set to rescue Germany's homeless and unemployed. Street magazines in Germany, Switzerland, and Austria have been given exclusive rights to publish the translation of the first chapter of HP5 ahead of release.[27] This is a significant double-edged strategy worthy of Bill Gates and Microsoft, creating a hunger for the whole work across the European continent with a free or low cost sampler. A more charitable reading would welcome this demonstration of Rowling's willingness to contribute to selected charities. But this is not a simple equation either. This emerging trait builds into the public persona of author as hero. Rowling received an OBE and an honorary Ph.D. after HP4 for her services to literature. The Queen even managed to drop by Bloomsbury Press to meet her personally.[28] This gifting role also inspires confidence in Rowling's essential positioning as creator of Harry Potter as a force for good, quite possibly the new patron saint of orphans and outcasts. Importantly, it continues to enlarge her public profile and her audience.

HP5: The Launch and the Law

Finally there is the biggest release in the history of grand releases, the launch of HP5, a highly coordinated marketing blitz. Number Five is placed under a

[22]British Tourist Authority, Report to Tourism Summit, Mar. 5, 2002. http://www.culture.gov.uk/PDF/3rd_tourism_summit_bta.pdf. Accessed Oct. 15, 2003.

[23]Andrew Blake. *The Irresistible Rise of Harry Potter*, London and New York: Verso, 2002.

[24]"Harry Potter to weave tourism magic," BBC News. Nov. 19, 2001. http://news.bbc.co.uk/l/hi/entertainment/film/1664005.stm. Accessed Dec. 8, 2003.

[25]"JK Rowling Biography and Harry Potter." JK Rowling and Harry Potter. http://freeuk.com.webbuk2/harrypotter.htm. Accessed Oct. 15, 2003.

[26]"Harry Potter wins English tourism 'Oscar.'" Press release. VisitBritain. Apr. 23, 2003. http://www.visitbritain.com/uk/presscentre/press_releases/archive/qpr-jun_2003/pfv2003_04. Accessed Aug. 12, 2003.

[27]"Harry Potter to rescue Germany's homeless." Reuters UK. Oct. 13, 2003. http://www.reuters.co.uk/newsPackageArticle.jhtml?type=entertainmentNews&storyID=. Accessed Oct. 15, 2003.

[28]Op cit. "JK Rowling Biography and Harry Potter."

strict embargo, a strategy increasingly used by publishers on high profile titles such as Donna Tartt's *The Little Friend* or Peter Carey's *My Life as a Fake*. Legal injunctions are lodged in courts across the globe barring the disclosure of any book summary or plot details before the launch. Rowling appears to enjoy the secrecy of the embargoed book, claiming that not knowing details of the next story is "part of the excitement" that her subplots and clues create for readers.[29] A global public is urged to play the game, "don't spoil the surprise."[30]

Whether or not this is a marketing initiative or the author's imposition, the embargo strengthens the alliance between the author and her audience, aimed at keeping the secrets safe for the good of children/readers everywhere. It also creates an unfamiliar bond between the publisher and the public. The embargo becomes an advertiser's dream-scheme used not only to protect the HP5 story, but also as a global media tool to educate the public about intellectual property law. Publishers have rights and they will be enforced across national boundaries. Publishers in the Netherlands, India, and China have already been prosecuted for publishing fake Potters or Potter parodies such as the Russian *Tanya Grotter and the Magic Double Bass* and the Chinese *Harry Potter and Leopard Walk Up to Dragon* and *Harry Potter and the Golden Turtle*. The Russian author, Dmitry Yemets, claims that his parody is an original work, part of a separate and legitimate genre, and is appealing the decision. It remained available in Russia, selling 600,000 copies in nine months.[31] In an unusually strong statement of support for Western copyright law, the Chinese publishing company was prosecuted, fined, and three men jailed for up to three years. The Indian publisher expressed disappointment at being forced to dump his fakes since he was doing "a rather nice job" with his Indian version of Hogwarts.[32] Illegal copies and clones are finding an enthusiastic audience. According to "pirate buster" Ian Taylor, ten unauthorized translations of HP5 will be available in Iran shortly after the launch.[33] Nevertheless, Rowling's band of lawyers is mounting a determined counter-charge. The force of law is being marshaled against all black-hearted transgressors.

As the launch date approaches, the media keep the public informed. Dogged police work tracks down the "shifty sounding man" who offered to sell three chapters to *The Sun* for $61,900. Four conspirators appear before the local Magistrate with the ringleader being sentenced to 180 hours community service.[34] In northern England a semi-trailer disappears with over seven thousand copies of the forbidden goods. Given a street value of $330,000 — that is, the size of a moderate drugs haul — there are unfortunately, no arrests.[35]

[29]Op cit. "JK Rowling: The Interview."

[30]Op cit. Kirkpatrick.

[31]Op cit. "Bulletin EdDesk Article." p. 5 of 6.

[32]Ibid.

[33]"Harry Potter's pirates," CBSNEWS.com. London. June 5, 2003. http://www.cbsnews.com/stories/2003/06/17/evening news/printable559002.shtml. Accessed Sept. 24, 2003.

[34]"Harry Potter thief sentenced." *The Sunday Mail*. Queensland Newspapers. June 5, 2003. http://www.thesundaymail.news.com.au/printpage/0,5942,6547254,00.html. Accessed Sept. 24, 2003.

[35]"Booknappers may blow secrets," *Gold Coast Bulletin*, June 19, 2003, p.6.

Now, this is a truck full of books, arguably for the children's market, and this is a remarkable environmental impact statement.

In the States, the embargo is taken equally seriously. A health food store in New York sells a copy to a *Daily News* reporter and details of the plot are published, "potentially spoiling publishing's most treasured secret."[36] The paper is being sued for $150 million for Intellectual Property damages for Rowling and damages to Scholastic's $4.5 million worldwide marketing campaign.[37] And what is amazing here is that in the midst of this campaign coordinated across multiple media channels (syndicated newspapers, magazines, television, and film networks), Scholastic still managed to spend $4.5 million on marketing, twice the budget for HP4.

Embargo restrictions on booksellers are unprecedented. Retailers sign detailed legal affidavits not to open boxes, display copies, or release plot details. Violators will be punished. In Australia, the Retailer Embargo Agreement carried a penalty for infringing booksellers of a $100,000 fine, court costs, and denial of future supplies of Potter books.[38] Local bookstores are urged to creatively promote Harry Potter events and consider crowd control arrangements.

In an unexpected spin-off, the imminent launch of HP5 single-handedly disrupts the Australian Book Fair at Darling Harbour, the annual showcase of the publishing industry. Allen & Unwin, the largest independent publishing house who distribute the Bloomsbury list, decide not to attend the Fair at all — a first for the usually prominent independent publisher. The second day's trading is seriously limited because interstate booksellers returned to home base to prepare for the early Saturday morning unwrapping of the 750,000 Potter books ordered for the Australian market.[39] Publishers at the Book Fair are more than usually despondent.

The scale of this book release rivals the fanfare opening of a blockbuster movie, redefining benchmarks in the book industry. In Australia proceedings are festive. An official countdown is held in Federation Square in Melbourne hosted by the Acting Premier John Thwaites and Lord Mayor John So.[40] The independent bookseller, Gleebooks, hosts a steam train ride for 800 enthusiasts. Snake charmers and fire-eaters entertain the crowded Platform Nine and pumpkin juice is served onboard.[41] Channel Nine's *Sixty Minutes* pays for an extra carriage to join the train so Charles Wooley can host an absolutely riveting Harry Potter reading group.

---

[36]"Security tight for Harry Potter book deliveries." *USA Today*. June 18, 2003. http://www.usatoday.com/life/books/news/2003-06-18-potter-security_x.htm. Accessed Sept. 24, 2003.

[37]"Rowling's wild about Harry." *Courier-Mail*, June 20, 2003, p. 6.

[38]Kirsty Sexton. "Magic moment for Potter fans," *Courier-Mail*, June 22, 2003, p. 5.

[39]Alexa Moses. "9.01: Harry's back after a long spell," SMH.com.au, June 21, 2003. http://www.smh.com.au/articles/2003/06/20/1055828487663.html. Accessed Jul. 8, 2003.

[40]"We're just wild about new Harry," *Townsville Bulletin*, June 21, 2003, p. 41.

[41]"Harry Potter magic hits Sydney," Ninemsn, June 22, 2003. http://news.ninemsn.com.au/Entertainment/story_49675.asp. Accessed July 8, 2008.

Dress-ups, wizards and quizzes, breakfasts and queues out into the street result in over 300,000 copies sold in Australia that first day and over 250,000 sold in the following week.[42] Borders in Brisbane sold 1000 copies in the first hour. In the States the venture sparked superlatives and hyperbole, one report terming it the "Woodstock for kids. . . . Instead of sleeping in the mud, they're sleeping in the aisles," a response that passed five million books into the hands of Yankee consumers that first weekend.[43] Within four months, eleven million books were sold, adding $170 million to Scholastic revenue, a 55 percent quarterly increase.[44]

The downside for booksellers is the massive discounts by chain stores who use books as a loss leader strategy. Bestsellers are sold at a discount of up to 40 percent — that is, at a loss — in order to attract the target demographic group into the stores to buy other products. In the USA, more than half the 8.5 million copies went to discount chains. In Australia the price at Grace Bros., Target, and Woolworths was less than the booksellers were charged wholesale by the publisher.[45] An independent Sydney bookseller ran out of copies early on launch day. Staff and friends combed the chain stores buying up what they could. One staff member was apprehended by the Big W security guard and kicked out of the store — for buying too many books![46] It is estimated that discounting cost retailers $9.12 million in missed revenue in Australia alone over the first eight days.[47] There is growing concern among both booksellers and publishers that this trend is turning the book trade into a loss leader industry.

Conclusion

The Harry Potter series has broken through conventional literary circuitry and become the Sumo wrestler of mass consumption. J. K. Rowling has reasserted the archetype of the book author as literary hero, a role cleverly framed by the media machine. At the same time the role of the individual author as content generator for multimedia cross-purposing is strongly affirmed.

The Harry Potter books are now written, produced, and marketed from a complex and interdependent literary and business infrastructure that is intently focused on maximizing opportunities in the marketplace. The scale of success is producing some surprising results such as the literacy campaign by Coca-Cola and the bonanza for optometrists. It is also reinforcing the use of

[42]"Harry Potter and the big book release," Australian *Bookseller & Publisher*. Aug. 2003, p.14.

[43]Paul Festa, "Latest Potter book scanned, swapped," CNETNews.com, June 26, 2003. http://asia.cnet.com/newstech/personaltech/0,39001147,39137966,00.htm. Accessed Sept. 24, 2003.

[44]"Scholastic's hero Harry Potter," LISNews.com, Sept. 24, 2003. http://harrypotter.lisnews.com/article.pl?sid=03/09/24/1353200&mode=thread&tid=62. Accessed Jan. 10, 2004.

[45]Mark Johnson. "Selling Harry Potter 5 — A view from a (very) small bookshop," Australian *Bookseller & Publisher*. Aug. 2003, p.17.

[46]Ibid.

[47]Op.cit., "Harry Potter & the big book release."

embargoes both as a marketing tool for publishers capitalizing on the suspense of the well-kept secret, and as an education strategy informing the world about intellectual property law. The extraordinary level of sales creates skews in the book marketplace as chain store discounts draw readers away from traditional points of sale and mask industry sales figures and profit margins. But the readers are happy.

Expert opinion is divided on the benefits of this series for the reader, the book industry, and society. Harry Potter is good for the eyes, but bad for the teeth. The books get kids reading, which probably means they will go to heaven, but it is feared that they promote witchcraft, which probably means something else again. Sadly, the series is also accused of promoting senseless consumerism and the British class system, of embedding hierarchical authoritarianism and negative stereotypes of gender. However, it is good for the British tourism and film industries.

Despite these many contradictions, the Harry Potter series has captured the imagination of a global audience. This is, after all, what the trade of publishing is all about. That it is so complexly interwoven into a realm of corporate and business strategies beyond the world of publishing is what makes the Harry Potter phenomenon so intriguing — what finally won my interest as a reluctant reader.

READING THE TEXT

1. What does Galligan mean by the "multi-purposing of content" (para. 3) and "building the brandname"?

2. What does Galligan mean by the "romance of the literary hero" (para. 3), and how does J. K. Rowling's personal history and involvement in marketing the *Harry Potter* industry exemplify that myth?

3. Describe in your own words how the *Harry Potter* industry changed after Rowling signed a contract with AOL-TimeWarner.

4. How can it be said that adult criticism of the *Harry Potter* books "feeds the increasingly broad marketing loop" (para. 12) surrounding them?

READING THE SIGNS

1. In your journal, explore your own response to *Harry Potter*, whether the books or the films. To what extent do you think you were influenced by the extensive merchandising? If you never paid much attention to *Harry Potter*, how do you explain your disinterest?

2. **CONNECTING TEXTS**   Galligan focuses on the business side of the *Harry Potter* industry, not the novels themselves, but she suggests that they are popular, in part, because Potter's character "fit[s] so many of the traditional stereotypes of the literary worlds" (para. 3). Using this claim as a critical framework, write an argument in which you analyze *Harry Potter*'s appeal. To develop your ideas, consult Robert B. Ray's "The Thematic Paradigm" (p. 342), Linda Seger's

"Creating the Myth" (p. 356), and David Denby's "High-School Confidential: Notes on Teen Movies" (p. 396).

3. Support, oppose, or complicate the proposition that the extensive merchandising of *Harry Potter* sullies the artistic integrity of Rowling's creation. Given the marketing that Galligan describes, are you persuaded, for instance, that Rowling has "struggled . . . to rein in the excesses of the merchandising megalords" (para. 9)?

4. **CONNECTING TEXTS**   Galligan refers to adult critics of *Harry Potter* who decry the way the series promotes the British class system. Read or reread Michael Parenti's "Class and Virtue" (p. 406) and assess the validity of this criticism.

ALISON SCHNEIDER

Frumpy or Chic? Tweed or Kente? Sometimes Clothes Make the Professor

Do you ever wonder whether your professors actually look at themselves in the mirror? Indeed, sometimes it may look as if their fashion sense was switched off at birth, but as Alison Schneider reports in this feature for Chronicle of Higher Education, *sometimes clothes do make, or unmake, the professor, from the successful English professor who wears torn T-shirts as conceptual art, to the woman in red taffeta and cowboy boots who may still be on the job market. In short, like everyone else in the world of work, your professors too are judged by the clothes they wear and the way they look. And please don't ask us how we got our jobs. Alison Schneider was formerly a senior writer for* Chronicle of Higher Education, *where this piece first appeared.*

There was just one problem with the English department's job candidate: his pants.

They were polyester, green polyester, and the members of the hiring committee considered that a serious offense. For 10 minutes they ranted about the cut, the color, the cloth. Then and only then did they move on to weightier matters.

He did not get the job.

Neither did a woman lugging an oversized tote bag (too working-class). Or a man sporting a jaunty sweater and scarf (too flaky). Or a woman in a red-taffeta dress and cowboy boots (too — well, too much).

In the world of academe, where the life of the mind prevails, does it really 5 matter if a scholar wears Gucci, gabardine, or grunge? What about good looks?

Can such things tip the scales in a job interview, weaken a bid for tenure, or keep you off the A list on the conference circuit? Many professors say they can, although there is quibbling over the reasons why. Talk about appearances might seem unjustified given the profession's showing in the arena of good looks and good taste. "Academics are still the worst-dressed middle-class occupational group in America," says Valerie Steele, chief curator at the museum of the Fashion Institute of Technology and editor of *Fashion Theory: The Journal of Body, Dress & Culture*.

But despite their threadbare reputation, scholars spend a lot of time thinking, talking, and writing about appearances. Last month, Elaine Showalter, an English professor at Princeton University, came out of the closet, so to speak, and admitted in *Vogue* magazine that she has a fetish for fashion. She waxed eloquent about her Cossack minidress and turquoise boots from Bologna. "For years," she wrote, "I've been trying to make the life of the mind coexist with the day at the mall."

She is not alone. Scholars squirm when the topic of appearance arises, but a growing number agree that even in the ivory tower, image and intellect are hopelessly intertwined. "I absolutely judge what people wear," says Wayne Koestenbaum, an English professor at the City University of New York's Graduate School and University Center, who dabs on specific perfumes to pay homage to particular writers. (He declined to provide an example. "It's much too personal," he says.) But "there are people who are excited as I am by certain ideas, certain artistic movements. There are semiotic codes of dress, makeup, and hair that say things about your allegiances." He should know. He dyed his hair red when he entered graduate school. "It was intimately connected to my intellectual advancement and my movement into feminist and gay theory."

That sounds like self-conscious gobbledygook to some professors. When it comes to appearances, academe breaks down into two camps: pro-frumpy and pro-fashion. Fans of frumpiness insist that if you want to prove you're intellectually a cut above the competition, think twice before parading around in an Italian-cut blazer. "If it's a choice between being chic or frumpy, I think it benefits academics more to be frumpy," says Emily Toth, a professor of English and women's studies at Louisiana State University. "If you look like you spend too much time on your clothes, there are people who will assume that you haven't put enough energy into your mind." Dr. Toth, who doubles in her off-hours as Ms. Mentor — the Miss Manners of academe — has dished out pithy advice for years, first in a column for *Concerns*, the journal of the Women's Caucus of the Modern Language Association, and now in a book, *Ms. Mentor's Impeccable Advice for Women in Academia*.

As for the taffeta dress and cowboy boots — which Ms. Mentor saw for herself — such an outfit may signal that a scholar doesn't grasp the right professional priorities, she says in an interview. "If you don't know how to dress, then what else don't you know? Do you know how to advise students or grade papers? The clothes *are* part of the judgment of the mind."

"Does it say I'm a Wittgenstein scholar?"

Clothes also help determine if someone will fit into a particular institu- 10 tion. Ask around, and you'll hear professors talk about regional norms for academics: The Midwest dresses down, the South dresses up. Tailored but casual wins the day in the Northeast, and anything goes in California — as long as it looks good. Not to mention the fact that individual universities have their own idiosyncratic norms, which professors ignore at their peril. "A lot depends on institutional context," explains Catharine R. Stimpson, dean of the graduate school of arts and sciences at New York University. "At a small, fraught department, where everybody is out to get everybody else, they'd use anything — they could even use a little Liz Claiborne — as a sign of overreaching."

Perhaps the biggest liability of looking too good is that colleagues and students may spend more time thinking about what a professor wears than what he or she says. When clothes become a distraction, the frumpiness faction contends, they do a disservice to young scholars who are trying to establish themselves in their field.

Men occasionally take flak for putting too much of a premium on their own appearance. People still talk about what Andrew Ross, the ultra-hip director of the American-studies program at N.Y.U., wore to the M.L.A.'s 1991 meeting: a yellow Comme des Garcons blazer, a Japanese hand-painted tie, and wedge-heeled suede shoes. Back then, Mr. Ross told *The New York Times* that the jacket was "a sendup of the academic male convention of yellow polyester," but these days he doesn't care to comment. Little wonder. The outfit made him a legend in some eyes and a laughingstock in others. Still, he says, "I don't think it's a bad thing that academics think more about their appearance right now, when the profession is under siege. It translates into a perception that they're not otherworldly, that they don't live in ivory towers, that they meet people where they are rather than tell them where they ought to be." His only fashion regret: removing his earrings when he went on the market. It didn't even land him a job.

"Dressing fashionably in academia is like clearing the four-foot high jump. The bar is not that high," says Michael Bérubé, an English professor at the University of Illinois at Urbana-Champaign. "Anything with some cut or color draws derision — and admiration — because the sartorial requirements of the business are so low." Mr. Bérubé may know whereof he speaks. He showed up at last month's M.L.A. meeting sporting an electric-blue suit of 100-per-cent polyester. He loves the outfit: "It's an amazing color, and it never loses its crease!"

A man may be able to pull off an electric-blue suit without raising eyebrows, but what about a woman? "I still think there's a predisposition to take men more seriously," says Domna C. Stanton, a professor of French and women's

Michael Bérubé, English professor at the U. of Illinois at Urbana-Champaign: "Dressing fashionably in academia is like clearing the four-foot high jump."

studies at the University of Michigan. Junior-faculty women face a particularly difficult quandary, she says. "How do they convey professional seriousness without looking like a man in drag?" Here's the short list of Ms. Mentor's do's and don'ts: For starters, younger women should play down their sexuality. Skirts should be knee-length or below. Pants are never appropriate for interviews. Steer clear of high-heeled shoes. Choose dark colors over light ones. Ms. Mentor recommends dark purple: "It looks good on everyone."

But some people think playing by the rules is the riskiest move of all. 15 "I don't think frumpy gets you anywhere except forgotten," says Jane Gallop, a professor of English and comparative literature at the University of Wisconsin at Milwaukee. She's made strong fashion statements for years. She wore velvet jeans and a sweater when she went on the job market; donned a now-legendary skirt made of men's ties when she lectured on psychoanalytic theory and the phallus; and slipped into suede fringed pants and cowboy boots to talk about Western civilization.

She hasn't toned down her look much since her junior-professor days. "I teach in torn T-shirts that I have actually torn myself," she says. And she still defends using clothing as conceptual art: "There's a stupid impression that a lack of style signifies seriousness, but anyone who comes from a literary sense of things knows that style is often the best way to convey complicated things. You should use everything you have to make people think." Dr. Showalter agrees: "Teaching is performance. We use everything we've got, and costume is part of it. That's not to say that you dress up like Emma Bovary, but a little liveliness is desirable."

"Give me a break," replies Camille Paglia, a humanities professor at the University of the Arts. "Yes, teaching is a performance art. But when the teacher hijacks the classroom for self-display — of fashion or mannerism or cult of personality — we have a corruption of education. Professors think, 'They're here because of me, because of my wonderful whimsy, my wonderful way of doing things.' It makes me want to throw up." Ms. Paglia favors pantsuits for public lectures — she's especially fond of her flowing, Donna Karan tuxedo suit — but sticks to simple slacks, a plain jacket, and rubber-soled shoes in the classroom.

What does all this sartorial sniping mean for scholars going on the job market and the people who are grooming them? Professors spend an inordinate amount of time fine-tuning not only what their proteges will say at interviews but also how they will look when they say it. Mentors criticize everything from the studs in the job-seekers' ears to the shoes on their feet.

The result: Scholars hunting for jobs are expected to look far better than those who have one, says Nancy K. Miller, an English professor at CUNY's graduate school. "I wonder if the emphasis on appearance at the hiring level isn't a displacement of the real issue: that these students aren't going to get jobs. We focus on their clothing as if the perfect suit or haircut, or the toning down of extravagant styles, will guarantee them a job." Alas, she says, it won't.

Karla F. C. Holloway, Duke U. director
of African and African-American studies:
"We can't afford" to be casual in "our
professional demeanor."

The deconstruction of dress weighs particularly heavily upon minority 20
professors. "There is a special turn of the knife for racial and ethnic women,"
says Nell Painter, a black historian at Princeton. "There are prejudices against
people who look too Jewish, too working-class, too Italian, too black, or too
much of anything different." She adds, however, that "if you look too WASPish,
that's probably all right."

The stakes are high for blacks, Ms. Painter says, because nothing they do
is neutral. "If you wear a pair of classic trousers and no kente cloth, that
makes a statement. And if you wear kente cloth, *that* makes a statement."
"My difficulty with that," says Karla F. C. Holloway, director of African and
African-American studies at Duke University, "is that it makes the other parts
of you invisible — your scholarship, your intellect, your seriousness." That's
why she favors formality. She doesn't repress her African-American roots —
she wears ethnic prints and wraps her hair in a braid, like her grandmother
did — but she steers clear of casual couture. "Casualness has never been part
of our professional demeanor," she says. "Maybe because we can't afford to
make it part of our professional demeanor."

The most glaring exception may be Robin D. G. Kelley, a historian at N.Y.U.
He does have some designer suits in his closet, but most days he pulls on a
pair of black jeans, black combat boots, and a "contemporary" — meaning

'50s-looking — shirt or sweater. Students think he's hip and approachable. But looking cool has its cost. "At every stage in my career, youth and informality — in dress, in appearance, in presentation — have been the bane of my existence. Professors take me less seriously." Fortunately, Dr. Kelley says he has found that "the one thing that speaks louder than dress is the work that you do." Hair, however, is something else entirely. "People lose their jobs over how they style their hair," he says. A big Afro is associated with late-'60s radicalism, while straightened hair signals that you're a "serious sell-out white wannabe." Braids, dreadlocks, and shaved heads give the impression that you've got a chip on your shoulder. "When I had my hair short, I was a safe Negro," Dr. Kelley says. Now he's growing dreadlocks, a decision that's cramping his style when it comes to his current work, a book about Thelonious Monk. He'd like to don the kind of funky hats that the jazz pianist wore, but he can't until his hair finishes "locking," he says. "It's really messing up my vibe."

Things are complicated in other ways for those professors — men or women, white or black — graced with exceptionally good looks. In academe, beauty is a double-edged sword. Scholars, like everybody else, sometimes assume that a sound mind isn't likely to be accompanied by a sexy body. Bennett Link, a physicist at Montana State University at Bozeman, posed bare-chested last year in the "Studmuffins of Science" calendar, a tongue-in-cheek tribute to good-looking geeks. The attention over his appearance as "Dr. April" has died down, but he admits that when the calendar came out, he wanted to keep it quiet. "The way a person looks doesn't play much of a role in the sciences," he says. In fact, he adds, it's a matter of pride among scientists to dress down. But image is critical. "It's important to appear smart and competent. I wasn't sure if the calendar would hurt my chances for tenure." (He went along with the idea after his girlfriend at the time had sent in the photos.)

Most people think good looks don't hurt. "Generally, looking attractive helps you get a job," Ms. Gallop says. "It's not supposed to be true — and it's nothing that ever gets said — but prejudices operate against people who are seriously overweight or have bad skin or are really unattractive. It produces a kind of discomfort." As Ms. Mentor puts it, if A is the cream of the academic crop when it comes to looks, and F is "wolf man," then "wolf man does not get a job." Fortunately, she says, most scholars fall somewhere between B+ and D+. But then, she's grading on a curve.

READING THE TEXT

1. What are the arguments in support of the "pro-frumpy" and "pro-fashion" camps in academia, according to Schneider?

2. Explain in your own words how institutional and geographical context might affect fashion norms at a college or university.

3. According to Schneider, how do gender and ethnic differences affect a professor's choices of fashion?

4. What does Elaine Showalter mean by saying that "teaching is performance" (para. 16)?

READING THE SIGNS

1. In your journal, write your own response to the question Schneider poses: "In the world of academe, where the life of the mind prevails, does it really matter if a scholar wears Gucci, gabardine, or grunge?" (para. 5).

2. **CONNECTING TEXTS**   Interview at least five professors of both genders, probing their opinions about whether different fashion norms exist for male and female professors on your campus. Use your results in an argument about whether a fashion double standard exists for professors at your school. To develop your ideas, read or reread Deborah Tannen's "There Is No Unmarked Woman" (p. 620).

3. In class, discuss the ways in which you semiotically read the physical appearance of your professors, especially in the beginning of a term when you may not know them. How do fashion and hair affect your assumptions about them as teachers, either favorably or unfavorably? What patterns do you see in the class's responses?

4. Write an essay in which you support, oppose, or complicate Camille Paglia's statement that "teaching is a performance art. But when the teacher hijacks the classroom for self-display — of fashion or mannerism or cult of personality — we have a corruption of education" (para. 17).

5. Schneider focuses on professors, but what about students and their fashion choices? Randomly observe students at your school congregating in a public place (say, the student union building), and note the predominant fashion styles. Then write a semiotic interpretation of the fashion trends you observe. Do you believe that institutional and geographical context might influence those trends, as Schneider suggests they do for faculty?

DAVID GOEWEY

"Careful, You May Run Out of Planet":
SUVs and the Exploitation of the American Myth

If you think that a car is just a car and that a sport utility vehicle is just a bigger car, then David Goewey's semiotic analysis of the SUV craze could be something of an eyeopener for you. Situating America's love affair with the automobile, in general, and the SUV, in particular, within a historical context, Goewey reveals how the sport utility vehicle is a full-fledged myth machine, symbolically incorporating many of America's ideological values and contradictions within its several tons of heavy metal. And with the explosive popularity of the Cadillac Escalade and GM's Hummer, Goewey's 1999 essay is still on target. An actor and teacher, Goewey wrote this essay, which won the Oliver Evans Undergraduate Essay Prize at California State University, Northridge, as a term paper in a class on popular culture. He published Crash Out *in 2005, about an escape from Sing Sing prison. He currently teaches at the Co-op City Campus of the School of New Resources at the College of New Rochelle.*

"For centuries man had fantasized about the glories of independent travel," wrote the thirteenth-century scientist and philosopher Roger Bacon. Although writing during the Middle Ages, Bacon predicted, with uncanny accuracy, that humanity "shall endow chariots with incredible speed, without the aid of any animal" (Pettifer and Turner 9). Bacon's prescient forecast conjured a vision that became a twentieth-century American fact of life: the ubiquitous automobile. By 1872, French inventor Amédée Bollée had developed steam-powered demonstration models (Flink 6), and within the next thirty-five years the United States dominated the world market for gasoline-powered automobiles (Pettifer and Turner 15). In the new century America itself — with a vast geography, scattered settlements, and relatively low population density — seemed best suited to the spread of a romanticized car culture (Flink 43). America, in short, took to the roads with relish.

The automobile quickly entered American popular culture. Tin Pan Alley devoted no fewer than six hundred songs to the pleasures of motoring (Pettifer and Turner 17). The futurist art movement, furthermore, appropriated the automobile as a specific symbol of modernity itself (Wernick 80), representative of speed, progress, and technology. As a token, the car embodied escapist fantasy (Pettifer and Turner 239), allowing the individual to conquer time and space. But it was America's unique values of freedom, individualism, and the pursuit of happiness that became manifested in the automobile — values that imbued the car with definitive mythic significance (Robertson 191).

Now, at the end of the twentieth century, the vehicle that combines the most potent mix of American mythologies is the sport utility vehicle (SUV) — hybrid passenger cars/light trucks with four-wheel drive. With sales expected to exceed one million units in 1998, the SUV is the fastest-growing segment of the automobile market (Storck 79). However, as a social phenomenon, SUVs contain both practical and mythic contradictions. For example, these vehicles are designed for rugged, off-road motoring, yet a mere 10 percent of drivers ever leave surface streets or highways (Storck 99). With their muscular styling and dominant height and weight, SUVs are almost ludicrously masculine in design, yet women account for 40 percent of sales (Storck 79). Furthermore, while SUV advertising campaigns often pose the vehicle in rural settings of woodlands or along lakesides, the SUV is anything but nature-friendly with its thirsty gasoline tank and lower emission standards (Pope 14). In short, the modern SUV represents a preeminent symbol of American popular culture.

A semiotic analysis of the contradictions inherent in the SUV phenomenon, as well as its historical and socioeconomic significance, therefore, reveals the intriguing ironies that underscore America's predominant ideology. American culture's faddish preoccupation with the SUV may be seen as deeply embedded in a national identity. Furthermore, a close look at the SUV trend also reveals America's understanding of reality and fantasy and its conflicting attitude toward human survival and environmental protection. As a cultural signifier, the SUV both reveals and reflects the principal components of America's popular mythology.

The most obvious ironies are perhaps best observed in the SUV model 5 names chosen by the manufacturers. Many vehicle names are directly evocative of America's western frontier mythology, such as the Jeep Wrangler or the Isuzu Rodeo. Others are linked to the Western European tradition of the exploration and settlement of foreign lands, such as the Ford Explorer or the Land Rover Discovery. Indeed, the GMC Yukon blends both American western imagery and the European exploratory drive and thus embodies the American notion of a frontier: remote, extremely wild, and to the average person unknown.

The fascination with the American frontier, which today's automakers so effectively exploit, is directly tied to America's historical beginnings. The idea of the frontier as both sacred and menacing is a principal tenet in the nation's mythology. The first Europeans, after all, encountered a daunting wilderness. *Mayflower* passenger William Bradford described a "hideous and desolate wilderness . . . represent[ing] a wild and savage hue" (Robertson 45). The Europeans, steeped in fairy-tale traditions of the forest as the dark dwelling place of witches and cannibals, therefore considered the woods intrinsically evil (Robertson 49). The forests were godless and had to be tamed before they could be inhabitable, leveled before they could be considered usable. The Native Americans, likewise, were viewed as the personification of this savage wasteland and therefore had to be subjugated along with the wilderness to ensure the spread of civilization (Robertson 50). And the early Americans' religious convictions justified this expansion.

"I'm changing the climate! Ask me how!" Robert Lind tags a Lincoln Navigator SUV with a bumper sticker in a parking lot in Corte Madera, California. Lind tags oversized SUVs with bumper stickers because he believes they harm the environment.

The notion that Americans were on a God-given mission to subdue this newfound jungle and expand Western civilization "into the limitless wilderness" (Robertson 44) became institutionalized in American mythology by the Jacksonian policy of Manifest Destiny. Americans were believed to be ordained by God to carry the noble virtues of democracy, freedom, and civilization westward across the continent (Robertson 72). This relentless expansionism, then, was suffused with religious significance and mission. The frontier was seen as the demarcation between order and disorder, between goodness and evil. To challenge the frontier, therefore, took supreme courage and zeal, and men like Daniel Boone, George Rogers Clark, and Andrew Jackson became outstanding western heroes (Robertson 80).

Corollary to this idea of an expansive frontier was the belief in the ever-abundant opportunities and riches available to whoever was brave and ambitious enough to pursue them. This idea of "more" was contingent on the belief in a limitless frontier and served as a motivating factor in the pursuit of happiness and the drive to succeed. Expansion, in a sense, became an end in itself (Shames 33–34). However, in late-twentieth-century America, the concept of more has suffered a practical setback. Diminishing economic expectations from the 1960s through the 1980s, including a shrinking productivity rate, a decrease in real earnings, and a growing national debt, all contributed to challenge the mythic notion of the frontier as fruitful with economic possibilities (Shames 34–36).

It is perhaps not coincidental, then, that the sport utility vehicle craze began in earnest in the early 1980s (Storck 79). In reaction to "the fear that the world may not be . . . big enough" (Shames 37), the decade's penchant for conspicuous consumption can be seen as a challenge to that anxiety. And the introduction of large, powerful vehicles into the mass market, with names like the Ford Bronco and the Chevy Blazer, may represent the reassertion of a courageous American defiance in response to threatened frontiers.

Furthermore, the growth of the SUV market through the 1990s, with this   10 segment comprising 23 percent of total auto sales (Storck 79), suggests the adaptability of the SUV's mythic significance. The expanding economy of the Clinton years — based on the globalization of economic interests and the consequent resurrection of expanding frontiers — recasts the SUV as a celebratory metaphor for power and control. The SUV, in this context, represents the resurgence of the conquering American.

The GMC Yukon, named for a region far from the American mainstream, can be seen to embody the cultural notion of the wild frontier as fearsome and therefore in need of civilization. And the vehicle is certainly well designed for the rugged task of settlement. Weighing in at over 5,300 pounds (with passengers), measuring over 16½ feet in length and just under 6 feet in height, the GMC Yukon is among the largest SUVs on the market (Storck 27). Its massive size arguably manifests the expansive idea of America's western frontier.

However, the GMC Yukon's heftiness necessarily affects its miles-per-gallon ratio. The average rounds off at a measly 13 miles per gallon (Storck 27), less than half what the U.S. government requires for passenger cars. And with a fuel tank capacity of 30 gallons and an estimated full tank mileage of under 400 miles, the GMC Yukon can be seen vehemently to declare the concept of more. Furthermore, juxtaposing the GMC Yukon with its namesake suggests an egregious symmetry. The Yukon Territory, north of British Columbia, Canada, abuts Prudhoe Bay. Exploratory oil drilling there in 1967 uncovered the largest oilfield in North America, with an estimated capacity of about 10 billion barrels (Yergin 571). The American myth of an ever-expansive frontier, then, is powerfully manifested in the heavyweight GMC Yukon, which locates and justifies its own mass production in the fact of a naturally oil-abundant Yukon Territory.

Another popular SUV that contains a doubly potent signifier within the manufacturer's title is the Jeep Cherokee. Considered the original SUV, the Jeep Cherokee dates all the way back to 1948. As a result, owners take a measure of purist's pride, believing their SUV is the one that started it all (Storck 41). But a closer look at this SUV's mythohistorical connections may provide the owners' pride with a deeper significance.

The Jeep Cherokee prototype — the General Purpose Vehicle, which was shortened to Jeep — was introduced during World War II in response to a U.S. Army–sponsored competition among automakers. It was first developed by the Bantam Motor Company, and the design was then completed by the Willys-Overland Company. The Ford Motor Company also assisted in the mass production of what was soon considered the "backbone of all Allied military transport" and the "crowning success of the war" (Flink 276). No doubt drawing on their heroic wartime performance, surplus military Jeeps were sold stateside and helped to introduce a market for four-wheel-drive recreational vehicles (Flink 276).

The usefulness and durability of four-wheel-drive vehicles, however, was recognized even earlier during World War I, and many automakers, including Packard, Peerless, and Nash motor companies, vied for government contracts. Manufacturers found that luxury car chassis were easily converted to 2 or 3 ton truck bodies (Flink 78) — a literal blending of automobiles and trucks that clearly prefigures the modern SUV. Along with the Jeep's victorious wartime service, then, the SUV conveys such powerful militaristic connotations as morally righteous patriotism, overwhelming industrial ingenuity and might, and the imperative conquest of evil.

An interesting link between automobility and the American frontier was provided approximately forty years earlier by a Civil War hero. On his retirement in 1903, Civil War veteran General Nelson A. Miles, who had successfully hunted Chief Joseph and the Nez Perce to ground in 1877 and to whom the Apache war leader Geronimo surrendered in 1886 (Josephy 416, 429), foresaw the military promise of motor vehicles. He urged Secretary of War Elihu Root to "replace five regiments of calvary" with troops on bicycles and in motor vehicles (Flink 74), believing that the horse was now obsolete. General Miles's foresight was ironic in light of the Jeep Cherokee's double significance.

The Jeep Cherokee's militaristic connotations become oppressive when considering the grotesquely racist misapplication of a Native American tribal name to a motor vehicle. Although the word *Cherokee* is a misnomer derived from the Choctaw definition for cave dwellers and actually has no meaning in the language of those to whom it is applied, it is nevertheless used to designate at least one group of Native Americans, the United Keetoowah Band of Cherokee, in Oklahoma (Josephy 323). This original misnaming indicates the indeterminability of language, especially in the traumatic context of Native American history. And while it may be argued that such indeterminacy freely allows a manufacturer's use of the name to sell a product, the word *Cherokee* nevertheless denotes a group of people still thriving today despite oppression.

In the 1820s, despite the fierce allegiance to tradition held by many Cherokee, a large number of them succumbed to the ongoing proselytizing efforts of Moravian missionaries to become the "most acculturated of southern tribes" (Josephy 320). The Cherokee learned the English alphabet and even innovated a Cherokee alphabet based on the English model. In 1828, this led to the remarkable publication, in English and Cherokee, of a native newspaper (Josephy 320). Cherokee efforts to assimilate into what could be seen even then as a dominant culture, in other words, were vigorous.

Nevertheless, also in 1828, President Andrew Jackson undertook an aggressive campaign of ethnic cleansing against the Cherokee. Capitalizing on white racism to pass anti-Cherokee legislation, and with the discovery of gold on Cherokee territory, Jackson made physical removal of the tribe a national issue (Josephy 325). This culminated in the infamous and tragic Trail of Tears, the forced march west to Oklahoma of eighteen thousand Cherokee men, women, and children under the armed escort of General Winfield Scott and seven thousand U.S. Army troops (Josephy 331).

The manufacturers of the Jeep Cherokee clearly ignore this dismal chapter 20 in U.S. history and instead evoke superficially positive components of a mythic American past. Drawing on traditional viewpoints of the western frontier as the border between civilization and wilderness (Robertson 92) and oblivious to the fact that the Cherokee were an enforced western tribe, the Jeep Cherokee manufacturer exploits mythic identifications of Native Americans with the fearsome and violent "imagery and logic of the frontier" (Robertson 106).

The Jeep Cherokee manufacturer also mines the symbol of the quintessential American hero, the cowboy. Pitted against the frontier, the cowboy was directly descended from the backwoodsmen and pathfinders who pioneered west to the Ohio River Valley and beyond to the Northwest Passage. As the frontier pushed on, the continent's western plains and mountains became the wilderness that was next in need of subjugation and control. The cowboy, and his close companions in the American mythic imagination of the Wild West, the U.S. Cavalry, became the defenders of civilization and the champions of progress (Robertson 161–62). As such, they symbolized law and order in a lawless land. Both the cowboy and the U.S. Cavalry were the good guys risking themselves to save civilization from the bad guys, most notably the wildly violent Indians (Robertson 162).

The Jeep Cherokee, then, is a multilayered symbol indeed. This SUV appropriates the token of a victorious American struggle over the frontier, won by American cowboys and cavalrymen, and combines it with the morally righteous conquest over evil achieved during World War II. The modern driver who slips behind the wheel of a Jeep Cherokee assumes the militaristically heroic mantle that is suffused within the vehicle's legend and manifested in the control available in the "tight and precise steering, easy maneuverability . . . and taut overall feel from the firm suspension" (Storck 41). Detached from historical truths, however, the SUV's "excellent visibility all around" and "superior driving position" (Storck 41), qualities essential to success in battle, capitalize on these military/frontier connotations and at the same time sublimate factual battlefield horrors into an aggressive game of on-the-road cowboys and Indians.

The SUV, with its rugged militaristic symbolism, magnifies the traditional association of the automobile as a masculine token. Yet women account for a sizable share of the SUV market (Storck 79). This appeal, in fact, extends and amplifies a traditional relationship between women and motor vehicles. The introduction of the automobile may well have affected the scope of women's societal role more than that of men. Unlike the horse and buggy, for instance, the automobile demanded skill over physical strength to operate, and so women were offered mobility and parity that driving a team of horses denied them (Flink 162).

However, middle-class women by the 1920s were still traditionally tied to the home, for the most part, although electrical household appliances had nevertheless increased leisure time. The refrigerator, for example, permitted the bulk buying of a week's worth of perishable food at one stop, leaving time for socializing or an afternoon movie matinee (Flink 164). The added spare time, combined with automobility's enhanced sense of individual freedom (Robertson 191), afforded women at least temporary escape from the confines of the home that defined their routine (Flink 163).

As the automobile helped to change women's role from that of home-based providers of food and clothing into consumers of mass-produced goods, car designers soon recognized the potential of the female market. Such comfort features as plush upholstery, heaters, and automatic transmissions were planned with women in mind (Flink 163). And advertising executives, quick to determine that women were disproportionately the nation's consumers (Marchand 66), began to target automobile ads at them. One of the most famous advertisements, for the Jordan Motor Company's Playboy automobile, began "Somewhere west of Laramie there's a broncho-busting, steer-roping girl" (Pettifer and Turner 130), clearly utilizing the familiar western imagery of freedom and control.

This relationship between women and their automobiles has grown even more complex in recent years. First, the car didn't so much redefine women's fundamental domestic role as increase the scope of its domain. Also, it is reasonable to assume that the automobile facilitated women's introduction into the workplace by easing transportation between the home and job. And yet in 1997, economic equality still eludes the American workforce: Working women earn less than 75 percent of men's average income (Jones et al. 49). A woman's job, furthermore, may include not only doing outside work but ferrying children to and from school and activities and shopping for the family. A subsequent feeling of disempowerment, then, may find relief behind the wheel of a physically powerful and symbolically potent SUV.

Advertisers evidently think so. They still acknowledge a woman's buying power and capitalize on the appeal SUVs hold for many female drivers. One current SUV advertisement aimed at women, promoting the Subaru Forester, both stresses its inherent power and rugged potential and notes the female-friendly design of this smaller vehicle. The larger photo in a . . . two-page spread in *Time* shows the Forester kicking up a dust trail as it barrels down a dirt track. The accompanying smaller picture presents a casually dressed young woman easily tying a kayak to the SUV's roof. The ad's dominant image is a rough and careless strength. And while the woman in the ad is proportionally submissive, she is capably preparing for an exciting outdoor adventure. The double message suggests a sense of diminishment that is compensated for with images of ability, ease, and the casual transference of power.

Perhaps the most logical and disarming association carmakers and advertisers exploit when designing and promoting an SUV is the vehicle's connection to nature. As previously noted, implicit within the SUV's frontier imagery is a confrontational attitude toward the wilderness. Accordingly, automakers design — and advertisers sell — SUVs capable of handling the roughest terrain.

And indeed, much of the appeal of SUVs is their promise of providing access to the farthest reaches of the globe. As a marketing gimmick, for instance, Land Rover cosponsors and participates in the annual Camel Trophy relay, pitting various SUVs against the jungle wilds of Borneo and South America. Besides the obvious British imperialistic connotations such a race implies, the challenge of maneuvering a Land Rover Discovery "over garbage can sized rocks" or "through streams where the entire vehicle is submerged" (Storck 6) positions the competitor in a naturally inharmonious contest.

Advertisers take a dual approach when exploiting the adversarial relationship between SUVs and nature. In some print ads this relationship is clothed in benign natural imagery, often with a warning text. The Mitsubishi Montero Sport, for example, pictures a gleaming silver vehicle perched prominently on the rocky shoreline of a wooded lakesite. The tall stand of evergreen trees are at a safe distance; the water surface is without a ripple. The bold black headline proclaims, "It Came to Comfort Earth," and the text goes on to inform the reader that "the planet wasn't exactly designed for your comfort."

So the Montero Sport offers a wondrous solution to an uncomfortable   30
world. The proximity of nature to the vehicle in the photo is remote, suggesting that the mere presence of the Montero Sport is enough to keep nature at bay. Furthermore, the SUV's silver color combines with the headline to imply that the Montero Sport carries an otherworldly salvation. Nature and its uncomfortability, therefore, are controlled by the SUV's omnipresence, and the driver is safe due to the vehicle's "car-like . . . civility."

Ads for the luxury Infiniti QX4 portray a similar oppositional message but with a more active approach. A silver SUV is pictured once again, but this time bolting through the shallow water of a black-rock lakeshore. The landpoint jutting into the water directly behind the QX4, as though in pursuit, is in silhouette and resembles a large black serpent lagging just behind. The text's message cautions: "careful, you may run out of planet." Although the threat is clear, the presentation is nevertheless one of SUV power in opposition to nature. Indeed, the QX4 appears to be riding atop the water, and the text ends with the admonishment, "resist the urge to circumnavigate the globe."

So while the Infiniti ad sells the promise of adventure, at the same time it positions the SUV's representational power as necessary and inevitable. The QX4 is vigorously slashing through the water on its way to points unknown because it has to; the natural environment is dangerous, hostile to civilization, and quite capable of destroying it if not met with even more superior power. And as if to drive home the point, both the Montero Sport and the Infiniti QX4 ads present a silver SUV as the symbol of modernity, thereby drawing on the traditional American mythology of progress in opposition to a hostile wilderness.

The design and marketing of SUVs are based on traditional American attitudes toward nature and the wilderness. The vehicles are at the same time built for access to the natural world and yet sold by exploiting that relationship as confrontational. The SUV, in other words, makes easily available a world that is threatening to the driver and its occupants. And yet underlying these contradictions, and compounding them, is the very real impact that SUVs make on the environment.

The GMC Suburban, big sister to the aforementioned GMC Yukon, asserts itself with a 42 gallon capacity fuel tank. With a curb-side weight pushing five thousand pounds and amenities like air conditioning, the Suburban's gas mileage is generously estimated at about 16 miles to the gallon (Storck 29). While the GMC Suburban is admittedly the largest SUV model on the market, poor gas mileage ratios are the norm for these vehicles. Where the Environmental Protection Agency has determined that automobiles must meet a fuel economy standard of 27.5 miles a gallon, light trucks, which include all SUVs, currently need only to clear 20.7 miles a gallon. And many don't even achieve that (Bradsher).

The world oil industry may keep billions of barrels in their inventories on any given day (Yergin 686), leading to the understandable public perception that supplies are unlimited. But fossil fuels are still a nonrenewable resource. Moreover, American gasoline use is expected to rise by 33 percent within the next fifteen years, indicating that fuel conservation is not much of an issue with consumers (Bradsher). 35

But perhaps the more pressing problem, and one that is directly exacerbated by the SUV craze, is the threat of global warming from the increased burning of fossil fuels. Carbon dioxide levels in the atmosphere have risen by about 25 percent in the last century and appear to coincide with a worldwide increase in the use of petroleum. Various cataclysmic effects are predicted as a result, including rising sea levels from melting ice caps, the spread of tropical diseases to normally temperate regions, and extreme weather fluctuations (McKibben 9, 18). Yet the booming SUV market belies any overwhelming concern on the part of American consumers. In fact, the vehicle's popularity in the face of such dire predictions seems the latest manifestation of an established confrontational relationship to nature.

As the world does indeed become more dangerous, the apparent protection that SUVs afford becomes more desirable, and the need to control the uncontrollable becomes more acute. Driving a five thousand pound, resource-devouring behemoth not only justifies the impact on the environment, as a means of revenge against an enemy, but it acts as a means of celebration— the exultation of victory over the savage beast of nature. The SUV, in its design and presentation, seeks to make safely available what it can ultimately dominate; as such, it attempts to reduce the entire world to the state of a drive-through wildlife nature preserve. At the end of the twentieth century, the SUV perfectly embodies an American mythology of conquest and control.

America's love affair with the sport utility vehicle shows the abiding power of traditional beliefs. The expansion of the frontiers continues despite facts that suggest there is nowhere left to go. This joyful faith in "more" feeds on the challenge of less. Indeed, a sport utility vehicle is the triumphant representation of denial—denial of the past, the present, and the future. American mythology is continuously reinvented and thereby endures in this pop cultural symbol.

WORKS CITED

Bradsher, Keith. "Light Trucks Increase Profits but Foul Air More Than Cars." *New York Times* 30 Nov. 1997, national ed., sec. 1:1+.

Flink, James J. *The Automobile Age.* Cambridge: MIT, 1988.

Jones, Barbara, Anita Blair, Barbara Ehrenreich, Arlie Russell Hochschild, Jeanne Lewis, and Elizabeth Perle McKenna. "Giving Women the Business." *Harper's* Dec. 1997: 47–58.

Josephy, Alvin M., Jr. *Five Hundred Nations: An Illustrated History of North American Indians.* New York: Knopf, 1994.

Marchand, Roland. *Advertising the American Dream: Making Way for Modernity 1920–1940.* Berkeley: University of California Press, 1985.

McKibben, Bill. *The End of Nature.* New York: Anchor, 1989.

Pettifer, Julian, and Nigel Turner. *Automania: Man and the Motorcar.* Boston: Little, Brown, 1984.

Pope, Carl. "Car Talks — Motown Walks." *Sierra Magazine* Mar./Apr. 1996: 14+.

Robertson, James Oliver. *American Myth, American Reality.* New York: Hill & Wang, 1980.

Shames, Laurence. "The More Factor." *Signs of Life in the U.S.A.: Readings on Popular Culture for Writers.* Ed. Sonia Maasik and Jack Solomon. Boston: Bedford, 1994.

Storck, Bob. *Sport Utility Buyer's Guide '98.* Milwaukee: Pace, 1998.

Wernick, Andrew. "Vehicles for Myth." *Signs of Life in the U.S.A.: Readings on Popular Culture for Writers.* Ed. Sonia Maasik and Jack Solomon. Boston: Bedford, 1994.

Yergin, Daniel. *The Prize: The Epic Quest for Oil, Money and Power.* New York: Simon & Schuster, 1991.

Reading the Text

1. What significance does Goewey see in the names automakers give to SUVs?

2. In your own words, explain why Goewey considers the popularity of SUVs to be full of "ironies" (para. 5) and "contradictions" (para. 4).

3. How does Goewey account for the SUV's appeal to women?

4. In Goewey's view, why does the imagery associated with SUVs have an adversarial relationship with nature?

5. Chart how Goewey uses the semiotic method. How does he explicate the system to which SUVs belong and the cultural mythologies that such vehicles evoke?

Reading the Signs

1. Write a journal entry in which you interpret how your own car (or that of a friend or relative) acts as a sign. What messages does it send about your identity?

2. Using Goewey's approach as a model, interpret a different category of automobile, such as pickup trucks or small two-seaters, or an individual model that has a distinctive image, such as the Smart Car.

3. Collect automobile advertising from several popular magazines, and analyze how the cars are promoted as signs. What slogans are used to catch your attention? What values and ideologies are linked to particular makes and models?

4. Since Goewey wrote this article, many models of SUVs have entered the market, both smaller makes such as the Saturn VUE and larger ones like the Cadillac Escalade. Study the imagery associated with such models, in both advertising and manufacturer Web sites. Then write an essay in which you argue whether Goewey's position that SUVs are linked with American frontier mythology applies to SUVs today.

THOMAS L. FRIEDMAN
Revolution Is U.S.

With the downfall of the Soviet Union and the end of the Cold War, a new historical era emerged that replaced superpower competition with a consumer-driven politico-economic dynamic generally referred to as globalization. And though America is not the sole player in this new global system, its domination of the world's consumer and entertainment markets, as Thomas L. Friedman points out in this selection, is often taken by the rest of the world as a kind of conspiracy to dominate, or Americanize, the world itself. But whether globalization equals Americanization, Friedman suggests, we seem to want a world in which there is "a Web site in every pot, a Pepsi on every lip, [and] Microsoft Windows in every computer," for in the end, "globalization is us." The winner of two Pulitzer Prizes for reporting and the winner of a National Book Award for From Beirut to Jerusalem *(1989), Friedman is the foreign affairs columnist for the* New York Times *and the author of* The Lexus and the Olive Tree *(2000), from which this reading is taken. His most recent book is* The World Is Flat: A Brief History of the Twenty-first Century *(2005).*

I believe in the five gas stations theory of the world.

That's right: I believe you can reduce the world's economies today to basically five different gas stations. First there is the Japanese gas station. Gas is $5 a gallon. Four men in uniforms and white gloves, with lifetime employment contracts, wait on you. They pump your gas. They change your oil. They wash your windows, and they wave at you with a friendly smile as you drive away in peace. Second is the American gas station. Gas costs only $1 a gallon, but you pump it yourself. You wash your own windows. You fill your own tires. And when you drive around the corner four homeless people try to steal your hubcaps. Third is the Western European gas station. Gas there also costs $5 a gallon. There is only one man on duty. He grudgingly pumps your gas and unsmilingly changes your oil, reminding you all the time that his union contract says he only has to pump gas and change oil. He doesn't do windows. He works only thirty-five hours a week, with ninety minutes off each day for lunch, during which time the gas station is closed. He also has six weeks' vacation every summer in the south of France. Across the street, his two brothers and uncle, who have not worked in ten years because their state unemployment insurance pays more than their last job, are playing boccie ball. Fourth is the developing-country gas station. Fifteen people work there and they are all cousins. When you drive in, no one pays any attention to you because they are all too busy talking to each other. Gas is only 35 cents a gallon because it is subsidized by the government, but only one of the six pumps actually works. The others are broken and they are waiting for the replacement parts to be flown in from Europe. The gas station is rather run-down because the absentee owner lives in Zurich and takes all the profits out of the country. The owner doesn't know that half his employees actually sleep in the repair shop at night and use the car wash equipment to shower. Most of the customers at the developing-country gas station either drive the latest-model Mercedes or a motor scooter — nothing in between. The place is always busy, though, because so many people stop in to use the air pump to fill their bicycle tires. Lastly there is the communist gas station. Gas there is only 50 cents a gallon — but there is none, because the four guys working there have sold it all on the black market for $5 a gallon. Just one of the four guys who is employed at the communist gas station is actually there. The other three are working at second jobs in the underground economy and only come around once a week to collect their paychecks.

What is going on in the world today, in the very broadest sense, is that through the process of globalization everyone is being forced toward America's gas station. If you are not an American and don't know how to pump your own gas, I suggest you learn. With the end of the Cold War, globalization is globalizing Anglo-American-style capitalism and the Golden Straitjacket. It is globalizing American culture and cultural icons. It is globalizing the best of America and the worst of America. It is globalizing the American Revolution and it is globalizing the American gas station.

But not everyone likes the American gas station and what it stands for, and you can understand why. Embedded in the Japanese, Western European, and communist gas stations are social contracts very different from the American one, as well as very different attitudes about how markets should operate and be controlled. The Europeans and the Japanese believe in the state exercising power over the people and over markets, while Americans tend to believe more in empowering the people and letting markets be as free as possible to sort out who wins and who loses.

Because the Japanese, Western Europeans, and communists are uncomfort- 5 able with totally unfettered markets and the unequal benefits and punishments they distribute, their gas stations are designed to cushion such inequalities and to equalize rewards. Their gas stations also pay more attention to the distinctive traditions and value preferences of their communities. The Western Europeans do this by employing fewer people, but paying them higher wages and collecting higher taxes to generously support the unemployed and to underwrite a goody bag of other welfare-state handouts. The Japanese do it by paying people a little less but guaranteeing them lifetime employment, and then protecting those lifetime jobs and benefits by restricting foreign competitors from entering the Japanese market. The American gas station, by contrast, is a much more efficient place to drive through: The customer is king; the gas station has no social function; its only purpose is to provide the most gas at the cheapest price. If that can be done with no employees at all — well, all the better. A flexible labor market will find them work somewhere else. Too cruel, you say? Maybe so. But, ready or not, this is the model that the rest of the world is increasingly being pressured to emulate.

America is blamed for this because, in so many ways, globalization is us — or is at least perceived that way by a lot of the world. The three democratizations were mostly nurtured in America. The Golden Straitjacket was made in America and Great Britain. The Electronic Herd is led by American Wall Street bulls. The most powerful agent pressuring other countries to open their markets for free trade and free investment is Uncle Sam, and America's global armed forces keep these markets and sea lanes open for this era of globalization, just as the British navy did for the era of globalization in the nineteenth century. Joseph Nye Jr., dean of the Harvard University Kennedy School, summarized

A street in Lahore, Pakistan.

this reality well when he noted: "In its recent incarnation, globalization can be traced in part back to American strategy after World War II and the desire to create an open international economy to forestall another depression and to balance Soviet power and contain communism. The institutional framework and political pressures for opening markets were a product of American power and policy. But they were reinforced by developments in the technology of transportation and communications which made it increasingly costly for states to turn away from global market forces." In other words, even within the Cold War system America was hard at work building out a global economy for its own economic and strategic reasons. As a result, when the information revolution, and the three democratizations, came together at the end of the 1980s, there was a power structure already in place that was very receptive to these trends and technologies and greatly enhanced their spread around the world. As noted earlier, it was this combination of American power and strategic interests, combined with the made-in-America information revolution, that really made this second era of globalization possible, and gave it its distinctly American face.

Today, globalization often wears Mickey Mouse ears, eats Big Macs, drinks Coke or Pepsi, and does its computing on an IBM PC, using Windows 98, with an Intel Pentium II processor, and a network link from Cisco Systems. Therefore, while the distinction between what is globalization and what is Americanization may be clear to most Americans, it is not — unfortunately — to many others around the world. In most societies people cannot distinguish anymore among American power, American exports, American cultural assaults, American cultural exports, and plain vanilla globalization. They are now all wrapped into one. I am not advocating that globalization should be Americanization — but pointing out that that is how it is perceived in many quarters. No wonder the Japanese newspaper *Nihon Keizai Shimbun* carried a headline on June 4, 1999, about a conference in Tokyo on globalization that referred to the phenomenon as "The American-Instigated Globalization." When many people in the developing world look out into this globalization system what they see first is a recruiting poster that reads: UNCLE SAM WANTS YOU (for the Electronic Herd).

Martin Indyk, the former U.S. ambassador to Israel, told me a story that illustrates this point perfectly. As ambassador, he was called upon to open the first McDonald's in Jerusalem. I asked him what he said on the occasion of McDonald's opening in that holy city, and he said, "Fast food for a fast nation." But the best part, he told me later, was that McDonald's gave him a colorful baseball hat with the McDonald's logo on it to wear as he was invited to eat the first ceremonial Big Mac in Jerusalem's first McDonald's — with Israeli television filming every bite for the evening news. The restaurant was packed with young Israelis eager to be on hand for this historic event. While Ambassador Indyk was preparing to eat Jerusalem's first official Big Mac, a young Israeli teenager worked his way through the crowd and walked up to him. The teenager was carrying his own McDonald's hat and he handed it to Ambassador Indyk with a pen and asked, "Are you the ambassador? Can I have your autograph?"

Somewhat sheepishly, Ambassador Indyk replied, "Sure. I've never been asked for my autograph before."

As Ambassador Indyk took the hat and prepared to sign his name on 10 the bill, the teenager said to him, "Wow, what's it like to be the ambassador from McDonald's, going around the world opening McDonald's restaurants everywhere?"

Stunned, Ambassador Indyk looked at the Israeli youth and said, "No, no. I'm the *American* ambassador — not the ambassador from McDonald's!"

The Israeli youth looked totally crestfallen. Ambassador Indyk described what happened next: "I said to him, 'Does this mean you don't want my autograph?' And the kid said, no, I don't want your autograph, and he took his hat back and walked away."

No wonder that the love-hate relationship that has long existed between America and the rest of the world seems to be taking on an even sharper edge these days. For some people Americanization-globalization feels more than ever like a highly attractive, empowering, incredibly tempting pathway to rising living standards. For many others, though, this Americanization-globalization can breed a deep sense of envy and resentment toward the United States — envy because America seems so much better at riding this tiger and resentment because Americanization-globalization so often feels like the United States whipping everyone else to speed up, Web up, downsize, standardize, and march to America's cultural tunes into the Fast World. While I am sure there are still more lovers of America than haters out there, this [essay] is about the haters. It is about the *other* backlash against globalization — the rising resentment of the United States that has been triggered as we move into a globalization system that is so heavily influenced today by American icons, markets, and military might.

As the historian Ronald Steel once pointed out: "It was never the Soviet Union but the United States itself that is the true revolutionary power. We believe that our institutions must confine all others to the ash heap of history. We lead an economic system that has effectively buried every other form of production and distribution — leaving great wealth and sometimes great ruin in its wake. The cultural messages we transmit through Hollywood and McDonald's go out across the world to capture and also undermine other societies. Unlike more traditional conquerors, we are not content merely to subdue others: We insist that they be like us. And of course for their own good. We are the world's most relentless proselytizers. The world must be democratic. It must be capitalistic. It must be tied into the subversive messages of the World Wide Web. No wonder many feel threatened by what we represent."

The classic American self-portrait is Grant Wood's *American Gothic*, the 15 straitlaced couple, pitchfork in hand, expressions controlled, stoically standing watch outside the barn. But to the rest of the world, American Gothic is actually two twentysomething American software engineers who come into your country wearing long hair, beads, and sandals, with rings in their noses and paint on their toes. They kick down your front door, overturn everything in the house, stick a Big Mac in your mouth, fill your kids' heads with ideas you've never had or can't understand, slam a cable box onto your television, lock the channel to MTV, plug an Internet connection into your computer, and tell you: "Download or die."

That's us. We Americans are the apostles of the Fast World, the enemies of tradition, the prophets of the free market, and the high priests of high tech. We want "enlargement" of both our values and our Pizza Huts. We want the world to follow our lead and become democratic, capitalistic, with a Web site in every pot, a Pepsi on every lip, Microsoft Windows in every computer and most of all — most of all — with everyone, everywhere, pumping their own gas.

READING THE TEXT

1. Summarize in your own words Friedman's five gas stations theory of the world (para. 2). What cultural values are implicit in each variety of station?

2. What did historian Ronald Steel mean when he argued that "It was never the Soviet Union but the United States itself that is the true revolutionary power" (para. 14)?

3. What, to the rest of the world, is the image of *American Gothic* (para. 15), according to Friedman?

4. Characterize Friedman's tone in outlining the five types of gas station. How does his tone affect your response to his piece?

READING THE SIGNS

1. To much of the rest of the world, the United States is responsible for globalization. Conduct an in-class debate arguing whether this assessment is accurate. To develop and support your team's position, you might interview some international students about the attitudes toward the United States that prevail in their country.

2. In America, there is a great deal of resentment, especially from labor unions, of international trade agreements like the North American Free Trade Agreement (NAFTA) that America has signed in the name of globalization. In light of this resentment, write an essay arguing for or against the proposition that globalization is beneficial for America. To enhance your argument, research the economic effects of such treaties as NAFTA on the American economy, and the discussions about NAFTA that were raised in the 2008 presidential primaries and election.

3. Evaluate the validity of Friedman's assertion that "we Americans are the apostles of the Fast World, the enemies of tradition, the prophets of the free market, and the high priests of high tech" (para. 16).

4. Write an argumentative essay that analyzes the validity of Friedman's five gas stations theory of the world. To what extent could Friedman be accused of stereotyping cultural patterns? To what extent could his discussion be considered serious or tongue-in-cheek?

THOMAS FRANK
Commodify Your Dissent

"Sometimes You Gotta Break the Rules." "This is different. Different is good." "The Line Has Been Crossed." "Resist the Usual." If you are guessing that these defiant declarations must come from the Che Guevara/Jack Kerouac Institute of World Revolution and Extreme Hipness, you're in for a surprise, because they are actually advertising slogans for such corporations as Burger King, Arby's, Toyota, Clash Clear Malt, and Young & Rubicam. Just why huge corporations are aping the language of the Beats and the 1960s counterculture is the centerpiece of Thomas Frank's thesis that the countercultural idea has become "the official aesthetic of consumer society." Commodifying the decades-long youth habit of dissenting against corporate America, corporate America has struck back by adopting the very attitudes that once meant revolution, Frank believes, thus turning to its own capitalist uses the postures of rebellion. Indeed, when Apple can persuade you to buy a computer because its guy is just plain cooler *than some IBM nerd, there may be no way out. Frank is the author of* Commodify Your Dissent: Salvos from the Baffler *(with Matt Weiland, 1997), from which this selection is taken;* The Conquest of Cool: Business Culture, Counterculture, and the Rise of Hip Consumerism *(1998);* One Market Under God: Extreme Capitalism, Market Populism, and the End of Economic Democracy *(2001), and* What's the Matter with Kansas?: How Conservatives Won the Heart of America *(2005).*

The public be damned! I work for my stockholders.
　　　　　　　　　　　　— WILLIAM H. VANDERBILT, 1879

Break the rules. Stand apart. Keep your head. Go with your heart.
　　　　　　　　　　　　— TV commercial for Vanderbilt perfume, 1994

Capitalism is changing, obviously and drastically. From the moneyed pages of the *Wall Street Journal* to TV commercials for airlines and photocopiers we hear every day about the new order's globe-spanning, cyber-accumulating ways. But our notion about what's wrong with American life and how the figures responsible are to be confronted haven't changed much in thirty years. Call it, for convenience, the "countercultural idea." It holds that the paramount ailment of our society is conformity, a malady that has variously been described as overorganization, bureaucracy, homogeneity, hierarchy, logocentrism, technocracy, the Combine, the Apollonian.[1] We all know what it is and what it does. It transforms humanity into "organization man," into "the man in the gray flannel suit." It is "Moloch[2] whose mind is pure machinery," the "incomprehensible prison" that consumes "brains and imagination." It is artifice, starched shirts, tailfins, carefully mowed lawns, and always, always, the consciousness of impending nuclear destruction. It is a stiff, militaristic order that seeks to suppress instinct, to forbid sex and pleasure, to deny basic human impulses and individuality, to enforce through a rigid uniformity a meaningless plastic consumerism.

As this half of the countercultural idea originated during the 1950s, it is appropriate that the evils of conformity are most conveniently summarized with images of 1950s suburban correctness. You know, that land of sedate music, sexual repression, deference to authority, Red Scares, and smiling white people standing politely in line to go to church. Constantly appearing as a symbol of arch-backwardness in advertising and movies, it is an image we find easy to evoke.

The ways in which this system are to be resisted are equally well understood and agreed-upon. The Establishment demands homogeneity; we revolt by embracing diverse, individual lifestyles. It demands self-denial and rigid adherence to convention; we revolt through immediate gratification, instinct uninhibited, and liberation of the libido and the appetites. Few have put it more bluntly than Jerry Rubin did in 1970: "Amerika says: Don't! The yippies say: Do It!" The countercultural idea is hostile to any law and every establishment. "Whenever we see a rule, we must break it," Rubin continued. "Only by breaking rules do we discover who we are." Above all rebellion consists of a sort of Nietzschean antinomianism,[3] an automatic questioning of rules, a rejection of whatever social prescriptions we've happened to inherit. Just Do It is the whole of the law.

The patron saints of the countercultural idea are, of course, the Beats, whose frenzied style and merry alienation still maintain a powerful grip on the American imagination. Even forty years after the publication of *On the Road*, the works of Kerouac, Ginsberg, and Burroughs remain the sine qua non of dissidence, the model for aspiring poets, rock stars, or indeed anyone who feels vaguely artistic or alienated. That frenzied sensibility of pure experience, life on the edge, immediate gratification, and total freedom from moral restraint, which the Beats first propounded back in those heady days when suddenly everyone could have their own TV and powerful V-8, has stuck with us through all the intervening years and become something of a permanent American style. Go to any poetry reading and you can see a string of junior

[1]**Apollonian**   An allusion to the god Apollo, a term for rational consciousness. –EDS.

[2]**Moloch**   An ancient idol to whom children were sacrificed, used by Allen Ginsberg as a symbol for industrial America in his poem "Howl." –EDS.

[3]**Nietzschean antinomianism**   An allusion to the German philosopher Friedrich Nietzsche's challenging of conventional Christian morality. –EDS.

Kerouacs go through the routine, upsetting cultural hierarchies by pushing themselves to the limit, straining for that gorgeous moment of original vice when Allen Ginsberg first read "Howl" in 1955 and the patriarchs of our fantasies recoiled in shock. The Gap may have since claimed Ginsberg and *USA Today* may run feature stories about the brilliance of the beloved Kerouac, but the rebel race continues today regardless, with ever-heightening shit-references calculated to scare Jesse Helms, talk about sex and smack that is supposed to bring the electricity of real life, and ever-more determined defiance of the repressive rules and mores of the American 1950s — rules and mores that by now we know only from movies.

But one hardly has to go to a poetry reading to see the countercultural 5 idea acted out. Its frenzied ecstasies have long since become an official aesthetic of consumer society, a monotheme of mass as well as adversarial culture. Turn on the TV and there it is instantly: the unending drama of consumer unbound and in search of an ever-heightened good time, the inescapable rock 'n' roll soundtrack, dreadlocks and ponytails bounding into Taco Bells, a drunken, swinging-camera epiphany of tennis shoes, outlaw soda pops, and mind-bending dandruff shampoos. Corporate America, it turns out, no longer speaks in the voice of oppressive order that it did when Ginsberg moaned in 1956 that *Time* magazine was

> always telling me about responsibility. Business-
> men are serious. Movie producers are serious.
> Everybody's serious but me.

Nobody wants you to think they're serious today, least of all Time Warner. On the contrary: the Culture Trust is now our leader in the Ginsbergian search for kicks upon kicks. Corporate America is not an oppressor but a sponsor of fun, provider of lifestyle accoutrements, facilitator of carnival, our slang-speaking partner in the quest for that ever-more apocalyptic orgasm. The countercultural idea has become capitalist orthodoxy, its hunger for transgression upon transgression now perfectly suited to an economic-cultural regime that runs on ever-faster cyclings of the new; its taste for self-fulfillment and its intolerance for the confines of tradition now permitting vast latitude in consuming practices and lifestyle experimentation.

Consumerism is no longer about "conformity" but about "difference." Advertising teaches us not in the ways of puritanical self-denial (a bizarre notion on the face of it), but in orgiastic, never-ending self-fulfillment. It counsels not rigid adherence to the tastes of the herd but vigilant and constantly updated individualism. We consume not to fit in, but to prove, on the surface at least, that we are rock 'n' roll rebels, each one of us as rule-breaking and hierarchy-defying as our heroes of the 60s, who now pitch cars, shoes, and beer. This imperative of endless difference is today the genius at the heart of American capitalism, an eternal fleeing from "sameness" that satiates our thirst for the New with such achievements of civilization as the infinite brands of identical cola, the myriad colors and irrepressible variety of the cigarette rack at 7-Eleven.

As existential rebellion has become a more or less official style of Information Age capitalism, so has the countercultural notion of a static, repressive Establishment grown hopelessly obsolete. However the basic impulses of the countercultural idea may have disturbed a nation lost in Cold War darkness, they are today in fundamental agreement with the basic tenets of Information Age business theory. . . .

Contemporary corporate fantasy imagines a world of ceaseless, turbulent change, of centers that ecstatically fail to hold, of joyous extinction for the craven gray-flannel creature of the past. Businessmen today decorate the walls of their offices not with portraits of President Eisenhower and emblems of suburban order, but with images of extreme athletic daring, with sayings about "diversity" and "empowerment" and "thinking outside the box." They theorize their world not in the bar car of the commuter train, but in weepy corporate retreats at which they beat their tom-toms and envision themselves as part of the great avant-garde tradition of edge-livers, risk-takers, and ass-kickers. Their world is a place not of sublimation and conformity, but of "leadership" and bold talk about defying the herd. And there is nothing this new enlightened species of businessman despises more than "rules" and "reason." The prominent culture-warriors of the right may believe that the counterculture was capitalism's undoing, but the antinomian businessmen know better. "One of the t-shirt slogans of the sixties read, 'Question authority,'" the authors of *Reengineering the Corporation* write. "Process owners might buy their re-engineering team members the nineties version: 'Question assumptions.'"

The new businessman quite naturally gravitates to the slogans and sensibility of the rebel sixties to express his understanding of the new Information World. He is led in what one magazine calls "the business revolution" by the office-park subversives it hails as "business activists," "change agents," and "corporate radicals." . . . In television commercials, through which the new American businessman presents his visions and self-understanding to the public, perpetual revolution and the gospel of rule-breaking are the orthodoxy of the day. You only need to watch for a few minutes before you see one of these slogans and understand the grip of antinomianism over the corporate mind:

> Sometimes You Gotta Break the Rules — Burger King
> If You Don't Like the Rules, Change Them — WXRT-FM
> The Rules Have Changed — Dodge
> The Art of Changing — Swatch
> There's no one way to do it. — Levi's
> This is different. Different is good. — Arby's
> Just Different From the Rest — Special Export beer
> The Line Has Been Crossed: The Revolutionary New Supra — Toyota
> Resist the Usual — the slogan of both Clash Clear Malt and Young & Rubicam
> Innovate Don't Imitate — Hugo Boss
> Chart Your Own Course — Navigator Cologne
> It separates you from the crowd — Vision Cologne

In most, the commercial message is driven home with the vanguard iconography of the rebel: screaming guitars, whirling cameras, and startled old timers who, we predict, will become an increasingly indispensable prop as consumers require ever-greater assurances that, Yes! You are a rebel! Just look at how offended they are! . . .

The structure and thinking of American business have changed enormously in the years since our popular conceptions of its problems and abuses were formulated. In the meantime the mad frothings and jolly apolitical revolt of Beat, despite their vast popularity and insurgent air, have become powerless against a new regime that, one suspects, few of Beat's present-day admirers and practitioners feel any need to study or understand. Today that beautiful countercultural idea, endorsed now by everyone from the surviving Beats to shampoo manufacturers, is more the official doctrine of corporate America than it is a program of resistance. What we understand as "dissent" does not subvert, does not challenge, does not even question the cultural faiths of Western business. What David Rieff wrote of the revolutionary pretensions of multiculturalism is equally true of the countercultural idea: "The more one reads in academic multiculturalist journals and in business publications, and the more one contrasts the speeches of CEOs and the speeches of noted multiculturalist academics, the more one is struck by the similarities in the way they view the world." What's happened is not co-optation or appropriation, but a simple and direct confluence of interest.

READING THE TEXT

1. In your own words, define what Frank means by "countercultural idea" (para. 1).
2. How does Frank explain the relationship between the countercultural idea and conformity?
3. How are the Beats early progenitors of today's countercultural ideas, according to Frank?
4. In what ways does Frank believe that modern business has co-opted the countercultural idea?
5. How do you characterize Frank's tone in this selection, and does it enhance or detract from the forcefulness of his argument?

READING THE SIGNS

1. Analyze some current advertising, either in a magazine or on television, asking whether the advertisements employ the countercultural idea as a marketing ploy. Use your observations as the basis for an essay in which you assess whether that idea and the associated "iconography of the rebel" still prevail in advertising as Frank suggests.

2. In class, brainstorm a list of today's cultural rebels, either marketing characters or real people such as actors or musicians, and discuss why these rebels are considered attractive to their intended audience. Use the class discussion as a springboard for your own essay in which you analyze how the status of cultural rebels is a sign of the mood of modern American culture.

3. **CONNECTING TEXTS**   Write an essay in which you agree, disagree, or modify Frank's contention that marketing no longer promotes conformity but, rather, "never-ending self-fulfillment . . . constantly updated individualism" (para. 6). To develop your ideas, consult the Introduction to Chapter 6, "American Paradox."

4. Visit a youth-oriented store such as Urban Outfitters and analyze its advertising, product displays, and both exterior design and interior decor. Write an essay in which you gauge the extent to which the store uses the iconography of the rebel as a marketing strategy.

5. Study a current magazine focused on business or on modern technology, such as *Business Week*, *Business 2.0*, or *Wired*. To what extent does the magazine exemplify Frank's claim that modern business eschews conformity and embraces rebellion and rule-breaking? Alternately, you might analyze some corporate Web sites, preferably several from companies in the same industry. Keep in mind that different industries may have very different corporate cultures; the values and ideals that dominate high tech, for instance, may differ dramatically from those in finance, entertainment, or social services.

"Mind if I smoke?"
"Care if I die?"
Van Wagner
EVIDEO
EUROWORLD
VIDEO

BROUGHT TO YOU B(U)Y
The Signs of Advertising

Advertising on the Edge

An attractive young woman runs frantically down a suburban street pursued by a ferocious pit bull. She leaps upward into the branches of a tree, but the dog leaps right after her and sinks his teeth into the pant leg of her jeans. With a wrench of his jaws, he peels the jeans right off her, then, abruptly, leaves her alone, running down the street with the jeans in his teeth. The woman follows him into a house where, clad only in bikini briefs, she sees the dog carry the jeans to a young man who puts them on and gives the girl a scolding glance as she shamefacedly watches him.

Sounds rather like the narrative for some especially nasty porno flick, doesn't it? But it's not. As you may have recognized, this is a summary of a television advertisement for Levi's jeans.

You might have seen the following ad as well: Two men stand in front of a rustic cabin with their dogs. One of the men is pale, slender, and expensively dressed in a fishing outfit that could have come from L.L. Bean. His dog is a purebred, highly trained terrier. The other man is husky, rugged looking, dressed in jeans and a plaid shirt. His dog is an unusually scruffy-looking mutt. The first man, in a supercilious voice, tells the second that his dog has been trained to fetch beer for him. With exaggerated self-confidence, he tells his dog to fetch, and the dog obediently runs to a cooler, pulls out a bottle of beer, and neatly brings it to his master. The second man looks on gruffly for a moment, then tells his dog to fetch. The dog rushes right at the other man and leaps straight for his crotch. The man screams and, backing away, flings his beer to the scruffy dog's master, who catches it with a rough gesture of victory.

This second ad, for Budweiser beer, was chosen by a viewers' poll as the best ad of Super Bowl XXXVII. And like the Levi's ad, it bears a cultural message.

To analyze these ads we need, as with all cultural signs, to establish the system that they belong to. Since both ads were made for television and feature dogs, we could begin with TV advertisements that feature animals, especially dogs. Of course there are a slew of such ads, especially for pet foods (remember Morris the 9-Lives cat, or that pooch that chases the chuckwagon across a kitchen floor?), but animals have been used to advertise a great many products, usually with the intention of lending a cute and cuddly image to the product (like the Charmin teddy bear). Budweiser used animal mascots in the 1980s with its Spuds Mackenzie campaign, which featured an anthropomorphic English pit bull who surfed, partied, and hung out with his own crew of bikini-clad Spudettes as he laid claim to the title of world's supreme "party animal." Shortly before the Spuds campaign appeared, the Stroh Brewing Company used a dog named Alex in its advertisements who, while behaving like an ordinary dog in most ways, seemed to have a taste for Stroh's himself.

Both Spuds and Alex were funny figures (as were the ants, frogs, lizards, and ferrets that succeeded Spuds in later Budweiser campaigns) and, like many such advertising animals, were designed to confer upon the products they fronted an aura of humorous fun through the sheer incongruity of their behavior. The Levi's and Budweiser ads we are analyzing here were also intended to be funny, and so they can be associated with the system of humorous animal-themed advertisements. But the source of their humor is quite different, and it is in that difference that we can find the significance of the ads.

In both ads the behavior of the animals is not incongruous nor, in itself, funny. The Levi's pit bull engages in the kind of aggressive behavior that, all too often, compels animal control authorities to put dogs down; the Budweiser mutt makes the kind of sudden attack out of which personal injury lawsuits

---

Discussing the Signs of Advertising

Bring to class a print ad from a newspaper, a magazine, or a commercial Web site and in small groups discuss your semiotic reading of it. Be sure to ask, "Why am I being shown this or being told that?" How do the characters in the ad function as signs? What sort of people don't appear as characters? What cultural myths are invoked in this ad? What relationship do you see between those myths and the intended audience of the publication? Which ads do your group members respond to positively and why? Which ads doesn't your group like?

are made. What makes their attacks funny (or at least potentially funny) is whom they attack. In one ad, it is an attractive young woman; in the other, a caricature of a yuppie. And the creators of the ads assume that their target audience will take pleasure in seeing such victims attacked and discomfited.

You've probably already guessed who that audience might be, but let's work through it semiotically. In determining the audience for a particular advertisement, it can be very useful to pick out the character or characters within the ad with whom its viewers are expected to identify. Since no one wishes to be chased into a tree by a dog and have one's clothing torn off, and because no one wants to be bitten in the crotch, we can assume that viewers are meant to identify with neither the young woman in the Levi's ad nor the yuppie in the Budweiser ad. But the matter goes deeper than that. In the case of the Budweiser ad, the yuppie is carefully coded to appeal to a populist class resentment of supercilious wealth. It is no accident that the hero of the ad is coded to appear as a kind of rural workingman's hero, an ordinary Joe, with his ordinary dog, who is revenged upon the upper-class snob who crosses him. The ad works very much like a carefully staged professional wrestling match in which a populist warrior beats up a wrestler who is coded to symbolize elite wealth or privilege. Playing to a traditional American mythology that celebrates the common man, the Budweiser ad, with its testosterone-driven vision of appropriate class vengeance, thus can be seen as appealing to male viewers who can identify not only with the ad's ordinary Joe but with his resentment of wealth and privilege as well.

The Levi's ad also appeals to men, but not in the same way. For one, class resentment does not factor into this ad. But another kind of resentment surfaces — and it isn't of people who borrow your jeans without permission. That the ad is intended to appeal to male viewers is evident in the entire point of view embodied in the ad, beginning with what film critics call the camera's "male gaze." The camera watches the woman flee, and then records her being stripped, carefully revealing her sexy underwear. When she limps back to the house where the dog's owner is putting on his restored jeans, his gaze, along with the camera's, rests upon her, in her humiliation, and her underwear. It is hardly likely that any woman would identify with the woman in this ad. But males (especially young males, given the relative youth of both characters) are expected to identify with the man in the ad, who, instead of being featured heroically rescuing the damsel in distress (as might have happened in a 1950s ad), smugly gives the woman a look that says, more or less, "don't do that again." One wonders if another version of the ad will feature music from the Rolling Stones's hit "Under My Thumb."

The Levi's ad signifies a profound misogyny that can be found throughout contemporary American popular culture, from women-despising pop and hip-hop lyrics (see Andre Mayer's "The New Sexual Stone Age" in Chapter 3) to fashion magazine spreads that feature women who look like they're about to be raped (or have already been raped). Such signifiers point to a profound resentment of, even hostility toward, young women on the part of young men, a resentment whose origins are not easy to identify. Whether caused by the advances women have made through the women's movement, by a growing feeling of helplessness in a corporate capitalist society (that causes men to lash out at women as scapegoats for the powerlessness they feel in a world that has made them expendable), or by whatever social causes that one might discover, the brutal humor presented in the Levi's ad is a sign of a new kind of gender gap in which women, once placed on a kind of pedestal in sexual relations, have been cast into the dirt.

The fact that both ads feature violence is a sign of a further social disaffection that is by no means confined to the United States. Does someone bother you? Sic your dog on him (it's no accident that attack dog breeds like Rottweilers and pit bulls have become massively popular). Your girlfriend borrows your jeans again? Send Bowser after her. Someone cut you off on the freeway? Don't just give him the finger, shoot the sucker. In short, if you've got a problem, let violence solve it. There's a lot of rage loose in the land and the world. And if this doesn't sound very serious to you, consider that it is just this kind of thinking that led to the destruction of the World Trade Center on September 11, 2001.

The Dove Dilemma

The remarkable success of the Dove Campaign for Real Beauty is a sign that it is not only young men who are angry these days, however. Orchestrating a consumer backlash against unrealistic and artificially constructed beauty standards, the Dove corporation has tapped into a widespread resentment among girls and women against the anorectic and air-brushed images conventionally employed by the cosmetics industry to sell its wares. Appreciated even by such feminist commentators as Jennifer L. Pozner (see her essay, "Dove's 'Real Beauty' Backlash," in this chapter), the Dove campaign—from its "Evolution" ad revealing the making of a billboard goddess, to its photographic displays of naked middle-aged and older women—appears to be a genuine interruption of business as usual in the advertising industry, an appeal to the reality principle rather than to fantasy and desire.

Indeed, even a cursory survey of any women's fashion magazine will reveal the uniqueness of Dove's approach and the reasons for the gratitude with which many of its target consumers have greeted it. But in the world of advertising and the consumerist system that it serves, unqualified revolutions are hard, if not impossible, to come by, and when analyzed within the perspective of traditional gender codes (see the Introduction to Chapter 7 for a discussion of this topic), the Dove Campaign for Real Beauty isn't really so very revolutionary after all. In fact, it is quite conventional.

According to the gender code that governs male and female behavior in our society, it is a woman's role to be beautiful, to be attractive to the gaze of men. Men, in contrast, are expected to be powerful—either in body or mind—

and while good looks certainly don't hurt, they aren't central to a man's self-conception within the code. For women, on the other hand, intelligence, if it is acknowledged, is secondary, with beauty being primary. (Consider in this regard the prominent attention paid to the belief that Professor Lisa Randall of Harvard University, a well-known expert in string-theory physics, resembles the attractive actress Jodie Foster. The physical appearance of male physicists is virtually never discussed.) And what the Dove campaign does is reinforce this primacy by telling girls and women not that beauty doesn't matter *but that they are already beautiful.*

In other words, the Dove campaign isn't challenging the gender codes at all; it is actually reinforcing them. The women's movement, especially in the 1970s, once sought to overthrow the gender codes that bound women into a stringent "beauty mythology," arguing for the freedom for a woman to develop herself intellectually without obsessive regard for her appearance. The Dove Campaign for Real Beauty, paradoxically, threatens to undermine this goal by making an apparently feminist argument against unrealistic beauty standards while actually continuing to tell women that their bodies come first. This is understandable because Dove's purpose is to sell cosmetics products, not physics textbooks, but that is why it is highly unlikely that you will find any genuine challenge to the status quo in an advertising campaign for mass-marketed goods.

And Here's the Pitch

The preceding analyses were brought to you by the advertising industry and were intended to illustrate how advertisements too are signs of cultural desire and consciousness. Indeed, advertising is not just show and tell. In effect, it's a form of behavior modification, a psychological strategy designed not only to inform you about products but also to persuade you to buy them by making associations between the product and certain pleasurable experiences or emotions that may have nothing to do with the product at all — like sex, or a promise of social superiority, or a simple laugh. Indeed, in no other area of popular culture can we find a purer example of the deliberate movement from objective *denotation* (the pictorial image of a product that appears in an advertisement) to subjective *connotation* (the feeling that the advertiser wishes to associate with the product), thereby transforming *things* into *signs*.

No one knows for sure just how effective a given ad campaign might be in inducing consumer spending by turning objects into signs, but no one is taking any chances either, as you can see by the annual increase in advertising costs for the Super Bowl: At last count it was some $2.7 million for a thirty-second spot. And it is the promise of ever-increasing advertising revenues that has turned Google into the Web 2.0 darling of Wall Street. As James B. Twitchell has written, America is indeed an "ad culture," a society saturated with advertising.

Exploring the Signs of Advertising

Select one of the products advertised in the "Portfolio of Advertise-ments" (in this chapter), and design in your journal an alternative ad for that product. Consider what different images or cast of characters you could include. What different myths — and thus different values — could you use to pitch this product? Then freewrite on the significance of your alternative ad. If you have any difficulty imagining an alterna-tive image for the product, what does that say about the power of advertising to control our view of the world? What does your choice of imagery and cultural myths say about you?

With all the advertising out there, it is getting harder and harder for ad-vertisers to get our attention, or keep it, so they are constantly experimenting with new ways of getting us to listen. In recent years, for example, advertisers who are out to snag the youth market have taken to staging their television ads as if they were MTV videos — complete with rapid jump-cut filming tech-niques, rap or rock background music, and dizzying montage effects — in order to grab the attention of their target audience and to cause their viewers to associate the product with the pleasures of MTV. Self-conscious irony has also been a popular advertising technique as advertisers strive to overcome the ad-savvy sophistication of generations of consumers who have become skeptical of the claims and techniques of advertising.

More recently, a marketing strategy known as "stealth advertising" has appeared in selected locations. For example, companies pay people to do things like sit in Starbucks and play computer games; when someone takes an inter-est, they talk about how cool it is and ask passersby on the street to take their photo with a really cool new camera — and by the way, they say, isn't this a really cool new camera?! The trick here is to advertise without having people actually know they're being marketed to — just what the ad doctor ordered for advertising-sick consumers.

As the years pass and the national mood shifts with the tides of history, new advertising techniques will emerge. So look around and ask yourself, as you're bombarded with advertising, "Why am I being shown *that*, or being told this?" Or cast yourself as the director of an ad, asking yourself what you would do to pitch a product; then look at what the advertiser has done. Pay attention to the way an ad's imagery is organized, its precise denotation. Every detail counts. Why are these colors used, or why is the ad in black and white? Why are cute stuffed animals chosen to pitch toilet paper? What are those people doing in that perfume commercial? Why the cowboy hat in an ad for jeans? Look too for what the ad doesn't include: Is it missing a clear view of the product itself or an ethnically diverse cast of characters? In short, when interpreting an ad, transform it into a text, going beyond what it denotes to what it connotes — to what it is trying to insinuate or say.

The Semiotic Foundation

There is perhaps no better field for semiotic analysis than advertising, for ads work characteristically by substituting signs for things, and by reading those signs you can discover the values and desires that advertisers seek to exploit. It has long been recognized that advertisements substitute images of desire for the actual products, selling images of fun, or popularity, or sheer celebrity, promising a gratifying association with the likes of Jessica Simpson if you get your next pizza from Pizza Hut. Automobile commercials, for their part, are notorious for selling not transportation but fantasies of power, prestige, and sexual potency.

By substituting desirable images for concrete needs, modern advertising seeks to transform desire into necessity. You need food, for example, but it takes an ad campaign to convince you through attractive images that you need a Big Mac. Your job may require you to have a car, but it's an ad that persuades you that a Land Rover is necessary for your happiness. If advertising

Today's Special: The Home Shopping Network.

worked otherwise, it would simply present you with a functional profile of a product and let you decide whether it will do the job.

From the early twentieth century, advertisers have seen their task as the transformation of desire into necessity. In the twenties and thirties, for example, voluminously printed advertisements created elaborate story lines designed to convince readers that they needed this mouthwash to attract a spouse or that caffeine-free breakfast drink to avoid trouble on the job. In such ads, products were made to appear not only desirable but absolutely necessary. Without them, your very survival as a socially competent being would be in question.

Many ads still work this way, particularly "guilt" ads that prey on your insecurities and fears. Deodorants and mouthwashes are typically pitched in such a fashion, playing on our fear of smelling bad in public. Can you think of any other products whose ads play on guilt or shame? Do you find them to be effective?

The Commodification of Desire

Associating a logically unrelated desire with an actual product (as in pitching beer through sexual come-ons) can be called the "commodification" of desire. In other words, desire itself becomes the product that the advertiser is selling. This marketing of desire was recognized as early as the 1950s in Vance Packard's *The Hidden Persuaders*. In that book, Packard points out how by the 1950s America was well along in its historic shift from a producing to a consuming economy. The implications for advertisers were enormous. Since the American economy was increasingly dependent on the constant growth of consumption, as discussed in the Introduction to Chapter 1 of this text, manufacturers had to find ways to convince people to consume ever more goods. So they turned to the advertising mavens on Madison Avenue, who responded with advertisements that persuaded consumers to replace perfectly serviceable products with "new and improved" substitutions within an overall economy of planned design obsolescence.

America's transformation from a producer to a consumer economy also explains that while advertising is a worldwide phenomenon, it is nowhere so prevalent as it is here. Open a copy of the popular French picture magazine *Paris Match*. You'll find plenty of paparazzi photos of international celebrities but almost no advertisements. Then open a copy of *Vogue*. It is essentially a catalogue, where scarcely a page is without an ad. Indeed, advertisers themselves call this plethora of advertising "clutter" that they must creatively "cut through" each time they design a new ad campaign. The ubiquity of advertising in our lives points to a society in which people are constantly pushed to buy, as opposed to economies like Japan's that emphasize constant increases in production. And desire is what loosens the pocketbook strings.

While the basic logic of advertising may be similar from era to era, the content of an ad, and hence its significance, differs as popular culture changes.

Reading Advertising on the Net

Many viewers watch the Super Bowl as much for the commercials as for the football game; indeed, the Super Bowl ads now have their own pregame public-relations hype and, in many a media outlet, their own postgame analysis and ratings. Visit *Advertising Age*'s report on the most recent Super Bowl (http://www.adage.com/), and study the ads and their commentary about them. What images and styles predominate, and what do the dominant patterns say about popular taste? What does the public's avid interest in Super Bowl ads say about the power of advertising and its role in American culture?

Looking at ads from different eras tells the tale. Advertising in the 1920s, for instance, focused especially on its market's desires for improved social status. Ads for elocution and vocabulary lessons appealed to working- and lower-middle-class consumers who were invited to fantasize that buying the product or service could help them enter the middle class. Meanwhile, middle-class consumers were invited to compare their enjoyment of the sponsor's product with that of the upper-class models shown happily slurping this coffee or purchasing that vacuum cleaner in the ad. Of course, things haven't changed that much since the twenties. Can you think of any ads that use this strategy today? How often are glamorous celebrities called in to make you identify with their "enjoyment" of a product? Have you heard ads for vocabulary-building programs that promise you a "verbal advantage" in the corporate struggle?

One particularly amusing ad from the twenties played on America's fear of communism in the wake of the Bolshevik Revolution in Russia. "Is your washroom breeding Bolsheviks?" asks a print ad from the Scott Paper Company. The ad's lengthy copy explains how it might be doing so: If your company restroom is stocked with inferior paper towels, it says, discontent will proliferate among your employees and lead to subversive activities. RCA Victor and Campbell's Soup, we are assured, are no such breeding grounds of subversion, thanks to their contracts with Scott. You, too, can fight the good fight against communism by buying Scott towels, the ad suggests. To whom do you think this ad was directed? What did they fear?

Populism vs. Elitism

American advertising tends to swing in a pendulum motion between the status-conscious ads that dominated the twenties and the more populist approach of decades like the seventies, when *The Waltons* was a top TV series and country music and truck-driving cowboys lent their popular appeal to Madison Avenue. This swing between elitist and populist approaches in advertising reflects a basic division within the American dream itself, a mythic promise that at once celebrates democratic equality and encourages you to rise above the crowd, to be better than anyone else. Sometimes Americans are more attracted to one side than to the other, but there is bound to be a shift back to the other side when the thrill wears off. Thus, the populist appeal of the seventies (even disco had a distinct working-class flavor: recall John Travolta's character in *Saturday Night Fever*) gave way to the elitist eighties, and advertising followed. Products such as Gallo's varietal wines, once considered barely a step up from jug wine, courted an upscale market through ads that featured classy yuppies serving it along with their salmon and asparagus, while Michelob light beer promised its fans that they "could have it all." Status advertising was all the rage in that glitzy, go-for-the-gold decade.

The nineties brought in a different kind of advertising that was neither populist nor elitist but was characterized by a cutting, edgy sort of humor. This humor was especially common in dot.com ads that typically addressed the sort of young, irreverent, and rather cocky souls who were the backbone of what was then called the "New Economy" and now "Web 1.0." More broadly, edgy advertising appealed to twentysomething consumers who were particularly coveted by the marketers who made possible such youth-oriented television networks as Fox and the WB. Raised in the *Saturday Night Live* era, such consumers were accustomed to cutting humor and particularly receptive to anything that smacked of attitude, and in the race to get their attention, advertisers followed with attitude-laden advertising.

The Levi's and Budweiser ads discussed earlier indicate that this sort of advertising and attitude is still very much alive in the first decade of the twenty-first century. Although there is, as we've seen, a touch of populism in the Budweiser commercial, the emphases are on attitude and schadenfreude; that is, taking pleasure in the suffering or misfortune of others (see a fuller analysis of this current trend in popular culture in the Introduction to Chapter 3). Look at the ads around you (they're impossible to miss): What moods and desires can you detect? Are Americans drawing together, or are we splintering into niche market groups and atomizing into single units of competitive consumption? The ads will tell.

The Readings

Our selections in this chapter include interpretations and analyses of the world of advertising, as well as advertisements for you to interpret yourselves. The chapter begins with a historical perspective: Roland Marchand's "The Parable of the Democracy of Goods" shows how advertisers in the 1920s played on the unconscious desires of their market by exploiting the fundamental myths of middle-class American culture. James B. Twitchell and Sandra Blakeslee follow with a paired set of readings on the "science" of advertising, revealing the elaborate social profiling schemes and neurological research through which marketers seek to categorize and control our consuming behavior. Next, Steve Craig offers four practical analyses of the ways in which television advertisers code their advertisements to appeal to men or women consumers, while Jennifer L. Pozner lambastes the male critics of the Dove Campaign for Real Beauty. Warren St. John reports on the ways in which marketers are cashing in on the metrosexual phenomenon, and Eric Schlosser looks at the world of children's advertising in which kids are manipulated to manipulate their parents. Gloria Steinem's insider's view of what goes on behind the scenes at women's magazines concludes the readings with an exposé of the often cozy relationship between magazine content and advertisers' desires. This chapter also includes a "Portfolio of Advertisements" for you to decode for yourself.

ROLAND MARCHAND
The Parable of the Democracy of Goods

Advertisements do not simply reflect American myths; they create them, as Roland Marchand shows in this selection from Advertising the American Dream *(1985). Focusing on elaborate advertising narratives, he describes "The Parable of the Democracy of Goods," which pitches a product by convincing middle-class consumers that, by buying this toilet seat or that brand of coffee, they can share an experience with the very richest Americans. The advertising strategies Marchand analyzes date from the 1920s to 1940s, and new "parables" have since appeared that reflect more modern times, but even the oldest are still in use today. A former professor of history at the University of California, Davis, Marchand also published* The American Peace Movement and Social Reform, 1898–1918 *(1973) and* Creating the Corporate Soul: The Rise of Public Relations and Corporate Imagery in American Big Business *(1998).*

As they opened their September 1929 issue, readers of the *Ladies' Home Journal* were treated to an account of the care and feeding of young Livingston Ludlow Biddle III, scion of the wealthy Biddles of Philadelphia, whose family coat-of-arms graced the upper right-hand corner of the page. Young Master Biddle, mounted on his tricycle, fixed a serious, slightly pouting gaze upon the reader, while the Cream of Wheat Corporation rapturously explained his constant care, his carefully regulated play and exercise, and the diet prescribed for him by "famous specialists." As master of Sunny Ridge Farm, the Biddles's winter estate in North Carolina, young Livingston III had "enjoyed every luxury of social position and wealth, since the day he was born." Yet, by the grace of a modern providence, it happened that Livingston's health was protected by a "simple plan every mother can use." Mrs. Biddle gave Cream of Wheat to the young heir for both breakfast and supper. The world's foremost child experts knew of no better diet; great wealth could procure no finer nourishment. As Cream of Wheat's advertising agency summarized the central point of the campaign that young Master Biddle initiated, "every mother can give her youngsters the fun and benefits of a Cream of Wheat breakfast just as do the parents of these boys and girls who have the best that wealth can command."[1]

While enjoying this glimpse of childrearing among the socially distinguished, *Ladies' Home Journal* readers found themselves schooled in one of the most pervasive of all advertising tableaux of the 1920s — the parable of

---

[1] *Ladies' Home Journal*, Sept. 1929, second cover; *JWT News Letter*, Oct. 1, 1929, p. 1, J. Walter Thompson Company (JWT) Archives, New York City.

the Democracy of Goods. According to this parable, the wonders of modern mass production and distribution enabled every person to enjoy the society's most significant pleasure, convenience, or benefit. The definition of the particular benefit fluctuated, of course, with each client who employed the parable. But the cumulative effect of the constant reminders that "any woman can" and "every home can afford" was to publicize an image of American society in which concentrated wealth at the top of a hierarchy of social classes restricted no family's opportunity to acquire the most significant products.[2] By implicitly defining "democracy" in terms of equal access to consumer products, and then by depicting the everyday functioning of that "democracy" with regard to one product at a time, these tableaux offered Americans an inviting vision of their society as one of incontestable equality.

In its most common advertising formula, the concept of the Democracy of Goods asserted that although the rich enjoyed a great variety of luxuries, the acquisition of their *one* most significant luxury would provide anyone with the ultimate in satisfaction. For instance, a Chase and Sanborn's Coffee tableau, with an elegant butler serving a family in a dining room with a sixteen-foot ceiling, reminded Chicago families that although "compared with the riches of the more fortunate, your way of life may seem modest indeed," yet no one— "king, prince, statesman, or capitalist"—could enjoy better coffee.[3] The Association of Soap and Glycerine Producers proclaimed that the charm of cleanliness was as readily available to the poor as to the rich, and Ivory Soap reassuringly related how one young housewife, who couldn't afford a $780-a-year maid like her neighbor, still maintained a significant equality in "nice hands" by using Ivory.[4] The C. F. Church Manufacturing Company epitomized this version of the parable of the Democracy of Goods in an ad entitled "a bathroom luxury everyone can afford": "If you lived in one of those palatial apartments on Park Avenue, in New York City, where you have to pay $2,000 to $7,500 a year rent, you still couldn't have a better toilet seat in your bathroom than they have—the Church Sani-white Toilet Seat which you can afford to have right now."[5]

Thus, according to the parable, no discrepancies in wealth could prevent the humblest citizens, provided they chose their purchases wisely, from retiring to a setting in which they could contemplate their essential equality, through possession of an identical product, with the nation's millionaires. In 1929, Howard Dickinson, a contributor to *Printers' Ink*, concisely expressed the social psychology behind Democracy of Goods advertisements: " 'With whom do the mass of people think they want to foregather?' asks the psychologist in advertising. 'Why, with the wealthy and socially distinguished, of

[2]*Saturday Evening Post*, Apr. 3, 1926, pp. 182–83; Nov. 6, 1926, p. 104; Apr. 16, 1927, p. 199; Scrapbook 54 (Brunswick-Balke-Collender), Lord and Thomas Archives, at Foote, Cone and Belding Communications, Inc., Chicago.

[3]*Chicago Tribune*, Nov. 21, 1926, picture section, p. 2.

[4]*Los Angeles Times*, July 14, 1929, part VI, p. 3; *Tide*, July 1928, p. 10; *Photoplay Magazine*, Mar. 1930, p. 1.

[5]*American Magazine*, Mar. 1926, p. 112.

course!' If we can't get an invitation to tea for our millions of customers, we can at least present the fellowship of using the same brand of merchandise. And it works."[6]

Some advertisers found it more efficacious to employ the parable's nega- 5
tive counterpart—the Democracy of Afflictions. Listerine contributed significantly to this approach. Most of the unsuspecting victims of halitosis in the
mid-1920s possessed wealth and high social position. Other discoverers of new
social afflictions soon took up the battle cry of "nobody's immune." "Body
Odor plays no favorites," warned Lifebuoy Soap. No one, "banker, baker, or
society woman," could count himself safe from B.O.[7] The boss, as well as the
employees, might find himself "caught off guard" with dirty hands or cuffs,
the Soap and Glycerine Producers assured readers of *True Story*. By 1930,
Absorbine Jr. was beginning to document the democratic advance of "athlete's foot" into those rarefied social circles occupied by the "daintiest member of the junior set" and the noted yachtsman who owned "a railroad or
two" (Fig. 1).[8]

The central purpose of the Democracy of Afflictions tableaux was to
remind careless or unsuspecting readers of the universality of the threat
from which the product offered protection or relief. Only occasionally did
such ads address those of the upper classes who might think that their status
and "fastidious" attention to personal care made them immune from common social offenses. In 1929 Listerine provided newspaper readers an opportunity to listen while a doctor, whose clientele included those of "the
better class," confided "what I know about *nice* women."[9] One might have
thought that Listerine was warning complacent, upper-class women that
they were not immune from halitosis—except that the ad appeared in the
Los Angeles Times, not *Harper's Bazaar*. Similarly, Forhan's toothpaste and
the Soap Producers did not place their Democracy of Afflictions ads in *True
Story* in order to reach the social elite. Rather, these tableaux provided enticing glimpses into the lives of the wealthy while suggesting an equalizing "fellowship" in shared susceptibilities to debilitating ailments. The parable of the
Democracy of Goods always remained implicit in its negative counterpart. It
assured readers that they could be as healthy, as charming, as free from
social offense as the very "nicest" (richest) people, simply by using a product
that anyone could afford.

Another variation of the parable of the Democracy of Goods employed
historical comparisons to celebrate even the humblest of contemporary
Americans as "kings in cottages." "No monarch in all history ever saw the day
he could have half as much as you," proclaimed Paramount Pictures. Even

[6]*Printers' Ink*, Oct. 10, 1929, p. 138.

[7]*Tide*, Sept. 15, 1927, p. 5; *American Magazine*, Aug. 1929, p. 93; *True Story*, June 1929,
p. 133; *Chicago Tribune*, Jan. 11, 1928, p. 16; Jan. 18, 1928, p. 15; Jan. 28, 1928, p. 7; *Photoplay Magazine*, Feb. 1929, p. 111.

[8]*True Story*, May 1928, p. 83; June 1929, p. 133; *American Magazine*, Feb. 1930, p. 110;
Saturday Evening Post, Aug. 23, 1930, p. 124.

[9]*Los Angeles Times*, July 6, 1929, p. 3.

FIGURE 1   A negative appeal transformed the Democracy of Goods into the Democracy of Afflictions. Common folk learned from this parable that they could inexpensively avoid afflictions that beset even the yachting set.

reigning sovereigns of the present, Paramount continued, would envy readers for their "luxurious freedom and opportunity" to enter a magnificent, bedazzling "palace for a night," be greeted with fawning bows by liveried attendants, and enjoy modern entertainment for a modest price (Fig. 2). The Fisher Body Corporation coined the phrase "For Kings in Cottages" to compliment ordinary Americans on their freedom from "hardships" that even kings had been forced to endure in the past. Because of a lack of technology, monarchs who traveled in the past had "never enjoyed luxury which even approached that of the present-day automobile." The "American idea," epitomized by the Fisher Body Corporation, was destined to carry the comforts and luxuries conducive to human happiness into "the life of even the humblest cottager."[10]

[10]*Saturday Evening Post*, May 8, 1926, p. 59; *American Magazine*, May 1932, pp. 76–77. See also *Saturday Evening Post*, July 18, 1931, pp. 36–37; Aug. 1, 1931, pp. 30–31; *Better Homes and Gardens*, Mar. 1930, p. 77.

FIGURE 2   Of course, real kings had never shared their status
with crowds of other "kings." But the parable of the Democracy
of Goods offered a brief, "packaged experience" of luxury and
preference.

Even so, many copywriters perceived that equality with past monarchs
might not rival the vision of joining the fabled "Four Hundred" that Ward
McAllister had marked as America's social elite at the end of the nineteenth century. Americans, in an ostensibly conformist age, hungered for exclusivity. So
advertising tableaux celebrated their ascension into this fabled and exclusive
American elite. Through mass production and the resulting lower prices, the
tableaux explained, the readers could purchase goods formerly available only
to the rich — and thus gain admission to a "400" that now numbered millions.

The Simmons Company confessed that inner-coil mattresses had once
been a luxury possessed only by the very wealthy. But now (in 1930) they

were "priced so everybody in the United States can have one at $19.95." Woodbury's Soap advised the "working girl" readers of *True Story* of their arrival within a select circle. "Yesterday," it recalled, "the skin you love to touch" had been "the privilege of one woman in 65," but today it had become "the beauty right of every woman."[11] If the Democracy of Goods could establish an equal consumer right to beauty, then perhaps even the ancient religious promise of equality in death might be realized, at least to the extent that material provisions sufficed. In 1927 the Clark Grave Vault Company defined this unique promise: "Not so many years ago the use of a burial vault was confined largely to the rich. . . . Now every family, regardless of its means, may provide absolute protection against the elements of the ground."[12] If it seemed that the residents of Clark vaults had gained equality with the "400" too belatedly for maximum satisfaction, still their loving survivors could now share the same sense of comfort in the "absolute protection" of former loved ones as did the most privileged elites.

The social message of the parable of the Democracy of Goods was clear. 10 Antagonistic envy of the rich was unseemly; programs to redistribute wealth were unnecessary. The best things in life were already available to all at reasonable prices. But the prevalence of the parable of the Democracy of Goods in advertising tableaux did not necessarily betray a concerted conspiracy on the part of advertisers and their agencies to impose a social ideology on the American people. Most advertisers employed the parable of the Democracy of Goods primarily as a narrow, nonideological merchandising tactic. Listerine and Lifebuoy found the parable an obvious, attention-getting strategy for persuading readers that if even society women and bankers were unconsciously guilty of social offenses, the readers themselves were not immune. Simmons Mattresses, Chevrolet, and Clark Grave Vaults chose the parable in an attempt to broaden their market to include lower-income groups. The parable emphasized the affordability of the product to families of modest income while attempting to maintain a "class" image of the product as the preferred choice of their social betters.

Most advertisers found the social message of the parable of the Democracy of Goods a congenial and unexceptionable truism. They also saw it, like the other parables prevalent in advertising tableaux, as an epigrammatic statement of a conventional popular belief. Real income was rising for nearly all Americans during the 1920s, except for some farmers and farmworkers and those in a few depressed industries. Citizens seemed eager for confirmation that they were now driving the same make of car as the wealthy elites and serving their children the same cereal enjoyed by Livingston Ludlow Biddle III. Advertisers did not have to impose the parable of the Democracy of

[11] *Saturday Evening Post*, Nov. 10, 1928, p. 90; *True Story*, Aug. 1934, p. 57. See also *Chicago Tribune*, Oct. 8, 1930, p. 17; *American Magazine*, Aug. 1930, p. 77; *Woman's Home Companion*, May 1927, p. 96.

[12] *American Magazine*, Feb. 1927, p. 130.

Goods on a contrary-minded public. Theirs was the easier task of subtly substituting this vision of equality, which was certainly satisfying *as a vision*, for
broader and more traditional hopes and expectations of an equality of self-
sufficiency, personal independence, and social interaction.

Perhaps the most attractive aspect of this parable to advertisers was that
it preached the coming of an equalizing democracy without sacrificing those
fascinating contrasts of social condition that had long been the touchstone of
high drama. Henry James, writing of Hawthorne, had once lamented the obstacles facing the novelist who wrote of an America that lacked such tradition-
laden institutions as a sovereign, a court, an aristocracy, or even a class of
country gentlemen. Without castles, manors, and thatched cottages, America
lacked those stark juxtapositions of pomp and squalor, nobility and peasantry,
wealth and poverty that made Europe so rich a source of social drama.[13] But
many versions of the parable of the Democracy of Goods sought to offset that
disadvantage without gaining James's desired "complexity of manners." They
dressed up America's wealthy as dazzling aristocrats, and then reassured
readers that they could easily enjoy an essential equality with such elites in
the things that really mattered. The rich were decorative and fun to look at,
but in their access to those products most important to comfort and satisfaction, as the magazine *Delineator* put it, "The Four Hundred" had become
"the four million."[14] Advertisers left readers to assume that they could gain
the same satisfactions of exclusiveness from belonging to the four million as
had once been savored by the four hundred.

While parables of consumer democracy frequently used terms like "everyone," "anyone," "any home," or "every woman," these categories were mainly
intended to comprise the audience of "consumer-citizens" envisioned by the
advertising trade, or families economically among the nation's top 50 percent. Thus the *Delineator* had more in mind than mere alliteration when it
chose to contrast the old "400" with the new "four million" rather than a new
"one hundred and twenty million." The standard antitheses of the Democracy
of Goods parables were "mansion" and "bungalow." Advertising writers rarely
took notice of the many millions of Americans whose standard of living fell
below that of the cozy bungalow of the advertising tableaux. These millions
might overhear the promises of consumer democracy in the newspapers or
magazines, but advertising leaders felt no obligation to show how their promises to "everyone" would bring equality to those who lived in the nation's
apartment houses and farmhouses without plumbing, let alone those who
lived in rural shacks and urban tenements.

In the broadest sense, the parable of the Democracy of Goods may be
interpreted as a secularized version of the traditional Christian assurances of
ultimate human equality. "Body Odor plays no favorites" might be considered

---

[13]Henry James, *Hawthorne*, rev. ed. (New York, 1967 [c. 1879]), p. 55.
[14]*Printers' Ink*, Nov. 24, 1927, p. 52.

a secular translation of the idea that God "sends rain on the just and on the unjust" (Matt. 5:45). Promises of the essential equality of those possessing the advertised brand recalled the promise of equality of access to God's mercy. Thus the parable recapitulated a familiar, cherished expectation. Far more significant, however, was the parable's insinuation of the capacity of a Democracy of Goods to redeem the already secularized American promise of political equality.

Incessantly and enticingly repeated, advertising visions of fellowship in a 15 Democracy of Goods encouraged Americans to look to similarities in consumption styles rather than to political power or control of wealth for evidence of significant equality. Francesco Nicosia and Robert Mayer describe the result as a "deflection of the success ethic from the sphere of production to that of consumption." Freedom of choice came to be perceived as a freedom more significantly exercised in the marketplace than in the political

FIGURE 3   Advertising such as this encouraged Americans to pursue consumption-oriented lifestyles.

arena. This process gained momentum in the 1920s; it gained maturity during the 1950s as a sense of class differences was nearly eclipsed by a fascination with the equalities suggested by shared consumption patterns and "freely chosen" consumer "lifestyles."[15]

READING THE TEXT

1. Summarize in your own words what Marchand means by the "parable of the Democracy of Goods" (para. 2).
2. What does Marchand mean by claiming that "the parable of the Democracy of Goods may be interpreted as a secularized version of the traditional Christian assurances of ultimate human equality" (para. 14)?
3. What is the "Democracy of Afflictions" (para. 5), in your own words?
4. According to Marchand, why were the 1920s an especially ripe era for the success of the advertising strategies that he describes?

READING THE SIGNS

1. Does the parable of the Democracy of Goods work to make society more egalitarian, or does it reinforce existing power structures? Write an essay arguing for one position or the other, focusing on particular ads for support.
2. Bring to class a popular magazine of your own choosing. In groups, study your selections. In which magazines is the myth of the Democracy of Goods most common? Do you find any relationship between the use of this myth and the magazines' intended readerships?
3. Obtain from your college library an issue of *Time* dating from the 1920s, and compare it with a current issue. In what ways, if any, have the social messages communicated in the advertising changed? Try to account for any changes you identify.
4. **CONNECTING TEXTS**   Compare and contrast the myth of the Democracy of Goods with the frontier myth that Laurence Shames describes in "The More Factor" (p. 86). Consider how the two myths shape our consuming behavior; you may also want to show how the myths appear in some current ads.

[15]Francesco M. Nicosia and Robert N. Mayer, "Toward a Sociology of Consumption," *The Journal of Consumer Research* 3 (1976): 73; Roland Marchand, "Visions of Classlessness; Quests for Dominion: American Popular Culture, 1945–1960," in *Reshaping America: Society and Institutions, 1945–1960,* ed. Robert H. Bremner and Gary W. Reichard (Columbus, Ohio, 1982), pp. 165–70.

When You Come Home

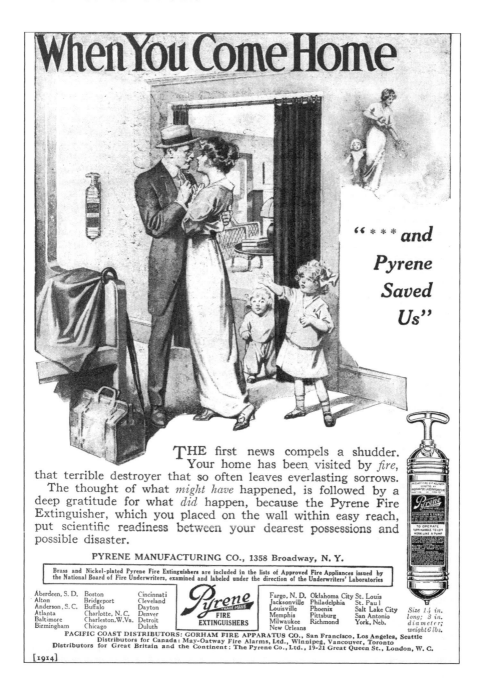

When You Come Home

"*** * *** *and* **Pyrene** *Saved* *Us*"

THE first news compels a shudder. Your home has been visited by *fire*, that terrible destroyer that so often leaves everlasting sorrows.

The thought of what *might have* happened, is followed by a deep gratitude for what *did* happen, because the Pyrene Fire Extinguisher, which you placed on the wall within easy reach, put scientific readiness between your dearest possessions and possible disaster.

PYRENE MANUFACTURING CO., 1358 Broadway, N. Y.

Brass and Nickel-plated Pyrene Fire Extinguishers are included in the lists of Approved Fire Appliances issued by the National Board of Fire Underwriters, examined and labeled under the direction of the Underwriters' Laboratories

Aberdeen, S. D.	Boston	Cincinnati	Fargo, N. D.	Oklahoma City	St. Louis
Alton	Bridgeport	Cleveland	Jacksonville	Philadelphia	St. Paul
Anderson, S. C.	Buffalo	Dayton	Louisville	Phoenix	Salt Lake City
Atlanta	Charlotte, N. C.	Denver	Memphis	Pittsburg	San Antonio
Baltimore	Charleston, W. Va.	Detroit	Milwaukee	Richmond	York, Neb.
Birmingham	Chicago	Duluth	New Orleans		

Pyrene TRADE MARK
FIRE EXTINGUISHERS

*Size 14 in.
long; 3 in.
diameter;
weight 6 lbs.*

PACIFIC COAST DISTRIBUTORS: GORHAM FIRE APPARATUS CO., San Francisco, Los Angeles, Seattle
Distributors for Canada: May-Oatway Fire Alarms, Ltd., Winnipeg, Vancouver, Toronto
Distributors for Great Britain and the Continent: The Pyrene Co., Ltd., 19-21 Great Queen St., London, W. C.

[1914]

READING THE SIGNS

1. The advertisement on page 191 tells a story. What is it? You might start with the title of the ad.

2. To whom is the ad directed? What emotions does it play on? Be sure to provide evidence for your answers. What are the "dearest possessions" the ad refers to?

3. This ad originally appeared in 1914. If you were to update it for a magazine today, what changes would you make? Why?

JAMES B. TWITCHELL

What We Are to Advertisers

Are you a "believer" or a "striver," an "achiever" or a "struggler," an "experiencer" or a "maker"? Or do you have no idea what we're talking about? If you don't, James Twitchell explains it all to you in this selection in which the psychological profiling schemes of American advertising are laid bare. For like it or not, advertisers have, or think they have, your number, and they will pitch their products according to the personality profile they have concocted for you. And the really spooky thing is that they're often right. A prolific writer on American advertising and culture, Twitchell's books include Adcult USA: The Triumph of Advertising in American Culture *(1996),* Twenty Ads That Shook the World *(2000),* Living It Up: Our Love Affair with Luxury *(2002),* Lead Us into Temptation: The Triumph of American Materialism *(1999), from which this selection is taken, and* Branded Nation *(2004). His most recent book is* Shopping for God: How Christianity Went from in Your Heart to in Your Face *(2007).*

Mass production means mass marketing, and mass marketing means the creation of mass stereotypes. Like objects on shelves, we too cluster in groups. We find meaning together. As we mature, we move from shelf to shelf, from aisle to aisle, zip code to zip code, from lifestyle to lifestyle, between what the historian Daniel Boorstin calls "consumption communities." Finally, as full-grown consumers, we stabilize in our buying, and hence meaning-making, patterns. Advertisers soon lose interest in us not just because we stop buying but because we have stopped changing brands.

The object of advertising is not just to brand parity objects but also to brand consumers as they move through these various communities. To explain his job, Rosser Reeves, the master of hard-sell advertising like the old Anacin ads, used to hold up two quarters and claim his job was to make you believe they were different, and, more importantly, that one was better than the other. Hence, at the macro level the task of advertising is to convince different sets of consumers — target groups — that the quarter they observe is somehow different in meaning and value than the same quarter seen by their across-the-tracks neighbors.

In adspeak, this is called *positioning*. "I could have positioned Dove as a detergent bar for men with dirty hands," David Ogilvy famously said, "but I chose to position it as a toilet bar for women with dry skin." Easy to say, hard to do. But if Anheuser-Busch wants to maximize its sales, the soccer mom driving the shiny Chevy Suburban must feel she drinks a different Budweiser than the roustabout in the rusted-out Chevy pickup.[1]

The study of audiences goes by any number of names: psychographics, ethnographics, macrosegmentation, to name a few, but they are all based on the ineluctable principle that birds of a feather flock together. The object of much consumer research is not to try to twist their feathers so that they will flock to your product, but to position your product in such a place that they will have to fly by it and perhaps stop to roost. After roosting, they will eventually think that this is a part of their flyway and return to it again and again.

Since different products have different meanings to different audiences, segmentation studies are crucial. Although agencies have their own systems 5 for naming these groups and their lifestyles, the current supplier of much raw data about them is a not-for-profit organization, the Stanford Research Institute (SRI).

The "psychographic" system of SRI is called acronymically VALS (now VALS2 +), short for Values and Lifestyle System. Essentially this schematic is based on the common-sense view that consumers are motivated "to acquire

[1]Cigarette companies were the first to find this out in the 1930s, much to their amazement. Blindfolded smokers couldn't tell what brand they were smoking. Instead of making cigarettes with different tastes, it was easier to make different advertising claims to different audiences. Cigarettes are hardly unique. Ask beer drinkers why they prefer a particular brand and invariably they tell you: "It's the taste," "This goes down well," "This is light and refreshing," "This is rich and smooth." They will say this about a beer that has been described as their brand, but is not. Anheuser-Busch, for instance, spent three dollars per barrel in 1980 to market a barrel of beer; now they spend nine dollars. Since the cost to reach a thousand television households has doubled at the same time the audience has segmented (thanks to cable), why not go after a particular market segment by tailoring ads emphasizing, in different degrees, the Clydesdales, Ed McMahon, Beechwood aging, the red and white can, dates certifying freshness, the spotted dog, the Eagle, as well as "the crisp, clean taste." While you cannot be all things to all people, the object of advertising is to be as many things to as many segments as possible. The ultimate object is to convince as many segments as possible that "This Bud's for you" is a sincere statement.

products, services, and experiences that provide satisfaction and give shape, substance, and character to their identities" in bundles. The more "resources" (namely money, but also health, self-confidence, and energy) each group has, the more likely they will buy "products, services, and experiences" of the group they associate with. But resources are not the only determinant. Customers are also motivated by such ineffables as principles, status, and action. When SRI describes these various audiences they peel apart like this (I have provided them an appropriate car to show their differences):

- Actualizers: These people at the top of the pyramid are the ideal of everyone but advertisers. They have "it" already, or will soon. They are sophisticated, take-charge people interested in independence and character. They don't need new things; in fact, they already have their things. If not, they already know what "the finer things" are and won't be told. They don't need a new car, but if they do they'll read *Consumer Reports*. They do not need a hood ornament on their car.

- Fulfilled: Here are mature, satisfied, comfortable souls who support the status quo in almost every way. Often they are literally or figuratively retired. They value functionality, durability, and practicality. They drive something called a "town car," which is made by all the big three automakers.

- Believers: As the word expresses, these people support traditional codes of family, church, and community, wearing good Republican cloth coats. As consumers they are predictable, favoring American products and recognizable brands. They regularly attend church and Wal-Mart, and they are transported there in their mid-range automobile like an Oldsmobile. Whether Oldsmobile likes it or not, they do indeed drive "your father's Oldsmobile."

Moving from principle-oriented consumers who look inside to status-driven consumers who look out to others, we find the Achievers and Strivers.

- Achievers: If consumerism has an ideal, here it is. Bingo! Wedded to job as a source of duty, reward, and prestige, these are the people who not only favor the establishment but *are* the establishment. They like the concept of prestige. Not only are they successful, they demonstrate their success by buying such objects as prestigious cars to show it. They like hood ornaments. They see no contradiction in driving a Land Rover in Manhattan.

- Strivers: A young Striver is fine; he will possibly mature into an Achiever. But an old Striver can be nasty; he may well be bitter. Since they are unsure of themselves, they are eager to be branded as long as the brand is elevating. Money defines success and they don't have enough of it. Being a yuppie is fine as long as the prospect of upward mobility is possible. Strivers like foreign cars even if it means only leasing a BMW.

Again, moving to the right are those driven less by the outside world but by their desire to participate, to be part of a wider world.

THE VALS2 NETWORK

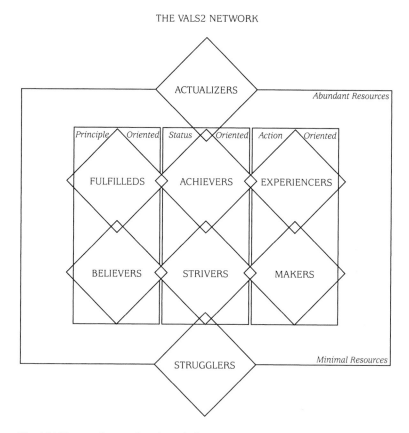

The VALS2 paradigm. Lifestyle styled: a taxonomy of taste and disposable income. (Stanford Research Institute)

- Experiencers: Here is life on the edge — enthusiastic, impulsive, and even reckless. Their energy finds expression in sports, social events, and "doing something." Politically and personally uncommitted, experiencers are an advertiser's dream come true as they see consumption as fulfillment and are willing to spend a high percent of their disposable income to attain it. When you wonder about who could possibly care how fast a car will accelerate from zero to sixty m.p.h., they care.

- Makers: Here is the practical side of Experiencers; they like to build things and they experience the world by working on it. Conservative, suspicious, respectful, they like to do things in and to their homes, like adding a room, canning vegetables, or changing the oil in their pickup trucks.

- Strugglers: Like Actualizers, these people are outside the pale of material- ism not by choice, but by low income. Strugglers are chronically poor. Their repertoire of things is limited not because they already have it all, but because they have so little. Although they clip coupons like Actualizers, theirs are from the newspaper. Their transportation is usually public, if any. They are the invisible millions.

As one might imagine, these are very fluid categories, and we may move through as many as three of them in our lifetimes. For instance, between ages 18–24 most people (61 percent) are Experiencers in desire or deed, while less than 1 percent are Fulfilled. Between ages 55 to 64, however, the Actualizers, Fulfilled, and Strugglers claim about 15 percent of the population each, while the Believers have settled out at about a fifth. The Achievers, Strivers, and Makers fill about 10 percent apiece, and the remaining 2 percent are Experiencers. The numbers can be broken down at every stage allowing for marital status, education, household size, dependent children, home ownership, household income, and occupation. More interesting still is the ability to accurately predict the appearance of certain goods in each grouping. SRI sells data on precisely who buys single-lens reflex cameras, who owns a laptop computer, who drinks herbal tea, who phones before five o'clock, who reads the *Reader's Digest*, and who watches *Beavis and Butthead*.

When one realizes the fabulous expense of communicating meaning for a product, the simple-mindedness of a system like VALS2 + becomes less risible. When you are spending millions of dollars for a few points of market share for your otherwise indistinguishable product, the idea that you might be able to attract the owners of socket wrenches by shifting ad content around just a bit makes sense. Once you realize that in taste tests consumers cannot tell one brand of cigarettes from another — including their own — nor distinguish such products as soap, gasoline, cola, beer, or what-have-you, it is clear that the product must be overlooked and the audience isolated and sold.

READING THE TEXT

1. What do marketers mean by "positioning" (para. 3), and why is it an important strategy to them?
2. What does the acronym VALS stand for, and what is the logic behind this system?
3. Why do marketers believe that the "product must be overlooked and the audience isolated and sold" (para. 8), according to Twitchell?

READING THE SIGNS

1. Consult the VALS2 network chart on page 195 and write a journal entry in which you place yourself on the chart. To what extent do you see yourself reflected in the VALS2 paradigm? What is your attitude toward being stereotyped by marketers?
2. In class, discuss whether the categories of consumers defined by the VALS2 paradigm are an accurate predictor of consumer behavior. Use the discussion as the basis of an essay in which you argue for or against the proposition that

stereotyping consumer lifestyles is an effective way of marketing goods and services.

3. Study the VALS2 paradigm in terms of the values it presumes. To what extent does it presume traditionally American values such as individualism? Use your analysis to formulate an argument about whether this marketing tool is an essentially American phenomenon.

4. **CONNECTING TEXTS** Twitchell, Sandra Blakeslee ("If You Have a 'Buy Button' in Your Brain, What Pushes It?" p. 197), Eric Schlosser ("Kid Kustomers," p. 222), and Malcolm Gladwell ("The Science of Shopping," p. 93) all describe marketing research strategies. Read these selections, and write an argument that supports, opposes, or modifies the proposition that marketers have misappropriated academic research techniques for manipulative and therefore ethically questionable purposes.

CREATING CONSUMERS

| SANDRA BLAKESLEE

If You Have a "Buy Button" in Your Brain, What Pushes It?

Inquiring advertisers want to know. And the reason is simple, for as Sandra Blakeslee reports in this news feature for the New York Times, *"at issue is whether marketers can exploit advances in brain science to make more effective commercials." Thus, using such technologies as functional magnetic resonance imaging machines, neuromarketers are testing the brain's response to everything from movie trailers to brand names like Coca-Cola and Pepsi to see if they can improve on their advertising effectiveness. With advertising rates approaching three million dollars for a thirty-second spot at the Super Bowl, one can hardly blame them, but, somehow, echoes of Aldous Huxley's* Brave New World *might be resonating in such studies as well. Blakeslee is the author of* Phantoms in the Brain: Probing the Mysteries of the Human Mind *(with V. S. Ramachandran and Oliver Sacks, 1999) and* The Body Has a Mind of Its Own: How Body Maps in Your Brain Help You Do (Almost) Everything Better *(with Matthew Blakeslee, 2007).*

Knowing what brand you are buying can influence your preferences by commandeering brain circuits involved with memory, decision making and self-image, researchers have found. When researchers monitored brain scans of 67 people who were given a blind taste test of Coca-Cola and Pepsi, each soft drink lit up the brain's reward system, and the participants were evenly split

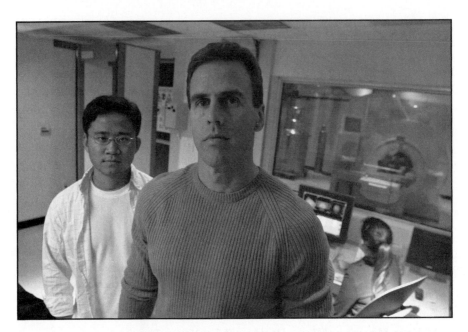

Dr. P. Read Montague, center, of Baylor College of Medicine, and Jian Li, left, a graduate student, used functional magnetic resonance imaging, which tracks blood flow as people perform mental tasks, to do a neurological taste test of Coca-Cola and Pepsi.

as to which drink they preferred. But when the same people were told what they were drinking, activity in a different set of brain regions linked to brand loyalty overrode their original preferences. Three out of four said that they preferred Coca-Cola. The study, published in the Oct. 14 issue of the journal *Neuron*, is the first to explore how cultural messages penetrate the human brain and shape personal preferences. Circulating in draft form over the last year, the study has been widely discussed by neuroscientists and advertisers, as well as people who worry about the power of commercials in determining consumer behavior.

At issue is whether marketers can exploit advances in brain science to make more effective commercials. Is there a "buy button" in the brain? Some corporations have teamed up with neuroscientists to find out. Recent experiments in so-called neuromarketing have explored reactions to movie trailers, choices about automobiles, the appeal of a pretty face and gut reactions to political campaign advertising, as well as the power of brand loyalty.

But the trend also has critics. For example, Commercial Alert, a consumer group that is highly critical of neuromarketing and has called it Orwellian, said that such studies were dangerous. In a July 12 letter to the Senate Committee on Commerce, Science and Transportation, the group's executive director, Gary Ruskin, asked for an investigation of neuromarketing. "What would happen in this country if corporate marketers and political consultants could literally peer inside our brains and chart the neural activity that leads to our selections in the supermarket and voting booth?" Mr. Ruskin wrote. "What if they then could trigger this neural activity by various means, so as to modify our behavior to serve their own ends?"

Defenders of the studies counter that Mr. Ruskin and others who express fears about the studies are overreacting and do not understand the research. Dr. Steven Quartz, a neuroscientist at the California Institute of Technology in Pasadena, Calif., said Mr. Ruskin's comments represented "gross misunderstandings and distortions of both the power of brain imaging technology and its use in marketing." "It's pure fantasy to suppose that neuromarketing is about embedding subliminal messages," Dr. Quartz continued.

Companies, however, see the chance to find out what their customers 5 really think as a great opportunity.

Corporate executives are the first to admit they do not really know how advertising works. They spend $117 billion a year on advertisements, but most people do not remember what product is featured in a given commercial. Four out of five new products flop. There is no conclusive evidence that advertising ever causes sales to go up. Worst of all, consumers tend to behave like finicky cats, making it difficult to fathom what they want.

Neuromarketing relies on a brain scanning device called functional magnetic resonance imaging or f.M.R.I., a machine that tracks blood flow as people perform mental tasks. Specific regions light up, showing increased blood flow when they recognize a face, hear a song, make a decision, perceive a reward, pay attention or sense deception. In the studies, the machines are being used to shed light on brain mechanisms that play a central role in consumer behavior: circuits that underlie reward, decision making, motivation, emotions and the senses of self. Anything that is novel, researchers have found, grabs the brain's attention system by tapping directly into reward pathways.

Being able to see how the brain responds to novelty and makes decisions is potentially a huge step forward for marketers, said Tim McPartlin, a senior vice president of Lieberman Research Worldwide in Los Angeles. Conventional techniques for learning consumer preferences are notoriously inadequate, Mr. McPartlin said. The traditional methods that companies use to explore consumer preferences do not always reflect actual buying patterns. "You use surveys when you want to test something—the reaction to an ad, package, new product name, or design," he said. "You ask questions scaled to gauge the response. But the scales are a blunt tool," he said. "They cannot capture the emotional responses beneath consumer preferences."

Complicating matters further, in focus groups, some people want to please, others to dominate—urges that can influence their choices. In interviews, consumers often say what they think the interviewer wants to hear. "You ask if they like a luxury product and their puritanical side comes out," Mr. McPartlin said. "They tell you 'I'm not interested in that' but their medial prefrontal cortex is saying they are." Cultural differences are also a big problem.

"In Latin cultures, they tell you they like everything," Mr. McPartlin said. A product rated as a 9 in Brazil gets a 6 in Germany.

Brain imaging experiments cut through these problems, Mr. McPartlin said,   10 making it possible for companies to see more quickly and accurately what their customers want, like and feel that they need. For example, Dr. Quartz is using f.M.R.I. to test movie trailers. Coming attractions make a big difference in getting people to buy movie tickets but movie studios need a way to tell which are most effective. It turns out, Dr. Quartz said, that a trailer's success is related to whether it engages people emotionally. But people have trouble verbalizing their emotions. The f.M.R.I. machine detects emotional responses that are of a clear value to Hollywood. Trailers make an ideal subject for brain imaging, Dr. Quartz said: "If I show you a commercial for a laundry detergent, I don't know if you are reacting to the product or to something funny or interesting about the commercial. But the movie trailer is the product itself. If you react well, you are reacting to the product."

Other studies have examined various types of everyday decision making. In Germany, DaimlerChrysler corporation took functional brain images of men as they looked at various kinds of cars, finding, perhaps not surprisingly, racy sports cars activated the men's reward centers. At Harvard, researchers found that in young heterosexual men a brain reward area was highly activated by beautiful female faces. Plain female faces and attractive male faces had no effect. And Dr. Gregory Berns of Emory University in Atlanta is studying how people's opinions are swayed by others. The research could shed light on products that become fads.

Dr. P. Read Montague, a neuroscientist at the Baylor College of Medicine in Houston who led the Coca-Cola versus Pepsi study, said he was fascinated by the way cultural images insinuated their way into people's choices. The study of Coke and Pepsi, financed by the National Institute on Drug Abuse and the Kane Family Foundation, showed that two different brain systems were at play. When subjects used their sense of taste alone to choose a preferred drink, an area of the brain called the ventrolateral prefrontal cortex lit up. When told they were drinking "the real thing," as Coke is widely known, a memory region call the hippocampus and another part of the prefrontal cortex lit up. The study showed that some people did not choose a drink based on taste alone, Dr. Montague said. They chose a drink plus what it conjured up to their medial prefrontal cortex, namely the strong brand identity of Coca-Cola, he said.

Researchers at the University of California, Los Angeles recently looked at how Democrats and Republicans differ in their neural responses to campaign commercials showing images of the Sept. 11 terrorist attacks. Democrats, they found, were more fearful.

Mr. Ruskin of Commercial Alert points to such studies as proof that they pose a threat to society. "They are probing the human psyche for the purpose of influencing it," he said. "At its best, neuromarketing would make advertising more effective. At its worst, neuromarketing could make propaganda more effective, potentially leading to new totalitarian regimes, civil strife, wars, genocide and countless deaths."

But defenders of neuromarketing say the technology cannot force people 15 to do something that they would not do otherwise. "If people realize they're being manipulated, they will start to question their choices," Dr. Berns said. "The more we know, the more executive control we can exert over our decisions." Dr. Sam McClure, a postdoctoral researcher at Princeton and a co-author of the soft drink study, suggested that neuromarketing might someday even be used to protect vulnerable brains. The prefrontal cortex, which helps mediate consumer choice, develops late in children and is impaired in older people, groups that are highly susceptible to advertising, he said. Young children are often sucked in by advertisements for sugary foods, while the elderly can fall victim to buying fake insurance policies. "If brain imaging studies clearly showed those vulnerabilities, laws could be passed to protect people from advertising," Dr. McClure said.

Reading the Text

1. Define neuromarketing in your own words.
2. Why does Commercial Alert label neuromarketing as "Orwellian"?
3. What arguments are presented to defend neuromarketing?
4. Why are traditional marketing strategies like consumer surveys considered ineffective?

Reading the Signs

1. In class, form teams and debate whether neuromarketing is indeed "Orwellian" or, instead, is an advance in the study of consumer behavior. Drawing on the debate for counterarguments, write an essay in which you present your own argument about this question.
2. **CONNECTING TEXTS**   In class, discuss your own response to brand names. Do you buy — or avoid — generic products? To what extent do you buy a product because of its label? Use the discussion as the basis of an essay in which you assess the importance of brand names in constructing a consumer's identity. To develop your ideas, consult Anne Norton's "The Signs of Shopping" (p. 101).
3. **CONNECTING TEXTS**   Defenders of neuromarketing claim that it can be used to "protect people from advertising" (para. 15), particularly vulnerable consumers such as children. Adopt the perspective of Eric Schlosser ("Kid Kustomers," p. 222) and critique this claim. To develop your ideas, you might consult Anne Galligan's "Pottermania: The Marketing behind the Magic" (p. 129).

STEVE CRAIG

Men's Men and Women's Women

Men and women both drink beer, but you wouldn't guess that from the television ads that pitch beer as a guy beverage and associate beer drinking with such guy things as fishing trips, bars, and babes. Conversely, both men and women can find themselves a few pounds overweight, but you wouldn't know that from the ads, which almost always feature women intended to appeal to women dieters. In this selection, Steve Craig provides a step-by-step analysis of four TV commercials, showing how advertisers carefully craft their ads to appeal, respectively, to male and female consumers. A professor in the department of radio, television, and film at the University of North Texas, Craig has written widely on television, radio history, and gender and media.

Gender and the Economics of Television Advertising

The economic structure of the television industry has a direct effect on the placement and content of all television programs and commercials. Large advertisers and their agencies have evolved the pseudo-scientific method of time purchasing based on demographics, with the age and sex of the consumer generally considered to be the most important predictors of purchasing behavior. Computers make it easy to match market research on product buying patterns with audience research on television viewing habits. Experience, research, and intuition thus yield a demographic (and even psychographic) profile of the "target audience." Advertisers can then concentrate their budgets on those programs which the target audience is most likely to view. The most economical advertising buys are those in which the target audience is most concentrated (thus, the less "waste" audience the advertiser must purchase) (Barnouw, 1978; Gitlin, 1983; Jhally, 1987).

Good examples of this demographic targeting can be seen by contrasting the ads seen on daytime television, aimed at women at home, with those on weekend sports telecasts. Ads for disposable diapers are virtually never seen during a football game any more than commercials for beer are seen during soap operas. True, advertisers of some products simply wish to have their commercials seen by the largest number of consumers at the lowest cost without regard to age, sex, or other demographic descriptors, but most consider this approach far too inefficient for the majority of products.

A general rule of thumb in television advertising, then, is that daytime is the best time to reach the woman who works at home. Especially important to advertisers among this group is the young mother with children. Older women, who also make up a significant proportion of the daytime audience, are generally considered less important by many advertisers in the belief that they spend far less money on consumer goods than young mothers.

Prime time (the evening hours) is considered a good time to reach women who work away from home, but since large numbers of men are also in the audience, it can also be a good time to advertise products with wider target audiences. Weekend sports periods (and, in season, "Monday Night Football") are the only time of the week when men outnumber women in the television audience, and therefore, become the optimum time for advertising products and services aimed at men.

Gendered Television, Gendered Commercials

In his book *Television Culture* (1987, Chs. 10, 11), John Fiske discusses "gen- 5 dered television," explaining that the television industry successfully designs some programs for men and others for women. Clearly, program producers and schedulers must consider the target audience needs of their clients (the advertisers) in creating a television program line up. The gendering of programming allows the industry to provide the proper audience for advertisers by constructing shows pleasurable for the target audience to watch, and one aspect of this construction is in the gender portrayals of characters.

Fiske provides the following example:

> Women's view of masculinity, as evidenced in soap operas, differs markedly from that produced from the masculine audience. The "good" male in the daytime soaps is caring, nurturing, and verbal. He is prone to making comments like "I don't care about material wealth or professional success, all I care about is us and our relationship." He will talk about feelings and people and rarely express his masculinity in direct action. Of course, he is still decisive, he still has masculine power, but that power is given a "feminine" inflection. . . . The "macho" characteristics of goal centeredness, assertiveness, and the morality of the strongest that identify the hero in masculine television, tend here to be characteristics of the villain. (p. 186)

But if the programming manipulates gender portrayals to please the audience, then surely so must the commercials that are the programs' reason for being. My previous research (Craig, 1990) supports the argument that advertisers also structure the gender images in their commercials to match the expectations and fantasies of their intended audience. Thus, commercials portraying adult women with children were nearly four times more likely to appear during daytime soap operas than during weekend sports (p. 50). Daytime advertisers exploit the image of women as mothers to sell products to mothers. Likewise, during the weekend sports broadcasts, only 18% of the primary male characters were shown at home, while during the daytime ads, 40% of them were (p. 42). For the woman at home, men are far more likely to be portrayed as being around the house than they are in commercials aimed at men on weekends.

Gendered commercials, like gendered programs, are designed to give pleasure to the target audience, since it is the association of the product with a pleasurable experience that forms the basis for much American television advertising. Yet patriarchy conditions males and females to seek their pleasure differently. Advertisers therefore portray different images to men and women in order to exploit the different deep-seated motivations and anxieties connected to gender identity. I would now like to turn to a close analysis of four television commercials to illustrate some of these differing portrayals. Variations in how men and women are portrayed are especially apparent when comparing weekend and daytime commercials, since ads during these day parts almost completely focus on a target audience of men or women respectively.

Analysis of Four Commercials

In order to illustrate the variation of gender portrayal, I have chosen four commercials. Each was selected to provide an example of how men and women are portrayed to themselves and to the other sex. The image of men and women in commercials aired during weekend sports telecasts I call "Men's Men" and "Men's Women." The portrayals of men and women in commercials aimed at women at home during the daytime hours I call "Women's Men" and "Women's Women." Although there are certainly commercials aired during these day parts which do not fit neatly into these categories, and even a few which might be considered to be counter-stereotypical in their gender portrayals, the commercials and images I have chosen to analyze are fairly typical and were chosen to permit a closer look at the practices revealed in my earlier content analysis. Further, I acknowledge that the readings of these commercials are my own. Others may well read them differently.

Men's Men

I would first like to consider two commercials originally broadcast during 10 weekend sports and clearly aimed at men. (These and the other commercials I will discuss were broadcast on at least one of the three major networks. I recorded them for analysis during January, 1990.)

COMMERCIAL 1: ACURA INTEGRA (:30)

MUSIC: Light rock guitar music runs throughout. Tropical elements (e.g., a steel drum) are added later.

A young, white, blond, bespectacled male wearing a plain sweatshirt is shown cleaning out the interior of a car. He finds an old photograph of himself and two male companions (all are young, slender, and white) posing with a trophy-sized sailfish. He smiles. Dissolve to what appears to be a flashback of the fishing trip. The three men are now seen driving down the highway in the car (we now see that it is a new black Acura Integra) in a Florida-like landscape. We see a montage of close-ups of the three men inside the car, then a view out the car window of what looks to be the Miami skyline.

ANNOUNCER (male): "When you think about all the satisfaction you get out of going places. . . . Why would you want to take anything less . . ."

Dissolve to a silhouette shot of a young woman in a bathing suit walking along the beach at sunset.

ANNOUNCER: ". . . than America's most satisfying car?"

On this last line, the three young men are seen in silhouette knee-deep in the water at the same beach, apparently watching the woman pass. One of the men drops to his knees and throws his arms up in mock supplication. A montage of shots of the three men follows, shots of a deep-sea fishing boat intercut with shots of the first man washing the car. The montage ends with the three posing with the trophy sailfish. The screen flashes and freezes and becomes the still photo seen at the first of the commercial. The final shot shows a long shot of the car, freshly washed. The first man, dressed as in the first shot, gives the car a final polish and walks away. The words "Acura" and "Precision Crafted Performance" are superimposed over the final shot.

ANNOUNCER: "The Acura Integra."

This ad, which ran during a weekend sports telecast, has a number of features that makes it typical of many other commercials aimed at men. First, it is for an automobile. My previous research found that 29% of the network commercials telecast in the weekend time period were for cars and other automotive products (compared to only 1% during the daytime sample) (Craig, 1990, p. 36). In our culture, automobiles are largely the male's province, and men are seen by the automotive industry as the primary decision makers when it comes to purchases. Further, cars are frequently offered as a means of freedom (literally so in this ad), and escapism is an important component in many weekend ads (only 16% of weekend ads are set at home compared to 41% of daytime ads) (p. 43).

Second, with the exception of a brief silhouette of the woman on the beach, there are no women in this commercial. Camaraderie in all-male or nearly all-male groupings is a staple of weekend commercials, especially those for automobiles and beer. Again, my earlier research indicates that fully one-third of weekend commercials have an all-adult male cast (but only 20% of daytime commercials have an all-adult female cast) (p. 36).

The escapism and male camaraderie promised in this commercial are simply an extension of the escapism and camaraderie men enjoy when they watch (and vicariously participate in) weekend sports on television. Messner

(1987) suggests that one reason for the popularity of sports with men is that it offers them a chance to escape from the growing ambiguity of masculinity in daily life.

> Both on a personal/existential level for athletes and on a symbolic/ideolog- ical level for spectators and fans, sport has become one of the "last bas- tions" of male power and superiority over—and separation from—the "feminization" of society. The rise of football as "America's number-one game" is likely the result of the comforting *clarity* it provides between the polarities of traditional male power, strength, and violence and the con- temporary fears of social feminization. (p. 54)

The Acura commercial acts to reinforce male fantasies in an environment of clear masculinity and male domination. Men's men are frequently por- trayed as men without women. The presence of women in the commercials might serve to threaten men's men with confusing uncertainty about the nature of masculinity in a sexist, but changing, society (Fiske, 1987, pp. 202–209, offers an extended psychoanalytic explanation of the absence of women in masculine television). On the other hand, the absence of women must *not* sug- gest homosexuality. Men's men are clearly heterosexual. To discourage any sus- picions, the Acura ad portrays three (rather than two) men vacationing together.

It is also at least partly for this reason that the single quick shot in which 15 the woman *does* appear in this commercial is important. She is nothing more than an anonymous object of desire (indeed, in silhouette, we cannot even see her face), but her presence both affirms the heterosexuality of the group while at the same time hinting that attaining sexual fulfillment will be made easier by the possession of the car. Men's men have the unchallenged free- dom of a fantasized masculinity—to travel, to be free from commitment, to seek adventure.

Men's Women

COMMERCIAL 2: MILLER BEER (:30)

> We see the interior of a cheap roadside cafe. It is lit with an almost blinding sunlight streaming in the windows. A young couple sits in a far booth holding hands. A young, blond waitress is crossing the room. A silent jukebox sits in the foreground. At first we hear only natural sounds. We cut to a close-up from a low angle from outside the cafe of male legs as they enter the cafe. The legs are clad in blue jeans and cow- boy boots. As the man enters, we cut to a close-up of the blond waitress looking up to see the man. We see a close-up of the man's body as he passes the silent jukebox. As if by magic, the jukebox begins to play the rhythm and blues number "I Put a Spell on You." We see the couple that was holding hands turn in surprise. The man in the booth's face is unlit and we can see no features, but the woman is young with long blond hair. She looks surprised and pulls her hand away from the man's. We

cut to an extreme close-up of the waitress's face. It is covered with sweat. As she watches the man pass, a smile appears on her face. She comes over to take the man's order. The camera takes the man's point of view.

MAN: "Miller Genuine Draft."
WAITRESS: "I was hopin' you'd say that."

We see a shot of a refrigerator door opening. The refrigerator is filled with sweating, backlit bottles of Miller beer. We then see a close-up of the man holding a bottle and opening it magically with a flick of his thumb (no opener). A montage of shots of the product amid blowing snow follows this. The sounds of a blizzard are heard.

ANNOUNCER: "Cold filtered. Never heat pasteurized. Miller Genuine Draft. For those who discover this real draft taste . . . the world is a *very* cool place."

On this last line we see close-ups of the woman in the booth and the waitress. Wind is blowing snow in their faces and they are luxuriating in the coolness. The waitress suddenly looks at the camera with shocked disappointment. We cut to an empty seat with the man's empty beer bottle rocking on the table. The music, snow, and wind end abruptly. We see the man's back as he exits the cafe. The final shot is of the waitress, elbow propped on the counter, looking after the man. The words "Tap into the Cold" are superimposed.

When women do appear in men's commercials, they seldom challenge the primary masculine fantasy. Men's women are portrayed as physically attractive, slim, and usually young and white, frequently blond, and almost always dressed in revealing clothing. Since most men's commercials are set in locations away from home, most men's women appear outside the home, and only infrequently are they portrayed as wives. There are almost always hints of sexual availability in men's women, but this is seldom played out explicitly. Although the sexual objectification of women characters in these ads is often quite subtle, my previous content analysis suggests that it is far more common in weekend than in daytime ads (Craig, 1990, p. 34). Men's women are also frequently portrayed as admirers (and at times, almost voyeurs), generally approving of some aspect of product use (the car he drives, the beer he drinks, the credit card he uses).

In these respects, the Miller ad is quite typical. What might have been a simple commercial about a man ordering and drinking a beer becomes an elaborate sexual fantasy, in many respects constructed like a porn film. The attractive, eager waitress is mystically drawn to the man who relieves her bored frustrations with an orgasmic chug-a-lug. She is "hot" while he (and the beer) is "*very* cool." But once he's satisfied, he's gone. He's too cool for conversation or commitment. We never see the man's face, but rather are invited, through the use of the point-of-view shot, to become a participant in the mystic fantasy.

There is, of course, considerable tongue-in-cheek intent in this ad. Males know that the idea of anonymous women lusting after them, eager for sex without commitment, is fantasy. But for many men, it is pleasurable fantasy, and common enough in weekend commercials. The main point is that the product has been connected, however briefly, with the pleasure of this fantasy. The physical pleasure of consuming alcohol (and specifically cold Miller beer) is tied to the pleasurable imaginings of a narrative extended beyond that which is explicitly seen.

One industry executive has explained this advertising technique. Noting the need for "an imaginary and motivating value" in ads, Nicolas (1988) argues that:

> Beyond the principle of utility, it becomes more and more important to associate a principle of pleasure to the value. The useful must be linked to the beautiful, the rational to the imaginary, the indispensable to the superfluous. . . . It is imperative that the image be seductive. (p. 7)

Although some research has documented changes in gender portrayals 20 in television advertising over the past few years (e.g., Bretl & Cantor, 1988; Ferrante, et al., 1988), such conclusions are based on across-the-schedule studies or of prime time rather than of specifically gendered day parts. While avoiding portraying women as blatant sex objects is doubtless good business in daytime or prime time, it would almost certainly inhibit male fantasies such as this one, commonly seen during weekend sports. The man's woman continues to be portrayed according to the rules of the patriarchy.

The next two commercials were originally aired during daytime soap operas. They represent Madison Avenue's portrayal of women and men designed for women.

Women's Women

COMMERCIAL 3: WEIGHT WATCHERS (:30)

The opening shot is a quick pan from toe to head of a young, thin, white woman with dark hair. She is dressed in a revealing red bathing suit and appears to be reclining on the edge of a pool. Her head is propped up with a pillow. She is wearing sunglasses and smiling.

ANNOUNCER (woman, voice-over): "I hate diets . . . but I lost weight fast with Weight Watchers' new program."

We see the same woman sitting at a dining table in a home kitchen eating a meal. She is wearing a red dress. The camera weaves, and we briefly glimpse a man and two small children also at the table. Another close-up of the woman's body at the pool. This time the camera frames her waist.

ANNOUNCER: "And I *hate* starving myself."

We see the same family group eating pizza at a restaurant. More close-ups of the woman's body at poolside.

ANNOUNCER: "But with their new 'fast and flexible' program I don't have to."

Shot of the woman dancing with the man, followed by a montage of more shots of the family at dinner and close-ups of the woman at poolside.

ANNOUNCER: "A new food plan lets me live the way I want . . . eat with my family and friends, still have fun."

Close-up shot of balance scales. A woman's hand is moving the balance weight downward.

ANNOUNCER: "And in no time . . . *here I am!*"

Shot of the woman on the scales. She raises her hands as if in triumph. The identical shot is repeated three times.

ANNOUNCER: "Now there's only one thing I hate . . . not joining Weight Watchers sooner."

As this last line is spoken, we see a close-up of the woman at the pool. She removes her sunglasses. The man's head comes into the frame from the side and kisses her on the forehead.

This commercial portrays the woman's woman. Her need is a common one in women's commercials produced by a patriarchal society — the desire to attain and maintain her physical attractiveness. Indeed, my previous research indicates that fully 44% of the daytime ads sampled were for products relating to the body (compared with only 15% of the ads during weekend sports). In this ad, her desire for an attractive body is explicitly tied to her family. She is portrayed with a husband, small children, and a nice home. It is her husband with whom she dances and who expresses approval with a kiss. Her need for an attractive body is her need to maintain her husband's interest and maintain her family's unity and security. As Coward (1985) has written:

> Most women know to their cost that appearance is perhaps the crucial way by which men form opinions of women. For that reason, feelings about self-image get mixed up with feelings about security and comfort. . . . It sometimes appears to women that the whole possibility of being loved and comforted hangs on how their appearance will be received. (p. 78)

But dieting is a difficult form of self-deprivation, and she "hates" doing it. Implicit also is her hatred of her own "overweight" body — a body that no longer measures up to the idealized woman promoted by the patriarchy (and seen in the commercial). As Coward explains:

> . . . advertisements, health and beauty advice, fashion tips are effective precisely because somewhere, perhaps even subconsciously, an anxiety, rather than a pleasurable identification [with the idealized body] is awakened. (p. 80)

Weight Watchers promises to alleviate the pain of dieting at the same time it relieves (or perhaps delays) the anxiety of being "overweight." She can diet and "still have fun."

A related aspect is this ad's use of a female announcer. The copy is writ- 25 ten in the first person, but we never see the model speaking in direct address. We get the impression that we are eavesdropping on her thoughts—being invited to identify with her—rather than hearing a sales pitch from a third person. My earlier research confirmed the findings of other content analyses that female voice-overs are relatively uncommon in commercials. My findings, however, indicated that while only 3% of the voice-overs during weekend sports were by women announcers, 16% of those during daytime were. Further, 60% of the women announcers during daytime were heard in commercials for body-related products (Craig, 1990, p. 52).

Women's Men

COMMERCIAL 4: SECRET DEODORANT (:30)

We open on a wide shot of a sailing yacht at anchor. It is sunrise and a woman is on deck. She descends into the cabin. Cut to a close-up of the woman as she enters the cabin.

WOMAN: "Four bells. Rise and shine!"

A man is seen in a bunk inside the cabin. He has just awakened. Both he and the woman are now seen to be young and white. She is thin and has bobbed hair. He is muscular and unshaven (and a Bruce Willis look-alike).

MUSIC: Fusion jazz instrumental (UNDER).
MAN (painfully): "Ohhhh . . . I can't move."
WOMAN: "Ohhhhh. I took a swim—breakfast is on—I had a shower. Now it's *your turn.*"

As she says this, she crosses the cabin and places a container of Secret deodorant on a shelf above the man. The man leans up on one elbow then falls back into bed with a groan.

MAN: "Ahhh, I can't."

She pulls him back to a sitting position then sits down herself, cradling him in her arms.

WOMAN: "Come onnn. You only changed *one* sail yesterday."
MAN (playfully): "Yeah, but it was a *big* sail."

Close-up of the couple. He is now positioned in the bed sitting with his back to her. He leans his head back on her shoulder.

WOMAN: "Didn't you know sailing's a sport? You know . . . an active thing."
MAN: "I just don't get it. . . . You're *so* together already. . . . Um. You smell
    great."
WOMAN: "Must be my Secret."

She looks at the container of Secret on the shelf. The man reaches over
and picks it up. Close-up of the Secret with the words "Sporty Clean
Scent" visible on the container.

MAN: "Sporty clean?"
WOMAN: "It's new."
MAN: "Sounds like something I could use."
WOMAN: "Unnnnn . . . I don't think so. I got it for me."

She takes the container from him and stands up and moves away. He
stands up behind her and holds her from behind.

WOMAN: "For these close quarters . . . ?"
MAN: "Well close is good."

He begins to kiss her cheek.

WOMAN: "I thought you said you couldn't move."

She turns to face him.

MAN: "I was saving my strength?"
WOMAN: "Mmmm."

We dissolve to a close-up of the product on the shelf.

ANNOUNCER (woman): "New Sporty Clean Secret. Strong enough for a man,
    but pH-balanced for an active woman."

This commercial portrays the woman's man. He's good looking, sensitive,
romantic, and he appreciates her. What's more, they are alone in an exotic
location where he proceeds to seduce her. In short, this commercial is a 30-
second romance novel. She may be today's woman, be "so together," and she
may be in control, but she still wants him to initiate the love-making. Her
man is strong, active, and probably wealthy enough to own or rent a yacht.
(Of course, a more liberated reading would have her as the owner of the
yacht, or at least sharing expenses.) Yet he is also vulnerable. At first she
mothers him, holding him in a Pietà-like embrace and cooing over his sore
muscles. Then he catches her scent — her Secret — and the chase is on.

As in the Weight Watchers commercial, it is the woman's body that is portrayed as the source of the man's attraction, and it is only through maintaining that attraction that she can successfully negotiate the relationship.
Although at one level the Secret woman is portrayed as a "new woman" —
active, "sporty," self-assured, worthy of her own deodorant — she still must
rely on special (even "Secret") products to make her body attractive. More to

the point, she still must rely on her body to attract a man and fulfill the fantasy of security and family. After all, she is still mothering and cooking breakfast.

Once again, the product is the source of promised fantasy fulfillment — not only sexual fulfillment, but also the security of a caring relationship, one that allows her to be liberated, but not too liberated. Unlike the women of the Acura and Miller's commercials who remained anonymous objects of desire, the men of the Weight Watchers and Secret commercials are intimates who are clearly portrayed as having relationships that will exist long after the commercial is over.

Conclusion

Gender images in television commercials provide an especially intriguing field of study. The ads are carefully crafted bundles of images, frequently designed to associate the product with feelings of pleasure stemming from deep-seated fantasies and anxieties. Advertisers seem quite willing to manipulate these fantasies and exploit our anxieties, especially those concerning our gender identities, to sell products. What's more, they seem to have no compunction about capitalizing on dehumanizing gender stereotypes to seek these ends.

A threat to patriarchy is an economic threat, not only to men who may   30
fear they will have their jobs taken by women, but also in a more fundamental way. Entire industries (automotive, cosmetics, fashion) are predicated on the assumption that men and women will continue behaving according to their stereotypes. Commercials for women therefore act to reinforce patriarchy and to co-opt any reactionary ideology into it. Ccmmercials for men need only reinforce masculinity under patriarchy and, at most, offer men help in coping with a life plagued by women of raised conscience. Betty Friedan's comments of 1963 are still valid. Those "deceptively simple, clever, outrageous ads and commercials" she wrote of are still with us. If anything, they have become more subtle and insidious. The escape from their snare is through a better understanding of gender and the role of mass culture in defining it.

WORKS CITED

Barnouw, E. (1978). *The sponsor*. NY: Oxford.

Bretl, D. J. & Cantor, J. (1988). The portrayal of men and women in U.S. television commercials: A recent content analysis and trends over 15 years. *Sex Roles, 18*(9/10), 595–609.

Coward, R. (1985). *Female desires: How they are sought, bought and packaged*. New York: Grove.

Craig, S. (1990, December). *A content analysis comparing gender images in network television commercials aired in daytime, evening, and weekend telecasts*. (ERIC Document Reproduction Service Number ED 329 217.)

Ferrante, C., Haynes, A., & Kingsley, S. (1988). Image of women in television advertising. *Journal of Broadcasting & Electronic Media, 32*(2), 231–37.

Fiske, J. (1987). *Television culture*. New York: Methuen.

Friedan, B. (1963). *The feminine mystique*. New York: Dell.

Gitlin, T. (1983). *Inside prime time*. New York: Pantheon.

Jhally, S. (1987). *The codes of advertising: Fetishism and the political economy of meaning in the consumer society*. New York: St. Martin's.

Messner, M. (1987). Male identity in the life course of the jock. In M. Kimmel (Ed.), *Changing men* (pp. 53–67). Newbury Park, CA: Sage.

Nicolas, P. (1988). From value to love. *Journal of Advertising Research, 28*, 7–8.

READING THE TEXT

1. How, according to John Fiske, is television programming gendered?

2. Why is male camaraderie such a common motif in "men's men" advertising, according to Craig?

3. What roles do women tend to play in the two types of commercials aimed at men? What roles do men tend to play in the two types of commercials aimed at women?

4. Why does Craig believe that "a threat to patriarchy is an economic threat" (para. 30)?

READING THE SIGNS

1. In class, discuss whether you agree with Craig's interpretations of the four commercials that he describes. If you disagree, what alternative analysis do you propose?

2. The four commercials Craig analyzes aired in 1990. View some current commercials broadcast during daytime and sports programs. Use your observations as the basis for an argument about whether the gendered patterns in advertising that Craig outlines exist today. If the patterns persist, what implications does that have for the tenacity of gender codes? If you see differences, how can you account for them?

3. Write an essay in which you support, refute, or modify Craig's belief that gendered advertising of the sort he describes is "dehumanizing" (para. 29).

4. **CONNECTING TEXTS**   Do metrosexuals fit any of the four patterns that Craig describes (see Warren St. John, "Metrosexuals Come Out," p. 217)? If so, explain your reasoning; if not, create your own fifth pattern to fit this type of consumer.

5. Watch TV programs that are not overtly geared toward one gender, such as prime-time drama or network news. To what extent does the advertising that accompanies these shows fit Craig's four categories of gender portrayal? How do you account for your findings?

6. **CONNECTING TEXTS**   Enter the debate over the origins of gender identity: Is it primarily biological or largely socially constructed? Write an essay in which you advance your position; you can develop your ideas by consulting Andre Mayer's "The New Sexual Stone Age" (p. 312), Aaron Devor's "Gender Role Behaviors and Attitudes" (p. 567), Deborah Blum's "The Gender Blur: Where Does Biology End and Society Take Over?" (p. 573), or Mariah Burton Nelson's "I Won. I'm Sorry" (p. 539).

JENNIFER L. POZNER

Dove's "Real Beauty" Backlash

*It sounds almost like the Macy's Santa Claus advising shoppers to look
for something at Gimbel's in Miracle on 34th Street, but there you have
it: Dove's "Campaign for Real Beauty" is actually telling ordinary girls
and women to feel good about themselves. And, for the most part, Jennifer L. Pozner is rather glad it is, even if the Dove ads are still aimed at
selling beauty products according to the implicit philosophy that "cellulite is unsightly, women's natural aging process is shameful, and
flabby thighs are flawed and must be fixed." No, what angers Pozner are
the male media figures who have voiced dismay at Dove's display of
women with realistic figures and faces, some of whom dare to be middle-
aged. Indeed, for Pozner, it is the commentary of such men that makes
the Dove campaign so necessary in the first place. Pozner is executive
director of Women In Media & News.*

When it comes to Madison Avenue misogyny, usually it's the ad that's objectionable (hello, *Advertising Week!*), rather than the product itself.

The opposite is true in the latest incarnation of Dove's "Campaign for
Real Beauty," which poses a bevy of full-figured babes in bras and boyshorts
on billboards throughout New York, Chicago, DC, LA and other top urban
markets . . . just in time for the rollout of their new line of "firming cremes."

If the same smiling size sixes (and eights, and tens) were hawking hair
dye or shilling for soap, the campaign would be revolutionary — but despite
the company's continued and commendable intent to expand notions of
female beauty to include the non-skinny and non-white, Dove's attempts are
profoundly limited by a product line that comes with its own underlying philosophy: cellulite is unsightly, women's natural aging process is shameful, and
flabby thighs are flawed and must be fixed . . . oh, so conveniently by Dove's
newest lotion.

The feel-good "women are ok at whatever size" message is hopelessly
hampered by the underlying attempt to get us to spend, spend, spend to "correct" those pesky "problem areas" advertisers have always told us to hate
about our bodies. As Salon.com's Rebecca Traister put it, the message is "love
your ass but not the fat on it."

Yet even though Dove's "Real Beauty" ads play to and subtly reinforce the 5
stereotypes they claim to be exposing, it's impossible not to feel inspired by
the sight of these attractive, healthy women smiling playfully at us from their
places of billboard honor, their voluptuous curves all the more luscious alongside the bags-of-bones in competitors' campaigns.

Gina Crisanti was featured in Dove's campaign.

Unless, of course, you're *Chicago Sun Times* columnist Richard Roeper, who reacted to Dove's "chunky women" with the sort of fear and loathing he should reserve for the cheesy Hollywood schlock he regularly "thumbs up" during his Ebert & Roeper film reviews. "I find these Dove ads a little unsettling. If I want to see plump gals baring too much skin, I'll go to Taste of Chicago, OK?," Roeper ranted, saying that while he knows he should probably praise Dove for breaking away from airbrushed, impossible-to-achieve, youth-obsessed ad imagery, he much prefers to bitch and moan. "When we're talking women in their underwear on billboards outside my living room windows, give me the fantasy babes, please. If that makes me sound superficial, shallow and sexist — well yes, I'm a man."

Unsettling? Try Roeper's implication that all men are just naturally sexist — and that a man who wears gender-based bigotry as a badge of pride has some of the most power in the media to determine which films succeed and which fail. (Remember Reoper's admission next time his thumb goes way up for a flick whose humor rarely rises above cheap gags about sperm as hair gel, or when he pans a promising movie centered around strong female characters.)

Dozens of major media outlets jumped on Roeper's comments as an excuse to run insulting headlines such as "Fab or Flab," with stories exploring the "controversy" over whether Dove's ads are, as *People* put it, "the best thing to happen to advertising since the free sample, or an eyesore of outsize proportions."

The tone of this debate turned nasty, quickly, with women's self esteem in one camp and men's fragile eyes in another as typified by a second *Sun Times* writer's comments that these "disturbing" and "frightening" women should "put on clothes (please, really)" because "ads should be about the beautiful people. They should include the unrealistic, the ideal or the unattainable look for which so many people strive." Besides, wrote Lucio Guerrero, "the only time I want to see a thigh that big is in a bucket with bread crumbs on it."

From there, print and broadcast outlets featured a stream of man-on-   10
the-street interviews begging Madison Avenue to bring back the starvation-saturated, silicone enhanced sweeties they'd come to expect seeing on their commutes to work, echoing Guerrero's mean-spirited musings.

Some masked their aesthetic objections under the guise of health concerns: "At the risk of sounding politically incorrect," Bill Zwecker, the balding, paunchy, middle-aged anchor of CBS's local newscast in Chicago, weighed in on his CBS blog, "In this day and age, when we are facing a huge obesity problem in this country, we don't need to encourage anyone — women OR men — to think it's okay to be out of shape." Perhaps this line of attack would have been more convincing if the women in the ads were unhealthily overweight (they're actually smaller-sized than the average American woman), or if Zwecker was a little more *GQ* and a little less *Couch Potato Quarterly*.

Certainly, these men so quick to demonize "the Dove girls" show no understanding that those "fantasy babes" of traditional ads have a profoundly negative impact on the health of girls and women in America. Advertising has never glorified obesity (though that problem is arguably a byproduct of McDonalds, M&Ms and other junk food ads), but the industry has equated starvation and drug addiction with women's beauty and value for decades.

The "real beauty" backlash underscores just how necessary Dove's campaign is — however hypocritical the product they're selling may be. What's "unsettling" is not that Roeper, Guerrero and Zwecker might have to look at empowerment-infused ads targeted to female consumers — it's that men with power positions in the media still think it's acceptable to demand that women be displayed only in the hyper-objectifying images they feel is somehow their due.

READING THE TEXT

1. Why does Pozner believe that Dove's "Real Beauty" ads "reinforce the stereotypes they claim to be exposing" (para. 5)?

2. In Pozner's view, what is the basis of the objections that Richard Roeper and some other male commentators have to the Dove "Campaign for Real Beauty"?

3. Characterize Pozner's tone in this selection, particularly in her comments regarding male critics of Dove's ads. What effect does it have on your response to her essay?

READING THE SIGNS

1. In a creative journal assignment, assume the perspective of one of the Dove "Real Beauty" models and write a letter in response to Richard Roeper's complaints about the Dove ads.

2. Write an argumentative essay that validates, rejects, or complicates Pozner's claim that "the 'real beauty' backlash underscores just how necessary Dove's campaign is — however hypocritical the product they're selling may be" (para. 13).

3. Write an essay evaluating Richard Roeper's response to the Dove ad campaign. To what extent is it "unsettling" (para. 7), as Pozner sees it, or do you find it to be simply honest?

4. **CONNECTING TEXTS**   Write an essay arguing whether ad campaigns such as Dove's "Real Beauty" and Nike's "My Butt Is Big" are indeed revolutionary or simply a new twist on advertising's tendency to objectify women's bodies. To develop your ideas, read or reread Courtney Martin's "The Famine Mystique" (p. 607).

WARREN ST. JOHN
Metrosexuals Come Out

They've been lampooned on The Simpsons *and pampered on* Queer Eye *for the Straight Guy — and Madison Avenue is taking notice. "They" are that category of consumers popularly known as "metrosexuals": straight young men whose fashion and grooming tastes have crossed over into areas once reserved for feminine consumption. As Warren St. John reports in this analysis of the metrosexual phenomenon on the eve of* Queer Eye's *debut in 2003, the metrosexual is a tempting target for marketers, offering a growing market for goods traditionally coded for women. St. John is a reporter for the* New York Times, *where this selection was first published, and the author of* Rammer, Jammer, Yellow Hammer *(2004).*

By his own admission, 30-year-old Karru Martinson is not what you'd call a manly man. He uses a $40 face cream, wears Bruno Magli shoes and custom-tailored shirts. His hair is always just so, thanks to three brands of shampoo and the precise application of three hair grooming products: Textureline Smoothing Serum, got2b styling glue and Suave Rave hairspray. Mr. Martinson likes wine bars and enjoys shopping with his gal pals, who have come to trust

Actor Jeffrey Donovan examines
skin care products at Kiehl's, an
upscale boutique.

his eye for color, his knack for seeing when a bag clashes with an outfit, and his understanding of why some women have 47 pairs of black shoes. ("Because they can!" he said.) He said his guy friends have long thought his consumer and grooming habits a little . . . different. But Mr. Martinson, who lives in Manhattan and works in finance, said he's not that different. "From a personal perspective there was never any doubt what my sexual orientation was," he said. "I'm straight as an arrow."

So it was with a mixture of relief and mild embarrassment that Mr. Martinson was recently asked by a friend in marketing to be part of a focus group of "metrosexuals" — straight urban men willing, even eager, to embrace their feminine sides. Convinced that these open-minded young men hold the secrets of tomorrow's consumer trends, the advertising giant Euro RSCG, with 233 offices worldwide, wanted to better understand their buying habits. So in a private room at the Manhattan restaurant Eleven Madison Park recently, Mr. Martinson answered the marketers' questions and schmoozed with 11 like-minded straight guys who were into Diesel jeans, interior design, yoga and Mini Coopers, and who would never think of ordering a vodka tonic without specifying Grey Goose or Ketel One. Before the focus group met, Mr. Martinson said he was suspicious that such a thing as a metrosexual existed. Afterward, he said, "I'm fully aware that I have those characteristics."

America may be on the verge of a metrosexual moment. On July 15, Bravo will present a makeover show, *Queer Eye for the Straight Guy*, in which a team of five gay men "transform a style-deficient and culture-deprived straight man from drab to fab," according to the network. Condé Nast is developing a shopping magazine for men, modeled after *Lucky*, its successful women's magazine, which is largely a text-free catalog of clothes and shoes. There is no end to the curious new vanity products for young men, from a *Maxim*-magazine-branded hair coloring system to Axe, Unilever's all-over body deodorant for guys. And men are going in for self-improvement strategies traditionally associated with women. For example, the number of plastic surgery procedures on men in the United States has increased threefold since 1997, to 807,000, according to the American Society for Aesthetic Plastic Surgery.

"Their heightened sense of aesthetics is very, very pronounced," Marian Salzman, chief strategy officer at Euro RSCG, who organized the gathering at Eleven Madison Park, said of metrosexuals. "They're the style makers. It doesn't mean your average Joe American is going to copy everything they do," she added. "But unless you study these guys you don't know where Joe American is heading."

Paradoxically, the term metrosexual, which is now being embraced by   5 marketers, was coined in the mid-90's to mock everything marketers stand for. The gay writer Mark Simpson used the word to satirize what he saw as consumerism's toll on traditional masculinity. Men didn't go to shopping malls, buy glossy magazines or load up on grooming products, Mr. Simpson argued, so consumer culture promoted the idea of a sensitive guy — who went to malls, bought magazines and spent freely to improve his personal appearance.

Within a few years, the term was picked up by British advertisers and newspapers. In 2001, Britain's Channel Four brought out a show about sensitive guys called *Metrosexuality*. And in recent years the European media found a metrosexual icon in David Beckham, the English soccer star, who paints his fingernails, braids his hair and poses for gay magazines, all while maintaining a manly profile on the pitch. Along with terms like "PoMosexual," "just gay enough" and "flaming heterosexuals," the word metrosexual is now gaining currency among American marketers who are fumbling for a term to describe this new type of feminized man.

America has a long tradition of sensitive guys. Alan Alda, John Lennon, even Al Gore all heard the arguments of the feminist movement and empathized. Likewise, there's a history of dashing men like Cary Grant and Humphrey Bogart who managed to affect a personal style with plenty of hair goop but without compromising their virility. Even Harrison Ford, whose favorite accessory was once a hammer, now poses proudly wearing an earring. But what separates the modern-day metrosexual from his touchy-feely forebears is a care-free attitude toward the inevitable suspicion that a man who dresses well, has good manners, understands thread counts or has opinions on women's fashion is gay.

"If someone's going to judge me on what kind of moisturizer I have on my shelf, whatever," said Marc d'Avignon, 28, a graduate student living in the East Village, who describes himself as "horrendously addicted to Diesel jeans" and living amid a chemistry lab's worth of Kiehl's lotions. "It doesn't bother me at all. Call it homosexual, feminine, hip, not hip—I don't care. I like draw-ing from all sorts of sources to create my own persona."

While some metrosexuals may simply be indulging in pursuits they had avoided for fear of being suspected as gay—like getting a pedicure or wear-ing brighter colors—others consciously appropriate tropes of gay culture the way white suburban teenagers have long cribbed from hip-hop culture, as a way of distinguishing themselves from the pack. Having others question their sexuality is all part of the game. "Wanting them to wonder and having them wonder is a wonderful thing," said Daniel Peres, the editor in chief of *Details*, a kind of metrosexual bible. "It gives you an air of mystery: could he be? It makes you stand out."

Standing out requires staying on top of which products are hip and which   10
are not. Marketers refer to such style-obsessed shoppers as prosumers, or urban influentials—educated customers who are picky or just vain enough to spend more money or to make an extra effort in pursuit of their personal look. A man who wants to buy Clinique for Men, for example, has to want the stuff so badly that he will walk up to the women's cosmetics counter in a department store, where Clinique for Men is sold. A man who wants Diesel jeans has to be willing to pay $135 a pair. A man who insists on Grey Goose has to get comfortable with paying $14 for a martini. "The guy who drinks Grey Goose is willing to pay extra," said Lee Einsidler, executive vice president of Sydney Frank Importing, which owns Grey Goose. "He does it in all things in his life. He doesn't buy green beans, he buys haricots verts."

Other retailers hope to entice the man on the fence to get in touch with his metrosexual side. Oliver Sweatman, the chief executive of Sharps, a new line of grooming products aimed at young urban men, said that to lure manly men to buy his new-age shaving gels—which contain Roman chamomile, gotu kola and green tea—the packaging is a careful mixture of old and new imagery. The fonts recall the masculinity of an old barber shop, but a funny picture of a goat on the label implies, he said, something out of the ordinary.

In an effort to out closeted metrosexuals, Ms. Salzman and her marketing team at Euro RSCG are working at perfecting polling methods that will iden-tify "metrosexual markers." One, she noted, is that metrosexuals like telling their friends about their new finds. Mr. Martinson, the Bruno Magli–wearing metrosexual, agreed. "I'm not in marketing," he said. "But when you take a step back, and say, 'Hey, I e-mailed my friends about a great vodka or a great Off Broadway show,' in essence I am a marketer and I'm doing it for free."

Most metrosexuals, though, see their approach to life as serving their own interests in the most important marketing contest of all: the battle for babes. Their pitch to women: you're getting the best of both worlds.

Some women seem to buy it. Alycia Oaklander, a 29-year-old fashion pub-licist from Manhattan, fell for John Kilpatrick, a Washington Redskins season ticket holder who loves Budweiser and grilling hot dogs, in part because of his passion for shopping and women's fashion shows. On their first dates,

Mr. Kilpatrick brought champagne, cooked elaborate meals and talked the talk about Ms. Oaklander's shoes. They were married yesterday. "He loves sports and all the guy stuff," Ms. Oaklander said. "But on the other hand he loves to cook and he loves design. It balances out."

The proliferation of metrosexuals is even having an impact in gay circles. 15 Peter Paige, a gay actor who plays the character Emmett on the Showtime series *Queer as Folk*, frequently complains in interviews that he's having a harder time than ever telling straight men from gays. "They're all low-slung jeans and working out with six packs and more hair product than I've ever used in my life, and they smell better than your mother on Easter," he said. Mr. Paige said there was at least one significant difference between hitting on metrosexuals and their less evolved predecessors. "Before, you used to get punched," he said. "Now it's all, 'Gee thanks, I'm straight but I'm really flattered.'"

READING THE TEXT

1. Write your own definition of the term *metrosexual*.

2. Summarize the typical buying habits that marketers ascribe to metrosexuals.

3. How, according to St. John, do metrosexuals compare with such "sensitive" men as Alan Alda and John Lennon (para. 7)?

4. In St. John's view, how do women and gay men typically view metrosexuals?

READING THE SIGNS

1. Analyze an issue of *Details*, studying both the advertising and the articles. To what extent does it fit St. John's description of the magazine as the "metrosexual bible" (para. 9)?

2. Write an essay in which you support, refute, or complicate St. John's claim that "America may be on the verge of a metrosexual moment" (para. 3). To support your position, study men's magazines or the advertising that accompanies TV programs with substantial male viewership; you might research as well grooming products available in drug or department stores and the strategies used to market them.

3. **CONNECTING TEXTS** Read or reread Nell Bernstein's "Goin' Gangsta, Choosin' Cholita" (p. 691), and write an essay in which you assess the phenomenon of "trying on" a different identity, whether it be ethnic, as in Bernstein's essay, or gendered, as St. John discusses. What explanation can you give for its popularity?

4. **CONNECTING TEXTS** Read or reread James B. Twitchell's "What We Are to Advertisers" (p. 192). Where in the VALS2 + system would you locate metrosexuals, and why? If you do not see this group fitting in this system, how would you alter it to include metrosexuals?

ERIC SCHLOSSER
Kid Kustomers

Children rarely have much money of their own to spend, but they have a great deal of "pester power," along with the "leverage" to get their parents to buy them what they want. And so, as Eric Schlosser reports in this reading, Madison Avenue has been paying a great deal of attention to "kid kustomers" in recent years, pitching them everything from toys and candy to cell phones and automobiles. With more and more working couples spending more money on their kids to compensate for spending less time with them, Schlosser suggests, we are likely to see only an increase in such advertising in the years to come. Hmmm . . . are preteen dating services next? A correspondent for The Atlantic, *Schlosser is the author of* Fast Food Nation *(2001), from which this selection is taken, and* Reefer Madness: Sex, Drugs, and Cheap Labor in the American Black Market *(2003). In 2006 he published, with Charles Wilson, a book for young readers titled* Chew on This: Everything You Don't Want to Know about Fast Food.*

Twenty-five years ago, only a handful of American companies directed their marketing at children — Disney, McDonald's, candy makers, toy makers, manufacturers of breakfast cereal. Today children are being targeted by phone companies, oil companies, and automobile companies as well as clothing stores and restaurant chains. The explosion in children's advertising occurred during the 1980s. Many working parents, feeling guilty about spending less time with their kids, started spending more money on them. One marketing expert has called the 1980s "the decade of the child consumer." After largely ignoring children for years, Madison Avenue began to scrutinize and pursue them. Major ad agencies now have children's divisions, and a variety of marketing firms focus solely on kids. These groups tend to have sweet-sounding names: Small Talk, Kid Connection, Kid2Kid, the Gepetto Group, Just Kids, Inc. At least three industry publications — *Youth Market Alert*, *Selling to Kids*, and *Marketing to Kids Report* — cover the latest ad campaigns and market research. The growth in children's advertising has been driven by efforts to increase not just current, but also future, consumption. Hoping that nostalgic childhood memories of a brand will lead to a lifetime of purchases, companies now plan "cradle-to-grave" advertising strategies. They have come to believe what Ray Kroc and Walt Disney realized long ago — a person's "brand loyalty" may begin as early as the age of two. Indeed, market research has found that children often recognize a brand logo before they can recognize their own name.

The discontinued Joe Camel ad campaign, which used a hip cartoon character to sell cigarettes, showed how easily children can be influenced by the right corporate mascot. A 1991 study published in the *Journal of the American Medical Association* found that nearly all of America's six-year-olds could identify Joe Camel, who was just as familiar to them as Mickey Mouse. Another study found that one-third of the cigarettes illegally sold to minors were Camels. More recently, a marketing firm conducted a survey in shopping malls across the country, asking children to describe their favorite TV ads. According to the CME KidCom Ad Traction Study II, released at the 1999 Kids' Marketing Conference in San Antonio, Texas, the Taco Bell commercials featuring a talking chihuahua were the most popular fast food ads. The kids in the survey also liked Pepsi and Nike commercials, but their favorite television ad was for Budweiser.

The bulk of the advertising directed at children today has an immediate goal. "It's not just getting kids to whine," one marketer explained in *Selling to Kids*, "it's giving them a specific reason to ask for the product." Years ago sociologist Vance Packard described children as "surrogate salesmen" who had to persuade other people, usually their parents, to buy what they wanted. Marketers now use different terms to explain the intended response to their ads — such as "leverage," "the nudge factor," "pester power." The aim of most children's advertising is straightforward: Get kids to nag their parents and nag them well.

James U. McNeal, a professor of marketing at Texas A&M University, is considered America's leading authority on marketing to children. In his book *Kids As Customers* (1992), McNeal provides marketers with a thorough analysis of "children's requesting styles and appeals." He classifies juvenile nagging tactics into seven major categories. A *pleading* nag is one accompanied by

Do Frosted Flakes plus Yoda equal a "sugar-coated nag"?

repetitions of words like "please" or "mom, mom, mom." A *persistent* nag involves constant requests for the coveted product and may include the phrase "I'm gonna ask just one more time." *Forceful* nags are extremely pushy and may include subtle threats, like "Well, then, I'll go and ask Dad." *Demonstrative* nags are the most high-risk, often characterized by full-blown tantrums in public places, breath-holding, tears, a refusal to leave the store. *Sugar-coated* nags promise affection in return for a purchase and may rely on seemingly heartfelt declarations like "You're the best dad in the world." *Threatening* nags are youthful forms of blackmail, vows of eternal hatred and of running away if something isn't bought. *Pity* nags claim the child will be heartbroken, teased, or socially stunted if the parent refuses to buy a certain item. "All of these appeals and styles may be used in combination," McNeal's research has discovered, "but kids tend to stick to one or two of each that proved most effective . . . for their own parents."

McNeal never advocates turning children into screaming, breath-holding monsters. He has been studying "Kid Kustomers" for more than thirty years and believes in a more traditional marketing approach. "The key is getting children to see a firm . . . in much the same way as [they see] mom or dad, grandma or grandpa," McNeal argues. "Likewise, if a company can ally itself with universal values such as patriotism, national defense, and good health, it is likely to nurture belief in it among children."

Before trying to affect children's behavior, advertisers have to learn about their tastes. Today's market researchers not only conduct surveys of children in shopping malls, they also organize focus groups for kids as young as two or three. They analyze children's artwork, hire children to run focus groups, stage slumber parties and then question children into the night. They send cultural anthropologists into homes, stores, fast food restaurants, and other places where kids like to gather, quietly and surreptitiously observing the behavior of prospective customers. They study the academic literature on child development, seeking insights from the work of theorists such as Erik Erikson and Jean Piaget. They study the fantasy lives of young children; they apply the findings in advertisements and product designs.

Dan S. Acuff—the president of Youth Market System Consulting and the author of *What Kids Buy and Why* (1997)—stresses the importance of dream research. Studies suggest that until the age of six, roughly 80 percent of children's dreams are about animals. Rounded, soft creatures like Barney, Disney's animated characters, and the Teletubbies therefore have an obvious appeal to young children. The Character Lab, a division of Youth Market System Consulting, uses a proprietary technique called Character Appeal Quadrant Analysis to help companies develop new mascots. The technique purports to create imaginary characters who perfectly fit the targeted age group's level of cognitive and neurological development.

Children's clubs have for years been considered an effective means of targeting ads and collecting demographic information; the clubs appeal to a child's fundamental need for status and belonging. Disney's Mickey Mouse Club, formed in 1930, was one of the trailblazers. During the 1980s and 1990s, children's clubs proliferated, as corporations used them to solicit the names, addresses, zip codes, and personal comments of young customers. "Marketing messages sent through a club not only can be personalized," James McNeal advises, "they can be tailored for a certain age or geographical group." A well-designed and well-run children's club can be extremely good for business. According to one Burger King executive, the creation of a Burger King Kids Club in 1991 increased the sales of children's meals as much as 300 percent.

The Internet has become another powerful tool for assembling data about children. In 1998 a federal investigation of Web sites aimed at children found that 89 percent requested personal information from kids; only 1 percent required that children obtain parental approval before supplying the information. A character on the McDonald's Web site told children that Ronald McDonald was "the ultimate authority in everything." The site encouraged kids to send Ronald an e-mail revealing their favorite menu item at McDonald's, their favorite book, their favorite sports team — and their name. Fast food Web sites no longer ask children to provide personal information without first gaining parental approval; to do so is now a violation of federal law, thanks to the Children's Online Privacy Protection Act, which took effect in April of 2000.

Despite the growing importance of the Internet, television remains the 10 primary medium for children's advertising. The effects of these TV ads have long been a subject of controversy. In 1978, the Federal Trade Commission (FTC) tried to ban all television ads directed at children seven years old or younger. Many studies had found that young children often could not tell the difference between television programming and television advertising. They also could not comprehend the real purpose of commercials and trusted that advertising claims were true. Michael Pertschuk, the head of the FTC, argued that children need to be shielded from advertising that preys upon their immaturity. "They cannot protect themselves," he said, "against adults who exploit their present-mindedness."

The FTC's proposed ban was supported by the American Academy of Pediatrics, the National Congress of Parents and Teachers, the Consumers Union, and the Child Welfare League, among others. But it was attacked by the National Association of Broadcasters, the Toy Manufacturers of America, and the Association of National Advertisers. The industry groups lobbied Congress to prevent any restrictions on children's ads and sued in federal court to block Pertschuk from participating in future FTC meetings on the subject. In April of 1981, three months after the inauguration of President Ronald Reagan, an FTC staff report argued that a ban on ads aimed at children would be impractical, effectively killing the proposal. "We are delighted by the FTC's reasonable recommendation," said the head of the National Association of Broadcasters.

The Saturday-morning children's ads that caused angry debates twenty years ago now seem almost quaint. Far from being banned, TV advertising aimed at kids is now broadcast twenty-four hours a day, closed-captioned and in stereo. Nickelodeon, the Disney Channel, the Cartoon Network, and the other children's cable networks are now responsible for about 80 percent of all television viewing by kids. None of these networks existed before 1979. The typical American child now spends about twenty-one hours a week watching television — roughly one and a half months of TV every year. That does not include the time children spend in front of a screen watching videos, playing video games, or using the computer. Outside of school, the typical American child spends more time watching television than doing any other activity except sleeping. During the course of a year, he or she watches more than thirty thousand TV commercials. Even the nation's youngest children are watching a great deal of television. About one-quarter of American children between the ages of two and five have a TV in their room.

READING THE TEXT

1. Why, according to Schlosser, did an "explosion in children's advertising" (para. 1) occur during the 1980s?

2. What is "pester power" (para. 3), and how is it used as a marketing strategy?

3. How has the Internet contributed to the expansion in advertising directed toward children, according to Schlosser?

4. What strategies does Schlosser say marketers use to determine children's tastes in products?

READING THE SIGNS

1. Watch a morning of Saturday cartoon shows on TV and make a list of all the products that are advertised. What products are directly tied in to the show? Use your observations as the basis for an essay in which you analyze the relationship between children's programming and the advertising that supports it.

2. Perform a semiotic analysis of an advertisement from any medium directed at children. What signifiers in the ad are especially addressed to children? Consider such details as the implied narrative of the ad, its characters, and their appearance, colors, music, and voice track.

3. Conduct an in-class debate over whether children's advertising should be more strictly regulated. To develop support for your team's position, watch some TV programs aimed at children and the advertising that accompanies it.

4. **CONNECTING TEXTS** Read or reread James B. Twitchell's "What We Are to Advertisers" (p. 192) and write an essay in which you analyze whether Twitchell's assertion that "mass marketing means the creation of mass stereotypes" (para. 1) applies to child consumers.

GLORIA STEINEM
Sex, Lies, and Advertising

One of the best-known icons of the women's movement, Gloria Steinem has been a leader in transforming the image of women in America. As a cofounder of Ms. *magazine, in which this selection first appeared, Steinem has provided a forum for women's voices for more than thirty years, but as her article explains, it has not been easy to keep this forum going. A commercial publication requires commercials, and the needs of advertisers do not always mesh nicely with the goals of a magazine like* Ms. *Steinem ruefully reveals the compromises* Ms. *magazine had to make over the years to satisfy its advertising clients, compromises that came to an end only when* Ms. *ceased to take ads. Steinem's publications include* Revolution from Within *(1992), a personal exploration of the power of self-esteem;* Moving beyond Words *(1994); and* Outrageous Acts and Everyday Rebellions *(2nd ed., 1995). Currently the president of Voters for Choice and a consulting editor for* Ms., *Steinem continues to combine her passion for writing and activism as an unflagging voice in American feminism.*

Goodbye to cigarette ads where poems should be.
Goodbye to celebrity covers and too little space.
Goodbye to cleaning up language so *Ms.* advertisers won't be boycotted by the Moral Majority.
In fact, goodbye to advertisers *and* the Moral Majority.
Goodbye to short articles and short thinking.
Goodbye to "post-feminism" from people who never say "post-democracy."
Goodbye to national boundaries and hello to the world.
Welcome to the magazine of the post-patriarchal age.
The turn of the century is *our turn!*

That was my celebratory mood in the summer of 1990 when I finished the original version of the exposé you are about to read. I felt as if I'd been released from a personal, portable Bastille. At least I'd put on paper the ad policies that had been punishing *Ms.* for all the years of its nonconforming life and still were turning more conventional media, especially (but not only) those directed at women, into a dumping ground for fluff.

Those goodbyes were part of a letter inviting readers to try a new, ad-free version of *Ms.* and were also a homage to "Goodbye to All That," a witty and lethal essay in which Robin Morgan bade farewell to the pre-feminist male Left of twenty years before. It seemed the right tone for the birth of a brand-new, reader-supported, more international form of *Ms.*, which Robin was heading as editor-in-chief, and I was serving as consulting editor. Besides,

I had a very personal kind of mantra running through my head: *I'll never have to sell another ad as long as I live.*

So I sent the letter off, watched the premiere issue containing my exposé go to press, and then began to have second thoughts: Were ad policies too much of an "inside" concern? Did women readers already know that magazines directed at them were filled with editorial extensions of ads — and not care? Had this deceptive system been in place too long for anyone to have faith in changing it? In other words: Would anybody give a damn?

After almost four years of listening to responses and watching the ripples spread out from this pebble cast upon the waters, I can tell you that, yes, readers do care; and no, most of them were not aware of advertising's control over the words and images around it. Though most people in the publishing industry think this is a practice too deeply embedded ever to be uprooted, a lot of readers are willing to give it a try — even though that's likely to mean paying more for their publications. In any case, as they point out, understanding the nitty-gritty of ad influence has two immediate uses. It strengthens healthy skepticism about what we read, and it keeps us from assuming that other women must want this glamorous, saccharine, unrealistic stuff.

Perhaps that's the worst punishment ad influence has inflicted upon us. 5 It's made us feel contemptuous of other women. We know we don't need those endless little editorial diagrams of where to put our lipstick or blush — we don't identify with all those airbrushed photos of skeletal women with everything about them credited, *even their perfume* (can you imagine a man's photo airbrushed to perfection, with his shaving lotion credited?) — but we assume there must be women out there somewhere who *do* love it; otherwise, why would it be there?

Well, many don't. Given the sameness of women's magazines resulting from the demands made by makers of women's products that advertise in all of them, we probably don't know yet what a wide variety of women readers want. In any case, we do know it's the advertisers who are determining what women are getting now.

The first wave of response to this exposé came not from readers but from writers and editors for other women's magazines. They phoned to say the pall cast by anticipated or real advertising demands was even more widespread than rebellious *Ms.* had been allowed to know. They told me how brave I was to "burn my bridges" (no critic of advertising would ever be hired as an editor of any of the women's magazines, they said) and generally treated me as if I'd written about organized crime instead of practices that may be unethical but are perfectly legal. After making me promise not to use their names, they offered enough additional horror stories to fill a book, a movie, and maybe a television series. Here is a typical one: when the freelance author of an article on moisturizers observed in print that such products might be less necessary for young women — whose skin tends to be not dry but oily — the article's editor was called on the carpet and denounced by her bosses as "anti-moisturizer." Or how about this: the film critic for a women's magazine asked

Gloria Steinem (left) and Patricia Carbine cofounded *Ms.* magazine.

its top editor, a woman who makes millions for her parent company, whether movies could finally be reviewed critically, since she had so much clout. No, said the editor; if you can't praise a movie, just don't include it; otherwise we'll jeopardize our movie ads. This may sound like surrealism in everyday life, or like our grandmothers advising, "If you can't say something nice, don't say anything," but such are the forces that control much of our information.

I got few negative responses from insiders, but the ones I did get were bitter. Two editors at women's magazines felt I had demeaned them by writing the article. They loved their work, they said, and didn't feel restricted by ads at all. So I would like to make clear in advance that my purpose was and is to change the system, not to blame the people struggling within it. As someone who has written for most women's magazines, I know that many editors work hard to get worthwhile articles into the few pages left over after providing all the "complementary copy" (that is, articles related to and supportive of advertised products). I also know there are editors who sincerely want exactly what the advertisers want, which is why they're so good at their jobs. Nonetheless, criticizing this ad-dominant system is no different from criticizing male-dominant marriage. Both institutions make some people happy, and both seem free as long as your wishes happen to fall within their traditional boundaries. But just as making more equal marital laws alleviates the suffering of many, breaking the link between editorial and advertising will help all media become more honest and diverse.

A second wave of reaction came from advertising executives who were asked to respond by reporters. They attributed all problems to *Ms.* We must have been too controversial or otherwise inappropriate for ads. I saw no stories that asked the next questions: Why had non-women's companies from Johnson & Johnson to IBM found our "controversial" pages fine for their ads? Why did desirable and otherwise unreachable customers read something so "inappropriate"? What were ad policies doing to *other* women's media? To continue my marriage parallel, however, I should note that these executives seemed only mildly annoyed. Just as many women are more dependent than men on the institution of marriage and so are more threatened and angry when it's questioned, editors of women's magazines tended to be more upset than advertisers when questioned about their alliance. . . .

Then came the third wave — reader letters which were smart, thoughtful, 10 innovative, and numbered in the hundreds. Their dominant themes were anger and relief: relief because those vast uncritical oceans of food/fashion/ beauty articles in other women's magazines weren't necessarily what women wanted after all, and also relief because *Ms.* wasn't going to take ads anymore, even those that were accompanied by fewer editorial demands; anger because consumer information, diverse articles, essays, fiction, and poetry could have used the space instead of all those oceans of articles about ad categories that had taken up most of women's magazines for years. . . .

Last and most rewarding was the response that started in the fall. Teachers of journalism, advertising, communications, women's studies, and other contemporary courses asked permission to reprint the exposé as a supplementary text. That's another reason why I've restored cuts, updated information, and added new examples — including this introduction. Getting subversive ideas into classrooms could change the next generation running the media.

The following pages are mostly about women's magazines, but that doesn't mean other media are immune.

Sex, Lies, and Advertising

Toward the end of the 1980s, when glasnost was beginning and *Ms.* magazine seemed to be ending, I was invited to a press lunch for a Soviet official. He entertained us with anecdotes about the new problems of democracy in his country; for instance, local Communist leaders who were being criticized by their own media for the first time, and were angry.

"So I'll have to ask my American friends," he finished pointedly, "how more subtly to control the press."

In the silence that followed, I said: "Advertising."   15

The reporters laughed, but later one of them took me aside angrily: How dare I suggest that freedom of the press was limited in this country? How dare I imply that *his* newsmagazine could be influenced by ads?

I explained that I wasn't trying to lay blame, but to point out advertising's media-wide influence. We can all recite examples of "soft" cover stories that newsmagazines use to sell ads, and self-censorship in articles that should have taken advertised products to task for, say, safety or pollution. Even television news goes "soft" in ratings wars, and other TV shows don't get on the air without advertiser support. But I really had been thinking about women's magazines. There, it isn't just a little content that's designed to attract ads; it's almost all of it. That's why advertisers — not readers — had always been the problem for *Ms.* As the only women's magazine that didn't offer what the ad world euphemistically describes as "supportive editorial atmosphere" or "complementary copy" (for instance, articles that praise food/fashion/beauty subjects in order to "support" and "complement" food/fashion/beauty ads), *Ms.* could never attract enough ads to break even.

"Oh, *women*'s magazines," the journalist said with contempt. "Everybody knows they're catalogs — but who cares? They have nothing to do with journalism."

I can't tell you how many times I've had this argument since I started writing for magazines in the early 1960s, and especially since the current women's movement began. Except as moneymaking machines — "cash cows," as they are so elegantly called in the trade — women's magazines are usually placed beyond the realm of serious consideration. Though societal changes being forged by women have been called more far-reaching than the industrial revolution by such nonfeminist sources as the *Wall Street Journal* — and though women's magazine editors often try hard to reflect these changes in the few pages left after all the ad-related subjects are covered — the magazines serving the female half of this country are still far below the journalistic and ethical standards of news and general-interest counterparts. Most depressing of all, this fact is so taken for granted that it doesn't even rate an exposé.

For instance: If *Time* and *Newsweek*, in order to get automotive and GM ads, had to lavish editorial praise on cars and credit photographs in which newsmakers were driving, say, a Buick from General Motors, there would be a scandal — maybe even a criminal investigation. When women's magazines from *Seventeen* to *Lear's* publish articles lavishing praise on beauty and fashion products, and credit in text, the cover, and other supposedly editorial photographs a particular makeup from Revlon or a dress from Calvin Klein because those companies also advertise, it's just business as usual.

When *Ms.* began, we didn't consider *not* taking ads. The most important reason was to keep the price of a feminist magazine low enough for most women to afford. But the second and almost equal reason was to provide a forum where women and advertisers could talk to each other and experiment with nonstereotyped, informative, imaginative ads. After all, advertising was (and is) as potent a source of information in this country as news or TV or movies. It's where we get not only a big part of our information but also images that shape our dreams.

We decided to proceed in two stages. First, we would convince makers of "people products" that their ads should be placed in a women's magazine: cars, credit cards, insurance, sound equipment, financial services — everything that's used by both men and women but was then advertised only to men. Since those advertisers were accustomed to the division between editorial pages and ads that news and general-interest magazines at least try to maintain, such products would allow our editorial content to be free and diverse. Furthermore, if *Ms.* could prove that women were important purchasers of "people products," just as men were, those advertisers would support other women's magazines, too, and subsidize some pages for articles about something other than the hothouse worlds of food/fashion/beauty. Only in the second phase would we add examples of the best ads for whatever traditional "women's products" (clothes, shampoo, fragrance, food, and so on) that subscriber surveys showed *Ms.* readers actually used. But we would ask those advertisers to come in *without* the usual quid pro quo of editorial features praising their product area; that is, the dreaded "complementary copy."

From the beginning, we knew the second step might be even harder than the first. Clothing advertisers like to be surrounded by editorial fashion spreads (preferably ones that credit their particular labels and designers); food advertisers have always expected women's magazines to publish recipes and articles on entertaining (preferably ones that require their products); and shampoo, fragrance, and beauty products in general insist on positive editorial coverage of beauty aids — a "beauty atmosphere," as they put it — plus photo credits for particular products and nothing too depressing; no bad news. That's why women's magazines look the way they do: saccharine, smiley-faced and product-heavy, with even serious articles presented in a slick and sanitized way.

But if *Ms.* could break this link between ads and editorial content, then we should add "women's products" too. For one thing, publishing ads only for gender-neutral products would give the impression that women have to become "like men" in order to succeed (an impression that *Ms.* ad pages sometimes *did* give when we were still in the first stage). For another, presenting a full circle of products that readers actually need and use would allow us to select the best examples of each category and keep ads from being lost in a sea of similar products. By being part of this realistic but unprecedented mix, products formerly advertised only to men would reach a growth market of women, and good ads for women's products would have a new visibility.

Given the intelligence and leadership of *Ms.* readers, both kinds of products would have unique access to a universe of smart consultants whose response would help them create more effective ads for other media too. Aside from the advertisers themselves, there's nobody who cares as much about the imagery in advertising as those who find themselves stereotyped or rendered invisible by it. And they often have great suggestions for making it better.

As you can see, we had all our energy, optimism, and arguments in good working order.

I thought at the time that our main problem would be getting ads with good "creative," as the imagery and text are collectively known. That was where the women's movement had been focusing its efforts, for instance, the National Organization for Women's awards to the best ads, and its "Barefoot and Pregnant" awards for the worst. Needless to say, there were plenty of candidates for the second group. Carmakers were still draping blondes in evening gowns over the hoods like ornaments that could be bought with the car (thus also making clear that car ads weren't directed at women). Even in ads for products that only women used, the authority figures were almost always male, and voice-overs for women's products on television were usually male too. Sadistic, he-man campaigns were winning industry praise; for example, *Advertising Age* hailed the infamous Silva Thin cigarette theme, "How to Get a Woman's Attention: Ignore Her," as "brilliant." Even in medical journals, ads for tranquilizers showed depressed housewives standing next to piles of dirty dishes and promised to get them back to work. As for women's magazines, they seemed to have few guidelines; at least none that excluded even the ads for the fraudulent breast-enlargement or thigh-thinning products for which their back pages were famous.

Obviously, *Ms.* would have to avoid such offensive imagery and seek out the best ads, but this didn't seem impossible. The *New Yorker* had been screening ads for aesthetic reasons for years, a practice that advertisers accepted at the time. *Ebony* and *Essence* were asking for ads with positive black images, and though their struggle was hard, their requests weren't seen as unreasonable. . . .

Let me take you through some of our experiences — greatly condensed, but just as they happened. In fact, if you poured water on any one of these, it would become a novel:

- Cheered on by early support from Volkswagen and one or two other car companies, we finally scrape together time and money to put on a major reception in Detroit. U.S. carmakers firmly believe that women choose the upholstery color, not the car, but we are armed with statistics and reader mail to prove the contrary: A car is an important purchase for women, one that is such a symbol of mobility and freedom that many women will spend a greater percentage of income for a car than will counterpart men.

But almost nobody comes. We are left with many pounds of shrimp on the table, and quite a lot of egg on our face. Assuming this near-total boycott is partly because there was a baseball pennant play-off the same day, we blame ourselves for not foreseeing the problem. Executives go out of their way to explain that they wouldn't have come anyway. It's a dramatic beginning for ten years of knocking on resistant or hostile doors, presenting endless documentation of women as car buyers, and hiring a full-time saleswoman in Detroit — all necessary before *Ms.* gets any real results.

This long saga has a semi-happy ending: Foreign carmakers understood better than Detroit that women buy cars, and advertised in *Ms.*; also years of research on the women's market plus door-knocking began to pay off. Eventually, cars became one of our top sources of ad revenue. Even Detroit began to take the women's market seriously enough to put car ads in other women's magazines too, thus freeing a few more of their pages from the food/fashion/beauty hothouse.

But long after figures showed that a third, even half, of many car models were being bought by women, U.S. makers continued to be uncomfortable addressing female buyers. Unlike many foreign carmakers, Detroit never quite learned the secret of creating intelligent ads that exclude no one and then placing them in media that overcome past exclusion. Just as an African American reader may feel more invited by a resort that placed an ad in *Ebony* or *Essence*, even though the same ad appeared in *Newsweek*, women of all races may need to see ads for cars, computers, and other historically "masculine" products in media that are clearly directed at them. Once inclusive ads are well placed, however, there's interest and even gratitude from women. *Ms.* readers were so delighted to be addressed as intelligent consumers by a routine Honda ad with text about rack-and-pinion steering, for example, that they sent fan mail. But even now, Detroit continues to ask: "Should we make special ads for women?" That's probably one reason why foreign cars still have a greater share of the women's market in the United States than of the men's.

• In the *Ms.* Gazette, we do a brief report on a congressional hearing into coal tar derivatives used in hair dyes that are absorbed through the skin and may be carcinogenic. This seems like news of importance: Newspapers and newsmagazines are reporting it too. But Clairol, a Bristol-Myers subsidiary that makes dozens of products, a few of which have just come into our pages as ads *without* the usual quid pro quo of articles on hair and beauty, is outraged. Not at newspapers or newsmagazines, just at us. It's bad enough that *Ms.* is the only women's magazine refusing to provide "supportive editorial" praising beauty products, but to criticize one of their product categories on top of it, however generically or even accurately — well, *that* is going too far.

We offer to publish a letter from Clairol telling its side of the story. In an excess of solicitousness, we even put this letter in the Gazette, not in Letters to the Editors, where it belongs. Eventually, Clairol even changes its hair-coloring formula, apparently in response to those same hearings. But in spite of surveys that show *Ms.* readers to be active women who use more of almost everything Clairol makes than do the readers of other women's magazines, *Ms.* gets almost no ads for those dozens of products for the rest of its natural life.

• Women of color read *Ms.* in disproportionate numbers. This is a source of pride to *Ms.* staffers, who are also more racially representative than the editors of other women's magazines (which may include some beautiful black models but almost no black decisionmakers; Pat Carbine hired the first black editor at *McCall's*, but she left when Pat did). Nonetheless, the reality of *Ms.*'s

Portfolio of Advertisements

READING THE SIGNS

Consider these questions as you analyze the advertisements on the following pages.

1. The robotic skateboarder featured in the Jeep ad is composed of many typical urban sights and symbols. Identify them and explain how they are intended to transform the image of a wilderness sport vehicle to an urban one.

2. The Mr. Rooter ad parodies the sort of article commonly found in women's magazines. What kind of article is that, and why do you think the ad makes use of it?

3. This ad by the American Egg Board can be associated with the ads run for milk consumption but is different in the way it specifies the interests and activities of its model. Without simply describing the ad, interpret the sort of consumer this ad would be likely to appeal to and why you think "Lisa Jones" was chosen for the campaign.

4. The Phoenix Wealth Management ad clearly appeals to female consumers. Study the models in the ad. What image of the target market is created, and to what attitudes toward gender roles and class is the ad appealing?

5. The San Diego Convention and Visitors Bureau ad is addressed to parents. What details, both pictorial and verbal, convey this? Why do you think the ad agency chose this comic take on family dynamics to achieve its purpose?

6. The Honda Pilot ad could be called a "piggy-back" ad because it plays on an already popular cultural phenomenon. Identify this piggy-back effect and describe the target market that the ad implies by using it.

7. What gender codes does the McCormick Gravy ad use to attract consumers to its product? Which generation is the presumed target of the ad? How can you tell?

INTRODUCING JEEP. COMPASS. THE URBAN RECREATIONAL VEHICLE.

It's time to start having fun with the city. The all new 2007 Jeep Compass comes with an advanced 172 hp 2.4L engi⸱

that gets up to 30 miles per gallon*, an available four-wheel-drive system, Electronic Stability Program (ESP) wi⸱

Brake Assist, as well as a Five-Star side-impact safety rating†. All for a starting price of $15,985‡

‡Limited model 4X4 as shown, $22,235. MSRPs exclude tax.
*2.4L engine EPA estimate of 26 city/30 highway for 5-speed manual-equipped 4X2 models.
†Based on NHTSA crash testing.
Jeep is a registered trademark of DaimlerChrysler Corporation.

Jeep

Is he right for you?

Is your plumber a keeper or should you throw him back? Take this quiz and find out.

When your plumber arrives he:
A. Parks on the street so he doesn't dirty your driveway
B. Parks in your driveway
C. Is dropped off by his mother

How would you describe your plumber's appearance?
A. Clean and professional
B. A tad messy
C. Cro-Magnon

When your plumber leaves, your home is:
A. As clean as when he arrived
B. Dirtier
C. A potential biohazard

When asked what the job is going to cost, your plumber:
A. Gives you a detailed pricing menu
B. Quotes a "round-about" figure
C. Asks, "How much ya' got?"

Ask Mr. Rooter®:

"My final bills never match the quotes my plumber gives me over the phone. What should I do?" – Amy, 35

Dear Amy,
Unless he has secret powers, no plumber can honestly know what a job's going to cost until he sees the problem for himself. A low estimate over the phone is just a way to win your business. You'd be better off with a plumber that comes and diagnoses your problem first. By the way, that's what I do. – Mr. Rooter

If you answered anything but A, it's time to find a new plumber.
If you answered nothing but A, you've obviously found Mr. Rooter®.
For the plumber you deserve visit MrRooter.com or call 877-Rooter-5.

Mr. Rooter™ PLUMBING

Lisa Jones is an
operations manager
kid dropper-offer
kid picker-upper
grocery shopper
garden planter
triathlon finisher
homework helper
Egg lover

The incredible edible egg.

Keep yourself going with the all-natural,
high quality protein only found in eggs.

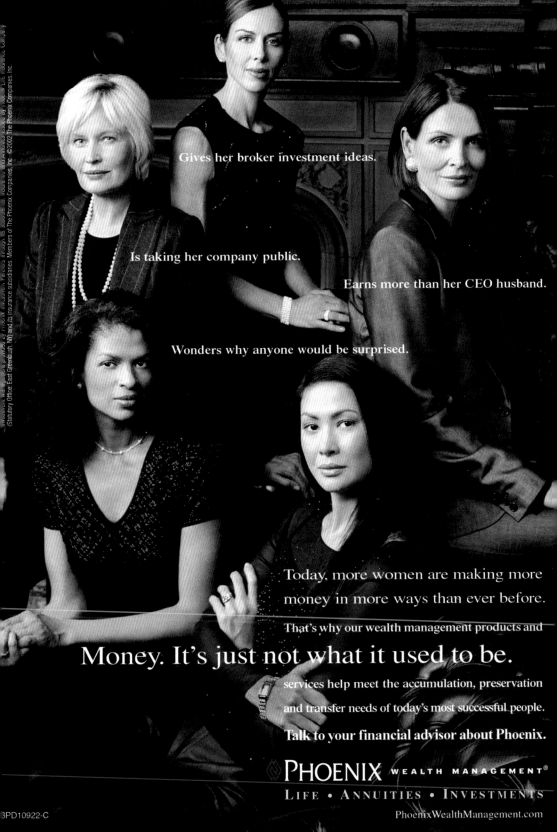

Don't take them on sucky vacations.

Remember, one day
they'll choose your

retirement home.

Book an extraordinary vacation at www.sandiego.org, the official travel resource for the San Diego region, and preserve your legacy before it's too late.

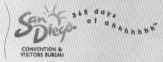

YourSpace.

he eight-passenger Honda Pilot. For those who need more than a home page to feel at ome, the Pilot's 244-hp engine, available heated leather seats and DVD Rear Entertainment ystem will give you a place to truly call your own.

The Pilot ⓗ **HONDA**

McCormick®

The Taste You Trust®

Three generations.

One secret ingredient.

Gravy you're proud to put on your holiday table.

All the makings of the
perfect holiday tradition.

The Taste You Trust™ **McCormick®**

Brown Gravy MIX

The Taste You Trust™ **McCormick®**

Turkey Gravy
MIX WITH OTHER NATURAL FLAVORS

©2007 McCormick & Co., Inc.

It was your mom's gravy. And some day, it'll be your daughter's.
But it will always start with McCormick®. Add your own personal
touch to our custom blend of herbs and spices, and pass down
the taste of McCormick Gravy from generation to generation.

**For great-tasting recipes, visit mccormick.com
or call 1-800-MEAL-TIPS**

staff and readership is obscured by ads filled with enough white women to make the casual reader assume *Ms.* is directed at only one part of the population, no matter what the editorial content is.

In fact, those few ads we are able to get that feature women of color — for instance, one made by Max Factor for *Essence* and *Ebony* that Linda Wachner gives us while she is president of Max Factor — are greeted with praise and relief by white readers, too, and make us feel that more inclusive ads should win out in the long run. But there are pathetically few such images. Advertising "creative" also excludes women who are not young, not thin, not conventionally pretty, well-to-do, able-bodied, or heterosexual — which is a hell of a lot of women.

- Our intrepid saleswomen set out early to attract ads for the product category known as consumer electronics: sound equipment, computers, calculators, VCRs, and the like. We know that *Ms.* readers are determined to be part of this technological revolution, not to be left out as women have been in the past. We also know from surveys that readers are buying this kind of stuff in numbers as high as those of readers of magazines like *Playboy* and the "male 18 to 34" market, prime targets of the industry. Moreover, unlike traditional women's products that our readers buy but don't want to read articles about, these are subjects they like to see demystified in our pages. There actually *is* a supportive editorial atmosphere.

"But women don't understand technology," say ad and electronics executives at the end of our presentations. "Maybe not," we respond, "but neither do men — and we all buy it."

"If women *do* buy it," counter the decisionmakers, "it's because they're 40 asking their husbands and boyfriends what to buy first." We produce letters from *Ms.* readers saying how turned off they are when salesmen say things like "Let me know when your husband can come in."

Then the argument turns to why there aren't more women's names sent back on warranties (those much-contested certificates promising repair or replacement if anything goes wrong). We explain that the husband's name may be on the warranty, even if the wife made the purchase. But it's also true that women are experienced enough as consumers to know that such promises are valid only if the item is returned in its original box at midnight in Hong Kong. Sure enough, when we check out hair dryers, curling irons, and other stuff women clearly buy, women don't return those warranties very often either. It isn't the women who are the problem, it's the meaningless warranties.

After several years of this, we get a few ads from companies like JVC and Pioneer for compact sound systems — on the grounds that women can understand compacts, but not sophisticated components. Harry Elias, vice president of JVC, is actually trying to convince his Japanese bosses that there is something called a woman's market. At his invitation, I find myself speaking at trade shows in Chicago and Las Vegas trying to persuade JVC dealers that electronics showrooms don't have to be locker rooms. But as becomes apparent, however, the trade shows are part of the problem. In Las Vegas, the only women working at technology displays are seminude models serving champagne. In Chicago, the big attraction is Marilyn Chambers, a porn star who followed Linda Lovelace of *Deep Throat* fame as Chuck Traynor's captive and/or employee, whose pornographic movies are being used to demonstrate VCRs.

In the end, we get ads for a car stereo now and then, but no VCRs; a welcome breakthrough of some IBM personal computers, but no Apple or no Japanese-made ones. Furthermore, we notice that *Working Woman* and *Savvy*, which are focused on office work, don't benefit as much as they should from ads for office equipment either. . . .

• Then there is the great toy train adventure. Because *Ms.* gets letters from little girls who love toy trains and ask our help in changing ads and box-top photos that show only little boys, we try to talk to Lionel and to get their ads. It turns out that Lionel executives *have* been concerned about little girls. They made a pink train and couldn't understand why it didn't sell.

Eventually, Lionel bows to this consumer pressure by switching to a photograph of a boy *and* a girl—but only on some box tops. If trains are associated with little girls, Lionel executives believe, they will be devalued in the eyes of little boys. Needless to say, *Ms.* gets no train ads. If even 20 percent of little girls wanted trains, they would be a huge growth market, but this remains unexplored. In the many toy stores where displays are still gender divided, the "soft" stuff, even modeling clay, stays on the girls' side, while the "hard" stuff, especially rockets and trains, is displayed for boys—thus depriving both. By 1986, Lionel is put up for sale. 45

We don't have much luck with other kinds of toys either. A *Ms.* department, Stories for Free Children, edited by Letty Cottin Pogrebin, makes us one of the very few magazines with a regular feature for children. A larger proportion of *Ms.* readers have preschool children than do the readers of any other women's magazine. Nonetheless, the industry can't seem to believe that feminists care about children—much less have them.

• When *Ms.* began, the staff decided not to accept ads for feminine hygiene sprays and cigarettes on the same basis: They are damaging to many women's health but carry no appropriate warnings. We don't think we should tell our readers what to do—if marijuana were legal, for instance, we would carry ads for it along with those for beer and wine—but we should provide facts so readers can decide for themselves. Since we've received letters saying that feminine sprays actually kill cockroaches and take the rust off metal, we give up on those. But antismoking groups have been pressuring for health warnings on cigarette ads as well as packages, so we decide we will accept advertising if the tobacco industry complies.

Philip Morris is among the first to do so. One of its brands, Virginia Slims, is also sponsoring women's tennis tournaments and women's public opinion polls that are historic "firsts." On the other hand, the Virginia Slims theme,

"You've come a long way, baby," has more than a "baby" problem. It gives the impression that for women, smoking is a sign of progress.

We explain to the Philip Morris people that this slogan won't do well in our pages. They are convinced that its success with *some* women means it will work with *all* women. No amount of saying that we, like men, are a segmented market, that we don't all think alike, does any good. Finally, we agree to publish a small ad for a Virginia Slims calendar as a test, and to abide by the response of our readers.

The letters from readers are both critical and smart. For instance: Would 50 you show a photo of a black man picking cotton next to one of an African American man in a Cardin suit, and symbolize progress from slavery to civil rights by smoking? Of course not. So why do it for women? But instead of honoring test results, the executives seem angry to have been proved wrong. We refuse Virginia Slims ads, thus annoying tennis players like Billie Jean King as well as incurring a new level of wrath: Philip Morris takes away ads for *all* its many products, costing *Ms.* about $250,000 in the first year. After five years, the damage is so great we can no longer keep track.

Occasionally, a new set of Philip Morris executives listens to *Ms.* saleswomen, or laughs when Pat Carbine points out that even Nixon got pardoned. I also appeal directly to the chairman of the board, who agrees it is unfair, sends me to another executive—and *he* says no. Because we won't take Virginia Slims, not one other Philip Morris product returns to our pages for the next sixteen years.

Gradually, we also realize our naïveté in thinking we could refuse all cigarette ads, with or without a health warning. They became a disproportionate source of revenue for print media the moment television banned them, and few magazines can compete or survive without them; certainly not *Ms.*, which lacks the support of so many other categories. Though cigarette ads actually inhibit editorial freedom less than ads for food, fashion, and the like —cigarette companies want only to be distant from coverage on the dangers of smoking, and don't require affirmative praise or photo credits of their product—it is still a growing source of sorrow that they are there at all. By the 1980s, when statistics show that women's rate of lung cancer is approaching men's, the necessity of taking cigarette ads has become a kind of prison.

Though I never manage to feel kindly toward groups that protest our ads and pay no attention to magazines and newspapers that can turn them down and still keep their doors open—and though *Ms.* continues to publish new facts about smoking, such as its dangers during pregnancy—I long for the demise of the whole tobacco-related industry. . . .

• General Mills, Pillsbury, Carnation, Del Monte, Dole, Kraft, Stouffer, Hormel, Nabisco: You name the food giant, we try to get its ads. But no matter how desirable the *Ms.* readership, our lack of editorial recipes and traditional homemaking articles proves lethal.

We explain that women flooding into the paid labor force have changed 55 the way this country eats; certainly, the boom in convenience foods proves that. We also explain that placing food ads *only* next to recipes and how-to-entertain articles is actually a negative for many women. It associates food with work — in a way that says only women have to cook — or with guilt over *not* cooking and entertaining. Why not advertise food in diverse media that don't always include recipes (thus reaching more men, who have become a third of all supermarket shoppers anyway) and add the recipe interest with specialty magazines like *Gourmet* (a third of whose readers are men)?

These arguments elicit intellectual interest but no ads. No advertising executive wants to be the first to say to a powerful client, "Guess what, I *didn't* get you complementary copy." Except for an occasional hard-won ad for instant coffee, diet drinks, yogurt, or such extras as avocados and almonds, the whole category of food, a mainstay of the publishing industry, remains unavailable to us. Period. . . .

• By the end of 1986, magazine production costs have skyrocketed and postal rates have increased 400 percent. Ad income is flat for the whole magazine industry. The result is more competition, with other magazines offering such "extras" as free golf trips for advertisers or programs for "sampling" their products at parties and other events arranged by the magazine for desirable consumers. We try to compete with the latter by "sampling" at what we certainly have enough of: movement benefits. Thus, little fragrance bottles turn up next to the dinner plates of California women lawyers (who are delighted), or wine samples lower the costs at a reception for political women. A good organizing tactic comes out of this. We hold feminist seminars in shopping centers. They may be to the women's movement what churches were to the civil rights movement in the South — that is, *where people are.* Anyway, shopping center seminars are a great success. Too great. We have to stop doing them in Bloomingdale's up and down the East Coast, because meeting space in the stores is too limited, and too many women are left lined up outside stores. We go on giving out fancy little liquor bottles at store openings, which makes the advertisers happy — but not us.

Mostly, however, we can't compete in this game of "value-added" (the code word for giving the advertisers extras in return for their ads). Neither can many of the other independent magazines. Deep-pocketed corporate parents can offer such extras as reduced rates for ad schedules in a group of magazines, free tie-in spots on radio stations they also own, or vacation junkets on corporate planes.

Meanwhile, higher costs and lowered income have caused the *Ms.* 60/40 preponderance of edit over ads — something we promised to readers — to become 50/50: still a lot better than most women's magazines' goals of 30/70, but not good enough. Children's stories, most poetry, and some fiction are casualties of reduced space. In order to get variety into more limited pages, the length (and sometimes the depth) of articles suffers. Though we don't solicit or accept ads that would look like a parody in our pages, we get so worn down that some slip through. Moreover, we always have the problem of working just as hard to get a single ad as another magazine might for a whole year's schedule of ads.

Still, readers keep right on performing miracles. Though we haven't been able to afford a subscription mailing in two years, they maintain our guaranteed circulation of 450,000 by word of mouth. Some of them also help to make up the advertising deficit by giving *Ms.* a birthday present of $15 on its fifteenth anniversary, or contributing $1,000 for a lifetime subscription — even those who can ill afford it.

What's almost as angering as these struggles, however, is the way the media report them. Our financial problems are attributed to lack of reader interest, not an advertising double standard. In the Reagan-Bush era, when "feminism-is-dead" becomes one key on the typewriter, our problems are used to prepare a grave for the whole movement. Clearly, the myth that advertisers go where the readers are — thus, if we had readers, we would have advertisers — is deeply embedded. Even industry reporters rarely mention the editorial demands made by ads for women's products, and if they do, they assume advertisers must be right and *Ms.* must be wrong; we must be too controversial, outrageous, even scatalogical to support. In fact, there's nothing in our pages that couldn't be published in *Time*, *Esquire*, or *Rolling Stone* — providing those magazines devoted major space to women — but the media myth often wins out. Though comparable magazines our size (say, *Vanity Fair* or the *Atlantic*) are losing more money in a single year than *Ms.* has lost in sixteen years, *Ms.* is held to a different standard. No matter how much never-to-be-recovered cash is poured into starting a magazine or keeping it going, appearances seem to be all that matter. (Which is why we haven't been able to explain our fragile state in public. Nothing causes ad flight like the smell of nonsuccess.)

My healthy response is anger, but my not-so-healthy one is depression, worry, and an obsession with finding one more rescue. There is hardly a night when I don't wake up with sweaty palms and pounding heart, scared that we won't be able to pay the printer or the post office; scared most of all that closing our doors will be blamed on a lack of readers and thus the movement, instead of the real cause. ("Feminism couldn't even support one magazine," I can hear them saying.)

We're all being flattened by a velvet steamroller. The only difference is that at *Ms.*, we keep standing up again.

Do you think, as I once did, that advertisers make decisions based on rational and uniform criteria? Well, think again. There is clearly a double standard. The same food companies that insist on recipes in women's magazines place ads in *People* where there are no recipes. Cosmetics companies support the *New Yorker*, which has no regular beauty columns, and newspaper pages that have no "beauty atmosphere."

Meanwhile, advertisers' control over the editorial content of women's   65
magazines has become so institutionalized that it is sometimes written into
"insertion orders" or dictated to ad salespeople as official policy — whether by
the agency, the client, or both. The following are orders given to women's
magazines effective in 1990. Try to imagine them being applied to *Time* or
Newsweek.

• Dow's Cleaning Products stipulated that ads for its Vivid and Spray 'n' Wash
products should be adjacent to "children or fashion editorial"; ads for Bathroom
Cleaner should be next to "home furnishing/family" features; with similar requirements for other brands. "If a magazine fails for ½ the brands or more,"
the Dow order warned, "it will be omitted from further consideration."

• Bristol-Myers, the parent of Clairol, Windex, Drano, Bufferin, and much
more, stipulated that ads be placed next to "a full page of compatible editorial."

• S. C. Johnson & Son, makers of Johnson Wax, lawn and laundry products,
insect sprays, hair sprays, and so on, insisted that its ads *"should not be opposite extremely controversial features or material antithetical to the nature/copy of
the advertised product."* (Italics theirs.)

• Maidenform, manufacturer of bras and other women's apparel, left a
blank for the particular product and stated in its instructions: "The creative
concept of the _____ campaign, and the very nature of the product itself,
appeal to the positive emotions of the reader/consumer. Therefore, it is imperative that all editorial adjacencies reflect that same positive tone. The editorial
must not be negative in content or lend itself contrary to the _____ product
imagery/message (e.g., *editorial relating to illness, disillusionment, large size
fashion, etc.*)." (Italics mine.)

• The De Beers diamond company, a big seller of engagement rings, pro-   70
hibited magazines from placing its ads with "adjacencies to hard news or anti-
love/romance themed editorial." . . .

• Kraft/General Foods, a giant with many brands, sent this message with an
Instant Pudding ad: "urgently request upbeat parent/child activity editorial,
mandatory positioning requirements — opposite full page of positive editorial —
right hand page essential for creative — minimum 6 page competitive separation (i.e., all sugar based or sugar free gelatins, puddings, mousses, creames
[sic] and pie filling) — Do not back with clippable material. Avoid: controver-
sial/negative topics and any narrow targeted subjects."

• An American Tobacco Company order for a Misty Slims ad noted that the
U.S. government warning must be included, but also that there must be: "no
adjacency to editorial relating to health, medicine, religion, or death."

• Lorillard's Newport cigarette ad came with similar instructions, plus:
"Please be aware that the Nicotine Patch products are competitors. The minimum six page separation is required."

Quite apart from anything else, you can imagine the logistical nightmare this creates when putting a women's magazine together, but the greatest casualty is editorial freedom. Though the ratio of advertising to editorial pages in women's magazines is only about 5 percent more than in *Time* or *Newsweek*, that nothing-to-read feeling comes from all the supposedly editorial pages that are extensions of ads. To find out what we're really getting when we pay our money, I picked up a variety of women's magazines for February 1994, and counted the number of pages in each one (even including table of contents, letters to the editors, horoscopes, and the like) that were not ads and/or copy complementary to ads. Then I compared that number to the total pages. Out of 184 pages, *McCall's* had 49 that were nonad or ad-related. Of 202, *Elle* gave readers 48. *Seventeen* provided its young readers with only 51 nonad or ad-related pages out of 226. *Vogue* had 62 out of 292. *Mirabella* offered readers 45 pages out of a total of 158. *Good Housekeeping* came out on top, though only at about a third, with 60 out of 176 pages. *Martha Stewart Living* offered the least. Even counting her letter to readers, a page devoted to her personal calendar, and another one to a turnip, only seven out of 136 pages had no ads, products, or product mentions. . . .

Within the supposedly editorial text itself, praise for advertisers' products 75 has become so ritualized that fields like "beauty writing" have been invented. One of its practitioners explained to me seriously that "It's a difficult art. How many new adjectives can you find? How much greater can you make a lipstick sound? The FDA restricts what companies can say on labels, but we create illusion. And ad agencies are on the phone all the time pushing you to get their product in. A lot of them keep the business based on how many editorial clippings they produce every month. The worst are products [whose manufacturers have] their own name involved. It's all ego."

Often, editorial becomes one giant ad. An issue of *Lear's* featured an elegant woman executive on the cover. On the contents page, we learn she is wearing Guerlain makeup and Samsara, a new fragrance by Guerlain. Inside, there just happen to be full-page ads for Samsara, plus a Guerlain antiwrinkle skin cream. In the article about the cover subject, we discover she is Guerlain's director of public relations and is responsible for launching, you guessed it, the new Samsara. . . .

When the *Columbia Journalism Review* cited this example in one of the few articles to include women's magazines in a critique of ad influence, Frances Lear, editor of *Lear's*, was quoted at first saying this was a mistake, and then shifting to the defense that "this kind of thing is done all the time."

She's right. Here's an example with a few more turns of the screw. Martha Stewart, *Family Circle*'s contributing editor, was also "lifestyle and entertaining consultant" for Kmart, the retail chain, which helped to underwrite the renovation of Stewart's country house, using Kmart products; *Family Circle* covered the process in three articles not marked as ads; Kmart bought $4 million worth of ad pages in *Family Circle*, including "advertorials" to introduce a line of Martha Stewart products to be distributed by Kmart; and finally, the "advertorials," which at least are marked and only *look* like editorial pages, were reproduced and distributed in Kmart stores, thus publicizing *Family Circle* (owned by the New York Times Company, which would be unlikely to do this kind of thing in its own news pages) to Kmart customers. This was so lucrative that Martha Stewart now has her own magazine, *Martha Stewart Living* (owned by Time Warner), complete with a television version. Both offer a happy world of cooking, entertaining, and decorating in which nothing critical or negative ever seems to happen.

I don't mean to be a spoilsport, but there are many articles we're very unlikely to get from that or any other women's magazine dependent on food ads. According to Senator Howard Metzenbaum of Ohio, more than half of the chickens we eat (from ConAgra, Tyson, Perdue, and other companies) are contaminated with dangerous bacteria; yet labels haven't yet begun to tell us to scrub the meat and everything it touches — which is our best chance of not getting sick. Nor are we likely to learn about the frequent working conditions of this mostly female work force, standing in water, cutting chickens apart with such repetitive speed that carpal tunnel syndrome is an occupational hazard. Then there's Dole Food, often cited as a company that keeps women in low-level jobs and a target of a lawsuit by Costa Rican workers who were sterilized by contact with pesticides used by Dole — even though Dole must have known these pesticides had been banned in the United States.

The consumerist reporting we're missing sometimes sounds familiar. Remember the *Ms.* episode with Clairol and the article about potential carcinogens in hair dye? Well, a similar saga took place with L'Oréal and *Mademoiselle* in 1992, according to an editor at Condé Nast. Now, editors there are supposed to warn publishers of any criticism in advance, a requirement that might well have a chilling effect. [80]

Other penalties are increasing. As older readers will remember, women's magazines used to be a place where new young poets and short story writers could be published. Now, that's very rare. It isn't that advertisers of women's products dislike poetry or fiction, it's just that they pay to be adjacent to articles and features more directly compatible with their products.

Sometimes, advertisers invade editorial pages — literally — by plunging odd-shaped ads into the text, no matter how that increases the difficulty of reading. When Ellen Levine was editor of *Woman's Day*, for instance, a magazine originally founded by a supermarket chain, she admitted, "The day the copy had to rag around a chicken leg was not a happy one."

The question of ad positioning is also decided by important advertisers, a rule that's ignored at a magazine's peril. When Revlon wasn't given the place of the first beauty ad in one Hearst magazine, for instance, it pulled its ads from *all* Hearst magazines. In 1990 Ruth Whitney, editor in chief of *Glamour*, attributed some of this pushiness to "ad agencies wanting to prove to a client that they've squeezed the last drop of blood out of a magazine." She was also "sick and tired of hearing that women's magazines are controlled by cigarette ads." Relatively speaking, she was right. To be as controlling as most advertisers of women's products, tobacco companies would have to demand articles in flat-out praise of smoking, and editorial photos of models smoking a credited brand. As it is, they ask only to be forewarned so they don't advertise in the same issue with an article about the dangers of smoking. But for a magazine like *Essence*, the only national magazine for African American women, even taking them out of one issue may be financially difficult, because other advertisers might neglect its readers. In 1993, a group called Women and Girls Against Tobacco, funded by the California Department of Health Services, prepared an ad headlined "Cigarettes Made Them History." It pictured three black singers — Mary Wells, Eddie Kendricks, and Sarah Vaughan — who died of tobacco-related diseases. *Essence* president Clarence Smith didn't turn the ad down, but he didn't accept it either. When I talked with him in 1994, he said with pain, "the black female market just isn't considered at parity with the white female market; there are too many other categories we don't get." That's in spite of the fact that *Essence* does all the traditional food-fashion-beauty editorial expected by advertisers. According to California statistics, African American women are more addicted to smoking than the female population at large, with all the attendant health problems.

Alexandra Penney, editor of *Self* magazine, feels she has been able to include smoking facts in health articles by warning cigarette advertisers in advance (though smoking is still being advertised in this fitness magazine). On the other hand, up to this writing in 1994, no advertiser has been willing to appear opposite a single-page feature called "Outrage," which is reserved for important controversies, and is very popular with readers. Another women's magazine publisher told me that to this day Campbell's Soup refuses to advertise because of an article that unfavorably compared the nutritional value of canned food to that of fresh food — fifteen years ago.

I don't mean to imply that the editors I quote here share my objections to 85 ad demands and/or expectations. Many assume that the women's magazines at which they work have to be the way they are. Others are justifiably proud of getting an independent article in under the advertising radar, for instance, articles on family violence in *Family Circle* or a series on child sexual abuse and the family courts in *McCall's*. A few insist they would publish exactly the same editorial, even if there were no ads. But it's also true that it's hard to be honest while you're still in the job. "Most of the pressure came in the form of direct product mentions," explained Sey Chassler, who was editor in chief of *Redbook* from the sixties to the eighties and is now out of the game. "We got threats from the big guys, the Revlons, blackmail threats. They wouldn't run ads unless we credited them."

What could women's magazines be like if they were as editorially free as good books? as realistic as the best newspaper articles? as creative as poetry and films? as diverse as women's lives? What if we as women — who are psychic immigrants in a public world rarely constructed by or for us — had the same kind of watchful, smart, supportive publications on our side that other immigrant groups have often had?

We'll find out only if we take the media directed at us seriously. If readers were to act in concert in large numbers for a few years to change the traditional practices of *all* women's magazines and the marketing of *all* women's products, we could do it. After all, they depend on our consumer dollars — money we now are more likely to control. If we include all the shopping we do for families and spouses, women make 85 percent of purchases at point of sale. You and I could:

- refuse to buy products whose ads have clearly dictated their surroundings, and write to tell the manufacturers why;

- write to editors and publishers (with copies to advertisers) to tell them that we're willing to pay *more* for magazines with editorial independence, but will *not* continue to pay for those that are editorial extensions of ads;

- write to advertisers (with copies to editors and publishers) to tell them that we want fiction, political reporting, consumer reporting, strong opinion, humor, and health coverage that doesn't pull punches, praising them when their ads support this, and criticizing them when they don't;

- put as much energy and protest into breaking advertising's control over what's around it as we put into changing the images within it or protesting harmful products like cigarettes;

- support only those women's magazines and products that take us seriously as readers and consumers;

- investigate new laws and regulations to support freedom from advertising influence. The Center for the Study of Commercialism, a group founded in 1990 to educate and advocate against "ubiquitous product marketing," recommends whistle-blower laws that protect any members of the media who disclose advertiser and other commercial conflicts of interest, laws that require advertiser influence to be disclosed, Federal Trade Commission involvement, and denial of income tax exemptions for advertising that isn't clearly identified — as well as conferences, citizen watchdog groups, and a national clearinghouse where examples of private censorship can be reported.

Those of us in the magazine world can also use this carrot-and-stick technique. The stick: If magazines were a regulated medium like television, the editorial quid pro quo demanded by advertising would be against the rules of the FCC, and payola and extortion would be penalized. As it is, there are potential illegalities to pursue. For example: A magazine's postal rates are determined by the ratio of ad pages to editorial pages, with the ads being charged at a higher rate than the editorial. Counting up all the pages that are *really* ads could make an interesting legal action. There could be consumer fraud cases lurking in subscriptions that are solicited for a magazine but deliver a catalog.

The carrot is just as important. In twenty years, for instance, I've found no independent, nonproprietary research showing that an ad for, say, fragrance is any more effective placed next to an article about fragrance than it would be when placed next to a good piece of fiction or reporting. As we've seen, there are studies showing that the greatest factor in determining an ad's effectiveness is the credibility and independence of its surroundings. An airtight wall between ads and edit would also shield corporations and agencies from pressures from both ends of the political spectrum and from dozens of pressure groups. Editors would be the only ones responsible for editorial content — which is exactly as it should be.

Unfortunately, few agencies or clients hear such arguments. Editors often 90 maintain the artificial purity of refusing to talk to the people who actually control their lives. Instead, advertisers see salespeople who know little about editorial, are trained in business as usual, and are usually paid on commission. To take on special controversy editors might also band together. That happened once when all the major women's magazines did articles in the same month on the Equal Rights Amendment. It could happen again — and regularly.

Meanwhile, we seem to have a system in which everybody is losing. The reader loses diversity, strong opinion, honest information, access to the arts, and much more. The editor loses pride of work, independence, and freedom from worry about what brand names or other critical words some sincere freelancer is going to come up with. The advertiser loses credibility right along with the ad's surroundings, and gets more and more lost in a sea of similar ads and interchangeable media.

But that's also the good news. Because where there is mutual interest, there is the beginning of change.

If you need one more motive for making it, consider the impact of U.S. media on the rest of the world. The ad policies we tolerate here are invading the lives of women in other cultures — through both the content of U.S. media and the ad practices of multinational corporations imposed on other countries. Look at our women's magazines. Is this what we want to export?

Should *Ms.* have started out with no advertising in the first place? The odd thing is that, in retrospect, I think the struggle was worth it. For all those years, dozens of feminist organizers disguised as *Ms.* ad saleswomen took their courage, research, slide shows, humor, ingenuity, and fresh point of view into every advertising agency, client office, and lion's den in cities where advertising is sold. Not only were sixteen years of *Ms.* sustained in this way, with all the changeful words on those thousands of pages, but some of the advertising industry was affected in its imagery, its practices, and its understanding of the female half of the country. Those dozens of women themselves were affected, for they learned the art of changing a structure from both within and without, and are now rising in crucial publishing positions where women have never been. *Ms.* also helped to open nontraditional categories of ads for women's magazines, thus giving them a little more freedom — not to mention making their changes look reasonable by comparison.

But the world of advertising has a way of reminding us how far there is 95 to go.

Three years ago, as I was finishing this exposé in its first version, I got a call from a writer for *Elle.* She was doing an article on where women parted their hair: Why, she wanted to know, did I part mine in the middle?

It was all so familiar. I could imagine this writer trying to make something out of a nothing assignment. A long-suffering editor laboring to think of new ways to attract ads for shampoo, conditioner, hairdryers, and the like. Readers assuming that other women must want this stuff.

As I was working on this version, I got a letter from Revlon of the sort we disregarded when we took ads. Now, I could appreciate it as a reminder of how much we had to disregard:

> We are delighted to confirm that Lauren Hutton is now under contract to Revlon.
>
> We are very much in favor of her appearing in as much editorial as possible, but it's important that your publication avoid any mention of competitive color cosmetics, beauty treatment, hair care or sun care products in editorial or editorial credits in which she appears.
>
> We would be very appreciative if all concerned are made aware of this.

I could imagine the whole chain of women — Lauren Hutton, preferring to be in the Africa that is her passion; the ad executive who signed the letter, only doing her job; the millions of women readers who would see the resulting artificial images; all of us missing sources of information, insight, creativity, humor, anger, investigation, poetry, confession, outrage, learning, and perhaps most important, a sense of connection to each other; and a gloriously diverse world being flattened by a velvet steamroller.

I ask you: Can't we do better than this?   100

READING THE TEXT

1. What does Steinem mean by "complementary copy" (para. 17) and "advertorial" (para. 78)?

2. Summarize the relationship Steinem sees between editorial content and advertising in women's magazines.

3. In Steinem's view, what messages about gender roles does complementary copy send readers of women's magazines?

4. What is the history of response to this article since its initial publication in 1990, according to Steinem?

READING THE SIGNS

1. Steinem asserts that virtually all content in women's magazines is a disguised form of advertising. Test her hypothesis in a detailed analysis of a single issue of a magazine such as *Cosmopolitan*, *Jane*, or *Elle*. Do you find instances of complementary copy and advertorials? How do you react as a potential reader of such a magazine?

2. Explore whether Steinem's argument holds for men's magazines such as *Maxim* or *GQ*. If you identify differences, how might they be based on different assumptions about gender roles?

3. Have each member of the class bring in a favorite magazine. In small groups, study the relationship between ads and articles. What magazines have the most complementary copy? How can you account for your findings?

4. In your journal, explore whether you believe advertisers infringe on the freedom of the press.

VITAMEATAVEGAMIN
FOR HEALTH

VIDEO DREAMS

Television, Music, and Cultural Forms

Interpreting the Televising of America

Even before the advent of cultural studies, writing about television was a common assignment in American classrooms, so this chapter's topic might be quite familiar to you. Indeed, in high school you may have been asked to write about a favorite TV program or music video, perhaps in a summary writing exercise, a descriptive essay, or an opinion piece on why such-and-such a program is your favorite show. But in college you will be asked to write critical interpretations of television, a somewhat different task than expressing an opinion about how entertaining a program is. In interpreting TV, you still need to rely on your skills in description and summary, because you need to describe the show for your reader, but your purpose will be to go beyond these writing tasks toward the construction of interpretive arguments about the cultural significance of your topic.

Television offers an especially rich field of possible writing topics, ranging from a historical analysis of a whole category of TV programming (such as the sitcom or detective show) to an interpretation of a single episode. Some topics, especially if you choose a historical approach, will require research. Let's say, for example, that you want to analyze the roles of women in situation comedies over the years. Comparing the women in *I Love Lucy*, *Father Knows Best*, *The Mary Tyler Moore Show*, *Murphy Brown*, *Roseanne*, and *The New Adventures of Old Christine* can reveal a great deal about the cultural contexts in which those programs appeared and so enable you to construct a thesis about American gender roles over the past fifty years. Such an analysis lends itself particularly well to the semiotic method of establishing a system of related, or associated, signs, and then noting the differences that distinguish your subject. All of the shows from *I Love Lucy* to *The New Adventures of Old Christine*, for example, feature comic female leads, but their characters are presented in very different ways. By analyzing those differences and situating each show within its cultural context, you can discover how the cultural perspective on women's roles in society has changed dramatically over the years. Indeed, such shows are particularly striking cultural barometers.

The interpretation of a single television episode is much like interpreting a short story. You should consider every potentially significant detail in the episode and subject it to a close reading. As with all semiotic analyses, your first step when preparing to analyze a TV program is to suspend your aesthetic opinions — that is, whether you like a show or not. What you are working toward is a critical analysis, what you think a program's underlying cultural significance may be. This process also differs from describing what you think the show's explicit message is. Many programs have clearly presented messages, or morals, but what you are looking for is the message beyond the message, so to speak, the implicit, often contradictory, signals the show is sending.

The Kids Aren't All Right

A clear example of this type of double message can be found in a single episode of the popular "dramedy" *Desperate Housewives*. "My Heart Belongs to Daddy" (Episode 204), which first aired on October 16, 2005, concluded with a voice-over from the show's ghostly narrator, Mary Alice, intoning about the good things that happen when families have good fathers and the bad things that happen when they don't — which appeared to be the explicit moral of an episode packed with family dysfunctionality due to absent fathers. But a

---

Discussing the Signs of Television

In class, choose a current television program, and have the entire class watch one episode (either watch the episode as "homework" or ask someone to tape it and then watch it in class). Interpret the episode semiotically. What values and cultural myths does the show project? What do the commercials broadcast during the show say about the presumed audience for it? Go beyond the episode's surface appeal or "message" to look at the particular images it uses to tell its story, always asking, "What is this program *really* saying?"

closer look at the details reveals a powerful undercurrent of meaning that the explicit moral does not state.

You may find a recap of "My Heart Belongs to Daddy" on the show's official Web site at http://abc.go.com/primetime/desperate/recaps/204.html. Given the soap-operatic nature of a dramedy like *Desperate Housewives* — the way that any individual episode is intertwined with past episodes and never achieves closure in itself — you should research the backstory of a series of this kind before attempting an analysis, as we did prior to our own analysis. But rather than attempting to summarize here the highly involved situation in which this particular episode is entwined, we shall treat it as a largely stand-alone story, focusing on three different subplots featuring the behavior of young boys.

These subplots center on the characters of Lynette, Susan, and Bree. Lynette has recently returned to her job in the corporate world because her husband lost *his* job, and she is unhappy about missing time with her young son Parker. Unmarried Susan, for her part, is pursuing a romantic relationship with Mike, who happens to be the secret father of Zach, a homicidal teenaged runaway who is looking for Paul, who is Zach's presumptive father and has gone missing for reasons of his own. Meanwhile, widow Bree is dating George, a relationship highly resented by her son Andrew since it is so soon after his father's death.

Got all that? Fans of the show will be aware of the excessively complicated story line that has taken the series to this point, but this will do for our purposes.

Let's begin with Lynette. She isn't simply unhappy; she is driven to tears by Parker's weird behavior in response to her absence. He has invented an "imaginary friend," whom he calls Mrs. Mulberry, and who is embodied in a black umbrella (obviously inspired by *Mary Poppins*) that he carries with him everywhere and insists on sleeping with. When his mother comes in to kiss him goodnight, Parker rejects her while expressing his deep affection for Mrs. Mulberry. The situation could make us very sympathetic for a young child who is going through severe separation anxiety, but he is really nasty about the whole matter. Not only does he callously reject Lynette's sincere attempts to connect with him, but he uses the umbrella to assault his teacher at school, an event that leads to Lynette's having to meet with the school principal.

In the end Lynette can't take it anymore and sneaks away the umbrella and tosses it in the trash. The next morning the trash collector accidentally drops the umbrella in the street rather than in the trash truck. When Lynette comes out shortly thereafter to take Parker (who is protesting that he can't leave until he finds Mrs. Mulberry) to school, she tells him that Mrs. Mulberry has gone on to help another child, but at this moment they both see the umbrella lying in the street. An expression of joy crosses Parker's face, soon to be replaced by one of horror when a car drives by and flattens the umbrella. Lynette looks relieved, as Parker finally turns to his mother for comfort. She's gotten him back, and she's back in control.

Then there's Bree. She has invited George over for dinner, and Andrew, trying to disgust George and drive him away from his mother, starts telling him about the noises his mother makes during sex. Bree, who is in the kitchen, doesn't hear this, and when George, understandably, erupts in anger, he is the one who looks bad to Bree as Andrew smirkingly looks on. The audience, however, can see very clearly who the jerk is and that Bree is being duped.

George gets his revenge at a swim meet, carefully planning things so that just at the beginning of Andrew's race, Andrew will look up into the stands to see Bree rapturously kissing George. Andrew jumps out of the pool and runs into the stands where he begins to slug George, which causes Bree to erupt at Andrew, to the great satisfaction of George. Andrew is subsequently packed off to a camp for troublesome children by his mother, who is firmly in control at the end of the episode.

Finally Susan, who has located the missing Zach, is on the verge of helping him find his "father," Paul, when Zach brings up his continuing romantic feelings for Susan's daughter, Julia. A homicidal near-maniac with a track record of threatening people with guns, Zach is not exactly any mother's idea of a good suitor for her daughter, and Susan understandably changes her mind and instead tricks Zach into leaving the state. As with Parker's shock and Andrew's comeuppance, the situation is presented in such a manner that the audience's sympathy is likely to be with the woman, not the boy, as Susan skillfully controls the situation.

To determine a semiotic significance for these details, one needs to keep in mind the program's target audience and what is likely to entertain that audience. Remember, commercial television exists to entertain, and analyzing what makes it entertaining is what leads us to its significance. In the case of *Desperate Housewives*, the target audience predominantly consists of women, often mothers, who can especially identify with the parenting difficulties of the women depicted in the program. An episode packed with conflicts with misbehaving boys who have taken control of various situations but who all get a comeuppance in the end points to an existing frustration in the mothers who enjoy the show. The entertainment value lies in the catharsis such viewers may feel in seeing the boys "punished." Note that none of the boys suffers any physical harm (mothers would not be entertained by *that*); the punishment lies in a restoration of maternal power: In each case the boy's comeuppance leaves the woman in control after she had lost it for a while. Evidently, a significant number of American women are feeling such desperation, or the scriptwriters would not have exploited it to write the story. Commercial TV exists to attract its audience, not repel it, and *Desperate Housewives* is not a show for young boys.

The episode of *Desperate Housewives* that we have just analyzed thus sends a signal beyond the explicit message. Recall that the explicit message was, in effect, patriarchal, a declaration of the need for good and strong fathers. But the underlying message, somewhat contradictorily, is matriarchal, presenting the cathartic triumph of women over young males. The potentially subversive significance of this counter-message is masked by Mary Alice's voice-over, which makes the episode appear completely conventional and thus avoids the sort of controversy that could sink a prime-time series. But it is that unconventional, subtle counter-signal in the plot that may account for much of the success of *Desperate Housewives*, an indicator that there are a good many desperate women eager to see their frustrations sympathetically dramatized and addressed.

The Flow

Whatever show you choose to analyze, remember why it is on TV in the first place: Television, whether network or cable, is there to make money. It is a major part of our consumer culture, and most of what appears on TV is there because advertisers who want to reach their intended markets sponsor it. The shows that command the highest share of viewers, accordingly, command the highest advertising rates, and so producers are keen to have their viewers emotionally connect with their programs—and a main strategy involves satisfying viewer fantasies, a version of which we uncovered in our analysis of *Desperate Housewives*. This is especially striking in teen-address shows that feature fashion-model-glamorous actors and actresses (often in their twenties) playing adolescents in the awkward years, but it is also true for adult-address shows, which invite their viewers to identify with high-status professionals like doctors (*ER*) and lawyers (*The Practice*). Identifying with their favorite characters, viewers—or so television sponsors hope—will identify with the products they see advertised on the shows. And buy them.

This is why one of the most revealing features in a television program analysis includes the advertising that accompanies the show. By paying attention to the ads, you can learn much about the intended audience. Ask yourself, then, why is the nightly news so often sponsored by over-the-counter pain killers? Why is daytime TV, especially in the morning, so often accompanied by cheesy ads for vocational training schools? Why are youth-oriented prime-time shows filled with fast-food commercials, while family programs have a lot of car ads?

Your analysis of a single episode of a television program can also usefully include a survey of where the show fits within what cultural studies pioneer Raymond Williams called the "flow" of an evening's TV schedule. Flow refers to the sequence of TV programs and advertisements, from, say, the five o'clock news, through the pre-prime-time 7:00 to 8:00 slot, through prime time and on through to the 11:00 news and the late-night talk shows. What precedes your program? What follows? Can you determine the strategy behind your show's scheduling?

Reality Bites

One kind of programming that you simply cannot miss anymore in the evening's flow is reality TV, a genre that seems to be on the verge of supplanting every other kind of television show. With its relatively low production costs and lack of superstar salary demands, reality TV was a producer's dream come true from the first, but audiences, especially in the coveted eighteen-to thirty-year-old market niche, have absolutely adored it. Despite its popularity, RTV is not without its critics, however, and there is certainly something about the genre that begs for cultural analysis. Let's conduct one here.

As with any semiotic analysis, a little history is helpful. One might say that reality television began in 1948 with Allen Funt's *Candid Camera*, which featured the filming of real people (who didn't know that they were on camera, unlike today's reality contestants) as they reacted to annoying situations concocted by the show's creators. The show's attraction lay in the humor viewers could enjoy in watching other people get into minor jams. There is a name for this kind of humor that comes from psychoanalytic theory: *schadenfreude*, or taking pleasure in the misfortunes of others, as when we laugh at someone slipping on a banana peel. And we shall see that this early appeal from the history of reality TV is very much a part of the current popularity of the genre.

After *Candid Camera* came the 1970s' PBS series *An American Family*. In this program a camera crew moved in with a suburban family named the Louds and filmed them in their day-to-day lives. The Louds were not contestants and there were no prizes to be won. The program was conceived as an experiment in *cinema verité* to see if it was possible for television to be authentically realistic. The experiment was a bit of a failure, however, as the Loud family members began to act out for the camera. The result was the eventual dissolution of the Louds as a family unit and a general sense of unease about such experiments.

The next, and probably most crucial step, was when MTV in effect revived the concept behind *An American Family* and launched *Real World* in 1992. Like *An American Family*, *Real World* attempted to be realistic, with its constant camera recording of the lives of a group of people living together in the same house, but unlike *An American Family*, *Real World* is a fantasy that caters to young adult viewers who can imagine themselves living in such glamorous circumstances while enjoying the vicarious experience of becoming instant TV stars like the people on the show. That there is a certain tampering with reality in *Real World*, a deliberate selection of participants based upon their appearance and how they can be cast into often contrived romances as well as antagonisms, constitutes a contradiction that differentiates *Real World* from *An American Family* (which was not scripted) and leads us to the dawning of the reality revolution.

The astounding success of the first versions of *Who Wants to Marry a Millionaire?* and *Survivor* established reality TV's full coming-of-age. In both programs we can see strong traces of what made their pioneering predecessors popular. But through their introduction of a game show element, complete with contestants competing for huge cash prizes, a whole new dimension was added that ultimately differentiates many of the new reality shows from those of the past and helps establish their significance.

The game show elements of such programs are obvious enough, and so part of their appeal is just that of the game show: the vicarious chance to imagine oneself as being in the shoes of the contestants (after all, anyone in principle can get on a game show) and winning lots of money. There is also an element of schadenfreude here if one takes pleasure in watching the losers in game show competitions. But by adding the real-life element of actual marriage to the mix, *Who Wants to Marry a Millionaire?* brought a whole new dimension of humiliation to the genre. It's one thing to be caught on camera during the emotional upheaval of competing for large cash prizes, but it's quite another to be in an erotic competition and lose, with millions watching you.

Shows like *Who Wants to Marry a Millionaire?* and all its progeny (*The Bachelor*, *The Bachelorette*, *Age of Love*, and so on and so forth) have their origins, in part, in the system of television programming that began with *The Dating Game* in the 1960s and the many dating programs that followed in its wake. But *The Dating Game* tried to reduce the inherent humiliation factor in such competitions through a split-screen effect that allowed the audience to see a single contestant, say, on the left, and three other contestants on the right, who would be concealed from the one on the left. That contestant would ask questions of the three concealed contestants (men if the questioner was a woman, women if it was a man) and pick one for a date. This sort of nicety looks rather quaint today in the aftermath of another pioneering RTV program, *Temptation Island*, a show that made the sexual humiliation of its protagonists the main attraction, along with voyeuristic sexual titillation. Thus, in *Temptation Island* voyeurism linked up with schadenfreude in a formula that is now common on sex-themed RTV programs.

Survivor, for its part, combines a game show element with an action-adventure theme that invites viewers to imagine themselves in exciting outdoor situations that are exaggerated versions of the sort of adventure-safari vacations that had become very popular in the 1990s and continue to be so today. With people spending $75,000 and upward to be guided to the top of Mount Everest, a show like *Survivor* is very much a reflection of the fantasies of its viewers. Indeed, it presents the ultimate fantasy of enjoying an extreme vacation, while becoming a television star overnight as contestants reemerge in civilization on the talk-show circuit and in milk commercials.

Survivor also includes elements of voyeurism and schadenfreude in its formula for success, as viewers can watch the weekly humiliation of contestants struggling to stay in the game, while ogling the younger female contestants in their often skimpy attire. But it adds yet another dimension to the mix by inviting viewers to identify with some contestants and to despise others (though the creators of the show deny this, there is evidence that contestants are directed to play out specified roles). One need only look at the weekly Internet commentary to see just how much the ordinary folk on *Survivor* can be hated, and the experience of watching contestants be voted off the show brings in a dimension of outright sadism as viewers take pleasure in the disappointments of the contestants they despise (indeed, some reality programs, like *American Idol* and *Dancing With the Stars*, take this element a step further by allowing viewers to participate in voting contestants off).

Finally, while game shows usually feature some sort of competition among the contestants, the *Survivor* series takes such competition to a new level by compelling its contestants to engage in back-stabbing conspiracies as they claw their way toward a million-dollar payoff. (The 2006 season even introduced an element of racial conflict by forming tribes according to race to really spice up the contest.) It isn't enough for tribe to compete against tribe; there has to be intratribal backbiting and betrayal as well. Such a subtext constitutes a kind of grotesque parody of American capitalism itself, in which the cutthroat competition of the workplace is moved to the wilderness. Not to miss out on a good thing, RTV soon brought it all back to the office with *The Apprentice*, a show that makes capitalist competition its major theme, while echoing the talent show elements of *American Idol*. Indeed, so successful was the formula that *The Apprentice* would be joined for a while by *My Big Fat Obnoxious Boss*, which really turned the evils of life under capitalism into schadenfreude-laden entertainment.

Then there are all the makeover shows, from *Queer Eye for the Straight Guy* to *Extreme Makeover* and every clone that you can think of. Though there are significant differences among such shows (not all, for example, feature the freak show overtones that *The Swan* did), they share the message that something is wrong with us that needs to be corrected by experts. Our houses aren't decorated properly; our clothes aren't right; our noses are all wrong; we're not beautiful enough. There doesn't seem to be anything in our lives that the makeover shows can't offer to improve. In effect, such shows send the message that a well-lived life is a matter of proper consumption, that spending money can make you the kind of person you've always wanted to be — or the kind of person that you think others want you to be. Indeed, makeover TV is the perfect companion to a consumer culture: No wonder advertisers love it.

Voyeurism. Schadenfreude. Sadism. Dog-eat-dog capitalist competitiveness. Conspicuous consumption. RTV's formula seems to appeal to some of the most primitive and socially disruptive of human instincts, violating taboos in the name of profits (for an example of *real* taboo tweaking, consider the *Jackass* franchise). Indeed, in the aftermath of an actual injury suffered by one of the *Survivor: Outback* contestants (he was burned by a fire), commentators wondered whether future installments would have to include the death of a contestant to satisfy their viewers' ever-greater desires for mayhem. But while there has been no such event (to date), reality TV continues to grow, covering every imaginable possible topic (spouse swapping, anyone?). Combining disdain with desire, RTV invites viewers to fantasize that they too can effortlessly become celebrities, or rich, or beautiful, while sneering at those who, by being contestants or characters on such shows, actually pursue the fantasy. We've come a long way from the "I'm OK. You're OK" era. Today, it's more like "I'm not OK. You're an idiot."

Crime Scene Imaginations

A fairly recent spin-off of the reality TV fervor has been the criminal mystery series in which the techniques of crime solving have been more important than the plot. Led by such shows as *CSI: Las Vegas*, these crime dramas share with their predecessors a story line centered on a murder mystery and the investigators who solve it. But in a crucial difference, the new shows feature crime solvers who aren't cops or detectives: They're forensic laboratory technicians (as in *CSI: Las Vegas*) or casino security employees (as in *Las Vegas*). These programs combine a scripted fictional story line with (presumably) realistic views into the world of forensic science, or whatever expertise the crime-solving team happens to have. The clinical realism of a show like *CSI: Las Vegas* suggests an audience interest in reality-based programming even when the program is a fiction. Part of this interest may well have been stimulated in the days of the O. J. Simpson murder trial, during which, for a year or so, audiences could witness daily the testimony of forensic technicians and scientists — rather nerdy sorts, actually, when compared with the dashing detectives of murder mystery tradition, but they seem to have struck a chord, if the many spin-offs from *CSI: Las Vegas* are any indicator.

A second source for the interest in reality-oriented crime dramas can probably be found in the aftermath of the September 11 attacks. With brutal suddenness, Americans became aware of the complex array of otherwise ordinary people who are responsible for maintaining national security. In the past, the threat from abroad lay in intercontinental ballistic missiles, weapons wielded by governments whom only the U.S. military could challenge. But after 9/11, the military has been joined by hosts of nonmilitary personnel whose mission is to prevent another catastrophe. The new crime dramas, without even referring directly to national security and terrorism (as programs like *24* do), show us these ordinary people and their equipment and subtly reassure their audiences that ordinary people like them are at work keeping track of the bad guys.

Altered States

Our point is that whether you are considering a fully scripted show, RTV, or any other sort of program, you can find a cultural message behind the entertaining facade shown on the screen. The facade is the fantasy that distracts its viewers from the ways in which television programmers use their programs to achieve their primary ends — which are, in effect, to get us to go out and buy the products that sponsor the shows. That is why TV shows reflect the attitudes and desires of their core audiences and why interpreting TV reveals what those attitudes and desires are.

Interpreting television programming is especially valuable at a time when TV is blurring the line between fantasy and reality in an ever-more-profound manner. A process accelerated by docudrama-style shows like *America's Most Wanted*, it reflects television's profound effect on the very way that we perceive our world. If television were to vanish today — no more shows, no more prime time — its effects would live on in the way it has altered our sense of reality. We expect instant visual access to every corner of the earth because of TV, and we want to get to the point quickly. It is often claimed that our attention spans have been shortened in a universe of televised sound bites, but at the same time our desire for information has expanded (inquiring minds want to know). Indeed, the television age has equally been an information age.

All the News That's Fit to Jeer

Television has not only blurred the line between fiction and reality; it has also effaced the traditional distinction between the "news" and "entertainment." In a shift that parallels the deconstruction of the line between high and low culture, television news broadcasts are increasingly being compelled to compete with such entertainment-based news "sources" as Comedy Central's *The Daily Show*, as comedic "anchor men" like Jon Stewart and Stephen Colbert take the once-hallowed places of such network anchors as Edward R. Murrow, Walter Cronkite, and Dan Rather. With younger viewers staying away from traditional network news broadcasts in droves, the "news" is being transformed to be more like the sources such viewers prefer. For their part, by bringing in new faces like Katie Couric, the traditional networks are struggling to make the news more entertaining, sexier, and edgier in order to compete, thus undermining the old distinction between information and entertainment that TV news once relied upon.

This movement towards a world of "infotainment" can be regarded from two different perspectives. On the one hand, it can be argued that young viewers have never been drawn to the network news and that the popularity of comedic news sources simply means that today's younger viewers are both savvier than viewers of their generation in the past and better informed because their attraction to shows like *The Daily Show* keeps them abreast of current events. A further argument for this position could be made by expanding the system in which we analyze the rise of infotainment to include the political and cultural implications of such programs as *The Simpsons* and *South Park*, both of which regularly address, and skewer, contemporary political and cultural issues, weighing in on current controversies with a directness and

Stephen Colbert.

daring that the conventional news never approaches. From such a perspective, it could be argued that thanks to making the news entertaining, television is raising a remarkably sophisticated, news-savvy generation of Americans.

Without dismissing such a position, it is still possible to offer a counterargument, however. That is, when there was still a clear distinction between entertainers whose material was based on current politics — like Mort Saul and Mark Russell — and news broadcasters — like Walter Cronkite and Chet Huntley and David Brinkley — the subject matter of the news could be taken more seriously and thus have a greater effect on viewers. For the fundamental nature of entertainment is precisely that it is not serious; it is a distraction from the grim realities of everyday life. We seek entertainment to escape reality, not engage with it. Thus, if our source of information about reality is packaged as entertainment, we are less likely to be actively affected by it and to get involved in the issues presented to us. Laughter is a great catharsis, a release of energy, but when we laugh at the grimly real issues of our day, we are all the less likely to expend that energy on doing anything about them.

So, whether we are watching *The Daily Show* or *South Park*, enjoying the points that such programs may be scoring against the political targets that we like to see attacked, our very enjoyment may be disempowering after all, allowing jeering to replace acting and laughter to replace outrage.

From Symbols to Icons

In semiotic terms, the ubiquity of television and video in our lives represents a shift from one kind of sign system to another. As Marshall McLuhan pointed out more than forty years ago in *The Gutenberg Galaxy* (1962), Western culture since the fifteenth century has defined itself around the printed word — the linear text that reads from left to right and top to bottom. The printed word, in the terminology of the American founder of semiotics, Charles Sanders Peirce, is a symbolic sign, one whose meaning is entirely arbitrary or conventional. A symbolic sign means what it does because those who use it have decided so. Words don't look like what they mean. Their significance is entirely abstract.

Not so with a visual image like a photograph or TV picture, which does resemble its object and is not entirely arbitrary. Though a photograph is not literally the thing it depicts and often reflects a good deal of staging and manipulation by the photographer, we often respond to it as if it were an innocent reflection of the world. Peirce called such signs "icons," referring by this term to any sign that resembles what it means. The way you interpret an icon, then, differs from the way you interpret a symbol or word. The interpretation of words involves your cognitive capabilities; the interpretation and reception of icons are far more sensuous, more a matter of vision than cognition. The shift from a civilization governed by the paradigm of the book to one dominated by television accordingly involves a shift in the way we "read" our world, as the symbolic field of the printed page yields to the iconic field of the video screen.

The shift from a symbolic, or word-centered, world to an iconic universe filled with visual images carries profound cultural implications. Such implications are not necessarily negative. The accessibility of video technology, for example, has created opportunities for personal expression that have never existed before. It is very difficult to publish a paper-and-ink book, but anyone can post to YouTube. The rapid transmissibility of video images speeds up communication and can bond groups of linguistically and culturally diverse people together, as MTV speaks to millions of people around the nation and world at once in the language of dance and music.

At the same time, video images may be used to stimulate political action. Rappers and their audiences particularly view rap and rap videos as subversions of the dominant society, just as baby boomers in the sixties used rock 'n' roll in challenging the Establishment. Indeed, while many critics of TV deplore the passivity of its viewers, the medium is not inherently passive. Look at it this way: TV has a visceral power that print does not. Words abstractly describe things; television shows concrete images. Dramatic television images of drowning polar bears, for example, have recently helped awaken people to the effects of global warming and climate change. Television, in short, has the potential to awaken the apathetic as written texts cannot.

But there is a price to be paid for the modes of perception that the iconic world of TV stimulates. For while one can read the signs of TV and video actively and creatively (which, of course, is the whole point of this book), and one *can* be moved to action by a video image, the sheer visibility of icons tempts one to receive them uncritically and passively. Icons look so much like the realities they refer to that it is easy to forget that icons, too, are signs: images that people can construct to carry ideological meanings. Just think of all those iconic images of the classic fifties-era sitcoms. *Leave It to Beaver*, *Father Knows Best*, *The Ozzie and Harriet Show*, and so on, established an American mythology of an idyllic era by the sheer persuasiveness of their images. In fact, the 1950s were not such idyllic years. Along with the McCarthyite hysteria of the Cold War and the looming specter of nuclear war and contamination from open-air nuclear testing, there were economic downturns; the Korean War; and a growing sense that American life was becoming sterile, conformist, and materialistic — though it wasn't until the sixties that this uneasiness broke into the open. Few fathers in the fifties had the kind of leisure that the sitcom dads had, and the feminist resurgence in the sixties demonstrated that not all women were satisfied with the housewifely roles assigned them in every screenplay. And yet, those constructed images of white middle-class contentment and security have become so real in the American imagination that they can be called on in quite concrete ways, as when political candidates refer to them as "evidence" of a lost world of "family values" that they promise to restore.

Niche Marketing

The emergence of cable TV in recent years has worked its own changes in the content of your viewing experience. The proliferation of cable channels has fostered a more finely targeted programming schedule by which producers can focus on narrowly defined audiences, from nature lovers to home shoppers. This is referred to as "niche marketing," and television today is far more divided into special niches than it was in the early days. For this reason today's Nielsen leaders, which have been designed to appeal to special niche markets, don't get nearly the numbers that sixties hits like *The Beverly Hillbillies* enjoyed, but they don't need to either. When there was less viewer choice, everyone watched the same shows, but now that there is more choice, producers target the most desirable audiences — that is, those who are perceived as commanding the most disposable income. Thus most prime-time television is aimed at middle-class to upper-middle-class viewers between the ages

---

Exploring the Signs of Music Videos

In your journal, explore the impact music videos have had on you. How have videos shaped your desires and expectations about life? How were your actions and behavior influenced by MTV? What videos were especially meaningful to you? What did you think about them when you were younger, and how do you see them now? (If you didn't watch MTV, you might focus instead on other types of television programs.)

---

of eighteen and forty-nine, with the upper-end age figure dropping to as low as twenty-nine or thirty on the Fox network.

The fine-tuning of audiences, then, simply reflects a fine-tuning of marketing: Specially defined audiences can be targeted for specially defined marketing campaigns. In this sense, the advent of cable TV repeats the same history as that of traditional commercial television, which became a medium primarily for the pitching of goods and services. But the proliferation of channels bears the potential to upset television's commercial monopoly. When NBC, CBS, ABC, and their affiliates ruled the airways, programming decisions for an entire nation were made by a tiny group of executives. Aside from the Nielsen ratings, viewers had little chance to let programmers know what they wanted to see. While certainly no revolution has occurred in the wake of cable, there has been some movement toward more audience participation in what gets broadcast.

The phenomenal success of MTV provides a good example of the increasing power of the television audience. In its early years, rock music appeared on TV in such programs as *American Bandstand*, *Shindig*, and *Hullabaloo*. In each case, a rock act had to be toned down considerably before it could be televised (Elvis was ordered not to bump and grind lest he be banned from the TV screens of the fifties). What amounted to censorship worked because the venues for the televising of rock were often adult oriented (consider how the Beatles first appeared to American audiences on the adult variety program *The Ed Sullivan Show*). MTV, on the other hand, is an entirely youth-oriented station. Though it too exists to promote products — through both the videos it displays and the commercials it runs — MTV must conform to the tastes of its audience to succeed, rather than simply dictate to that audience what it will broadcast.

Hey Hey, Oh My, Will Rock 'n' Roll Ever Die?

Rock performers from The Who to Neil Young have written songs about the enduring destiny of rock 'n' roll, but while news of the death of rock is certainly premature, it has been surpassed in recent years by rap and rhythm and blues as the most popular youth music in America. Once an authentic urban street phenomenon culturally coded as the music of African Americans (which is why early white rappers like Vanilla Ice and Marky Mark were regarded as something of a joke), rap has fully crossed over to be the preferred pop entertainment of teens of all ethnicities, making it possible for white rappers like Eminem to succeed — though his act is carefully designed to appear as "authentically black."

Eminem's success repeats, in its own fashion, the rise of Elvis Presley in the 1950s, when disc jockeys in the still-segregated South refused to include black musicians on their playlists, thus excluding such rock pioneers as Chuck Berry, Bo Diddley, and Little Richard. Elvis was regarded at the time as "a white boy who sounded black," and he soared to stardom as black artists were reclassified as "rhythm-and-blues" performers and were largely exiled to marginal radio stations.

There is an interesting cultural question involved in the early co-optation of black rock 'n' roll, and the contemporary co-optation of rap by such performers as Eminem. That question is why mainstream white middle-class youths continue to turn to the music of marginalized black America to express and entertain themselves. The simplest answer is that in the last fifty years or so, white teens have identified with the African American subculture, viewing the music of black America as an authentic medium for the expression of their own resentments and desires. In the 1940s and 1950s, Beat hipsters like Jack Kerouac turned to the cultural forms of black America (especially hot jazz and bebop) as an alternative to a society that they found repressive and sterile, while young white audiences found in the more sexually expressive music of rhythm and blues an outlet for their own sexual desires in a sexually repressed era. Today, the commodified anger and violence that can be found in many hip-hop numbers are embraced by white teens as an expression of

Reading Music on the Net

Many popular musicians and groups boast their own Web site or host special "concert" events on the Internet. Find the site of a favorite artist by using a search engine such as Yahoo! (**www.yahoo.com/ Entertainment/Music/Artists**) or trying a commercial site, **artistdirect .com**. Then study your artist's site, and analyze the images created for him or her. How is the artist "packaged" on the Net, and does that packaging differ from that used in other media? What sort of relationship is established between the artist and you, the fan, and how does the electronic medium affect that relationship?

their own anger — against their parents, against rules and restrictions, against any form of authority, not to mention hostility against women for many a male rap fan.

Indeed, no cultural form in America today is more identified with youth than rap, with most adults detesting it. Wedded to television through the auspices of MTV, rap embodies the collective consciousness of young consumers, forming lasting bonds of generational identity. But with generational change will come changes in expression, and today's cutting edge top-ten single will likely be on tomorrow's "classic rap" playlist, prompting future young listeners to smile in derision as they contemplate the doddering musical tastes of their elders (that is, you), while enjoying their own forms of musical rebellion.

The Readings

We begin the readings in this chapter with Francine Prose's provocative analysis of reality TV, arguing that the ruthless Machiavellian behavior we can watch every night on such shows as *Survivor* and *The Apprentice* is really no different from — in fact, is a reflection of — the behavior of America's corporate and political leadership. James Harold follows with a philosophical meditation on the guilty pleasures of *The Sopranos*. In a paired set of readings on television's favorite animated series, Carl Matheson looks at *The Simpsons* — one of TV's longest-running institutions — and explores what happens when self-conscious irony overrides just about everything else, while David Valleau Curtis and Gerald J. Erion argue that the no-holds-barred irreverence of *South Park* is actually good for American democracy. Next, Jaime J. Weinman reports on the Fox network's ideologically motivated attempt to take on Comedy Central. Susan Douglas next argues that behind the progressive surfaces of *NYPD Blue* and *ER* lies a less-than-enlightened ideology, and Andre Mayer offers a scathing critique of the misogynistic tendencies in contemporary pop music. Marissa Connolly then analyzes how *Will and Grace* makes gay-themed television "safe" for network viewing, while Cynthia Tucker concludes the chapter with an indictment of what she sees as the self-destructive tendencies of gangsta rap.

FRANCINE PROSE

Voting Democracy off the Island:
Reality TV and the Republican Ethos

*It is an essential semiotic principle that, one way or another, everything
connects up in a society. In this provocative analysis of the underlying
ideology of reality television (RTV), Francine Prose discovers what may
seem a surprising connection between the RTV craze and current trends
in American politics. When millions of Americans tune in to watch Donald Trump dump, one by one, the frantic contenders for a dazzling corporate job, or cheer as the quasi-democracies of* Survivor *vote each other
out until only one "winner" is left, we can see the Social Darwinism that
seems to guide, as Prose argues, the current crop of national leaders at
work. The author of fourteen books of fiction — including* Hunters and
Gatherers *(1996),* Guided Tours of Hell: Novellas *(1997), and* A Changed
Man *(2005) — and five nonfiction books — including the best-selling* Reading Like a Writer *(2006) — Prose is a contributing editor at* Harper's *and
a writer on art for the* Wall Street Journal. *This article originally appeared
in* Harper's *in 2004.*

Not even Melana can believe it's real. As the "former NFL cheerleader and
beauty queen looking to fall in love with the perfect guy" swans a bit dazedly
through the Palm Springs mansion in which she will soon undertake the task
of selecting Mr. Right from among sixteen eligible bachelors, she coos about
the thrill of living a "dream come true."

It's the premiere episode of NBC's *Average Joe*, one of the extremely popular and profitable "reality-based" television shows that, in recent years, have
proliferated to claim a significant share of major-network prime time. Featuring ordinary people who have agreed to be filmed in dangerous, challenging,
or embarrassing situations in return for the promise of money, romance, or
fame, these offerings range from *Who Wants to Marry a Millionaire?* to *Who
Wants to Marry My Dad?*, from long-run hits such as *Survivor* and *The Real
World* to the short-lived *Are You Hot?* and *Boy Meets Boy*.

The title *Average Joe* has evidently alerted Melana to the possibility that
her bachelor pool may not be stocked with the same species of dazzling
hunks, those walking miracles of body sculpting, cosmetic dentistry, and hair-
gel expertise who courted *The Bachelorette*. Clearly, she's expecting to meet
the more routinely, unself-consciously attractive sort of guy one might spot on
the street or at the water cooler.

But, as frequently happens, the audience is privy to an essential truth —
or, in the argot of reality programming, a "reveal" — concealed from the hapless

participants. Now, as the cameras whisk us to the bachelors' quarters, we instantly get the visual joke that is, even by the standards of reality TV, sadistic.

The men about to compete for Melana's affections are not merely Joe 5 Well Below Average but Joe Out of the Question. Several are obese; others have tics, dermatological or dental problems, or are short, bespectacled, balding, stooped. Racial and cultural diversity is provided by a diminutive "university professor" from Zimbabwe with a penchant for intellectual boasting and grave fashion miscalculations.

Although the sight of Melana's suitors is intended to amuse and titillate rather than to touch us, it would (to paraphrase Dickens amid this Dickensian crowd) take a heart of stone not to be moved by the moment when the men take a look at one another and realize that their inclusion in this confraternity of nerds is probably not a mistake.

Meanwhile, night has fallen on the desert, and the lovely Melana, all dressed up and as starry-eyed as a kid on Christmas morning, comes out to meet the guys. A white limousine pulls up. A male model emerges, and Melana's face brightens, only to darken seconds later when he announces that, sadly, he is not one of her bachelors.

The white limo carries the tease away. Presently a bus arrives.

The bus doors open. They send the fat guys out first. And by the time a half-dozen sorry specimens are lined up, grinning their hearts out, even Melana gets it. Her shock and dismay are genuine. The men cannot help but notice. "This is *bad*," she whispers, and we can read her lips. "Someone's messing with my head."

What lends the scene its special poignancy is that Melana knows, as do 10 we, that what has befallen her is not some cruel accident of fate. Rather, she has brought misfortune on herself. In filling out the questionnaire that led to her being selected as the heroine of *Average Joe*, she indicated that "a good personality" mattered more to her than did appearance. And in doing so, she violated one of the cardinal rules, a basic article of faith, one of the values that this new version of reality pumps out, hour after hour, night after night, into the culture. Had Melana watched more reality-based TV, she would have learned that surface beauty (preferably in concert with a strong manipulative instinct, a cunning ability to play the game, and vast quantities of money) is all that counts. Melana has transgressed. And now, as we sit back and watch, she is about to be punished.

If this — a dash of casual brutality, a soupçon of voyeurism — is your recipe for entertainment, it's a taste you can satisfy, in the privacy of your living room, nearly every evening. In fact, unless you own one of those televisions that allow you to watch two programs at once, you may be forced to make some hard choices.

On a typical night — Thanksgiving Eve, November 26, 2003 — you could, at eight, watch a contestant on CBS's *Survivor Pearl Islands* secure himself some

Landing the big one: a scene from the début of the RTV hit
Survivor.

sympathy by misleading his fellow tribe members into thinking that his grand-mother has just died. But witnessing the "biggest lie ever told on *Survivor*" would mean missing the episode of NBC's *Queer Eye for the Straight Guy* in which a quintet of homosexual fashion and lifestyle advisers convince a bald-ing lawyer to lose his unflattering hairpiece. At nine, you could shop along with ABC's Trista for *Trista and Ryan's Wedding*, an account of the big-ticket ceremony that would solemnize the love affair spawned, as America watched, on *The Bachelorette*. And at ten, on *Extreme Makeover*, the most literally inva-sive series so far, two lucky souls (chosen from more than 10,000 applicants) have their lives transformed by plastic surgery. On this night a man whose 200-pound weight loss has left him looking like a shar-pei, and a rather pretty grade-school teacher — who believes that she is only a rhinoplasty and a chin implant away from rivaling her beautiful sisters — will go under the knife.

In the event that three hours of watching your fellow humans suffer and squirm and endure surgical procedures has left you feeling uneasy about how you have spent your time, or what you have found amusing, you can be reassured — as are the network executives, it would seem — by the fact that you are not alone. In January 2003 the premiere of Fox Network's *Joe Million-aire*, in which a construction worker courted women tricked into believing that he possessed a vast personal fortune, attracted 18.6 million viewers; 40 million tuned in for its conclusion. *American Idol*, the talent show that asks fans to vote for their favorite contestants by telephone, received 110 million calls in its first season and 15.5 million calls during the final show alone. By contrast, the most popular national news program — NBC's *Nightly News* — averages around 11 million viewers per night.

Like Melana, network accountants were quick to see reality shows as a dream come true. For although production values and costs have risen, reality-based programs are still relatively cheap to produce, mostly because they avoid the expense of hiring actors whose salary demands can rise astronomically if the show becomes a hit. One consequence is that television actors have seen a radical reduction in the number and range of available roles.

Despite the fact that journalists periodically hail the death of reality TV, it has proved remarkably long-lived. MTV's *The Real World*, which sends seven attractive young strangers to spend six months turning their luxury housing into a Petri dish of sexual, racial, and interpersonal tension, has been running since 1992. Now in its eighth season, *Survivor* has airlifted a succession of warring "tribes" from the Amazon to the jungles of Thailand. During the week of November 17–23, 2003, the only shows more popular than *Survivor Pearl Islands* (which drew 19.9 million viewers) were *CSI*, *ER*, and *Friends*.

On aesthetic grounds alone, it's arguable that reality-based shows are no better or worse than *CSI*, *ER*, and *Friends*. But the most obvious difference is the most crucial one. Fans of *Friends* understand that they are watching a sit-com, cast with celebrity actors. Watching *Survivor* and *The Real World*, they believe that they are observing *real* men and women.

Viewers do, of course, realize that some of what they're seeing has been instigated or exacerbated by the show's producers. Yet the fact is that viewers *are* watching people who, regardless of their career ambitions or masochistic exhibitionism, are amateurs who may have been chosen *for* their fragility and instability. Many of the "Average Joes" could never get hired as character actors. And observing their response to stress and humiliation generates a gladiatorial, bread-and-circus atmosphere that simply does not exist when we see movie stars in scrubs sail a gurney down the halls of *ER*.

Reality-based TV, then, is not a scripted fiction but an improvisation, an apparently instructive improvisation that doles out consistent and frequently reinforced lessons about human nature and, yes, reality. These programs also generate a jittery, adrenalized buzz that produces a paradoxically tranquilized numbness in which our defenses relax and leave us more receptive to the "information" we are receiving. For this reason alone, even those who take pride in never looking at TV, except for the occasional peek at PBS, might want to tune in and see what reality their fellow citizens have been witnessing.

What might future anthropologists (or, for that matter, contemporary TV-addicted children and adults) conclude about our world if these programs constituted their primary source of information? The most obvious lesson to be drawn from reality TV, the single philosophical pole around which everything else revolves, is that the laws of natural selection are even more brutal, inflexible, and *sensible* than one might suppose from reading *Origin of Species*. Reality is a Darwinian battlefield on which only the fittest survive, and it's not merely logical but admirable to marshal all our skills and resources to succeed in a struggle that only one person can win.

Compelling its testy, frequently neurotic castaways to operate as if they were several rungs down the evolutionary ladder, grubbing roots and berries and forced to earn such basic necessities as blankets by performing acrobatic stunts, *Survivor* is the prototype. The show urges its participants to labor for their tribe but always, ultimately, for themselves. Because at the end of the day — in this case, the final episode — only one person will walk away with a million dollars. And in case we lose sight of first principles, the show's motto, which appears in its logo, is "Outwit. Outplay. Outlast."

Survivor is the younger American cousin of the 1997 Swedish *Expedition Robinson*, a title judged too literary for the U.S. market. It's probably just as well that the series wasn't called *Expedition Robinson*. *Robinson Crusoe* and *Swiss Family Robinson* extol the virtues and advantages of fellowship and cooperation, whereas on *Survivor* such considerations are useful only to a point. *Survivor* could be Defoe's masterpiece rewritten by Ayn Rand. And for all its Darwinian trappings, the series offers a skewed view of the *purpose* of the struggle for dominance. Propagating the species is the last thing on these people's minds.

And so the steps that lead toward that goal aren't determined by physical combat or brilliant displays of plumage. Rather, contestants are eliminated by a democratic process; every few days, tribe members vote on which of their fellows will be forced to leave the island. As we watch, the loser trudges across a rope bridge or rock ledge and off to a dismal future without a million dollars.

Observant readers may already have noted that the guiding principles to which I've alluded — flinty individualism, the vision of a zero-sum society in which no one can win unless someone else loses, the conviction that altruism and compassion are signs of folly and weakness, the exaltation of solitary striving above the illusory benefits of cooperative mutual aid, the belief that certain circumstances justify secrecy and deception, the invocation of a reviled common enemy to solidify group loyalty — are the exact same themes that underlie the rhetoric we have been hearing and continue to hear from the Republican Congress and our current administration.

Of course, no sensible person would imagine that Donald Rumsfeld is sitting down with the producers of reality-based TV to discuss the possibility that watching the contestants sweat and strain to bring civilization to the jungle will help us accept the sacrifices we have been and are still being asked to make in Iraq. On the other hand, there is the unsettling precedent set by *Profiles from the Front Line*, a series that aired around the time of the war in Iraq and was produced for ABC Entertainment by Jerry Bruckheimer, whose credits include *Black Hawk Down*.

According to an advance release from the network,

the Pentagon and the Department of Defense lent their full support and cooperation to this unique production. . . . As America prepares for a possible war with Iraq, the country continues to wage a perilous war on terrorism. ABC will transport viewers to actual battlefields in Central Asia with a six-episode series that will feature actual footage of the elite U.S. Special Operations forces apprehending possible terrorists, as well as compelling, personal stories of the U.S. military men and women who bear the burden and risks of this fighting.

Indeed, ABC News complained that — in order to film the soldiers arresting a "big-time" Taliban leader, disarming rockets, providing medical care to Afghan civilians, capturing fuel-truck hijackers, and accepting the love and gratitude of the Afghan people — the show's producers were being granted a level of access to the troops that Pentagon officials denied the network's actual reporters.

But even when the collaboration between the military, the government, and the entertainment industry is not nearly so overt, these shows continue to transmit a perpetual, low-frequency hum of agitprop. The ethics (if one can call them that) and the ideals that permeate these programs at once reflect and reinforce the basest, most mindless and ruthless aspects of the current political zeitgeist. If the interests of the corporate culture that controls our television stations are at heart the same as those that fund and support lobbyists and politicians, it stands to reason that — when network executives do meet to determine what is appropriate, entertaining, profitable, what people want and need to see — they are unlikely to flinch at portraying stylized versions of the same behavior we read about in the press, or can observe on the Senate floor.

If reality TV does turn out to be not only the present but also the future of prime-time television, it seems more than likely that a steady, high-intake, long-term diet of *Survivor* and *The Bachelorette* will subtly, or not so subtly, affect the views and values of the audiences that tune in week after week. Watching a nightly Darwinian free-for-all cannot help but have a desensitizing effect. Once you've absorbed and assimilated the idea that civility is, at best, a frill, you may find yourself less inclined to suppress an eruption of road rage or the urge to ridicule the homely Average Joe who dares to approach a pretty girl. If the lesson of reality TV is that anyone will do anything for money, that every human interaction necessarily involves the swift, calculated formation and dissolution of dishonest, amoral alliances, it seems naive to be appalled by the fact that our government has been robbing us to pay off its supporters in the pharmaceutical industry and among the corporations profiting from the rebuilding of Iraq. After you've seen a "real person" lie about his grandmother's death, you may be slightly less shocked to learn that our leaders failed to come clean about the weapons of mass destruction.

After all, it's the way the world works; it's how people behave. We can't have witnessed all that reality without having figured that out by now. How foolish it would be to object to the billing practices of companies such as Halliburton, or to the evidence that our government has been working behind the scenes to dismantle the social security system and to increase (in the guise of reducing) what the elderly will have to pay for health care. *Everybody* acts like that, given half the chance. And we all admire a winner, regardless of how the game was won.

Which is the message we get, and are meant to be getting, every time a bachelor outsmarts his rivals, every time the castaways vote a contender off the island and inch one rung up the ladder. Indeed, those weekly tribal councils at which the voting occurs, held in a cavern or cave decorated to evoke the palm-fringed exotica of the tiki lounge or the Bugs Bunny cartoon, are arguably the most disturbing and pernicious moments in the reality-TV lineup. They're a travesty of democracy so painfully familiar, so much like what our political reality is actually becoming, that it's far more unnerving than watching Donald Trump brutally fire each week's losers, or ugly single guys made to feel even more unattractive than they are.

The castaways vote, as we do, but it's a democracy that might have been 30 conceived if the spirit of Machiavelli had briefly possessed the mind of Thomas Jefferson; indeed, the reasons behind the survivors' ballots might puzzle our Founding Fathers. Because this fun-house version of the electoral process seeks to dismantle civilization rather than to improve it, the goal is neither a common good nor the furthering of life, liberty, or the pursuit of happiness. It's a parody of democracy, robbed of its heart and soul, a democracy in which everyone always votes, for himself.

READING THE TEXT

1. What explanations does Prose provide for the recent dramatic increase in the number of reality TV programs?

2. How does Prose contrast reality TV with other sorts of programming, such as sitcoms and dramas?

3. Summarize in your own words the guiding social and philosophical principles that underlie reality television.

4. What is the relationship that Prose sees between reality TV and Republican politics?

5. What effect does Prose believe a long-term diet of reality TV will have on the American consciousness?

READING THE SIGNS

1. In an argumentative essay, support, refute, or modify Prose's proposition that the guiding principles that underlie reality TV are the same that shape the policies of the George W. Bush administration.

2. Interview several fans of reality TV about their attraction to such programs. Do they like all reality TV shows, or do they discriminate among them? If the latter, what is their pattern of preference? Then use your findings as the basis of an argumentative essay about why this genre has developed such a large following in early twenty-first-century America.

3. Read or reread the Introduction to this chapter, and write an essay in which you analyze whether the appeal of the episode of *Average Joe* that Prose describes is based on schadenfreude. Alternately, watch another current RTV program, particularly one that is based on voting contestants out of a contest, and conduct the same sort of analysis.

4. In class, brainstorm responses to Prose's question, "What might future anthropologists . . . conclude about our world if [reality] programs constituted their primary source of information?" (para. 19). Then write an essay in which you propose your own response to this question.

5. Write an essay in which you support, challenge, or complicate Prose's claim that the contestant voting ritual that occurs on many reality TV programs is "a parody of democracy, robbed of its heart and soul, a democracy in which everyone always votes, for himself" (para. 30).

"You're Fired."

READING THE SIGNS

1. What is *The Apprentice*? To what does "You're Fired" refer? Provide reasons why this expression has become a popular catchphrase.
2. What is the purpose of this banner? What does it promote? Is it, in your opinion, effective?

JAMES HAROLD

A Moral Never-Never Land: Identifying with Tony Soprano

Tony Soprano kills people. He breaks their legs and threatens to castrate them. Yet, somehow, James Harold likes Tony Soprano. He knows this might seem odd, and he wonders whether there is anything morally wrong with it. Since Harold is also a philosopher, he is well equipped to reflect on the matter, as he does in this philosophical exploration, which first appeared in The Sopranos and Philosophy *(2004), of the moral effect of* The Sopranos. *Arguing that* The Sopranos *offers a multifaceted view of gangster life that combines both sympathetic and repulsive elements, Harold concludes that it is indeed beneficial for such a TV show to stimulate viewers to think deeply about the nature of good and evil. An assistant professor of philosophy at Mount Holyoke College, Harold's essays have been published in the* Journal of Aesthetics and Art Criticism, Philosophical Investigations, *and the* British Journal of Aesthetics.

I like Tony Soprano; I can't help it. I like him despite the fact that I recognize that he's a vicious and dangerous criminal. I don't particularly *want* to like him, and I certainly don't think I would like him if he were a real person who lived down the street from me. If he were really my neighbor, I think I'd feel for him what the Cusamanos do: a mixture of fear, fascination, and disgust. Nonetheless, recognizing that he is fictional, I like him. I find myself sympathizing with him: when he is depressed, I pity him; when he is wronged, I feel anger towards those who have betrayed him; and when he is successful, I share in his happiness. I want him to do well. I root for him to defeat his opponents, and, at the end of Season Four, for him to win back his wife Carmela.

Is there anything *morally* wrong with caring about Tony Soprano in this way? If Tony Soprano were a real person, then most people would agree that liking him is at least a little bit morally unsavory. This is Charmaine Bucco's opinion, for example, especially with regard to her husband Artie's friendship with Tony, and it's also the view of most of the other non-Mafia related characters on the show, such as Dr. Melfi's friends and family, the Cusamanos, and so on. But Tony Soprano isn't real — he's fictional, and I know that even if the Cusamanos don't. So what could be wrong with my liking Tony Soprano, given that I know that *The Sopranos* is a work of fiction?

From time to time, as political winds change, politicians, including, for example, Tipper Gore, Joseph Lieberman, and Bob Dole, have weighed in against various artworks in popular culture on the grounds that these artworks are morally dangerous. *The Sopranos* has attracted its fair share of this kind of

Dr. Melfi and Tony Soprano.

criticism. Usually these criticisms are answered by proponents of freedom of expression, and the discussion turns to censorship and the necessity of toleration and diversity of viewpoints. What often gets left behind in these debates is the crucial issue of whether or not there really is any reason to think that a series like *The Sopranos* can be morally corrupting. It is often unclear exactly how artworks like *The Sopranos* are supposed to be bad for us. One of the things that worries some of us is that television shows like *The Sopranos* make very bad people seem, well, likeable.

When Is Art Dangerous?

The first Western philosopher to worry seriously about the moral effects of fiction on its audience was Plato. Plato worried about the way that the dramatic poets like Homer played on the emotions of audience members in ways that could be dangerous and manipulative. Poetry, Plato believed, evokes strong emotion in ways that could undermine social stability. In Plato's time, a dramatic poem like *The Odyssey* would be read aloud or sung in a public performance, and so poetry, for Plato, is more like theater for us. An ideal society, Plato thought, would be governed by principles of reason, and our willingness to follow through on these rational principles could be weakened by desires arising from strong emotion — the province of poetry. Poetry was supposed to be dangerous because it can lead us to sympathize with fictional characters, and thus the feelings of the fictional characters come to infect the audience. Plato wrote:

> When even the best of us hear Homer or one of the other tragedians imitating one of the heroes sorrowing and making a long lamenting speech or singing and beating his breast, you know that we enjoy it, give ourselves up to following it, sympathize with the hero, take his sufferings seriously, and praise as a good poet the one who affects us most in this way.[1]

In the end, the feelings of the audience and the feelings of the character are the same, and the audience may feel pity, or grief, even when it's not appropriate to do so. Further, we may carry these inappropriate emotions home with us, and they can become part of our character, and affect the way we act. Plato recognized how strongly we can feel about poetry, and the power that this passion can have: sympathetic attention to art, he said, "nurtures and waters them and establishes them as rulers in us."[2] These passions can become so strong that we can no longer control them in our everyday lives. Plato's example is of a man who enjoys comic plays and who then comes to act like a buffoon at home; but someone who enjoyed a show like *The Sopranos* could well be possessed by more dangerous emotions, like rage, revenge, or contempt for ordinary people. If you are inclined to think that Plato's arguments don't apply to modern audiences, consider the following quote, taken from a fan Web site discussion of "University," which speaks to just this kind of worry.

> When my boyfriend and I watch *The Sopranos*, he gets so caught up, you would think it was happening to him. This gentle man, who wouldn't harm a fly. It's strange phenomena [*sic*], and not unlike soap addicts who confuse TV with reality.[3]

In the nineteenth century, Leo Tolstoy expressed similar concerns about art (including much of his own writing) in his book *What Is Art?* Tolstoy had undergone a deep religious experience late in his life, and he came to believe that most art was morally corrupt. Like Plato, he held that art evoked strong emotions in its audience, and he believed that many such emotions are, in his view, morally corrupting. Only art motivated by true Christian feeling, according to Tolstoy, could be morally acceptable. Tolstoy therefore rejected virtually all art, except popular Christian peasant art, which, he believed, conveyed only simple Christian love. Other artworks transmitted corrupt feelings to their audiences — feelings of unjust pride or lust, for example.[4] These feelings

---

[1] Plato, *Republic* (605c–d), translated by G. M. A. Grube and C. D. C. Reeve (Indianapolis: Hackett, 1992).

[2] Plato, 606d.

[3] <http://www.the-sopranos.com/db/ep32_review.htm>. The post was anonymous.

[4] One important difference between Plato and Tolstoy is that Tolstoy thought that the feelings transmitted were the feelings of the artist or author, whereas Plato thought that they were the feelings of the character.

make people worse morally, because the feelings are selfish, and they alienate people from one another.

Plato and Tolstoy are separated by thousands of years, but their views share certain features in common: they both hold that art corrupts its audience by playing on emotion; they both hold that some art is worse than others in doing so; they believe that the emotional impact of art is great enough to influence how we act and what kind of people we become, so that art can make us bad people; they were both particularly critical of the most popular artists of their day. There is little doubt that both of them would have disapproved of *The Sopranos*. Should we, like Plato and Tolstoy, be worried that we might be infected by watching *The Sopranos*, and caring about the immoral protagonists?

Plato and Tolstoy have their present-day counterparts, too. Some cognitive scientists believe that when we watch a television show like *The Sopranos*, we simulate the feelings of the characters portrayed on screen. That is, we use our own minds to imitate what we imagine is going on in the minds of characters, and we feel an emotion that is in some ways like the emotion that the character feels. This emotion can then affect us in a number of ways. We sometimes call this "sympathizing" or "identifying" with a character onscreen. Though in many cases we are able to separate the character's emotion from our own feelings, sometimes our imaginings of the fictional character's emotions infect and affect our own.[5]

Tony Soprano does this himself in "Proshai, Livushka." After the death of his mother, Tony watches his favorite film, *Public Enemy*. In this movie, Jimmy Cagney's character is a gangster with a gentle, loving mother. As Tony watches, he sympathizes with the Cagney character, and imagines having a loving, trusting relationship with his mother. This makes him smile, at first, and then cry, as he compares this imagined mother-son relationship with his own experience. We understand why Tony is so deeply affected by this film, because we can also be affected by works of fiction. Tony is moved by identifying with the Cagney character, and we are moved by identifying with Tony.

A key feature of this view is that we pick out a character to identify with, and we focus on that person's feelings and emotions. It is this character that we identify with; he or she is the one that we know the best, and often, he or she is the one that we like the most. In the case of *The Sopranos*, despite a large, strong ensemble cast, the primary character with whom audiences identify is Tony himself. This is how I come to care about Tony, and why I feel relief when he is successful, even when his "success" consists in murder, as when he strangles the mob informant Febby Petrulio in "College."

The problem with this sympathetic identification is that sometimes the character with whom we identify has thoughts and feelings which are morally

[5]This phenomenon is discussed by Robert Gordon in his "Sympathy, Simulation, and the Impartial Spectator," in *Mind and Morals: Essays on Ethics and Cognitive Science*, edited by Larry May, Marilyn Friedman, and Andy Clark (Boston: MIT Press, 1996), pp. 165–80.

reprehensible, and by identifying with that character, we risk being infected by these vicious sentiments. We might start to think that Tony's views about violence and vengeance are reasonable, or we might come to share his propensity for anger, jealousy, rage, and suspicion. If imagining these feelings leads us to share them (even to a small extent), then liking Tony could make a person morally worse.

Why *The Sopranos*?

There are so many works of popular art that feature gangsters — not to mention other kinds of vicious people — as protagonists that it hardly seems fair to pick on *The Sopranos*. *Godfather Parts I, II*, and *III, Goodfellas, Carlito's Way, Scarface, Casino*, and *Public Enemy* are just a few examples of films that feature gangsters as main characters. (Most of these movies are referenced and discussed by the characters in *The Sopranos*, especially by Silvio Dante, who loves to imitate Al Pacino's character from *The Godfather*.) But *The Sopranos* distinguishes itself from these other works in three ways. First, *The Sopranos* is an ongoing television series, not a two-hour movie. As of this writing, four seasons comprising fifty-two episodes have been shown, and at least two more seasons are planned. That will make more than three *days* worth of material if one were to sit down and watch them all back-to-back. By contrast, all the films of the *Godfather* series, taken together, would take fewer than ten hours to watch. So loyal viewers of *The Sopranos* spend a long time with these characters, getting to know much more about them, and potentially, to care much more about them than viewers ever could with a film character. Not surprisingly, we are more deeply affected by characters we spend more time with and get to know better, and we get to spend a lot of time with Tony and friends.

Second, the gangsters in *The Sopranos*, especially Tony, are portrayed in deeply psychological and often quite intimate ways. We often get to see Tony's dreams (occasionally we see other characters' dreams, such as Christopher's and Dr. Melfi's, but not often). Through Tony's sessions with Dr. Melfi, we get to know Tony's feelings much better than we could otherwise. In those sessions, we get to understand his childhood (through flashbacks), his hopes and concerns, and his fears. We get a very strong picture of Tony as a complete human being. The character himself is a rich and complex one. In addition to being a gangster (with all that implies) we also learn that Tony tries, in his own way, to be a good father and husband, that he cares deeply about his children and wants them to do well. We learn that he loves his friends deeply, even those (like Big Pussy) that he ends up killing. He has a strong sense of responsibility, and when he says he will do something, he feels bound to do it. Despite (perhaps because of) his evil, vicious qualities, Tony has some good features, as well. Tony Soprano is a more fully developed character than any other fictional gangster ever created, and we get to know him intimately.

Third, *The Sopranos* strives for verisimilitude. It does not have the ironic stylishness of *Goodfellas*, nor is it an idealized period piece like *The Godfather*. With one major exception — the number of gang killings[6] — the show is strikingly realistic. Virtually every element, including the psychoanalysis, the New Jersey settings, the language used by the characters, Tony and Carmela's family dynamics, the FBI surveillance techniques, and the mob structure and organization is very close to what is found in the real world. The show is set in our own time and many of the phenomena that the characters deal with — for example, Prozac, 9/11, Attention Deficit Disorder, coaches sexually assaulting student athletes, the competitiveness of college acceptance, teen drug use — are phenomena that we deal with as well. The characters on *The Sopranos* are aware of the fictional portrayals of gangsters and they discuss these. In "Christopher," Carmela and her friends attend a lecture about the portrayal of Italian-American women as mob wives; Dr. Melfi's ex-husband Richard complains over and over again about the stereotyped portrayal of Italian-Americans in gangster films. The psychiatrist who Tony consults when Dr. Melfi won't see him makes a reference to the Robert DeNiro comedy *Analyze This*. *The Sopranos* thus continues the tradition of gangster fictions, but in a deeper, more reflective way than most do: like us, the characters on *The Sopranos* know that these other stories are fictional.

All of these features conspire to make Tony Soprano a very sympathetic character. When Plato says, "We enjoy it, give ourselves up to following it, sympathize with the hero, take his sufferings seriously," the hero he describes could be Tony. But sympathizing with Tony is not like sympathizing with Artie Bucco; Tony is a terribly vicious and violent man. Tony personally commits five murders that we see on screen: he strangles Febby Petrulio in "College"; he shoots one of Junior's hired killers in "I Dream of Jeanie Cusamano" (this one, at least, is self-defense); in "From Where to Eternity," he kills Matt Bevilaqua with Big Pussy; and then he, Paulie, and Silvio turn around and shoot Big Pussy in "Funhouse"; finally, he kills Ralph Cifaretto in "Whoever Did This." On top of these five, he orders many, many other killings which are carried out by other members of his gang (some shown onscreen and some off). He loses his temper continually, administering beatings to girlfriends (Irina, Gloria) and business associates (Mikey Palmice, Georgie the bartender, Ralphie Cifaretto, Assemblyman Zellman). He doesn't ever hit Dr. Melfi, but he comes quite close. On top of his propensity for personal violence, we have his virulent racism and homophobia, his profiting from corruption, gambling, drugs, and other enterprises that presumably ruin the lives of people we never see on screen. There is no doubt that Tony Soprano is evil, vicious, and morally bankrupt. Yet we like him.

[6]One fan Web site counts thirty-nine deaths over the first four seasons (http://www.the-sopranos .com/db/bodycount.htm). The number of killings on the show far exceeds the number in real life for similar mobs.

Is It Morally Wrong to Watch *The Sopranos*?

The Sopranos leads its audience to identify with a terrible person. Is it then wrong to watch the show? Could identifying with Tony make us worse people too? In the end, I doubt it. There are a number of reasons why *The Sopranos* as a whole does more than just make bad people look good. First, although Tony Soprano is the main character on the show, some of the main characters of *The Sopranos* who are quite sympathetic are not gangsters and are pretty good people, particularly Dr. Melfi and Meadow Soprano. Many other characters, if not good, at least suffer pangs of conscience for the evil they do (or the evil men they love), and they try to do good from time to time: Carmela, Artie Bucco,[7] and Adriana, for example. These characters struggle continually with their moral positions, and their complicity in the crimes being committed all around them. Even some thoroughly bad characters like Christopher and Paulie are forced from time to time to reflect on the moral consequences of what they do ("From Where to Eternity").

But the primary moral center of the show, which serves to balance out the immoral facets of these attractive characters, is Jennifer Melfi's psychiatrist's office. It is here that the viewer is most often led to identify not just with Tony, but with his victims, and to see Tony's life in a richer, more morally sophisticated way. In a long-running series like *The Sopranos*, we see things from more than just one point of view. Tony's psychoanalysis sessions with Dr. Melfi afford us an opportunity to see Tony from the outside as well as from the inside, and to remind us of the self-deception and flimsy justifications that Tony uses in order to continue his life of crime and violence. Tony likes to compare himself to a soldier at war, or a "captain of industry," but he doesn't convince anyone with these analogies (perhaps not even himself). Dr. Melfi's facial expressions make clear her contempt for these facile attempts at justification.

Consider the episode entitled "House Arrest." In this episode, on the advice of his lawyer, Tony has decided to distance himself from criminal activity and spend his time with his legitimate businesses. He grows increasingly restless and agitated; he develops a serious rash; he becomes irritable and frustrated, and he complains of this to Dr. Melfi. Dr. Melfi asks him: "Do you know why a shark keeps moving? . . . There's a psychological condition known as alexithymia,[8] common in certain personalities. The individual craves almost ceaseless action, which enables them to avoid acknowledging the abhorrent

[15]

---

[7]Artie is a very interesting character, morally speaking. For the most part, he is not involved in Tony's activities. Artie did have a brief fling with loan sharking in season four, but it didn't work out, and he wasn't really up to the nasty side of it. But he does indirectly profit from Tony's business, and he keeps silent about some of his wrongdoings.

[8]Alexithymia, strictly speaking, is somewhat different than Jennifer Melfi's account of it here. Ordinarily, alexithymia refers to a condition wherein the patient has difficulty in recognizing her or his own emotions. Melfi is describing how alexithymia manifests itself in sociopathic personalities like Tony's.

things they do." When Tony asks what happens when such people are forced to stop and reflect, she answers, "They have time to think about their behavior. How what they do affects other people. About feelings of emptiness and self-loathing, haunting them since childhood. And they crash." Tony gets her point, but he chooses to respond to this lesson not by reflecting, but by returning to Satriale's with the other mobsters and getting back into action — thus, the shark gets back in motion rather than think about the ethical consequences of how he lives.

Jennifer Melfi continually reminds us as an audience of the dangers of seeing things exclusively from Tony's point of view, and her character provides an alternative point of view on Tony's life and actions. When she complains to her psychiatrist, Elliot Kupferberg, that she is in a "moral never-never land" with Tony Soprano, "Not wanting to judge but to treat," we know exactly how she feels ("From Where to Eternity"). Dr. Melfi, and sometimes other characters such as the Buccos, Meadow, or even Carmela, provide us with an alternative moral center that allows us to see Tony and his actions from the outside, and they remind us of the moral consequences of what Tony does. After Dr. Melfi's rapist goes free, she realizes that she could tell Tony about her rapist, and be revenged on him, but she does not do so ("Employee of the Month"). During this sequence, we sympathize with Melfi, and her moral choice, not with Tony. The finale of the second season ("Funhouse") concludes with one of the few montage sequences ever used in the series.[9] We see alternating shots of the Soprano family celebrating Meadow's graduation, and various shots of the criminal activities that will be paying Meadow's tuition. By juxtaposing these two scenes, the producers of *The Sopranos* remind us that what we like about Tony cannot be separated from the evil he does.

The problem with Plato's and Tolstoy's moral criticism of art is that their emotional theories of artistic identification are simplistic. We do not just take on one character or one point of view, and we do not respond emotionally in only one way. *The Sopranos* provides us with many different ways of seeing the life of a gangster, and it also invites us to feel in a variety of ways about it. Sometimes the show does make Tony and his crew look quite sympathetic; but it also provides us with other perspectives, and permits us, if we try, to formulate a complex and sophisticated personal moral response to gangster life, and not merely to imitate Tony.

This does not mean that Plato's and Tolstoy's concerns about art should be dismissed lightly. They are right that artworks can affect us deeply, and sometimes cause audiences to identify with immoral characters. But whether

---

[9]The second season has more of these moments of moral reflection and serious moral examination than any other season: from the very beginning of the season, when Dr. Melfi has to decide whether she has a moral responsibility to take Tony back as a patient, to this final sequence, the characters and the creators grapple with right and wrong in a very direct way. None of the other seasons has as much sustained, direct attention to morality.

or not these artworks are morally corrupting depends on other factors as well. Television shows like *The Sopranos* which provide multiple moral perspectives on evil characters, and which offer room for moral reflection, might even be good for us, rather than evil.

READING THE TEXT

1. Explain in your own words why Plato and Tolstoy believed that art could be "dangerous."

2. How, according to Harold, does the depiction of the mob in *The Sopranos* compare with other cinematic portrayals of gangsters?

3. Why does Harold believe that Dr. Melfi is the "moral center" (para. 15) of the program?

4. In class, discuss the effect of Harold's first-person opener, "I like Tony Soprano; I can't help it" (para. 1). Why do you think he begins with this confession?

READING THE SIGNS

1. Write an essay supporting, opposing, or modifying Harold's contention that *The Sopranos* has a moral center and that it is Dr. Melfi.

2. Watch an episode of *The Sopranos*, and assess the validity of Harold's claim that programs like it "might even be good for us, rather than evil" (para. 19).

3. **CONNECTING TEXTS**   Read or reread Vivian Sobchak's "The Postmorbid Condition" (p. 414), and write an essay in which you argue whether or not *The Sopranos* displays the trend toward "carelessness toward violence" that Sobchak believes dominates contemporary cinema.

4. Compare and contrast *The Sopranos* with one of the gangster films that Harold lists in paragraph 10. How is the mob represented in each work, and what does that representation suggest about the values and interests of the era in which it was created?

5. **CONNECTING TEXTS**   Read or reread Robert B. Ray's "The Thematic Paradigm" (p. 342), and write an essay in which you argue whether Tony Soprano can be considered a hero. If so, what kind of hero is he? If not, why not?

| CARL MATHESON

The Simpsons, *Hyper-Irony, and the Meaning of Life*

Don't have a cow or anything, but most comedy, as Carl Matheson points out in this analysis of The Simpsons, *which first appeared in* The Simpsons and Philosophy *(2001), is based in cruelty. And while Matheson doesn't "mean to argue that the makers of* The Simpsons *intended the show primarily as a theater of cruelty," he does "imagine that they did." At any rate, Matheson suggests, the pervasive irony that makes the program funny should serve as a warning to anyone who believes that this ever-popular cartoon sitcom is a warm endorser of family values. Carl Matheson is a professor in, and chair of, the department of philosophy at the University of Manitoba. He has published essays in the* British Journal of Aesthetics, *the* Journal of Aesthetics and Art Criticism, *and* Philosophy and Literature.

DISAFFECTED YOUTH #1: Here comes that cannonball guy. He's cool.
DISAFFECTED YOUTH #2: Are you being sarcastic, dude?
DISAFFECTED YOUTH #1: I don't even know anymore.
— "Homerpalooza," Season 7

What separates the comedies that were shown on television fifty, forty, or even twenty-five years ago from those of today? First, we may notice technological differences, the difference between black-and-white and color, the difference between film stock (or even kinescope) and video. Then there are the numerous social differences. For instance, the myth of the universal traditional two-parent family is not as secure as it was in the 1950s and 1960s, and the comedies of the different eras reflect changes in its status — although even early comedies of the widow/widower happy fifties, sixties, and seventies were full of nontraditional families, such as are found in *The Partridge Family*, *The Ghost and Mrs. Muir*, *Julia*, *The Jerry van Dyke Show*, *Family Affair*, *The Courtship of Eddie's Father*, *The Andy Griffith Show*, *The Brady Bunch*, *Bachelor Father*, and *My Little Margie*. Also, one may note the ways in which issues such as race have received different treatments over the decades.

But I would like to concentrate on a deeper transformation: today's comedies, at least most of them, are funny in different ways from those of decades past. In both texture and substance the comedy of *The Simpsons* and *Seinfeld* is worlds apart from the comedy of *Leave It to Beaver* and *The Jack Benny Show*, and is even vastly different from much more recent comedies, such as *MASH* and *Maude*. First, today's comedies tend to be highly *quotational*: many of today's comedies essentially depend on the device of referring to or quoting other works of popular culture. Second, they are *hyper-ironic*: the flavor of

283

humor offered by today's comedies is colder, based less on a shared sense of humanity than on a sense of world-weary cleverer-than-thouness. In this essay I would like to explore the way in which *The Simpsons* uses both quotational-ism and hyper-ironism and relate these devices to currents in the contemporary history of ideas.

Quotationalism

Television comedy has never completely foregone the pleasure of using pop culture as a straight man. However, early instances of quotation tended to be opportunistic; they did not comprise the substance of the genre. Hence, in sketch comedy, one would find occasional references to popular culture in *Wayne and Shuster* and *Johnny Carson*, but these references were really treated as just one more source of material. The roots of quotationalism as a main source of material can be found in the early seventies with the two visionary comedies, *Mary Hartman Mary Hartman*, which lampooned soap operas by being an ongoing soap opera, and *Fernwood 2Night*, which, as a small-budget talk show, took on small-budget talk shows. Quotationalism then came much more to the attention of the general public between the mid-seventies and early eighties through *Saturday Night Live*, *Late Night with David Letterman*, and *SCTV*. Given the mimical abilities of its cast and its need for weekly material, the chief comedic device of *SNL* was parody — of genres (the nightly news, television debates), of particular television shows (*I Love Lucy*, *Star Trek*) and of movies (*Star Wars*). The type of quotationalism employed by Letterman was more abstract and less based on particular shows. Influenced by the much earlier absurdism of such hosts as Dave Garroway, Letterman immediately took the formulas of television and cinema beyond their logical conclusions (*The Equal-izer Guy*, chimp cam, and spokesperson Larry "Bud" Melman).

However, it was *SCTV* that gathered together the various strains of quota-tionalism and synthesized them into a deeper, more complex, and more mys-terious whole. Like *Mary Hartman*, and unlike *SNL*, it was an ongoing series with recurring characters such as Johnny Larue, Lola Heatherton, and Bobby Bittman. However, unlike *Mary Hartman*, the ongoing series was about the workings of a television station. *SCTV* was a television show about the pro-cess of television. Through the years, the models upon which characters like Heatherton and Bittman were based vanished somewhat into the background, as Heatherton and Bittman started to breathe on their own, and therefore, came to occupy a shadowy space between real (fictional) characters and simu-lacra. Furthermore, *SCTV*'s world came to intersect the real world as some of the archetypes portrayed (such as Jerry Lewis) were people in real life. Thus, *SCTV* eventually produced and depended upon patterns of inter-textuality and cross-referencing that were much more thoroughgoing and subtle than those of any program that preceded it.

The Simpsons was born, therefore, just as the use of quotationalism was ⁵ maturing. However, *The Simpsons* was not the same sort of show as *SNL* and *SCTV*. One major difference, of course, was that *The Simpsons* was animated while the others were (largely) not, but this difference does not greatly affect the relevant potential for quotationalism — although it may be easier to draw the bridge of the *U.S.S. Enterprise* than to rebuild it and re-enlist the entire original cast of *Star Trek*. The main difference is that as an ostensibly ongoing family comedy, *The Simpsons* was both plot and character driven, where the other shows, even those that contained ongoing characters, were largely sketch driven. Furthermore, unlike *Mary Hartman Mary Hartman*, which existed to parody soap operas, *The Simpsons* did not have the *raison d'être* of parodying the family-based comedies of which it was an instance. The problem then was this: how does one transform an essentially non-quotational format into an essentially quotational show?

The answer to the above question lies in the form of quotationalism employed by *The Simpsons*. By way of contrast, let me outline what it was definitively not. Take, for instance, a *Wayne and Shuster* parody of Wilde's *The Picture of Dorian Gray*. In the parody, instead of Gray's sins being reflected in an artwork, while he remains pure and young in appearance, the effects of Gray's overeating are reflected in the artwork, while he remains thin. The situation's permissions and combinations are squeezed and coaxed to produce the relevant gags and ensuing yuks. End of story. Here the quotationalism is very direct; it is the source both of the story line and of the supposedly humorous contrast between the skit and the original novel. Now, compare this linear and one-dimensional use of quotation for the purposes of parody with the pattern of quotation used in a very short passage from an episode from *The Simpsons* entitled "A Streetcar Named Marge." In the episode, Marge is playing Blanche Dubois opposite Ned Flanders's Stanley in *Streetcar!*, her community theatre's musical version of the Tennessee Williams play. In need of day care for little Maggie, she sends Maggie to the Ayn Rand School for Tots, which is run by the director's sister. Headmistress Sinclair, a strict disciplinarian and believer in infant self-reliance, confiscates all of the tots' pacifiers which causes an enraged Maggie to lead her classmates in a highly organized reclamation mission, during which the theme from *The Great Escape* plays in the background. Having re-acquired the pacifiers the group sits, arrayed in rows, making little sucking sounds, so that when Homer arrives to pick up Maggie, he is confronted with a scene from Hitchcock's *The Birds*.

The first thing that one can say about these quotations is that they are very funny. . . . To see that these quotations are funny just watch the show again. Second, we note that these quotations are not used for the purpose of parody.[1]

---

[1] I don't mean to say that *The Simpsons* does not make use of parody. The episode currently under discussion contains a brilliant parody of Broadway adaptations, from its title to the show-stopping tune "A Stranger Is Just a Friend You Haven't Met!"

Rather, they are allusions, designed to provide unspoken metaphorical elaboration and commentary about what is going on in the scene. The allusion to Ayn Rand underscores the ideology and personal rigidity of Headmistress Sinclair. The theme music from *The Great Escape* stresses the determination of Maggie and her cohort. The allusion to *The Birds* communicates the threat of the hive-mind posed by many small beings working as one. By going outside of the text via these nearly instantaneous references, *The Simpsons* manages to convey a great deal of extra information extremely economically. Third, the most impressive feature of this pattern of allusion is its pace and density, where this feature has grown more common as the series has matured. Early episodes, for instance the one in which Bart saws the head off the town's statue of Jebediah Springfield, are surprisingly free of quotation. Later episodes derive much of their manic comic energy from their rapid-fire sequence of allusions. This density of allusion is perhaps what sets *The Simpsons* most apart from any show that has preceded it.

However, the extent to which *The Simpsons* depends on other elements of pop culture is not without cost. Just as those readers who are unfamiliar with Frazer's *Golden Bough* will be hindered in their attempt to understand Eliot's "The Waste Land," and just as many modern-day readers will be baffled by many of the Biblical and classical allusions that play important roles in the history of literature, many of today's viewers won't fully understand much of what goes on in *The Simpsons* due to an unfamiliarity with the popular culture that forms the basis for the show's references. Having missed the references, these people may interpret *The Simpsons* as nothing more than a slightly off-base family comedy populated with characters who are neither very bright nor very interesting. From these propositions they will probably derive the theorem that the show is neither substantial nor funny, and also the lemma that the people who like the show are deficient in taste, intelligence, or standards of personal mental hygiene. However, not only do the detractors of the show miss a great deal of its humor, they also fail to realize that its pattern of quotations is an absolutely essential vehicle for developing character and for setting a tone. And, since these people are usually not huge fans of popular culture to begin with, they will be reluctant to admit that they are missing something significant. Oh well. It is difficult to explain color to a blind man, especially if he won't listen. On the other hand, those who enjoy connecting the quotational dots will enjoy their task all the more for its exclusivity. There is no joke like an in-joke: the fact that many people don't get *The Simpsons* might very well make the show both funnier and better to those who do.

Hyper-Ironism and the Moral Agenda

Without the smart-ass, comedy itself would be impossible. Whether one subscribes, as I do, to the thesis that all comedy is fundamentally cruel, or merely to the relatively spineless position that only the vast majority of comedy is fundamentally cruel, one has to admit that comedy has always relied upon the joys to be derived from making fun of others. However, usually the cruelty has been employed for a positive social purpose. In the sanctimonious *MASH*, Hawkeye and the gang were simply joking to "dull the pain of a world gone mad," and the butts of their jokes, such as Major Frank Burns, symbolized threats to the liberal values that the show perpetually attempted to reinforce in the souls of its late-twentieth-century viewers. In *Leave It to Beaver*, the link between humor and the instillation of family values is didactically obvious. A very few shows, most notably *Seinfeld*, totally eschewed a moral agenda.[2] *Seinfeld*'s ability to maintain a devoted audience in spite of a cast of shallow and petty characters engaged in equally petty and shallow acts is miraculous. So, as I approach *The Simpsons*, I would like to resolve the following questions. Does *The Simpsons* use its humor to promote a moral agenda? Does it use its humor to promote the claim that there is no justifiable moral agenda? Or, does it stay out of the moral agenda game altogether?

These are tricky questions, because data can be found to affirm each of them. To support the claim that *The Simpsons* promotes a moral agenda, one usually need look no further than Lisa and Marge. Just consider Lisa's speeches in favor of integrity, freedom from censorship, or any variety of touchy-feely social causes, and you will come away with the opinion that *The Simpsons* is just another liberal show underneath a somewhat thin but tasty crust of nastiness. One can even expect Bart to show humanity when it counts, as when, at military school, he defies sexist peer pressure to cheer Lisa on in her attempt to complete an obstacle course. The show also seems to engage in self-righteous condemnation of various institutional soft targets. The political system of Springfield is corrupt, its police chief lazy and self-serving, and its Reverend Lovejoy ineffectual at best. Property developers stage a fake religious miracle in order to promote the opening of a mall. Mr. Burns tries to increase business at the power plant by blocking out the sun. Taken together, these examples seem to advocate a moral position of caring at the level of the individual, one which favors the family over any institution.

However, one can find examples from the show that seem to be denied accommodation within any plausible moral stance. In one episode, Frank Grimes (who hates being called "Grimey") is a constantly unappreciated model worker, while Homer is a much beloved careless slacker. Eventually, Grimes breaks down and decides to act just like Homer Simpson. While "acting like Homer" Grimes touches a transformer and is killed instantly. During the funeral oration by Reverend Lovejoy (for "Gri-yuh-mee, as he liked to be called") a snoozing Homer shouts out "Change the channel, Marge!" The rest of the service breaks into spontaneous and appreciative laughter, with Lenny saying "That's our Homer!" End of episode. In another episode, Homer is unintentionally responsible for the death of Maude Flanders, Ned's wife. In the

10

---

[2]For a different view, see Robert A. Epperson, "Seinfeld and the Moral Life," in William Irwin, ed., *Seinfeld and Philosophy: A Book about Everything and Nothing* (Chicago: Open Court, 2000), pp. 163–74.

crowd at a football game, Homer is eager to catch a T-shirt being shot from little launchers on the field. Just as one is shot his way, he bends over to pick up a peanut. The T-shirt sails over him and hits the devout Maude, knocking her out of the stands to her death. These episodes are difficult to locate on a moral map; they certainly do not conform to the standard trajectory of virtue rewarded.

Given that we have various data, some of which lead us towards and others away from the claim that *The Simpsons* is committed to caring, liberal family values, what should we conclude? Before attempting to reach a conclusion, I would like to go beyond details from various episodes of the show to introduce another form of possibly relevant evidence. Perhaps, we can better resolve the issue of *The Simpsons'* moral commitments by examining the way it relates to current intellectual trends. The reader should be warned that, although I think that my comments on the current state of the history of ideas are more or less accurate, they are greatly oversimplified. In particular, the positions that I will outline are by no means unanimously accepted.

Let's start with painting. The influential critic, Clement Greenberg, held that the goal of all painting was to work with flatness as the nature of its medium and he reconstructed the history of painting so that it was seen to culminate in the dissolution of pictorial three-dimensional space and the acceptance of total flatness by the painters of the mid-twentieth century. Painters were taken to be like scientific researchers whose work furthered the progress of their medium, where the idea of artistic progress was to be taken as literally as that of scientific progress. Because they were fundamentally unjustifiable and because they put painters into a straitjacket, Greenberg's positions gradually lost their hold, and no other well-supported candidates for the essence of painting could be found to take their place. As a result painting (and the other arts) entered a phase that the philosopher of art, Arthur Danto, has called "the end of art." By this Danto did not mean that art could no longer be produced, but rather that art could no longer be subsumed under a history of progress towards some given end.[3] By the end of the 1970s, many painters had turned to earlier, more representational styles, and their paintings were as much commentaries on movements from the past, like expressionism, and about the current vacuum in the history of art, as they were about their subject matter. Instead of being about the essence of painting, much of painting came to be about the history of painting. Similar events unfolded in the other artistic media as architects, filmmakers, and writers returned to the history of their disciplines.

However, painting was not the only area in which long-held convictions concerning the nature and inevitability of progress were aggressively challenged. Science, the very icon of progressiveness, was under attack from a number of quarters. Kuhn held (depending on which interpreter of him you agree with) either that there was no such thing as scientific progress, or that if there

---

[3]See Arthur Danto, *After the End of Art* (Princeton: Princeton University Press, 1996).

was, there were no rules for determining what progress and scientific rationality were. Feyerabend argued that people who held substantially different theories couldn't even understand what each other was saying, and hence that there was no hope of a rational consensus; instead he extolled the anarchistic virtues of "anything goes." Early sociological workers in the field of science studies tried to show that, instead of being an inspirational narrative of the disinterested pursuit of truth, the history of science was essentially a story of office-politics writ large, because every transition in the history of science could be explained by appeal to the personal interests and allegiances of the participants.[4] And, of course, the idea of philosophical progress has continued to be challenged. Writing on Derrida, the American philosopher Richard Rorty argues that anything like *the* philosophical truth is either unattainable, nonexistent, or uninteresting, that philosophy itself is a literary genre, and that philosophers should reconstrue themselves as writers who elaborate and reinterpret the writings of other philosophers. In other words, Rorty's version of Derrida recommends that philosophers view themselves as historically aware participants in a conversation, as opposed to quasi-scientific researchers.[5] Derrida himself favored a method known as deconstruction, which was popular several years ago, and which consisted of a highly technical method for undercutting texts by revealing hidden contradictions and unconscious ulterior motives. Rorty questions whether, given Derrida's take on the possibility of philosophical progress, deconstruction could be used only for negative purposes, that is, whether it could be used for anything more than making philosophical fun of other writings.

Let me repeat that these claims about the nature of art, science, and philosophy are highly controversial. However, all that I need for my purposes is the relatively uncontroversial claim that views such as these are now in circulation to an unprecedented extent. We are surrounded by a pervasive crisis of authority, be it artistic, scientific or philosophical, religious or moral, in a way that previous generations weren't. Now, as we slowly come back to earth and *The Simpsons*, we should ask this: if the crisis I described were as pervasive as I believe it to be, how might it be reflected generally in popular culture, and specifically in comedy?

We have already discussed one phenomenon that may be viewed as a consequence of the crisis of authority. When faced with the death of the idea of progress in their field, thinkers and artists have often turned to a reconsideration of the history of their discipline. Hence artists turn to art history, architects to the history of design, and so on. The motivation for this turn is natural; once one has given up on the idea that the past is merely the inferior pathway to a

---

[4]Thomas Kuhn, *The Structure of Scientific Revolutions*, second edition (Chicago: University of Chicago Press, 1970). Paul Feyerabend, *Against Method* (London: NLB, 1975). For a lively debate on the limits of the sociology of knowledge, see James Robert Brown (ed.), *Scientific Rationality: The Sociological Turn* (Dordrecht: Reidel, 1984).

[5]Richard Rorty, "Philosophy as a Kind of Writing," pp. 90–109 in *Consequences of Pragmatism* (Minneapolis: University of Minnesota Press, 1982).

better today and a still better tomorrow, one may try to approach the past on its own terms as an equal partner. Additionally, if the topic of progress is off the list of things to talk about, an awareness of history may be one of the few things left to fill the disciplinary conversational void. Hence, one may think that quotationalism is a natural offshoot of the crisis of authority, and that the prevalence of quotationalism in *The Simpsons* results from that crisis.

The idea that quotationalism in *The Simpsons* is the result of "something in the air" is confirmed by the stunning everpresence of historical appropriation throughout popular culture. Cars like the new Volkswagen Beetle and the PT Cruiser quote bygone days, and factories simply can't make enough of them. In architecture, New Urbanist housing developments try to re-create the feel of small towns of decades ago, and they have proven so popular that only the very wealthy can buy homes in them. The musical world is a hodgepodge of quotations of styles, where often the original music being quoted is simply sampled and re-processed.

To be fair, not every instance of historical quotationalism should be seen as the result of some widespread crisis of authority. For instance, the New Urbanist movement in architecture was a direct response to a perceived erosion of community caused by the deadening combination of economically segregated suburbs and faceless shopping malls; the movement used history in order to make the world a better place for people to live with other people. Hence the degree of quotationalism in *The Simpsons* could point towards a crisis in authority, but it could also stem from a strategy for making the world better, like the New Urbanism, or it could merely be a fashion accessory, like retro-khaki at the Gap.

No, if we want to plumb the depths of *The Simpsons'* connection with the crisis in authority we will have to look to something else, and it is at this point that I return to the original question of this section: does *The Simpsons* use its humor to promote a moral agenda? My answer is this: *The Simpsons* does not promote anything, because its humor works by putting forward positions only in order to undercut them. Furthermore, this process of undercutting runs so deeply that we cannot regard the show as merely cynical; it manages to undercut its cynicism too. This constant process of undercutting is what I mean by "hyper-ironism."

To see what I mean, consider "Scenes from the Class Struggle in Spring-field," an episode from the show's seventh season. In this episode Marge buys a Coco Chanel suit for $90 at the Outlet Mall. While wearing the suit, she runs into an old high-school classmate. Seeing the designer suit and taking Marge to be one of her kind, the classmate invites Marge to the posh Springfield Glen Country Club. Awed by the gentility at the Club, and in spite of sniping from club members that she always wears the same suit, Marge becomes bent on social climbing. Initially alienated, Homer and Lisa fall in love with the club for its golf course and stables. However, just as they are about to be inducted into the club, Marge realizes that her newfound obsession with social standing has taken precedence over her family. Thinking that the club also probably doesn't want them anyway, she and the family walk away. However, unbeknownst to the Simpsons, the club has prepared a lavish welcome party for them, and is terribly put out that they haven't arrived—Mr. Burns even "pickled the figs for the cake" himself.

At first glance, this episode may seem like another case of the show's reaffirmation of family values: after all, Marge chooses family over status. Furthermore, what could be more hollow than status among a bunch of shallow inhuman snobs? However, the people in the club turn out to be inclusive and fairly affectionate, from golfer Tom Kite who gives Homer advice on his swing despite that fact that Homer has stolen his golf clubs—and shoes—to Mr. Burns, who thanks Homer for exposing his dishonesty at golf. The jaded cynicism that seems to pervade the club is gradually shown to be a mere conversational trope; the club is prepared to welcome the working-class Simpsons with open arms—or has it realized yet that they are working class? Further complicating matters are Marge's reasons for walking away. First, there is the false dilemma between caring for her family and being welcomed by the club. Why should one choice exclude the other? Second is her belief that the Simpsons just don't belong to such a club. This belief seems to be based on a classism that the club itself doesn't have. This episode leaves no stable ground upon which the viewer can rest. It feints at the sanctity of family values and swerves closely to class determinism, but it doesn't stay anywhere. Furthermore, upon reflection, none of the "solutions" that it momentarily holds is satisfactory. In its own way, this episode is as cruel and cold-blooded as the Grimey episode. However, where the Grimey episode wears its heartlessness upon its sleeve, this episode conjures up illusions of satisfactory heart-warming resolution only to undercut them immediately. In my view, it stands as a paradigm of the real *Simpsons*.

I think that, given a crisis of authority, hyper-ironism is the most suitable form of comedy. Recall that many painters and architects turned to a consideration of the history of painting and architecture once they gave up on the idea of fundamental trans-historical goal for their media. Recall also that once Rorty's version of Derrida became convinced of the non-existence of transcendent philosophical truth, he reconstructed philosophy as an historically aware conversation which largely consisted of the deconstruction of past works. One way of looking at all of these transitions is that, with the abandonment of *knowledge* came the cult of *knowingness*. That is, even if there is no ultimate truth (or method for arriving at it) I can still show that I understand the intellectual rules by which you operate better than you do. I can show my superiority over you by demonstrating my awareness of what makes you tick. In the end, none of our positions is ultimately superior, but I can at least show myself to be in a superior position for now on the shifting sands of the game we are currently playing. Hyper-irony is the comedic instantiation of the cult of knowingness. Given the crisis of authority, there are no higher purposes to which comedy can be put, such as moral instruction, theological revelation, or showing how the world is. However, comedy can be used to attack anybody at all who thinks that he or she has any sort of handle on the answer to any major question, not to replace the object of the attack with a better way of looking at things, but merely for the pleasure of the attack, or perhaps for the sense of momentary superiority mentioned earlier. *The Simpsons* revels in the attack. It treats nearly everything as a target, every stereotypical character, every foible, and every institution. It plays games of one-upmanship with its audience members by challenging them to identify the avalanche of allusions it throws down to them. And, as "Scenes from the Class Struggle in Springfield" illustrates, it refrains from taking a position of its own.

However, to be fair to those who believe *The Simpsons* takes a stable moral stance, there are episodes which seem not to undercut themselves at all. Consider, for instance, the previously mentioned episode in which Bart helps Lisa at military school. In that episode, many things are ridiculed, but the fundamental goodness of the relationship between Bart and Lisa is left unquestioned. In another episode, when Lisa discovers that Jebediah Springfield, the legendary town founder, was a sham, she refrains from announcing her finding to the town when she notices the social value of the myth of Jebediah Springfield. And, of course, we must mention the episode in which jazzman Bleeding Gums Murphy dies, which truly deserves the Simpsonian epithet "worst episode ever." This episode combines an uncritical sentimentality with a naive adoration of art-making, and tops everything off with some unintentionally horrible pseudo-jazz which would serve better as the theme music for a cable-access talk show. Lisa's song "Jazzman" simultaneously embodies all three of these faults, and must count as the worst moment of the worst episode ever. Given these episodes and others like them, which occur too frequently to be dismissed as blips, we are still left with the conflicting data with which we started. . . . Is *The Simpsons* hyper-ironic or not? One could argue that the hyper-ironism is a trendy fashion accessory, irony from the Gap, which does not reflect the ethos of the show. Another critically well-received program, *Buffy the Vampire Slayer* is as strongly committed to a black and white distinction between right and wrong as only teenagers can be. Its dependence on wisecracks and subversive irony is only skin deep. Underneath the surface, one will find angst-ridden teens fighting a solemn battle against evil demons who want to destroy the world. Perhaps, one could argue, beneath the surface irony of *The Simpsons* one will find a strong commitment to family values.

I would like to argue that Simpsonian hyper-ironism is not a mask for an underlying moral commitment. Here are three reasons, the first two of which are plausible but probably insufficient. First, *The Simpsons* does not consist of a single episode, but of over two hundred episodes spread out over more than ten seasons. There is good reason to think that apparent resolutions in one episode are usually undercut by others.[6] In other words, we are cued to respond ironically to one episode, given the cues provided by many other episodes. However, one could argue that this inter-episodic undercutting is itself under-cut by the show's frequent use of happy family endings.

Second, as a self-consciously hip show, The Simpsons can be taken to be aware of and to embrace what is current. Family values are hardly trendy, so there is little reason to believe that The Simpsons would adopt them whole-heartedly. However, this is weak confirmation at best. As a trendy show, The Simpsons could merely flirt with hyper-irony without fully adopting it. After all, it is hardly hyper-ironic to pledge allegiance to any flag, including the flag of hyper-ironism. Also, in addition to being a self-consciously hip show, it is also a show that must live within the constraints of prime-time American net-work television. One could argue that these constraints would force The Simp-sons towards a commitment to some sort of palatable moral stance. Therefore, we cannot infer that the show is hyper-ironic from the lone premise that it is self-consciously hip.

The third and strongest reason for a pervasive hyper-ironism and against the claim that The Simpsons takes a stand in favor of family values is based on the perception that the comedic energy of the show dips significantly when-ever moral closure or didacticism rise above the surface (as in the Bleeding Gums Murphy episodes). Unlike Buffy the Vampire Slayer, The Simpsons is fun-damentally a comedy. Buffy can get away with dropping its ironic stance, be-cause it is an adventure focused on the timeless battle between good and evil. The Simpsons has nowhere else to go when it stops being funny. Thus, it's very funny when it celebrates physical cruelty in any given Itchy and Scratchy Show. It's very funny when it ridicules Krusty and the marketing geniuses who broadcast Itchy and Scratchy. It's banal, flat, and not funny when it tries to deal seriously with the issue of censorship arising from Itchy and Scratchy. The lifeblood of The Simpsons, and its astonishing achievement, is the pace of cru-elty and ridicule that it has managed to sustain for over a decade. The preva-lence of quotationalism helps to sustain this pace, because the show can look beyond itself for a constant stream of targets. When the target-shooting slows down for a wholesome message or a heart-warming family moment, the pro-gram slows to an embarrassing crawl with nary a quiver from the laugh-meter.

I don't mean to argue that the makers of The Simpsons intended the show primarily as a theater of cruelty, although I imagine that they did. Rather, I want to argue that, as a comedy, its goal is to be funny, and we should read it in a way that maximizes its capability to be funny. When we interpret it as a wacky but earnest endorsement of family values, we read it in a way that ham-strings its comedic potential. When we read it as a show built upon the twin pillars of misanthropic humor and oh-so-clever intellectual one-upmanship, we maximize its comedic potential by paying attention to the features of the show

---

[6]Thanks to my colleague and co-contributor, Jason Holt, for first suggesting this to me.

that make us laugh. We also provide a vital function for the degree of quota-tionalism in the show, and as a bonus, we tie the show into a dominant trend of thought in the twentieth century.

But, if the heart-warming family moments don't contribute to the show's comedic potential, why are they there at all? One possible explanation is that they are simply mistakes; they were meant to be funny but they aren't. This hypothesis is implausible. Another is that the show is not exclusively a com-edy, but rather a family comedy — something wholesome and not very funny that the whole family can pretend to enjoy. This is equally implausible. Alter-natively, we can try to look for a function for the heart-warming moments. I think there is such a function. For the sake of argument, suppose that the engine driving *The Simpsons* is fueled by cruelty and one-upmanship. Its view-ers, although appreciative of its humor, might not want to come back week after week to such a bleak message, especially if the message is centered on a family with children. *Seinfeld* never really offered any hope; its heart was as cold as ice. However, *Seinfeld* was about disaffected adults. A similarly bleak show containing children would resemble the parody of a sitcom in Oliver Stone's *Natural Born Killers*, in which Rodney Dangerfield plays an alcoholic child-abuser. Over the years, such a series would lose a grip on its viewers, to say the least. I think that the thirty seconds or so of apparent redemption in each episode of *The Simpsons* is there mainly to allow us to soldier on for twenty-one and a half minutes of maniacal cruelty at the beginning of the next episode. In other words, the heart-warming family moments help *The Simpsons* to live on as a series. The comedy does not exist for the sake of a message; the occasional illusion of a positive message exists to enable us to tolerate more comedy. Philosophers and critics have often talked of the para-dox of horror and the paradox of tragedy. Why do we eagerly seek out art forms that arouse unpleasant emotions in us like pity, sadness, and fear? I think that, for at least certain forms of comedy, there is an equally important paradox of comedy. Why do we seek out art that makes us laugh at the plight of unfortunate people in a world without redemption? The laughter here seems to come at a high price. *The Simpsons*' use of heart-warming family endings should be seen as its attempt to paper over the paradox of comedy that it exemplifies so well.

I hope to have shown that quotationalism and hyper-ironism are preva-lent, inter-dependent, and jointly responsible for the way in which the humor in *The Simpsons* works. The picture I have painted of *The Simpsons* is a bleak one, because I have characterized its humor as negative, a humor of cruelty and condescension — but really funny cruelty and condescension. I have left out a very important part of the picture however. *The Simpsons*, consisting of a not-as-bright version of the Freudian id for a father, a sociopathic son, a prissy daughter, and a fairly dull but innocuous mother, is a family whose members love each other. And, we love them. Despite the fact that the show strips away any semblance of value, despite the fact that week after week it offers us little comfort, it still manages to convey the raw power of the irrational (or nonrational) love of human beings for other human beings, and it makes us play along by loving these flickering bits of paint on celluloid who live in a flickering hollow world. Now *that's* comedy entertainment.

READING THE TEXT

1. Write an outline of Matheson's essay, being sure to note how Matheson establishes differences and similarities in relation to other pop culture phenomena. Compare your outline with those produced by the rest of the class.
2. Explain in your own words what Matheson means by "quotationalism" and "hyper-ironism" (para. 2).
3. What does Matheson mean by "historical appropriation" (para. 17)?
4. Matheson outlines recent intellectual trends in the study of art, science, and philosophy. What are those trends, and what relationship does Matheson find between them and a TV program such as *The Simpsons*?
5. What connection does Matheson see between the "crisis of authority" (para. 15) and hyper-irony?

READING THE SIGNS

1. Write an argumentative essay that supports, challenges, or complicates Matheson's position that "heart-warming family moments" appear in *The Simpsons* "mainly to allow us to soldier on for twenty-one and a half minutes of maniacal cruelty" (para. 28).
2. In class, brainstorm other TV shows and films that are hyper-ironic and use the list as the basis for your own essay in which you argue whether their popularity is a barometer of the current cultural mood in America or whether it is an aberration.
3. Watch an episode of *The Simpsons* and analyze the extent to which it supports Matheson's belief that, rather than promoting a moral stance, the show "does not promote anything" (para. 19).
4. Visit a Web site devoted to *The Simpsons*, such as **www.thesimpsons.com**, and study the comments fans make about the program. To what extent do your observations support Matheson's belief that "those who enjoy connecting the quotational dots will enjoy their task all the more for its exclusivity" (para. 8)?
5. Compare and contrast the humor in *The Simpsons* with that of another TV show such as *SpongeBob SquarePants*. Do the shows appeal to different audiences, and if so, why? To develop your discussion, you might interview viewers of both programs about their responses to each.
6. **CONNECTING TEXTS** Using Matheson's concept of hyper-irony, analyze an episode of *South Park*. To what extent does it display the hyper-ironic style that Matheson believes characterizes *The Simpsons*? To develop your ideas, consult David Valleau Curtis and Gerald J. Erion, "*South Park* and the Open Society" (p. 296).

DAVID VALLEAU CURTIS AND GERALD J. ERION
South Park *and the Open Society*

Well, Kyle, we all know that South Park *doesn't have, you know, exactly the highest reputation out there for good taste and maturity, but these philosopher dudes think that we're right up there with Thomas Jefferson when it comes to upholding "the fundamental principles of democratic political philosophy." Whatever. But really, David Valleau Curtis and Gerald J. Erion argue that the way we, um, diss everybody from "right-wing fascist types" to "sanctimonious liberal celebrities" is a great example of "not tolerating a tolerance for intolerance." I mean, cool! David Valleau Curtis is a professor of communications at Blackburn College, and Gerald J. Erion is assistant professor of philosophy at Medaille College.*

Unfettered Intellectual Inquiry or Potty Humor?

At first glance, *South Park* seems to offer little more than crude animation and tasteless jokes expressed with a juvenile and offensive vulgarity. However, as media theorist Douglas Rushkoff argues in his book *Media Virus!*, a sophisticated social criticism sometimes lurks beneath the surface of seemingly inane cartoons, comics, video games, and the like.[1] Such is the case with *South Park*; indeed, we can draw an oblique social criticism from the show that illustrates some of the fundamental principles of democratic political philosophy introduced by such great thinkers as Karl Popper and Thomas Jefferson.

For instance, consider *South Park*'s treatment of overzealous political activists. Though the show's core duo of Kyle and Stan play relatively centered roles, many of the remaining cast members are caricatured extremists who serve as objects of the show's funniest and most clever jokes. Cartman, for example, often plays a buffoonish exaggeration of a right-wing conservative. On the other hand, Hollywood celebrities like Rob Reiner appear as liberal fanatics whose views have little connection to the mainstream. And religious extremists of all types receive particularly harsh ridicule; indeed, anyone familiar with *South Park* knows this is one of the main reasons the show is so regularly targeted for censorship, boycott, or cancellation.

Perhaps extremists receive such unflattering portrayals on *South Park* because of the threat that they can sometimes pose to the very free expression that makes the show possible. Consider this pronouncement from *South Park* co-creator Trey Parker, made during an extended interview with his partner Matt Stone on the PBS program *The Charlie Rose Show*: "What we say with

---

[1]Douglas Rushkoff, *Media Virus! Hidden Agendas in Popular Culture* (New York: Ballantine Books, 1994); see especially chapter 4, "Kids' TV," pp. 100–125 and chapter 6, "Alternative Media," pp. 179–209.

the show is not anything new, but I think it is something that is great to put out there. It is that the people screaming on this side and the people screaming on that side are the same people, and it's OK to be someone in the middle, laughing at both of them."[2] So, it could be noteworthy that *South Park*'s scripts do not silence extremists; instead, extremists are allowed to express their views (or in some cases, allowed to express caricatured versions of their views), which are then held up for examination and subsequent ridicule. While extremists are tolerated, then, they are not permitted to suppress the sort of free expression that is vital to the show itself.

In this chapter, we'll examine characters and situations from *South Park* to explore such possibilities. Along the way, we'll consider some of the important democratic concepts and arguments presented by thinkers like Popper and Jefferson. Of particular interest will be the role of free expression and unfettered intellectual inquiry — even when such expression and inquiry are offensive — in a democratic society. In the end, we'll see that Popper and others have understood this sort of freedom to be absolutely *essential* to a healthy democracy.

Karl Popper, the Open Society, and Its Enemies

Though his name might be unfamiliar to most, Karl Popper (1902–1994) was one of the most important and influential philosophers of the twentieth century. An Austrian by birth, Popper made major contributions to philosophical thinking about knowledge and science. However, it is his celebrated critique of totalitarian governments that most concerns us here, since we can see important elements of this critique in numerous *South Park* episodes.

Popper's critique of totalitarianism is based upon his distinction between a *closed society* and an *open society*. To Popper, a closed society is one in which social customs are especially rigid and resistant to criticism. The most significant characteristic of a closed society is "the lack of distinction between the customary or conventional regularities of social life and the regularities found in 'nature'; and this goes often together with the belief that both are enforced by a supernatural will."[3] Consequently, the rules and customs of closed societies are relatively clear and uncontested. "The right way is always determined by taboos, by magical tribal institutions which can never become objects of critical consideration" (*OS*, p. 168). It's no surprise, then, that ways of life in closed societies rarely change. When changes do occur, they are more like "religious conversions" or "the introduction of new magical taboos" than careful, rational attempts to improve the lives of the society's members (*OS*, p. 168).

---

[2]*The Charlie Rose Show*, September 26, 2005; abbreviated hereafter as *CRS*.

[3]Karl Popper, *The Open Society and Its Enemies* (London: G. Routledge and Sons, 1945), p. 168; abbreviated hereafter as *OS*.

On the other hand, Popper's *open society* is one where customs are open to the "rational reflection" of its members (*OS*, p. 169). In an open society, this reflection and its associated public discussion can be significant and con- sequential, and ultimately can produce changes in the society's taboos, rules, and codified laws. In fact, this power extends even to whole governments, as Popper maintains that the key mark of a democracy is its ability to facilitate wholesale governmental changes without violence.[4]

Popper's critique of closed totalitarian societies is, in large part, a practical one. To Popper, the most successful societies will be those that are able to apply the uninhibited criticism at the heart of the scientific method to what- ever new social problems they may face. As Bryan Magee writes, "because problem-solving calls for the bold propounding of trial solutions which are then subjected to criticism and error elimination, [Popper] wants forms of society which permit of the untrammeled assertion of differing proposals, fol- lowed by criticism, followed by the genuine possibility of change in the light of criticism."[5] So, open societies are preferable because they permit — or even better, *promote* — a free and critical exchange of ideas. This ultimately leaves them more flexible than closed societies, and thus more capable of dealing in creative ways with all of the problems that inevitably confront them.

Of course, not every society is an open society, nor is every open society as open as it should be. Given his experiences in Europe just before World War II, Popper was particularly interested in the question of why democracies are sometimes attracted to the closed totalitarianism of, for instance, Nazism or Fascism. As a result, he devotes considerable attention to this issue in both *The Open Society and Its Enemies* and his later book, *The Poverty of Historicism*. The bulk of Popper's work here investigates the political philosophies of Plato (427–347 BCE) and Karl Marx (1818–1883), but what's most important is that Popper generally seems to understand those on both the extreme right wing and the extreme left wing of the political spectrum as "enemies of the open society." Representatives of both extremes have difficulty tolerating the free and open public discussion that is so essential to an open society. Moreover, both are impatient with the imperfections inherent in the democratic process, and both are too quick to reject the possibility that their views might be mistaken.

South Park and the "Enemies"

Despite the over-the-top presentation of most *South Park* episodes, it seems likely that co-creators Parker and Stone would share Popper's distrust of politi- cal extremism. Time and time again, they develop characters and situations

---

[4]"Prediction and Prophecy in the Social Sciences," in *Popper's Conjectures and Refutations* (New York: Basic Books, 1962), pp. 344–45. See also Popper's "Public Opinion and Liberal Principles" con- tained in the same volume, pp. 346–54.

[5]Bryan Magee, *Karl Popper* (New York: Viking, 1973), pp. 70–71.

aimed at ridiculing various "enemies" of the open society. For Parker and Stone, as much as for Popper, democracy is endangered by totalitarian threats from both the political right and the political left. Recall Parker's claim during the *Charlie Rose* interview that "the people screaming on this side and the people screaming on that side are the same people, and it's OK to be someone in the middle, laughing at both of them." While the strategy of Parker and Stone is not so much to argue with extremists as to mock them, there is no question that they consistently single out fanatics of all sorts for especially vicious treatment.

Consider Cartman. He is typically portrayed as a ridiculous, albeit unusually young, right-wing fanatic. Anti-democratic and authoritarian, Cartman is a selfish bully who finds heartless humor in the misfortunes of others. He makes fun of Kenny for being poor, and for having an alcoholic father. He teases Kyle for being Jewish; indeed, his anti-Semitism is so strong that he sees nothing wrong with dressing up as Adolf Hitler for Halloween. Cartman also has a curious hostility for those he sees as "hippies," and he abuses his pets Mister Kitty and Fluffy the Pig. In fantasizing about a career in law enforcement, Cartman yearns not to help people or serve his community, but to have others, he drawls, "respect my authorita." (To our horror and amusement, Cartman actually manages to get himself deputized in the episode "Chickenlover.") For these and countless other sins and character defects, Cartman rarely makes it through an episode without being mocked or otherwise punished (and with penalties up to and including crucifixion).

Parker and Stone satirize the political left as well, especially when left-wing politics lead to the sort of hypocrisy inconsistent with a proper open society. For example, in the episode, "Ike's Wee Wee," Mr. Mackey attempts to convince Kyle, Stan, and the rest of Mr. Garrison's class that smoking, alcohol, and drugs are bad. Alas, his presentation does not reveal a sophisticated understanding of substance abuse or addiction. Instead, in a rather paternalistic and condescending lecture, Mr. Mackey simply tells the children: "Smoking's bad, you shouldn't smoke. And, uh, alcohol is bad; you shouldn't drink alcohol. And, uh, as for drugs, well, drugs are bad; you shouldn't do drugs." Eager to enhance the drug awareness of South Park's children, Mr. Mackey then passes around a sample of marijuana for their examination. The sample disappears (at the hands of Mr. Garrison, it turns out), and Mr. Mackey is promptly fired by Principal Victoria. With no money, no job, and ultimately nowhere to live, Mr. Mackey becomes a drug addict himself. (His recovery at the Betty Ford Clinic is, ironically, facilitated by a counselor who has him repeat the slogan, "Drugs are bad.")

The left-wing liberalism of many Hollywood celebrities also receives brutal treatment on *South Park*. Indeed, Parker and Stone seem to reserve some of their most merciless attacks for outspoken stars like Tom Cruise and Rob Reiner. For his part, Reiner appears willing to lie, cheat, and sacrifice Cartman's life in order to further his heavy-handed anti-tobacco agenda in the episode "Butt Out." And just after the disputed November 2000 Presidential election, Rosie O'Donnell visits South Park to resolve an unsettled kindergarten election involving her nephew in the episode "Trapper Keeper." After O'Donnell suggests some questionable vote recount strategies, Mr. Garrison erupts: "People like you preach tolerance and open-mindedness all the time, but when it comes to Middle America, you think we're all evil and stupid country yokels who need your political enlightenment! Well, just because you're on TV doesn't mean you know crap about the government!" Thus, *South Park* exhibits a clear pattern of criticism for extremist "enemies of the open society," whether right-wing fascist types or sanctimonious liberal celebrities.

Not Tolerating a Tolerance for Intolerance

Our discussion of Popper's contributions to democratic political philosophy must include one last component, which Popper dubs the *paradox of intolerance*. According to Popper, the sort of tolerance required to keep a democracy healthy requires, ironically, an *intolerance* for intolerance. In other words, those who refuse to let others ask questions and speak their minds ought to be prevented from doing so; otherwise, the open discussion that is so essential to a healthy democracy will become impossible to maintain. As he puts it: "If we extend unlimited tolerance even to those who are intolerant, if we are not prepared to defend a tolerant society against the onslaught of the intolerant, then the tolerant will be destroyed, and tolerance with them" (*OS*, p. 546).

A special concern for criticizing and countering intolerance might explain   15
South Park's surprisingly nasty treatment of groups like the Church of Scientology. Popularized by the endorsement of such celebrities (and *South Park* foils) as Tom Cruise and John Travolta, the Church of Scientology also suffers from the widely held perception that it seeks to silence former members and others who criticize its beliefs and practices. In fact, Isaac Hayes, the Scientologist who had long provided the voice for the beloved character Chef, left the show in 2006 because of its treatment of Scientology in episodes like "Trapped in the Closet." (One can only imagine his horror had he stuck around for "The Return of Chef," an episode produced just after his departure in which Chef joins a cult-like group called "The Super Adventure Club." Moreover, his lines in "The Return of Chef" were voiced by splicing together bits of his singing and dialogue from earlier episodes in a particularly awkward but clever way.)

Indeed, *South Park*'s willingness to criticize intolerance earned the show a Peabody Award in April of 2006. According to Peabody Awards Program director Horace Newcomb: "We see [*South Park*] as a bold show that deals with issues of censorship and social and cultural topics. My line on *South Park* is that it properly offends everybody by design and by doing so it reminds us all that it's probably a good idea to be tolerant."[6]

[6]Interview with Josh Grossberg, "'South Park,' 'Galactica,' Peabody'd," *E! Online*, April 5, 2006.

Thomas Jefferson and the Foundations of Modern Democracy

Before we conclude, let's connect Popper's ideas to those of his predecessors, especially since Popper self-consciously viewed himself in the tradition of earlier philosophers. For instance, students of American history may notice similarities between Popper's views on free and open expression and those of the great political leader and scholar, Thomas Jefferson (1743–1826). Jefferson was the primary author of the American Declaration of Independence (1776) and was among the foremost intellectuals of the revolutionary era. Under the influence of some of the same thinkers who later inspired Popper — especially Francis Bacon (1561–1626) and John Locke (1632–1704) — Jefferson pursued a wide range of philosophical interests throughout his lifetime. He was by all accounts deeply committed to freedom of thought and expression, a commitment manifested most notably in his steadfast defense of religious freedom and tolerance.

While it may be easy for us to take religious freedom for granted these days, Jefferson lived shortly after the very long and very bloody conflict that engulfed Europe following the Protestant Reformation. He knew very well, then, the high social and political costs of religious discrimination, coercion, and war. Jefferson's preeminent contribution to the defense of religious liberty was his Virginia Bill for Establishing Religious Freedom, a document first drafted in 1777 and passed into law in 1786. So proud of the Bill was Jefferson that it was one of the three items he listed in his self-penned "Epitaph" of 1826.[7]

Rereading the Bill today, it's easy to discern a Popper-like conviction that free and unfettered inquiry is the only satisfactory method for gaining knowledge, whether regarding important matters of science, politics, religion, or anything else. "Truth," Jefferson writes, "is great and will prevail if left to herself; she is the proper and sufficient antagonist to error, and has nothing to fear from the conflict unless by human interposition disarmed of her natural weapons, free argument and debate." Moreover, Jefferson continues, "errors cease to be dangerous when it is freely permitted to contradict them." There is even something of a divine justification for free inquiry here, as when Jefferson proclaims in his preamble that "God hath created the mind free." Jefferson concludes the Bill with the bold universal declaration that "the rights hereby asserted are of the natural rights of mankind."[8] Thus, Boyd writes in his editor's footnotes to the Bill: "The Preamble to [Jefferson's] Bill provided philosophical justification, as of natural right, not merely to the ideas of religious toleration and separation of state and church but also for the right of the

---

[7]The other two items were his writing of the Declaration of Independence and his founding of the University of Virginia; it is interesting to note the omission from this list of his two terms as President of the United States. See the "Epitaph" in Jefferson's *Writings*, ed. by Merrill D. Peterson (New York: Literary Classics of the US, 1984), pp. 706–7.

[8]All quotations from *Writings*, pp. 346–48.

individual to complete intellectual liberty — 'the opinions of men are not the object of civil government, nor under its jurisdiction.'"[9]

Someone in the Middle

Given our earlier discussion of *South Park*'s treatment of the Church of Scien- [20] tology, and given the show's infamous and insensitive ridicule of Christianity, Judaism, Islam, Mormonism, and other faiths, these are points worth remembering. According to Jefferson, who lived in the aftermath of tremendous religious violence, "free argument and debate" are the proper means for settling contentious issues. And according to Popper, "rational reflection" supplemented by open public discussion is the most effective way to solve complex social problems. As for *South Park*'s creators, consider Stone's comments during his interview with Parker on *The Charlie Rose Show*: "Where we live is, like, the liberalest liberal part of the world. There's a groupthink, and you only get to some new truth by argument and by dissent, and so we just play devil's advocate all of the time." We can therefore understand *South Park* within a wider intellectual context that champions free — and sometimes offensive — investigation and expression, just as the Peabody judges have done. Instead of limiting discussion about difficult issues when it becomes uncomfortable, Popper, Jefferson, Parker, Stone, and others are willing to tolerate such expression for its greater benefits.

To summarize, then, *South Park* offers us much more than vulgar language, crude potty humor, and shock for shock's sake. We learn something by paying close attention to the show's tacit criticism of overzealous left-wing and right-wing political extremists: "It's OK to be someone in the middle, laughing at both of them."

READING THE TEXT

1. In class, discuss how Curtis and Erion use philosophical concepts proposed by Karl Popper and Thomas Jefferson as a critical tool to interpret *South Park*, particularly the program's portrayal of extremist characters. In what ways do these concepts enhance your appreciation of their overall argument about *South Park*?

2. In your own words, summarize Karl Popper's distinction between a closed society and an open society.

3. Why would extremists, both on the left and the right, be "enemies of the open society" (para. 9), according to the authors?

4. Why does Karl Popper believe that a democratic society needs the paradoxical "*intolerance* for intolerance" (para. 14)?

[9]From Julian P. Boyd (ed.), *The Papers of Thomas Jefferson* (Princeton, NJ: Princeton University Press, 1950), vol. 2, p. 547.

5. How do the authors connect Jefferson's views on free expression to Popper's ideas on the same subject, and why do you think they make that connection?

READING THE SIGNS

1. Write your own semiotic analysis of a *South Park* episode. Does it make the sort of political statements that Curtis and Erion suggest?

2. Write an essay in which you assess the authors' underlying assumption that the creators of *South Park* would share Karl Popper's critique of totalitarianism, especially in their creation of extremist characters. If you adopt a skeptical position, be sure to suggest an alternative explanation for their use of extremists.

3. **CONNECTING TEXTS**   The selection quotes *South Park* creator Matt Stone as characterizing American culture as "the liberalist liberal part of the world" dominated by "groupthink" (para. 20). Write a response to this claim, supporting, refuting, or complicating it. To develop your ideas, you might consult Jaime J. Weinman, "Fox News Attempts to Get Funny" (p. 304) and David Brooks, "One Nation, Slightly Divisible" (p. 487).

4. Curtis and Erion believe that *South Park* does offer "more than crude animation and tasteless jokes expressed with a juvenile and offensive vulgarity" (para. 1). To what extent do you agree with this assumption? Does the program offer genuine political commentary, or does its humor and vulgarity undercut the possibility of any such message?

5. **CONNECTING TEXTS**   To what extent do you believe that an entertainment medium such as television can send serious political messages? To formulate your response, analyze an episode of *South Park* and of at least one other program that seems to offer political commentary, such as *The Simpsons* or *The Daily Show*. Be sure to study not only what the political messages might be but the strategies the programs use to communicate them. To develop your ideas, you might consult Carl Matheson's "*The Simpsons*, Hyper-Irony, and the Meaning of Life" (p. 283).

JAIME J. WEINMAN
Fox News Attempts to Get Funny

In the summer of 2007, The Daily Show *sent a correspondent to Iraq, which isn't especially funny, but it is paradoxical because at the same time the Fox News network debuted a couple of news shows intended to compete with* The Daily Show *by adopting its comedic style, though delivered from the opposite end of the ideological spectrum. Jaime J. Weinman's media report on Fox's new strategy highlights a profound You-Decade phenomenon: the fact that youthful viewers are overwhelmingly choosing overtly entertainment-based sources for news information, thus further blurring the traditional distinctions between objective reporting and propaganda, as well as between entertainment and reality. Indeed, as one conservative columnist has noted, the stakes are high when no one can afford to ignore "a crowd that will, in short order, be influencing our nation after you take the big dirt nap, conservative mom and dad." Jaime J. Weinman writes on popular culture for such journals as* Macleans *and* Salon.com.

Why are the producers of Fox News so desperate to be funny? This past month, the conservative cable news channel added two shows that attempt to make fun of liberals, instead of just calling them traitors the way Fox News' regular anchors do. You don't see CNN trying to come up with a comedy show, but then Fox News' new programming ventures may be more about a political movement than news — or, for that matter, comedy.

The 1/2 Hour News Hour, Fox's answer to *The Daily Show*, comes from Joel Surnow, creator of the comedy-challenged hit *24*. The first episode included a guest appearance by Surnow's friend Rush Limbaugh and comparisons between Barack Obama and Oprah. If that's not enough liberal-bashing comedy for you, Fox News has also come up with a late-night talk show called *Red Eye*, starring former *Maxim UK* editor Greg Gutfeld. Gutfeld, who once called liberals "patriotic terrorists," tried to prove how cutting-edge *Red Eye* was by informing his co-panelists that Fox News was allowing him to say the word "douche."

An article by Doug Giles, a columnist for the conservative site Townhall .com, may provide a clue about why Fox News is trying to get hilarious. Giles warned his ideological comrades that they would lose the culture wars unless they learned to make viewers laugh. Pointing out that demographic trends strongly favor consumers of Comedy Central, he wrote: "Blowing off this bunch that's not listening to conservative talk radio, watching Bill [O'Reilly], or logging on to Townhall.com is to dis a crowd that will, in short order, be influencing our nation after you take the big dirt nap, conservative mom and dad."

This isn't just about trying to fill up some time on a 24-hour news channel. With the popularity of liberal-leaning humor among young people, and the liberal-Democratic tilt of young voters in the 2006 mid-term elections, conservatives are worried that the future belongs to people who have been brought up to think that tax cuts and preventive war are for dorks. Fox News, a network formed to assist the conservative movement, found itself faced with a choice: Find the funny, or watch its movement slip into irrelevance.

Will the combination of humor and Republican party boosting ever take off? Gavin McNett, a writer for the liberal humor blog Sadlyno.com, doesn't think so. He says today's conservatives have a "hermetic, self-referential world view" that leads them to mistake talking points for jokes. "Referencing one of their common shibboleths often serves the purpose that humor would serve," he continues. "There has to be an element of surprise in humor — and conservatives hate surprise. It's just how they're wired." 5

Sure enough, most of the jokes on *The 1/2 Hour News Hour* aren't really jokes at all: They're Fox News segments with a laugh track. A typical remark from the pilot episode is that Democratic National Committee chairman Howard Dean is mentally ill and "getting the medical attention he has so desperately needed." We're expected to laugh not because there was any amusing spin on the talking point, but just because we agree. Anyone who doesn't already agree will be flipping the channel to a real comedy show.

But contrary to what McNett says, there have always been successful right-leaning comedians and comedy writers; today's most prominent examples are Trey Parker and Matt Stone, the creators of *South Park*. Their episodes carry titles like "Die, Hippie, Die!" and make fun of environmentalists, hybrid cars, and liberal atheist Richard Dawkins. A typical episode of *South Park* produces more laughter at the expense of liberal sacred cows than anything Fox News can come up with.

The difference is that Parker and Stone are not party men; like liberal comics, they have a political philosophy that they incorporate into their work. Much of today's conservative movement, on the other hand, is based on partisan politics: Fox News or Townhall.com are unofficial organs of the Republican party. It's hard to be an effective comedian while being an advocate for a party, any party: Al Franken hasn't been particularly funny since he stopped being a political satirist and became a Democratic candidate for the Senate.

But Fox News will keep trying to entice young viewers with *The 1/2 Hour News Hour*'s mental illness jokes. As Doug Giles wrote, if conservatives can't crack wise, they may lose "our ideological battle with the secularists who whiz on traditional American values."

That's comedy gold right there. 10

READING THE TEXT

1. Summarize in your own words Weinman's answer to her opening question, "Why are the producers of Fox News so desperate to be funny?" (para. 1).

2. What is the nature of the humor that dominates Fox News and *Red Eye*, and what is Weinman's assessment of that humor?

3. Why does Weinman say that "it's hard to be an effective comedian while being an advocate for a party, any party" (para. 8)?

READING THE SIGNS

1. In your journal, reflect on your own consumption of news. What are your principle sources of news, and why? What sort of news do you pay attention to and what sort do you ignore? What are the implications of your habits and tastes?

2. In class, form teams and debate whether programs like Fox's *The 1/2 Hour News Hour* and *The Daily Show* represent an advance in news programming because their style is attractive to a demographic group — young people — that tends not to watch news, or whether they are a dangerous assault on traditional journalistic values of objectivity and fairness. To prepare your team's position, be sure to study segments of both traditional news shows and the newer, more comedic news shows.

3. Compare and contrast a conservative news program with one that has a more liberal slant, focusing not only on the humor but on the content and style of presentation as well.

4. **CONNECTING TEXTS**   In class, brainstorm media — news shows, TV programs, films — that most students agree are humorous. Analyze the results and write your own essay proposing your definition of what constitutes humor for young people today. To develop your ideas, consult the Introduction to this chapter and Carl Matheson's "*The Simpsons*, Hyper-Irony, and the Meaning of Life" (p. 283).

SUSAN DOUGLAS
Signs of Intelligent Life on TV

Do you look for television programming that reflects an enlightened view of American women? Susan Douglas does, and in this essay that originally appeared in Ms. *in 1995, she reports her findings, which are mixed, at best. Although popular TV dramas like* ER *and* NYPD Blue *appear to present characters and plotlines that defy gender stereotypes, Douglas still finds the telltale signs of cultural bias against women in such programs — especially a bias against strong professional women. When not watching TV, Douglas is chair of the department of communication studies at the University of Michigan and media critic for* The Progressive. *She is the author of* Where the Girls Are: Growing Up Female with the Mass Media *(1994),* Inventing American Broadcasting, 1899–1922 *(1987),* Listening In: Radio and the American Imagination *(1999), and, with Meredith Michaels,* The Mommy Myth: The Idealization of Motherhood and How It Undermines Women *(2004).*

When the hospital show *ER* became a surprise hit, the pundits who had declared dramatic television "dead" were shocked. But one group wasn't surprised at all.

Those of us with jobs, kids, older parents to tend to, backed-up toilets, dog barf on the rug, and friends/partners/husbands we'd like to say more than "hi" to during any diurnal cycle don't have much time to watch television. And when we do — usually after 9:38 P.M. — we have in recent years been forced to choose between Diane Sawyer interviewing Charles Manson or Connie Chung chasing after Tonya [Harding] and Nancy [Kerrigan]. People like me, who felt that watching the newsmagazines was like exposing yourself to ideological smallpox, were starved for some good escapist drama that takes you somewhere else yet resonates with real life and has ongoing characters you care about.

When *NYPD Blue* premiered in the fall of 1993 with the tough-but-sensitive John Kelly, and featuring strong, accomplished women, great lighting, bongo drums in the sound track, and male nudity, millions sighed with relief. When *ER* hit the air, we made it one of the tube's highest rated shows. Tagging farther behind, but still cause for hope, is another hospital drama, *Chicago Hope*.

All three shows acknowledge the importance of the adult female audience by featuring women as ongoing characters who work for a living and by focusing on contemporary problems in heterosexual relationships (no, we haven't yet achieved everyday homosexual couples on TV). More to the point, hound-dog-eyed, emotionally wounded yet eager-to-talk-it-through guys are center stage. So what are we getting when we kick back and submerge ourselves in these dramas? And what do they have to say about the ongoing project of feminism?

For those of you who don't watch these shows regularly, here's a brief ⁵ précis: *NYPD Blue* is a cop show set in New York City and has producer Steven Bochco's signature style — lots of shaky, hand-held camera work, fast-paced editing (supported by the driving, phallic backbeat in the sound track), and multiple, intersecting plots about various crimes and the personal lives of those who work in the precinct. Last season there were more women in the show; and last season there was John Kelly.

This year, the show is more masculinized. Watching Bobby Simone, played by Jimmy Smits, earn his right to replace Kelly was like witnessing a territorial peeing contest between weimaraners. Bobby had to be as sensitive and emotionally ravaged as Johnny, so in an act of New Age male one-upmanship, the scriptwriters made him a widower who had lost his wife to breast cancer. But Bobby had to be one tough customer too, so soon after we learn of his wife's death, we see him throwing some punks up against a fence, warning them that he will be their personal terminator unless they stop dealing drugs.

ER has the same kind of simultaneous, intersecting story lines, served up with fast-tracking cameras that sprint down hospital corridors and swirl around operating tables like hawks on speed. And there are the same bongo drums and other percussive sounds when patients are rushed in for treatment. *Chicago Hope* is *ER* on Valium: stationary cameras, slower pace, R&B instead of drumbeats. It's also *ER* on helium or ether, kind of a *Northern Exposure* goes to the hospital, with more offbeat plots and characters, like a patient who eats his hair or a kid whose ear has fallen off.

Whenever I like a show a lot — meaning I am there week in and week out — I figure I have once again embraced a media offering with my best and worst interests at heart. Dramatic TV shows, which seek a big chunk of the middle- and upper-income folks between 18 and 49, need to suck in those women whose lives have been transformed by the women's movement (especially women who work outside the home and have disposable income) while keeping the guys from grabbing the remote. What we get out of these twin desires is a blend of feminism and antifeminism in the plots and in the female characters. And for the male characters we have an updated hybrid of masculinity that crossbreeds decisiveness, technical expertise, and the ability to throw a punch or a basketball, with a soft spot for children and a willingness to cry.

On the surface, these shows seem good for women. We see female cops, lawyers, doctors, and administrators, who are smart, efficient, and successful. But in too many ways, the women take a backseat to the boys. In *NYPD Blue*, for example, we rarely see the women actually doing their jobs. The overall message in the three shows is that, yes, women can be as competent as men, but their entrance into the workforce has wrecked the family and made women so independent and hard-hearted that dealing with them and understanding them is impossible. Despite this, they're still the weaker sex.

In *ER* it is Carol Hathaway (Julianna Margulies), the charge nurse, who [10] tried to commit suicide. It is Dr. Susan Lewis (Sherry Stringfield) who is taken in by an imposter who claims to be a hospital administrator. Dr. Lewis is also the only resident who has trouble standing up to white, male authority figures: She is unable to operate while the head cardiologist watches her. In *Chicago Hope*, a psychiatrist prevails upon a female nurse to dress up like Dorothy (ruby slippers, pigtails, and all) because a patient refusing surgery is a *Wizard of Oz* junkie. Even though she points out that no male doctor would be asked to do anything like it, the shrink insists she continue the masquerade because the patient's life is at stake. Here's the crucial guilt-shifting we've all come to know and love — this patient's illness is somehow more her responsibility than anyone else's. Her humiliation is necessary to save him.

The Ariel Syndrome — Ariel was the name of Walt Disney's little mermaid, who traded her voice for a pair of legs so that she could be with a human prince she'd seen from afar for all of ten seconds — grips many of the women, who have recurring voice problems. Watch out for female characters who "don't want to talk about it," who can't say no, who don't speak up. They make it even harder for the women who do speak their minds, who are, of course, depicted as "bitches."

One major "bitch" is the wife of *ER*'s Dr. Mark Greene (Anthony Edwards). He's a doctor who's barely ever home, she's a lawyer who lands a great job two hours away, and they have a seven-year-old. Those of us constantly negotiating about who will pick up the kids or stay late at work can relate to this. The problem is that *ER* is about *his* efforts to juggle, *his* dreams and ambitions. We know this guy, we like him, we know he's a great doctor who adores his wife and child. Her, we don't know, and there's no comparable female doctor to show the woman's side of this equation. As a result, when conflicts emerge, the audience is primed to want her to compromise (which she's already done, so he can stay at the job he loves). When she insists he quit his job and relocate, she sounds like a spoiled child more wedded to a rigid quid pro quo than to flexibility, love, the family. It's the conservative view of what feminism has turned women into — unfeeling, demanding blocks of granite.

One of the major themes of all three shows is that heterosexual relationships are a national disaster area. And it's the women's fault. Take *NYPD Blue*. Yes, there's the fantasy relationship between Andy Sipowicz (Dennis Franz) and Sylvia Costas (Sharon Lawrence), in which an accomplished woman helps a foul-mouthed, brutality-prone cop with really bad shirts get in touch with his feelings and learn the pleasures of coed showering. While this affair has become the emotional anchor of the show, it is also the lone survivor in the ongoing gender wars.

It looks like splitsville for most of the show's other couples. Greg Medavoy (Gordon Clapp) infuriates Donna Abandando (Gail O'Grady) by his behavior, which includes following her to see whom she's having lunch with. She's absolutely right. But after all the shots of Greg looking at her longingly across the office (again, we're inside his head, not hers), the audience is encouraged to think that she should give the guy a break. By contrast, her explanations of why she's so angry and what she wants have all the depth and emotional warmth of a Morse code message tapped out by an iguana. Of course Greg doesn't understand. She won't help him.

In this world, female friendships are nonexistent or venomous. And there is 15 still worse ideological sludge gumming up these shows. Asian and Latina women are rarely seen, and African American women are also generally absent except as prostitutes, bad welfare moms, and unidentified nurses. In the *ER* emergency room, the black women who are the conscience and much-needed drill ser-geants of the show don't get top billing, and are rarely addressed by name. There is also an overabundance of bad mothers of all races: adoptive ones who desert their kids, abusive ones who burn their kids, and hooker ones (ipso facto bad). Since the major female characters — all upper-middle-class — don't have kids, we don't see their struggles to manage motherhood and work. And we cer-tainly don't see less privileged moms (the real majority in the United States), like the nurses or office workers, deal with these struggles on a lot less money.

One of the worst things these shows do, under a veneer of liberalism and feminism, is justify the new conservatism in the United States. The suspects brought in for questioning on *NYPD Blue* are frequently threatened and some-times beaten, but it's O.K. because they all turn out to be guilty, anyway. Legal representation for these witnesses is an unspeakable evil because it hides the truth. After a steady diet of this, one might assume the Fourth Amendment, which prohibits unreasonable search and seizure, is hardly worth preserving.

So why are so many women devoted to these shows? First off, the women we do see are more successful, gutsy, more fully realized than most female TV characters. But as for me, I'm a sucker for the men. I want to believe, despite all the hideous evidence to the contrary, that some men have been human-ized by the women's movement, that they have become more nurturing, sen-sitive, and emotionally responsible. I want to believe that patriarchy is being altered by feminism. Since I get zero evidence of this on the nightly news, I want a few hours a week when I can escape into this fantasy.

Of course, we pay a price for this fantasy. TV depicts "real men" being feminized for the better and women masculinized for the worse. The message from the guys is, "We became the kind of men you feminists said that you wanted, and now you can't appreciate us because you've forgotten how to be a 'real' woman." It's a bizarre twist on the real world, where many women have changed, but too many men have not. Nevertheless, in TV land femi-nism continues to hoist itself with its own petard. Big surprise.

READING THE TEXT

1. What does Douglas mean by saying that "watching the newsmagazines was like exposing yourself to ideological smallpox" (para. 2), and what attitude toward the media does this comment reveal?

2. Why, in Douglas's view, are professional women attracted to programs such as *ER* and *NYPD Blue*?

3. What, according to Douglas, is the overt message about gender roles that the TV shows she discusses communicate? What is the hidden message?

4. How are non-Caucasian women presented in *ER* and *NYPD Blue*, according to Douglas, and what is her opinion about their presentation?

5. How does Douglas view the "new conservatism in the United States" (para. 16)?

READING THE SIGNS

1. Watch an episode of *ER* or *NYPD Blue* (on cable or at your school's media library), and write an essay in which you support, refute, or modify Douglas's belief that the show, despite superficial nods at feminism, perpetuates traditional gender roles.

2. In class, brainstorm TV shows that portray women as professionals or in other responsible, intelligent roles. Then, using Douglas's argument as your starting point, discuss whether the shows adopt a feminist or an antifeminist stance in portraying female characters.

3. In your journal, discuss your favorite prime-time TV show, exploring exactly what you find attractive about the program.

4. Watch a TV show that focuses on young adult characters. Do you see evidence of the covert antifeminism that Douglas describes? What does the treatment of female characters say about the show's presumed audience? Use your findings as evidence in an analytic essay about the show's portrayal of women.

5. **CONNECTING TEXTS**   Do you see evidence of covert antifeminism in advertising? Write an essay in which you explore the depiction of women in advertising, focusing perhaps on ads in a woman's magazine such as *Elle* or *Jane*. To develop your argument, consult Steve Craig's "Men's Men and Women's Women" (p. 202).

ANDRE MAYER

The New Sexual Stone Age

*More than thirty years after the beginning of the modern women's move-
ment, the traditional codes that govern gender behavior and identity are
being replaced by new notions of what it means to be a man or woman.
But you wouldn't know it by listening to contemporary pop music, especially rap-metallists like Kid Rock and Limp Bizkit, who, Andre Mayer
argues, have returned "to an age of rampant chauvinism, where men
swagger about in a testosterone rage and women are reduced to sexual
ornaments." Suddenly, it's "pimp culture" time on the pop airwaves,
where men are men and women are, well—maybe you should watch a
videotape of the Britney Spears Pepsi commercial run during Super Bowl
XXXVI. Mayer is a columnist for* Shift.com *magazine, where this piece
first appeared in 2001.*

Everywhere you look, people are taking a more open-minded stance on gender roles. In October 2000, the Dutch parliament implemented legislation that
would make it the first country in the world to recognize gay marriages. Ohio
University announced it would designate thirty campus bathrooms "unisex"
to accommodate transgendered students. The number of male nurses is rising, as is the overall viewership of women's sports. Outmoded notions about
the roles of men and women are relaxing; except, that is, in pop music, where
quite the opposite is true. Glance at magazine covers, at videos, at lyric sheets:
We've returned to an age of rampant chauvinism, where men swagger about
in a testosterone rage and women are reduced to sexual ornaments.

The most visible advocates are artists like Kid Rock, Limp Bizkit, and
Crazy Town, who not only resemble eighties hair metal in their thudding
guitar assault, but in their celebration of male debauchery and female sub-
servience. In song, females are oppugned; in videos, they're totted up like
bimbos and objectified. Limp Bizkit's "Nookie" does both: The track is a
misogynistic kiss-off to a girlfriend, and when singer Fred Durst shouts "I did
it all for the nookie," he's blatantly admitting that he exploited her for sex.
Critics have long reproved hip hop for its too-enthusiastic use of words like
"bitches" and "hos," but rappers could always deflect accountability for claiming that their lyrics were a stark reflection of ghetto reality. With the advent of
rap-metal, however, artists like Kid Rock and Limp Bizkit have taken the gritty
argot of their hip hop heroes and are passing it off as their own. With widespread use, such hateful language becomes more accepted.

The same can be said for the current prevalence of pimp iconography.
Echoing rappers like the Notorious B.I.G. and Too $hort, Kid Rock fancies him-

self an "American pimp," but he's part of a greater trend that includes apparel (Phat Pimp Clothing, Pimpdaddy.com), movies (the Hughes brothers' documentary *American Pimp* and the upcoming comedy *Lil' Pimp*, about a nine-year-old procurer), and staged events, like Boston's annual "Pimps and Hos Ball." It stems from the general nostalgia for blaxploitation flicks like *Cleopatra Jones* and *The Mack*, in which pimps are the pinnacle of camp, dressing in garish attire and spouting comical jive. Real pimps are far less cuddly — as we know, they insult, abuse, and unscrupulously lord over their female charges. Most people would agree that pimping is abhorrent, but the image has become so widespread — and in many cases, sentimentalized — that a new generation of pop culture consumers blithely embraces it.

Unfortunately, the current contingent of female stars is doing little to correct these primitive attitudes. Many of them — the Britneys, the Christinas, the Jessicas — dress like prostitutes, or at the very least, extras in a Van Halen video. When these chirpy, vacuous singers swept into vogue, they knocked more intelligent and progressive gals like Tori Amos and Alanis Morissette off the charts. Every new video or awards show is an opportunity for immodest types like Mariah Carey and Toni Braxton to set new standards for libidinous spectacle, and while they pay lip service to positive messages, the only thing they offer their distaff fans is an unattainable image of female sexuality.

So what's the cause of this retrograde sexism? Many critics have pointed 5 to the feelings described by Susan Faludi in her book *Stiffed: The Betrayal of the American Man*, in which she claims that feelings of emasculation (due to a number of factors, including joblessness and feminism) have spurred many men to reassert their manhood. The most glaring consequence of this may be the popularity of so-called "lad mags," of which *Maxim* was arguably the catalyst. Started in the mid-nineties, *Maxim* captured an immense demographic of horny males by offering *Playboy*-type titillation (stopping just short of pornography) and insolent commentary. The effect inevitably snowballed into other media — while pop has always used sex to help sell albums, record executives undoubtedly felt that increasing the T&A in the marketing of female artists would also satisfy the booming *Maxim* niche.

The music press seems eerily complicit with the problem. While some writers have commented on the inherent virgin-whore complex in Britney Spears's image, for example, many seem only too happy to defend it, or at the very least excuse it. The Spears profile in the September 13th issue of *Rolling Stone* typifies the music press's soft treatment of gender. The cover features Spears with trademark bared midriff and salacious leer and carries the kicker "Britney talks back: Don't treat me like a little girl." Like most Spears interviews, it's a shameless red herring. The story is punctuated with Spears's cheerily oblivious musings on the nature of her appeal, and in lieu of any remotely revealing quotes, writer Jenny Eliscu comes to the shrugging conclusion that "Britney and her image are one and the same — she is as much of a delightful contradiction as she seems." The title of Spears's single, "I'm a Slave 4 U," suggests that her provocative image shows no signs of flagging.

Meanwhile, those females who assert their strength often seem misguided. The catchphrase "independent women" is as hollow as the shrieks of "girl power!" back in 1997.

Destiny's Child equate self-sufficiency with having the wherewithal to buy their own clothes, shoes, and cars. Then again, any assertion of dignity seems practical at a time when Eminem protégés D12 spout, "Independent women in the house / Show us your tits and shut your motherfucking mouth" ("Ain't Nuttin' But Music").

This prevailing machismo not only denigrates women, but inherently scorns anyone whom it deems less than "manly" (i.e., impervious to sensitivity and militantly hetero). Barring gender benders like Marilyn Manson and Placebo's Brian Molko, few artists seem interested in exploring the androgyny of David Bowie and Freddie Mercury. And why would they? Right now, pop seems not only unreceptive but hostile to such liberalism.

The easiest qualification of music's current homophobia is taking a tally   10 of the number of openly gay stars. There are few beyond Elton John, k.d. lang, Melissa Etheridge, and Rufus Wainwright. Has anyone heard from George Michael lately? He's probably wary of returning to this increasingly homophobic milieu. Given the current indication for close-mindedness, sitting out until pop emerges from the Stone Age seems like a sound idea.

READING THE TEXT

1. What contradiction does Mayer see in the evolution of gender roles and the content and style of contemporary pop music?

2. What does Mayer mean by "pimp iconography" (para. 3)?

3. Characterize Mayer's tone in this essay. How does it affect your response to his argument?

4. According to Mayer, what is the significance of the relative dearth of gay performers in today's pop music world?

READING THE SIGNS

1. Write an essay defending, refuting, or modifying Mayer's contention that much of popular music reinforces outmoded notions about gender roles.

2. **CONNECTING TEXTS**   Mayer describes a trend he sees in popular music, but he does not offer his own explanation for it. Write an essay in which you present your thesis for why so much modern pop music is sexist. To develop support for your stance, you might analyze some current music videos, paying attention to both lyrics and the personal style of the artists you watch. You might also consult Cynthia Tucker's "Thug Culture Is a Cancer Destroying Black America" (p. 326) and Joan Morgan's "Sex, Lies, and Videos" (p. 616).

3. **CONNECTING TEXTS**   Mayer cites Maxim as a current magazine that exploits the desire of "many men to reassert their manhood" (para. 5). Analyze an issue

of *Maxim*, and write an essay that disputes or supports Mayer's characterization of it. To develop your ideas, you might interview some men who are regular readers of the magazine and some men who find no interest in it; in
addition, you might read or reread Courtney Martin's "The Famine Mystique"
(p. 607).

4. Write an essay in which you analyze the style of female rappers. To what
   extent do they share the "primitive attitudes" (para. 4) that Mayer ascribes to
   such stars as Britney Spears and Mariah Carey? How do you account for any
   differences that you may observe?

5. Form teams and conduct an in-class debate on whether the patterns Mayer
   sees in pop music are indeed chauvinistic and dangerous or, instead, a sign of
   liberation. Use the debate to generate ideas for an essay in which you formulate your own argument about this question.

MARISA CONNOLLY

Homosexuality on Television:
The Heterosexualization of Will and Grace

> *Network TV is on the cutting edge of social change, right? Courageously
> challenging long-standing prejudices on behalf of progressive new view-
> points? After all, it has brought us* Will and Grace, *a perennial hit sitcom
> featuring gay characters that shatter the homophobic history of popular
> culture. So why, Marisa Connolly asks, is the relationship between gay Will
> and straight Grace so, well, romantic? Why did the show maintain an
> erotic tension between the two that continued from season to season? Why
> did Will take so long to get a boyfriend? Could it be that* Will and Grace
> *isn't really so very courageous after all? Connolly, who is an area director
> of Communications for the American Cancer Society, thinks not.*

He's single, successful and good-looking. She's independent, strong-willed and
attractive. They'd make the perfect couple, except for one teensy problem —
he's gay, she's straight.

Such is the premise of NBC's *Will and Grace*, a half-hour situation comedy
in its fifth season that serves two purposes. First, the show attempts to
explore a totally platonic relationship between two best friends of opposite
sexes. Secondly, the show features two gay male leads with polar-opposite
personalities in order to destigmatize the representation of the homosexual

man. The show has been one of NBC's most successful since its debut, garnering both critical and public praise for its portrayal of homosexuality as just another aspect of the lives of the four main characters.

However, in order to make a show with such controversial subject matter palatable for the masses, both scriptwriters and the mainstream media have taken to talking about the show's two leads more like a romantic couple rather than a pair of best friends. For the purposes of this analysis, "couple" will refer specifically to a romantic pairing. This metaphor, which plays out on screen in both word and action, also carries over into the language used to describe the show and its characters in mainstream print media. Metaphors that misclassify this relationship can make a television show with a gay male lead easier to digest for the viewing audience, but it can also have negative effects on the inroads the show has made in making homosexuality more acceptable on mainstream television.

This analysis will explore the extent to which reviews in mainstream print media reflect the heterosexual undercurrent apparent in *Will and Grace*. Common representations of homosexuality on television will be explained, followed by an examination of how *Will and Grace* heterosexualizes the relationship between the two lead characters. Finally, the paper will examine how those metaphors translate into print media, and how that translation affects the viewing public.

None of this discussion is meant to demean the accomplishments of *Will and Grace* as the first vehicle to tackle homosexuality naturally in prime time. However, it is important to evaluate the discourse about an important program such as this one, in order to understand how the public uses old metaphors to make sense of new representations that push the envelope of what has been previously accepted. 5

Background

During television's 1997–1998 season, viewers watched as ABC's *Ellen* became the first television show ever to feature an openly gay lead character — Ellen Morgan, played by actress/comedienne Ellen DeGeneres. The actress timed her personal coming out with the coming out of her character amidst an onslaught of controversy, protest, and criticism from right-wing conservatives such as Jerry Falwell. Initial viewer and public reaction to Ellen's revealed sexuality was positive. But as the season continued and the episodes continued to delve into Ellen's self-discovery and the hardships she faced as a lesbian in today's society, the audience slipped away while criticism continued, forcing ABC to cancel the program at the end of the season.

TV critics and reviewers attributed the failure of *Ellen* not to the public's inability to embrace an openly gay character, but more to the show's almost preachy overtones in the episodes following Ellen's initial coming out. The consensus among scholars was that *Ellen* was too political and didactic, containing "veritable lessons in queer socio-politics."[1] As a result of the negative feedback and criticism with which ABC had to deal, it seemed unlikely that any network would be willing to take a risk with a homosexual character again anytime soon.

Will and Grace: More Accessible Homosexuality

However, in September 1998, NBC launched *Will and Grace*. Created by writers Max Mutchnick and David Kohan and directed by James Burrows (of *Cheers*, *Friends*, and *Frasier* fame), the program featured the first openly gay male character in a lead role on prime-time television. The move was risky — airing a program like *Will and Grace* so soon after *Ellen* crashed and burned could have plunged the show and the network into boundless controversy.

But NBC was confident that *Will and Grace* would be a more successful vehicle for an openly gay character for a few reasons. First, the show did not focus around a homosexual man's coming out, but rather homosexuality as a way of life. There was no pilot episode that depicted Will coming to terms with his sexuality, although flashback episodes have explored this moment in Will's life. Will's homosexuality has been a given from the very beginning of the series. Additionally, the character of Will was not portrayed with any common stereotypical "gay" behavior. The final reason NBC could be more confident in the show's success was that the producers threw a heterosexual woman into the mix.

The show revolves around Will Truman (Eric McCormack), a young 10 lawyer living in New York City who just ended a seven-year relationship with another man. His best friend, Grace Adler (Debra Messing), is an interior designer who, in the pilot episode, leaves her fiancé at the altar. The two friends had dated in college, until Will revealed his sexuality to Grace, and they'd been the best of friends ever since.

The relationship between Will and Grace was based on the real-life friendship between Mutchnick, who is himself openly gay, and his friend Janet, who is straight. Mutchnick and Kohan wanted to explore the male-female relationship dynamic "when sex doesn't get in the way," but they also wanted to present a more true-to-life representation of a gay man in Will, who is good-looking, successful, and less effeminate than most stereotypes.

They balanced that representation with the addition of Will's friend Jack McFarland (Sean Hayes), who is flamboyantly gay and serves as comic relief along with Grace's assistant, Karen Walker (Megan Mullally). The combination of all four players created an aesthetically pleasing representation of single life in New York City, and resulted in a much less controversial success for NBC.

[1] James R. Keller. "*Will and Grace*: The Politics of Inversion." *Queer (Un)Friendly Film and Television* (London: McFarland & Company, 2002): 122.

The show debuted in a Monday night timeslot, moved to Tuesdays after it showed promise, and ended up in the coveted "Must See TV" line-up on Thursday night before its first season had even ended. It garnered critical praise from both mainstream sources and homosexual interest groups. GLAAD (the Gay and Lesbian Alliance Against Defamation) hailed the show for its portrayal of two different representations of gay men. The show even found itself competing for the same advertising dollars as ABC's *Dharma and Greg*, a program based on the lives of a heterosexual couple. It seemed that mainstream society had grown to accept the gay community on its television programs.[2]

Criticism from Other Sources

In the years since *Will and Grace* premiered to great success on NBC, so soon after the negativity swirled around *Ellen*, media critics have tried to understand why the show did not come under the fire of public outcry. The overwhelming consensus is that though *Will and Grace* has been monumental in bringing homosexuality as a reality into the living rooms of houses around the world, it "negotiates with the dominant culture by making the most important relationships between the two gay characters heterosocial and quasi-heterosexual."[3] It has been clear since the show's first season that the most important relationship has been the friendship between Will and Grace. Though the program is about a homosexual male and his heterosexual best friend, scripts and comic devices have often made it seem that Will and Grace were the perfect heterosexual couple, separated only by sexual orientation. Battles and Hilton-Morrow present this situation as yet another example of delayed consummation — a plot line that puts off the matchup of the leading male and female characters in order to keep the audience tuning in on a weekly basis. Will and Grace are often positioned as a couple, as well as subject to the barbs of Karen, who often chides their bickering or displays of affection with lines like "Oh, just climb on top of each other and get it over with already!"[4]

It is this placement of Will and Grace as a heterosexual couple almost destined to be together that seems to be the reason for its widespread appeal and lack of criticism from right-wing groups. Even though the show contains openly gay and sometimes raunchy humor, provided by Jack and Karen, according to Battles and Hilton-Morrow, this behavior is shown as almost infantile, playing to a familial relationship among the four characters. Karen

15

---

[2]Kathleen Battles and Wendy Hilton-Morrow. "Gay Characters in Conventional Spaces: *Will and Grace* and the Situation Comedy Genre." *Critical Studies in Media Communication.* 19 (2002): 89.

[3]Keller, 123.

[4]Battles and Hilton-Morrow, 93.

and Jack are the children to Will and Grace's parental figures.[5] That fact alone plays into the inherent heterosexual relationship between gay Will and straight Grace.

Media Representation

Since *Will and Grace*'s first season, print media and other forums have run many reviews, criticisms and praises for the program. In looking at the representation of homosexuals in this program, it became clear that these reviews may look at the relationship between Will and Grace similarly to the way the relationship is portrayed on the program itself. Specifically, to what extent does the print media heterosexualize the characters? Focusing specifically on the language used to describe their friendship, does the print media use words like "couple," "romance" and "sexual tension" when they comment on Will and Grace? Do they use any metaphors or comparisons to past television couples that carry a heterosexual connotation?

Television reviews in print media sources play a large role in creating the general buzz around a show, as well as contribute to the total viewership of a program. If these reviews are presenting the relationship between Will and Grace as heterosexual, they could be responsible for detracting from the audience's understanding of the show as an exploration of a homosexual lifestyle.

Of course, the media would not be entirely to blame for any misrepresentations of the relationship between Will and Grace — the writers of the program have come under some degree of fire for keeping Will out of any real romantic relationship with another man. The media can only comment on what is presented to them in a weekly episode. This paper explores how much of that veiled metaphor of heterosexuality translated itself into the print media.

Methodology

In order to analyze the extent to which the print media perpetuates the idea that *Will and Grace* depicts a successful homosexual television vehicle because it masquerades Will and Grace as a quasi-heterosexual couple, this study examined certain metaphors and phraseology used in various articles and reviews in newspapers during the show's lifetime. Because the show has been on the air for five seasons at the writing of this paper, it has accumulated quite a bit of press. Therefore, in order to make the research more manageable the search was limited to two time periods: articles written in U.S. newspapers and magazines during the show's first season — 1998–1999 — and

---

[5]Battles and Hilton-Morrow, 97.

articles written to commemorate the show's fifth season and 100th episode—September 2002–December 9, 2002. A new television program always receives much media attention in its early days in order for producers to introduce the show, its characters, and its premise, but also so television critics can make their opinions known on whether the program will be a success or a flop. *Will and Grace* was a product of NBC—whose "Must See TV" line-ups are among television's most successful—and it featured the first homosexual male lead on American television; therefore print media pieces filled with character description and analysis were easy to find during this time period.

In addition, looking at articles written around a commemorative event [20] like a sitcom's 100th episode is a helpful way to monitor the changes in media perception of the show between its first season and its current one. Have the metaphors changed with the show's writing as the years have gone by?

The articles used in the analysis were located using two different news index sources: Lexis-Nexis and EBSCO Host through Academic Search Premier. Searches for "will and grace" in Arts and Sports News/Entertainment News from September 1998 through June 1999 turned up over 200 matches. A search from September 2002 through December 2002 turned up about 124 articles. Filtering out the one-sentence blurbs and weekly ratings reports, the data set included 27 articles that could be classified as reviews, trend stories, and actor interviews, each of which used in some way the metaphors and phraseology discovered in the analysis. These articles also came from all over the country, in papers as large as the *Washington Post* to smaller papers such as the *Bergen County Record* (New Jersey).

In the analysis of these articles, it is important to note that many articles written during the first season of *Will and Grace* highlighted and discussed the same criticisms of the show explored in this analysis. The metaphors and language used as examples here are separate examples of metaphors or language used by the media to describe the relationship between lead characters Will and Grace, and have nothing to do with articles or sections of articles that use this language to further discussion about the show's interpretation of homosexuality. To do so would obviously have skewed the analysis in one direction.

Findings

Research has uncovered a few common metaphors used by print media to describe the relationship between Will and Grace as heterosexual. In each instance the form the metaphor takes is different. Sometimes the metaphor appears in one sentence as a one-time comparison or description; in other examples it permeates the entire paragraph like a literary device, perhaps repeating one word or playing off the creation of a mental image earlier in the paragraph. The metaphor use also differs between simple word choice and the writer's personal opinion. Word choice tends to reflect what the writer has seen in that evening's particular episode. A review that carries the writer's opinion of the show as a whole, and not simply one specific episode, tends to tie everything it critiques to the larger picture of the show as a whole. When the writer's opinion colors the review, the metaphor can set a tone for the entire article, focusing on Grace, for example, "still harboring hopes for a man who has his eye on other men."[6]

Specifically, three metaphors occurred frequently within the data set. Two focus explicitly on making Will and Grace's relationship heterosexual, while the third is a more general classification of relationships between gay men and straight women and how print media relates to them. Following are several examples from the data set where each metaphor demonstrates how these metaphors are used in each article.

THE "ROMANCE" METAPHOR

Many reviews during the first season have classified Will and Grace's relation- 25 ship as a "romantic" one, using words like "love," "lovers" and "romance" when describing what these characters mean to each other. The use of a metaphor involving "love" in some way is not out of the ordinary to describe these characters. After all, the show is meant to explore a strong platonic love between a man and a woman. Similarly, most writers are quick to point out, subsequently, that it is "not that kind of love."[7] However, the reader is often set up from the beginning of the review to think that Will and Grace are just another couple. For example, the first part of the previous example reads, "Will (Eric McCormack) and Grace (Debra Messing), they're in love."[8]

The problem with using such romance-heavy terminology in describing Will and Grace is that it cements the characters into a position of physical, romantic love. There have been too many sitcoms to count that have focused on a pair or group of friends that did not hinge on this idea of subliminal love. In a program that is trying to make the relationship between these four people seem as mainstream as possible, it takes away from that idea to continuously refer to the obvious love Will and Grace share for one another.

The "romance" metaphor also tends to make much more of the physical nature of Will and Grace's relationship. For example, an article in *The Nation* makes this reference: "Grace has already moved in, at his insistence, as his new roommate, which will give them many opportunities to hug each other after they've resolved whatever antics come between them. . . ."[9] This quote is a good example of how the author's opinion colors the metaphor used. Here, the writer is clearly making the hugs between Will and Grace more romantic than they are perhaps intended to be, labeling certain experiences "excuses" to hug.

---

[6]Matthew Gilbert. "Will Success Ruin NBC's *Will & Grace?*" *Boston Globe* 8 Apr. 1999: El.

[7]Drew Jubera. "Ready or Not, It's Time for Fall Season to Open." *Atlanta Journal and Constitution* 21 Sept. 1998: 01C.

[8]Jubera, 01C.

[9]Alyssa Katz. "Beyond Ellen." *The Nation* 2 Nov. 1998: 32–34.

Entering into the fifth season, the "romance" metaphor has not disappeared. Another article in the *Boston Globe* compared Will and Grace's gay-straight relationship as "a sexless love affair."[10] This metaphor takes "romance" to another level by marking it as forbidden love, and brings even more complex connotations to the relationship.

Another example of the romance metaphor was paired with the second major metaphor, which will be described in the next section: "Do Will and Grace love each other? Clearly. They live together; they depend on and bicker with each other; they share their hopes, desires and neuroses; they praise, criticize and tease each other relentlessly."[11] Each one of these behaviors is associated with the state of being in love. Again, there are many kinds of love that can be described in this way, but the writer of this review makes it clear he is referring to only romantic love between a man and a woman.

THE "COUPLE" METAPHOR

The example above segues nicely into the "couple" metaphor. The review follows that quote with a segment from that week's episode in which Will and Grace are fighting in public and a stranger mistakes them for a married couple:

> "We're not married!" Grace fires back. "And I'm gay!" Will snaps.
> "Well, if you're not married, and you're gay," the man says, nodding toward Will, "what the hell's all this about?"
> What, indeed.[12]

It is obvious, from the last line of this quote, that the writer of this review has a clear opinion that Will and Grace should be a classical heterosexual couple. Many times, Will and Grace are described as "the perfect couple," with only one major barrier keeping them apart: "Will's gayness is the only thing that stands between the devoted pair and lifelong happiness."[13]

A second example of this insinuation: "They are the perfect couple. But they aren't lovers, nor will they be."[14] With no real label for a platonic relationship between a heterosexual woman and a homosexual man, it seems as though writers can only refer to the characters by the strongly marked word "couple," risking the romantic connotation. The only label writers seem to be able to come up with is "perfect," idealizing to some extent the relationship between these two characters as something that neither homosexuality nor

[10]Matthew Gilbert. "Pop Music: More Than Friends. Forget the Naysayers, with Its Unique Wit and Style, *Will and Grace* Remains One of TV's Elite Comedies." *Boston Globe* 17 Nov. 2002: Nl.

[11]Eric Mink. "*Will and Grace* Top of Class of '99: Bright Season Finale Proves It's Not Just Another Sitcom." *New York Daily News* 13 May 1999: 106.

[12]Ibid, 106.

[13]Katz, 32–34.

[14]Tom Walter. "New-Season Shopping? Start with *Will and Grace*." *Commercial Appeal (TN)* 21 Sept. 1998, C2.

heterosexuality can completely emulate: "the perfectly committed no-commit couple,"[15] and "the boy and the girl are too perfect for each other to ever get it on."[16] This kind of idealization leads to the ultimate end in coupledom, that Will and Grace belong together: "Naturally, the show puts them together. More importantly, it makes us believe they belong together."[17]

Some uses of the metaphor even go as far to suggest that Will's gayness is something that he can "get over," in order to bring Will and Grace together in the end:

> They are, in short, a perfect match except that they are sexually incompatible and there is a strange but unmistakably romantic tone to the show. Is it possible that the producers actually want viewers to hope, unconsciously, that these two terrific and very good-looking people will, eventually, somehow, overcome that little sexual, uh, glitch?[18]

THE "ODD COUPLE" METAPHOR

Some writers, however, have made an attempt to put a different label on the relationship — a new spin on the term "couple" which works well for developing a trend in popular culture that seems to enjoy pairing homosexual men with heterosexual women. Just before *Will and Grace* hit television airwaves, Hollywood had made a few movies following this formula. First coined in an article appearing in *Entertainment Weekly*, the "Odd Couple" metaphor relates Will and Grace, and other gay man–straight woman relationships to the opposites attract relationship between the characters on the original *Odd Couple* television show: "Gay men and straight women are to the '90s what Oscar and Felix were to the '70s."[19] In the first season, this metaphor does not exactly speak to the heterosexual nature of Will and Grace's relationship, because Oscar and Felix were two same-sex friends, but it does seem to make the idea of homosexuality friendlier to the viewing audience, which is, again, one of the major criticisms of *Will and Grace* as a groundbreaking television program. Another example of the "Odd Couple" metaphor: "If only she'd had a pal like Will Truman, half of television's latest odd couple in *Will and Grace.* . . ."[20]

The motivation behind the word "odd" in this metaphor, however, raises a 35 few questions, and begins to mark where the mainstream media has stopped

---

[15]Jubera, 01C.

[16]Katz, 34.

[17]Robert Bianco. "16 New Series Premiere This Week, NBC's *Will & Grace* Leads the Lineup." *USA Today* 21 Sept. 1998: 1D.

[18]Eric Mink. "Peacock's Got the 'Will'." *New York Daily News* 21 Sept. 1998: 71.

[19]A. Jacobs. "When Gay Men Happen to Straight Women." *Entertainment Weekly*. Retrieved November 14, 2002 from www.ew.com.

[20]Stephen McCauley. "He's Gay, She's Straight, They're a Trend." *New York Times* 20 Sept. 1998, 31.

feeling the influence of the show's scripts and intentions. From the beginning, Mutchnick and Kohan were trying to create a show about homosexuality that made it more mainstream, blending homosexual and heterosexual life into one seamless world. Marking Will and Grace's relationship as "odd" is not something one could believe Mutchnick would find acceptable. The "odd" can only really refer to the neuroses and behaviors of the "bickering, superficial, relationship-impaired foursome,"[21] and not to the social status of their relationship.

But later repetition of the metaphor makes a few changes. Rather than specifically relating Will and Grace to same-sex friends Oscar and Felix, the "couple" part of "Odd Couple" starts to take on comparisons to other television pairings: "They rank with some of TV's classic couples, including Sam and Diane [*Cheers*], and Oscar and Felix."[22] The most interesting aspect of this morphing of the "Odd Couple" metaphor is now we have Will and Grace paired with one of television's most well-known pairs of frustrated lovers — Sam and Diane from James Burrows's *Cheers*. In season five, Will and Grace are not considered "odd" as much as they are considered "fated" never to be together, yet always to be together, as good friends.

Conclusion

The consequences of metaphors like the ones discussed above still carry heavily on the future of *Will and Grace*. To date, the show is still one of NBC's most popular, holding down the 9 p.m. timeslot in the "Must-See TV" lineup. Megan Mullally, Sean Hayes, and Eric McCormack have each gone on to win supporting and lead acting trophies, respectively, and the show itself earned the Emmy for Outstanding Comedy Series in 2000. However, Will's character has yet to have a serious on-screen romantic relationship with another man comparable to those of Grace, and a more recent plot line has revolved around Will and Grace's attempts to have a child together.

If the program continues to push Will and Grace together with pseudo-romantic overtones, then the print media will most likely continue to discuss the characters' exploits with heterosexual metaphors. The media can only represent the images, words and storylines a television program shows them. Perhaps a look at the metaphors used to describe the relationship between supporting players Karen and Jack would turn more favorably towards a platonic gay man–straight woman relationship, but until the show changes its name to *Karen and Jack*, the emphasis will be on Will, Grace, and the love that almost constantly seems to speak its name.

[21] Gilbert, 2002, NI.
[22] Gilbert, 2002, NI.

READING THE TEXT

1. Why, according to Connolly, did *Ellen* fail?

2. How did *Will and Grace*'s creators work to defuse the controversy over the show's focus on gay characters?

3. In Connolly's view, how are Will and Grace made to appear like a heterosexual couple?

4. What is Connolly's methodology in her research of the media's response to *Will and Grace*?

READING THE SIGNS

1. Watch an episode of *Will and Grace* and analyze the relationship between the two lead characters. Have things changed since Connolly wrote her essay? If so, how would you explain those changes?

2. **CONNECTING TEXTS**   Adopt Susan Douglas's ("Signs of Intelligent Life on TV," p. 307) perspective on TV's treatment of gender roles and analyze the treatment of gender in *Will and Grace*.

3. Analyze another TV program that features gay characters, such as *Queer Eye for the Straight Guy*. Do you see evidence of the soft-peddling of homosexuality?

4. **CONNECTING TEXTS**   Write an argumentative essay in response to the proposition that, despite the heterosexualization of the two lead characters, *Will and Grace* still represented a milestone in the media's depiction of gay characters and culture when it first appeared. To develop your ideas, consult Andy Medhurst, "Batman, Deviance, and Camp" (p. 592) and Sean Cahill, "The Case for Marriage Equality" (p. 586).

CYNTHIA TUCKER
Thug Culture Is a Cancer Destroying Black America

Hey hey, my my, gangsta rap will never die, but it might tone it down some if it doesn't want to contribute any longer to the sort of real-world violence that young urban African Americans face every day. In fact, Cynthia Tucker argues in this op-ed piece, gangsta rap is fueling a "thug culture" that is destroying the lives of black Americans by "glorifying violence, misogyny, and thuggery." Well aware of the argument that gangsta rap is marketed to white consumers by white music industry executives, Tucker still believes that "blaming The Man seems shallow and irresponsible" when rap numbers like T. I.'s "Hurt" seem intent on glamorizing the slaughter of entire black families in their homes by black gangs clad in ski masks and armed with AK-47s and Mac 10s. Cynthia Tucker is a Pulitzer Prize–winning syndicated columnist and is the editorial page editor for The Atlanta Constitution.

Clifford Harris Jr. would have been celebrated last Saturday night at the BET Hip-Hop Awards, had he made it to the ceremony. Instead, he was in police custody, charged with illegal possession of firearms. The young rapper could have stood before a cheering audience in downtown Atlanta and accepted his award for Best CD of the Year, had he steered clear of machine guns and silencers. Instead, he was handcuffed, fingerprinted, photographed, incarcerated. Harris — whose stage name is T. I. — should be riding the wave of his incredible success, enjoying freedom, fame, and fortune. Instead, he's looking at the prospect of several years in prison. He was arrested Saturday afternoon after he was allegedly caught trying to take possession of the weapons from his bodyguard, who was apparently cooperating with authorities. Already a convicted crack dealer, Harris faces a potentially lengthy sentence.

Somewhere along the way, a cadre of young black men and women began glorifying violence, misogyny, and thuggery, accepting incarceration as inevitable, resigning themselves to lives on the margins of mainstream society. They created a thug culture that has been commodified — celebrated in music and movies, sold to poor adolescents in wretched neighborhoods as well as affluent teenagers in upscale communities. But the violence isn't just playacting; it's not just teenagers trying on a rebellious facade. Young adults — many of them men, most of them black — get arrested. They go to prison. They die on the streets.

There is now a cottage industry dedicated to defending rap music, a group of enablers who glorify hard-core rap as a legitimate art form reflecting the bitter real-life experiences of ghetto inhabitants. But I have no patience for the academic exegeses. This so-called music and the lifestyle it glorifies is a malignancy destroying black America. What does it take for mothers and fathers, ministers and teachers, music executives and TV moguls to turn it off?

Last year, T. I. attended the funeral of Philant Johnson, 26, his best friend and personal assistant, who was shot dead in a gun battle among moving cars on I-75 near Cincinnati. Police said the gunfire followed an argument involving unidentified locals and T. I.'s entourage at a Cincinnati nightclub. If Harris had regrets about Johnson's death, they apparently didn't manifest as pacifism. He kept a small arsenal at his Atlanta home, according to police.

The criminal justice system — notorious for grinding black men down — gave the young rapper T. I. a second chance after he was convicted for selling cocaine. Not only has he launched a highly successful music career, but he has also won notice as an actor. He has a role in the new movie *American Gangster*, starring Denzel Washington and Russell Crowe. But given that second chance, what did Harris do? If he had machine guns, as police say, at whom did he intend to point them?

Homicide is the leading cause of death among black men between the ages of 15 and 30. And it is a fratricidal enterprise. Young black men are killed by other young black men. If white entertainers were making millions singing about the slaughter of black men and mistreatment of black women, city streets would clog with protesters. Demonstrators would pack the halls of Congress. Commerce would grind to a halt as black activists demanded boycotts. But somehow, the violence and misogyny of T. I., 50 Cent, and Nelly are less inflammatory.

Yes, a lot of their music is purchased by white consumers, as a lot of it is marketed by white executives. But blaming The Man seems shallow and irresponsible when black Americans are abetting their own destruction.   5

READING THE TEXT

1. Define in your own words what Tucker means by "thug culture."
2. What does Tucker mean by saying that "thug culture . . . has been commodified" (para. 2)?
3. Why does Tucker find the actions of rapper T. I. so reprehensible?
4. Characterize Tucker's style in this selection, including her choice of words such as "cancer" and "malignancy." How does it affect your response to her argument?

READING THE SIGNS

1. In an essay, propose your own answer to Tucker's question, "What does it take for mothers and fathers, ministers and teachers, music executives and TV moguls to turn [hard-core rap] off?" (para. 3).

2. As Tucker mentions, her indictment of hard-core rap contrasts with the position of those who defend rap "as a legitimate art form reflecting the bitter real-life experiences of ghetto inhabitants" (para. 3). In class, form teams and debate which view of rap is more accurate. To develop support for your team's position, base your arguments on both specific rap songs and the biographies of the artists who produced them.

3. Do a semiotic comparison of the work of an earlier hip-hop artist, such as Tupac Shakur, and a current hip-hop performer such as 50 Cent. Do you find differences in their depiction of the hip-hop community? If so, how do you account for those differences?

4. **CONNECTING TEXTS**   Tucker claims that a double standard exists whereby white entertainers are not allowed to glorify violence and misogyny as some black entertainers do. In an essay, present your own argument about whether or not such a double standard does indeed exist, supporting your claims with evidence drawn from entertainers of both ethnicities. To develop your ideas, consult Andre Meyer, "The New Sexual Stone Age" (p. 312), Corey Williams, "NAACP Symbolically Buries N-Word" (p. 500), and Joan Morgan, "Sex, Lies, and Videos" (p. 616).

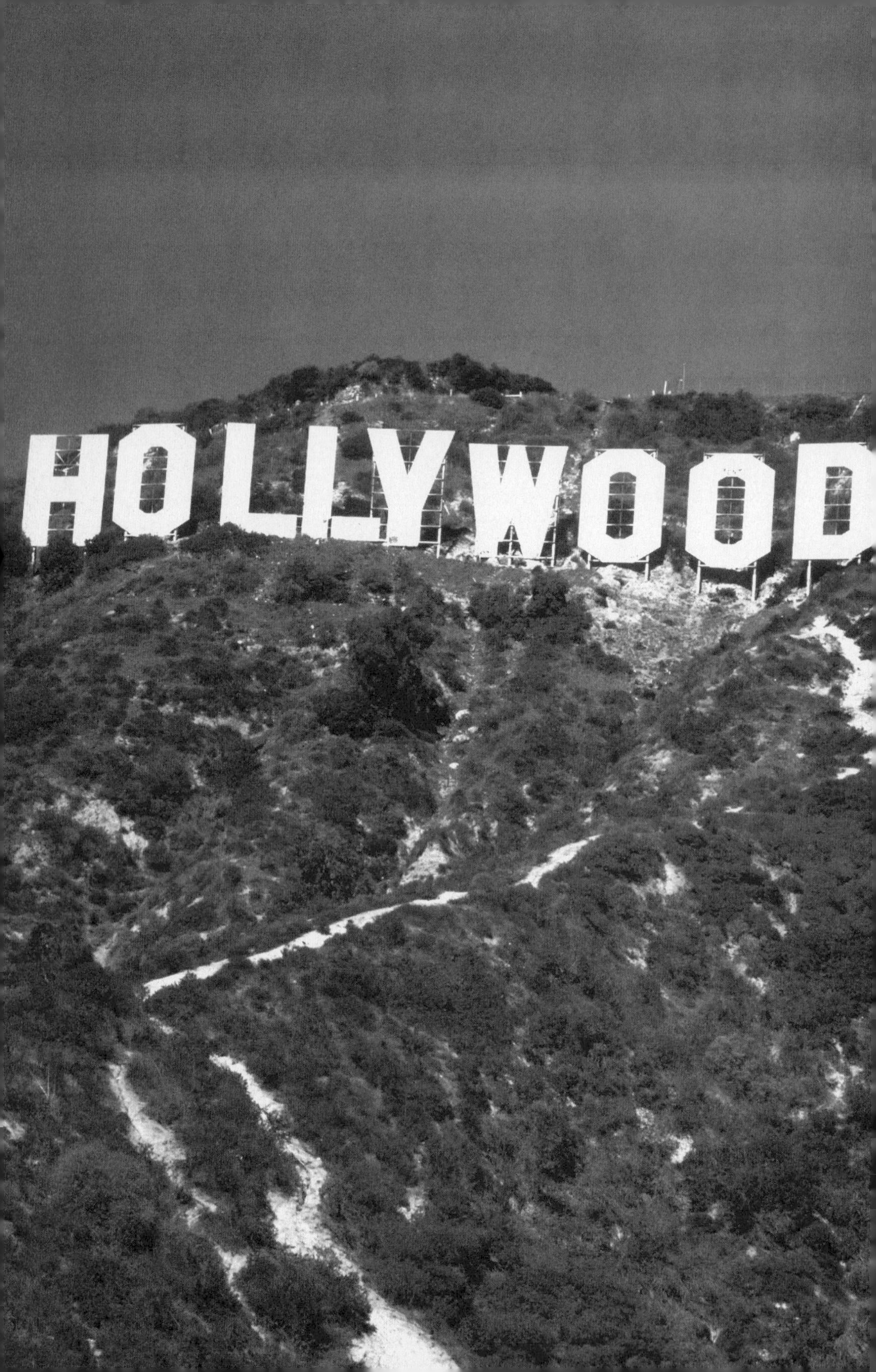
HOLLYWOOD

THE HOLLYWOOD SIGN

The Culture of American Film

The Prequel

Let's play Jeopardy. Category: Hollywood movies for $250. Buzzers ready? In recent years the following movies all shared something in common: *Harry Potter and the Order of the Phoenix, Shrek the Third, Spider-Man 3, Pirates of the Caribbean: At World's End, Ocean's Eleven, Ocean's Twelve, Ocean's Thirteen, Rocky Balboa, Rambo, Live Free or Die Hard, Alien vs. Predator — Requiem, Meet the Fockers, Exorcist: The Beginning, The Bourne Ultimatum, Star Trek, Fantastic Four: Rise of the Silver Surfer, The Dark Knight, I Am Legend, Saw, Saw II, Saw III, Saw IV.*

Time's up. And the correct response is: What are some recent Hollywood sequels, prequels, remakes, and adaptations?

And now a daily double for $500. He said, "It looks like déjà vu all over again."

Time's up. And the correct response is: Who was Yogi Berra? You can say that again. And again.

The Sequel

Now, seriously, do you ever get the impression that Hollywood is stuck on replay? That there's nothing to watch except for reruns? That the creative departments of America's movie industry are all on summer vacation? It's true that not everything on the silver screen is a rehash of an old warhorse, but certainly a lot of duplication has come out of Hollywood these days. Even

331

the 2007 Academy Award winner for Best Picture, *The Departed*, was a re-make of a Hong Kong film. And, as is usually the case when a pattern appears in popular culture, we can find a semiotic message behind it.

Once again, the first step in conducting a semiotic analysis is to establish the system within which the sign to be analyzed may be associated with other similar signs. Such systems are frequently historical in nature, and in the case of the Hollywood remake, the system is quite venerable. Film classics like *Wuthering Heights*, *Hamlet*, *Rebecca*, *Moby Dick*, and any film based on a Jane Austen novel have all been made and remade. Such remakes may signify nothing more than a given director's desire to pay homage to a revered prede-cessor or to appeal to audiences' desire to see a favorite story retold with more modern faces. And in the case of Gus Van Sant's 1998 remake of Alfred Hitchcock's *Psycho* (1960), which put Anne Heche in Janet Leigh's shoes (or, one should say, shower), both motivations are apparent.

But the sheer number of Hollywood remakes, sequels, prequels, and adap-tations in recent years suggests an intensification of the phenomenon that is not easily explained in such terms. This difference within the system points to at least two semiotic meanings, the first of which involves the postmodern context in which the contemporary Hollywood remake appears, and the sec-ond involves the commercial imperatives behind filmmaking.

Flashback: The Postmodern System

Postmodernism is, in effect, both a historical period and an attitude. As a his-torical period, postmodernism refers to the culture that has emerged in the wake of the media age, one obsessed with electronic imagery and the prod-ucts of mass culture. As an attitude, postmodernism rejects the values of the past, not in favor of new values but instead to ironize value systems as such. Thus, in the postmodern worldview, our traditional hierarchical distinctions valuing high culture over low culture, say, or creativity over imitation, tend to get flattened out. What was once viewed in terms of an oppositional hierar-chy (origination is opposed to emulation and is superior to it) is reconceived and deconstructed. Postmodern artists, accordingly, tend to reproduce, with an ironic or parodic twist, already existing cultural images in their work, especially if they can be drawn from mass culture and mass society — as Roy Lichten-stein's cartoon canvasses parody popular cartoon books and Andy Warhol's tomato soup cans repeat the familiar labels of the Campbell Soup Company — thus mixing high culture and mass culture in a new, nonoppositional, relation.

Similarly, postmodern filmmakers frequently allude to existing films in their work, as in the final scene of Tim Burton's *Batman*, which directly alludes to Alfred Hitchcock's *Vertigo*, or Oliver Stone's and Quentin Tarantino's *Natural Born Killers*, which recalls *Bonnie and Clyde*. Such allusions to, and repetitions of, existing cultural images in postmodern cinema are called double-coding, because of the way that the postmodern artifact simultaneously refers to

---

Exploring the Signs of Film

In your journal, list your favorite movies. Then consider your list: What does it say about you? What cultural myths do the movies tend to reflect, and why do you think those myths appeal to you? What signs particularly appeal to your emotions? What sort of stories about human life do you most respond to?

---

existing cultural codes and recasts them in new contexts. The conclusion of *Batman*, for example, while echoing *Vertigo*'s climactic scene, differs dramatically in its significance (turning in this case from tragedy to farce).

To put this another way, the postmodern worldview holds that it is no longer possible or desirable to create new images; rather, one surveys the vast range of available images that mass culture has to offer, and repeats them, but with a difference. Such a formula would seem to explain the age of the remake rather nicely, and certainly some of today's remakes reflect postmodern sophistication in their creation. But, somehow, too often such productions lack that ironic wink of self-consciousness that identifies postmodern artistry, that sense of parody that begs you not to take it too seriously.

Thus, there is a second explanation, for as virtually every movie industry commentator has observed, the rage to remake is most often a commercial rather than a creative decision. Simply put, it is safer to go with the tried-and-true than to trust an innovation, as we see in all those movies that are spin-offs of successful television series, like *The Simpsons Movie*, or popular books, like the *Harry Potter* films. And that's what the spate of recent remakes and whatnot signifies: that the movie industry has become so beholden to the profit motive that risk taking and imagination take a back seat to bottom-line imperatives, with Accounting calling the shots instead of Creative. Why come up with something new when you can be sure of a hit by rehashing an existing hit?

Indeed, wherever one looks in popular culture today, one can read the same semiotic message, with music companies and television producers (especially reality TV producers) alongside their cinematic brethren all producing clones of what has already worked (more Britneys, more Makeovers, more Fockers), making money if not art along a yellow brick road paved with gold.

Here's to You, Mrs. Robinson

A particularly interesting spin on the adaptation front can be found in the 2005 movie *Rumor Has It. . . .* Neither a commercial nor a critical success, this Rob Reiner effort might appear as little more than a vehicle for Jennifer Aniston's post-*Friends* career, but it actually offers an especially rich field for cultural semiotic analysis. We won't present a full analysis of the film here but will show, instead, how a single image in a movie may be a striking sign of cultural change.

Should you not have seen *Rumor Has It . . .* , a brief plot summary is in order (remember, while plot summaries are often necessary in semiotic analyses, they should not loom large in an essay and should be as succinct as possible). The key to the plot of *Rumor Has It . . .* is that it is based on an unusual concept that establishes it as a kind of romantic-comic sequel to the 1967 cinematic icon *The Graduate. That* movie (which was based on a novel of the same title) presented a devastating critique of the sterile lives of upper-middle-class suburbanites, centering on the experiences of one Benjamin Braddock (played by Dustin Hoffman), who returns from college to his parents' home and is seduced by a family friend, Mrs. Robinson (played by Anne Bancroft and immortalized by Paul Simon's theme song for the movie). Benjamin ends up falling in love with Mrs. Robinson's daughter, Elaine (played by Katharine Ross), and eventually runs off with her, literally carrying her out of the opulent church wedding where she is about to marry a respectable young medical student. The crucial final image shows Ben and Elaine (still in her wedding dress) ecstatically riding in the back of the bus that is carrying them from the sterile world of the Robinsons and the Braddocks into a presumably more meaningful future.

Katharine Ross and Dustin Hoffman in *The Graduate*, 1967.

Now, keep your eye on that image, because the *difference* between that final scene and the final scene of *Rumor Has It . . .* is sufficient to cue us in to the profound cultural difference marked by this peculiar "sequel."

The premise of *Rumor Has It . . .* is that a real family living in Pasadena, California, served as the model for the characters in *The Graduate*. The model for Mrs. Robinson, Catherine (played by Shirley MacLaine), is now the grandmother of Sarah Huttinger (played by Jennifer Aniston). Catherine's daughter is now dead, but she really did run off with the model for Benjamin Braddock, whose "real name" is Beau Burroughs (played by Kevin Costner), but left him after a few days to return home and marry the respectable Earl Huttinger, who is Sarah's father. Or is he? For in the course of the movie, Sarah learns that she may have been conceived during Beau and Elaine's brief elopement and that, therefore, Beau Burroughs is her real father. Upon investigating, Sarah finds Beau — now an extremely glamorous dot.com millionaire — and, in a twist that could be the subject of an entirely different analysis, is seduced by him. Obvious complications ensue.

Just in case you're wondering, we finally learn that Beau is not Sarah's father, but that's not what concerns us here. What we want to study is the final scene of *Rumor Has It. . . .* In *this* final scene, we see the huge, opulent celebration of Sarah's marriage to Jeff (played by Mark Ruffalo), a respectable lawyer, for Sarah decides to leave the ultra-rich Beau to return to her upper-middle-class

Mark Ruffalo and Jennifer Aniston in *Rumor Has It . . . ,* 2005.

family and fiancé. A nice, sentimental, romantic-comic ending. Cut to the credits.

But let's look at the difference between those two endings. *The Graduate* concluded with a triumphant image of *escape* from the plastic world of upper-middle-class affluence (indeed, *The Graduate* made *plastic* the operative term among the 1960s youth counterculture to describe the sterile values of suburban life). *Rumor Has It . . .*, by contrast, concludes with a triumphant image of an *embrace* of upper-middle-class suburban life (it is also significant that Jeff is a lawyer: a solid upper-middle-class profession). The significance of this difference is profound. That is, the almost forty years between 1967 and 2005 witnessed a shift from the countercultural rejection of middle-class, materialistic values to an enthusiastic adoption of them. The baby boomers (a generation to which Rob Reiner belongs) who made sex, drugs, and rock 'n' roll the keynotes of 1960s' popular culture are now grown up, are now the "plastic" Establishment themselves, and their children (who are of Jennifer Aniston's generation), rather than rebelling against their parents' values, have embraced them. We can see this in the movie's happy ending, which is a fantasy playing to the desires of its target audience. Baby boomers gone respectable can take satisfaction in Earl Huttinger's final triumph over Beau Burroughs, while their Gen X children can feel all warm and fuzzy over Sarah's sentimental return to her fiancé, Jeff. That the triumph of middle-class respectability is what is entertaining about the film — just as the defiance of middle-class respectability was what was entertaining about *The Graduate* — is the crucial sign of a profound cultural shift. In effect, *Rumor Has It . . .* is an ideological remake of *The Graduate* to suit a very different era.

The fact that, in spite of its all-star cast, *Rumor Has It . . .* was not a commercial success is probably not significant in itself. Failures at the aesthetic level (such as poorly executed plot, bad dialogue, and shoddy acting) often lead to a film's commercial or critical failure. What counts is the thinking behind the movie, the "concept," which presumed that a story that effectively reverses the whole message of a prior movie (and an especially iconic movie at that) would be a successful moneymaker. Good-bye *Mother Jones*; hello *Wall Street Journal*.

Discussing the Signs of Film

In any given year, one film may dominate the Hollywood box office, becoming a blockbuster that captures that public's cinematic imagination. In class, discuss which film would be your choice as this year's top hit. Then analyze the film semiotically. Why has *this* film so successfully appealed to so many moviegoers?

The Culture Industry

Hollywood moviemakers have been providing America, and world audiences, with entertainments that have both reflected and shaped audience desires for roughly a century. Long before the advent of TV, movies were providing their viewers with the glamour, romance, and sheer excitement that modern life seems to deny. So effective have movies been in molding audience desire that such early culture critics as Theodor Adorno and Max Horkheimer[1] have accused them of being part of a vast, Hollywood-centered "culture industry" whose products have successfully distracted their audiences from the inequities of modern life, and so have effectively maintained the social status quo by drawing everyone's attention away from it.

More recent analysts, however, are far less pessimistic. Indeed, for many cultural studies "populists," films, along with the rest of popular culture, can represent a kind of mass resistance to the political dominance — or what is often called the *hegemony* — of the social and economic powers-that-be. For such critics, films can provide utopian visions of a better world, stimulating their viewers to imagine how their society might be improved, and so, perhaps, inspiring them to go out and do something about it.

Whether you believe that films distract us from the real world or inspire us to imagine a better one, their central place in contemporary American culture demands interpretation. For their impact goes well beyond the movie theater or video screen. Far from being mere entertainments, movies constitute a profound part of our everyday lives, with every film festival and award becoming major news, and each major release becoming the talk of the country, splashed across the entire terrain of American media from newspapers to television to the Internet. Just think of the pressure you feel to be able to discuss the latest film sensation among your friends. Consider how, if you decide to save a few bucks and wait for the DVD release, you would lose face and be seriously on the social outs. No, there is nothing frivolous about the movies. You've been watching them all your life: Now's the time to start thinking about them semiotically.

Interpreting the Signs of American Film

Interpreting a movie or a group of movies is not unlike interpreting a television program or group of programs. Here too you must suspend your personal feelings or aesthetic judgments about your subject. As with any semiotic analysis, your goal is to interpret the cultural significance of your topic, not to give it a thumbs up or a thumbs down. Thus, you may find it more rewarding

---

[1]**Theodor Adorno** (1903–1969) and **Max Horkheimer** (1895–1973) authored *Dialectic of Enlightenment* (1947), a book whose analyses included a scathing indictment of the culture industry.–EDS.

A row of Oscar statues. Oscar award–winning films are often good subjects for semiotic analysis.

to interpret those films that promise to be culturally meaningful rather than simply choosing your favorite flick. Determining whether a movie is culturally meaningful in the prewriting stage, of course, may be a hit-or-miss affair; you may find that your first choice does not present any particularly interesting grounds for interpretation. That's why it can be helpful to consider factors that suggest a particular movie is special, such as enormous popularity or widespread critical attention. Of course, cult favorites, while often lacking in critical or popular attention, can also be signs pointing toward their more self-selected audiences and so are perfectly good candidates for analysis. Academy Award candidates are also reliable as cultural signs.

Your interpretation of a movie or group of movies should begin with a construction of the system in which it belongs — that is, those movies, past and present, with which it can be associated. While tracing those associations, be on the lookout for striking differences from what is otherwise like what you are analyzing — in the case of our sequels/remakes analysis above, a significant increase in the sheer volume of Hollywood redos — because those differences are what often identify the significance of your subject.

Archetypes are useful features for film analysis as well. An archetype is anything that has been repeated in storytelling from ancient times to the present. There are character archetypes, such as the wise old man, which include such figures as Yoda and Gandalf, and plot archetypes, as in the heroic quest, which is the archetypal backbone of films like *The Lord of the Rings* trilogy. All those male buddy films — from *Butch Cassidy and the Sundance Kid* to *Lethal Weapon* to *Men in Black* — hark back to archetypal male bonding stories as old as *The Epic of Gilgamesh* (from the third millennium B.C.) and the *Iliad*, while Cruella de Vil from *101 Dalmatians* is sister to the Wicked Witch of the West, Snow White's evil stepmother, and every other witch or crone dreamed up by the patriarchal imagination. All those sea monsters, from Jonah's "whale" to Moby Dick to Jaws, are part of the same archetypal phylum, and every time a movie hero struggles to return home after a long journey — Dorothy to Kansas, Lassie to Timmie — a story as old as *Exodus* and the *Odyssey* is retold.

Hollywood is well aware of the enduring appeal of archetypes (see Linda Seger's selection in this chapter for a how-to description of archetypal script writing), and director George Lucas's reliance on the work of anthropologist Joseph Campbell in his creation of the *Star Wars* saga is widely known. But it is not always the case that either creators or consumers are consciously aware of the archetypes before them. Part of a culture's collective unconscious, archetypal stories can send messages that their audiences only subliminally understand. A heavy dosage of male-bonding films in a given Hollywood season, for instance, can send the unspoken cultural message that a man can't really make friends with a woman and that women are simply the sexual reward for manly men. Similarly, too many witches in a given Hollywood season can send the antifeminist message that there are too many bitches (think of *Fatal Attraction* and *Basic Instinct*).

Movies as Metaphors

Sometimes movies can also be seen as metaphors for larger cultural concerns. Consider the grade-B horror flicks of the 1950s, such as the original *Godzilla*. If we study only its plot, we would see little more than a cheesy horror story featuring a reptilian monster that is an archetypal kin of the dragons

---

Reading Film on the Net

Most major films now released in the United States receive their own Web site. You can find them listed in print ads for the film (check your local newspaper). Select a current film, find the Web address, log on, and analyze the film's site semiotically. What images are used to attract your interest in the film? What interactive strategies, if any, are used to increase your commitment to the film? If you've seen the movie, how does the Net presentation of it compare with your experience viewing it either in a theater or on video? Alternatively, analyze the posters designed to attract attention to a particular film; a useful resource is the Movie Poster Page (www.musicman.com/mp/mp.html).

in medieval literature. But Godzilla was no mere dragon transported to the modern world. The dragons that populated the world of medieval storytelling were themselves often used as metaphors for the satanic serpent in the Garden of Eden, but Godzilla was a wholly different sort of metaphor. Created by Japanese filmmakers, Godzilla was originally a metaphor for the nuclear era. A female mutant creation of nuclear poisoning, Godzilla rose over her Japanese audiences like a mushroom cloud, symbolizing the potential for future mushroom clouds both in Japan and around the world in the Cold War era.

For their part, American filmmakers in the 1950s had their own metaphors for the nuclear era. Whenever some "blob" threatened to consume New York or some especially toxic slime escaped from a laboratory, the suggestion that science — especially nuclear science — was threatening to destroy the world filled the theater along with the popcorn fumes. And if it wasn't science that was the threat, Cold War filmmakers could scare us with communists, as films like *Invasion of the Body Snatchers* metaphorically suggested through its depiction of a town in which everyone looked the same but had really been taken over by aliens. "Beware of your neighbors," the movie warned, "they could be communists."

In such ways, an entire film can be a kind of metaphor, but you can find many smaller metaphors at work in the details of a movie as well. Early filmmakers, for example, used to put a tablecloth on the table in dining scenes to signify that the characters at the table were good, decent people (you can find such a metaphor in Charlie Chaplin's *The Kid*, where an impoverished tramp who can't afford socks or a bathrobe still has a nice tablecloth on the breakfast table). Sometimes a director's metaphors have a broad political significance, as at the end of the James Dean classic *Giant*, where the parting shot presents a tableau of a white baby goat standing next to a black baby goat, which is juxtaposed with the image of a white baby standing in a crib side by side with a brown baby. Since the human babies are both the grandchildren of the film's protagonist (one of whose sons has married a Mexican woman, the other an Anglo), the goats are added to underscore metaphorically the message of racial reconciliation that the director wanted to send.

Reading a film, then, is much like reading a novel. Both are texts filled with intentional and unintentional signs, metaphors, and archetypes, and both are cultural signifiers. The major difference is in their medium of expression. Literary texts are cast entirely in written words; films combine verbal language, visual imagery, and sound effects. Thus, we perceive literary and cinematic texts differently, for the written sign is perceived in a linear fashion that relies on one's cognitive and imaginative powers, while a film primarily targets the senses: One sees and hears (and sometimes even smells!). That film is such a sensory experience often conceals its textuality. One is tempted to sit back and go with the flow, to say that it's only entertainment and doesn't have to "mean" anything at all. But as cinematic forms of storytelling overtake written forms of expression, the study of movies as complex texts bearing cultural messages and values is becoming more and more important. Our "libraries" are increasingly to be found in theaters and from Netflix, where the texts of Hollywood can be read for eight dollars (or so) a view or rented for even less. There's a lot to read out there.

The Readings

A paired set of readings on heroes as they appear in the movies opens this chapter, with Robert B. Ray's analysis of the "official" and "outlaw" hero complementing Virginia Postrel's exploration of cinematic superheroes and the glamour they project to their fans. Linda Seger offers a screenwriter's how-to guide for the creation of the kind of archetypal characters that make *Star Wars* one of the most popular movies of all time, while Lisa Kernan provides a framework for the rhetorical analysis of movie trailers. Todd Boyd is next with an essay that situates the "gangsta" film within a history of gangster movies, focusing on the politics of such films as *Boyz N the Hood*, and Jessica Hagedorn surveys a tradition of American filmmaking in which Asian women are presented as either tragic or trivial. David Denby's "High-School Confidential" explains why generations of teenagers flock to all those jocks-and-cheerleaders-versus-the-nerds movies. Then Tom Moore explains how movies like *Freedom Writers* misrepresent the realities of teaching in America's urban classrooms. Michael Parenti takes a social-class-based approach to the codes of American cinema, noting the caste biases inherent in such popular hits as *Pretty Woman*, while Aeon J. Skoble takes *Forrest Gump* to task for undermining the American work ethic, showing how even the most popular movies among middle Americans can be viewed as subversive. Finally, Vivian C. Sobchack concludes the chapter with an almost-unflinching analysis of screen violence, then and now.

ROBERT B. RAY
The Thematic Paradigm

Usually we consider movies to be merely entertainment, but as Robert Ray demonstrates in this selection from his book A Certain Tendency of the Hollywood Cinema *(1985), American films have long reflected fundamental patterns and contradictions in our society's myths and values. Whether in real life or on the silver screen, Ray explains, Americans have always been ambivalent about the value of civilization, celebrating it through official heroes like George Washington and Jimmy Stewart, while at the same time questioning it through outlaw heroes like Davy Crockett and Jesse James. Especially when presented together in the same film, these two hero types help mediate America's ambivalence, providing a mythic solution. Ray's analyses show how the movies are rich sources for cultural interpretation; they provide a framework for decoding movies as different as* Lethal Weapon *and* Malcolm X. *Ray is a professor and director of film and media studies at the University of Florida at Gainesville. His publications include* The Avant Garde Finds Andy Hardy *(1995),* How a Film Theory Got Lost and Other Mysteries in Cultural Studies *(2001) and, most recently,* The ABCs of Classic Hollywood *(2008).*

The dominant tradition of American cinema consistently found ways to overcome dichotomies. Often, the movies' reconciliatory pattern concentrated on a single character magically embodying diametrically opposite traits. A sensitive violinist was also a tough boxer (*Golden Boy*); a boxer was a gentle man who cared for pigeons (*On the Waterfront*). A gangster became a coward because he was brave (*Angels with Dirty Faces*); a soldier became brave because he was a coward (*Lives of a Bengal Lancer*). A war hero was a former pacifist (*Sergeant York*); a pacifist was a former war hero (*Billy Jack*). The ideal was a kind of inclusiveness that would permit all decisions to be undertaken with the knowledge that the alternative was equally available. The attractiveness of Destry's refusal to use guns (*Destry Rides Again*) depended on the tacit understanding that he could shoot with the best of them, Katharine Hepburn's and Claudette Colbert's revolts against conventionality (*Holiday, It Happened One Night*) on their status as aristocrats.

Such two-sided characters seemed particularly designed to appeal to a collective American imagination steeped in myths of inclusiveness. Indeed, in creating such characters, classic Hollywood had connected with what Erik Erikson has described as the fundamental American psychological pattern:

The functioning American, as the heir of a history of extreme contrasts and abrupt changes, bases his final ego identity on some tentative com-

bination of dynamic polarities such as migratory and sedentary, individualistic and standardized, competitive and co-operative, pious and free-
thinking, responsible and cynical, etc. . . .

　　To leave his choices open, the American, on the whole, lives with two
sets of "truths."[1]

The movies traded on one opposition in particular, American culture's
traditional dichotomy of individual and community that had generated the
most significant pair of competing myths: the outlaw hero and the official
hero.[2] Embodied in the adventurer, explorer, gunfighter, wanderer, and loner,
the outlaw hero stood for that part of the American imagination valuing self-
determination and freedom from entanglements. By contrast, the official
hero, normally portrayed as a teacher, lawyer, politician, farmer, or family
man, represented the American belief in collective action, and the objective
legal process that superseded private notions of right and wrong. While the
outlaw hero found incarnations in the mythic figures of Davy Crockett, Jesse
James, Huck Finn, and all of Leslie Fiedler's "Good Bad Boys" and Daniel
Boorstin's "ring-tailed roarers," the official hero developed around legends
associated with Washington, Jefferson, Lincoln, Lee, and other "Good Good
Boys."

　　An extraordinary amount of the traditional American mythology adopted
by Classic Hollywood derived from the variations worked by American ideology around this opposition of natural man versus civilized man. To the extent
that these variations constituted the main tendency of American literature
and legends, Hollywood, in relying on this mythology, committed itself to
becoming what Robert Bresson has called "the Cinema."[3] A brief description
of the competing values associated with this outlaw hero–official hero opposition will begin to suggest its pervasiveness in traditional American culture.

　　1. *Aging*: The attractiveness of the outlaw hero's childishness and pro-   5
pensity to whims, tantrums, and emotional decisions derived from America's
cult of childhood. Fiedler observed that American literature celebrated "the
notion that a mere falling short of adulthood is a guarantee of insight and
even innocence." From Huck to Holden Caulfield, children in American literature were privileged, existing beyond society's confining rules. Often, they
set the plot in motion (e.g., *Intruder in the Dust*, *To Kill a Mockingbird*), acting
for the adults encumbered by daily affairs. As Fiedler also pointed out, this
image of childhood has impinged upon adult life itself, has become a 'career'

---

[1]Erik H. Erikson, *Childhood and Society* (New York: Norton, 1963), p. 286.

[2]Leading discussions of the individual-community polarity in American culture can be
found in *The Contrapuntal Civilization: Essays Toward a New Understanding of the American Ex-
perience*, ed. Michael Kammen (New York: Crowell, 1971). The most prominent analyses of
American literature's use of this opposition remain Leslie A. Fiedler's *Love and Death in the
American Novel* (New York: Stein and Day, 1966) and A. N. Kaul's *The American Vision* (New
Haven: Yale University Press, 1963).

[3]Robert Bresson, *Notes on Cinematography*, trans. Jonathan Griffin (New York: Urizen Books,
1977), p. 12.

The "outlaw hero," Davy Crockett, portrayed by Fess Parker.

like everything else in America,"[4] generating stories like *On the Road* or *Easy Rider* in which adults try desperately to postpone responsibilities by clinging to adolescent lifestyles.

While the outlaw heroes represented a flight from maturity, the official heroes embodied the best attributes of adulthood: sound reasoning and judgment, wisdom and sympathy based on experience. Franklin's *Autobiography* and *Poor Richard's Almanack* constituted this opposing tradition's basic texts, persuasive enough to appeal even to outsiders (*The Great Gatsby*). Despite the legends surrounding Franklin and the other Founding Fathers, however, the scarcity of mature heroes in American literature and mythology indicated American ideology's fundamental preference for youth, a quality that came to be associated with the country itself. Indeed, American stories often distorted the stock figure of the Wise Old Man, portraying him as mad (Ahab), useless (Rip Van Winkle), or evil (the Godfather).

2. *Society and Women*: The outlaw hero's distrust of civilization, typically represented by women and marriage, constituted a stock motif in American mythology. In his *Studies in Classic American Literature*, D. H. Lawrence detected

[4]Leslie A. Fiedler, *No! In Thunder* (New York: Stein and Day, 1972), pp. 253, 275.

the recurring pattern of flight, observing that the Founding Fathers had come to America "largely to get *away*. . . . Away from what? In the long run, away from themselves. Away from everything."[5] Sometimes, these heroes undertook this flight alone (Thoreau, *Catcher in the Rye*); more often, they joined ranks with other men: Huck with Jim, Ishmael with Queequeg, Jake Barnes with Bill Gorton. Women were avoided as representing the very entanglements this tradition sought to escape: society, the "settled life," confining responsibilities. The outlaw hero sought only uncompromising relationships, involving either a "bad" woman (whose morals deprived her of all rights to entangling domesticity) or other males (who themselves remained independent). Even the "bad" woman posed a threat, since marriage often uncovered the clinging "good" girl underneath. Typically, therefore, American stories avoided this problem by killing off the "bad" woman before the marriage could transpire (*Destry Rides Again*, *The Big Heat*, *The Far Country*). Subsequently, within the all-male group, women became taboo, except as the objects of lust.

The exceptional extent of American outlaw legends suggests an ideological anxiety about civilized life. Often, that anxiety took shape as a romanticizing of the dispossessed, as in the Beat Generation's cult of the bum, or the characters of Huck and "Thoreau," who worked to remain idle, unemployed, and unattached. A passage from Jerzy Kosinski's *Steps* demonstrated the extreme modern version of this romanticizing:

> I envied those [the poor and the criminals] who lived here and seemed so free, having nothing to regret and nothing to look forward to. In the world of birth certificates, medical examinations, punch cards, and computers, in the world of telephone books, passports, bank accounts, insurance plans, wills, credit cards, pensions, mortgages and loans, they lived unattached.[6]

In contrast to the outlaw heroes, the official heroes were preeminently worldly, comfortable in society, and willing to undertake even those public duties demanding personal sacrifice. Political figures, particularly Washington and Lincoln, provided the principal examples of this tradition, but images of family also persisted in popular literature from *Little Women* to *Life with Father* and *Cheaper by the Dozen*. The most crucial figure in this tradition, however, was Horatio Alger, whose heroes' ambition provided the complement to Huck's disinterest. Alger's characters subscribed fully to the codes of civilization, devoting themselves to proper dress, manners, and behavior, and the attainment of the very things despised by the opposing tradition: the settled life and respectability.[7]

---

[5]D. H. Lawrence, *Studies in Classic American Literature* (New York: Viking/Compass, 1961), p. 3. See also Fiedler's *Love and Death in the American Novel* and Sam Bluefarb's *The Escape Motif in the American Novel: Mark Twain to Richard Wright* (Columbus: Ohio State University Press, 1972).

[6]Jerzy Kosinski, *Steps* (New York: Random House, 1968), p. 133.

[7]See John G. Cawelti, *Apostles of the Self-Made Man: Changing Concepts of Success in America* (Chicago: University of Chicago Press, 1965), pp. 101–23.

3. *Politics and the Law*: Writing about "The Philosophical Approach of the   10
Americans," Tocqueville noted "a general distaste for accepting any man's
word as proof of anything." That distaste took shape as a traditional distrust
of politics as collective activity, and of ideology as that activity's rationale. Such
a disavowal of ideology was, of course, itself ideological, a tactic for discouraging systematic political intervention in a nineteenth-century America whose
political and economic power remained in the hands of a privileged few. Tocqueville himself noted the results of this mythology of individualism which
"disposes each citizen to isolate himself from the mass of his fellows and
withdraw into the circle of family and friends; with this little society formed to
his taste, he gladly leaves the greater society to look after itself."[8]

This hostility toward political solutions manifested itself further in an
ambivalence about the law. The outlaw mythology portrayed the law, the sum
of society's standards, as a collective, impersonal ideology imposed on the
individual from without. Thus, the law represented the very thing this mythology sought to avoid. In its place, this tradition offered a natural law discovered
intuitively by each man. As Tocqueville observed, Americans wanted "To escape from imposed systems . . . to seek by themselves and in themselves for
the only reason for things . . . in most mental operations each American relies
on individual effort and judgment" (p. 429). This sense of the law's inadequacy
to needs detectable only by the heart generated a rich tradition of legends celebrating legal defiance in the name of some "natural" standard: Thoreau went
to jail rather than pay taxes, Huck helped Jim (legally a slave) to escape, Billy
the Kid murdered the sheriff's posse that had ambushed his boss, Hester
Prynne resisted the community's sexual mores. This mythology transformed
all outlaws into Robin Hoods, who "correct" socially unjust laws (Jesse James,
Bonnie and Clyde, John Wesley Harding). Furthermore, by customarily portraying the law as the tool of villains (who used it to revoke mining claims,
foreclose on mortgages, and disallow election results — all on legal technicali-
ties), this mythology betrayed a profound pessimism about the individual's
access to the legal system.

If the outlaw hero's motto was "I don't know what the law says, but I do
know what's right and wrong," the official hero's was "We are a nation of laws,
not of men," or "No man can place himself above the law." To the outlaw hero's
insistence on private standards of right and wrong, the official hero offered the
admonition, "You cannot take the law into your own hands." Often, these official heroes were lawyers or politicians, at times (as with Washington and Lincoln), even the executors of the legal system itself. The values accompanying

---

[8]Alexis de Tocqueville, *Democracy in America*, ed. J. P. Mayer, trans. George Lawrence
(Garden City, N.Y.: Anchor/Doubleday, 1969), pp. 430, 506. Irving Howe has confirmed Tocqueville's point, observing that Americans "make the suspicion of ideology into something approaching a national creed." *Politics and the Novel* (New York: Avon, 1970), p. 337.

such heroes modified the assurance of Crockett's advice, "Be sure you're right, then go ahead."

In sum, the values associated with these two different sets of heroes contrasted markedly. Clearly, too, each tradition had its good and bad points. If the extreme individualism of the outlaw hero always verged on selfishness, the respectability of the official hero always threatened to involve either blandness or repression. If the outlaw tradition promised adventure and freedom, it also offered danger and loneliness. If the official tradition promised safety and comfort, it also offered entanglements and boredom.

The evident contradiction between these heroes provoked Daniel Boorstin's observation that "Never did a more incongruous pair than Davy Crockett and George Washington live together in a national Valhalla." And yet, as Boorstin admits, "both Crockett and Washington were popular heroes, and both emerged into legendary fame during the first half of the nineteenth century."[9]

The parallel existence of these two contradictory traditions evinced the general pattern of American mythology: the denial of the necessity for choice. In fact, this mythology often portrayed situations requiring decision as temporary aberrations from American life's normal course. By discouraging commitment to any single set of values, this mythology fostered an ideology of improvisation, individualism, and ad hoc solutions for problems depicted as crises. American writers have repeatedly attempted to justify this mythology in terms of material sources. Hence, Irving Howe's "explanation":

> It is when men no longer feel that they have adequate choices in their styles of life, when they conclude that there are no longer possibilities of honorable maneuver and compromise, when they decide that the time has come for "ultimate" social loyalties and political decisions — it is then that ideology begins to flourish. Ideology reflects a hardening of commitment, the freezing of opinion into system. . . . The uniqueness of our history, the freshness of our land, the plenitude of our resources — all these have made possible, and rendered plausible, a style of political improvisation and intellectual free-wheeling.[10]

Despite such an account's pretext of objectivity, its language betrays an acceptance of the mythology it purports to describe: "honorable maneuver and compromise," "hardening," "freezing," "uniqueness," "freshness," and "plenitude" are all assumptive words from an ideology that denies its own status. Furthermore, even granting the legitimacy of the historians' authenticating causes, we are left with a persisting mythology increasingly discredited by historical developments. (In fact, such invalidation began in the early nineteenth century, and perhaps even before.)

---

[9]Daniel J. Boorstin, *The Americans: The National Experience* (New York: Random House, 1965), p. 337.

[10]*Politics and the Novel*, p. 164.

The American mythology's refusal to choose between its two heroes went beyond the normal reconciliatory function attributed to myth by Lévi-Strauss. For the American tradition not only overcame binary oppositions; it systematically mythologized the certainty of being able to do so. Part of this process involved blurring the lines between the two sets of heroes. First, legends often brought the solemn official heroes back down to earth, providing the sober Washington with the cherry tree, the prudent Franklin with illegitimate children, and even the upright Jefferson with a slave mistress. On the other side, stories modified the outlaw hero's most potentially damaging quality, his tendency to selfish isolationism, by demonstrating that, however reluctantly, he would act for causes beyond himself. Thus, Huck grudgingly helped Jim escape, and Davy Crockett left the woods for three terms in Congress before dying in the Alamo for Texas independence. In this blurring process, Lincoln, a composite of opposing traits, emerged as the great American figure. His status as president made him an ex officio official hero. But his Western origins, melancholy solitude, and unaided decision-making all qualified him as a member of the other side. Finally, his ambivalent attitude toward the law played the most crucial role in his complex legend. As the chief executive, he inevitably stood for the principle that "we are a nation of laws and not men"; as the Great Emancipator, on the other hand, he provided the prime example of taking the law into one's own hands in the name of some higher standard.

Classic Hollywood's gallery of composite heroes (boxing musicians, rebellious aristocrats, pacifist soldiers) clearly derived from this mythology's rejection of final choices, a tendency whose traces Erikson detected in American psychology:

> The process of American identity formation seems to support an individual's ego identity as long as he can preserve a certain element of deliberate tentativeness of autonomous choice. The individual must be able to convince himself that the next step is up to him and that no matter where he is staying or going he always had the choice of leaving or turning in the opposite direction if he chooses to do so. In this country the migrant does not want to be told to move on, nor the sedentary man to stay where he is; for the life style (and the family history) of each contains the opposite element as a potential alternative which he wishes to consider his most private and individual decision.[11]

The reconciliatory pattern found its most typical incarnation, however, in one particular narrative: the story of the private man attempting to keep from being drawn into action on any but his own terms. In this story, the reluctant hero's ultimate willingness to help the community satisfied the official values. But by portraying this aid as demanding only a temporary involvement, the story preserved the values of individualism as well.

---

[11] *Childhood and Society*, p. 286.

Like the contrasting heroes' epitomization of basic American dichotomies, the reluctant hero story provided a locus for displacement. Its most famous version, for example, *Adventures of Huckleberry Finn*, offered a typically individualistic solution to the nation's unresolved racial and sectional anxieties, thereby helping to forestall more systematic governmental measures. In adopting this story, Classic Hollywood retained its censoring power, using it, for example, in *Casablanca* to conceal the realistic threats to American self-determination posed by World War II.

Because the reluctant hero story was clearly the basis of the Western, American literature's repeated use of it prompted Leslie Fiedler to call the classic American novels "disguised westerns."[12] In the movies, too, this story appeared in every genre: in Westerns, of course (with *Shane* its most schematic articulation), but also in gangster movies (*Angels with Dirty Faces, Key Largo*), musicals (*Swing Time*), detective stories (*The Thin Man*), war films (*Air Force*), screwball comedy (*The Philadelphia Story*), "problem pictures" (*On the Waterfront*), and even science fiction (the Han Solo character in *Star Wars*). *Gone with the Wind*, in fact, had two selfish heroes who came around at the last moment, Scarlett (taking care of Melanie) and Rhett (running the Union blockade), incompatible only because they were so much alike. The natural culmination of this pattern, perfected by Hollywood in the 1930s and early 1940s, was *Casablanca*. Its version of the outlaw hero–official hero struggle (Rick versus Laszlo) proved stunningly effective, its resolution (their collaboration on the war effort) the prototypical Hollywood ending.

The reluctant hero story's tendency to minimize the official hero's role (by [20] making him dependent on the outsider's intervention) suggested an imbalance basic to the American mythology: Despite the existence of both heroes, the national ideology clearly preferred the outlaw. This ideology strove to make that figure's origins seem spontaneous, concealing the calculated, commercial efforts behind the mythologizing of typical examples like Billy the Kid and Davy Crockett. Its willingness, on the other hand, to allow the official hero's traces to show enables Daniel Boorstin to observe of one such myth, "There were elements of spontaneity, of course, in the Washington legend, too, but it was, for the most part, a self-conscious product."[13]

The apparent spontaneity of the outlaw heroes assured their popularity. By contrast, the official values had to rely on a rational allegiance that often wavered. These heroes' different statuses accounted for a structure fundamental to American literature, and assumed by Classic Hollywood: a split between the moral center and the interest center of a story. Thus, while the typical Western contained warnings against violence as a solution, taking the law into one's own hands, and moral isolationism, it simultaneously glamorized the outlaw hero's intense self-possession and willingness to use force to

---

[12]*Love and Death in the American Novel*, p. 355.
[13]*The Americans: The National Experience*, p. 337.

settle what the law could not. In other circumstances, Ishmael's evenhanded philosophy paled beside Ahab's moral vehemence, consciously recognizable as destructive.

D. H. Lawrence called this split the profound "duplicity" at the heart of nineteenth-century American fiction, charging that the classic novels evinced "a tight mental allegiance to a morality which all [the author's] passion goes to destroy." Certainly, too, this "duplicity" involved the mythology's pattern of obscuring the necessity for choosing between contrasting values. Richard Chase has put the matter less pejoratively in an account that applies equally to the American cinema:

> The American novel tends to rest in contradictions and among extreme ranges of experience. When it attempts to resolve contradictions, it does so in oblique, morally equivocal ways. As a general rule it does so either in melodramatic actions or in pastoral idylls, although intermixed with both one may find the stirring instabilities of "American humor."[14]

Or, in other words, when faced with a difficult choice, American stories resolved it either simplistically (by refusing to acknowledge that a choice is necessary), sentimentally (by blurring the differences between the two sides), or by laughing the whole thing off.

READING THE TEXT

1. What are the two basic hero types that Ray describes in American cinema?

2. How do these two hero types relate to America's "psychological pattern" (para. 2)?

3. Explain why, according to Ray, the outlaw hero typically mistrusts women.

READING THE SIGNS

1. **CONNECTING TEXTS**   Read Andy Medhurst's "Batman, Deviance, and Camp" (p. 592) and write an essay that defines what sort of hero Batman is, according to Ray's schema.

2. What sort of hero is Russell Crowe in *3:10 to Yuma*? Write an essay in which you apply Ray's categories of hero to the Crowe character, supporting your argument with specific references to the film.

3. In class, brainstorm on the blackboard official and outlaw heroes you've seen in movies. Then categorize these heroes according to characteristics they share (such as race, gender, profession, or social class). What patterns emerge in your categories, and what is the significance of those patterns?

[14]Richard Chase, *The American Novel and Its Tradition* (Garden City, N.Y.: Anchor/Doubleday, 1957), p. 1.

4. Ray focuses on film, but his categories of hero can be used as a critical framework to analyze other media, including television. What kind of heroes are the heroes in the program *Heroes*?

5. Cartoon television series like *The Simpsons* and *South Park* feature characters that don't readily fit Ray's categories of hero. Invent a third type of hero to accommodate such characters.

6. A third type of character that has been popular in recent years is the out-and-out outlaw, someone who breaks the law without any regard for society, like Tony Soprano and Hannibal Lecter, as well as numerous gangsters, hit men, and cops gone bad. Write a paper identifying a number of such characters and construct a semiotic argument explaining their appeal to contemporary audiences.

INVENTING HEROES

VIRGINIA POSTREL
Superhero Worship

With three Spider-Man *movies already in the can with no end in sight to the potential sequels, and a seemingly endless series of* Batman, *Super-man,* X-Men, Iron Man, *and* Whatever-Man *films on the horizon, a serious look at the widespread appeal of these seemingly trivial productions is certainly in order. Virginia Postrel provides such an analysis in this article that originally appeared in* The Atlantic. *Her thesis is simple: "On a fundamental, emotional level, superheroes . . . serve the same function for their audience as Golden Age movie stars did for theirs: they create glamour." Seeking escape from a drab, mundane life, the superhero fan is invited to* identify *with the hero, sharing both his special powers and his human frailties — as in the vicarious pleasure enjoyed by watching* Spider-Man's *aerial acrobatics while at the same time identifying with his financial and romantic problems. Postrel is a contributing editor for* The Atlantic *and the author of* The Future and Its Enemies *(1998) and* The Substance of Style *(2003).*

When *Superman* debuted in 1978, it invented a whole new movie genre — and a new kind of cinematic magic. Today, hundreds of millions of dollars depend on the heroic box-office performances of costumed crusaders whom Hollywood once thought worthy only of kiddie serials or campy parodies. The two *Spider-Man* movies rank among the top ten of all time for gross domestic receipts, and *X-Men: The Last Stand* and *Superman Returns* are among this year's biggest hits.

Superhero comics have been around since Irving Thalberg and Louis B. Mayer ruled the back lot, but only recently has Hollywood realized the natural connection between superhero comics and movies. It's not just that both are simultaneously visual and verbal media; that formal connection would apply equally to the "serious" graphic novels and sequential art that want nothing to do with crime fighters in form-fitting outfits. Cinema isn't just a good medium for translating graphic novels. It's specifically a good medium for *superheroes*. On a fundamental, emotional level, superheroes, whether in print or on film, serve the same function for their audience as Golden Age movie stars did for theirs: they create glamour.

If that sounds crazy, it's because we tend to forget what glamour is really about. Glamour isn't beauty or luxury; those are only specific manifestations for specific audiences. Glamour is an imaginative process that creates a specific, emotional response: a sharp mixture of projection, longing, admiration, and aspiration. It evokes an audience's hopes and dreams and makes them seem attainable, all the while maintaining enough distance to sustain the fantasy. The elements that create glamour are not specific styles — bias-cut gowns or lacquered furniture — but more general qualities: grace, mystery, transcendence. To the right audience, Halle Berry is more glamorous commanding the elements as Storm in the *X-Men* movies than she is walking the red carpet in a designer gown.

"You'll believe a man can fly," promised *Superman*'s trailers. Brian Chase, a forty-year-old Los Angeles lawyer and comic-book enthusiast, recalls, "They *did* make you believe it." He says that after seeing the movie for the first time, when he was thirteen, he "ran back from the theater jumping over things. I was embarrassingly convinced. I projected myself into it, and I was not going to let it go for the world." That is the emotional effect of glamour, and it's something superhero comics have delivered since Superman hit print in 1938. The *Superman* movie's marketing slogan was thus more than a promise of convincing special effects. It was a pledge to engage the audience's dreams without ridicule. In *Superman*, only the villains were silly. A decade later, Tim Burton's operatic *Batman* made even the clown-faced Joker seem genuinely scary. Influenced by Frank Miller's reinvention of Batman as the Dark Knight, Burton's *Batman* movies portrayed a dangerous world in desperate need of a masked hero. Instead of the campy straight man of the 1960s television series or the tame Mister Rogers of the 1950s comic books, Batman was once again a glamorous creature of the night, powerful and mysterious.

The superhero movies that have followed, like the comics from which they 5 were derived, have engaged their subjects without emotional reservation. They may have humor (Marvel comics like *Spider-Man* and *The Fantastic Four* are famous for it), but they lack the kind of irony that punctures glamour and makes the audience feel foolish for its suspension of disbelief, the sort of campy mockery exemplified by the *Batman* television show or Joel Schumacher's disastrous *Batman & Robin*, featuring a smirking George Clooney in the lead.

The superhero fans who wear costumes to comics conventions, buy miniatures of their favorite characters, or line up for artists' autographs aren't themselves glamorous. But neither were the Depression-era housewives who bought knockoffs of Joan Crawford's gowns or wrote fan letters to Gary Cooper. And neither are the *InStyle* readers who copy Natalie Portman's latest haircut or wear a version of Halle Berry's Oscar dress to the prom. Glamour is, to quote a fashion blurb, "all about transcending the everyday." The whole point of movie glamour was — and is — escape. "What the adult American female chiefly asks of the movies is the opportunity to escape by reverie from an existence which she finds insufficiently interesting," wrote Margaret Farrand Thorp in *America at the Movies* (1939). Movies are "the quickest release from a drab, monotonous, unsatisfying environment in dreaming of an existence which is rich, romantic, glamorous."

Superheroes appeal to a different sort of romanticism. Brian Chase draws a distinction between himself and other members of a hip e-mail list called Glamour: "Their idea of glamour would be to get invited to the right party. To me growing up, the idea of glamour was to be the guy who could save the right party from a meteor." Says Richard Neal, owner of Zeus Comics, an upscale comics store in Dallas, "It's not just superpowers but dashing good looks, villains you can fight, getting aggression out." (Buff and business-savvy, Neal bears no resemblance to the classic comics-store proprietor, represented so memorably on *The Simpsons*.)

Superheroes are masters of their bodies and their physical environment. They often work in teams, providing an ideal of friendship based on competence, shared goals, and complementary talents. They're special, and they know it. "Their *true* identities, the men in colorful tights, were so elemental, so universal, so transcendent of the worlds that made them wear masks that they carried with them an unprecedented optimism about the value of one's inner reality," writes Gerard Jones in *Men of Tomorrow: Geeks, Gangsters and the Birth of the Comic Book*. "We all knew that Clark Kent was just a game played by Superman and that the only guy who mattered was that alien who showed up in Metropolis with no history and no parents."

Comic-book heroes, like all glamorous icons, cater to "dreams of flight and transformation and escape." Those words are from one of the best books ever written on glamour: Michael Chabon's 2000 novel, *The Amazing Adventures of Kavalier and Clay*. Like many a Hollywood story, *Kavalier and Clay* is wise to the perils of trying to live out glamorous dreams in the real world, again and again showing the tragicomic effects of such attempts. Early on, for instance, young Joe Kavalier almost drowns while attempting a Houdini-like escape designed to gain entrance to what he imagines is a glamorous private club for magicians. (It is, in fact, a rather run-down place whose dining room "smelled of liver and onions.") On the eve of World War II, Joe and his cousin Sammy create a successful comic-book hero called the Escapist, whose villainous foes include Hitler himself. Their glamorous illusion is that such fights are easy to win.

Chabon explicitly defends the escapism of comics. After the war, his Kava- 10
lier reflects:

> Having lost his mother, father, brother, and grandfather, the friends and
> foes of his youth, his beloved teacher Bernard Kornblum, his city, his his-
> tory — his home — the usual charge leveled against comic books, that they
> offered *merely an easy escape from reality*, seemed to Joe actually to be a
> powerful argument on their behalf. . . . It was a mark of how fucked-up
> and broken was the world — the reality — that had swallowed his home
> and his family that such a feat of escape, by no means easy to pull off,
> should remain so universally despised.

Still, glamour is always vulnerable to those who love it. The more we're
drawn to a glamorous person, place, or thing, the more we scrutinize it, seeking to fill in the details — which ultimately destroys the mystery and grace.
Someone will always look for the hidden flaws, the seamy side of the story.
Hence the demand for gossip about Princess Diana's bulimia or Jennifer
Lopez's romantic problems. These *Behind the Music*–style revelations replace
the transcendence of glamour with the mundane problems of mere celebrity.
Beyond these grubby details is a more mythic kind of debunking: the artistic
revisionism that warns of glamour's dangers and disappointments. The power
of such revisionism, however, depends on the emotional pull of the original.
Someone who knows little and cares even less about Hollywood dreams will
miss the pity and terror of *Sunset Boulevard*. Someone who scorns superheroes as infantile won't understand the scary wonder of *Watchmen*, the brilliant 1987 graphic novel in which Alan Moore and Dave Gibbons deconstruct
superheroes. To the wrong audience, glamour, even revisionist glamour, will
seem like camp.

One way to balance the real ideal while preserving glamour is to give
the audience an insider's view. So superhero comics now tend to situate their
stories in a world like our own, with ubiquitous, sensationalist media and inescapable trade-offs between personal and professional life. To their audience
inside the comics, the superheroes are powerful and mysterious celebrities
subject to public adulation and tabloid attacks. The real-world audience, by
contrast, gets a glimpse behind the mask, a chance to identify with the character and to experience glamour once removed — to imagine *what it would be
like to be glamorous*, and how much hard work, sacrifice, and attention to detail that seemingly effortless power requires. This double vision acknowledges
the art behind the illusion. Glamour may look easy, but it never is.

READING THE TEXT

1. Explain in your own words what Postrel means by glamour and how it attracts
   an audience.
2. Why does Postrel believe that glamour creates a "natural connection between
   superhero comics and movies" (para. 2)?

3. What does Postrel mean when she suggests that audiences view superheroes with a "double vision" (para. 13)?

4. Summarize Brian Chase's reasons for being such a fan of Superman.

5. Why is glamour "always vulnerable to those who love it" (para. 11)?

READING THE SIGNS

1. Before reading Postrel's essay, brainstorm your own definition of glamour. Then compare your definition to Postrel's: What similarities and differences do you see?

2. For her essay, Postrel interviewed a random fan of Superman about his enthusiasm for this superhero. Borrowing her methodology, interview at least four fans of superheroes, asking about the reasons for their responses to these characters. To what extent do they illustrate Postrel's argument about glamour? Use your results as the basis of an argument about the appeal of superheroes.

3. **CONNECTING TEXTS** According to Postrel's definition, is Harry Potter a superhero? To develop your ideas, consult Anne Galligan's "Pottermania: The Marketing behind the Magic" (p. 129).

4. **CONNECTING TEXTS** Write an essay in which you present your own distinction between a cinematic hero and a superhero, being sure to ground your argument in a consideration of specific hero characters from both categories. To develop your ideas, you might read or reread Robert B. Ray's "The Thematic Paradigm" (p. 342), Linda Seger's, "Creating the Myth" (p. 356), Tom Moore's "Movie Fantasy vs. Classroom Reality" (p. 402), and Anne Galligan's "Pottermania: The Marketing behind the Magic" (p. 129).

5. Using Postrel's definition of a superhero as a critical framework, analyze the latest Spider-Man movie. Does Spidey demonstrate her sense of glamour? If you believe that he does, use specific details from the film to illustrate how that happens; if you believe that he does not, explain how he complicates Postrel's argument for a superhero's appeal.

LINDA SEGER
Creating the Myth

To be a successful screenwriter, Linda Seger suggests in this selection from Making a Good Script Great *(1987), you've got to know your archetypes. Seger reveals the secret behind the success of such Hollywood creations as* Star Wars' *Luke Skywalker and tells you how you can create such heroes yourself. In this how-to approach to the cinema, Seger echoes the more academic judgments of such semioticians of film as Umberto Eco — the road to popular success in mass culture is paved with cultural myths and clichés. A script consultant and author who has given professional seminars on filmmaking around the world, Seger has also published* Creating Unforgettable Characters *(1990) and* When Women Call the Shots: The Developing Power and Influence of Women in Television and Film *(1996).*

All of us have similar experiences. We share in the life journey of growth, development, and transformation. We live the same stories, whether they involve the search for a perfect mate, coming home, the search for fulfillment, going after an ideal, achieving the dream, or hunting for a precious treasure. Whatever our culture, there are universal stories that form the basis for all our particular stories. The trappings might be different, the twists and turns that create suspense might change from culture to culture, the particular characters may take different forms, but underneath it all, it's the same story, drawn from the same experiences.

Many of the most successful films are based on these universal stories. They deal with the basic journey we take in life. We identify with the heroes because we were once heroic (descriptive) or because we wish we could do what the hero does (prescriptive). When Joan Wilder finds the jewel and saves her sister, or James Bond saves the world, or Shane saves the family from the evil ranchers, we identify with the character, and subconsciously recognize the story as having some connection with our own lives. It's the same story as the fairy tales about getting the three golden hairs from the devil, or finding the treasure and winning the princess. And it's not all that different a story from the caveman killing the woolly beast or the Roman slave gaining his freedom through skill and courage. These are our stories — personally and collectively — and the most successful films contain these universal experiences.

Some of these stories are "search" stories. They address our desire to find some kind of rare and wonderful treasure. This might include the search for outer values such as job, relationship, or success; or for inner values such as respect, security, self-expression, love, or home. But it's all a similar search.

Some of these stories are "hero" stories. They come from our own experiences of overcoming adversity, as well as our desire to do great and special acts. We root for the hero and celebrate when he or she achieves the goal because we know that the hero's journey is in many ways similar to our own.

We call these stories *myths*. Myths are the common stories at the root of our universal existence. They're found in all cultures and in all literature, ranging from the Greek myths to fairy tales, legends, and stories drawn from all of the world's religions.

A myth is a story that is "more than true." Many stories are true because one person, somewhere, at some time, lived it. It is based on fact. But a myth is more than true because it is lived by all of us, at some level. It's a story that connects and speaks to us all.

Some myths are true stories that attain mythic significance because the people involved seem larger than life, and seem to live their lives more intensely than common folk. Martin Luther King, Jr., Gandhi, Sir Edmund Hillary, and Lord Mountbatten personify the types of journeys we identify with, because we've taken similar journeys — even if only in a very small way.

Other myths revolve around make-believe characters who might capsulize for us the sum total of many of our journeys. Some of these make-believe characters might seem similar to the characters we meet in our dreams. Or they might be a composite of types of characters we've met.

In both cases, the myth is the "story beneath the story." It's the universal pattern that shows us that Gandhi's journey toward independence and Sir Edmund Hillary's journey to the top of Mount Everest contain many of the same dramatic beats. And these beats are the same beats that Rambo takes to set free the MIAs, that Indiana Jones takes to find the Lost Ark, and that Luke Skywalker takes to defeat the Evil Empire.

In *Hero with a Thousand Faces*, Joseph Campbell traces the elements that form the hero myth. "In their own work with myth, writer Chris Vogler and seminar leader Thomas Schlesinger have applied this criteria to *Star Wars*. The myth within the story helps explain why millions went to see this film again and again."

The hero myth has specific story beats that occur in all hero stories. They show who the hero is, what the hero needs, and how the story and character interact in order to create a transformation. The journey toward heroism is a process. This universal process forms the spine of all the particular stories, such as the *Star Wars* trilogy.

The Hero Myth

1. In most hero stories, the hero is introduced in ordinary surroundings, in a mundane world, doing mundane things. Generally, the hero begins as a nonhero; innocent, young, simple, or humble. In *Star Wars*, the first time we see Luke Skywalker, he's unhappy about having to do his chores, which consists of picking out

Star Wars, 1977.

some new droids for work. He wants to go out and have fun. He wants to leave his planet and go to the Academy, but he's stuck. This is the setup of most myths. This is how we meet the hero before the call to adventure.

2. Then something new enters the hero's life. It's a catalyst that sets the story into motion. It might be a telephone call, as in *Romancing the Stone*, or the German attack in *The African Queen*, or the holograph of Princess Leia in *Star Wars*. Whatever form it takes, it's a new ingredient that pushes the hero into an extraordinary adventure. With this call, the stakes are established, and a problem is introduced that demands a solution.

3. Many times, however, the hero doesn't want to leave. He or she is a reluctant hero, afraid of the unknown, uncertain, perhaps, if he or she is up to the challenge. In *Star Wars*, Luke receives a double call to adventure. First, from Princess Leia in the holograph, and then through Obi-Wan Kenobi, who says he needs Luke's help. But Luke is not ready to go. He returns home, only to find that the Imperial Stormtroopers have burned his farmhouse and slaughtered his family. Now he is personally motivated, ready to enter into the adventure.

4. In any journey, the hero usually receives help, and the help often comes ₁₅ from unusual sources. In many fairy tales, an old woman, a dwarf, a witch, or a wizard helps the hero. The hero achieves the goal because of this help, and because the hero is receptive to what this person has to give.

There are a number of fairy tales where the first and second son are sent to complete a task, but they ignore the helpers, often scorning them. Many times they are severely punished for their lack of humility and unwillingness to accept help. Then the third son, the hero, comes along. He receives the help, accomplishes the task, and often wins the princess.

In *Star Wars*, Obi-Wan Kenobi is a perfect example of the "helper" character. He is a kind of mentor to Luke, one who teaches him the Way of the Force and whose teachings continue even after his death. This mentor character appears in most hero stories. He is the person who has special knowledge, special information, and special skills. This might be the prospector in *The Treasure of the Sierra Madre*, or the psychiatrist in *Ordinary People*, or Quint in *Jaws*, who knows all about sharks, or the Good Witch of the North who gives Dorothy the ruby slippers in *The Wizard of Oz*. In *Star Wars*, Obi-Wan gives Luke the light saber that was the special weapon of the Jedi Knight. With this, Luke is ready to move forward and do his training and meet adventure.

5. The hero is now ready to move into the special world where he or she will change from the ordinary into the extraordinary. This starts the hero's transformation, and sets up the obstacles that must be surmounted to reach the goal. Usually, this happens at the first Turning Point of the story, and leads into Act Two development. In *Star Wars*, Obi-Wan and Luke search for a pilot to take them to the planet of Alderaan, so that Obi-Wan can deliver the plans to Princess Leia's father. These plans are essential to the survival of the Rebel Forces. With this action, the adventure is ready to begin.

6. Now begin all the tests and obstacles necessary to overcome the enemy and accomplish the hero's goals. In fairy tales, this often means getting past witches, outwitting the devil, avoiding robbers, or confronting evil. In Homer's *Odyssey*, it means blinding the Cyclops, escaping from the island of the Lotus-Eaters, resisting the temptation of the singing Sirens, and surviving a shipwreck. In *Star Wars*, innumerable adventures confront Luke. He and his cohorts must run to the *Millennium Falcon*, narrowly escaping the Stormtroopers before jumping into hyperspace. They must make it through the meteor shower after Alderaan has been destroyed. They must evade capture on the Death Star, rescue the Princess, and even survive a garbage crusher.

7. At some point in the story, the hero often hits rock bottom. He often has 20 a "death experience," leading to a type of rebirth. In *Star Wars*, Luke seems to have died when the serpent in the garbage-masher pulls him under, but he's saved just in time to ask R2D2 to stop the masher before they're crushed. This is often the "black moment" at the second turning point, the point when the worst is confronted, and the action now moves toward the exciting conclusion.

8. Now, the hero seizes the sword and takes possession of the treasure. He is now in charge, but he still has not completed the journey. Here Luke has the Princess and the plans, but the final confrontation is yet to begin. This starts the third-act escape scene, leading to the final climax.

9. The road back is often the chase scene. In many fairy tales, this is the point where the devil chases the hero and the hero has the last obstacles to overcome before really being free and safe. His challenge is to take what he has learned and integrate it into his daily life. He *must* return to renew the mundane world. In *Star Wars*, Darth Vader is in hot pursuit, planning to blow up the Rebel Planet.

10. Since every hero story is essentially a transformation story, we need to see the hero changed at the end, resurrected into a new type of life. He must face the final ordeal before being "reborn" as the hero, proving his courage and becoming transformed. This is the point, in many fairy tales, where the Miller's Son becomes the Prince or the King and marries the Princess. In *Star Wars*, Luke has survived, becoming quite a different person from the innocent young man he was in Act One.

At this point, the hero returns and is reintegrated into his society. In *Star Wars*, Luke has destroyed the Death Star, and he receives his great reward.

This is the classic "Hero Story." We might call this example a *mission* or *task* 25 *myth*, where the person has to complete a task, but the task itself is not the real treasure. The real reward for Luke is the love of the Princess and the safe, new world he had helped create.

A myth can have many variations. We see variations on this myth in James Bond films (although they lack much of the depth because the hero is not transformed), and in *The African Queen*, where Rose and Allnutt must blow up the *Louisa*, or in *Places in the Heart*, where Edna overcomes obstacles to achieve family stability.

The *treasure myth* is another variation on this theme, as seen in *Romancing the Stone*. In this story, Joan receives a map and a phone call which forces her into the adventure. She is helped by an American birdcatcher and a Mexican pickup truck driver. She overcomes the obstacles of snakes, the jungle, waterfalls, shootouts, and finally receives the treasure, along with the "prince."

Whether the hero's journey is for a treasure or to complete a task, the elements remain the same. The humble, reluctant hero is called to an adventure. The hero is helped by a variety of unique characters. S/he must overcome a series of obstacles that transform him or her in the process, and then faces the final challenge that draws on inner and outer resources.

The Healing Myth

Although the hero myth is the most popular story, many myths involve healing. In these stories, some character is "broken" and must leave home to become whole again.

The universal experience behind these healing stories is our psychological 30 need for rejuvenation, for balance. The journey of the hero into exile is not all that different from the weekend in Palm Springs, or the trip to Hawaii to get away from it all, or lying still in a hospital bed for some weeks to heal. In all cases, something is out of balance and the mythic journey moves toward wholeness.

Being broken can take several forms. It can be physical, emotional, or psychological. Usually, it's all three. In the process of being exiled or hiding out in the forest, the desert, or even the Amish farm in *Witness*, the person becomes whole, balanced, and receptive to love. Love in these stories is both a healing force and a reward.

Think of John Book in *Witness*. In Act One, we see a frenetic, insensitive man, afraid of commitment, critical and unreceptive to the feminine influences in his life. John is suffering from an "inner wound" which he doesn't know about. When he receives an "outer wound" from a gunshot, it forces him into exile, which begins his process of transformation.

At the beginning of Act Two, we see John delirious and close to death. This is a movement into the unconscious, a movement from the rational, active police life of Act One into a mysterious, feminine, more intuitive world. Since John's "inner problem" is the lack of balance with his feminine side, this delirium begins the process of transformation.

Later in Act Two, we see John beginning to change. He moves from his highly independent life-style toward the collective, communal life of his Amish hosts. John now gets up early to milk the cows and to assist with the chores. He uses his carpentry skills to help with the barn building and to complete the bird-house. Gradually, he begins to develop relationships with Rachel and her son, Samuel. John's life slows down and he becomes more receptive, learning important lessons about love. In Act Three, John finally sees that the feminine is worth saving, and throws down his gun to save Rachel's life. A few beats later, when he has the opportunity to kill Paul, he chooses a nonviolent response instead. Although John doesn't "win" the Princess, he has nevertheless "won" love and wholeness. By the end of the film, we can see that the John Book of Act Three is a different kind of person from the John Book of Act One. He has a different kind of comradeship with his fellow police officers, he's more relaxed, and we can sense that somehow, this experience has formed a more integrated John Book.

Combination Myths

Many stories are combinations of several different myths. Think of *Ghostbusters*, 35 a simple and rather outrageous comedy about three men saving the city of New York from ghosts. Now think of the story of "Pandora's Box." It's about the woman who let loose all manner of evil upon the earth by opening a box she was told not to touch. In *Ghostbusters*, the EPA man is a Pandora figure. By shutting off the power to the containment center, he inadvertently unleashes all the ghosts upon New York City. Combine the story of "Pandora's Box" with a hero story, and notice that we have our three heroes battling the Marshmallow Man. One of them also "gets the Princess" when Dr. Peter Venkman finally receives the affections of Dana Barrett. By looking at these combinations, it is apparent that even *Ghostbusters* is more than "just a comedy."

Tootsie is a type of reworking of many Shakespearean stories where a woman has to dress as a man in order to accomplish a certain task. These

Shakespearean stories are reminiscent of many fairy tales where the hero becomes invisible or takes on another persona, or wears a specific disguise to hide his or her real qualities. In the stories of "The Twelve Dancing Princesses" or "The Man in the Bearskin," disguise is necessary to achieve a goal. Combine these elements with the transformation themes of the hero myth where a hero (such as Michael) must overcome many obstacles to his success as an actor and a human being. It's not difficult to understand why the *Tootsie* story hooks us.

Archetypes

A myth includes certain characters that we see in many stories. These characters are called *archetypes*. They can be thought of as the original "pattern" or "character type" that will be found on the hero's journey. Archetypes take many forms, but they tend to fall within specific categories.

Earlier, we discussed some of the helpers who give advice to help the hero — such as the *wise old man* who possesses special knowledge and often serves as a mentor to the hero.

The female counterpart of the wise old man is the *good mother*. Whereas the wise old man has superior knowledge, the good mother is known for her nurturing qualities, and for her intuition. This figure often gives the hero particular objects to help on the journey. It might be a protective amulet, or the ruby slippers that Dorothy receives in *The Wizard of Oz* from the Good Witch of the North. Sometimes in fairy tales it's a cloak to make the person invisible, or ordinary objects that become extraordinary, as in "The Girl of Courage," an Afghan fairy tale about a maiden who receives a comb, a whetstone, and a mirror to help defeat the devil.

Many myths contain a *shadow figure*. This is a character who is the opposite 40 of the hero. Sometimes this figure helps the hero on the journey; other times this figure opposes the hero. The shadow figure can be the negative side of the hero which could be the dark and hostile brother in "Cain and Abel," the stepsisters in "Cinderella," or the Robber Girl in "The Snow Queen." The shadow figure can also help the hero, as the whore with the heart of gold who saves the hero's life, or provides balance to his idealization of woman.

Many myths contain *animal archetypes* that can be positive or negative figures. In "St. George and the Dragon," the dragon is the negative force which is a violent and ravaging animal, not unlike the shark in *Jaws*. But in many stories, animals help the hero. Sometimes there are talking donkeys, or a dolphin which saves the hero, or magical horses or dogs.

The *trickster* is a mischievous archetypical figure who is always causing chaos, disturbing the peace, and generally being an anarchist. The trickster uses wit and cunning to achieve his or her ends. Sometimes the trickster is a harmless prankster or a "bad boy" who is funny and enjoyable. More often, the trickster is a con man, as in *The Sting*, or the devil, as in *The Exorcist*, who demanded all the skills of the priest to outwit him. The "Till Eulenspiegel" stories revolve around the trickster, as do the Spanish picaresque novels. Even the tales of Tom Sawyer have a trickster motif. In all countries, there are stories that revolve around this figure, whose job it is to outwit.

"Mythic" Problems and Solutions

We all grew up with myths. Most of us heard or read fairy tales when we were young. Some of us may have read Bible stories, or stories from other religions or other cultures. These stories are part of us. And the best way to work with them is to let them come out naturally as you write the script.

Of course, some filmmakers are better at this than others. George Lucas and Steven Spielberg have a strong sense of myth and incorporate it into their films. They both have spoken about their love of the stories from childhood, and of their desire to bring these types of stories to audiences. Their stories create some of the same sense of wonder and excitement as myths. Many of the necessary psychological beats are part of their stories, deepening the story beyond the ordinary action-adventure.

Myths bring depth to a hero story. If a filmmaker is thinking only about the 45 action and excitement of a story, audiences might fail to connect with the hero's journey. But if the basic beats of the hero's journey are evident, a film will often inexplicably draw audiences, in spite of critics' responses to the film.

Take *Rambo*, for instance. Why was this violent, simple story so popular with audiences? I don't think it was because everyone agreed with its politics. I do think Sylvester Stallone is a master at incorporating the American myth into his filmmaking. That doesn't mean it's done consciously. Somehow he is naturally in sync with the myth, and the myth becomes integrated into his stories.

Clint Eastwood also does hero stories, and gives us the adventure of the myth and the transformation of the myth. . . . Eastwood's films have given more attention to the transformation of the hero, and have been receiving more serious critical attention as a result.

All of these filmmakers — Lucas, Spielberg, Stallone, and Eastwood — dramatize the hero myth in their own particular ways. And all of them prove that myths are marketable.

Application

It is an important part of the writer's or producer's work to continually find opportunities for deepening the themes within a script. Finding the myth beneath the modern story is part of that process.

To find these myths, it's not a bad idea to reread some of Grimm's fairy tales 50 or fairy tales from around the world to begin to get acquainted with various myths. You'll start to see patterns and elements that connect with our own human experience.

Also, read Joseph Campbell and Greek mythology. If you're interested in Jungian psychology, you'll find many rich resources within a number of books on the subject. Since Jungian psychology deals with archetypes, you'll find many new characters to draw on for your own work.

With all of these resources to incorporate, it's important to remember that the myth is not a story to force upon a script. It's more a pattern which you can bring out in your own stories when they seem to be heading in the direction of a myth.

As you work, ask yourself:

> Do I have a myth working in my script? If so, what beats am I using of the hero's journey? Which ones seem to be missing?
>
> Am I missing characters? Do I need a mentor type? A wise old man? A wizard? Would one of these characters help dimensionalize the hero's journey?
>
> Could I create new emotional dimensions to the myth by starting my character as reluctant, naive, simple, or decidedly "unheroic"?
>
> Does my character get transformed in the process of the journey?
>
> Have I used a strong three-act structure to support the myth, using the first turning point to move into the adventure and the second turning point to create a dark moment, or a reversal, or even a "near-death" experience?

Don't be afraid to create variations on the myth, but don't start with the myth itself. Let the myth grow naturally from your story. Developing myths are part of the rewriting process. If you begin with the myth, you'll find your writing becomes rigid, uncreative, and predictable. Working with the myth in the rewriting process will deepen your script, giving it new life as you find the story within the story.

READING THE TEXT

1. How does Seger define the "hero myth" (para. 11)?
2. In your own words, explain what Seger means by "the healing myth" (para. 29).
3. What is an "archetype" (para. 37) in film?

READING THE SIGNS

1. Seger is writing to aspiring screenwriters. How does her status as an industry insider affect her description of heroic archetypes?
2. **CONNECTING TEXTS**   Focusing on gender issues, compare Seger's formulation of heroes with Robert B. Ray's in "The Thematic Paradigm" (p. 342). To what extent do Seger and Ray adequately explain the role of women — and men — in movies?
3. **CONNECTING TEXTS**   Review Michael Parenti's "Class and Virtue" (p. 406) and write an essay identifying the myths behind the modern stories *Pretty Woman* and *Indecent Proposal*.

4. Rent a DVD of *Titanic* or a segment of the *Lord of the Rings* trilogy, and write an essay in which you explain the myths and archetypal characters the film includes. How might archetypal and mythic patterns explain the film's success?

5. Seger recommends that aspiring screenwriters read Grimm's fairy tales for inspiration. You can find them online. Read some of Grimm's tales, and then write an argument assessing the suitability of such tales as inspiration for films today.

6. **CONNECTING TEXTS**   What myths about social class, race, and gender do you see in *Forrest Gump*? Brainstorm these myths in class, and then use your list of myths to write an essay in which you explain why the film has developed such a loyal fan base. To develop your ideas, consult Aeon J. Skoble's "*Forrest Gump*: A Subversive Movie" (p. 410).

LISA KERNAN
Trailer Rhetoric

If anything would seem to be a throwaway pop cultural artifact, it would be the movie trailer, that teasing snippet that is supposed to pique your interest in an upcoming film. But as Lisa Kernan demonstrates in this scholarly analysis of the rhetoric of movie trailers, a trailer is really a very complex production, carefully constructed to appeal to the generic expectations of its target audiences. For example, the fans of the Western expect to see dramatic horseback chases across a recognizable scenic terrain, and trailers for such films accordingly feature high-energy horseback chases through iconographically Western scenery. Using a number of devices from classical rhetoric, the movie trailer thus offers a surprising text for rhetorical analysis. The author of Coming Attractions: Reading American Movie Trailers *(2004), where this selection was originally published, Kernan was a librarian for film, television, and theater in the UCLA Arts Library until her death in 2006.*

The Rhetoric of Genre: Trailer Space

Genres have long been called on to differentiate artworks within a framework of similarities, and have proven to be an effective means for the film industry to encapsulate and promote the particular type of experience a given film will provide. At the same time, one of the principal goals of Hollywood film promotion, as emphasized by Rick Altman, Janet Staiger, and others, is product differentiation.[1] Promoting films on the basis of a rhetoric of genre would appear to contradict this goal — in its emphasis, literally, on the generic. It is this apparent contradiction that informs and animates appeals to audience interest in genre in Hollywood trailers. In those trailers where the rhetoric of genre is dominant, product differentiation is mediated by a comforting familiarity in representations of those elements of a film that producers are assuming the audience will want to see.

The promotional appeal of genre as a whole rests heavily on familiarity, on the lure and comfort of the known. Generic worlds are instances of a particular kind of cinematic place where we want to go again and again, whether by re-viewing favorite genre films or by revisiting such a place via a new film of the same genre. The decision to attend, rent or buy a film is at times determined by the kind of (known) generic place we may desire to inhabit or revisit, and it is their oneiric[2] and/or ritual aspect of moviegoing that the rhetoric of genre exploits.[3] At the same time, the promotional category of genre is a key method by which films are efficiently packaged as commodities.[4]

Recognizing this process of ideological containment or boundary-policing is key to the discernment of Hollywood's implied audiences through trailers' rhetoric of genre. Like all systems of communication, rhetoric, and particularly rhetoric's figure of the enthymeme (where assumptions about the listener or audience are structured into an argument), relies on the setting and recognition of boundaries between self and other, or in this case producer and audience (the trailer producers' assumptions of where the audience's shared understandings of a given topic are likely to start and stop). Protecting the industry's investments in its control of these boundaries is the domain of ideology. Trailers highlight such attempts at boundary-policing through their formal properties. As perhaps the most montage-driven signifying system in the regime of popular cinema, their discontinuity editing comprising a sort of

---

[1]See, for example, Rick Altman, *Film/Genre* (London: British Film Institute, 1999); Janet Staiger, "Announcing Wares, Winning Patrons, Voicing Ideals: Thinking about the History and Theory of Film Advertising," *Cinema Journal* 29, no. 3 (spring 1990): 3–31; Mark Stuart Miller, "Promoting Movies in the Late 1930s: Pressbooks at Warner Bros." (Ph.D. diss., University of Texas, Austin, 1994); Mary Beth Haralovich, "Motion Picture Advertising: Industrial and Social Forces and Effects, 1930–1948" (Ph.D. diss., University of Wisconsin-Madison, 1984).

[2]**oneiric** Dreamlike.–EDS.

[3]Some video rental stores reinforce the prominence of genre and stardom as selection parameters in spectatorial decision making, often disguising the familiarity aspect of genre by fragmenting categories as much as possible, offering the consumer a seemingly vast range of selections and emphasizing the centrality of the consumer's role as selector (disguising also the limitations of choices). See Robert Eberwein, "Ideology and Video Rental Stores," presented at Society for Cinema Studies, Pittsburgh, 1992.

[4]As Steve Neale characterizes, the function of genres is "to institutionalize a set of expectations which [the industry] will be able, within the limits of its economic and ideological practices, to fulfill. . . . Genres . . . provide a means of regulating memory and expectation, a means of containing the possibilities of reading. Overall, they offer the industry a means of controlling demand, and the institution a means of containing coherently the effects that its products produce." Stephen Neale, *Genre* (London: British Film Institute, 1980), 54–55.

"metamontage," the rhetoric of trailers trades heavily in boundaries, edges, and the spaces between where meaning happens (or is assumed to happen). Looking in particular at how generic boundaries are policed, whether by containment or expansion, gives us an idea of the parameters of trailers' assumptions about audiences.

Even as the lure of familiarity in the rhetoric of genre in trailers can be seen as a strategy of ideological containment, it strikes a chord with real audience desires for certain kinds of generic "spatial" containment — the feeling of being "in the mood" for film noir, for a romantic comedy, or for fifties science fiction, for example. Trailers do things to generic space. While the "metamontage" structure of most trailers makes their temporality arguably more important to their signification than their spatiality (since they do not generally provide spatial continuity), trailers still enable a reading of the forces at work in the Hollywood culture system in relation to social space. The conceptual generic "spaces" that movie audiences crave and that the industry attempts to configure or contain are at once *products* of a social imaginary and material industrial *products*, and we can conceive of trailers as a "production" of space that encompasses both of these aspects of the word.[5] By analyzing the ways that trailers' discontinuous representations of generic space rhetorically display industry assumptions about audiences' desires for these spaces, we can think of these "representations of space" dialectically, neither reducing them to *just* an "effect" of capitalist marketing tactics nor treating them as an unproblematic fulfillment of real audience desires. In turn, analysis of the promotion of generic space can begin to illuminate other features of actual social space in each of the three eras of trailer production.

Spatial analogies are also explored in relation to movie marketing by Janet Harbord, to characterize the role of genre in the "reconfigured landscape" of the contemporary market-driven film industry. She points out that genre is a key means by which the industry attempts to manage the "tangential paths, alleyways and flights of passage" that contemporary film texts take during the course of their construction as commodities. "In effect, genre creates the unifying principle of the hyper-text" (Harbord uses this term to refer to the contemporary film text's no longer unitary identity as a constellation incorporating promotional and ancillary texts as well as the film proper),

[5]The interaction between audiences' experiential knowledge of generic cinematic space and the industry's impulses to police the boundaries of cinematic meaning in trailers can be illuminated by reference to Henri Lefebvre's concept of "representations of space." Lefebvre's monumental reconceptualization of spatiality in human imagination and experience, *The Production of Space*, addresses the quest for an antimetaphoric "science of space," which attempts to express the relationship between space, social organization, and modes of production. He argues that each mode of production "offers up its own peculiar space, as it were, as an 'object' for analysis and overall theoretical explication" (31). Within Lefebvre's schema, cinema would be considered a "representation of space," or social space as "conceived" (as opposed to space as "perceived" or space as "lived," both categories of experience rather than represented experience) (40). *The Production of Space*, trans. Donald Nicholson-Smith (Oxford: Basil Blackwell, 1991).

"facilitating the role of marketing in pre-selling audiences to a film; genre presents overarching continuity for the audience and the historically proven formula for the production company."[6] This perspective is consistent with my argument that trailers' appeals to audience interest in genres are the highest logical type of the three rhetorical appeals.

Genre has become an increasingly problematic and nuanced category of film analysis in recent years, as critical discourse has begun to make a stronger attempt to take into account both reception practices and the studio production discourse of the process of genre formation. As Rick Altman and Steve Neale (among others) point out, genre is a multiply and historically determined category, and often what critics define as one genre, the studios might define as another.[7] Altman, moreover, has also argued that movie posters demonstrate that classical-era films were often promoted by invoking multiple genres. Altman offers the example of two generic promotional hooks frequently utilized for classical adventure films besides that of the adventure genre itself: these are "romance" and "travel." Characterizing a poster for *Only Angels Have Wings* (1939), Altman argues,

> Hollywood has no interest, as this poster clearly suggests, in explicitly identifying a film with a single genre. On the contrary, the industry's publicity purposes are much better served by implying that a film offers "Everything the Screen can give you." Typically, this means offering something for the men ("EACH DAY a Rendezvous with Peril!"), something for the women ("EACH NIGHT a Meeting with Romance!"), and an added something for that tertium quid audience that prefers travel to adventure or romance ("the mighty tapestry of the FOG-SHROUDED ANDES").[8]

In trailers, however, this multiplicity tends to play out more as an inclusiveness *within* genres. Once we look at trailers, elements that might appear as divisive or segmented appeals to different markets in print promotions can contribute to a perception that studios are offering audiences a more inclusive construction of individual genres by virtue of the trailer's inevitably more "holistic" presentation of these same diverse filmic elements within a single cinematic text — one that apes and reproduces (small portions of) the film itself.

The trailer for *Only Angels Have Wings*, for example, repeats the poster's "each day" and "each night" lines in its titles, and appeases the tourist faction in its introduction, where a narrator states, "This is Barranca, a South Ameri-

[6]Janet Harbord, *Film Cultures* (London: Sage Publications, 2002), 79.

[7]Neale cites an article by Charles Musser showing that *The Great Train Robbery* (1903), which critics have come to canonize as the first Western, was perceived within the industry at the time as pertaining to the crime genre. Charles Musser, "The Travel Genre in 1903–04: Moving toward Fictional Narratives," *Iris* 2, no. 1 (1984): 56–57, cited in Steve Neale, "Questions of Genre," *Screen* 31, no. 1 (1990): 55.

[8]Rick Altman, "Reusable Packaging: Generic Products and the Recycling Process," in *Refiguring American Film Genres: Theory and History*, ed. Nick Browne (Berkeley: University of California Press, 1998), 9.

can banana port where men live by their daring, and women by their charm." Overall, the trailer functions within the rhetoric of stardom, folding all three of the generic elements the poster calls to our attention into a text that keeps returning to images, scenes and titles promoting stars Cary Grant and Jean Arthur, as well as the "return to the screen" of Richard Barthelmess. While genre is not the principal focus of the trailer's rhetoric, the film is promoted as an adventure film, and the titles (which in the poster, Altman felt, appeared to fragment generic coherence) here function as assumptions that audiences want romance and exotic locations to be *incorporated into* the adventure genre.

The most obvious way that many trailers invoke specific genres is through *iconography*. Most trailers show live-action clips from the film, so it is hard to avoid presenting genre iconography in any trailer, but those with strong genre appeal will often underline familiar generic iconography by presenting it in hyperbolic fashion, such as opening a Western trailer with dynamically inter-cut shots from a horseback chase scene over picturesque Western terrain, or by allowing an iconographically significant but narratively insignificant scene, such as an extreme long shot of a group of people — for example, a chorus line dancing on stage in a musical — to play under the trailer's titles. This is a frequent trailer trope used to create visual generalizations and place locations generically.[9]

Hyperbole and *generalization* work together in genre appeals to differenti- 10 ate each film within an overall fabric of familiarity. Their interaction is also evident in trailer graphics. Titles may announce the film as "the most spectacular singing-dancing entertainment ever produced" (*Brigadoon*, 1954), or tell us that "It has the burning brand of greatness on it!" (*The Big Country*, 1958), often in letters that themselves evoke generalized generic associations, such as sparkling title lettering for classical musical trailers; wavy, jagged, or soft-focus lettering for horror film trailers; or big square early printing press fonts that connote "Wanted" posters for Western trailers. Graphic genre generalization in classical and transitional-era trailers also takes the form of generically cued drawings accompanying titles, such as musical instruments or musical notes, lassos or cacti, skeletons or gravestones, flowers and birds or other "feminine" motifs (for romantic comedy or melodrama trailers). Contemporary trailers also use graphics, heavily interwoven with sound effects, to signal genre, such as the flashing titles and percussive sounds punctuating trailers for action films.

Another pervasive trailer convention often marshaled for the rhetoric of genre is *repetition*. Frequent repetition within narration, titles and visual motifs connotes both sameness (again and again) and newness (unprecedented abundance). Repetition also generates rhythm, and rhythm is an important

---

[9]My discussions of the three rhetorical conventions have omitted, for reasons of length, many of the examples from which I constructed these arguments, but they are detailed in the dissertation from which this book is drawn. See my "A Cinema of (Coming) Attractions: American Movie Trailer Rhetoric" (Ph.D. diss., University of California, Los Angeles, 2000).

structural feature of trailers' sensory appeal. Examples of rhyming, alliteration, visual doubling and other refrains of return and repetition abound in the case studies that follow, even when the trailers are not for sequels or cycle films (which of course capitalize on repetition in numerous ways).[10] Repetition is at the heart of the concept of genre in mass culture, a point emphasized by Fredric Jameson: "The atomized or serial 'public' of mass culture wants to see the same thing over and over again, hence the urgency of the generic structure and the generic signal."[11] The fact that repetition functions within trailers' rhetoric of genre in overdetermined ways redoubles and reinforces a conception of audiences as craving repetition and familiarity in genre films. Strong figures of repetition also remind audiences of their own attachment to this kind of rhetoric and ritualized spectatorship.

Within trailer rhetoric, repetition generally functions to reinforce existing genres. That is most obviously demonstrated in trailers for sequels, films that belong to cycles, and double-bill trailers, or the more frequent rerelease double-bill trailers. Trailers for sequels (and sequels themselves) emphasize repetition throughout the sound era but become more prevalent in the contemporary era, and their use of repetition continues to draw audiences in with a promise of familiarity and novelty.

The prevalence of sequels in genre films of the late seventies and eighties enables even a trailer sequel, elucidating the importance of repetition. The trailer for *Friday the 13th Part 2* (1981) is a sequel to the trailer for *Friday the 13th* (1980). The first film's trailer establishes a graphic motif of counting days, with screen-filling titles that list the numbers 1 to 12, each followed by a clip from the film, the clips building in suspense to the final title, "Friday, the 13th," followed by an announcement, "You may only see it once, but that will be enough." The sequel's trailer announces, "On a June night in 1980, Friday the 13th . . . ," followed by a clip from the original film, then, "Why should Friday the 13th, 1981, be any different? The body count continues." The numbering motif is reprised (14 to 23). The clips following each number decrease in length as the numbers ascend, then the trailer's tagline announces: "The day you count on for terror is not over!" The idea of repetition and the notion of sequel are overdetermined in this trailer series in a clever way that links repetition with terror (and thus with genre appeals) — and manages to create anticipation for the next film out of dread of the next murder. Even the first trailer's remark about seeing the film only once can be read in this context as a challenge to see it, and its sequel(s), more than once. (The film ultimately spawned six sequels.)

The *Friday the 13th* trailers hyperbolically illustrate the way in which sequels reinforce audience viewing of genre films by linking the repetition of

---

[10]Vivian Sobchack calls attention to the function of repetition as a promotional strategy specifically within the historical epic film in her essay "'Surge and Splendor': A Phenomenology of the Hollywood Historical Epic," *Representations*, no. 29 (winter 1990): 24–49.

[11]Fredric Jameson, "Reification and Utopia in Mass Culture," *Social Text* 1, no. 1 (winter 1979): 137.

production with the repetition of reception (repeat viewing). The rhetorical logic of sequel and cycle trailers entails a textual demonstration of the producers' knowledge that audiences liked the original film by asserting in the sequel trailer their desire to make another one like it, which in turn creates an assumption that audiences will want to come see the latest episode or version since they are assumed to have liked the first one. However, this logic can succeed only if novelty is asserted along with the original film's proven likability. The rhetoric of sequel and cycle trailers dovetails with the rhetoric of genre in part because sequels tend to be genre films, but also because genre, as previously mentioned, is the packaging of a circumscribed generic world, as opposed to story elements or stars in situations. Sequels and cycles thus duplicate the precise generic worlds of their predecessors more consistently than they do their story elements or stars — thus, trailers that assert the rhetoric of genre reinforce existing genres almost as if genres were sequels on a grander scale.

"Generic sequels" are posited in trailers that capitalize on generic "sameness" by explicitly reminding audiences of similar successful films within the same genre that have preceded the film being promoted, a strategy common to trailers throughout the sound era (as exemplified by the frequent classical-era trope of "From the studio which gave you . . ."; in *The Last Outpost* [1935] trailer, for example, a title proclaims "Produced by the studio which gave you 'The Lives of a Bengal Lancer'" [also 1935], another empire-building war drama).[12] Trailers can refer even more obliquely to earlier films and thus assert genre by using the earlier films' music, such as the *Sliver* (1993) trailer's use of the *Basic Instinct* (1992) score.[13]

Repetition is related to another convention common to the rhetoric of genre, *the equation*. Through narration or titles and at times visual linking, trailers often assert an equation between the film and its generic subject matter, or between the spectator's (assumed) experience and the characters' experiences.[14] Puns might link characters' desires or actions to assumptions about audience desires to view the film, such as the reference to "Dangerous curves ahead for . . . [cast members]" followed by the tagline "It's the entertainment 'pick-up' of the year!" in the trailer for *They Drive by Night* (1940). In this case both the reference to "dangerous curves," which at once equates driving with sex and sex with danger, and that to an "entertainment 'pick-up,'" which equates hitchhiking with sex and both with spectatorship, assume spectators' interest in the perilous sexuality of film noir. Trailers utilize such equations to allow audiences to link particular generic features with their anticipated spectatorial experience.

[12]This example also demonstrates how studio branding can be interwoven with, yet subordinated to, rhetorical appeals.

[13]Since trailers are generally produced before the film's music is completed, they often use music from the soundtracks of other films. In this case, the trailer also reinforces the film's identity as a Sharon Stone vehicle.

[14]This convention is also utilized within the rhetoric of story.

Beyond merely invoking genres, trailers also contribute to genre definition. Much has been made in recent work on genre of the hybridity of contemporary genres in the pervasive postmodern media climate of pastiche and recombination of earlier popular narratives and myths. Trailers are a historical precedent for generic recombination and quotation, even as they illustrate the industry's attempts to force unusual or anomalous films into familiar generic molds. In addition to repetition, which allows genres to be reinforced in close continuity with audience expectations based on prior experiences, trailers reinforce genres by bringing in "new blood," while making comparisons with earlier generic models. The reconfiguring of established genres to accommodate new kinds of filmmaking usually takes the form of associating new elements with a genre, fitting odd films or smaller market films such as "art films" into established genres, or even positing a new subgenre to consolidate audience familiarity with something new. Trailers for many 1980s films characterized by nostalgia and quotation maximized the appeal of the old genre *and* the film's revisions of it, such as a trailer for *One from the Heart* (1982), which opens with citations of Coppola's credits and calls the film "a new kind of old-fashioned romance."

Another way trailers reinforce genre is to promote anomalous or one-of-a-kind films under familiar generic rubrics. A type of anomalous film that became institutionalized as such within the Hollywood film market after the demise of the studio system was the "art film." These films are occasionally promoted within the rhetorical terms of established genres, but more prevalent is the emergence of new generic conventions in the attempt to promote the art film as a genre in the late fifties and early sixties, such as the *Pawnbroker* (1965) trailer's innovative stylized graphics and use of a dissonant jazz soundtrack. Moreover, artistry itself becomes a selling point for such films, as exemplified by the frequent citation of critics and references to the film's director as an artist, such that certain ways of flagging the director mark the film as an art film and thus as belonging to a genre.

Trailers also differentiate films with regard to genre by labeling a new cycle within a genre, or at least helping a cycle to become familiar to audiences. This latter aspect backs up Rick Altman's argument that studios employed promotional discourses in the service of their project to "initiate film cycles that [would] provide successful, easily exploitable models associated with a single studio."[15] A cycle, of course, is a group of films within a genre that possess strong plot and/or star continuities, such as the *Dead End Kids* or *Star Wars* films. In the more commodity-oriented contemporary market these have come to be called "franchises."

From the 1950s onward, trailers have demonstrated a self-awareness [20] of their status as a genre, and many evidence a *self-referentiality* generally thought to be prevalent only in later postmodern popular media texts. This self-awareness of trailers as a genre is illustrated by numerous examples that parody classical trailer rhetoric, such as the self-conscious tabloid-style block titles

[15]Altman, *Film/Genre*, 60.

in the trailer for Kubrick's *The Killing* (1956), which start as pseudonews headlines: "Daring hold-up nets $2 million! / Police baffled by fantastic crime! / Masked bandit escapes with race track loot! / Suspense! / Terror! / Violence! / Will grip you as no other picture since *Scarface* and *Little Caesar*!" Other trailers that overtly satirize classical trailer form include those for *Fritz the Cat* (1972), *Young Frankenstein* (1974), *The Wanderers* (1978), and *Tag: The Assassination Game* (1982). More recently, trailers also demonstrate awareness of their own generic status by presenting self-contained "minimovies" — such as the dialogue-free montage trailers for *Cliffhanger* (1993), *Desperado* (1995), or *Eyes Wide Shut* (1999) — or using extra footage and telling their own "story" to promote their source films. These latter cases are examples of a recent trend in trailer production, where two factors — increased interest in promotional discourses, reflected in popular and trade press articles and in awards such as the Hollywood Reporter Key Art Awards; and the generally increased "buzz" factor of contemporary Hollywood — combine to encourage a newly self-aware artistry in trailermaking, along with a greater competitiveness among the various ad agencies that produce trailers. As promotional budgets have become a higher percentage of a film's total budget, and as technology has enabled cost-effective electronic editing, studios have responded to the higher stakes by at times hiring competing ad agencies to produce more than one trailer campaign for a film, increasing the mandate to dazzle and attract.[16]

Through iconography, hyperbole and generalization, repetition, equations (or other comparisons), and self-referentiality, the rhetoric of genre utilizes assumptions about audience desires for familiar generic spaces to enhance their desires for something new. The conventions of the rhetoric of genre demonstrate that, allowing for some historical variation, this balancing act took place throughout the three periods of the sound era in Hollywood. Indeed, the similarities of the promotional message in trailers of different eras are, paradoxically, almost as striking as their differences.

READING THE TEXT

1. Why does Kernan say that by promoting a film's genre a movie trailer appears to contradict the marketing goal of distinguishing a film from competitors?

2. Briefly define in your own words the rhetorical techniques that Kernan believes characterize most trailers: iconography, hyperbole and generalization, repetition, and equation.

3. How does repetition work as a rhetorical strategy in both trailers and sequels, according to Kernan?

4. In Kernan's view, what effect can trailers have on a potential audience's perception of unconventional films?

5. What does Kernan mean by saying that some post-1950s trailers are self-referential?

---

[16]David Finkle, "Sleek Previews: Tales behind the Trailers," *Village Voice*, Apr. 7, 1998.

READING THE SIGNS

1. In your journal, reflect on your own response to trailers. Do they influence your decisions about what films to see? If so, what kind of trailers have more impact on you, and why? If not, how do you account for your resistance to them?

2. Watch a trailer for a current film, and do an in-depth analysis of it. Does it use some or all of the rhetorical strategies Kernan describes, and, if so, how? To what extent does it achieve the two goals Kernan claims for trailers: to differentiate a film from other films and to locate the film within a familiar genre? To view a trailer, you can check a film's Web site or consult a cinematic database, such as www.imdb.com.

3. Kernan argues that one goal of movie trailers is to situate the films within a particular cinematic genre. Watch at least four trailers for movies in one genre (such as suspense or romantic comedy). What similarities do you see? Use your results to propose the specific formulas typically used to promote films in this genre. If you do not find similarities, use your results to rebut Kernan's argument.

4. Underlying Kernan's analysis of trailers is the assumption that mass audiences are attracted to the familiar and the conventional. Write an essay in which you demonstrate, refute, or modify this assumption, being sure to base your argument on a discussion of specific films.

5. **CONNECTING TEXTS**   Write a journal entry in which you list and discuss movie trailers that make use of violent clips to attract an audience. Do violent trailers desensitize viewers to violence? Consult Vivian C. Sobchack's "The Postmorbid Condition" (p. 414) to inform your discussion.

TODD BOYD

So You Wanna Be a Gangsta?

Before there were "gangstas" there were gangsters, and as Todd Boyd points out in this selection from Am I Black Enough for You? Popular Culture *from the 'Hood and Beyond (1997), both have played their part in American and cinematic history. From the Italian gangsters of* Scarface *and the* Godfather *films to the Latino and African American gangstas of* American Me *and* Boyz N the Hood, *the gang movie has provided a dramatic setting for an ongoing contest in which the American underclass both resists and embraces the values of mainstream society. Boyd holds the Price Chair for Study of Race and Popular Culture in the School of Cinema-Television at the University of Southern California, and is coeditor (with Aaron Baker) of* Out of Bounds: Sports, Media, and the Politics of Identity *(1997) and (with Kenneth Shropshire) of* Basketball Jones: America above the Rim *(2000). He has written for such journals as* Wide Angle, Cinéaste, Film-forum, *and* Public Culture. *His most recent books are* Young, Black, Rich, and Famous: The Rise of the NBA, the Hip Hop Invasion, and the Transformation of American Culture *(2003) and* The Notorious Ph.D.'s Guide to the Super Fly '70s *(2007).*

The gangster film and the Western are two of the most important genres in the history of Hollywood, especially with respect to articulation of the discourse of American history and masculinity. Whereas the Western concentrated on the mythic settling of the West and a perceived notion of progression, it was primarily concerned with the frontier mentality of the eighteenth through the late nineteenth century. The gangster genre, on the other hand, is about the evolution of American society in the twentieth century into a legitimate entity in the world economy.

Though the Western covertly articulated the politics of oppression against Native Americans during the settling of the West, the gangster genre focused on questions of ethnicity — e.g., Italian, Irish — and how these are transformed over time into questions of race — Black, Latino, etc. This ideological shift provided an interesting representation of the significant position that race has come to occupy in the discourse of American society. We must look at the transformation of the linguistic sign "gangster" and its slow transition to its most recent embodiment as "gangsta" as an instructive historical metaphor. . . .

Americans have always had a fascination with the underworld society populated by those who openly resisted the laws of dominant society and instead created their own world, living by their own rules. Gangsters have in many ways been our version of revolutionaries throughout history. Whereas Europe has always had real-life political revolutionaries, twentieth-century American discourse, upheld by police and government activity, seems to have found ways of perverting for the public the political voices that exist outside the narrow traditions of allowed political expression.

The displacement of these political voices by the forces of oppression has created a renegade space within American culture that allows for the expression of gangster culture. Gangsters indeed function as somewhat revolutionary in comparison to the rest of society, as demonstrated by their open defiance of accepted societal norms and laws, existence in their own environment, and circulation of their own alternative capital. This allows them to remain part of the larger society but to fully exist in their own communities at the same time. This lifestyle has been a consistent media staple throughout the twentieth century, particularly in film.

From as early as D. W. Griffith's *Musketeers of Pig Alley* (1912) and the celebrated studio films of the 1930s — e.g., *Little Caesar* (1930), *Public Enemy* (1931), and *Scarface* (1932) — through the epic treatment rendered in the first two *Godfather* films (1972, 1974), the gangster has enjoyed a vivid screen life. What is important here is that these criminals, as they are deemed by the dominant society, are defined as deviant primarily because of issues of ethnicity, as opposed to issues of race, though to some extent all definitions of ethnicity in this context are inevitably influenced by a subtle definition of race.

This emphasis on ethnicity as it functions in opposition to the standard "white Anglo-Saxon Protestant" is summarized in the first two *Godfather* films. As the United States, both at and immediately after the turn of the century, increasingly became a nation of European immigrants, incoming Italians were consigned to the bottom of the social ladder. In the opening segment of *Godfather II*, Michael Corleone is berated and verbally abused by Senator Geery of Nevada because of his Italian heritage. The word "Italian" is set in opposition to "American" constantly in this segment so as to highlight the ethnic hierarchy which remains a foundational issue in this film. Corleone's ascension to power is complicated by his inability to fully surmount this societal obstacle, at least at this point in the film, and by extension that point in American history — the early 1950s.

It is Francis Ford Coppola's argument that such oppression forced these Italian immigrants into a subversive lifestyle and economy much like that practiced throughout southern Italy, especially in Sicily. Borrowing from their own cultural tradition, some of these new Americans used the underground economy as a vital means of sustenance in the face of ethnic, religious, and cultural oppression. And though their desire, being heavily influenced by the discourse of an "American dream," was to ultimately be fully assimilated into American society, the achievement of this desire was revealed to be at the cost of losing their ethnic and cultural heritage. . . .

At a larger level, the film's historical themes indicate the assimilation of ethnicity into a homogeneous American society, yet foreground the continued rejection of race as a component of the metaphoric "melting pot" — because it is the challenge of race that accelerates the assimilative process of ethnicity.

In the first *Godfather* film, we see this same social dynamic at play regarding ethnicity over race. Near the film's conclusion, we witness the memorable meeting of the "heads of the five families," where the dilemmas of drug trafficking are being discussed by the various Mafia leaders. Vito Corleone is characterized as opposing this potentially lucrative venture for moral reasons, while many of the other members are excited about the possible financial benefits. The chieftain from Kansas City suggests that the Mafia should engage in selling drugs, but only at a distance, leaving the underside of this environment to be experienced by what he describes as the "dark people" because, as he adds, "they're animals anyway, let them lose their souls." His use of the phrase "dark people" and his labeling of them as "animals" clearly reference African Americans, and by extension racialized others in general. This line of dialogue is viewed by many African Americans as prophetic, seeing that the release of *The Godfather* in the early 1970s closely paralleled the upsurge in underworld drug activity throughout African American ghetto communities.

In relation to the assimilation of ethnicity at the expense of race, this line 10 also signifies the way in which the previously mentioned structural hierarchy exists aside from the racial hierarchy, which many African Americans have been unable to transcend because of the difference in skin color. Though Italians through this perverted formulation could be considered inferior to "wasps," those traits that make them different can be easily subsumed when contrasted with the obvious difference of skin color and the history that goes along with being darker. It is in this context that the thematic progression of the *Godfather* films signals the end of the public fascination with the Italian gangster and his ethnically rich underworld.

Furthermore, this line indicates that the drug culture would be an important turning point in the historical discourse specific to the question of race as time moved forward. This line of reasoning has been pursued in numerous texts, most recently through Bill Duke's film *Deep Cover* (1992), which comments on the conspiracy involved in both furnishing and addicting segments of the Black community with drugs as a political maneuver by the government to keep these individuals sedated and oppressed so as to quell any potential political resistance. Mario Van Peebles's film *Panther* (1995) asserts the same theory in connection with the attempted destruction of the Black Panther Party by J. Edgar Hoover and the FBI. In both cases, crime can be seen as affirming capitalism, yet in specifically racial terms.

With this assimilation of ethnicity as signified through the Coppola films, America finds the need to fulfill this otherwise empty space with the next logical descending step on the social ladder, that being race.[1] Two other films from the 1980s effectively mark the shift away from the ethnic gangster to the racialized gangsta. Brian De Palma's remake of *Scarface* (1983) is an obvious rewriting of the genre from the perspective of race. Whereas the main character in the 1932 film was an Italian, in the De Palma version we deal with a racialized Cuban.

Drawing from real political events, De Palma's film begins with the Mariel boat lift of Cuban refugees into south Florida during the latter part of the 1970s, an event which many still consider a lingering legacy of Jimmy Carter's presidency. The film's main character, Tony Montana, is clearly foregrounded as a racialized other. His Cuban identity, broken accent, penchant for garishness, and overall ruthless approach to wealth and human life served as the basis for the popular media representation of Latin American drug dealers that came to dominate the 1980s.

With an increase in drug paranoia from the conservative Reagan and Bush administrations, this form of representation would nearly erase past images of Italian mob figures from the popular memory. While John Gotti was a celebrated folk hero for his stylish media-friendly disposition, individuals such as Carlos Lader Rivas, Pablo Escobar, and Manuel Noriega, who became common sights on the evening news and network news magazine programs, were depicted as threats to the very fabric of our society. To add to this popular form of representation, NBC's series *Miami Vice* drew many of its story lines and criminal figures from this newly accepted version of racialized representation.[2] . . .

The other major filmic event that reflected this obsession with the drug culture and the question of race was Dennis Hopper's *Colors* (1988). Hopper's film offered an intricate look at the gang culture that existed in both South Central and East Los Angeles. Its main characters were two white Los

15

---

[1]The popular 1990 Martin Scorsese film *Goodfellas* is different from the gangster films which preceded it. At the conclusion of this film, the main character, Henry Hill, turns state's evidence on his former colleagues, thus violating one of the most stringent codes of the gangster lifestyle. And though some would argue that this film is a revisionist gangster film, it is sufficiently separated from other examples of the genre so as not to be confused. Scorsese's *Casino* (1995) continues this move to a contemporary gangster epic.

Another example of this revisionist trend would be Barry Levinson's fictional account of the life of Benjamin "Bugsy" Siegel, with its emphasis on Siegel's mistress, Virginia Hill, and the way in which her influence can be read as substantial, though detrimental, to Siegel in the financial decisions that he makes. *Bugsy* (1991) presents a sentimental underworld figure who has been "softened" by this female presence, which goes against the masculinist approach normally associated with the gangster. This rereading of the central character, with an emphasis on the female, adds to my notion of a revisionist trend in the genre, though in this case it is gender, not race, that is the point of transition.

[2]For a detailed discussion of the drug trade in Los Angeles, see Mike Davis, "The Political Economy of Crack," in *City of Quartz* (New York: Verso, 1990), and for a larger discussion of the role played by the media, the politics of Reagan/Bush, and the drug culture of the 1980s, see Jimmie Reeves and Richard Campbell, *Cracked Coverage* (Durham: Duke Univ. Press, 1994).

Angeles police officers who were commissioned with the monumental task of eliminating the urban crime being perpetrated by African American and Latino youth. This film tied in neatly with the increasing commentary presented by national news programs about what had begun as a regional situation and was later argued to have spread throughout the country. Using the police, and by extension the rest of white society, as its victims, the film endorsed the racial paranoia concerning criminality that at this time was in full swing.

Colors, for all intents and purposes, made the gangbanger America's contemporary criminal of choice, turning a localized problem into a national epidemic that once again linked crime with specific notions of race. In many ways, *Colors* served the same function for gangsta culture that *Birth of a Nation* served for the early stages of African American cinema. Both films, through their overt racial paranoia, and in both cases using armed militia as an answer to the perceived Black threat — in one case the Ku Klux Klan, in the other a racist police department — inspired a series of African American cinematic responses. This regressive film engendered a public fascination with the newly defined "gangsta."

With the traditional white ethnic gangster film having all but disappeared, the way was clear for the entrance of a new popular villain to be screened across the mind of American society. The ideological link between crime and race would be made worse, and the image of the African American gangbanger would become not only popular in the sense of repeated representation, but financially lucrative as well. In addition to the changing history of the Hollywood gangster film, several other historical factors specific to African American culture would contribute to the emergence and eventual proliferation of the African American "gangsta."

From the Black Godfather to the Black Guerrilla Family

The late 1960s and early 1970s saw an increase in underworld activity, especially involving drugs, throughout many lower-class Black communities. In many ways more important than the drugs themselves was the culture that accompanied this underworld lifestyle and the way in which it was represented visually. The garish fashions popularized by Eleganza and Flag Brothers, heavily adorned, ornament-laden Cadillacs, and other materialistic excesses helped to define this cultural terrain as "cool" during this period. . . .

In several of the films that define this period, eventually known as the "Blaxploitation" era of Hollywood (1970–73), the Black protagonist was presented in opposition to a stereotypical white menace who was bent on destroying the African American community, primarily through the influx of drugs and the accompanying culture of violence. For the most part, evil in the films was personified in the form of a corrupt police or mafia figure, if not both at the same time. Thus much of the narrative action appeared in battles between some faction of the white mafia, who had traditionally been in control of the ghetto, albeit from a distance, and the emerging Black underworld figures who were striving to wrest control of this alternative economy from their white counterparts.

It was as if the loosening of societal restrictions gained during the civil [20] rights movement permitted exploitation of the community through control of underworld vices, though the actual control was in the hands of manipulative outsiders, who used the Black gangster as their foil. The Black gangster, whether he was a pimp, dope dealer, or hustler, through these films became a prominent example of what it meant to be an entrepreneur. The tension between outside influence and inside control is represented in many of the films of the period, most notably *Cotton Comes to Harlem*, *Across 110th Street*, *Superfly*, and *The Mack*. The African American gangster had become a media staple by the mid-1970s. . . .

Many of the films of this period were based on the dynamics of an African American underworld existence (e.g., *Sweetsweetback's Badass Song*, *The Mack*, *Willie Dynamite*, *Coffy*, *Cleopatra Jones*), and in conjunction with the popular ghetto literature of Iceberg Slim and Donald Goines, as well as the more esoteric works of author Chester Himes and playwright Charles Gordone, this form of representation remained viable long after this period had passed. In line with Nelson George's argument that "Blaxploitation movies are crucial to the current '70's retro-nuevo phase," this historical period left a series of low-budget films which would eventually be perfect for transfer to the home video format. The "Blaxploitation" films would leave an indelible imprint on African American popular culture as the "gangsta" continued to rise in prominence and position.

A Small Introduction to the "G" Funk Era

With the historical antecedents of the Hollywood gangster film and 1970s Blaxploitation films, along with popular African American literature that explored the culture, the stage was set for the flowering of gangsta culture in the late 1980s and early 1990s. The contemporary manifestation continued to appear in the form of cinema, but also gained increasing visibility in the world of rap music, to the point of establishing its own genre and forming a solid cultural movement. This transition from genre to cultural movement included representations in film, music, and literature, and involved multiple layers of society: communal, political, and corporate. From the regular individuals whose personal narratives drew heavily from gangster culture, to rap artists whose real-life antics coincided with the fictional rhetoric of their lyrics, and finally to the highest levels of government, where questions of moral integrity, community debasement, and freedom of speech were constantly being posed, this cultural movement had a great deal of currency with respect to African Americans in society, especially the African American male. . . .

Boyz N the Hood, 1991.

Though there are glimpses of the gangster lifestyle in a number of films that appeared throughout the late 1980s and especially in the early 1990s, the two films most relevant to an understanding of gangsta culture are John Singleton's *Boyz N the Hood* (1991) and Allen and Albert Hughes's *Menace II Society* (1993). Not to ignore such a popular film as Mario Van Peebles's *New Jack City* (1991) or Abel Ferrera's cult video classic *The King of New York* (1990), but these texts are more directly influenced by the traditional gangster paradigm, in addition to being set in New York City. The filmic representation of gangsta culture draws many of its influences from rap music, and in turn rap music assumes a great deal of identity with the work of Singleton and the Hughes brothers. Contemporary gangsta culture is undoubtedly a West Coast phenomenon.

The other film that holds a vital position in the representation of gangsta culture is Edward James Olmos's *American Me* (1992). This film addresses the culture from a Latino perspective as opposed to an African American one. This is of utmost importance, for while gangsta culture is publicly regarded as an African American entity, much of the culture derives from the close proximity in which African Americans and Latinos coexist in racialized Los Angeles. . . .

Hispanics Causin' Panic

American Me demonstrates that aspects of African American gangsta life and   25
Mexican American gangsta culture are in dialogue with one another, though it
can at times be a highly contested dialogue. There are two distinct instances
in the film where a potential clash between the races is openly criticized as
being counterproductive to someone's coming to consciousness and ultimate
cultural empowerment. As the Mexican mafia (La Eme) smuggles drugs into
the prison, we witness a Black inmate who steals the cocaine intended for
another inmate. Upon revelation of the culprit, Santana, the leader of La Eme,
instructs his soldiers to burn the man as an act of punishment. This triggers a
cell-block confrontation that borders on a riot between La Eme and the Black
Guerrilla Family (BGF). As the prison guards descend, the riot is aborted, but
not without critical commentary. Santana informs the leader of the BGF that
the situation was not racially motivated, but simply an action of retribution
to forestall any future attempts at hindering their drug-trafficking efforts in
prison. In other words, "business, never personal." This is a case in which the
interest of underground capitalism supersedes any specific racial agenda.

Yet this scene is important as the setup for a similar situation that occurs
later in the film. When La Eme attempts to sever its tie with the traditional
Italian Mafia, the move is met with much resistance. Scagnelli, the mob boss,
refuses to relinquish his end of the drug business in East L.A. As a result, several members of La Eme rape and murder Scagnelli's son while he is in
prison. In response, Scagnelli sends uncut heroin into the barrio, causing several overdoses. This creates a chain reaction of retribution, which eventually

American Me, 1992.

culminates in Santana's death at the hands of his own men. At a certain point during this series of events, J.D., the only white member of La Eme, who slowly attempts to wrest control of the gang from Santana, orders a hit on the BGF by using the Aryan Brotherhood, the white gang represented in the film. Santana objects to this action and criticizes J.D. for "sending out the wrong message."

Santana's objection is based on his increasing awareness of racial and social consciousness, which has been facilitated by the politically empowered female character Julie. Julie, like the female character of Ronnie in *Menace*, helps Santana to realize the error of his misguided ways. On several occasions she criticizes his violent philosophy in ways that other characters cannot for fear of death. In a pivotal scene late in the film, Julie exposes Santana's position in all its limitations. After a series of extremely critical remarks about Santana's hypocritical use of crime as a way of arguing for *la raza*, he tells her, "If you were a man, I'd . . ." His incomplete sentence is cut short by Julie's own completion of it: "You'd kill me; no, you'd fuck me in the ass." Having witnessed several scenes in which men were raped because of Santana's power over them, in addition to his rape of Julie, we can feel the magnitude of her statement. She not only criticizes his politics, she has criticized his masculinity by alluding to the latent homosexuality of his supposed gestures of power.

Ultimately, she forces Santana to understand that the power struggles which often take place between those who are marginalized permit the continued oppression of their voices by those in power. Santana even says to J.D., "We spend all our time dealing with the miatas [their slang term for Blacks], and the Aryan Brotherhood, only to be dealing with ourselves." In other words, ideological distractions ultimately leave us in the same place, with no advancement in consciousness or power.

These ideas eventually separate Santana's newfound political consciousness from J.D.'s "business as usual" approach to crime and the underlying destruction of the community. It is not coincidental that J.D.'s whiteness, which is endorsed by Santana early in the film, looms as the final authority once he has ordered the killing of Santana and presumably taken control of the gang. At the beginning of the film, as expressed through the American military oppression of the Mexican American citizens, and at the conclusion, with J.D.'s murdering of Santana, thus destroying any possibility for an overall group consciousness, we can see that racism and white supremacy are the root causes of the chaos that permeates much of the present-day urban landscape. It is this fundamental understanding of race, racism, and complicity in one's own oppression that substantiates the importance of *American Me*. *American Me* engages history and politics to subtly yet convincingly argue that the real root of evil in American society as it relates to oppressed minorities is the bondage of systemic and institutionalized racism. This understanding also distinguishes it as a political statement from the rather limited bourgeois politics of *Boyz N the Hood* and the nihilistically apolitical *Menace II Society*. . . .

Boyz Will Be Boyz

Either they don't know, won't show, or don't care what's going on in the hood.

— DOUGHBOY, *Boyz N the Hood*

While *American Me* serves as an "objective third party" against which to eval- 30
uate *Boyz* and *Menace*, the similarities notwithstanding, to engage the culturally specific tenets of Black popular culture we must look at texts which are
firmly situated in the domain of African American cinema in order to study
the class politics of each film. In this regard, the political position of *Boyz N the
Hood* can be defined as either a bourgeois Black nationalist or an Afrocentric
model that focuses on the "disappearing" Black male, yet also fits easily into
the perceived pathology of the culture in a modernized version of the legendary Moynihan report of the late 1960s. This report regarded the typically
broken African American family as a cause of societal dysfunction at the highest level.

Singleton's film was integral to the politically charged period of resurgent
Black nationalism in the late 1980s and early 1990s. This cultural resurgence
of Black nationalism, most closely associated with the work of Public Enemy,
KRS-One, and Sister Souljah, also set the tone for the discourse that informed
Do the Right Thing, as well as many of the debates that emerged after the film's
release.

From the outset it is obvious that Singleton's film is conversant with the
Afrocentric discourse that permeates much of Black intellectual and cultural life.
The film opens by establishing South Central Los Angeles as its geographical,
cultural, and political center. Yet the landscape of Los Angeles is a historically
specific one. The film begins in 1984, as we quickly spot several campaign
posters that support the re-election of President Ronald Reagan — the obvious
contradiction of this image being seen in a community such as South Central,
which is the type of community most victimized by the racial and class politics
of Reagan's first term. Another contradiction is signaled as a young Black male,
while looking at an abandoned dead body lying in an alley, gives this political
image "the finger." This young character is identified as being closely associated
with gang culture. He declares that both of his brothers have been shot, and in
turn they are heroic in his mind because they have yet to be killed. His marginal
status allows him to recognize at some level that this supreme image of white
male authority is in stark contrast to his own existence.

As we enter the classroom, we are presented with another contradiction.
The camera pans the student drawings that cover the wall. These pictures
contain images of people being shot, police brutality, and other acts that
emphasize the daily violence that defines many of the lives in this poor Black
community. These images are contradicted by the speech being delivered by the
white teacher about the historical importance of the first European "settlers" or
"pilgrims" on American soil. Her lecture is on the reasons this country cele-

brates the Thanksgiving holiday, yet by implication it also articulates the exploitation of America and Native Americans and the ensuing colonization, which was a helpful instrument in establishing the societal hierarchy that we inhabit today.

The ideology that is being discussed is being put into practice through the attitudes and policies of Ronald Reagan. Reagan clearly felt the need to return to some form of these earlier examples of oppression in the course of his presidential career, as his repeated attacks on affirmative action, his support of states' rights, and his overall embrace of positions consistent with right-wing conservatism about race clearly indicated. In a sense, the actions of those who are being celebrated by the teacher, the "pilgrims," have contributed to the conditions of the people depicted in the children's drawings. The film sets up a binary opposition between the conservative politics of America and African Americans' rejection of these oppressive policies. This scene is one of the few in the film in which racism and white supremacy are directly critiqued.

As the scene develops, Tre, the film's main character, confronts his ele- 35 mentary school teacher, asserting that humankind originated in Africa and not in Europe. Yet in his presentation, Tre is criticized not only by his teacher, but by other students as well. The same student who gave Reagan "the finger" completely dissociates himself from Tre's Afrocentric assertion, "We're all from Africa." In response, this child declares, "I ain't from Africa, I'm from Crenshaw Mafia," further linking himself to gang culture through his identification with the set known as "Crenshaw Mafia." The obvious irony of this scene is that gang affiliation is set in direct conflict with one's racial and cultural identity. It is as if being a gangsta supersedes race, as opposed to being a result of racial and class hierarchies in America.

In this same exchange, we can also hear echoes of Tre's father, Furious, and his lessons on life that recur throughout the film. This is once again set in opposition to the words of the aspiring gangsta's older brothers. This exchange leads to a fight between the two children, underscoring the incompatibility of progressive politics and existence in gangsta culture. Yet through the setting of gangsta culture in opposition to nationalist politics, it becomes clear that this bourgeois understanding ignores the fact that gangsters historically are easily transformed into revolutionaries because of their marginal status in society.

Remarks about the plight of the "Black man" dominate much of Furious's commentary in the film. As critic Michael Dyson has alluded, these comments fit well with the male-centered Afrocentric ideals of thinkers such as Jawanza Kanjufu, Haki Madhabuti, and Molefi Asante. *Boyz* uses gangsta culture as an alluring spectacle, which is underscored by the film's exaggeratedly violent trailer, but this spectacle is used to engage an Afrocentric critique that denounces the routine slaying of Black men, whether by other gang members or by the police. *Boyz* makes interesting use of many of the icons of gangsta culture while conducting its Black nationalist critique. The film straddles both areas, opening the door to the ensuing onslaught of gangsta imagery.

In this sense, *Boyz* is much like the imagery connected with one of its co-stars, Ice Cube. As a rapper, Ice Cube has consistently combined signs of gangsta culture with an ideological perspective that emphasizes a perverted Black nationalist agenda, borrowed primarily from the Nation of Islam. Similarly, *Boyz* combines gangsta icons with Afrocentrism, ultimately privileging the ideological critique over the iconography. This strain of political discourse was popular during the late 1980s and early 1990s, with *Boyz* providing a cinematic counterpart to rap music. Singleton's film, though visualizing gangsta culture on a mass scale, is really more acceptable as a political text than as a thesis on the complex gangsta mentality. In many ways, *Boyz* represents the culmination of this politically resurgent period, as the theme of Black nationalism slowly disappeared from most popular forms shortly thereafter.

Though the film is overtly political, it reflects a bourgeois sense of politics. At the conclusion of the film we see a didactic scroll which tells us that Tre and Brandi, the one utopic Black male/female relationship presented in the film, have ventured off to Morehouse and Spelman College in Atlanta, respectively, to pursue their middle-class dreams far away from South Central L.A. Morehouse and Spelman have often been thought of as the Black equivalent of Harvard or Yale, the historical breeding ground for bourgeois Blackness. The fact that the two colleges are located in Atlanta, the current "mecca" of Black America, underscores the film's flimsy political position. *Boyz N the Hood* demonizes the landscape of Los Angeles while uncritically offering middle-class Atlanta as a metaphoric space where future generations of African Americans can exist free of the obstacles that are depicted in this film.

READING THE TEXT

1. What, according to Boyd, has been the cultural and political significance of the gangster underworld in American history and popular culture?
2. How did Hollywood in the late 1960s and early 1970s respond to the emergence of a drug culture in impoverished black communities, in Boyd's analysis?
3. Why does Boyd believe that *Boyz N the Hood* reflects both black nationalist and conventional bourgeois values?
4. How did *American Me* reflect the conflicts between Mexican American and African American gang subcultures?
5. What is the difference, according to Boyd, between race and ethnicity?

READING THE SIGNS

1. Write an essay supporting, complicating, or refuting the proposition that Hollywood's depiction of gangstas glorifies criminal behavior.
2. Rent a film like *Scarface* or *The Godfather*, and write an analysis comparing its treatment of ethnic "others" with the treatment of black gang members in a movie like *Boyz N the Hood*.

3. **CONNECTING TEXTS**   Write an essay in which you explore the reasons gangsta films and culture are so popular among middle-class white teens. To develop your ideas, consult Nell Bernstein's "Goin' Gangsta, Choosin' Cholita" (p. 691).

4. In class, form teams and debate the proposition that Hollywood exploits the black community in making gang films.

5. Watch a film featuring African Americans that Boyd does not discuss, such as *Waiting to Exhale*, *Dream Girls*, or *Diary of a Mad Black Woman*. Then write a response to Boyd in which you address the importance of gender in film analysis.

JESSICA HAGEDORN

Asian Women in Film: No Joy, No Luck

Why do movies always seem to portray Asian women as tragic victims of history and fate? Jessica Hagedorn asks in this essay, which originally appeared in Ms. *Even such movies as* The Joy Luck Club, *based on Amy Tan's breakthrough novel that elevated Asian American fiction to best-seller status, reinforce old stereotypes of the powerlessness of Asian and Asian American women. A screenwriter and novelist, Hagedorn calls for a different kind of storytelling that would show Asian women as powerful controllers of their own destinies. Hagedorn's publications include the novels* Dogeaters *(1990),* The Gangster of Love *(1996), and* Dream Jungle *(2001);* Danger and Beauty *(1993), a collection of poems;* Charlie Chan Is Dead: An Anthology of Contemporary Asian American Fiction *(1993); and* Fresh Kill *(1994), a screenplay.*

Pearl of the Orient. Whore. Geisha. Concubine. Whore. Hostess. Bar Girl. Mamasan. Whore. China Doll. Tokyo Rose. Whore. Butterfly. Whore. Miss Saigon. Whore. Dragon Lady. Lotus Blossom. Gook. Whore. Yellow Peril. Whore. Bangkok Bombshell. Whore. Hospitality Girl. Whore. Comfort Woman. Whore. Savage. Whore. Sultry. Whore. Faceless. Whore. Porcelain. Whore. Demure. Whore. Virgin. Whore. Mute. Whore. Model Minority. Whore. Victim. Whore. Woman Warrior. Whore. Mail-Order Bride. Whore. Mother. Wife. Lover. Daughter. Sister.

As I was growing up in the Philippines in the 1950s, my fertile imagination was colonized by thoroughly American fantasies. Yellowface variations on the exotic erotic loomed larger than life on the silver screen. I was mystified and enthralled by Hollywood's skewed representations of Asian women: sleek, evil goddesses with slanted eyes and cunning ways, or smiling, sarong-clad South

Seas "maidens" with undulating hips, kinky black hair, and white skin darkened by makeup. Hardly any of the "Asian" characters were played by Asians. White actors like Sidney Toler and Warner Oland played "inscrutable Oriental detective" Charlie Chan with taped eyelids and a singsong, chop suey accent. Jennifer Jones was a Eurasian doctor swept up in a doomed "interracial romance" in *Love Is a Many Splendored Thing*. In my mother's youth, white actor Luise Rainer played the central role of the Patient Chinese Wife in the 1937 film adaptation of Pearl Buck's novel *The Good Earth*. Back then, not many thought to ask why; they were all too busy being grateful to see anyone in the movies remotely like themselves.

Cut to 1960: *The World of Suzie Wong*, another tragic East/West affair. I am now old enough to be impressed. Sexy, sassy Suzie (played by Nancy Kwan) works out of a bar patronized by white sailors, but doesn't seem bothered by any of it. For a hardworking girl turning nightly tricks to support her baby, she manages to parade an astonishing wardrobe in damn near every scene, down to matching handbags and shoes. The sailors are also strictly Hollywood, sanitized and not too menacing. Suzie and all the other prostitutes in this movie are cute, giggling, dancing sex machines with hearts of gold. William Holden plays an earnest, rather prim, Nice Guy painter seeking inspiration in The Other. Of course, Suzie falls madly in love with him. Typically, she tells him, "I not important," and "I'll be with you until you say — Suzie, go away." She also thinks being beaten by a man is a sign of true passion and is terribly disappointed when Mr. Nice Guy refuses to show his true feelings.

Next in Kwan's short-lived but memorable career was the kitschy 1961 musical *Flower Drum Song*, which, like *Suzie Wong*, is a thoroughly American commercial product. The female roles are typical of Hollywood musicals of the times: women are basically airheads, subservient to men. Kwan's counterpart is the Good Chinese Girl, played by Miyoshi Umeki, who was better playing the Loyal Japanese Girl in that other classic Hollywood tale of forbidden love, *Sayonara*. Remember? Umeki was so loyal, she committed double suicide with actor Red Buttons. I instinctively hated *Sayonara* when I first saw it as a child; now I understand why. Contrived tragic resolutions were the only way Hollywood got past the censors in those days. With one or two exceptions, somebody in these movies always had to die to pay for breaking racial and sexual taboos.

Until the recent onslaught of films by both Asian and Asian American 5 filmmakers, Asian Pacific women have generally been perceived by Hollywood with a mixture of fascination, fear, and contempt. Most Hollywood movies either trivialize or exoticize us as people of color and as women. Our intelligence is underestimated, our humanity overlooked, and our diverse cultures treated as interchangeable. If we are "good," we are childlike, submissive, silent, and eager for sex (see France Nuyen's glowing performance as Liat in the film version of *South Pacific*) or else we are tragic victim types (see *Casualties of War*, Brian De Palma's graphic 1989 drama set in Vietnam). And if we are not silent, suffering doormats, we are demonized dragon ladies — cunning,

Anna May Wong.

deceitful, sexual provocateurs. Give me the demonic any day — Anna May Wong as a villain slithering around in a slinky gown is at least gratifying to watch, neither servile nor passive. And she steals the show from Marlene Dietrich in Josef von Sternberg's *Shanghai Express*. From the 1920s through the 1930s, Wong was our only female "star." But even she was trapped in limited roles, in what filmmaker Renee Tajima has called the dragon lady/lotus blossom dichotomy.

Cut to 1985: There is a scene toward the end of the terribly dishonest but weirdly compelling Michael Cimino movie *Year of the Dragon* (cowritten by Oliver Stone) that is one of my favorite twisted movie moments of all time. If you ask a lot of my friends who've seen that movie (especially if they're Asian), it's one of their favorites too. The setting is a crowded Chinatown nightclub. There are two very young and very tough Jade Cobra gang girls in a shoot-out with Mickey Rourke, in the role of a demented Polish American cop who, in spite of being Mr. Ugly in the flesh — an arrogant, misogynistic bully devoid of any charm — wins the "good" Asian American anchorwoman in the film's absurd and implausible ending. This is a movie with an actual disclaimer as its lead-in, covering its ass in advance in response to anticipated complaints about "stereotypes."

My pleasure in the hard-edged power of the Chinatown gang girls in *Year of the Dragon* is my small revenge, the answer to all those Suzie Wong "I want to be your slave" female characters. The Jade Cobra girls are mere background to the white male foreground/focus of Cimino's movie. But long after the movie has faded into video-rental heaven, the Jade Cobra girls remain defiant, fabulous images in my memory, flaunting tight metallic dresses and spiky cock's-comb hairdos streaked electric red and blue.

Mickey Rourke looks down with world-weary pity at the unnamed Jade Cobra
girl (Doreen Chan) he's just shot who lies sprawled and bleeding on the
street: "You look like you're gonna die, beautiful."

JADE COBRA GIRL: "Oh yeah? [blood gushing from her mouth] I'm proud of it."

ROURKE: "You are? You got anything you wanna tell me before you go, sweetheart?"

JADE COBRA GIRL: "Yeah. [pause] Fuck you."

Cut to 1993: I've been told that like many New Yorkers, I watch movies
with the right side of my brain on perpetual overdrive. I admit to being grouchy
and overcritical, suspicious of sentiment, and cynical. When a critic like Richard
Corliss of *Time* magazine gushes about *The Joy Luck Club* being "a fourfold
Terms of Endearment," my gut instinct is to run the other way. I resent being
told how to feel. I went to see the 1993 eight-handkerchief movie version
of Amy Tan's bestseller with a group that included my ten-year-old daughter.
I was caught between the sincere desire to be swept up by the turbulent
mother-daughter sagas and my own stubborn resistance to being so obviously
manipulated by the filmmakers. With every flashback came tragedy. The music
soared; the voice-overs were solemn or wistful; tears, tears, and more tears
flowed onscreen. Daughters were reverent; mothers carried dark secrets.

I was elated by the grandness and strength of the four mothers and the
luminous actors who portrayed them, but I was uneasy with the passivity of
the Asian American daughters. They seemed to exist solely as receptors for
their mothers' amazing life stories. It's almost as if by assimilating so easily
into American society, they had lost all sense of self.

Michelle Yeoh, *Tomorrow Never
Dies*, 1997.

In spite of my resistance, my eyes watered as the desperate mother played   10
by Kieu Chinh was forced to abandon her twin baby girls on a country road in
war-torn China. (Kieu Chinh resembles my own mother and her twin sister,
who suffered through the brutal Japanese occupation of the Philippines.) So far
in this movie, an infant son had been deliberately drowned, a mother played
by the gravely beautiful France Nuyen had gone catatonic with grief, a concubine had cut her flesh open to save her dying mother, an insecure daughter
had been oppressed by her boorish Asian American husband, another insecure
daughter had been left by her white husband, and so on. . . . The overall effect
was numbing as far as I'm concerned, but a man sitting two rows in front of us
broke down sobbing. A Chinese Filipino writer even more grouchy than me
later complained, "Must ethnicity only be equated with suffering?"

Because change has been slow, *The Joy Luck Club* carries a lot of cultural
baggage. It is a big-budget story about Chinese American women, directed by
a Chinese American man, cowritten and coproduced by Chinese American
women. That's a lot to be thankful for. And its box office success proves that
an immigrant narrative told from female perspectives can have mass appeal.
But my cynical side tells me that its success might mean only one thing in
Hollywood: more weepy epics about Asian American mother-daughter relationships will be planned.

That the film finally got made was significant. By Hollywood standards
(think white male; think money, money, money), a movie about Asian Americans even when adapted from a bestseller was a risky proposition. When I
asked a producer I know about the film's rumored delays, he simply said, "It's
still an *Asian* movie," surprised I had even asked. Equally interesting was director Wayne Wang's initial reluctance to be involved in the project; he told
the *New York Times*, "I didn't want to do another Chinese movie."

Maybe he shouldn't have worried so much. After all, according to the
media, the nineties are the decade of "Pacific Overtures" and East Asian chic.
Madonna, the pop queen of shameless appropriation, cultivated Japanese
high-tech style with her music video "Rain," while Janet Jackson faked kitschy
orientalia in hers, titled "If." Critical attention was paid to movies from China,
Japan, and Vietnam. But that didn't mean an honest appraisal of women's
lives. Even on the art house circuit, filmmakers who should know better took
the easy way out. Takehiro Nakajima's 1992 film *Okoge* presents one of the
more original film roles for women in recent years. In Japanese, "okoge"
means the crust of rice that sticks to the bottom of the rice pot; in pejorative
slang, it means fag hag. The way "okoge" is used in the film seems a reappro-
priation of the term; the portrait Nakajima creates of Sayoko, the so-called fag
hag, is clearly an affectionate one. Sayoko is a quirky, self-assured woman in
contemporary Tokyo who does voice-overs for cartoons, has a thing for Frida
Kahlo paintings, and is drawn to a gentle young gay man named Goh. But the
other women's roles are disappointing, stereotypical "hysterical females" and
the movie itself turns conventional halfway through. Sayoko sacrifices herself

to a macho brute Goh desires, who rapes her as images of Frida Kahlo paintings and her beloved Goh rising from the ocean flash before her. She gives birth to a baby boy and endures a terrible life of poverty with the abusive rapist. This sudden change from spunky survivor to helpless, victimized woman is baffling. Whatever happened to her job? Or that arty little apartment of hers? Didn't her Frida Kahlo obsession teach her anything?

Then there was Tiana Thi Thanh Nga's *From Hollywood to Hanoi*, a self-serving but fascinating documentary. Born in Vietnam to a privileged family that included an uncle who was defense minister in the Thieu government and an idolized father who served as press minister, Nga (a.k.a. Tiana) spent her adolescence in California. A former actor in martial arts movies and fitness teacher ("Karaticize with Tiana"), the vivacious Tiana decided to make a record of her journey back to Vietnam.

From Hollywood to Hanoi is at times unintentionally very funny. Tiana includes a quick scene of herself dancing with a white man at the Metropole hotel in Hanoi, and breathlessly announces: "That's me doing the tango with Oliver Stone!" Then she listens sympathetically to a horrifying account of the My Lai massacre by one of its few female survivors. In another scene, Tiana cheerfully addresses a food vendor on the streets of Hanoi: "Your hairdo is so pretty." The unimpressed, poker-faced woman gives a brusque, deadpan reply: "You want to eat, or what?" Sometimes it is hard to tell the difference between Tiana Thi Thanh Nga and her Hollywood persona: the real Tiana still seems to be playing one of her B-movie roles, which are mainly fun because they're fantasy. The time was certainly right to explore postwar Vietnam from a Vietnamese woman's perspective; it's too bad this film was done by a Valley Girl. 15

Nineteen ninety-three also brought Tran Anh Hung's *The Scent of Green Papaya*, a different kind of Vietnamese memento — this is a look back at the peaceful, lush country of the director's childhood memories. The film opens in Saigon, in 1951. A willowy ten-year-old girl named Mui comes to work for a troubled family headed by a melancholy musician and his kind, stoic wife. The men of this bourgeois household are idle, pampered types who take naps while the women do all the work. Mui is male fantasy: she is a devoted servant, enduring acts of cruel mischief with patience and dignity; as an adult, she barely speaks. She scrubs floors, shines shoes, and cooks with loving care and never a complaint. When she is sent off to work for another wealthy musician, she ends up being impregnated by him. The movie ends as the camera closes in on Mui's contented face. Languid and precious, *The Scent of Green Papaya* is visually haunting, but it suffers from the director's colonial fantasy of women as docile, domestic creatures. Steeped in highbrow nostalgia, it's the arty Vietnamese version of *My Fair Lady* with the wealthy musician as Professor Higgins, teaching Mui to read and write.

And then there is Ang Lee's tepid 1993 hit, *The Wedding Banquet* — a clever culture-clash farce in which traditional Chinese values collide with contemporary American sexual mores. The somewhat formulaic plot goes like this: Wai-Tung, a yuppie landlord, lives with his white lover, Simon, in a chic Manhattan brownstone. Wai-Tung is an only child and his aging parents in Taiwan long for a grandchild to continue the family legacy. Enter Wei-Wei, an artist who lives in a grungy loft owned by Wai-Tung. She slugs tequila straight from the bottle as she paints and flirts boldly with her young, uptight landlord, who brushes her off. "It's my fate. I am always attracted to handsome gay men," she mutters. After this setup, the movie goes downhill, all edges blurred in a cozy nest of happy endings. In a refrain of Sayoko's plight in *Okoge*, a pregnant, suddenly compla-cent Wei-Wei gives in to family pressures — and never gets her life back.

> "It takes a man to know what it is to be a real woman."
> — SONG LILING in *M. Butterfly*

Ironically, two gender-bending films in which men play men playing women reveal more about the mythology of the prized Asian woman and the superficial trappings of gender than most movies that star real women. The slow-moving *M. Butterfly* presents the ultimate object of Western male desire as the spy/opera diva Song Liling, a Suzie Wong/Lotus Blossom played by actor John Lone with a five o'clock shadow and bobbing Adam's apple. The best and most profound of these forays into cross-dressing is the spectacular melodrama *Farewell My Con-cubine*, directed by Chen Kaige. Banned in China, *Farewell My Concubine* shared the prize for Best Film at the 1993 Cannes Film Festival with Jane Campion's *The Piano*. Sweeping through 50 years of tumultuous history in China, the story revolves around the lives of two male Beijing Opera stars and the woman who marries one of them. The three characters make an unforgettable trian-gle, struggling over love, art, friendship, and politics against the bloody back-drop of cultural upheaval. They are as capable of casually betraying each other as they are of selfless, heroic acts. The androgynous Dieyi, doomed to play the same female role of concubine over and over again, is portrayed with great vulnerability, wit, and grace by male Hong Kong pop star Leslie Cheung. Dieyi competes with the prostitute Juxian (Gong Li) for the love of his childhood pro-tector and fellow opera star, Duan Xiaolou (Zhang Fengyi).

Cheung's highly stylized performance as the classic concubine-ready-to-die-for-love in the opera within the movie is all about female artifice. His side-long glances, restrained passion, languid stance, small steps, and delicate, refined gestures say everything about what is considered desirable in Asian women — and are the antithesis of the feisty, outspoken woman played by Gong Li. The characters of Dieyi and Juxian both see suffering as part and parcel of love and life. Juxian matter-of-factly says to Duan Xiaolou before he agrees to marry her: "I'm used to hardship. If you take me in, I'll wait on you hand and foot. If you tire of me, I'll . . . kill myself. No big deal." It's an echo of Suzie Wong's servility, but the context is new. Even with her back to the wall, Juxian is not helpless or whiny. She attempts to manipulate a man while admitting to the harsh reality that is her life.

Dieyi and Juxian are the two sides of the truth of women's lives in most 20 Asian countries. Juxian in particular — wife and ex-prostitute — could be seen as a thankless and stereotypical role. But like the characters Gong Li has played in

Chinese director Zhang Yimou's films, *Red Sorghum, Raise the Red Lantern*, and especially *The Story of Qiu Ju*, Juxian is tough, obstinate, sensual, clever, oafish, beautiful, infuriating, cowardly, heroic, and banal. Above all, she is resilient. Gong Li is one of the few Asian Pacific actors whose roles have been drawn with intelligence, honesty, and depth. Nevertheless, the characters she plays are limited by the possibilities that exist for real women in China.

"Let's face it. Women still don't mean shit in China," my friend Meeling reminds me. What she says so bluntly about her culture rings painfully true, but in less obvious fashion for me. In the Philippines, infant girls aren't drowned, nor were their feet bound to make them more desirable. But sons were and are cherished. To this day, men of the bourgeois class are coddled and prized, much like the spoiled men of the elite household in *The Scent of Green Papaya*. We do not have a geisha tradition like Japan, but physical beauty is over-treasured. Our daughters are protected virgins or primed as potential beauty queens. And many of us have bought into the image of the white man as our handsome savior: G.I. Joe.

Buzz magazine recently featured an article entitled "Asian Women/L.A. Men," a report on a popular hangout that caters to white men's fantasies of nubile Thai women. The lines between movies and real life are blurred. Male screenwriters and cinematographers flock to this bar-restaurant, where the waitresses are eager to "audition" for roles. Many of these men have been to Bangkok while working on film crews for Vietnam War movies. They've come back to L.A., but for them, the movie never ends. In this particular fantasy the boys play G.I. Joe on a rescue mission in the urban jungle, saving the whore from herself. "A scene has developed here, a kind of R-rated *Cheers*," author Alan Rifkin writes. "The waitresses audition for sitcoms. The customers date the waitresses or just keep score."

Colonization of the imagination is a two-way street. And being enshrined on a pedestal as someone's Pearl of the Orient fantasy doesn't seem so demeaning, at first; who wouldn't want to be worshipped? Perhaps that's why Asian women are the ultimate wet dream in most Hollywood movies; it's no secret how well we've been taught to play the role, to take care of our men. In Hollywood vehicles, we are objects of desire or derision; we exist to provide sex, color, and texture in what is essentially a white man's world. It is akin to what Toni Morrison calls "the Africanist presence" in literature. She writes: "Just as entertainers, through or by association with blackface, could render permissible topics that otherwise would have been taboo, so American writers were able to employ an imagined Africanist persona to articulate and imaginatively act out the forbidden in American culture." The same analogy could be made for the often titillating presence of Asian women in movies made by white men.

Movies are still the most seductive and powerful of artistic mediums, manipulating us with ease by a powerful combination of sound and image. In many ways, as females and Asians, as audiences or performers, we have learned to settle for less — to accept the fact that we are either decorative, invisible, or one-dimensional. When there are characters who look like us represented in a movie, we have also learned to view between the lines, or to add what is missing. For many of us, this way of watching has always been a necessity. We fill in the gaps. If a female character is presented as a mute, willowy beauty, we convince ourselves she is an ancestral ghost — so smart she doesn't have to speak at all. If she is a whore with a heart of gold, we claim her as a tough feminist icon. If she is a sexless, sanitized, boring nerd, we embrace her as a role model for our daughters, rather than the tragic whore. And if she is presented as an utterly devoted saint suffering nobly in silence, we lie and say she is just like our mothers. Larger than life. Magical and insidious. A movie is never just a movie, after all.

READING THE TEXT

1. Summarize in your own words Hagedorn's view of the traditional images of Asian women as presented in American film.

2. What is the chronology of Asian women in film that Hagedorn presents, and why do you think she gives us a historical overview?

3. Why does Hagedorn say that the film *The Joy Luck Club* "carries a lot of cultural baggage" (para. 11)?

4. What sort of images of Asian women does Hagedorn imply that she would prefer to see?

READING THE SIGNS

1. Watch *The Joy Luck Club* and write an essay in which you support, refute, or modify Hagedorn's interpretation of the film. Alternately, view another film featuring Asian characters, such as *The Fast and the Furious*, *Balls of Fury*, or *Rising Sun*, and use Hagedorn's article as a critical framework for analyzing the film's representation of Asian characters.

2. **CONNECTING TEXTS** In class, form teams and debate the proposition that Hollywood writers and directors have a social responsibility to avoid stereotyping ethnic characters. To develop your team's arguments, brainstorm films that depict various ethnicities, and then discuss whether the portrayals are damaging or benign. You might also consult Michael Omi's "In Living Color: Race and American Culture" (p. 655).

3. Study a magazine that targets Asian American readers, such as *Transpacific*, *Hyphen*, or *Yolk*. Then write an essay in which you analyze whether Asian women in the magazine fit the stereotypes that Hagedorn describes, keeping in mind the magazine's intended readership (businessmen, twentysomethings of both sexes, and so forth).

4. **CONNECTING TEXTS** Watch one of the gender-bending films Hagedorn mentions (such as *M. Butterfly*), and write your own analysis of the gender roles portrayed in the film. To develop your ideas, consult Aaron Devor's "Gender Role Behaviors and Attitudes" (p. 567).

DAVID DENBY

High-School Confidential: Notes on Teen Movies

Face it: High school for most of us is one extended nightmare, a long-playing drama starring cheerleaders and football players who sneer at the mere mortals who must endure their haughty reign. So it's little wonder that, as David Denby argues in this New Yorker *essay from 1999, teen movies so often feature loathsome cheerleaders and football stars who, one way or another, get theirs in this ever-popular movie genre. Indeed, Denby asks, "Who can doubt where Hollywood's twitchy, near-sighted writers and directors ranked—or feared they ranked—on the high-school totem pole?" Nerds at the bottom, where else, like the millions of suffering kids who flock to their films. A staff writer and film critic for the* New Yorker, *Denby is the author of* The Great Books: My Adventures with Homer, Rousseau, Woolf, and Other Indestructible Writers of the Western World *(1996) and* American Sucker *(2003).*

The most hated young woman in America is a blonde—well, sometimes a redhead or a brunette, but usually a blonde. She has big hair flipped into a swirl of gold at one side of her face or arrayed in a sultry mane, like the magnificent pile of a forties movie star. She's tall and slender, with a waist as supple as a willow, but she's dressed in awful, spangled taste: her outfits could have been put together by warring catalogues. And she has a mouth on her, a low, slatternly tongue that devastates other kids with such insults as "You're vapor, you're Spam!" and "Do I look like Mother Teresa? If I did, I probably wouldn't mind talking to the geek squad." She has two or three friends exactly like her, and together they dominate their realm—the American high school as it appears in recent teen movies. They are like wicked princesses, who enjoy the misery of their subjects. Her coronation, of course, is the senior prom, when she expects to be voted "most popular" by her class. But, though she may be popular, she is certainly not liked, so her power is something of a mystery. She is beautiful and rich, yet in the end she is preëminent because . . . she is preëminent, a position she works to maintain with Joan Crawford-like tenacity. Everyone is afraid of her; that's why she's popular.

She has a male counterpart. He's usually a football player, muscular but dumb, with a face like a beer mug and only two ways of speaking—in a conspiratorial whisper, to a friend; or in a drill sergeant's sudden bellow. If her weapon is the snub, his is the lame but infuriating prank—the can of Sprite emptied into a knapsack, or something sticky, creamy, or adhesive deposited in a locker. Sprawling and dull in class, he comes alive in the halls and in the cafeteria. He hurls people against lockers; he spits, pours, and sprays; he has a projectile relationship with food. As the crown prince, he claims the best-looking girl for himself, though in a perverse display of power he may invite an outsider or an awkward girl — a "dog" — to the prom, setting her up for some special humiliation. When we first see him, he is riding high, and virtually the entire school colludes in his tyranny. No authority figure — no teacher or administrator — dares correct him.

Thus the villains of the recent high-school movies. Not every American teen movie has these two characters, and not every social queen or jock shares all the attributes I've mentioned. (Occasionally, a handsome, dark-haired athlete can be converted to sweetness and light.) But as genre figures these two types are hugely familiar; that is, they are a common memory, a collective trauma, or at least a social and erotic fantasy. Such movies of the past year [1999] as *Disturbing Behavior*, *She's All That*, *Ten Things I Hate about You*, and *Never Been Kissed* depend on them as stock figures. And they may have been figures in the minds of the Littleton shooters, Eric Harris and Dylan Klebold, who imagined they were living in a school like the one in so many of these movies — a poisonous system of status, snobbery, and exclusion.

Do genre films reflect reality? Or are they merely a set of conventions that refer to other films? Obviously, they wouldn't survive if they didn't provide emotional satisfaction to the people who make them and to the audiences who watch them. A half century ago, we didn't need to see ten Westerns a year in order to learn that the West got settled. We needed to see it settled ten times a year in order to provide ourselves with the emotional gratifications of righteous violence. By drawing his gun only when he was provoked, and in the service of the good, the classic Western hero transformed the gross tangibles of the expansionist drive (land, cattle, gold) into a principle of moral order. The gangster, by contrast, is a figure of chaos, a modern, urban person, and in the critic Robert Warshow's formulation he functions as a discordant element in an American society devoted to a compulsively "positive" outlook. When the gangster dies, he cleanses viewers of their own negative feelings.

High-school movies are also full of unease and odd, mixed-up emotions. 5 They may be flimsy in conception; they may be shot in lollipop colors, garlanded with mediocre pop scores, and cast with goofy young actors trying to make an impression. Yet this most commercial and frivolous of genres harbors a grievance against the world. It's a very specific grievance, quite different from the restless anger of such fifties adolescent-rebellion movies as *The Wild One*, in which someone asks Marlon Brando's biker "What are you rebelling against?" and the biker replies "What have you got?" The fifties teen outlaw was against anything that adults considered sacred. But no movie teenager now revolts against adult authority, for the simple reason that adults have no authority. Teachers are rarely more than a minimal, exasperated presence, administrators get turned into a joke, and parents are either absent or distantly benevolent. It's a teen world, bounded by school, mall, and car, with occasional moments set in the fast-food outlets where the kids work, or in the kids' upstairs bedrooms, with their pinups and rack stereo systems. The enemy is not authority; the enemy is other teens and the social system that they impose on one another.

The bad feeling in these movies may strike grownups as peculiar. After all, from a distance American kids appear to be having it easy these days. The teen audience is facing a healthy job market; at home, their parents are stuffing the den with computers and the garage with a bulky S.U.V. But most teens aren't thinking about the future job market. Lost in the eternal swoon of late adolescence, they're thinking about their identity, their friends, and their clothes. Adolescence is the present-tense moment in American life. Identity and status are fluid: abrupt, devastating reversals are always possible. (In a teen movie, a guy who swallows a bucket of cafeteria coleslaw can make himself a hero in an instant.) In these movies, accordingly, the senior prom is the equivalent of the shoot-out at the O.K. Corral; it's the moment when one's worth as a human being is settled at last. In the rather pedestrian new comedy *Never Been Kissed*, Drew Barrymore, as a twenty-five-year-old newspaper reporter, goes back to high school pretending to be a student, and immediately falls into her old, humiliating pattern of trying to impress the good-looking rich kids. Helplessly, she pushes for approval, and even gets herself chosen prom queen before finally coming to her senses. She finds it nearly impossible to let go.

Genre films dramatize not what happens but how things feel — the emotional coloring of memory. They fix subjectivity into fable. At actual schools, there is no unitary system of status; there are many groups to be a part of, many places to excel (or fail to excel), many avenues of escape and self-definition. And often the movies, too, revel in the arcana of high-school cliques. In last summer's *Disturbing Behavior*, a veteran student lays out the cafeteria ethnography for a newcomer: Motorheads, Blue Ribbons, Skaters, Micro-geeks ("drug of choice: Stephen Hawking's *A Brief History of Time* and a cup of jasmine tea on Saturday night"). Subjectively, though, the social system in *Disturbing Behavior* (a high-school version of *The Stepford Wives*) and in the other movies still feels coercive and claustrophobic: humiliation is the most vivid emotion of youth, so in memory it becomes the norm.

The movies try to turn the tables. The kids who cannot be the beautiful ones, or make out with them, or avoid being insulted by them — these are the heroes of the teen movies, the third in the trio of character types. The female outsider is usually an intellectual or an artist. (She scribbles in a diary, she draws or paints.) Physically awkward, she walks like a seal crossing a beach, and is prone to drop her books and dither in terror when she stands before a handsome boy. Her clothes, which ignore mall fashion, scandalize the social queens. Like them, she has a tongue, but she's tart and grammatical, tending toward feminist pungency and precise diction. She may mask her sense of vulnerability with sarcasm or with Plathian rue (she's stuck in the bell jar), but even when she lashes out she can't hide her craving for acceptance.

The male outsider, her friend, is usually a mass of stuttering or giggling sexual gloom: he wears shapeless clothes; he has an undeveloped body, either stringy or shrimpy; he's sometimes a Jew (in these movies, still the generic outsider). He's also brilliant, but in a morose, preoccupied way that suggests masturbatory absorption in some arcane system of knowledge. In a few special cases, the outsider is not a loser but a disengaged hipster, either saintly or satanic. (Christian Slater has played this role a couple of times.) This outsider wears black and keeps his hair long, and he knows how to please women. He sees through everything, so he's ironic by temperament and genuinely indifferent to the opinion of others — a natural aristocrat, who transcends the school's contemptible status system. There are whimsical variations on the outsider figure, too. In the recent *Rushmore*, an obnoxious teen hero, Max Fischer (Jason Schwartzman), runs the entire school: he can't pass his courses but he's a dynamo at extracurricular activities, with a knack for staging extraordinary events. He's a con man, a fund-raiser, an entrepreneur — in other words, a contemporary artist.

In fact, the entire genre, which combines self-pity and ultimate vindication, might be called "Portrait of the Filmmaker as a Young Nerd." Who can doubt where Hollywood's twitchy, nearsighted writers and directors ranked — or feared they ranked — on the high-school totem pole? They are still angry, though occasionally the target of their resentment goes beyond the jocks and cheerleaders of their youth. Consider this anomaly: the young actors and models on the covers of half the magazines published in this country, the shirtless men with chests like burnished shields, the girls smiling, glowing, tweezed, full-lipped, full-breasted (but not too full), and with skin so honeyed that it seems lacquered — these are the physical ideals embodied by the villains of the teen movies. The social queens and jocks, using their looks to dominate others, represent an American barbarism of beauty. Isn't it possible that the detestation of them in teen movies is a veiled strike at the entire abs-hair advertising culture, with its unobtainable glories of perfection? A critic of consumerism might even see a spark of revolt in these movies. But only a spark.

My guess is that these films arise from remembered hurts which then get recast in symbolic form. For instance, a surprising number of the outsider heroes have no mother. Mom has died or run off with another man; her child, only half loved, is ill equipped for the emotional pressures of school. The motherless child, of course, is a shrewd commercial ploy that makes a direct appeal to the members of the audience, many of whom may feel like outsiders, too, and unloved, or not loved enough, or victims of some prejudice or exclusion. But the motherless child also has powers, and will someday be a success, an artist, a screenwriter. It's the wound and the bow all over again, in cargo pants.

As the female nerd attracts the attention of the handsomest boy in the senior class, the teen movie turns into a myth of social reversal — a Cinderella fantasy. Initially, his interest in her may be part of a stunt or a trick: he is leading her on, perhaps at the urging of his queenly girlfriend. But his gaze lights her up, and we see how attractive she really is. Will she fulfill the eternal American fantasy that you can vault up the class system by removing your specs? She wants her prince, and by degrees she wins him over, not just with her looks but with her superior nature, her essential goodness. In the male version of the Cinderella trip, a few years go by, and a pale little nerd (we see him at a reunion) has become rich. All that poking around with chemicals paid off. Max Fischer, of *Rushmore*, can't miss being richer than Warhol.

So the teen movie is wildly ambivalent. It may attack the consumerist ethos that produces winners and losers, but in the end it confirms what it is attacking. The girls need the seal of approval conferred by the converted jocks; the nerds need money and a girl. Perhaps it's no surprise that the outsiders can be validated only by the people who ostracized them. But let's not be too schematic: the outsider who joins the system also modifies it, opens it up to the creative power of social mobility, makes it bend and laugh, and perhaps this turn of events is not so different from the way things work in the real world, where merit and achievement stand a good chance of trumping appearance. The irony of the Littleton shootings is that Klebold and Harris, who were both proficient computer heads, seemed to have forgotten how the plot turns out. If they had held on for a few years they might have been working at a hip software company, or have started their own business, while the jocks who oppressed them would probably have wound up selling insurance or used cars. That's the one unquestionable social truth the teen movies reflect: geeks rule.

There is, of course, a menacing subgenre, in which the desire for revenge turns bloody. Thirty-one years ago, Lindsay Anderson's semi-surrealistic *If . . .* was set in an oppressive, class-ridden English boarding school, where a group of rebellious students drive the school population out into a courtyard and open fire on them with machine guns. In Brian De Palma's 1976 masterpiece *Carrie*, the pale, repressed heroine, played by Sissy Spacek, is courted at last by a handsome boy but gets violated — doused with pig's blood — just as she is named prom queen. Stunned but far from powerless, Carrie uses her telekinetic powers to set the room afire and burn down the school. *Carrie* is the primal school movie, so wildly lurid and funny that it exploded the clichés of the genre before the genre was quite set: the heroine may be a wrathful avenger, but the movie, based on a Stephen King book, was clearly a grinning-gargoyle fantasy. So, at first, was *Heathers*, in which Christian Slater's satanic outsider turns out to be a true devil. He and his girlfriend (played by a very young Winona Ryder) begin gleefully knocking off the rich, nasty girls and the jocks, in ways so patently absurd that their revenge seems a mere wicked dream. I think it's unlikely that these movies had a direct effect on the actions of the Littleton shooters, but the two boys would surely have recognized the emotional world of *Heathers* and *Disturbing Behavior* as their own. It's a place where feelings of victimization join fantasy, and you experience the social élites as so powerful that you must either become them or kill them.

But enough. It's possible to make teen movies that go beyond these fixed 15 polarities — insider and outsider, blond-bitch queen and hunch-shouldered nerd.

In Amy Heckerling's 1995 comedy *Clueless*, the big blonde played by Alicia Silverstone is a Rodeo Drive clotheshorse who is nonetheless possessed of extraordinary virtue. Freely dispensing advice and help, she's almost ironically good—a designing goddess with a cell phone. The movie offers a sun-shiny satire of Beverly Hills affluence, which it sees as both absurdly swollen and generous in spirit. The most original of the teen comedies, *Clueless* casts away self-pity. So does *Romy and Michele's High School Reunion* (1997), in which two gabby, lovable friends, played by Mira Sorvino and Lisa Kudrow, review the banalities of their high-school experience so knowingly that they might be criticizing the teen-movie genre itself. And easily the best American film of the year so far is Alexander Payne's *Election*, a high-school movie that inhabits a different aesthetic and moral world altogether from the rest of these pictures. *Election* shreds everyone's fantasies and illusions in a vision of high school that is bleak but supremely just. The movie's villain, an over-achieving girl (Reese Witherspoon) who runs for class president, turns out to be its covert heroine, or, at least, its most poignant character. A cross between Pat and Dick Nixon, she's a lower-middle-class striver who works like crazy and never wins anyone's love. Even when she's on top, she feels excluded. Her loneliness is produced not by malicious cliques but by her own implacable will, a condition of the spirit that may be as comical and tragic as it is mysterious. *Election* escapes all the clichés; it graduates into art.

READING THE TEXT

1. Describe in your own words the stereotypical male and female villains common in teen movies.
2. What does Denby mean by the comment, "Adolescence is the present-tense moment in American life" (para. 6)?
3. What sort of characters are typically the heroes in teen films, in Denby's view?
4. In what ways does a Cinderella fantasy inform teen films?
5. What is the "menacing subgenre" (para. 14) of teen movies?

READING THE SIGNS

1. Using Denby's description of stock character types in teen movies as your critical framework, analyze the characters in a current teen TV program, such as *Friday Night Lights* or *One Tree Hill*. Do you see the same conventions at work? How do you account for any differences you might see?
2. In class, brainstorm a list of current teen films. Then, using the list as evidence, write an essay in which you assess the validity of Denby's claim: "The enemy [in teen films] is not authority; the enemy is other teens and the social system that they impose on one another" (para. 5).
3. Rent a video or DVD of *American Beauty*, and write an essay in which you argue whether it can be categorized as a teen film, at least as Denby defines the genre.

4. **CONNECTING TEXTS**   Denby asks, "Do genre films reflect reality? Or are they merely a set of conventions that refer to other films?" (para. 4). Write an essay in which you propose your own response to these questions, using as evidence your high school experience and specific teen films. To develop your ideas, consult Tom Moore, "Movie Fantasy vs. Classroom Reality" (p. 402).

TOM MOORE

Movie Fantasy vs. Classroom Reality

Hollywood loves heroic teachers, educators like Jaime Escalante in Stand and Deliver *and Erin Gruwell in* Freedom Writers. *But as Tom Moore explains in this personal look at the challenges of teaching today, such movies can be both misleading and "dangerous," promoting what Moore calls the "Myth of the Great Teacher." What public school teachers need, Moore argues, are safe and adequately supplied classrooms, not Hollywood portrayals of teacher superheroes who are more missionary than professional, "eager to give up their lives and comfort for the benefit of others, without need of compensation." Tom Moore is a tenth-grade history teacher at a public school in the Bronx.*

In the past year or so, I have seen Matthew Perry drink 30 cartons of milk, Ted Danson explain the difference between a rook and a pawn, and Hilary Swank remind us that white teachers still can't dance or jive talk. In other words, I have been confronted by distorted images of my own profession — teaching. Teaching the post-desegregation urban poor, to be precise.

Although my friends and family (who should all know better) continue to ask me whether my job is similar to these movies, I find it hard to recognize myself or my students in them.

So what are these films really about? And what do they teach us about teachers? Are we heroes, villains, bullies, fools? The time has come to set the class record straight.

At the beginning of Ms. Swank's recent movie, *Freedom Writers*, her character, a teacher named Erin Gruwell, walks into her Long Beach, Calif., classroom, and the camera pans across the room to show us what we are supposed to believe is a terribly shabby learning environment. Any experienced educator will have already noted that not only does she have the right key to get into the room but, unlike the seventh-grade science teacher in my current school, she has a door to put the key into. The worst thing about Ms. Gruwell's classroom seems to be graffiti on the desks, and crooked blinds.

Freedom Writers, 2007.

I felt like shouting, Hey, at least you have blinds! My first classroom didn't, 5
but it did have a family of pigeons living next to the window, whose pane was
a cracked piece of plastic. During the winter, snowflakes blew in. The pigeons
competed with the mice and cockroaches for the students' attention.

This is not to say that all schools in poor neighborhoods are a shambles,
or that teaching in a real school is impossible. In fact, thousands of teachers in
New York City somehow manage to teach every day, many of them in schools
more underfinanced and chaotic than anything you've seen in movies or on
television (except perhaps the most recent season of *The Wire*).

Ms. Gruwell's students might backtalk, but first they listen to what she says.
And when she raises her inflection just slightly, the class falls silent. Many of
the students I've known won't sit down unless they're repeatedly asked to
(maybe not even then), and they don't listen just because the teacher is
speaking; even "good teachers" are occasionally drowned out by the din of 30
students simultaneously using language that would easily earn a movie an
NC-17 rating.

When a fight breaks out during an English lesson, Ms. Gruwell steps into
the hallway and a security guard immediately materializes to break it up. Forget the teacher — this guy was the hero of the movie for me.

If I were to step out into the hallway during a fight, the only people I'd see
would be some students who'd heard there was a fight in my room. I'd be
wasting my time waiting for a security guard. The handful of guards where I
work are responsible for the safety of five floors, six exits, two yards, and four
schools jammed into my building.

Although personal safety is at the top of both teachers' and students' lists ₁₀ of grievances, the people in charge of real schools don't take it as seriously as the people in charge of movie schools seem to.

The great misconception of these films is not that actual schools are more chaotic and decrepit — many schools in poor neighborhoods are clean and orderly yet still don't have enough teachers or money for supplies. No, the most dangerous message such films promote is that what schools really need are heroes. This is the Myth of the Great Teacher.

Films like *Freedom Writers* portray teachers more as missionaries than professionals, eager to give up their lives and comfort for the benefit of others, without need of compensation. Ms. Gruwell sacrifices money, time, and even her marriage for her job.

Her behavior is not represented as obsessive or self-destructive, but driven — necessary, even. She is forced into making these sacrifices by the aggressive neglect of the school's administrators, who won't even let her take books from the bookroom. The film applauds Ms. Gruwell's dedication, but also implies that she has no other choice. In order to be a good teacher, she has to be a hero.

Freedom Writers, like all teacher movies this side of *The Prime of Miss Jean Brodie*, is presented as a celebration of teaching, but its message is that poor students only need love, idealism, and martyrdom.

I won't argue the need for more of the first two, but I'm always surprised ₁₅ at how, once a Ms. Gruwell wins over a class with clowning, tears, rewards, and motivational speeches, there is nothing these kids can't do. It is as if all the previously insurmountable obstacles students face could be erased by a 10-minute pep talk or a fancy dinner. This trivializes not only the difficulties many real students must overcome, but also the hard-earned skill and tireless effort real teachers must use to help those students succeed.

Every year young people enter the teaching profession hoping to emulate the teachers they've seen in films. (Maybe in the back of my mind I felt that I could be an inspiring teacher like Howard Hesseman or Gabe Kaplan.[1]) But when you're confronted with the reality of teaching not just one class of misunderstood teenagers (the common television and movie conceit), but four or five every day, and dealing with parents, administrators, mentors, grades, attendance records, standardized tests, and individual education plans for children with learning disabilities, not to mention multiple daily lesson plans — all without being able to count on the support of your superiors — it becomes harder to measure up to the heroic movie teacher you thought you might be.

It's no surprise that half the teachers in poor urban schools, like Erin Gruwell herself, quit within five years. (Ms. Gruwell now heads a foundation.)

I don't expect to be thought of as a hero for doing my job. I do expect to be respected, supported, trusted, and paid. And while I don't anticipate that

---

[1]Hesseman starred in *Head of the Class*, Kaplan in *Welcome Back Kotter*.

Hollywood will stop producing movies about gold-hearted mavericks who play by their own rules and show the suits how to get the job done, I do hope that these movies will be kept in perspective.

While no one believes that hospitals are really like *ER* or that doctors are anything like *House*, no one blames doctors for the failure of the healthcare system. From No Child Left Behind to City Hall, teachers are accused of being incompetent and underqualified, while their appeals for better and safer workplaces are systematically ignored.

Every day teachers are blamed for what the system they're just a part of 20 doesn't provide: safe, adequately staffed schools with the highest expectations for all students. But that's not something one maverick teacher, no matter how idealistic, perky, or self-sacrificing, can accomplish.

READING THE TEXT

1. Define in your own words what Moore means by the "Myth of the Great Teacher" (para. 11).

2. What are some of the real-life consequences of the idealized depiction of teachers in films, according to Moore?

3. Moore grounds his argument in his own experience as a teacher. What impact does that information have on your response to his essay?

READING THE SIGNS

1. Watch another film that takes an inner-city school as its primary setting, such as *Stand and Deliver*, and analyze it using Moore's critique of such films as a critical framework. To what extent does it present the teacher as a romanticized hero, as Moore describes? Alternately, watch a film set in a suburban school, such as *The Breakfast Club* or *American Pie*. Do you see the same pattern of mythic teacher? If not, try to account for the difference.

2. **CONNECTING TEXTS**   Both Moore and Aeon J. Skoble ("*Forrest Gump*: A Subversive Movie," p. 410) find cinematic depictions that distort reality to be dangerous. Write an argumentative response to this position, supporting, refuting, or complicating it.

3. In class, form teams and debate the question of whether the idealized school films that Moore critiques are dangerous, on the one hand, or inspirational, on the other. Use the class debate as a source of counterarguments for your own essay that addresses this question.

4. In class, brainstorm films that depict college life, then create a list of stock characters and motifs. What roles do students tend to play, and what is their attitude toward schoolwork? How are professors characterized? What is the physical setting's appearance? Using Moore's essay as a model, write an analysis of the representation of college life, basing your essay on several specific examples of films.

MICHAEL PARENTI
Class and Virtue

In 1993, a movie called Indecent Proposal *presented a story in which a billionaire offers a newly poor middle-class woman a million dollars if she'll sleep with him for one night. In Michael Parenti's terms, what was really indecent about the movie was the way it showed the woman falling in love with the billionaire, thus making a romance out of a class outrage. But the movie could get away with it, partly because Hollywood has always conditioned audiences to root for the ruling classes and to ignore the inequities of class privilege. In this selection from* Make-Believe Media: The Politics of Entertainment *(1992), Parenti argues that Hollywood has long been in the business of representing the interests of the ruling classes. Whether it is forgiving the classist behavior in* Pretty Woman *or glamorizing the lives of the wealthy, Hollywood makes sure its audiences leave the theater thinking you can't be too rich. Parenti is a writer who lectures widely at university campuses around the country. His publications include* Power and the Powerless *(1978),* Inventing Reality: The Politics of the News Media *(1986),* Against Empire *(1995),* Dirty Truths *(1996),* America Besieged *(1998),* The Culture Struggle *(2006), and* Democracy for the Few *(2007).*

Class and Virtue

The entertainment media present working people not only as unlettered and uncouth but also as less desirable and less moral than other people. Conversely, virtue is more likely to be ascribed to those characters whose speech and appearance are soundly middle- or upper-middle class.

Even a simple adventure story like *Treasure Island* (1934, 1950, 1972) manifests this implicit class perspective. There are two groups of acquisitive persons searching for a lost treasure. One, headed by a squire, has money enough to hire a ship and crew. The other, led by the rascal Long John Silver, has no money — so they sign up as part of the crew. The narrative implicitly assumes from the beginning that the squire has a moral claim to the treasure, while Long John Silver's gang does not. After all, it is the squire who puts up the venture capital for the ship. Having no investment in the undertaking other than their labor, Long John and his men, by definition, will be "stealing" the treasure, while the squire will be "discovering" it.

To be sure, there are other differences. Long John's men are cutthroats. The squire is not. Yet, one wonders if the difference between a bad pirate and a good squire is itself not preeminently a matter of having the right amount of disposable income. The squire is no less acquisitive than the conspirators. He just does with money what they must achieve with cutlasses. The squire and his associates dress in fine clothes, speak an educated diction, and drink brandy. Long John and his men dress slovenly, speak in guttural accents, and drink rum. From these indications alone, the viewer knows who are the good guys and who are the bad. Virtue is visually measured by one's approximation to proper class appearances.

Sometimes class contrasts are juxtaposed within one person, as in *The Three Faces of Eve* (1957), a movie about a woman who suffers from multiple personalities. When we first meet Eve (Joanne Woodward), she is a disturbed, strongly repressed, puritanically religious person, who speaks with a rural, poor-Southern accent. Her second personality is that of a wild, flirtatious woman who also speaks with a rural, poor-Southern accent. After much treatment by her psychiatrist, she is cured of these schizoid personalities and emerges with a healthy third one, the real Eve, a poised, self-possessed, pleasant woman. What is intriguing is that she now speaks with a cultivated, affluent, Smith College accent, free of any low-income regionalism or ruralism, much like Joanne Woodward herself. This transformation in class style and speech is used to indicate mental health without any awareness of the class bias thusly expressed.

Mental health is also the question in *A Woman under the Influence* (1974), the story of a disturbed woman who is married to a hard-hat husband. He cannot handle — and inadvertently contributes to — her emotional deterioration. She is victimized by a spouse who is nothing more than an insensitive, working-class bull in a china shop. One comes away convinced that every unstable woman needs a kinder, gentler, and above all, more *middle-class* hubby if she wishes to avoid a mental crack-up.

Class prototypes abound in the 1980s television series *The A-Team*. In each episode, a Vietnam-era commando unit helps an underdog, be it a Latino immigrant or a disabled veteran, by vanquishing some menacing force such as organized crime, a business competitor, or corrupt government officials. As always with the make-believe media, the A-Team does good work on an individualized rather than collectively organized basis, helping particular victims by thwarting particular villains. The A-Team's leaders are two white males of privileged background. The lowest ranking members of the team, who do none of the thinking nor the leading, are working-class palookas. They show they are good with their hands, both by punching out the bad guys and by doing the maintenance work on the team's flying vehicles and cars. One of them, "B.A." (bad ass), played by the African American Mr. T., is visceral, tough, and purposely bad-mannered toward those he doesn't like. He projects an image of crudeness and ignorance and is associated with the physical side of things. In sum, the team has a brain (the intelligent white leaders) and a body with its simpler physical functions (the working-class characters), a hierarchy that corresponds to the social structure itself.[1]

[1]Gina Marchetti, "Class, Ideology and Commercial Television: An Analysis of *The A-Team*," *Journal of Film and Video* 39, Spring 1987, pp. 19–28.

Sometimes class bigotry is interwoven with gender bigotry, as in *Pretty Woman* (1990). A dreamboat millionaire corporate raider finds himself all alone for an extended stay in Hollywood (his girlfriend is unwilling to join him), so he quickly recruits a beautiful prostitute as his playmate of the month. She is paid three thousand dollars a week to wait around his super-posh hotel penthouse ready to perform the usual services and accompany him to business dinners at top restaurants. As prostitution goes, it is a dream gig. But there is one cloud on the horizon. She is low-class. She doesn't know which fork to use at those CEO power feasts, and she's bothersomely fidgety, wears tacky clothes, chews gum, and, y'know, doesn't talk so good. But with some tips from the hotel manager, she proves to be a veritable Eliza Doolittle in her class metamorphosis. She dresses in proper attire, sticks the gum away forever, and starts picking the right utensils at dinner. She also figures out how to speak a little more like Joanne Woodward without the benefit of a multiple personality syndrome, and she develops the capacity to sit in a poised, wordless, empty-headed fashion, every inch the expensive female ornament.

She is still a prostitute but a classy one. It is enough of a distinction for the handsome young corporate raider. Having liked her because she was charmingly cheap, he now loves her all the more because she has real polish and is a more suitable companion. So suitable that he decides to do the right thing by her: set her up in an apartment so he can make regular visits at regular prices. But now she wants the better things in life, like marriage, a nice house, and, above all, a different occupation, one that would allow her to use less of herself. She is furious at him for treating her like, well, a prostitute. She decides to give up her profession and get a high-school diploma so that she might make a better life for herself — perhaps as a filing clerk or receptionist or some other of the entry-level jobs awaiting young women with high school diplomas.[2]

After the usual girl-breaks-off-with-boy scenes, the millionaire prince returns. It seems he can't concentrate on making money without her. He even abandons his cutthroat schemes and enters into a less lucrative but supposedly more productive, caring business venture with a struggling old-time entrepreneur. The bad capitalist is transformed into a good capitalist. He then carries off his ex-prostitute for a lifetime of bliss. The moral is a familiar one, updated for post-Reagan yuppiedom: A woman can escape from economic and gender exploitation by winning the love and career advantages offered by a rich male. Sexual allure goes only so far unless it develops a material base and becomes a class act.[3]

READING THE TEXT

1. According to Parenti, what characteristics are typically attributed to working-class and upper-class film characters?

[2]See the excellent review by Lydia Sargent, *Z Magazine*, April 1990, pp. 43–45.
[3]Ibid.

2. How does Parenti see the relationship between "class bigotry" and "gender bigotry" (para. 7) in *Pretty Woman*?

3. What relationship does Parenti see between mental health and class values in films?

READING THE SIGNS

1. Rent a DVD of *Wall Street* or *There Will Be Blood*, and analyze the class issues that the movie raises. Alternately, watch an episode of *The Apprentice*, and perform the same sort of analysis.

2. Do you agree with Parenti's interpretation of *Pretty Woman*? Write an argumentative essay in which you defend, challenge, or complicate his reading of the film.

3. **CONNECTING TEXTS**   Read or reread Aaron Devor's "Gender Role Behaviors and Attitudes" (p. 567). How would Devor explain the gender bigotry that Parenti finds in *Pretty Woman*?

4. Rent the 1954 film *On the Waterfront* and watch it with your class. How are labor unions and working-class characters portrayed in that film? Does the film display the class bigotry that Parenti describes?

5. **CONNECTING TEXTS**   Read Michael Omi's "In Living Color: Race and American Culture" (p. 655). Then write an essay in which you create a category of cinematic racial bigotry that corresponds to Parenti's two categories of class and gender bigotry. What films have you seen that illustrate your new category?

AEON J. SKOBLE
Forrest Gump: *A Subversive Movie*

A perennially popular Hollywood icon in many parts of the country,
Forrest Gump *would appear to be anything but a subversive movie. A
southern rural innocent with a talent for football, ping-pong, corporate
capitalism, military heroism, and pithy aphorisms, ole Forrest is certainly no Michael Moore. But as Aeon J. Skoble argues in this film review
that originally appeared in* The Freeman *in 1995, his story is "unambiguously antiintellectual, and subversive in its power to make one enjoy
it anyway." The trouble, for Skoble, is that Forrest does not appear to
earn any of his achievements in life — including a successful business
career that can be attributed to the good fortune that his shrimp boat
just happens to be the only one in the fleet that is "left intact after a hurricane." Whatever happened to good old personal enterprise and initiative, Skoble wonders. Aeon J. Skoble teaches philosophy at the University
of Central Arkansas.*

A Hollywood movie is like a box of chocolates: it tastes good, but it's really
bad for you. Of course, it isn't bad to eat a small amount of chocolates; likewise, not all Hollywood movies are bad for you. But after seeing *Forrest Gump*,
the charming aphorism that was central to the film ("My momma says that
life is like a box of chocolates") metamorphosed in my mind in this fashion. I
caught myself enjoying the film while realizing that I was enjoying something
unhealthy. As time passes since the film's release, it not only grows in popularity, but the associated merchandising increases. One can buy collections of
Gump sayings, tins of "BubbaGump Shrimp," Gump t-shirts, and so on. As the
film's appeal grows, so does the need to examine its message. The movie won
six Academy Awards (including Best Picture and Best Actor for Tom Hanks) —
so the film is clearly an influential social and cultural item.

Before criticizing the film's vices, I first praise its virtues. It is very well
executed. The by-now-well-known special effects that make Tom Hanks appear in old newsreel footage and play championship ping-pong, and that
make Gary Sinise's legs disappear, are outstanding. Hanks adds another finely
crafted performance to his resume. The film's narrative structure is tight, and
strikes the right balance between serious drama and light comedy. Indeed it is
truly an excellent film, in the sense that it tells a story well and conveys a
message. But the values portrayed, like a box of chocolates, are too sweet and
not entirely healthy.

This film is subversive. It doesn't subvert the Constitution of the United
States, but rather it is subversive of the human spirit. This claim will come as a
spoilsport voice-in-the-wilderness to the many who are trumpeting the film as

410

Tom Hanks as the title character in *Forrest Gump,* 1994.

a triumph of the human spirit. *Forrest Gump* is unambiguously anti-intellectual, and subversive in its power to make one enjoy it anyway.

The naive innocent who prospers in a wicked world is an old standard, and a very seductive device. Even Wagner, after announcing the coming of the superman, found refuge in this archetype in *Parsifal.* Here Hanks portrays a man with an I.Q. of 75 who becomes a national hero and a millionaire through . . . what? The purity of his spirit and the grace of God, or something like that. The message is that intelligence, indeed ability generally, is unimportant. Providence will watch out for those without gifts, therefore everyone is gifted. Some of Gump's achievements are due to his being a nice guy. He wins the Medal of Honor for rescuing his company because he is unwilling to abandon his friend. But he becomes a great runner by divine fiat. His shrimp boat survives a hurricane. He becomes a champion ping-pong player simply by not taking his eye off the ball. It's not quite like *Being There*, to which this film is frequently compared. The character Chance in *Being There* receives his fortunes through the misinterpretations of his idiocy by a sick society, hence the satire. *Gump* is satire-free. But the film makes us ask, what's the point of having talents if talent is unimportant?

The film portrays talent not only as unimportant, but literally as an im- 5 pediment to the good life. Consider the intelligent and intellectually curious Jenny. She is an independent thinker who questions authority and social standards, and who is experimental and adventuresome. Jenny is punished with a series of abusive relationships; she finally dies of AIDS. I've rarely seen a characterization so hostile to inquiry. It is revealed that the roots of her eagerness to question authority and think independently are having a dysfunctional family. So an evil force drives her to independence of thought, and the results of the consequent life are drugs, abusive boyfriends, and AIDS.

The contrast with Gump is clear enough. His mother loves him. He always does as he's told, and prospers as a result. In response to the command, "just run," he is able to score touchdowns. This trait also makes him a natural for military service. To be sure that we do not interpret all this as anti-Christian, Jenny, despite her sins, is forgiven and rewarded in the afterlife in the form of a perfect child conceived with Forrest. When Lieutenant Dan loses his legs, he rails against God, but when he makes his peace with God, he walks again.

Gump's mother, played well by Sally Field, keeps admonishing him that he's no different from everyone else. The film insistently advances the idea that there is "nothing wrong with being stupid." Honestly, could there be a more dangerous message to promulgate? It should go without saying that people should not be cruel to those with less ability, and we may indeed wish to care for those incapable of taking care of themselves. But is there really *nothing wrong* with being less able, less smart? This is not about self-esteem for the disabled, it is actually about radical leveling, a devaluation of ability. How is Gump no different from anyone else? This claim seems innocent enough, and might follow from the idea that those of less ability are still humans deserving respect and dignity. But of course he is different — he is a great runner, a football star, a war hero, a millionaire. Most of us are none of those things. And he has a 75 I.Q., which most of us don't have either. So he is different from most people. By downplaying that, the critique of ability is made more subtle.

There's no secret to excelling, the film tells us, just do what you're supposed to do.

In real life, people must earn their achievements. Of course, some steal and some inherit, but in general, people have to achieve through their efforts. At any rate, that would be a better lesson to teach, I submit, than that if you just blunder about, God or fate will take care of everything. No ability is necessary to make a fortune in the shrimp business — just make sure that your shrimp boat is the only one left intact after a hurricane. No ability is necessary to be a football hero — just run until they tell you to stop running.

Of course, all these bits in the film are funny and charming. I laughed and 10 smiled on cue with everyone else. Hanks is always likable, and Gump especially so, being the sweet innocent that he is. But I am disturbed that a film could attain such popularity and appeal by advancing the view that ability is not an important component of business success and that critical thinking is not essential to achieve prosperity. Despite Gump being a successful businessman, the film thereby conveys a tacit anti-commerce message.

The anti-commerce message derives from the more general anti-ability theme. If intelligence and analytic ability are not portrayed in the most popular film of the year as important components of the good life, an intellectually lazy generation will tacitly take this as support for their disengaged condition.

The majority of teens cannot locate the Pacific Ocean on a world map, or the Civil War by half-century. The fastest growing trend in criminal defense is diminished responsibility. Books are out, MTV is in. Critical reasoning is on the decline not only as a skill but as a desideratum. And now comes *Forrest Gump* to reinforce the idea that we are not responsible for our destinies, that intelligence is not important, that independent thought will be punished. That's dangerous.

Forrest Gump is not a bad film, but it is subversive. The film is subversive because it is so well made and enjoyable. I enjoyed it even as I was aware of the unhealthiness of its message. If anyone tells me that it was a good film, or that he or she enjoyed it, I won't disagree. But if anyone tells me that it was profound or that it changed his life, I shall weep.

READING THE TEXT

1. In your own words, explain how Skoble uses the word "subversive" in this essay.

2. What evidence does Skoble advance to demonstrate his belief that *Forrest Gump* is "unhealthy" and "subversive" (paras. 1 and 3)?

3. Explain how, in Skoble's view, *Forrest Gump* can send an "anti-commerce message" (para. 10).

4. Chart the occasions when Skoble employs the rhetorical strategy of *concession*. How does that affect your response to his essay?

READING THE SIGNS

1. In an argumentative essay, respond to Skoble's underlying belief that "the idea that there is 'nothing wrong with being stupid'" sends a "dangerous message" (para. 7).

2. **CONNECTING TEXTS**   Forrest Gump is clearly the protagonist of the film, but is he a hero? If he is, how do you define his heroism; if you think he is not, why not? To develop your response to this question, read or reread Robert B. Ray's "The Thematic Paradigm" (p. 342), Linda Seger's "Creating the Myth" (p. 356), and Virginia Postrel's "Superhero Worship" (p. 351).

3. Watch another film that features a low-IQ protagonist, such as *Rainman*. Analyze the role that intelligence — or lack thereof — plays in the film. Does the film ultimately champion mediocrity or sentimentalize disability at the expense of intelligence and ability, as Skoble finds in *Forrest Gump*? Or does it send a different message about the value of intelligence and ability altogether?

4. Skoble focuses on *Forrest Gump*'s dismissal of intelligence and ability as the reason he sees the movie as problematic, but he does not discuss other aspects of the movie, such as its portrayal of ethnicity and gender. Write an essay in which you analyze that portrayal, focusing on particular characters and scenes.

VIVIAN C. SOBCHACK
The Postmorbid Condition

When Bonnie and Clyde *shuddered to a spectacular conclusion with the slow-motion machine-gunning of its main characters, the point was that in a society plagued by random and senseless violence Hollywood had a responsibility to make some kind of meaning out of it. But when Quentin Tarantino uses senseless violence for comic effect, the point, Vivian C. Sobchack argues in this essay originally published in* Screening Violence, *is that there is no point at all, or rather, that the human body has lost its meaning in contemporary life and has become little more than a machine whose destruction is on a par with an exploding automobile. Offering a profound and disturbing explanation for the popularity of movies like* Pulp Fiction *and* Natural Born Killers, *Sobchack reveals the forces behind the dehumanization of Hollywood violence. A professor and associate dean in the School of Theater, Film, and Television at UCLA, Sobchack is the author of* Screening Space: The American Science Fiction Film *(1987),* Address of the Eye: A Phenomenology of Film Experience *(1991),* The Persistence of History: Cinema, Television, and the Modern Event *(1995),* Meta-Morphing: Visual Transformation and the Culture of Quick-Change *(1999), and* Carnal Thoughts: Embodiment and Moving Image Culture *(2004).*

In an essay I wrote twenty-five years ago, I argued that screen violence in American films of the late 1960s and early 1970s was new and formally different from earlier "classical" Hollywood representations of violence. This new interest in violence and its new formal treatment not only literally satisfied an intensified cultural desire for "close-up" knowledge about the material fragility of bodies, but also — and more important — made increasingly senseless violence in the "civil" sphere sensible and meaningful by stylizing and aestheticizing it, thus bringing intelligibility and order to both the individual and social body's increasingly random and chaotic destruction. Indeed, I argued that random and senseless violence was elevated to meaning in these then "new" movies, its "transcendence" achieved not only by being up there on the screen, but also through long lingering gazes at carnage and ballets of slow motion that conferred on violence a benediction and the grace of a cinematic "caress."

Today, most American films have more interest in the presence of violence than in its meaning. There are very few attempts to confer order or perform a benediction upon the random and senseless death, the body riddled with bullets, the laying waste of human flesh. (The application of such order, benediction, and transcendental purpose is, perhaps, one of the explicit achievements of Steven Spielberg's high-tech but emotionally anachronistic

414

Saving Private Ryan, and it is no accident that its context is a morally intelligible World War II.) Indeed, in today's films (and whatever happened started happening sometime in the 1980s), there is no transcendence of "senseless" violence: It just *is*. Thus, the camera no longer caresses it or transforms it into something with more significance than its given instance. Instead of caressing violence, the cinema has become increasingly *careless* about it: either merely nonchalant or deeply lacking in care. Unlike medical melodramas, those films that describe violent bodily destruction evoke no tears in the face of mortality and evidence no concern for the fragility of flesh. Samuel L. Jackson's violent role and religious monologues in Quentin Tarantino's *Pulp Fiction* notwithstanding, we see no grace or benediction attached to violence. Indeed, its very intensity seems diminished: we need noise and constant stimulation and quantity to make up for a lack of significant meaning.

Perhaps this change in attitude and treatment of violence is a function of our increasingly *technologized* view of the body and flesh. We see this view dramatized outside the theater in the practices and fantasies of "maintenance" and "repair" represented by the "fitness center" and cosmetic surgery. Inside the theater, we see it dramatized in the "special effects" allowed by new technological developments and in an increasingly hyperbolic and quantified treatment of violence and bodily damage that is as much about "more" as it is about violence. It seems to me that this quantitative move to "more" in relation to violence — more blood, more gore, more characters (they're really not people) blown up or blown away — began with the contemporary horror film, with "slasher" and "splatter" films that hyperbolized violence and its victims in terms of quantity rather than through exaggerations of form. Furthermore, unlike in the "New Hollywood" films of the late 1960s and 1970s (here one thinks of Peckinpah or Penn), excessive violence in these "low" genre films, while eliciting screams, also elicited laughter, too much becoming, indeed, "too much": incredible, a "gross-out," so "outrageous" and "over the top" that ironic reflexivity set in (for both films and audiences) and the mounting gore and dead bodies became expected — and funny. (Here *Scream* and its sequel are recent examples.)

This heightened sense of reflexivity and irony that emerges from quantities of violence, from "more," is not necessarily progressive nor does it lead to a "moral" agenda or a critique of violence. (By virtue of its excesses and its emphasis on quantity and despite his intention, Oliver Stone's *Natural Born Killers* is quite ambiguous in this regard.) Indeed, in its present moment, this heightened reflexivity and irony merely leads to a heightened sense of representation: that is, care for the film as experience and text, perhaps, but a lack of any real concern for the bodies blown away (or up) upon the screen. In recent "splatter" films, in Tarantino films like *Reservoir Dogs* and *Pulp Fiction*, and in quite a number of action thrillers, bodies are more carelessly *squandered* than carefully stylized. Except, of course, insofar as excess, and hyperbole, itself constitutes stylization. Thus, most of the violence we see on screen today suggests Grand Guignol rather than Jacobean tragedy. However, in our current cultural moment, tiredly described as "postmodern" but filled with new forms of violence like "road rage," the exaggeration and escalating quantification of violence and gore are a great deal less transgressive than they were — and a great deal more absurd. Thus, Tarantino has said on various occasions that he doesn't take violence "very seriously" and describes it as "funny" and "outrageous."

This hyperbolic escalation and quantification of violence also has become quite common to the action picture and thriller, where the body count only exceeds the number of explosions and neither matters very much to anyone: here violence and the laying waste of bodies seems more "naturalized": that is, it regularly functions to fill up screen space and time in lieu of narrative complexity, and to make the central character look good by "virtue" of his mere survival (see, for example, *Payback*). Again, there seems no moral agenda or critique of violence here — only wisecracks and devaluation uttered out of the sides of a Bruce Willis–type mouth. Indeed, here is the careless violence and laconic commentary of comic books (where the panels crackle with zaps and bullets and explosions and the body count is all that counts).

On a more progressive note, I suppose it is possible to see this new excessive and careless treatment of violence on screen as a satiric form of what Russian literary theorist Mikhail Bakhtin has called "grotesque realism." That is, excessive representations of the body and its messier aspects might be read as containing critical and liberatory potential — this, not only because certain social taboos are broken, but also because these excessive representations of the grotesquerie of being embodied are less "allegorical" and fantastic than they are exaggerations of concrete conditions in the culture of which they are a part. In this regard, and particularly relevant to "indie" crime dramas and the action thriller (a good deal of it science-fictional), much has been written recently about the "crisis of the body" and a related "crisis of masculinity." Both of these crises are no longer of the *Bonnie and Clyde* or *Wild Bunch* variety: They are far too much inflected and informed by *technological* concerns and confusions and a new sense of the body as a technology, altered by technology, enabled by technology, and disabled by technology. Indeed, along with the Fordist assembly line and its increasing production of bodies consumed as they are violently "wasted" on the screen, comes the production of bodies as both technological *subjects* and *subjected to* technology: enhanced and extended, but also extinguished by Uzis, bombs, whatever the latest in firepower. Thus, we might argue, the excessive violence we see on the screen, the carelessness and devaluation of mere human flesh, is both a recognition of the high-tech, powerful, and uncontrollable subjects we (men, mostly) have become through technology — and an expression of the increasing frustration and rage at what seems a lack of agency and effectiveness as we have become increasingly controlled by and subject to technology.

This new quantification of and carelessness toward violence on the screen also points to other aspects of our contemporary cultural context. We have come both a long way and not so far from the assassins, serial killers, and madmen who made their mass presence visibly felt in the late 1960s and

John Travolta and Samuel L. Jackson are buddies and professional killers in *Pulp Fiction*, which takes a cartoonish approach to graphic violence, using a character's exploding head as the basis for an extended comic sketch.

early 1970s. They, like the bodies wasted on the screen, have proliferated at an increasingly faster and decreasingly surprising rate. They and the violence that accompanies them are now a common, omnipresent phenomenon of daily life—so much so that, to an unprecedented degree, we are resigned to living with them in what has become an increasingly uncivil society. "Senseless" and "random" violence pervades our lives and is barely remarkable or specific any longer—and while "road rage" and little children killed by stray bullets of gang bangers do elicit a moral *frisson*, for the most part we live in and suspect the absence of a moral context in this decade of extreme relativism. Violence, like "shit," happens—worth merely a bumper sticker nod that reconciles it with a general sense of helplessness (rather than despair).

No longer elevated through balletic treatment on narrative purpose, violence on the screen is sensed—indeed, appreciated—as senseless. But then so is life under the extremity of such technologized and uncivil conditions. Indeed, what has been called the "postmodern condition" might be more accurately thought of as the "postmorbid condition." There's a kind of meta-sensibility at work here: life, death, and the movies are a "joke" or an "illusion" and everyone's in on it. Violence on the screen and in the culture is not related to a moral context, but to a proliferation of images, texts, and spectacle. And, given that we cannot contain or stop this careless proliferation, violence and death both on the street and in *Pulp Fiction* become reduced to the practical—and solvable—problem of cleanup.

Pain, too, drops out of the picture. The spasmodic twitching that ends *Bonnie and Clyde* has become truly lifeless. The bodies now subjected to violence are just "dummies": multiple surfaces devoid of subjectivity and gravity, "straw men," if you will. "Wasting" them doesn't mean much. Hence, the power (both appealing and off-putting) of those few films that remind us that bodily damage hurts, that violently wasting lives has grave consequences. Hence, the immense popularity of *Saving Private Ryan*, a movie in which the massive quantity of graphic physical damage and the violent "squandering" of bodies and lives is "redeemed" to social purpose and meaning, its senselessness made sensible by its (re)insertion in a clearly defined (and clearly past) moral context. Hence, also, the popular neglect of *Beloved* or *Affliction*, movies in which violence is represented "close up" as singularly felt: graphically linked to bodily pain and its destruction of subjectivity. In these films, violence is not dramatized quantitatively or technologically and thus becomes extremely difficult to watch: that is, even though an image, understood by one's own flesh as *real*.

I am not sure how to end this particular postmortem on my original essay. 10 I still can't watch the eyeball being slit in *Un Chien Andalou*. But, as with *Straw Dogs* and *The French Connection*, I could and did watch all the violence in *Pulp Fiction*. Nonetheless, there's been a qualitative change as well as a quantitative one: while I watched those earlier violent films compulsively, with some real need to know what they showed me, I watch the excesses of the current ones casually, aware they won't show me anything real that I don't already know.

Reading the Text

1. What was Sobchack's argument in the essay on screen violence that she wrote now thirty years ago?

2. How does contemporary screen violence differ from that of the sixties and seventies, according to Sobchack?

3. What does Sobchack mean by referring to "our increasingly *technologized* view of the body" (para. 3)?

4. In what ways do irony and satire contribute to the desensitizing of contemporary audiences in the face of extreme screen violence, according to Sobchack?

Reading the Signs

1. Media violence is one of the most controversial issues in current cultural politics. Referring to a selection of current violent films, write an essay arguing for or against the proposition that screen violence desensitizes viewers to the realities of violence.

2. Write an argumentative essay in which you support, refute, or modify Sobchak's claim that films such as *Beloved* failed to attract audiences because, unlike most violent films, they depict pain and violence as *"real"* (para. 9). To develop support for your position, interview acquaintances who watched such a film and those who chose to avoid it.

3. In class, stage a debate on the proposition that the film industry should restrict its depictions of violence.

4. Watch *The Hills Have Eyes*, *High Tension*, *300*, or another violent film. To what extent does the film illustrate Sobchak's view that "we need noise and constant stimulation and quantity to make up for a lack of significant meaning" (para. 2)?

5. **CONNECTING TEXTS**   Watch *Boyz N the Hood* and analyze it semiotically. Use your observations as evidence for an essay in which you argue whether the film's violence is desensitizing, as Sobchak argues is the case for most contemporary films, or whether it strikes the viewer as "real." How does the film's genre — gangster film — affect your interpretation of the violence? To develop your ideas, read or reread Todd Boyd's "So You Wanna Be a Gangsta?" (p. 375).

6. In class, discuss the reasons many moviegoers find violence to be entertaining. What does the prevalence of violence say about modern American cultural values?

Reservoir Dogs

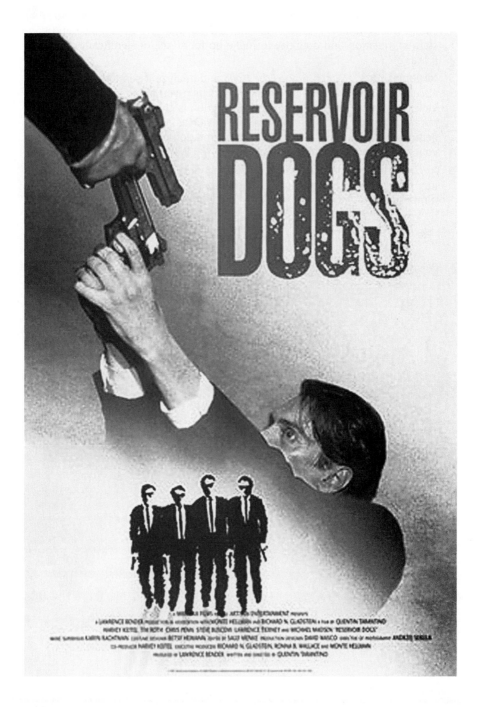

READING THE SIGNS

1. Based on the *Reservoir Dogs* poster, how would you characterize the subject matter of this film? Does the poster make you want to see the film? Why or why not? What is the effect of including one figure with part of his face obscured and the other with only his arm visible? What does the image of the four men at the bottom suggest? How do you interpret the splattering on the letters of the title?

2. Who, in your opinion, is the intended audience for this film? Why? What elements in this poster appeal to that intended audience?

3. A version of this poster includes the caption, "Four perfect killers. One perfect crime. Now all they have to fear is each other." In your opinion, is the ad more or less effective with this added text? Why or why not?

4. If you haven't seen *Reservoir Dogs*, rent it (though be warned that parts are quite violent). How well does this poster represent the film? If you had to design your own poster for this movie, what would it look like?

YOU-TOPIAN DREAMS

*MySpace, YourSpace, and the
Semiotics of Web 2.0*

Whose Space?

The first chat rooms were rather primitive places. Austere, you might say, with no images, music, or decoration of any kind, just plain text boxes where ghostly words materialized as if from out of nowhere. Visiting such places was a bit of an adventure then, a pioneering voyage into cyberspace and the uncharted expanses of the electronic frontier.

Things are a lot more cozy now in the world of online social networking. Homelike. In fact, if you happen to have a MySpace or Facebook page of your own — and the odds are overwhelming that you do — you've probably been furnishing it as if it was your own room for some years now, complete with images of not just your favorite people and entertainers but with your favorite music and videos as well.

All of which raises an interesting question: Is your personal space on the Internet a private or a public place, a space that completely belongs to you or only appears to through some strange illusion on the World Wide Web? To put this another way, when you are online socializing with others, are you "inside" or "outside," at home in your private territory or out on the streets in some sort of vast cybermall?

The paradoxical answer is that you are both inside *and* outside. On the one hand, you can set up and visit your MySpace or Facebook page within the confines of your home, but on the other hand, MySpace and Facebook are public sites on the Internet that anyone can visit at any time. Your page not only does not belong to you but others can access it and make comments within it or show it to other people without your knowledge. Even you are

423

likely to visit your page when you are somewhere else — at school or work or virtually anywhere thanks to your iPhone, laptop, or whatever multitasking communications device you own.

This inside/outside, public/private space challenges all of the traditional rules that govern three-dimensional space, codes that define the way we move and that tell us, quite literally, where we may and may not go and what we may do when we get there. Consider an ordinary street, a clearly marked "outside" or public space. You may walk down it, but you need to stick to the side (or sidewalk if there is one), and it's best to stay to the right to avoid oncoming foot traffic. If there are private houses on the street, you may approach the front door, but you're not supposed to cut through the yard, and you're certainly not allowed to enter without permission. You may enter the public space of a store, shopping center, or post office, but you might need to pay to enter a museum, and you need to pass through a security checkpoint if you are entering a courthouse or an airline terminal.

Now consider your own personal space: There, you set the rules. You determine who enters it and what can be done there. You might actually write out the rules that govern your space (as in posting a PLEASE REMOVE YOUR SHOES or NO SMOKING sign), but there is a greater likelihood of enforcing them if you are personally present. Indeed, the most basic personal space rule of all is that no unauthorized person should be in it when you are absent.

The spaces of everyday life, both public and private, are, in short, packed with complex codes that we violate or ignore at our peril. These codes all originate in the way that human beings define their territories. A *territory* is a space that has been given meaning through having been claimed by an individual or group of individuals. Unclaimed, unmarked space is socially meaningless, but put up a building or a fence, and the uncircumscribed landscape becomes a bounded territory, a human habitat with its own rules for permitted and unpermitted behavior. Anyone unaware of those rules can't survive for long in human society.

But what sort of territory is a social networking site, and what rules govern it? In a sense, it is a place where its users are all hosts and guests simultaneously, with the rules being accordingly quite confusing. A host is hospitable; a guest is polite and follows the host's guidance. But with no one on the Net

---

Exploring the Signs of Web 2.0

If you have a MySpace or Facebook page, describe it in your journal and discuss why you designed it as you did. What signs did you choose to communicate your identity, and why? Did you deliberately avoid including some signs? If so, why?

being entirely host or entirely guest, things can easily go wrong. You don't insult people in their own homes, but flaming on the Internet occurs all too often and has inspired a whole vocabulary for the "trolls" who break the as-yet-unwritten rules of good netiquette. Indeed, many sites and forums where people gather to socialize and communicate are often described as being like the Wild West — at one time a new and wide open place known for its lack of clear rules of conduct and the way in which it challenged traditional concep-tions of social space.

Thus, the new technologies that have created the virtual social spaces of the Internet are redefining our entire experience of space and the ways in which we interact with others within it, and this offers an exciting new subject for semiotic analysis.

From Being Lonely in a Crowd to Crowded while Alone

In previous editions of *Signs of Life in the U.S.A.*, we included a chapter on the traditional three-dimensional spaces of the built environment. But while such spaces still form the central core of our spatial experience, the emergent social spaces of virtual reality have prompted us to substitute this chapter to offer you a new field in which to exercise your semiotic intuitions and inter-pretations. So new is this field that no one can fully understand its effects on our behavior, but since you belong to the first generation to have grown up within this new social space, you are already well equipped to come to terms with it.

So let's begin with the reasons you may have set up your own social net-working page. Perhaps it was to promote your band or some other product or service. Realtors, construction firms, and even politicians use MySpace and Facebook for promotional purposes, and plenty of books are available to show you how to exploit these sites to promote yourself. Indeed, we can make an important association between social networking sites and traditional adver-tising media: Both are used to promote something that is for sale in some way. But at the same time there is a crucial difference insofar as the self-advertising you do on MySpace or Facebook is free: You do not have to pur-chase it and you can control its content and its dissemination. This difference semiotically connects social networking sites to the overall reversal of media control that we discuss in the general introduction to this book: the way in which an increasing proportion of media content is delivered from the bottom up rather than from the top down.

But it is more likely that your social networking page is much more per-sonal than that, that it is simply your place where you can share your life with others, especially your friends. If that is the case, your page can be associated with any place where you socialize with others, whether at school or work, or at more casual sites such as shopping malls, clubs, or your friends' homes. What both kinds of space have in common are the personal desires of those

---

Discussing the Signs of Web 2.0

Critics of online social networking sites have expressed concern that excessive online networking will diminish participants' ability to socialize normally in face-to-face environments. In class, discuss the legitimacy of this concern, drawing upon your personal experiences with social networking.

---

who frequent them to be popular, to have lots of friends. This is one reason MySpace and Facebook, in spite of their adult users, are still overwhelmingly sites for the young, for youth is that period of life when popularity and having lots of friends are particularly desirous.

But there is a vital difference between the social space of an online networking site and the traditional sites where people gather to socialize. While it is an obvious difference, it bears close attention: While online socializing may supplement face-to-face encounters, it can be conducted in complete isolation as well. No one else need be present for you to interact with others. This is also true of socializing by telephone, letters, and e-mail, of course, but social networking sites greatly magnify the paradoxical experience of being in a crowded space, while alone, online.

The immense popularity of sites like MySpace and such competitors as Facebook and Friendster demonstrates the enormous appeal of this ability to socialize without face-to-face contact. Part of this appeal obviously lies in its 24/7 immediacy: You can interact with your friends at any time and in any place. Part of it also may lie in the way one can broadcast just how popular one is by literally enumerating the number of one's online "friends," many of whom you may have never met before. But there is also the way that online socializing enables you to *control* the entire situation, literally enabling you to turn your friends on and off at will without giving offense (kind of hard to do that when someone is dragging you someplace where you don't really want to go), and, perhaps more importantly, allowing you to appear exactly the way you want to appear to others on your personal Web page.

Web 2 Lets U Be U

One thing you can be on MySpace is a star. After all, your MySpace page is your personal public relations center. There you can present yourself much as *People* presents celebrities, complete with the details of your latest romance and, if you happen to be in a band, your latest CD. YouTube, for its part, lets you be your own auteur, a budding Woody Allen who both directs and stars in your own productions. And in some cases, you can make yourself a real star, of sorts, if your YouTube creation is a hit and is spun out from computer to computer in a viral explosion of shared content. And you can even create your own online "television program" if enough people are attracted to your site. Hey, it worked for *lonelygirl15*.

A casual survey of the videos posted to YouTube alone reveals the enormous appeal of Web-based self-expression to a generation that has been raised in an entertainment culture within which media fame and celebrity have been presented as being among life's highest goals — if not *the* highest goal. Though most contributors will never see more than a smattering of responses to their videos, the fact remains that anyone can at least make a bid for glory on YouTube, and everyone has the chance to communicate with a worldwide audience.

In this sense, Web 2.0 bears a striking resemblance to reality television (indeed, YouTube has its roots in *America's Funniest Home Videos*), for in RTV, too, ordinary people can be transformed into overnight celebrities. But there is a crucial difference in that you don't have to audition for anything on the Internet and you can be your own impresario. No one need ever see you in person; no casting director stands in your way; no one can judge you except on the precise terms that you establish yourself. And all this is possible because of the profoundly different nature of self-presentation on the Internet. Indeed, one could call it a proxemic revolution.

Proxemics, a field loosely related to semiotics, is the study of the ways in which we communicate with others in face-to-face situations, including such factors as body language, facial expression, and tone of voice. But because body language, facial expression, and tone of voice are absent on the Internet, social interaction on the Web requires a very different approach. The visual cues of face-to-face interaction are so important to us in ordinary communication that we often simulate such cues online with photographs and videos of ourselves, MP3s, and, more simply, with emoticons, creating a whole new kind of communication.

The fact that we can control exactly what information we present to others while online offers us a freedom — even a fantasy freedom — to be whatever we want to be with others: more attractive, better natured, just plain more cool than we may really be. Virtual worlds like Second Life and SimCity demonstrate this freedom clearly, with an unusual proportion of participants looking awfully glamorous. This, too, is an important phenomenon to consider in our interpretation of the cultural significance of social networking sites.

So consider for a moment traditional media involving video images and projection screens. Both television and cinema, whether through programming, movies, or advertising, have always broadcast images of beautiful people living more romantic or adventurous lives than most people, in reality, can ever experience. This dream machine has provided generations of viewers with vicarious images of fantasy lives, and, through advertising, has promised the accomplishment of such lives if you only purchase the advertised product.

Reading Web 2.0 on the Net

YouTube allows users to create their own "television" content, yet the site is filled with content taken from other sources, such as television clips, concert footage, and the like. Conduct a survey of YouTube content to estimate the ratio of user-created content to postings of professional performers. Analyze and interpret your results semiotically. What are the implications of your findings for the bottom-up versus top-down debate over Web 2.0 "democracy"?

But the enthusiasm with which hundreds of millions of people from around the world have embraced the opportunities that interactive media have offered — from role-playing games like World of Warcraft to simulated reality sites like Second Life — demonstrates a craving to actually live the sort of lives that the traditional media have, either directly or indirectly, indicated that we *should* be living.

This is, paradoxically, why so many game-playing and world-building sites have striven, and continue to strive, to be more and more realistic, for if the fantasy is to be truly effective, it must feel real. Indeed, such virtual worlds as The Sims enable you not only to imagine your own life as you'd like to live it but to rehearse it — that is, building a simulated life, under the conditions of a game that can be played and replayed with ever-improving skill until you get everything just right — offering the ultimate fantasy of control. Because while real life is a messy affair, whose beginning and end we have no control over at all and whose middle can be played through only once without correction or second chance, simulated life fixes all that. Online, we can, in effect, play God with our own lives.

You-Topian Communities

Perhaps this ability to control our online lives in ways that real life forbids accounts for the almost utopian feel of many online communities. A utopia — from the Greek *ou* (no)-*topos* (place) — is an idealized vision of a perfected world, a world almost always set in some unattainable future. And with the real world becoming increasingly dystopian (or anti-utopian), plagued by social and political alienation, the virtual communities of the Net can be particularly attractive. Indeed, as the traditional village-based neighborhoods of the preindustrial era break down in the face of rampant urbanization (and are further disrupted by the geographical instabilities impelled by the modern job market), Web 2.0 technology offers a virtual village experience whose vast popularity attests to a deep desire for community in an alienated world.

If you have ever participated in an online community, even one that was not originally designed to be a community at all (like the astronomy and bird-watching forums that the authors of this book participate in), then you are likely to have experienced the surprisingly warm friendships that can spring up among people whose only connections are cybernetic. Commonly, these online friendships lead to actual face-to-face meetings wherein the participants can be pleasantly surprised by just how much their friends are like their online personas. Sometimes such meetings lead to lifelong friendships, even romances and marriages. And sometimes they lead to trouble. Bad trouble.

To Catch a Predator

For quite some time the world of MySpace and the many sites like it attracted little attention beyond the tens of millions of young people who frequented them. But, as with so many utopias, there was a snake in the garden all along. In this case, it was online predation. With gruesome tales of pedophiles trolling MySpace and taking advantage of the vast amounts of personal information that children naively post about themselves, parents and politicians began to take notice — hostile notice — demanding that protections be built into the system.

The fact that predators do use the Internet to lure unsuspecting victims (a tendency that even launched a reality television program called *To Catch a Predator*) gives a good deal of credence to the sort of backlash that has compelled MySpace to demonstrate its dedication to preventing online predation. But with so much of the appeal of the MySpace world lying in its independence from adult supervision — indeed standing as a kind of youthful utopia free from parental and other adult authority — the attempt to regulate popular social networking sites has been controversial. Many defenders of an unregulated MySpace point out that telephones and phone books have been used for predatory purposes too — and they aren't regulated — so they argue that the call for new restrictions reflects less a real danger than a typical adult reaction to the unfamiliar social mores of their children. After all, rock 'n' roll was once much mistrusted in the fifties, as were the freewheeling fashions and attitudes of the sixties. It is possible, then, that much of the suspicion directed at the social networking world is really a generational rather than a personal safety issue.

But then again, maybe not. Many naive users do post a huge amount of personal information on the Internet, often complete with provocative photographs and cell-phone numbers. What information about yourself have you posted — or elected not to post? Why? What do your younger siblings post? Do their choices ever concern you?

Top Down Meets Bottom Up

One thing, however, is certain. In a mass consumer society, even entirely grassroots phenomena can be appropriated by corporate elites if they become popular enough. Accordingly, it did not take long for the top-down component of society to recognize the potential profits to be made in social networking sites. Rupert Murdoch's purchase of MySpace, Google's acquisition of YouTube, and Microsoft's stake in Facebook are not acts of charity. With so many people visiting such sites, the revenue potential from advertising is enormous, and Web 2.0 capitalism has been quick to recognize the parallel between freely provided commercial television and freely provided Web sites where the users create their own content. Thus, side-by-side with that high school band that is using its MySpace page to promote its career is a marketer using MySpace (or Facebook or another such site) to promote an existing company's products or services, either directly on the site itself or indirectly by culling user information for targeted advertising. Top down meets bottom up in a site that is at once democratic and hierarchical, your space and corporate space.

So once again, we have a paradox. The democratic, user-generated spaces of the Internet are simultaneously revolutionary and business as usual. Users create their own content and actively build their own virtual spaces, but they do so on sites that are owned by huge corporations and that are maintained for profit. In its famous 1984 Super Bowl commercial that introduced the Macintosh, Apple Computer promised that the future was going to belong to the people, not to rigid, profit-seeking corporate powers. Web 1.0 and Web 2.0 were both built, in large part, by people who believed in this vision of a sort of anticorporate utopia. But when you are in the coils of a cultural mythology, it is very difficult to get out. Corporate capitalism and the ideology of the free market constitute the economic mythology of American culture. Thus, it is not surprising that the builders of the brave new worlds of the Internet have often gotten very rich and now sit on the boards of the companies that bought their once-modest and profitless Web creations. So, is Web 2.0 the portal to a new society, or just another way to make money, or the harbinger of a new social consciousness, or the same old hypercapitalist scramble in a glittering new package?

Yes.

The Readings

Henry Jenkins begins the chapter with an analysis of that emerging phenomenon that he calls "convergence culture," a world where old media and new come together to connect people in ways that they have never been connected before. Steven Johnson and Brian Williams follow with a paired set of opinion pieces on the democratic vistas of the Web 2.0 world: One's for it and the other isn't so sure. Next, Ted Friedman explores The Sims, a life-simulation game that has been especially attractive to women gamers. Alana Semuels's newspaper feature on the second thoughts that marketers are having about Second Life shows how even the best-laid plans of mice and marketers can go awry, while Clive Thompson reveals the astonishing economic powerhouses that are being generated by the players of such online games as EverQuest. A. B. Harris's call for a more mature, less adolescent, profile for online gamers is next, followed by Joanne Cavanaugh Simpson's bird's-eye view of the new consciousness of contemporary college students, which suggests that convergence culture may be getting out of hand. David Teten and Scott Allen conclude the chapter with a legal analysis of online free-speech rights: Hint, if you're a troll, you're out of luck.

HENRY JENKINS
Convergence Culture

You're watching American Idol *and a text message comes in informing you that AmericanIdolWatch.com reports that the guy who sings like Alvin the Chipmunk is outpolling your favorite contestant, so you log in to check the report and then phone in your vote to* American Idol *before "Alvin" can move on to the next level. Though it may seem pretty routine to you, your movement from television screen, to text-messaging, to the Internet, to cell phone constitutes a newly emerging mixture of old and new media that Henry Jenkins calls "convergence culture." In this selection from his book of the same title, Jenkins describes the new multi-mixed media and their possible effects on society and human consciousness. A self-avowed fan of the new media, Jenkins is the founder and director of MIT's Comparative Media Studies Program and author of numerous books, including* Textual Poachers: Television Fans and Participatory Culture *(1998),* Convergence Culture: Where Old and New Media Collide *(2006), and* The Wow Climax: Tracing the Emotional Impact of Popular Culture *(2007).*

Worship at the Altar of Convergence
— Slogan, the New Orleans Media Experience (2003)

The story circulated in the fall of 2001: Dino Ignacio, a Filipino-American high school student created a Photoshop collage of *Sesame Street*'s (1970) Bert interacting with terrorist leader Osama Bin Laden as part of a series of "Bert is Evil" images he posted on his homepage. Others depicted Bert as a Klansman, cavorting with Adolph Hitler, dressed as the Unabomber, or having sex with Pamela Anderson. It was all in good fun.

In the wake of September 11, a Bangladesh-based publisher scanned the Web for Bin Laden images to print on anti-American signs, posters, and T-shirts. *Sesame Street* is available in Pakistan in a localized format; the Arab world, thus, had no exposure to Bert and Ernie. The publisher may not have recognized Bert, but he must have thought the image was a good likeness of the al-Qaeda leader. The image ended up in a collage of similar images that was printed on thousands of posters and distributed across the Middle East.

CNN reporters recorded the unlikely sight of a mob of angry protestors marching through the streets chanting anti-American slogans and waving signs depicting Bert and Bin Laden (Fig. 1). Representatives from the Children's Television Workshop, creators of the *Sesame Street* series, spotted the CNN footage and threatened to take legal action: "We're outraged that our

FIGURE 1   Ignacio's collage surprisingly appeared in CNN
coverage of anti-American protests following September 11.

characters would be used in this unfortunate and distasteful manner. The people responsible for this should be ashamed of themselves. We are exploring
all legal options to stop this abuse and any similar abuses in the future." It
was not altogether clear whom they planned to sic their intellectual property
attorneys on — the young man who had initially appropriated their images, or
the terrorist supporters who deployed them. Coming full circle, amused fans
produced a number of new sites, linking various *Sesame Street* characters with
terrorists.

From his bedroom, Ignacio sparked an international controversy. His
images crisscrossed the world, sometimes on the backs of commercial media,
sometimes via grassroots media. And, in the end, he inspired his own cult following. As the publicity grew, Ignacio became more concerned and ultimately
decided to dismantle his site: "I feel this has gotten too close to reality. . . .
'Bert Is Evil' and its following has always been contained and distanced from
big media. This issue throws it out in the open."[1] Welcome to convergence
culture, where old and new media collide, where grassroots and corporate
media intersect, where the power of the media producer and the power of the
media consumer interact in unpredictable ways. . . .

By convergence, I mean the flow of content across multiple media plat- 5
forms, the cooperation between multiple media industries, and the migratory
behavior of media audiences who will go almost anywhere in search of the
kinds of entertainment experiences they want. Convergence is a word that

---

[1]Josh Grossberg, "The Bert-Bin Laden Connection?" E Online, October 10, 2001, http://
www.eonline.com/News/Items/0,1,8950,00.html. For a different perspective on Bert and Bin
Laden, see Roy Rosenzweig, "Scarcity or Abundance? Preserving the Past in a Digital Era,"
American Historical Review 108 (June 2003).

manages to describe technological, industrial, cultural, and social changes depending on who's speaking and what they think they are talking about. . . .

In the world of media convergence, every important story gets told, every brand gets sold, and every consumer gets courted across multiple media platforms. Think about the circuits that the Bert is Evil images traveled—from *Sesame Street* through Photoshop to the World Wide Web, from Ignacio's bedroom to a print shop in Bangladesh, from the posters held up by anti-American protestors that are captured by CNN and into the living rooms of people around the world. Some of its circulation depended on corporate strategies, such as the localization of *Sesame Street* or the global coverage of CNN. Some of its circulation depended on tactics of grassroots appropriation, whether in North America or in the Middle East.

This circulation of media content—across different media systems, competing media economies, and national borders—depends heavily on consumers' active participation. I . . . argue here against the idea that convergence should be understood primarily as a technological process bringing together multiple media functions within the same devices. Instead, convergence represents a cultural shift as consumers are encouraged to seek out new information and make connections among dispersed media content. . . .

The term, participatory culture, contrasts with older notions of passive media spectatorship. Rather than talking about media producers and consumers as occupying separate roles, we might now see them as participants who interact with each other according to a new set of rules that none of us fully understands. Not all participants are created equal. Corporations—and even individuals within corporate media—still exert greater power than any individual consumer or even the aggregate of consumers. And some consumers have greater abilities to participate in this emerging culture than others.

Convergence does not occur through media appliances, however sophisticated they may become. Convergence occurs within the brains of individual consumers and through their social interactions with others. Each of us constructs our own personal mythology from bits and fragments of information extracted from the media flow and transformed into resources through which we make sense of our everyday lives. Because there is more information on any given topic than anyone can store in their head, there is an added incentive for us to talk among ourselves about the media we consume. This conversation creates buzz that is increasingly valued by the media industry. Consumption has become a collective process—and that's what [I mean] by collective intelligence, a term coined by French cybertheorist Pierre Lévy. None of us can know everything; each of us knows something; and we can put the pieces together if we pool our resources and combine our skills. Collective intelligence can be seen as an alternative source of media power. We are learning how to use that power through our day-to-day interactions within convergence culture. Right now, we are mostly using this collective power through our recreational life, but soon we will be deploying those skills for more "serious" purposes. . . .

Convergence Talk

Another snapshot of convergence culture at work: In December 2004, a hotly 10 anticipated Bollywood film, *Rok Sako To Rok Lo* (2004), was screened in its entirety to movie buffs in Delhi, Bangalore, Hyderabad, Mumbai, and other parts of India through EDGE-enabled mobile phones with live video streaming facility. This is believed to be the first time that a feature film had been fully accessible via mobile phones.[2] It remains be to be seen how this kind of distribution fits into people's lives. Will it substitute for going to the movies or will people simply use it to sample movies they may want to see at other venues? Who knows?

Over the past several years, many of us have watched as cell phones have become increasingly central to the release strategies of commercial motion pictures around the world, as amateur and professional cell phone movies have competed for prizes in international film festivals, as mobile users have been able to listen in to major concerts, as Japanese novelists serialize their work via instant messenger, and as game players have used mobile devices to compete in augmented and alternative reality games. Some functions will take root; others will fail.

Call me old-fashioned. The other week I wanted to buy a cell phone — you know, to make phone calls. I didn't want a video camera, a still camera, a Web access device, an MP3 player, or a game system. I also wasn't interested in something that could show me movie previews, would have customizable ring tones, or would allow me to read novels. I didn't want the electronic equivalent of a Swiss army knife. When the phone rings, I don't want to have to figure out which button to push. I just wanted a phone. The sales clerks sneered at me; they laughed at me behind my back. I was told by company after mobile company that they don't make single-function phones anymore. Nobody wants them. This was a powerful demonstration of how central mobiles have become to the process of media convergence.

You've probably been hearing a lot about convergence lately. You are going to be hearing even more.

The media industries are undergoing another paradigm shift. It happens from time to time. In the 1990s, rhetoric about a coming digital revolution contained an implicit and often explicit assumption that new media were going to push aside old media, that the Internet was going to displace broadcasting, and that all of this would enable consumers to more easily access media content that was personally meaningful to them. A best-seller in 1990, Nicholas Negroponte's *Being Digital* drew a sharp contrast between "passive old media" and "interactive new media," predicting the collapse of broadcast networks in favor of an era of narrowcasting and niche media on demand: "What will

---

[2]"RSTRL to Premier on Cell Phone," IndiaFM News Bureau, December 6, 2004, http://www.indiafm.com/scoop/04/dec/0612rstrlcell/index.shtml.

FIGURE 2   Microsoft Corp. researchers Larry Zitnick, *left*, and Richard Hughes demonstrate "Lincoln," Windows Mobile 5 mobile phone technology that lets users take a cell-phone photo of a DVD cover and then receive Amazon.com reviews and other multimedia content relating to the DVD back on their phones.

happen to broadcast television over the next five years is so phenomenal that it's difficult to comprehend."[3] At one point, he suggests that no government regulation will be necessary to shatter the media conglomerates: "The monolithic empires of mass media are dissolving into an array of cottage industries. . . . Media barons of today will be grasping to hold onto their centralized empires tomorrow. . . . The combined forces of technology and human nature will ultimately take a stronger hand in plurality than any laws Congress can invent."[4] Sometimes, the new media companies spoke about convergence, but by this term, they seemed to mean that old media would be absorbed fully and completely into the orbit of the emerging technologies. George Gilder, another digital revolutionary, dismissed such claims: "The computer industry is converging with the television industry in the same sense that the automobile converged with the horse, the TV converged with the nickelodeon, the word-processing program converged with the typewriter, the CAD program converged with the drafting board, and digital desktop publishing converged with the linotype machine and the letterpress."[5] For Gilder, the computer had come not to transform mass culture but to destroy it.

[3]Nicholas Negroponte, *Being Digital* (New York: Alfred A. Knopf, 1995), p. 54.
[4]Ibid., pp. 57–58.
[5]George Gilder, "Afterword: The Computer Juggernaut: Life after *Life after Television*," added to the 1994 edition of *Life after Television: The Coming Transformation of Media and American Life* (New York: W. W. Norton), p. 189. The book was originally published in 1990.

The popping of the dot-com bubble threw cold water on this talk of a digi- 15
tal revolution. Now, convergence has reemerged as an important reference
point as old and new media companies try to imagine the future of the entertainment industry. If the digital revolution paradigm presumed that new media
would displace old media, the emerging convergence paradigm assumes that
old and new media will interact in even more complex ways. The digital revolution paradigm claimed that new media were going to change everything.
After the dot-com crash, the tendency were to imagine that new media had
changed nothing. As with so many things about the current media environment, the truth lay somewhere in between. More and more, industry leaders
are returning to convergence as a way of making sense of a moment of disori-
enting change. Convergence is, in that sense, an old concept taking on new
meanings. . . .

The Prophet of Convergence

If *Wired* magazine declared Marshall McLuhan the patron saint of the digital
revolution, we might well describe the late MIT political scientist Ithiel de Sola
Pool as the prophet of media convergence. Pool's *Technologies of Freedom*
(1983) was probably the first book to lay out the concept of convergence as a
force of change within the media industries:

> A process called the "convergence of modes" is blurring the lines be-
> tween media, even between point-to-point communications, such as the
> post, telephone and telegraph, and mass communications, such as the
> press, radio, and television. A single physical means — be it wires, cables
> or airwaves — may carry services that in the past were provided in sepa-
> rate ways. Conversely, a service that was provided in the past by any one
> medium — be it broadcasting, the press, or telephony — can now be pro-
> vided in several different physical ways. So the one-to-one relationship
> that used to exist between a medium and its use is eroding.[6]

Some people today talk about divergence rather than convergence, but Pool
understood that they were two sides of the same phenomenon.

"Once upon a time," Pool explained, "companies that published newspapers, magazines, and books did very little else; their involvement with other
media was slight."[7] Each medium had its own distinctive functions and markets, and each was regulated under different regimes, depending on whether
its character was centralized or decentralized, marked by scarcity or plentitude,
dominated by news or entertainment, and owned by governmental or private
interests. Pool felt that these differences were largely the product of political
choices and preserved through habit rather than any essential characteristic

---

[6]Ithiel de Sola Pool, *Technologies of Freedom: On Free Speech in an Electronic Age* (Cambridge, Mass.: Harvard University Press, 1983), p. 23.
[7]Ibid.

of the various technologies. But he did see some communications technologies as supporting more diversity and a greater degree of participation than others: "Freedom is fostered when the means of communication are dispersed, decentralized, and easily available, as are printing presses or microcomputers. Central control is more likely when the means of communication are concentrated, monopolized, and scarce, as are great networks."[8]

Several forces, however, have begun breaking down the walls separating these different media. New media technologies enabled the same content to flow through many different channels and assume many different forms at the point of reception. Pool was describing what Nicholas Negroponte calls the transformation of "atoms into bytes" or digitization.[9] At the same time, new patterns of cross-media ownership that began in the mid-1980s, during what we can now see as the first phase of a longer process of media concentration, were making it more desirable for companies to distribute content across the various channels rather than within a single media platform. Digitization set the conditions for convergence; corporate conglomerates created its imperative.

Much writing about the so-called digital revolution presumed that the outcome of technological change was more or less inevitable. Pool, on the other hand, predicted a period of prolonged transition, during which the various media systems competed and collaborated, searching for the stability that would always elude them: "Convergence does not mean ultimate stability or unity. It operates as a constant force for unification but always in dynamic tension with change. . . . There is no immutable law of growing convergence; the process of change is more complicated than that."[10]

As Pool predicted, we are in an age of media transition, one marked by tactical decisions and unintended consequences, mixed signals and competing interests, and most of all, unclear directions and unpredictable outcomes.[11] Two decades later, I find myself reexamining some of the core questions Pool raised — about how we maintain the potential of participatory culture in the wake of growing media concentration, about whether the changes brought about by convergence open new opportunities for expression or expand the power of big media. Pool was interested in the impact of convergence on political culture; I am more interested in its impact on popular culture, but . . . the lines between the two have now blurred.

It is beyond my abilities to describe or fully document all of the changes that are occurring. My aim is more modest. I want to describe some of the ways that convergence thinking is reshaping American popular culture and, in particular, the ways it is impacting the relationship between media audiences,

---

[8]Ibid., p. 5.

[9]Negroponte, *Being Digital.*

[10]Pool, *Technologies of Freedom*, pp. 53–54.

[11]For a fuller discussion of the concept of media in transition, see David Thorburn and Henry Jenkins, "Towards an Aesthetics of Transition," in David Thorburn and Henry Jenkins (eds.), *Rethinking Media Change: The Aesthetics of Transition* (Cambridge, Mass.: MIT Press, 2003).

producers, and content. Although this chapter will outline the big picture (insofar as any of us can see it clearly yet), subsequent chapters will examine these changes through a series of case studies focused on specific media franchises and their audiences. My goal is to help ordinary people grasp how convergence is impacting the media they consume and, at the same time, to help industry leaders and policymakers understand consumer perspectives on these changes. . . . This . . . has been challenging because everything seems to be changing at once and there is no vantage point that takes me above the fray. Rather than trying to write from an objective vantage point, I describe . . . what this process looks like from various localized perspectives — advertising executives struggling to reach a changing market, creative artists discovering new ways to tell stories, educators tapping informal learning communities, activists deploying new resources to shape the political future, religious groups contesting the quality of their cultural environs, and, of course, various fan communities who are early adopters and creative users of emerging media.

I can't claim to be a neutral observer in any of this. For one thing, I am not simply a consumer of many of these media products; I am also an active fan. The world of media fandom has been a central theme of my work for almost two decades — an interest that emerges from my own participation within various fan communities as much as it does from my intellectual interests as a media scholar. During that time, I have watched fans move from the invisible margins of popular culture and into the center of current thinking about media production and consumption. For another, through my role as director of the MIT Comparative Media Studies Program, I have been an active participant in discussions among industry insiders and policymakers; I have consulted with some of the companies discussed . . . ; my earlier writings on fan communities and participatory culture have been embraced by business schools and are starting to have some modest impact on the way media companies are relating to their consumers; many of the creative artists and media executives I interviewed are people I would consider friends. At a time when the roles between producers and consumers are shifting, my job allows me to move among different vantage points. . . . Yet, readers should also keep in mind that my engagement with fans and producers alike necessarily colors what I say. My goal here is to document conflicting perspectives on media change rather than to critique them. I don't think we can meaningfully critique convergence until it is more fully understood; yet if the public doesn't get some insights into the discussions that are taking place, they will have little to no input into decisions that will dramatically change their relationship to media.

The Black Box Fallacy

Almost a decade ago, science fiction writer Bruce Sterling established what he calls the Dead Media Project. As his Web site (http://www.deadmedia.org) explains, "The centralized, dinosaurian one-to-many media that roared and trampled through the twentieth century are poorly adapted to the postmodern technological environment."[12] Anticipating that some of these "dinosaurs" were heading to the tar pits, he constructed a shrine to "the media that have died on the barbed wire of technological change." His collection is astounding, including relics like "the phenakistoscope, the telharmonium, the Edison wax cylinder, the stereopticon . . . various species of magic lantern."[13]

Yet, history teaches us that old media never die — and they don't even necessarily fade away. What dies are simply the tools we use to access media content — the 8-track, the Beta tape. These are what media scholars call *delivery technologies*. Most of what Sterling's project lists falls under this category. Delivery technologies become obsolete and get replaced; media, on the other hand, evolve. Recorded sound is the medium. CDs, MP3 files, and 8-track cassettes are delivery technologies.

To define media, let's turn to historian Lisa Gitelman, who offers a model of media that works on two levels: on the first, a medium is a technology that enables communication; on the second, a medium is a set of associated "protocols" or social and cultural practices that have grown up around that technology.[14] Delivery systems are simply and only technologies; media are also cultural systems. Delivery technologies come and go all the time, but media persist as layers within an ever more complicated information and entertainment stratum.

A medium's content may shift (as occurred when television displaced radio as a storytelling medium, freeing radio to become the primary showcase for rock and roll), its audience may change (as occurs when comics move from a mainstream medium in the 1950s to a niche medium today), and its social status may rise or fall (as occurs when theater moves from a popular form to an elite one), but once a medium establishes itself as satisfying some core human demand, it continues to function within the larger system of communication options. Once recorded sound becomes a possibility, we have continued to develop new and improved means of recording and playing back sounds. Printed words did not kill spoken words. Cinema did not kill theater. Television did not kill radio.[15] Each old medium was forced to coexist with the emerging media. That's why convergence seems more plausible as a way of understanding the past several decades of media change than the old digital revolution paradigm had. Old media are not being displaced. Rather, their functions and status are shifted by the introduction of new technologies.

---

[12]Bruce Sterling, "The Dead Media Project: A Modest Proposal and a Public Appeal," http://www.deadmedia.org/modest-proposal.html.

[13]Ibid.

[14]Lisa Gitelman, "Introduction: Media as Historical Subjects," in *Always Already New: Media, History and the Data of Culture* (Cambridge, Mass.: MIT Press, 2006).

[15]For a useful discussion of the recurring idea that new media kill off old media, see Priscilla Coit Murphy, "Books Are Dead, Long Live Books," in David Thorburn and Henry Jenkins (eds.), *Rethinking Media Change: The Aesthetics of Transition* (Cambridge, Mass.: MIT Press, 2003).

The implications of this distinction between media and delivery systems become clearer as Gitelman elaborates on what she means by "protocols." She writes: "Protocols express a huge variety of social, economic, and material relationships. So telephony includes the salutation 'Hello?' (for English speakers, at least) and includes the monthly billing cycle and includes the wires and cables that materially connect our phones. . . . Cinema includes everything from the sprocket holes that run along the sides of film to the widely shared sense of being able to wait and see 'films' at home on video. And protocols are far from static."[16] [I] have less to say about the technological dimensions of media change than about the shifts in the protocols by which we are producing and consuming media.

Much contemporary discourse about convergence starts and ends with what I call the Black Box Fallacy. Sooner or later, the argument goes, all media content is going to flow through a single black box into our living rooms (or, in the mobile scenario, through black boxes we carry around with us everywhere we go). If . . . folks . . . could just figure out which black box will reign supreme, then everyone can make reasonable investments for the future. Part of what makes the black box concept a fallacy is that it reduces media change to technological change and strips aside the cultural levels we are considering here.

I don't know about you, but in my living room, I am seeing more and more black boxes. There are my VCR, my digital cable box, my DVD player, my digital recorder, my sound system, and my two game systems, not to mention a huge mound of videotapes, DVDs and CDs, game cartridges and controllers, sitting atop, laying alongside, toppling over the edge of my television system. (I would definitely qualify as an early adopter, but most American homes now have, or soon will have, their own pile of black boxes.) The perpetual tangle of cords that stands between me and my "home entertainment" center reflects the degree of incompatibility and dysfunction that exists between the various media technologies. And many of my MIT students are lugging around multiple black boxes — their laptops, their cells, their iPods, their Game Boys, their Blackberrys, you name it.

As Cheskin Research explained in a 2002 report, "The old idea of conver- 30 gence was that all devices would converge into one central device that did everything for you (à la the universal remote). What we are now seeing is the hardware diverging while the content converges. . . . Your email needs and expectations are different whether you're at home, work, school, commuting, the airport, etc., and these different devices are designed to suit your needs for accessing content depending on where you are — your situated context."[17] This pull toward more specialized media appliances coexists with a push

---

[16]Gitelman, "Introduction."

[17]Cheskin Research, "Designing Digital Experiences for Youth," *Market Insights Series*, Fall 2002, pp. 8–9.

toward more generic devices. We can see the proliferation of black boxes as symptomatic of a moment of convergence: because no one is sure what kinds of functions should be combined, we are forced to buy a range of specialized and incompatible appliances. On the other end of the spectrum, we may also be forced to deal with an escalation of functions within the same media appliance, functions that decrease the ability of that appliance to serve its original function, and so I can't get a cell phone that is just a phone.

Media convergence is more than simply a technological shift. Convergence alters the relationship between existing technologies, industries, markets, genres, and audiences. Convergence alters the logic by which media industries operate and by which media consumers process news and entertainment. Keep this in mind: convergence refers to a process, not an endpoint. There will be no single black box that controls the flow of media into our homes. Thanks to the proliferation of channels and the portability of new computing and telecommunications technologies, we are entering an era where media will be everywhere. Convergence isn't something that is going to happen one day when we have enough bandwidth or figure out the correct configuration of appliances. Ready or not, we are already living within a convergence culture.

Our cell phones are not simply telecommunications devices; they also allow us to play games, download information from the Internet, and take and send photographs or text messages. Increasingly they allow us to watch previews of new films, download installments of serialized novels, or attend concerts from remote locations. All of this is already happening in northern Europe and Asia. Any of these functions can also be performed using other media appliances. You can listen to the Dixie Chicks through your DVD player, your car radio, your Walkman, your iPod, a Web radio station, or a music cable channel.

Fueling this technological convergence is a shift in patterns of media ownership. Whereas old Hollywood focused on cinema, the new media conglomerates have controlling interests across the entire entertainment industry. Warner Bros. produces film, television, popular music, computer games, Web sites, toys, amusement park rides, books, newspapers, magazines, and comics.

In turn, media convergence impacts the way we consume media. A teenager doing homework may juggle four or five windows, scan the Web, listen to and download MP3 files, chat with friends, word-process a paper, and respond to e-mail, shifting rapidly among tasks. And fans of a popular television series may sample dialogue, summarize episodes, debate subtexts, create original fan fiction, record their own soundtracks, make their own movies — and distribute all of this worldwide via the Internet.

Convergence is taking place within the same appliances, within the same 35 franchise, within the same company, within the brain of the consumer, and within the same fandom. Convergence involves both a change in the way media are produced and a change in the way media are consumed.

The Cultural Logic of Media Convergence

Another snapshot of the future: Anthropologist Mizuko Ito has documented the growing pace of mobile communications among Japanese youth, describing young couples who remain in constant contact with each other throughout the day, thanks to their access to various mobile technologies.[18] They wake up together, work together, eat together, and go to bed together even though they live miles apart and may have face-to-face contact only a few times a month. We might call it telecocooning.

Convergence doesn't just involve commercially produced materials and services traveling along well-regulated and predictable circuits. It doesn't just involve the mobile companies getting together with the film companies to decide when and where we watch a newly released film. It also occurs when people take media in their own hands. Entertainment content isn't the only thing that flows across multiple media platforms. Our lives, relationships, memories, fantasies, desires also flow across media channels. Being a lover or a mommy or a teacher occurs on multiple platforms.[19] Sometimes we tuck our kids into bed at night and other times we Instant Message them from the other side of the globe.

And yet another snapshot: Intoxicated students at a local high school use their cell phones spontaneously to produce their own soft-core porn movie involving topless cheerleaders making out in the locker room. Within hours, the movie is circulating across the school, being downloaded by students and teachers alike and watched between classes on personal media devices.

When people take media into their own hands, the results can be wonderfully creative; they can also be bad news for all involved.

For the foreseeable future, convergence will be a kind of kludge — a jerry- 40 rigged relationship among different media technologies — rather than a fully integrated system. Right now, the cultural shifts, the legal battles, and the economic consolidations that are fueling media convergence are preceding shifts in the technological infrastructure. How those various transitions unfold will determine the balance of power in the next media era.

The American media environment is now being shaped by two seemingly contradictory trends: on the one hand, new media technologies have lowered production and distribution costs, expanded the range of available delivery channels, and enabled consumers to archive, annotate, appropriate, and recirculate media content in powerful new ways. At the same time, there has been alarming concentration of the ownership of mainstream commercial media,

[18]Mizuko Ito, "Mobile Phones, Japanese Youth and the Re-placement of the Social Contract," in Rich Ling and Per Petersen (eds.), *Mobile Communications: Re-Negotiation of the Social Sphere* (forthcoming). http://www.itofisher.com/mito/archives/mobileyouth.pdf.

[19]For a useful illustration of this point, see Henry Jenkins, "Love Online," in Henry Jenkins (ed.), *Fans, Gamers, and Bloggers* (New York: New York University Press, 2005).

with a small handful of multinational media conglomerates dominating all sectors of the entertainment industry. No one seems capable of describing both sets of changes at the same time, let alone show how they impact each other. Some fear that media are out of control, others that it is too controlled. Some see a world without gatekeepers, others a world where gatekeepers have unprecedented power. Again, the truth lies somewhere in between.

Another snapshot: People around the world are affixing stickers showing yellow arrows (http://global.yellowarrow.net) alongside public monuments and factories, beneath highway overpasses, onto lamp posts. The arrows provide numbers others can call to access recorded voice messages — personal annotations on our shared urban landscape. They use it to share a beautiful vista or criticize an irresponsible company. And increasingly, companies are co-opting the system to leave their own advertising pitches.

Convergence, as we can see, is both a top-down corporate-driven process and a bottom-up consumer-driven process. Corporate convergence coexists with grassroots convergence. Media companies are learning how to accelerate the flow of media content across delivery channels to expand revenue opportunities, broaden markets, and reinforce viewer commitments. Consumers are learning how to use these different media technologies to bring the flow of media more fully under their control and to interact with other consumers. The promises of this new media environment raise expectations of a freer flow of ideas and content. Inspired by those ideals, consumers are fighting for the right to participate more fully in their culture. Sometimes, corporate and grassroots convergence reinforce each other, creating closer, more rewarding relations between media producers and consumers. Sometimes, these two forces are at war and those struggles will redefine the face of American popular culture.

Convergence requires media companies to rethink old assumptions about what it means to consume media, assumptions that shape both programming and marketing decisions. If old consumers were assumed to be passive, the new consumers are active. If old consumers were predictable and stayed where you told them to stay, then new consumers are migratory, showing a declining loyalty to networks or media. If old consumers were isolated individuals, the new consumers are more socially connected. If the work of media consumers was once silent and invisible, the new consumers are now noisy and public.

Media producers are responding to these newly empowered consumers in contradictory ways, sometimes encouraging change, sometimes resisting what they see as renegade behavior. And consumers, in turn, are perplexed by what they see as mixed signals about how much and what kinds of participation they can enjoy.

As they undergo this transition, the media companies are not behaving in a monolithic fashion; often, different divisions of the same company are pursuing radically different strategies, reflecting their uncertainty about how to proceed. On the one hand, convergence represents an expanded opportunity for media conglomerates, since content that succeeds in one sector can spread across other platforms. On the other, convergence represents a risk since most of the media fear a fragmentation or erosion of their markets. Each time they move a viewer from television to the Internet, say, there is a risk that the consumer may not return.

Industry insiders use the term "extension" to refer to their efforts to expand the potential markets by moving content across different delivery systems, "synergy" to refer to the economic opportunities represented by their ability to own and control all of those manifestations, and "franchise" to refer to their coordinated effort to brand and market fictional content under these new conditions. Extension, synergy, and franchising are pushing media industries to embrace convergence. . . .

You are now entering convergence culture. It is not a surprise that we are not yet ready to cope with its complexities and contradictions. We need to find ways to negotiate the changes taking place. No one group can set the terms. No one group can control access and participation.

Don't expect the uncertainties surrounding convergence to be resolved anytime soon. We are entering an era of prolonged transition and transformation in the way media operate. Convergence describes the process by which we will sort through these options. There will be no magical black box that puts everything in order again. Media producers will only find their way through their current problems by renegotiating their relationship with their consumers. Audiences, empowered by these new technologies, occupying a space at the intersection between old and new media, are demanding the right to participate within the culture. Producers who fail to make their peace with this new participatory culture will face declining goodwill and diminished revenues. The resulting struggles and compromises will define the public culture of the future.

READING THE TEXT

1. Define in your own words what Henry Jenkins means by "convergence culture," and create a list of media examples that would constitute that culture.
2. What contradictions does Jenkins find in convergence culture?
3. Explain how convergence culture is both top down and bottom up.
4. Describe Jenkins's tone, considering the extent to which it may be neutral or biased. How does it affect your response to the concept of convergence culture?
5. In your own words, define what industry insiders mean by "extension," "synergy," and "franchise," and explain how they apply to the new media.

READING THE SIGNS

1. In your journal, reflect on your own experience with Web 2.0. What participatory media do you engage in, and why? If you avoid such media, what are the reasons behind your behavior?

2. Jenkins's claim that "When people take media into their own hands, the re-sults can be wonderfully creative; they can also be bad news for all involved" (para. 39) presents the two outcomes as equally possible. Write an essay in which you support Jenkins's assumption or weigh the outcomes and decide that one is more likely. If you argue the latter position, what tips the balance in favor of the side you chose?

3. **CONNECTING TEXTS**   Write an essay arguing for or against the proposition that "concentration of the ownership of mainstream commercial media" (para. 41) is turning you-topia into just another way for the corporate world to make money. To develop your ideas, consult Brian Williams's "Enough about You" (p. 449) and Steven Johnson's "It's All about Us" (p. 446).

4. **CONNECTING TEXTS**   A significant proportion of the videos on YouTube and simi-lar sites consists of copyrighted material. Write an essay in which you sup-port, oppose, or modify the position that ordinary copyright law should apply to the use of such material on YouTube. To develop your ideas, consult David Teten and Scott Allen, "Free Speech and Censorship in Online Communities" (p. 473).

CELEBRATING YOU

| STEVEN JOHNSON

It's All about Us

"If Web 1.0 was organized around pages, Web 2.0 is organized around people" such as online "hobbyists, diarists, [and] armchair pundits," Steven Johnson argues in this opinion piece that originally appeared in the Time *issue that named "You" Person of the Year in January 2007. Acknowledging the suspicion with which traditional professional jour-nalists and scholars regard such amateur sites as blogs and Wikipedia, Johnson still believes that the democratic opportunities of the Internet offer a chance for ordinary people to converse about the local issues in their lives that the professionals largely ignore. Rather than challenging the experts, the conversations taking place in Web 2.0 are supplementing them, Johnson believes, opening up a vast new discourse where ordinary people themselves are the experts. Steven Johnson is the author of* The Ghost Map *(2006).*

If Web 1.0 was organized around pages, Web 2.0 is organized around people. And not just those special people who appear on TV screens and in Op-Ed columns. Web 2.0 is made up of ordinary people: hobbyists, diarists, arm-chair pundits, people adding their voice to the Web's great evolving conversa-tion for the sheer love of it.

Amateurs, in other words. And to a certain extent, how you feel about the broader cultural implications of the Web revolves around the response this permanent amateur hour triggers in you. For some, it has power-to-the-people authenticity. For others, it signals the end of quality and professionalism, as though the history of electronic media turned out to be one long battle between Edward R. Murrow and *America's Funniest Home Videos*, and *Home Videos* won.

I happen to be a great believer in this wave, but there's no avoiding the reality that the shift from pro to am comes at some cost. There is undeniably a vast increase in the sheer quantity of accessibility of pure crap, even when measured against the dregs of the newsstand and the cable spectrum. That decreased signal-to-noise ratio means that filters — search tools, recommendation engines, RSS feeds — become increasingly important to us as a society, and so it's crucial that we have a public discussion about who designs those tools and what values are encoded in them.

If you read through the arguments and Op-Eds over the past few years about the impact of Web amateurism, you'll find that the debate keeps cycling back to two refrains: the impact of blogging on traditional journalism and the impact of Wikipedia on traditional scholarship. In both cases, a trained, institutionally accredited élite has been challenged by what the blogger Glenn Reynolds called an "army of Davids," with much triumphalism, derision and defensiveness on both sides.

This is a perfectly legitimate debate to have, since bloggers and Wikipedi- 5 ans are likely to do some things better than their professional equivalents and some things much worse, and we may as well figure out which is which. The problem with spending so much time hashing out these issues is that it overstates the importance of amateur journalism and encyclopedia authoring in the vast marketplace of ideas that the Web has opened up. The fact is that most user-created content on the Web is not challenging the authority of a traditional expert. It's working in a zone where there are no experts or where the users themselves are the experts.

The most obvious example of this is in the prominence of diary-style pages like those on LiveJournal and MySpace. These people aren't challenging David Brooks or George Will; they're just writing about their lives and the lives of their friends. The overwhelming majority of photographers on Flickr harbor no dream of becoming the next Annie Leibovitz. They just want to share with their extended family the pics they snapped over the holidays.

A few months ago, I helped launch a new service called outside.in that filters and organizes conversations happening online about neighborhoods around the country. Outside.in is a classic Web 2.0 company. We couldn't have built it 10 years ago because we are drawing upon the expertise of thousands of amateurs — the "placebloggers" who have emerged in the past few years to write about their neighborhoods and the issues that are most important to the people living in them. They're writing about the mugging last week, the playground that's opening up next week, the overpriced house that finally went off the market, the impact of No Child Left Behind on the local public school. There are thousands of these conversations going on every day on the Web — virtual discussions that are grounded in real places. We've tried to make it easier to find those conversations and add your voice to the mix. But without that extraordinary wave of placeblogging, we'd have nothing to work with. It would be like trying to launch Google back when there were still only a few hundred websites.

What's so interesting about those local conversations is that they involve experiences that the experts in traditional media have largely ignored — for good reason. Those experts realize that they can't compete with the real experts: the people who live in these communities and know all the issues — small and large — that shape their daily lives.

There's some irony in that lack of media coverage because the zone of experience that people care the most passionately about — beyond the intimate zone of family life — is the zone of their local community. Every successful neighborhood has always had its mavens and connectors, the true experts of the sidewalk, the playground and the backyard barbecue. But that local knowledge has been limited historically to the personal contact of word-of-mouth. Now, on the Web, it has a megaphone.

READING THE TEXT

1. What is the central difference between Web 1.0 and Web 2.0, according to Johnson?

2. What evidence does Johnson advance to support his belief that user-generated media are largely benign, if not liberating?

3. Why does Johnson believe that online "conversations" create access to information that professional journalists have ignored?

4. Johnson notes that he is a cofounder of a Web 2.0 company, outside.in. How might his relationship to a corporate entity affect his argument?

READING THE SIGNS

1. **CONNECTING TEXTS** Compare and contrast Johnson's and Brian Williams's ("Enough about You," p. 449) discussions of Web 2.0, considering both their characterization of the technology itself and their argument about its cultural consequences. Do you find that they are talking about the same phenomena, or do they have somewhat different focuses?

2. **CONNECTING TEXTS** As Johnson points out, much concern has been raised about the effect of Wikipedia on traditional scholarship, but he feels that such concern is unfounded. Interview at least five writing instructors and/or librarians at your school about their position on Wikipedia. Do they encourage or discourage their students to use it as a resource, and why? Does your school have any policies regarding students' reliance on Wikipedia? Use your results as the basis of an essay in which you support, oppose, or complicate Johnson's

take on Wikipedia. You might consult Scott Jaschik's "A Stand against Wikipedia" (p. 43).

3. Write an essay in which you argue whether Web 2.0's challenge to a "trained, institutionally accredited élite" has positive or negative consequences.

BRIAN WILLIAMS
Enough about You

Not everyone is certain that the democratic vistas of the you-centered world of Web 2.0 are entirely beneficial, and in this opinion piece by Brian Williams, which Time *originally published as a direct counterpoint to Steven Johnson's celebration of Web 2.0, a professional journalist considers what may be lost when everyone is a potential expert and everyone is "talking at once." What is more, Williams worries, with the ability to tailor our media consumption today to only those sources that reflect our already held views, we may be missing out on alternative perspectives "that citizens in an informed democracy need to know." After all, the cover of the* Time *issue in which Williams's selection appeared was a reflective surface intended to resemble a mirror. Brian Williams is the anchor and managing editor of the NBC* Nightly News.

While the mainstream media were having lunch, members of the audience made other plans. They scattered and are still on the move, part of a massive migration. The dynamic driving it? It's all about you. Me. And all the various forms of the First Person Singular. Americans have decided the most important person in their lives is . . . them, and our culture is now built upon that idea. It's the User-Generated Generation.

For those times when the 900 digital options awaiting us in our set-top cable box can seem limiting and claustrophobic, there's the Web. Once inside, the doors swing open to a treasure trove of video: adults juggling kittens, ill-fated dance moves at wedding receptions, political rants delivered to camera with venom and volume. All of it exists to fill a perceived need. Media executives — some still not sure what *it* is — know only that they want it. And they're willing to pay for it.

The larger dynamic at work is the celebration of self. The implied message is that if it has to do with you, or your life, it's important enough to tell someone. Publish it, record it . . . but for goodness' sake, share it — get it out there so that others can enjoy it. Or not. The assumption is that an audience of strangers will be somehow interested, or at the very worst not offended.

Intimacies that were once whispered into the phone are now announced unabashedly into cell phones as loud running conversations in public places. Diaries once sealed under lock and key are now called blogs and posted daily for all those who care to make the emotional investment.

We've raised a generation of Americans on a mantra of love and the 5 importance of self as taught by brightly colored authority figures with names like Barney and Elmo. On the theory that celebrating only the winners means excluding those who place, show, or simply show up, parents-turned-coaches started awarding trophies — entire bedrooms full — to all those who compete. Today everyone gets celebrated, in part to put an end to the common cruelties of life that so many of us grew up with.

Now the obligatory confession: in an irony of life that I've not yet fully reconciled myself to, I write a daily blog full of intimate details about one of the oldest broadcasts on television. While the media landscape of my youth, with its three television networks, now seems like forced national viewing by comparison, and while I anchor a broadcast that is routinely viewed by an audience of 10 million or more, it's nothing like it used to be. We work every bit as hard as our television-news forebears did at gathering, writing, and presenting the day's news but to a smaller audience, from which many have been lured away by a dazzling array of choices and the chance to make their own news.

It is now possible — even common — to go about your day in America and consume only what you wish to see and hear. There are television networks that already agree with your views, iPods that play only music you already know you like, Internet programs ready to filter out all but the news you want to hear.

The problem is that there's a lot of information out there that citizens in an informed democracy *need* to know in our complicated world with U.S. troops on the ground along two major fronts. Millions of Americans have come to regard the act of reading a daily newspaper — on *paper* — as something akin to being dragged by their parents to Colonial Williamsburg. It's a tactile visit to another time . . . flat, one-dimensional, unexciting, emitting a slight whiff of decay. It doesn't refresh. It offers no choice. Hell, it doesn't even move. Worse yet: nowhere does it greet us by name. It's for *everyone*.

Does it endanger what passes for the national conversation if we're all talking at once? What if "talking" means typing on a laptop, but the audience is too distracted to pay attention? The whole notion of "media" is now much more democratic, but what will the effect be on democracy?

The danger just might be that we miss the next great book or the next 10 great idea, or that we fail to meet the next great challenge . . . because we are too busy celebrating ourselves and listening to the same tune we already know by heart.

READING THE TEXT

1. Why does Williams believe that users of the new media are motivated largely by a desire to celebrate the self, and what evidence does he offer to support that belief?

2. Describe Williams's tone. What effect does it, and his "obligatory confession," have on the persuasiveness of his argument?

3. Why does Williams consider people's ability to customize the news and entertainment that they consume to be problematic?

READING THE SIGNS

1. **CONNECTING TEXTS**   Write an essay that proposes your own answer to Williams's concluding question: "The whole notion of 'media' is now much more democratic, but what will the effect be on democracy?" (para. 9). To develop your ideas, consult Henry Jenkins's "Convergence Culture" (p. 432) and Steven Johnson's "It's All about Us" (p. 446).

2. **CONNECTING TEXTS**   In class, form teams and debate the impact of Web 2.0, with one team taking Williams's position and the other adopting the perspective of Steven Johnson ("It's All about Us," p. 446). To develop your ideas, you might consult the Introduction to this chapter.

3. Locate Williams's blog on the Internet and analyze its content. To what extent does it simply share Williams's experiences with broadcast news? Do you see that it may serve any commercial purpose for NBC's *Nightly News*?

4. Write an essay in which you support, refute, or complicate Williams's contention that an overly democratic media environment might cause us to miss important information or a truly great idea or book amidst all the media clutter.

TED FRIEDMAN

From the Forest to the Trees: The Sims

Before there was Second Life, there was SimCity, a world-simulating game that first appeared in 1987, long before the Internet had become a household word. The success of SimCity led to a sequel in 2001, The Sims, a new role-playing game that, in Ted Friedman's words, "would transform the simulation genre." A game that focuses on people and interpersonal relationships, The Sims, and its numerous reinventions, has opened the world of computer gaming to large numbers of women and girls who are not attracted to the often violent and conflict-oriented realms of fantasy and science-fiction games, enabling them to experiment with different life choices and priorities in a controlled environment in which losing means only that you get to start over and try again until you win. Indeed, in games like The Sims, not only can you go home again but you can change the cast of characters a second time, or third, or fourth. The author of Electric Dreams: Computers in American Culture *(2005), from which this selection is taken, Friedman is an associate professor in the Department of Communications at Georgia State University.*

. . . Computer games are designed to be played until they are mastered. You succeed by learning how the software is put together. You win the game by deconstructing it. Unlike a book or film that is engaged only once or twice, a computer game is played over and over until every subtlety is exposed, every hidden choice obvious to the savvy player. The moment the game loses its interest is when all its secrets have been discovered, its boundaries revealed. That's when the game can no longer suck you in. No game feels fresh forever; eventually, you run up against the limits of its perspective, and move on to other games.

In the years after its debut in 1987, SimCity inspired numerous sequels and spin-offs. These games for the most part built on the original's gameplay rather than reinventing it. In 2000, however, SimCity creator Will Wright released a game that would transform the simulation genre. The Sims is a "people simulator." You control a household of characters, who can be roommates, lovers, or combinations of parents and children. You are responsible for each character's every activity — sleeping, eating, working, socializing, even using the toilet. The result is like a dollhouse come to life, and it's a truly engrossing experience. The Sims is the inverse of SimCity. While SimCity is about the big picture, The Sims allows you to drill down to the level of individual "Sims." The latest version of SimCity, in fact, SimCity 4, links the two levels, allowing you to import characters from The Sims into SimCity.

The Sims quickly became a top-selling computer game in the United States. In 2003 four of the top six best-selling computer games were Sims products, including The Sims Deluxe and three expansion packs. (SimCity 4 was number seven.)[1] The Sims 2, released in September 2004, was an even bigger hit. It sold more than one million copies in just its first ten days of release, marking the biggest videogame launch in the history of Electronic Arts, the game's publisher. Combined cumulative sales of all Sims games topped 41 million units by October 2004. This discussion will concentrate on the original Sims game, while keeping in mind subsequent developments.[2]

Part of the success of The Sims can be explained by how it has reached a deeply underserved audience: women gamers. While most computer games, from Doom to Civilization, prioritize violence and conflict,[3] The Sims emphasizes interpersonal relationships. It also presents female characters of less outsized proportions than Tomb Raider's Lara Croft. Women make up 56 percent of Sims players, compared to 43 percent of games overall.[4]

Prior to The Sims, there had been some American computer games with a focus on character, such as games in the role-playing genre. But these characters were almost always heroic archetypes thrust into larger-than-life fantasy and science fiction scenarios. There is also a tradition of romance-oriented "relationship simulation" computer games in Japan, but none of these games had been successfully imported into the American market. The Sims was the first American game to allow you to explore a character not through the modalities of fantasy or adventure, but of drama — the everyday.

So, how does The Sims construct this imaginary everyday world? The game is designed to be flexible and open-ended, but it does set some core rules. The primary measure of your moment-to-moment success is each character's "Mood" bar. When the Mood bar is full, the Sim is happy, and is more responsive, energetic, and productive. When the bar runs low, the Sim is sad, and grows lethargic and unresponsive. The key to your long-term goals for the Sim — whether they center on career, family, or whatever you choose to value — is making sure that the Sim stays happy as she or he goes about his or her daily tasks.

The Sim's mood, in turn, is a reflection of the state of satisfaction of eight basic "Needs": Hunger, Comfort, Hygiene, Bladder, Energy, Fun, Social, and Room. (The Sims 2 adds more existential needs, called "Aspirations.") Each one of these needs is tracked on a separate bar. A filled bar means the need is totally fulfilled at the moment; an empty bar means the need is totally

5

---

[1]Entertainment Software Association, "2004 Sales, Demographics and Usage Data."

[2]"Electronic Arts Posts Record Sims 2 Sales."

[3]On the gender politics of computer games, see Cassell and Jenkins, *From Barbie to Mortal Kombat*. For one designer's account of her own attempts to build games for girls, see Laurel, *Utopian Entrepreneur*.

[4]"Women Get in the Game."

unfulfilled. Various actions satisfy a Sim's needs. Eating satisfies hunger, washing satisfies hygiene, and so on. As time goes by, each bar runs down, until the need is again satisfied.

In order to satisfy many of these needs, you need to buy products. To buy products, you need money. You start the game with a set amount of money, then get a job and go to work to earn more. (Kids go to school instead of work, and "earn" grades instead of money.) Work and school are represented in the game only through their absence. The Sims take off for their jobs and classes, but the game interface stays at the house. If nobody's left at home, the hours rush by at accelerated speed, until the Sims return.

So, to get ahead in the game, you need to buy stuff. Much of the gameplay is spent in "Buy Mode." The game clock pauses, and a menu of consumer options pops up: appliances, furniture, decorations, and so on. Each item has a game function. A stove is needed to cook food, for example. The more expensive the stove, the more satisfying the food, filling the "Hunger" meter more fully.

The economics of The Sims has inspired one easy criticism: that it's a consumerist fantasy that turns life into one big shopping spree. A review of the game in the *New York Times*, for example, was titled "The Sims Who Die with the Most Toys Win."[5] Given the large number of women who play The Sims, this critique fits snugly with familiar gender stereotypes about women as shopping-obsessed overconsumers. But this analysis misses a complicating factor: the critical currency in The Sims is not money, but *time*. The gameplay is a continuous balancing act, a race to juggle multiple needs before time runs out and the day is over. Misallocate time, and the results are disastrous. If you miss too much work, you're fired. If you skip too much school, a truant officer hauls you off to military school. If you go too long without using the bathroom, you pee your pants. If you don't eat, you die.

The Sims, then, is a reflection not only of consumerism, but also of what sociologist Arlie Russell Hochschild calls "the time bind" — the constant pressure on Americans today, particularly working mothers, to juggle the competing demands of work and home.[6] The game is even grittily pessimistic about the possibilities of raising children in a two-income family. A Sim couple can make a child (the sex is chastely blurred out — the game is rated T by the Entertainment Software Ratings Board, for "content that may be suitable for persons ages 13 and older").[7] But with the new responsibilities a baby brings, if both Sim parents work outside the home, inevitably either one of the characters will miss work and get fired, or the baby will end up so neglected that a social worker shows up and takes it away. (In Sims 2, you can hire a nanny, but as in real life, this requires substantial funds.)

---

[5]Herz, "Game Theory."
[6]Hochschild, *The Time Bind*.
[7]For more on sexuality in The Sims, see Consalvo, "Hot Dates and Fairy Tale Romances."

A third economy in The Sims is personal relationships. In order for a Sim to advance in his or her job and make more money, the Sim needs to collect friends. Sims make friends by interacting with other Sims, both within the household (controlled by the player) and in the neighborhood (controlled by the computer). Sims talk to each other, but they don't speak English; rather, they speak "SimSpeak," gibberish that conveys emotion through intonation, but not precise meaning. They can also engage in a wide range of social behaviors, such as dancing, back rubbing, tickling, and kissing. A group of bars just like the eight Mood bars track how well the Sim is liked by each of his/her acquaintances. Another challenge of the game, then, is to orchestrate relationships to build up each Sim's number of friends, as well as find romantic partners for each Sim. (Taking a progressive stand, the game includes the possibility of gay and lesbian as well as straight romances. Gay couples can't make babies, but may adopt.)[8]

Given these themes, the appeal of the game to girls and women struggling to define their roles in contemporary America makes sense. The Sims is not simply an escapist fantasy, but a model with which to experiment with different sets of personal priorities, as reflected in different game strategies.

There's plenty of room to experiment, since you control not just one member of the household, but all of them, commanding them individually while coordinating their interactions with each other. Gameplay is not just a constant juggling act from task to the next, but from one character to another. The currently "active" character in any moment of gameplay is represented by a diamond over the character's head. (In a twist on that Tetris commercial, recent commercials for The Sims represent everyday real-life situations as if they were taking place in the world of the game, complete with diamonds floating overhead. Like the Tetris ad, the commercials highlight how playing the game restructures your perception of the world outside the game.)

Identification in The Sims, then, is multiple and shifting. You can bounce 15 from one side of a flirtation to the other, conducting a romance. Unlike SimCity, however, the identification remains personalized, even through the shifts. The game interface may present a god's-eye perspective — it's a third-person overhead view, never POV — but the game never disengages to the Olympian heights of the main map screens in SimCity and Civilization. More than any adventure game, The Sims allows you to develop characters you can really care about.

BIBLIOGRAPHY

Cassell, Justine, and Henry Jenkins. *From Barbie to Mortal Kombat: Gender and Computer Games*. Cambridge, MA: MIT University Press, 1998.
Consalvo, Mia. "Hot Dates and Fairy Tale Romances: Studying Sexuality in Video Games." In *The Video Game Theory Reader*. Ed. Mark J. P. Wolf and Bernard Perron. New York: Routledge, 2003. 171–94.

[8]See Consalvo, "Hot Dates and Fairy Tale Romances."

"Electronic Arts Posts Record Sims 2 Sales." Associated Press. September 29, 2004.

Entertainment Software Association. "2004 Sales, Demographics and Usage Data: Essential Facts about the Computer and Video Game Industry." < http://www.theesa.com/ EFBrochure.pdf > .

Herz, J. C. "Game Theory: The Sims Who Die with the Most Toys Win." *New York Times* 10 Feb. 2000.

Hochschild, Arlie Russell. *The Time Bind.* New York: Metropolitan Books, 1997.

"Women Get in the Game." *Microsoft Presspass.* 8 Jan. 2004. < http://www.microsoft .com/presspass/features/2004/Jan04/01-08WomanGamers.asp > .

READING THE TEXT

1. What is the difference between SimCity and its sequel The Sims?

2. Why does The Sims appeal in particular to women gamers?

3. What role do consumer products play in The Sims?

4. What is the "time bind," and how is it reflected in the structure of The Sims?

READING THE SIGNS

1. **CONNECTING TEXTS** Friedman observes that The Sims has been criticized for being "a consumerist fantasy that turns life into one big shopping spree" (para. 10). Drawing on this selection and Alana Semuels's "Virtual Marketers Have Second Thoughts about Second Life" (p. 457), write an essay arguing for or against the proposition that virtual reality games like The Sims are continuing a tradition of constructing willing consumers within a consumer society.

2. In an analytic essay, support, oppose, or modify the position that, rather than being progressive, The Sims — with its emphasis on personal relationships and its domestic setting — reinforces traditional gender roles.

3. **CONNECTING TEXTS** In class, form teams and debate whether it is healthy to play at life online (including simulated romances). To develop your ideas, consult Clive Thompson's "Game Theories" (p. 460).

4. **CONNECTING TEXTS** Study a role-playing fantasy game like World of Warcraft and compare and contrast it with The Sims. What gender-related patterns do you find? To develop your ideas, consult Aaron Devor, "Gender Role Behaviors and Attitudes" (p. 567).

5. Analyze a gaming Web site designed specifically for female gamers, such as **www.fragdolls.com**. In what ways does it replicate or alter the gender codes typically seen in Web sites designed for male gamers?

ALANA SEMUELS

Virtual Marketers Have Second Thoughts about Second Life

It all seemed so obvious: "Build" a shop on Second Life and the customers will come, moving seamlessly from virtual shopping to actual shopping in the real world. But as Alana Semuels discusses in this marketing report for the Los Angeles Times, *it doesn't appear to be working out that way, as Second Life denizens are displaying everything from indifference to outright hostility toward the commercial sites that have invaded their fantasies. You know that something is amiss when angry avatars begin to take "virtual action," such as nuking a Second Life Reebok outlet and shooting customers "outside the American Apparel store." No wonder some companies want out. Semuels is a staff writer for the* Los Angeles Times.

Second Life — a three-dimensional online society where publicity is cheap and the demographic is edgy and certainly computer-savvy — should be a marketer's paradise. But it turns out that plugging products is as problematic in the virtual world as it is anywhere else.

At http://www.secondlife.com — where the cost is $6 a month for premium citizenship — shopping, at least for real-world products, isn't a main activity. Four years after Second Life debuted, some marketers are second-guessing the money and time they've put into it. "There's not a compelling reason to stay," said Brian McGuinness, vice president of Aloft, a brand of Starwood Hotels & Resorts Worldwide Inc. that is closing its Second Life shop and donating its virtual land to the nonprofit social-networking group TakingITGlobal.

Linden Lab, the San Francisco firm that created Second Life, sells companies and people pieces of the landscape where they can build stores, conference halls, and gardens. Individuals create avatars, or virtual representations of themselves, that travel around this online society, exploring and schmoozing with other avatars. Land developed by users, rather than real-world companies, is among the most popular places in Second Life.

But the sites of many of the companies remaining in Second Life are empty. During a recent in-world visit, Best Buy Co.'s Geek Squad Island was devoid of visitors and the virtual staff that was supposed to be online. The schedule of events on Sun Microsystems Inc.'s site was blank, and the green landscape of Dell Island was deserted. Signs posted on the window of the empty American Apparel store said it had closed up shop.

McGuinness said Starwood's venture into Second Life did accomplish something. Feedback from denizens gave Aloft ideas for its physical hotels. 5

457

The suggestions included putting radios in showers and painting the lobbies in earth tones rather than primary colors. But now that the design initiative is over, he said, it's difficult to attract people to the virtual hotel to help build the real-world brand.

For some advertisers, the problem is that Second Life is a fantasyland, and the representations of the people who play in it don't have human needs. Food and drink aren't necessary, teleporting is the easiest way to get around and clothing is optional. In fact, the human form itself is optional. Avatars can play games, build beach huts, dress up like furry animals, flirt with strangers — sometimes all at once.

Their interests seem to tend toward the risque. Ian Schafer, chief executive of online marketing firm Deep Focus, which advises clients about entering virtual worlds, said he recently toured Second Life. He started at the Aloft hotel and found it empty. He moved on to casinos, brothels, and strip clubs, and they were packed. Schafer said he found in his research that "one of the most frequently purchased items in Second Life is genitalia."

Another problem for some is that Second Life doesn't have enough active residents. On its website, Second Life says the number of total residents is more than 8 million. But that counts people who signed in once and never returned, as well as multiple avatars for individual residents. Even at peak times, only about 30,000 to 40,000 users are logged on, said Brian Haven, an analyst with Forrester Research. "You're talking about a much smaller audience than advertisers are used to reaching," Haven said.

Some in the audience don't want to be reached. After marketers began entering Second Life, an avatar named Urizenus Sklar — in the real world, University of Toronto philosophy professor Peter Ludlow — wrote in the public-relations blog Strumpette that the community was "being invaded by an army of old world meat-space corporations." He and other residents accused companies of lacking creativity by setting up traditional-looking stores that didn't fit in. His column was reproduced in the *Second Life Herald*.

Nissan Motor Co., a subject of such protests, has since transformed its 10 presence in Second Life from a car vending machine to an "automotive amusement park," where avatars can test gravity-defying vehicles and ride hamster balls. Sun Micro has made its participation more interactive and fanciful, Chief Gaming Officer Chris Melissinos said. Ludlow isn't impressed. He said most firms were more interested in the publicity they received from their ties with Second Life than in the digital world itself. "It was a way to brand themselves as being leading-edge," he said.

Angry avatars have taken virtual action. Reebok weathered a nuclear bomb attack and customers were shot outside the American Apparel store. Avatars are creating fantasy knockoffs of brand-name products too.

Some buying and selling does go on in Second Life. An avatar can acquire currency — called Linden dollars — by earning it or buying it with U.S. dollars. (The exchange rate is 268 Lindens to $1.) With a stack of Linden dollars, an avatar can spice up his or her look or while away the time in a casino. Only a few other virtual worlds allow avatars to create and sell content as Second Life does. But users are flocking to the other worlds, in part because some don't require people to download software to take up residence.

Others just want to access a larger community than Second Life offers. Between May and June, the population of active avatars declined 2.5%, and the volume of U.S. money exchanged within the world fell from a high of $7.3 million in March to $6.8 million in June. Companies are following them. IBM Corp., which has an extensive presence in Second Life, is expanding into the other environments, including There, which features a digital version of the popular TV show *Laguna Beach*, and Entropia Universe, which pits users against one another in a sci-fi civilization.

Consulting firms that were set up to bring brands into Second Life are busy helping clients explore other worlds. One such agency, Millions of Us, recently announced that it had formed a partnership with Gaia Online, a site popular with teenagers, and CEO Reuben Steiger said it would be unveiling more soon. Millions of Us had previously worked only with Second Life. "It's not about whether Second Life is good or bad," Steiger said. "It's just that there are a lot of alternatives."

READING THE TEXT

1. According to Semuels, what are the reasons for advertising's failure to capture a market on Second Life?

2. In what ways have Second Life citizens expressed their resistance to marketing efforts on the site?

3. How have Second Life marketers sought to improve their advertising efforts?

READING THE SIGNS

1. One explanation for the failure of marketing efforts on Second Life is that the site is a "fantasyland," but traditional print and television advertising also engages in fantasy. Compare and contrast the ways in which fantasy is a marketing tool used in traditional and virtual reality venues. To what extent are the fantasies that are evoked similar? To develop your ideas, consult the Introduction to Chapter 2, "Brought to You B(u)y: The Signs of Advertising" (p. 171).

2. **CONNECTING TEXTS**   Second Life is a major player in a You-topian world that is supposedly built by its grassroots users, but, as Semuels's article suggests, it also has a corporate presence that may turn Web 2.0 into just another form of advertising. Write an essay arguing whether or not Second Life and similar sites can be authentic user-run worlds when advertising plays such a large role in their existence. To develop your ideas, consult Henry Jenkins's "Convergence Culture" (p. 432) and the Introduction to this chapter.

3. Semuels quotes a marketing analyst who claims that "one of the most frequently purchased items in Second Life is genitalia" (para. 7). Write an essay analyzing the appeal of Second Life and other virtual reality sites. Does that appeal go beyond sexual experimentation?

4. Visit Second Life and study its current advertising and marketing efforts. Do you see evidence, as Semuels suggests, of attempts at changing the style and impact of such marketing? If so, what are those changes, and how do they encourage the avatars that visit the site to become interested in their products and companies?

CLIVE THOMPSON
Game Theories

> Many online games involve a kind of internal economy within which players exchange game-related commodities for units of artificial currency. But it took a professional economist to realize that the accumulation of property in online gaming isn't simply a matter of play money. Indeed, as Clive Thompson reports in this article that originally appeared in The Walrus, economist Edward Castronova followed the movement of game-related property from the game EverQuest to eBay, where it was sold for real money, and he crunched the numbers to arrive at an astonishing conclusion: "The average player was generating . . . the equivalent of $3.42 (US) per hour." Such a discovery enabled Castronova to pioneer a new area of economic research that treats online economies as experimental spaces in which to analyze and test economic theories. So who said economics has to be the dismal science? Clive Thompson writes about science and technology for the New York Times Magazine, Wired, and Details, and blogs at collisiondetection.net.

Edward Castronova had hit bottom. Three years ago, the thirty-eight-year-old economist was, by his own account, an academic failure. He had chosen an unpopular field — welfare research — and published only a handful of papers that, as far as he could tell, "had never influenced anybody." He'd scraped together a professorship at the Fullerton campus of California State University, a school that did not even grant Ph.D.s. He lived in a lunar, vacant suburb. He'd once dreamed of being a major economics thinker but now faced the grim sense that he might already have hit his plateau. "I'm a schmo at a state school," he thought. And since his wife worked in another city, he was, on top of it all, lonely.

To fill his evenings, Castronova did what he'd always done: he played video games. In April 2001, he paid a $10 monthly fee to a multiplayer online game called EverQuest. More than 450,000 players worldwide log into EverQuest's "virtual world." They each pick a medieval character to play, such as a warrior or a blacksmith or a "healer," then band together in errant quests to slay magical beasts; their avatars appear as tiny, inch-tall characters striding across a Tolkienesque land. Soon, Castronova was playing EverQuest several hours a night. . . .

Then he noticed something curious: EverQuest had its own economy, a bustling trade in virtual goods. Players generate goods as they play, often by killing creatures for their treasure and trading it. The longer they play, the more powerful they get — but everyone starts the game at Level 1, barely strong enough to kill rats or bunnies and harvest their fur. Castronova would sell his fur to other characters who'd pay him with "platinum pieces," the artificial currency inside the game. It was a tough slog, so he was always stunned by the opulence of the richest players. EverQuest had been launched in 1999, and some veteran players now owned entire castles filled with treasures from their quests.

Things got even more interesting when Castronova learned about the "player auctions." *EverQuest* players would sometimes tire of the game, and decide to sell off their characters or virtual possessions at an online auction site such as eBay. When Castronova checked the auction sites, he saw that a Belt of the Great Turtle or a Robe of Primordial Waters might fetch $40; powerful characters would go for several hundred or more. And sometimes people would sell off 500,000-fold bags of platinum pieces for as much as $1,000.

As Castronova stared at the auction listings, he recognized with a shock 5 what he was looking at. It was a form of currency trading. Each item had a value in virtual "platinum pieces"; when it was sold on eBay, someone was paying cold, hard American cash for it. That meant the platinum piece was worth something in real currency. EverQuest's economy actually had real-world value.

He began calculating frantically. He gathered data on 616 auctions, observing how much each item sold for in US dollars. When he averaged the results, he was stunned to discover that the EverQuest platinum piece was worth about one cent US — higher than the Japanese yen or the Italian lira. With that information, he could figure out how fast the EverQuest economy was growing. Since players were killing monsters or skinning bunnies every day, they were, in effect, creating wealth. Crunching more numbers, Castronova found that the average player was generating 319 platinum pieces each hour he or she was in the game — the equivalent of $3.42 (US) per hour. "That's higher than the minimum wage in most countries," he marvelled.

Then he performed one final analysis: the Gross National Product of EverQuest, measured by how much wealth all the players together created in a single year inside the game. It turned out to be $2,266 per capita. By World Bank rankings, that made EverQuest richer than India, Bulgaria, or China, and nearly as wealthy as Russia.

It was the seventy-seventh richest country in the world. And it didn't even exist.

Castronova sat back in his chair in his cramped home office, and the weird enormity of his findings dawned on him. Many economists define their careers by studying a country. He had discovered one. . . .

When he finished his research, Castronova assembled it in a paper called 10
"Virtual Worlds: A First-Hand Account of Market and Society on the Cyberian
Frontier." He submitted it to an academic website, the Social Science Research Network, that distributes working papers, free for anyone to read. The
site has 43,982 papers by more than 37,000 authors. He didn't expect too
much. "I thought maybe seventy-five people would read it," he recalls, "and
that'd be great."

He was wrong. The paper sent a shock wave through the online world.
EverQuest players pounced on it and wrote up excited descriptions on game-
discussion boards. That led to a flurry of posts on popular blog sites. Soon,
academics and pundits in Washington were rushing to read it. Barely a few
months later, Castronova's paper became the most downloaded paper in the
entire database — beating out works by dozens of Nobel laureates. Today, it's
still in the top three.

Why the rush of interest? What can a game filled with elves and warrior
dwarves tell us about the real world?

Quite a lot, if you believe the economist Edward Chamberlin. In 1948,
Chamberlin admitted that all economists face a critical problem: they have no
clean "laboratory" in which to study behavior. "The social scientist . . . cannot
observe the actual operation of a real model under controlled circumstances,"
he wrote. "Economics is limited by the fact that resort cannot be had to the
laboratory techniques of the natural sciences." Instead, classical economics
tries to predict economic behavior by theorizing about a completely fair marketplace in which people are rational actors and all things are equal.

The problem with this — as plenty of left-wing critics have pointed out — is
that all things aren't equal. Some people are born into rich families, and blessed
with great opportunities. Others are born into dirt-poor neighborhoods where
even the most brilliant mind coupled with hard work may not forge success. As
a result, economists have warred for centuries over two diverging visions.
Adam Smith argued that people inherently prefer a free market and the ability
to rise above others; Karl Marx countered that capital was inherently unfair and
those with power would abuse it. But no pristine world exists in which to test
these theories — there is no country with a truly level playing field.

Except, possibly, for EverQuest, the world's first truly egalitarian polity. 15
Everyone begins the same way: with nothing. You enter with pathetic skills,
no money, and only the clothes on your back. Wealth comes from working
hard, honing your skills, and clever trading. It is a genuine meritocracy, which
is precisely why players love the game, Castronova argues. "It undoes all the
inequities in society. They're wiped away. Sir Thomas More would have dreamt
about that possibility, that kind of utopia," he says.

Virtual worlds have produced some surreal rags-to-riches stories. When
the online world Second Life launched, the players were impressed to see a
female avatar industriously building a sprawling monster home. An in-game
neighbor stopped by to say hello only to discover she was a homeless person

in British Columbia, logging on using her single remaining possession, a laptop. Penniless in the real world, she belonged to a social elite in the fake one.

Not all social inequities are absent, of course. For instance, Castronova discovered that women in the game are worth less than men, in a very measurable way: when he compared the sale of male and female avatars, he found that female characters sold for 10 percent less than male ones at precisely the same power level. Players with female avatars also say it's harder to advance in the game, at least initially — even though the female characters are often being played, in real life, by men. (A study by the game academic Nick Yee found that male players "cross-dress" as female characters at least one-third of the time.) Men play as women characters partly for the kinky thrill, but also because female characters are given random presents of free stuff by other players, a chivalric custom known as "gifting." "Personally, you receive a lot more stuff when you start out as a female," as one male cross-dresser wrote to Yee.

Ultimately, Castronova says, EverQuest supports one of Adam Smith's main points, which is that people actually prefer unequal outcomes. In fact, EverQuest eerily mirrors the state of modern free-market societies: only a small minority of players attain Level 65 power and own castles; most remain quite poor. When game companies offer socialist alternatives, players reject them. "They've tried to make games where you can't amass more property than someone else," says Castronova, "but everybody hated it. It seems that we definitely do not want everybody to have the same stuff all the time; people find it boring." It is a result that would warm the heart of a conservative.

Yet progressives, too, have been drawn to Castronova's research. Robert Shapiro, formerly an undersecretary of commerce for Bill Clinton, views the economist's findings as nothing less than a liberal call-to-arms. EverQuest players tolerate the massive split between the virtual rich and the poor, Shapiro tells me, only because they know that this is a level playing field. If you work hard enough, you'll eventually grow wealthy. In Shapiro's view, Castronova's research proves that the only way to create a truly free market is to support programs that give everyone a fair chance at success, such as good education and health care. "This may provide the most important lesson of all from the EverQuest experiment," he wrote in an essay. "Real equality can obviate much of a democratic government's intervention in a modern economy. . . . If EverQuest is any guide, the liberal dream of genuine equality would usher in the conservative vision of truly limited government." In other words, maybe the best way to save the real world is to make it more like EverQuest.

READING THE TEXT

1. Describe in your own words EverQuest's "economy."
2. Summarize the economic positions held by Adam Smith and Karl Marx, as Thompson describes them, and how those positions are reflected in the world of gaming.

3. Summarize Edward Castronova's procedure for calculating EverQuest's gross national product.

4. How does Castronova's analysis of EverQuest appeal to both liberals and conservatives?

5. What sort of role do female avatars play in EverQuest?

READING THE SIGNS

1. Thompson begins his selection with a very personal description of Edward Castronova and his life. How does that information affect your response to the article? Why do you think Thompson included it?

2. Write an essay arguing for, opposing, or complicating the assumption that EverQuest is a "meritocracy" (para. 15).

3. **CONNECTING TEXTS**   Compare and contrast the appeal of EverQuest with that of a game like The Sims, analyzing both gender roles and the role of consumerism in each. To develop your ideas, you might interview some fans of both games; in addition, consult Ted Friedman's "From the Forest to the Trees: The Sims" (p. 452).

4. **CONNECTING TEXTS**   Using Laurence Shames's "The More Factor" (p. 86) as a critical framework, analyze EverQuest's "economy." To what extent does it fuel its players' hunger for more?

5. Some successful gamers who are able to reach high levels of status in EverQuest exit the game and sell their status level to the highest bidder for real money on auction sites like eBay. Write an essay that evaluates this practice. Should game rules encourage a free-market approach to players' skill levels, or should the rules disqualify those who enter the game with a prepurchased high ranking?

A. B. HARRIS

Average Gamers Please Step Forward

Are you an "average gamer"? If you are, you must be a "male head-of-household professional" in your early thirties and "read books or daily newspapers on a regular basis," at least according to the Entertainment Software Association. Sound peculiar? It does to A. B. Harris, who really is an average gamer but who is well aware that, according to common opinion, gamers are mostly over-sexed male adolescents with a penchant for violence. Arguing in this "Speak Out" piece for Computer Games *that game magazines and gamers themselves are at least partly responsible for their "sordid and seedy" reputation, Harris calls for his fellow average game players to make themselves heard and demonstrate that they are "far more credible and intelligent" than their public image would suggest. Maybe this calls for a new World of Warcraft chess playing character. A. B. Harris is an average reader of* Computer Games.

According to the Entertainment Software Association, I'm the average gamer. I'm a male head-of-household professional in my early 30s, and I play games almost eight hours a week. I even fit some of the ESA's more obscure data, such as "devoting more than triple the amount of time spent playing games each week to exercising . . . creative endeavors . . . [and] cultural activities," as well as "reading books or daily newspapers on a regular basis." Is this sufficiently average?

How about — hold on to your hats — "exhibit a high level of interest in current events . . . [and] vote in most of the elections for which they are eligible"?

That's me, the ESA's poster child for gaming.

So why is it that, when I attempt a nonpartisan appraisal of my alleged brethren in the gaming populace at large, I feel so different? So alone? Consider the recent next-generation console launches: All across the country myriad gamers queued up outside their favorite big-box retailers, sometimes up to a week in advance. Surely within this dedicated group, I thought to myself, I'd find a generous sampling of the average gamer. But in the amateur, shaky-cam event coverage, I saw not professional early-30s heads of household, but a motley group of Mountain Dew–addicted juveniles who had somehow shirked life's responsibilities for a week-long urban camp-out. Wondering whether my initial judgment was biased, I watched on, as people in line were briefly interviewed. Unsettling snatches of conversation, tantamount to leet-speak, confirmed my fears — I was certainly not a member of this stratum of the population, be they average gamers or potential eBay sellers. ⁵

Dumbfounded, I silently asked where exactly the ESA had gathered its data.

465

Perhaps it was merely pandering to the mainstream press and its portrayal of gaming. But this assertion was promptly nullified, for I knew all too well that the plebeian view of gaming is rife with Hot Coffee–style shenanigans and ghastly tales of game-induced violence. Games are, according to mainstream media and the general public, a sordid and seedy form of entertainment, debauching our youth with sex and violence — which is a far cry from what the ESA suggests.

I therefore shifted my attention away from the mainstream to focus on the gaming press itself. Certainly our industry has a responsibility to represent the average gamer, to be able to define its veritable consumer base? Or so one would think!

But, after scrutinizing game magazine advertisements and fan forums, gamer interviews and reviews, I found no solace in what I discovered. Aside from occasional clever advertisements and infrequent constructive commentary, I found brainless ads and immature journalism. Sex and violence? Check. Tasteless banter? You bet. Shallow visual appeal? All present and accounted for. A sophisticated and insightful manner? Bueller? Bueller?

Years ago, when the videogaming industry was in its infancy, the brainless ads and immature journalism might have been more acceptable, for all young industries have a learning curve. More importantly, the average gamer certainly wasn't the professional, early-30s head of household, but was more likely to be a teenage technology enthusiast that the mainstream would deem a "nerd."

But this is the year 2007, not 1982. Within that quarter-century, this industry has seen an untold degree of technological evolution, surpassing anything before. More than ever, we have seemingly limitless options in the games available to us. We are closer than ever to creating truly virtual worlds that permit us to indulge the desire for personal experiences impossible in real life. And as time goes on, this evolution will assuredly continue unabated.   10

But some perplexing questions remain: If gaming has evolved to such a great degree, why have the culture surrounding gaming and the mainstream's opinion of that culture remained inert? And if indeed our industry's culture is stagnant or, worse yet, actually devolving, who exactly is to blame? Furthermore, what steps can be taken to rectify the debasement?

I alone can offer no solid answers to the above inquiries. Nor can the gaming magazines, journalists, and marketers; they simply cater to the perceived gamer demographic, the "average" gamer.

And what about the ESA's gamer profile? Although my findings suggest an entirely different profile, I still maintain the ESA in high regard. In fact, I consider their Game Player Data to be a paradigm to which we should all aspire. Dear friends, consider this a call to arms to demonstrate to not only our fellow gamers but also the general public that we are far more credible and intelligent than our perceived demographic suggests. Consider this a plea for us to serve as ambassadors, whether among our own or in foreign company. To maintain our awareness of gaming academia and share this knowledge with non-gamers. To live up to our average gamer profile. As a group of responsible gamers, we can change the mainstream.

READING THE TEXT

1. Summarize the profile of the average gamer, as described by the Entertainment Software Association.
2. According to Harris, what is the mainstream image of gamers?
3. How has advertising contributed to the mainstream image of gamers?

READING THE SIGNS

1. Write a semiotic analysis of a gaming magazine like *Computer Games*, focusing on the image of gamers that the magazine, including its advertising and editorial content, projects. Does the magazine reflect the identity of the "average gamer," as Harris would wish, or of the mainstream stereotype that he decries?
2. If you are an online game player, write a journal entry in which you assess whether you and your acquaintances fit the popular image of a gamer. How might your choice of game sites affect the image that is constructed?
3. **CONNECTING TEXTS** The mainstream image of a gamer is male. Visit a fan forum for a game that appeals to women or to both genders, and study the image of gamers it presents. To what extent does it reflect or deviate from the stereotype that Harris describes? To develop your ideas, you might consult Ted Friedman's "From the Forest to the Trees: The Sims" (p. 452).
4. **CONNECTING TEXTS** Harris issues a "call to arms" (para. 12) to fellow gamers, much in the way Gloria Steinem ("Sex, Lies, and Advertising," p. 227) and Joan Morgan ("Sex, Lies, and Videos," p. 616) also conclude their selections with an appeal to readers for social and political changes. Study the appeal for change in the three selections. To what extent do you find them effective, and why? In what ways might the intended readership of the selections affect their persuasiveness?

Master Chief Waits in Line

READING THE SIGNS

1. Jim Cush, of Babylon, New York, was photographed waiting in line dressed as Master Chief, the hero of the video game Halo 3, with other fans waiting to buy the game in Manhattan on September 24, 2007. What is your initial reaction to this photograph?

2. What, typically, is the purpose of putting on a costume? What does it allow the wearer to do? In what ways is a gaming avatar, which the user can personalize (such as those in Second Life), like a costume?

3. **CONNECTING TEXTS** Cush says he spent several thousand dollars creating his Master Chief outfit; he was not paid by Microsoft to promote the release of the game. What statement does that make about the intersection of commercial culture with personal identity? Speculate on reasons why Cush may have worn this outfit. Would you ever feel so devoted to a product that you would dress as a character derived from it? Why or why not? You might enrich your analysis by consulting Linda Seger's "Creating the Myth" (p. 356).

4. Consider the meaning of the name "Master Chief" and try to account for the purposes of the parts of the Master Chief outfit. Then consider what associations you can make with the Master Chief costume. What other costumes, outfits, or uniforms does it remind you of? What elements of the human body does it exaggerate? What elements does it hide? To what end?

JOANNE CAVANAUGH SIMPSON

Multitasking State of Mind

Do you ever wonder what your professors think of you when you do something really dumb like e-mail them to ask what your grade is in a class that you neither attended nor registered for? If you have, this essay by Joanne Cavanaugh Simpson may be something of an eyeopener. For here you will find the flip side of the You-topian, convergence culture world, a nagging belief that days spent "distracted by cell phones, iPods, text messaging, chat rooms, and social Web sites like Facebook or My-Space" are producing a scattered, fragmentary consciousness that may be affecting not only your schoolwork but your ability to communicate effectively with your instructors. Call it a generation gap, if you will, but Simpson is not alone in her concern that the "multitasking . . . state of mind" may be adding up to an "ADD Nation." Simpson is a lecturer and essayist who teaches at Johns Hopkins University.

Professor,
I did not turn in my final assignments. I would really like to do so. . . . I am won-dering if you have already turned in my grade, and if not will you tell me what my grade is before you turn it in. I need to graduate next semester . . . and I can't get a D or F. I would rather get a W and take the class again. Please let me know.

That e-mail arrived a week after the semester was over. Though this student had missed a few classes, she cited no health or family crisis. When I got the final grade roster, I realized she wasn't even *registered* for my fall writing course.

Did she just forget?

Sometimes phenomena or trends ripple through society; other times they create tidal waves. This past school year, I witnessed a tidal wave hit the Johns Hopkins Homewood campus. Call it ADD Nation or IM Generation, but a dif-ferent batch of students has arrived on college campuses.

In a faculty meeting in December, a few of my colleagues said there had 5 been a big shift recently. It's been a particularly bad semester, they said. More students are zoning out, less able to complete assignments. Others are uncon-cerned with details, more likely to skim the surface.

The art of communication, especially, seems to be suffering. Students send fragmented e-mails that border on rudeness. (One student wrote that I should regularly e-mail the class reminders about what assignments are due each week.) Others request final grade adjustments as though they were dis-gruntled consumers. One student, who wondered why he didn't get an A, raised his hand each week in class and whined, "Can we take a break?" My not-even-on-the-roster student had piped up during class one day, "Oh, yeah. I owe you a paper."

I have been teaching for nearly 10 years, and I've never seen anything like it.

What's going on?

The rudeness doesn't appear to be wholly intentional. Students seem more distracted than disrespectful. Some even come to class in a zombie-like state that surpasses sleep deprivation. To me it resembles the frazzled fallout of addiction, and — during a three-hour lecture or discussion class — slack-jawed, eye-glazed withdrawal. Really, mouths hanging open and everything.

For some students, attention spans hover around 1 minute, 45 seconds. 10 To them, I am just another click-and-skim Web site.

As I looked around, I saw that students indeed have little tolerance for anything that doesn't have the split-second, image-splashing pace of a Spike TV commercial or an Internet pop-up ad. Antsy with mere existence, they are often tuned everywhere but where they actually are. Multitaskers extraordinaire, many spend their days — and nights — distracted by cell phones, iPods, text messaging, chat rooms, and social Web sites like Facebook or MySpace. Seems to me, our youth are just too connected to the technological ether.

I'm not the only one noticing. *Time* magazine, the American trend meter, ran a cover story in March titled "Are Kids Too Wired for Their Own Good?" As the story notes, "media multitasking" has hit warp speed in the past few years: "The mental habit of dividing one's attention into many small slices has significant implications for the way young people learn, reason, socialize, do creative work, and understand the world." Apparently, the brain can "toggle" quickly from one task to another. Many of these students are master togglers. As *Time* points out, "Decades of research (not to mention common sense) indicate that the quality of one's output and depth of thought deteriorate as one tends to ever more tasks."

Not all students are in such a distracted state, of course. On the trend's upside, this technologically literate generation manipulates vast amounts of data with lightning dexterity. Hopkins students are smart — they use computers to design everything from heart surgery devices to engineering prototypes that can extract every ounce of ketchup from a bottle. Increasingly, however, my already overcommitted students complain about not having enough time or energy to focus.

The repercussions from such synaptic juggling, apparently, are just surfacing. I spoke with Vernon Savage, associate director of the Counseling Center at Homewood. Distraction has surged since Hopkins went online in dorms a few years ago, he says. "You sit in your room with an iPod and all of the technology available, so you can escape more easily," he said. "Procrastination is very sinister. It works for a few minutes to alleviate anxiety about the task pending. Then, as a result, you don't have much time to finish the task." Maybe that's why papers seem more thrown together at the last minute.

But didn't we all have distractions as college students? TV. Significant 15 others. CDs. Wine coolers with Skittles chasers. As I remember it, I still paid attention to one thing at a time: When I was with friends, I didn't try to work, too. Yet I asked one of my writing classes in the spring, "How many of you do several things at once?" Everyone raised his or her hand. One student says it takes him forever to finish a calculus assignment when his computer keyboard is in reach. Another student said that she cooks, watches TV, instant messages, and does her homework all at the same time. And those who are overtaxed don't seem to like it very much. "I'm stressed all the time," one student told me.

Still, I wondered why there was such a big shift now. Then I started counting on my fingers: College students today are among the first generation raised on the Internet — which became widely accessible starting in the early 1990s — when sophomores were just 6 or 7 years old. These students are trained to toggle, and their attention spans reflect their new mode of communication. I talked to Ben Locke, an expert in technology on college campuses and assistant director at Penn State University's counseling center. "The generation coming into school now grew up with this technology, and they don't know how to live without it," he says. "Technology has gone from sitting on a shelf to being on a person all day long." As a result, he notes: "Multitasking used to be a way of getting things done. Now it's a state of mind."

When students can't go the few minutes between classes without flipping open cell phones, it's as though they can't bear the silence. "Students don't disengage, they don't slow down," Locke says. "When they aren't connected, they don't know quite what to do with themselves."

In the end, students are experiencing life secondhand — text messaging each other at a concert, for example, instead of focusing on the music. Life increasingly seems to be All About Chat. As Locke and other researchers have noted, students are losing face-to-face communication skills, or not even developing those skills at all.

As was the case with my absentee student, the inability to pay attention translated into an inability to talk about a problem. E-mail creates more distance and requires less courage. (Apparently, she also faced bad grades in other courses, writing to me that she just didn't know what to tell her professors.) Having no other contact information, I e-mailed her back about whether she was registered for the course. I never heard from her again.

Because I teach elements of communication — literature and writing — 20 I'm wondering how to help my students focus. Multitasking, after all, is the anti-Zen. Living — *really living* and connecting with people — requires concentration, not distraction.

So instead of keeping pace with the Multimedia Madness, I want to alter the rhythm — bring in a yoga instructor and assign more readings in transcendental meditation. The late author J. Krishnamurti, in his 1964 book, *Think on These Things*, advised people to pay attention to the silence: "It is very important to have space in the mind. If the mind is not overcrowded, not ceaselessly occupied, then it can listen to that dog barking, to the sound of the train crossing the distant bridge, and also be fully aware of what is being said by a person talking here. Then the mind is a living thing, it is not dead."

READING THE TEXT

1. Why does Simpson say that her current students are members of "ADD Nation or IM Generation" (para. 4)?

2. According to Simpson, what are the consequences of "media multitasking"?

3. How do the distractions Simpson experienced as a college student compare with the distractions her students face today?

4. Why does Simpson say that "multitasking . . . is the anti-Zen" (para. 20)?

5. What effect does Simpson's use of anecdotal experience with students have on the persuasiveness of her essay, and with what sort of reader do you think it would be most effective?

READING THE SIGNS

1. In your journal, reflect on your own tendency either to multitask or to concentrate on one activity at a time. If you find yourself "addicted" to media, do you see any impact, positive or negative, on your schoolwork and relations with others? If you avoid media multitasking, do you find you are out of sync with most of your peers?

2. Write an argument supporting, refuting, or complicating counselor Ben Locke's claim that "students don't disengage, they don't slow down" (para. 17). To develop support for your position, you might interview several acquaintances about their own multitasking habits and observe students randomly as they leave lecture halls and other public buildings. Do they immediately turn to one or more electronic devices after class is over? Do they surreptitiously use such devices in class?

3. Simpson's essay reveals a distinct generation gap between herself and her students. Discuss in class the ways in which generational differences shape Simpson's argument and point of view.

4. Write an essay defending, opposing, or modifying Simpson's position that media multitasking is damaging today's students' mastery of the art of communication and ability to concentrate and focus.

DAVID TETEN AND SCOTT ALLEN

Free Speech and Censorship in Online Communities

Participants in online forums and communities are well acquainted with the phenomenon called "moderation": the fact that certain members of the community, moderators, are able to edit or delete comments that they find objectionable or in violation of the site's codes of conduct. And the response to such acts of moderation, as David Teten and Scott Allen note in this legal analysis for fastcompany.com, is "Censorship! You're violating my First Amendment Rights!" Such passions arise because Americans are accustomed to freedom of speech, particularly within the virtual spaces of the electronic frontier. But as Teten and Allen also note, anyone who demands unlimited online freedom of expression is out of luck: The law allows both public and private online communities to establish their own rules, and if a user doesn't like them, perhaps a move to a more congenially run site is in order. Teten and Allen are marketing consultants and the coauthors of The Virtual Handshake: Opening Doors and Closing Deals Online *(2005).*

Is free speech an absolute right in online communities? Yes, but community owners have the right to establish and enforce codes of conduct.

"Censorship! You're violating my First Amendment Rights!"

Students of online communities joke that most online debates eventually devolve into either comparisons to Hitler or allegations of violation of free speech rights. The person or people raising cries of censorship and assertions of the right to free speech are usually testing or pushing the envelope of the acceptable boundaries within the community — going off topic, profanity, flame wars, and so on.

Is free speech an absolute right within online communities? Can an online community, regardless of its size and membership requirements, establish and enforce a more restrictive code of conduct?

There is a long, well-established precedent for moderation/governance in 5 online communities — both ones that are open to the public and private ones. Online communities have for years been in the practice of having codes of conduct that were far more restrictive than constitutional protections. Even large, open membership communities have moderators who are able to edit or delete posts and suspend or eject members who violate those codes of conduct. To say that the boundaries of constitutionally protected free speech are applicable to any privately owned online community is to go contrary to decades of business practices.

Do blogs change this? What about sites like YouTube, Ecademy, or AlwaysOn, in which individual blogs or channels are aggregated or displayed in the front page and other pages? One could make the argument that blogs are somehow different because of the fact that they are an individual voice rather than a community space. However, the aggregation of them on the front page and the nature of the threaded comments, we believe, negates any such argument. The site may call them blogs, but if they're aggregated and allow comments, they're still really just one big threaded discussion forum. We doubt a court would see a substantial difference simply based on the slight technical difference.

Even so, most hosting companies, including blog hosting companies, also have terms of service that are more restrictive than free speech limits, typically restricting hate speech and pornography, among other things. For example, WordPress prohibits the use of PayPerPost (a service which allows advertisers to pay bloggers to post about their product) on blogs hosted on its service. Is that a violation of a blogger's right to free speech?

Under the Uniform Commercial Code, we all have the right to voluntarily restrict our free speech by contract, and when we join an online community we are doing just that — subject to whatever the terms of service are. In fact, the contract doesn't even have to be explicitly signed in order to be in effect. Consider that when you walk into a theater or restaurant, you give up some of your free speech rights. Do anything that is significantly unpleasant to other patrons — talk too loudly, let your kids run wild, etc. — and you'll be warned and eventually ejected.

Why would anyone expect an online community to be any different?

You do have the right of free speech, but the owners of a community also 10 have the right to establish and enforce codes of conduct within the community. In fact, the very same First Amendment jurisprudence that allows free speech allows the community owners not to be forced to "carry" that free speech. Further, by joining that community, your right of contract supersedes your right of free speech.

Many of these issues were ironed out in the early days of the Internet with the 1995 Stratton Oakmont v. Prodigy decision and its subsequent reversal by the U.S. Congress as part of the Communications Decency Act. The end result of this was two-fold: first, it grants online community providers a near-blanket immunity from liability for content posted by users, whether the community attempts to control the content or not. Secondly, under this legal protection, communities have been allowed to exercise control over content they consider objectionable in order to best serve the needs of the particular community.

However, the emergence of virtual worlds like The Sims Online and Second Life has brought the issue to the forefront again with several much-publicized cases. Santa Clara University Assistant Professor Eric Goldman has covered this in his 2005 paper, "Speech Showdowns at the Virtual Corral," in which he writes: Neither free speech rights nor private property and contract rights are absolute. Where they intersect in the physical world, confusing legal doctrines usually emerge, such as the U.S. Supreme Court cases addressing private speech at privately owned company towns and shopping centers. Though a bright-line rule has emerged (the First Amendment pertains only to state actors) the rule provides little prospective guidance because private actors can be characterized as state actors in some circumstances. In the online world, the speech/rights dichotomy also raises complex issues. Online private actors routinely use their private property (such as computers and networks) to create virtual spaces designed for speech, though speaker access is usually controlled by contract. An online provider exercising its property or contract rights inevitably squelches a speaker's rights. Nevertheless, despite online providers' capacity to exercise their rights capriciously, courts so far have unanimously held that private online providers are not state actors for First Amendment purposes.

So when you find yourself bumping up against the boundaries of behavior in an online community, you might want to consider whether that community is really the right community for you. If so, then you can either adapt your behavior to the code of conduct or you can use persuasive means to try to change the code of conduct. But don't make cries of "Censorship!" — you gave up that right when you joined.

Got something to say? Join the discussion.

READING THE TEXT

1. Why are online communities exempt from strict First Amendment protections of free speech, according to the authors?

2. Why do Teten and Allen categorize blogs as being similar to discussion forums, at least where the free speech controversy is concerned?

3. Summarize in your own words Eric Goldman's explanation of how free speech exists in the physical world and in the online world.

READING THE SIGNS

1. Write your own response to Teten and Allen's central question, "Is free speech an absolute right in online communities?" (para. 1). To develop your ideas, interview participants in online forums about whether they find codes of conduct unnecessarily restrictive or conducive to a sense of community.

2. The Internet has long been championed as a grassroots, democratic frontier where individual expression and creativity can reign. In an essay, argue whether codes of conduct contradict this image or whether they in fact are an instance of successful self-regulation.

3. **CONNECTING TEXTS** To what extent are virtual worlds affected by the free-speech debate? To develop your ideas, consult Ted Friedman's "From the Forest to the Trees: The Sims" (p. 452).

4. Compare and contrast a moderated and an unmoderated forum that are addressed to people with the same sort of interests. For instance, one might study two sites that target amateur astronomers: **www.cloudynights.com,** which is moderated, and **http://groups.google.com/group/sci.astro.amateur,** which is not. What differences do you see in both content and style of posts, and how can you explain those differences?

AMERICAN PARADOX

Culture and Contradiction in the U.S.A.

The Paris Paradox

On May 4, 2007, Paris Hilton received a forty-five day prison sentence for a driving-related parole violation. On June 3 of the same year, she began to serve that sentence. On June 7, she was released from prison by the Los Angeles County sheriff to serve the remainder of her term in home confinement. On June 8 she was ordered back to court and then returned to prison. On June 26, she was released after a total of twenty-two days in confinement.

Meanwhile, the world went crazy.

It was hard to avoid the story, as Hilton's legal woes made headlines around the globe, and Hilton herself became the object of worldwide derision. Soon to be joined in scandal by Lindsay Lohan and Nicole Richie, Hilton still somehow stood out, eclipsing her sisters in party-girl hijinks, sheer media hysteria, and mass condemnation. The strikingly vitriolic nature of much of that condemnation is, for the purposes of this chapter, the most significant part of the whole sorry story. There was little sympathy for the pathetic images of Hilton wailing in court and weeping in custody, and much mockery and ridicule — all of which was somewhat paradoxical insofar as it came from the same public that had made Hilton a celebrity in the first place. Something had clearly hit a nerve, but what was it?

A semiotic approach to this question can lead us to a profound realization about American culture that goes far beyond Paris Hilton and her antics, bringing us face to face with some of America's stickiest contradictions — that is, with the opposing tendencies within our culture that make us an extraordinarily complex, and sometimes even perplexing, society. This chapter introduces

---

Exploring the Signs of American Contradictions

The Janet Jackson–Justin Timberlake "wardrobe malfunction" during the 2004 Super Bowl half-time show led to heightened sensitivity to supposedly offensive episodes in the media, with increased FCC monitoring of programming and with Congress increasing fines for indecency. In your journal, explore the consequences of these responses. Do you regard them as a contradiction between the need to protect audiences, especially children, on the one hand, and the constitutional guarantee of freedom of speech, on the other?

---

you to those contradictions, and the "Paris Paradox" is a good place to begin as it is a sign of deeper currents within our everyday lives.

To interpret this sign, we must first set aside any personal attitudes we may have toward Paris Hilton one way or another. All we need are some facts and an understanding of the mythologies within which her story is entangled. So here are some facts: A member of one of the world's richest families and once a presumptive heiress to a personal fortune, Paris Hilton is also an entertainment celebrity who has starred in her own reality television series, has been a professional model, and has played small roles in a number of movies. At the same time, she is notorious for the release of a homemade sex video on the eve of the debut of the first season of her reality television show *The Simple Life*. That the circumstances surrounding the release of that video are clouded in mystery is simply another fact to be considered. In the end it doesn't matter whether Hilton herself had anything to do with it; what matters is that many people believe that she did and that the whole thing was a career-propelling public relations stunt.

These facts are really all that we need to start. So, what can we make of them?

First, there is Hilton's inherited social-class status. A wealthy socialite and debutante, Hilton belongs to an elite upper class that has always existed in American society, but which historically has been rejected, or even denied, by the grounding American mythology that America is a land of equal opportunity devoid of inherited distinctions and aristocratic privileges. The fact that America *has* families that enjoy inherited distinctions and aristocratic privileges hasn't fazed the mythology a bit and has instead produced a desire for representations of privileged families in popular culture as being morally inferior or contemptible — as exemplified in television series like *Dallas*, *Arrested Development*, and *My Super Sweet Sixteen*. At once fascinated by inherited privilege and repelled by it, Americans tend to have a love/hate relationship with their own aristocracy, and this contradictory tendency has a great deal to do with the reaction to Paris Hilton, the celebrity whom almost everyone, it sometimes appears, loves to hate.

To a certain degree, the often negative public reaction toward Lindsay Lohan and Nicole Richie can be related to that of Paris Hilton, for they also belong to prosperous families. Still, there is a certain difference in the degree of hostility that Hilton excites, a greater level of vitriolic outrage than is directed at her sisters in high-profile misbehavior. And this difference, as is always the case in the interpretation of a sign, is crucial to understanding the precise nature of Paris Hilton's cultural significance.

The difference here lies in the fact that while Lohan's parents were well-to-do, they were never a famously aristocratic clan as are the Hiltons, and Lohan's father has even spent a fair amount of time in prison. Richie, for her part, is the daughter of Lionel Richie, a very popular African American entertainer who worked his way up — a fact that helps mollify the public's reaction to his daughter's antics. Americans don't mind rich people as long as they make their own way, because that is an essential part of the mythology that we call the American dream (consider the huge popularity of self-made men like Lee Iacocca and Sam Walton); what they mind are people who inherit their wealth and make the mistake of flaunting it. And that's what makes Hilton different: the degree to which she openly flaunts and exploits her aristocratic background as the granddaughter of the famously and extravagantly wealthy Conrad Hilton. Her conduct, her very being, is a walking signifier of the sheer contradiction at the heart of one of America's most cherished mythologies; that is, while Americans value a level playing field and democratic vistas of opportunity, they also nurture a hereditary upper class that isn't on the same playing field at all. Hilton wouldn't be a celebrity without mass cooperation, and the unbridled hostility she faces (often from fellow entertainment celebrities who worked *their* way up) is a paradoxical sign of both compunction and catharsis. That is, Hilton makes America feel at once guilty for not being true to its class mythologies and relieved to be able to vent its mortification upon someone who, consciously or unconsciously, so openly flaunts her contradiction of them.

But wait, there's more.

There's that video. It is widely believed that its "leak" played a big role in winning instant notoriety for its "star," the kind of publicity that entertainment wannabes would sell their souls for in an environment where even bad publicity is good publicity. And that video openly flaunts another paradoxical contradiction in American culture: the contradiction between our puritanical, sexually repressive cultural roots and our common tendency to commodify sex and turn it into a marketing tool to sell just about anything and anybody. It isn't that women entertainers aren't sexually commodified all the time; they just aren't supposed to commodify *themselves*. *That* gives the game away too much, makes too obvious the contradiction, perhaps even the hypocrisy, within American culture.

One might say that Madonna pioneered this sort of thing, but her modest social origins and the fact that her sexual self-promotion was originally contained within nonpornographic dance videos shielded her from any significant backlash. But Hilton at least *appeared* to be her own sexual impresario, manipulating the mass media in a calculated manner for her own success. And that went too far, highlighting the fact that puritan America harbors its own commercial sexual contradiction, and there is nothing like the revelation of a cultural contradiction to trigger an angry reaction.

Indeed, when American mass culture gets particularly riled up about something, there is often a good chance that some sort of cultural contradiction has boiled to the surface. American culture is filled with contradictions, and when those contradictions clash in highly visible and scandalous situations, the result can be near hysteria. For another example, consider what happened at the half-time show during Super Bowl XXXVII.

Janet-Gate

Everything was proceeding routinely enough, with two MTV stars providing the entertainment amidst a carefully choreographed musical extravaganza, when suddenly something went wrong. In the aftermath of the catastrophe, both of the stars insisted that there had been an accident — a "wardrobe malfunction" to be exact — but the damage had been done. Before you could say "Janet Jackson's breast," the nation had risen up in wrath. Anti-indecency legislation began to pour out of Washington, D.C., Justin Timberlake pouted and apologized, Janet Jackson canceled an appearance or two, and Howard Stern decided that life would be easier on satellite radio.

As we write this introduction more than four years later, the dust is still settling on the Jackson-Timberlake fiasco, with CBS making a court challenge to the $550,000 fine from the FCC that it received for the incident, following upon an earlier successful legal appeal of the government's post–Super Bowl XXXVII ratcheting down on broadcast indecency. But, somehow, the whole

---

Discussing the Signs of American Contradictions

In class, discuss the results of the 2008 presidential and other recent national elections. Do you find in the results a fundamental divide between the values and political positions of the so-called blue and red states? If students hail from different states, compare the political climates in your home states; if most of the class comes from one state, consider whether your state has an internal red-blue divide. If you see differences in political attitudes, what are they, and who is aligned with which positions?

The "wardrobe malfunction" heard 'round the world.

matter seems a little askew, because if you had watched the onscreen promotions for the half-time show for Super Bowl XXXVII prior to the actual event, you would have seen just about as much of Janet Jackson as you could see when her bustier came off. In fact, in an environment saturated with images of skimpily clad women, you can hardly look anywhere without seeing pretty much what so upset the nation at half-time.

So what's going on? With Americans using female sexuality to sell just about everything (Super Bowl XXXVI featured an intensely hyped Pepsi ad with Britney Spears), and women's fashions featuring low waists and plunging necklines, the Timberlake-Jackson snafu seems to be pretty bland stuff. But it clearly struck a nerve, and, once again, it involved a contradiction between a highly eroticized commercial culture and a puritanical tradition.

For puritanism and capitalism, usually kept in separate spheres in America, collided that Super Bowl evening. On the one hand, there was the football game: America's favorite secular ritual that is cast as a celebration of the most traditional national values — not puritanism precisely, but certainly wholesome athletic competition and family entertainment. On the other hand, there was the money: the $2 million-plus per half-minute advertising charges and the money CBS put up for the broadcast rights. With so much money on the line (the bottom line, not the goal line), the Super Bowl has to guarantee its advertisers a large audience, and in recent years that has meant letting the kings of pop music, from Michael Jackson to U2 to the Rolling Stones, handle the half-time show in MTV-inspired extravaganzas. But what is commonplace on MTV (and that's a lot raunchier than what happened at half-time) is still shocking to the puritanical heartland, wherein the Super Bowl is still a symbol of traditionalism and family values. So it was really no surprise at all that something could go wrong. What was surprising was that it took so long for such a collision to happen.

The larger story here, then, is the story of America's many contradictions, including the fact that while America was founded on universal principles of freedom and human equality, slave owners helped write a constitution that guaranteed the rights of slaveholders. It took a civil war that killed more than 650,000 people to settle the matter, the most terrible war in American history. On a different front, while Americans have been among the most resource-voracious people in history, gobbling up and destroying much of what was an unspoiled continent when the nation was founded, we also invented environmentalism. Look at it this way: The country that gave the world Standard Oil is also the birthplace of the Sierra Club.

To the rest of the world, Americans look like crazy, mixed-up hypocrites, but we hardly notice it ourselves because we live our many contradictions within the texture of our everyday lives. These contradictions can make us look rather silly, as both the Super Bowl XXXVII brouhaha and the Paris Hilton story did, but they also make us very interesting, certainly worthy of cultural analysis.

Reading the Signs of American Contradictions on the Net

Despite the explosion in the number of media outlets in the last decade, critics have charged that the increased consolidation of media has in fact homogenized the mass media, with Americans paradoxically now having a narrower range of options available to them. Does the Internet — an environment that allows for blogs, chat rooms, discussion forums, and the like — manage to cut through this paradox? Or, with the rise of powerhouses like Amazon.com, Google, and eBay, do you see signs of corporate control threatening the much-heralded democratic freedom that the Internet offers?

Six Big American Contradictions

America presents enough cultural contradictions to fill an entire volume of analyses, but we'll look briefly here at six very basic ones that, at least in part, can help explain the notorious division between "red" and "blue" states that David Brooks writes about in this chapter. We have already looked at one of these contradictions: America's curious dichotomy between cultural puritanism and a capitalistic tendency to exploit sexuality on behalf of corporate profits. We inherit that puritanism from the Puritans themselves, who founded the Massachusetts Bay Colony in the 1620s. Deeply repressive of any expression of human sexuality, puritanism in America had become so striking by the nineteenth century that British visitors began to joke about finding the legs of American pianos draped in woolen stockings to avoid the exposure of a bare leg. It was this puritanical streak that caused the notorious filming of Elvis Presley from the waist up when he first performed on *The Ed Sullivan Show* in the 1950s (broadcasters objected to the King's vigorous pelvic gyrations). And it prompted a cultural backlash against such early rock 'n' rollers as Chuck Berry (arrested on a Mann Act violation), Little Richard (who performed in drag), and Jerry Lee Lewis (who married his thirteen-year-old cousin) that led to the popularization of squeaky-clean performers like Pat Boone and Debbie Reynolds.

An America that once judicially banned James Joyce's classic novel *Ulysses* because it contained a brothel scene, a soliloquy on oral sex, and the "F" word now can transform a classic children's story like *The Cat in the Hat* into a movie filled with off-color humor, while selling to preteen girls revealing tops and trousers that might have once embarrassed a prostitute. Prime-time network TV programs like *Desperate Housewives* (which staged its own sexually revealing NFL stunt in 2004 on behalf of some free publicity) turn the asexual suburbs of the classic sitcoms upside down, while in the aftermath of such early reality TV hits as *Temptation Island* and *The Bachelor* it's hard to miss a steamy scene somewhere when one turns on the television.

The second American contradiction, which was also at least partially involved in our interpretation of the Paris Hilton phenomenon, is described in detail in one of this chapter's readings, "Masters of Desire." This contradiction concerns our tendency to embrace cultural populism and cultural elitism simultaneously. That is to say, Americans at once value the democratic society "of the people, by the people, and for the people" that Abraham Lincoln so eloquently described in the Gettysburg Address, while at the same time we embrace an American dream that urges us to rise above the crowd to achieve elite status, power, and money. Thus, in the eighteenth century, a French writer named St. Jean de Crevecoeur could celebrate an American society that, unlike aristocratic Europe, did not contain large gaps between rich and poor (or so he claimed); and yet, Americans can turn the television show *The Apprentice*, which stars a billionaire who got his start by inheriting millions, into a hit, and subscribe to a magazine like *Fortune*, whose primary purpose is to let us know about who really has the bucks.

Then America's tradition of self-reliant individualism runs side by side with a tendency toward conformity that prompts us to be just like everybody else. Thus, where Ralph Waldo Emerson and Henry David Thoreau propounded the virtues of self-reliance and marching to the beat of a different drummer, and Americans to this day tend to mistrust centralized governmental institutions that limit personal freedom, America is also the country that in the McCarthyite 1950s compelled its citizens to conform to a middle-class standard of conduct and appearance, threatening the odd individual who happened to grow a beard or refuse to wear a business suit with an accusation of being a communist. And even today in small-town America, individuals can experience enormous social pressures to join the same churches as their neighbors and, generally, to live the same sort of lives.

Paradoxically, when Americans do rebel against the forces of conformism, they tend to do so in ways that only reproduce the ways of conformity through mass consumption. That is, the consumer marketplace is filled with mass-produced goods and services whose advertisements promise that your individual uniqueness will be assured if you (and a few million other consumers) buy this or that product, as in the Reebok campaign that insisted that, if you bought a shoe just like the shoes that millions of other consumers were buying, it would "let U be you."

A fourth contradiction lies in the conflict between American altruism (most dramatically embodied in the sacrifices made by New York City firefighters during the September 11 attacks on the World Trade Center) and the libertarianism that draws Americans to the novels of Ayn Rand and the politics of a sort of neo–Social Darwinism. We like to think of ourselves as a caring, charitable people, but we don't like welfare and we especially hate paying taxes. We like social services, but we don't like to make personal sacrifices to pay for them. If you happen to attend a public college, you know about this contradiction firsthand: Your tuition is going up because the people of your state will not pay higher taxes to support higher education, conveniently placing the burden on you.

A fifth contradiction can be found in America's simultaneous adoration of money and possessions and its commitment to religion and spirituality. The same land that attracted John Smith to Jamestown in 1607 in search of instant and easy wealth also attracted the Pilgrims in 1620 in search of religious freedom, along with Puritans in search of a place to build a theocratic "city on a hill." The most consumer-oriented society in history, America is also a place where some 80 percent of the population claims to be religious. Perhaps nothing in America better exemplifies this contradiction than the American Christmas, which combines the rituals of Christianity with the rituals of rampant consumerism. Every year everyone complains about this, but no one does anything about it — which is probably a good thing because, with a quarter of the nation's retail sales taking place during the Christmas season, the economy would collapse if anything were actually done to change it.

And finally, last but by no means least, there is that already mentioned contradiction between America's grand declaration of universal human freedom and equality and its racial history, which has witnessed institutionalized African slavery, the destruction of indigenous peoples, and the general marginalization of nonwhite Americans. That this is a contradiction and not a singularity, that it coexists with a genuine history of promoting freedom and equality, does not erase its painful existence, nor does it reduce its continuing potential to divide rather than unite us.

What's Red and Blue and Mad All Over?

These contradictions, which have been part of the fabric of American culture from the nation's beginning, have recently been displayed on a grand scale in successive presidential elections in which the country split almost exactly down the middle between what have come to be called the "red states" (roughly the South, the Midwest, and the noncoastal West) and the "blue states" (the East Coast north of Virginia, the Old Northwest, and the West Coast). Although these terms run the risk of overgeneralization, the red states tend to reflect religiosity, small-town conformism, relative racial homogeneity (or polarity), and puritanism, whereas the blue states tend to be more secular, less socially restrictive, more multicultural, and anti-puritan. Of course, folks in the red states can exemplify blue-state traits, and vice versa, but a general sense that these two electoral sections of the country are parting ways around a fundamental split of basic values persists, profoundly worrying those who fear that a fundamental split is occurring within American culture.

Privatizing the Public Sphere

The contradictions we have surveyed thus far might be called ethical contradictions — that is, contradictions in our value systems. In recent years, however, a new American contradiction has emerged that might best be referred to as a lifestyle contradiction: It can be found in the emerging number of gated residential communities, the explosion of cell-phone ownership, the popularity of humongous SUVs, and the advent of the iPod and iPhone. What all of these apparently unrelated phenomena share is their reflection of a new attitude toward the public sphere, one that, in effect, privatizes it through the creation of personalized lifestyle cocoons. Whenever someone retreats into a guard-gated neighborhood, or purchases a giant SUV because such cars are more likely to "prevail" over smaller vehicles in a traffic accident, or gabs on a cell phone while driving, dining in a restaurant, or sitting in class, one is effectively denying the existence of all those other people who occupy the same public space. Even the iPod, which enables you to personalize your own private musical playlist, creates a singular auditory realm that differs substantially from the shared realm of broadcast radio.

The contradiction here lies in the way that the inclusive embrace of America's official Latin slogan *e pluribus unum* ("in many, one") is transposed into an oppositional relationship between the private individual and the public commonweal. In the early 1960s, President John F. Kennedy thrilled Americans when he exhorted, "Ask not what your country can do for you, ask what you can do for your country." It is hard to imagine such a slogan even being uttered today, much less revered, in an era when the lifestyle choices of more and more Americans signify a withdrawal from, mistrust of, and even hostility toward their fellow citizens.

The system in which the signs of American communal disaffection may be discerned can be expanded to include the types of entertainment that are especially popular today. As analyzed in the Introduction to Chapter 3, the schadenfreude-ridden realm of reality TV, in which viewers take pleasure in the humiliation and discomfort of others, also signifies an increasingly atomized society. This is not an exclusively American phenomenon by any means, however, as similar signs of social decay are visible globally today. The causes of such social disaffection are quite complex and lie beyond the scope of this book — for popular culture certainly is not the source of global alienation. But we may find the effects of this contradiction reflected throughout popular culture, indicating once again how the apparently trivial circumstances of everyday life can be signifiers of serious social issues.

The Readings

David Brooks begins our survey of American contradictions with an ultimately optimistic exploration of the cultural divide that has made the terms "red America" and "blue America" household words. Randall Kennedy and Corey Williams follow with a paired set of readings relating to the contradictory legacy of America's racial history, looking, respectively, at racial profiling and the paradoxical use of the "N-word" in black speech and popular culture. Next, Tim Kasser scientifically probes the contradictions inherent in American materialism, while Jack Solomon's analysis of some of the fundamental mythologies that underlie American advertising highlights the contradiction between American populism and the elitism at the heart of the American dream. Shelley Fralic reports on the paradoxical phenomenon of rich celebrities marketing low-cost lines of consumer goods, and Mariah Burton Nelson critiques the cultural double standard that compels female athletes to be as concerned about their femininity as they are about winning. Alfred Lubrano offers a personal reflection on what it was like to move from working-class commonality to the Ivy League elite, and Richard Corliss concludes the chapter by taking up the contradiction between America's evangelical traditions and an often irreverent popular culture, showing how a new synthesis between old opponents is now forming.

DAVID BROOKS
One Nation, Slightly Divisible

Red is red, and blue is blue, and never the twain shall meet — or so one might conclude after presidential elections in which the American electorate divided decisively between so-called "red states" and "blue states." Shortly after the 2000 election, which first introduced the red state–blue state division, David Brooks went on the road (he didn't have to go far) to see whether Americans were so hopelessly culturally divided after all. He found that, while red America may have fewer Starbucks and Pottery Barn outlets than does blue America, the feared divide may not go so deep after all. Brooks is a columnist for the New York Times *and a commentator on* The NewsHour with Jim Lehrer. *This selection was first published in 2001 in the* Atlantic Monthly. *He is the author of* Bobos in Paradise: The New Upper Class and How They Got There *(2000) and* On Paradise Drive: How We Live Now (and Always Have) in the Future Tense *(2004).*

Sixty-five miles from where I am writing this sentence is a place with no Starbucks, no Pottery Barn, no Borders or Barnes & Noble. No blue *New York Times* delivery bags dot the driveways on Sunday mornings. In this place people don't complain that Woody Allen isn't as funny as he used to be, because they never thought he was funny. In this place you can go to a year's worth of dinner parties without hearing anyone quote an aperçu he first heard on *Charlie Rose*. The people here don't buy those little rear-window stickers when they go to a summer-vacation spot so that they can drive around with "MV" decals the rest of the year; for the most part they don't even go to Martha's Vineyard.

The place I'm talking about goes by different names. Some call it America. Others call it Middle America. It has also come to be known as Red America, in reference to the maps that were produced on the night of the 2000 presidential election. People in Blue America, which is my part of America, tend to live around big cities on the coasts. People in Red America tend to live on farms or in small towns or small cities far away from the coasts. Things are different there.

Everything that people in my neighborhood do without motors, the people in Red America do with motors. We sail; they powerboat. We cross-country ski; they snowmobile. We hike; they drive ATVs. We have vineyard tours; they have tractor pulls. When it comes to yard work, they have rider mowers; we have illegal aliens.

Different sorts of institutions dominate life in these two places. In Red America churches are everywhere. In Blue America Thai restaurants are everywhere. In Red America they have QVC, the Pro Bowlers Tour, and hunting. In

Blue America we have NPR, Doris Kearns Goodwin, and socially conscious investing. In Red America the Wal-Marts are massive, with parking lots the size of state parks. In Blue America the stores are small but the markups are big. You'll rarely see a Christmas store in Blue America, but in Red America, even in July, you'll come upon stores selling fake Christmas trees, wreath-decorated napkins, Rudolph the Red-Nosed Reindeer collectible thimbles and spoons, and little snow-covered villages.

We in the coastal metro Blue areas read more books and attend more 5 plays than the people in the Red heartland. We're more sophisticated and cosmopolitan — just ask us about our alumni trips to China or Provence, or our interest in Buddhism. But don't ask us, please, what life in Red America is like. We don't know. We don't know who Tim LaHaye and Jerry B. Jenkins are, even though the novels they have co-written have sold about 40 million copies over the past few years. We don't know what James Dobson says on his radio program, which is listened to by millions. We don't know about Reba or Travis. We don't know what happens in mega-churches on Wednesday evenings, and some of us couldn't tell you the difference between a fundamentalist and an evangelical, let alone describe what it means to be a Pentecostal. Very few of us know what goes on in Branson, Missouri, even though it has seven million visitors a year, or could name even five NASCAR drivers, although stock-car races are the best-attended sporting events in the country. We don't know how to shoot or clean a rifle. We can't tell a military officer's rank by looking at his insignia. We don't know what soy beans look like when they're growing in a field.

All we know, or all we think we know, about Red America is that millions and millions of its people live quietly underneath flight patterns, many of them are racist and homophobic, and when you see them at highway rest stops, they're often really fat and their clothes are too tight.

And apparently we don't want to know any more than that. One can barely find any books at Amazon.com about what it is like to live in small-town America — or, at least, any books written by normal people who grew up in small towns, liked them, and stayed there. The few books that do exist were written either by people who left the heartland because they hated it (Bill Bryson's *The Lost Continent*, for example) or by urbanites who moved to Red America as part of some life-simplification plan (*Moving to a Small Town: A Guidebook for Moving from Urban to Rural America*; National Geographic's *Guide to Small Town Escapes*). Apparently no publishers or members of the Blue book-buying public are curious about Red America as seen through Red America's eyes.

Crossing the Meatloaf Line

Over the past several months, my interest piqued by those stark blocks of color on the election-night maps, I have every now and then left my home in Montgomery County, Maryland, and driven sixty-five miles northwest to Franklin County, in south-central Pennsylvania. Montgomery County is one of the steaming-hot centers of the great espresso machine that is Blue America. It is just over the border from northwestern Washington, D.C., and it is full of upper-middle-class towns inhabited by lawyers, doctors, stockbrokers, and establishment journalists like me — towns like Chevy Chase, Potomac, and Bethesda (where I live). Its central artery is a burgeoning high-tech corridor with a multitude of sparkling new office parks housing technology companies such as United Information Systems and Sybase, and pioneering biotech firms such as Celera Genomics and Human Genome Sciences. When I drive to Franklin County, I take Route 270. After about forty-five minutes I pass a Cracker Barrel — Red America condensed into chain-restaurant form. I've crossed the Meatloaf Line; from here on there will be a lot fewer sun-dried-tomato concoctions on restaurant menus and a lot more meatloaf platters.

Franklin County is Red America. It's a rural county, about twenty-five miles west of Gettysburg, and it includes the towns of Waynesboro, Chambersburg, and Mercersburg. It was originally settled by the Scotch-Irish, and has plenty of Brethren and Mennonites along with a fast-growing population of evangelicals. The joke that Pennsylvanians tell about their state is that it has Philadelphia on one end, Pittsburgh on the other, and Alabama in the middle. Franklin County is in the Alabama part. It strikes me as I drive there that even though I am going north across the Mason-Dixon line, I feel as if I were going south. The local culture owes more to Nashville, Houston, and Daytona than to Washington, Philadelphia, or New York.

I shuttled back and forth between Franklin and Montgomery Counties 10 because the cultural differences between the two places are great, though the geographic distance is small. The two places are not perfect microcosms of Red and Blue America. The part of Montgomery County I am here describing is largely the Caucasian part. Moreover, Franklin County is in a Red part of a Blue state: overall, Pennsylvania went for Gore. And I went to Franklin County aware that there are tremendous differences within Red America, just as there are within Blue. Franklin County is quite different from, say, Scottsdale, Arizona, just as Bethesda is quite different from Oakland, California.

Nonetheless, the contrasts between the two counties leap out, and they are broadly suggestive of the sorts of contrasts that can be seen nationwide. When Blue America talks about social changes that convulsed society, it tends to mean the 1960s rise of the counterculture and feminism. When Red America talks about changes that convulsed society, it tends to mean World War II, which shook up old town establishments and led to a great surge of industry.

Red America makes social distinctions that Blue America doesn't. For example, in Franklin County there seems to be a distinction between those fiercely independent people who live in the hills and people who live in the valleys. I got a hint of the distinct and, to me, exotic hill culture when a hill dweller asked me why I thought hunting for squirrel and rabbit had gone out of fashion. I thought maybe it was just more fun to hunt something bigger. But he said, "McDonald's. It's cheaper to get a hamburger at McDonald's than to go out and get it yourself."

There also seems to be an important distinction between men who work outdoors and men who work indoors. The outdoor guys wear faded black T-shirts they once picked up at a Lynyrd Skynyrd concert and wrecked jeans that appear to be washed faithfully at least once a year. They've got wraparound NASCAR sunglasses, maybe a NAPA auto parts cap, and hair cut in a short wedge up front but flowing down over their shoulders in the back — a cut that is known as a mullet, which is sort of a cross between Van Halen's style and Kenny Rogers's, and is the ugliest hairdo since every hairdo in the seventies. The outdoor guys are heavily accessorized, and their accessories are meant to show how hard they work, so they will often have a gigantic wad of keys hanging from a belt loop, a tape measure strapped to the belt, a pocket knife on a string tucked into the front pants pocket, and a pager or a cell phone affixed to the hip, presumably in case some power lines go down somewhere and need emergency repair. Outdoor guys have a thing against sleeves. They work so hard that they've got to keep their arm muscles unencumbered and their armpit hair fully ventilated, so they either buy their shirts sleeveless or rip the sleeves off their T-shirts first thing, leaving bits of fringe hanging over their BAD TO THE BONE tattoos.

The guys who work indoors can't project this rugged proletarian image. It's simply not that romantic to be a bank-loan officer or a shift manager at the local distribution center. So the indoor guys adopt a look that a smart-ass, sneering Blue American might call Bible-academy casual — maybe Haggar slacks, which they bought at a dry-goods store best known for its appliance department, and a short-sleeved white Van Heusen shirt from the Bon-Ton. Their image projects not "I work hard" but "I'm a devoted family man." A lot of indoor guys have a sensitive New Age demeanor. When they talk about the days their kids were born, their eyes take on a soft Garth Brooks expression, and they tear up. They exaggerate how sinful they were before they were born again. On Saturdays they are patio masters, barbecuing on their gas grills in full Father's Day–apron regalia.

At first I thought the indoor guys were the faithful, reliable ones: the ones who did well in school, whereas the outdoor guys were druggies. But after talking with several preachers in Franklin County, I learned that it's not that simple. Sometimes the guys who look like bikers are the most devoted community-service volunteers and church attendees. 15

The kinds of distinctions we make in Blue America are different. In my world the easiest way to categorize people is by headroom needs. People who went to business school or law school like a lot of headroom. They buy humongous sport-utility vehicles that practically have cathedral ceilings over the front seats. They live in homes the size of country clubs, with soaring entry atriums so high that they could practically fly a kite when they come through the front door. These big-headroom people tend to be predators: their jobs have them negotiating and competing all day. They spend small fortunes on dry cleaning. They grow animated when talking about how much they love their blackberries. They fill their enormous wall space with huge professional family portraits — Mom and Dad with their perfect kids (dressed in light-blue oxford shirts) laughing happily in an orchard somewhere.

Small-headroom people tend to have been liberal-arts majors, and they have liberal-arts jobs. They get passive-aggressive pleasure from demonstrating how modest and environmentally sensitive their living containers are. They hate people with SUVs, and feel virtuous driving around in their low-ceilinged little Hondas, which often display a RANDOM ACTS OF KINDNESS bumper sticker or one bearing an image of a fish with legs, along with the word "Darwin," just to show how intellectually superior to fundamentalist Christians they are.

Some of the biggest differences between Red and Blue America show up on statistical tables. Ethnic diversity is one. In Montgomery County 60 percent of the population is white, 15 percent is black, 12 percent is Hispanic, and 11 percent is Asian. In Franklin County 95 percent of the population is white. White people work the gas-station pumps and the 7-Eleven counters. (This is something one doesn't often see in my part of the country.) Although the nation is growing more diverse, it's doing so only in certain spots. According to an analysis of the 2000 census by Bill Frey, a demographer at the Milken Institute, well over half the counties in America are still at least 85 percent white.

Another big thing is that, according to 1990 census data, in Franklin County only 12 percent of the adults have college degrees and only 69 percent have high school diplomas. In Montgomery County 50 percent of the adults have college degrees and 91 percent have high school diplomas. The education gap extends to the children. At Walt Whitman High School, a public school in Bethesda, the average SAT scores are 601 verbal and 622 math, whereas the national average is 506 verbal and 514 math. In Franklin County, where people are quite proud of their schools, the average SAT scores at, for example, the Waynesboro area high school are 495 verbal and 480 math. More and more kids in Franklin County are going on to college, but it is hard to believe that their prospects will be as bright as those of the kids in Montgomery County and the rest of upscale Blue America.

Because the information age rewards education with money, it's not surprising that Montgomery County is much richer than Franklin County. According to some estimates, in Montgomery County 51 percent of households have annual incomes above $75,000, and the average household income is $100,365. In Franklin County only 16 percent of households have incomes above $75,000, and the average is $51,872. 20

A major employer in Montgomery County is the National Institutes of Health, which grows like a scientific boomtown in Bethesda. A major economic engine in Franklin County is the interstate highway Route 81. Trucking companies have gotten sick of fighting the congestion on Route 95, which runs up the Blue corridor along the northeast coast, so they move their stuff along 81, farther inland. Several new distribution centers have been built along 81 in Franklin County, and some of the workers who were laid off when their factories closed, several years ago, are now settling for $8.00 or $9.00 an hour loading boxes.

The two counties vote differently, of course—the differences, on a nation-wide scale, were what led to those red-and-blue maps. Like upscale areas everywhere, from Silicon Valley to Chicago's North Shore to suburban Connecticut, Montgomery County supported the Democratic ticket in last year's presidential election, by a margin of 63 percent to 34 percent. Meanwhile, like almost all of rural America, Franklin County went Republican, by 67 percent to 30 percent.

However, other voting patterns sometimes obscure the Red-Blue cultural divide. For example, minority voters all over the country overwhelmingly supported the Democratic ticket last November. But—in many respects, at least—blacks and Hispanics in Red America are more traditionalist than blacks and Hispanics in Blue America, just as their white counterparts are. For example, the Pew Research Center for the People and the Press, in Washington, D.C., recently found that 45 percent of minority members in Red states agree with the statement "AIDS might be God's punishment for immoral sexual behavior," but only 31 percent of minority members in Blue states do. Similarly, 40 percent of minorities in Red states believe that school boards should have the right to fire homosexual teachers, but only 21 percent of minorities in Blue states do.

From Cracks to a Chasm?

These differences are so many and so stark that they lead to some pretty troubling questions: Are Americans any longer a common people? Do we have one national conversation and one national culture? Are we loyal to the same institutions and the same values? How do people on one side of the divide regard those on the other?

I went to Franklin County because I wanted to get a sense of how deep the 25 divide really is, to see how people there live, and to gauge how different their lives are from those in my part of America. I spoke with ministers, journalists, teachers, community leaders, and pretty much anyone I ran across. I consulted with pollsters, demographers, and market-research firms.

Toward the end of my project the World Trade Center and the Pentagon were attacked. This put a new slant on my little investigation. In the days immediately following September 11 the evidence seemed clear that despite our differences, we are still a united people. American flags flew everywhere in Franklin County and in Montgomery County. Patriotism surged. Pollsters started to measure Americans' reactions to the events. Whatever questions they asked, the replies were near unanimous. Do you support a military response against terror? More than four fifths of Americans said yes. Do you support a military response even if it means thousands of U.S. casualties? More than three fifths said yes. There were no significant variations across geographic or demographic lines.

A sweeping feeling of solidarity was noticeable in every neighborhood, school, and workplace. Headlines blared, "A NATION UNITED" and "UNITED STATE." An attack had been made on the very epicenter of Blue America—downtown Manhattan. And in a flash all the jokes about and seeming hostility toward New Yorkers vanished, to be replaced by an outpouring of respect, support, and love. The old hostility came to seem merely a sort of sibling rivalry, which means nothing when the family itself is under threat.

But very soon there were hints that the solidarity was fraying. A few stray notes of dissent were sounded in the organs of Blue America. Susan Sontag wrote a sour piece in *The New Yorker* about how depressing it was to see what she considered to be a simplistically pro-American reaction to the attacks. At rallies on college campuses across the country speakers pointed out that America had been bombing other countries for years, and turnabout was fair play. On one NPR talk show I heard numerous callers express unease about what they saw as a crude us-versus-them mentality behind President Bush's rhetoric. Katha Pollitt wrote in *The Nation* that she would not permit her daughter to hang the American flag from the living-room window, because, she felt, it "stands for jingoism and vengeance and war." And there was evidence that among those with less-strident voices, too, differences were beginning to show. Polls revealed that people without a college education were far more confident than people with a college education that the military could defeat the terrorists. People in the South were far more eager than people in the rest of the country for an American counterattack to begin.

It started to seem likely that these cracks would widen once the American response got under way, when the focus would be not on firemen and rescue workers but on the Marines, the CIA, and the special-operations forces. If the war was protracted, the cracks could widen into a chasm, as they did during Vietnam. Red America, the home of patriotism and military service (there's a big military-recruitment center in downtown Chambersburg), would undoubtedly support the war effort, but would Blue America (there's a big gourmet dog bakery in downtown Bethesda) decide that a crude military response would only deepen animosities and make things worse?

A Cafeteria Nation

These differences in sensibility don't in themselves mean that America has become a fundamentally divided nation. As the sociologist Seymour Martin Lipset pointed out in *The First New Nation* (1963), achievement and equality are the two rival themes running throughout American history. Most people, most places, and most epochs have tried to intertwine them in some way.

Moreover, after bouncing between Montgomery and Franklin Counties, I became convinced that a lot of our fear that America is split into rival camps arises from mistaken notions of how society is shaped. Some of us still carry the old Marxist categories in our heads. We think that society is like a layer cake, with the upper class on top. And, like Marx, we tend to assume that wherever there is class division there is conflict. Or else we have a sort of *Crossfire* model in our heads: where would people we meet sit if they were guests on that show?

But traveling back and forth between the two counties was not like crossing from one rival camp to another. It was like crossing a high school cafeteria. Remember high school? There were nerds, jocks, punks, bikers, techies, druggies, God Squadders, drama geeks, poets, and Dungeons & Dragons weirdoes. All these cliques were part of the same school: they had different sensibilities; sometimes they knew very little about the people in the other cliques; but the jocks knew there would always be nerds, and the nerds knew there would always be jocks. That's just the way life is.

And that's the way America is. We are not a divided nation. We are a cafeteria nation. We form cliques (call them communities, or market segments, or whatever), and when they get too big, we form subcliques. Some people even get together in churches that are "nondenominational" or in political groups that are "independent." These are cliques built around the supposed rejection of cliques.

We live our lives by migrating through the many different cliques associated with the activities we enjoy and the goals we have set for ourselves. Our freedom comes in the interstices; we can choose which set of standards to live by, and when.

We should remember that there is generally some distance between 35 cliques — a buffer zone that separates one set of aspirations from another. People who are happy within their cliques feel no great compulsion to go out and reform other cliques. The jocks don't try to change the nerds. David Rawley, [a] Greencastle minister . . . , has been to New York City only once in his life. "I was happy to get back home," he told me. "It's a planet I'm a little scared of. I have no desire to go back."

What unites the two Americas, then, is our mutual commitment to this way of life — to the idea that a person is not bound by his class, or by the religion of his fathers, but is free to build a plurality of connections for himself. We are participants in the same striving process, the same experimental journey. . . .

READING THE TEXT

1. Summarize in your own words the typical characteristics of red and blue America, as Brooks presents them.

2. What does Brooks mean by saying that, in blue America, "the easiest way to categorize people is by headroom needs" (para. 16)?

3. What ethnic and economic patterns does Brooks see in red and blue America?

4. How did the September 11 attacks affect Brooks's view of the two Americas?

READING THE SIGNS

1. In class, form groups and debate whether Brooks could be accused of stereotyping Americans and whether he is identifying a fundamental contradiction in American culture.

2. Would Brooks characterize your community as red or blue? Provide specific details to demonstrate your position. If you believe your community escapes Brooks's dichotomy, explain why.

3. Brooks wrote this article in 2001. To what extent does the red/blue divide still exist after the 2008 presidential election? If you believe that it remains, has the divide become larger or smaller? You might analyze media coverage of that election for evidence in support of your position.

4. **CONNECTING TEXTS**   In an analytic essay, write your own response to Brooks's question "Are Americans any longer a common people?" (para. 24). To develop your ideas, you might consult the Introduction to Chapter 8, "Constructing Race: Readings in Multicultural Semiotics" (p. 647).

RANDALL KENNEDY
Blind Spot

Racial profiling has been a hot-button issue in recent years, eliciting such sardonic condemnations as the claim that for many Americans it has become a crime to be caught "driving while black." Randall Kennedy, a professor of law at Harvard Law School, enters the controversy here from an unusual angle, finding a fundamental contradiction in the positions of both supporters and opponents of racial profiling. With supporters of racial profiling asserting the rights of the community over those of the individual, while at the same time endorsing the rights of the individual over those of the community when it comes to affirmative action, and opponents of racial profiling doing just the reverse, it is time, Kennedy suggests, for both sides to listen to what the other has to say. Kennedy is the author of Race, Crime, and the Law *(1997),* Nigger: The Strange Career of a Troublesome Word *(2002),* Interracial Intimacies: Sex, Marriage, Identity, and Adoption *(2003), and* Sellout: The Politics of Racial Betrayal *(2008). This selection originally appeared in the April 2002 issue of the* Atlantic.

What is one to think about "racial profiling"? Confusion abounds about what the term even means. It should be defined as the policy or practice of using race as a factor in selecting whom to place under special surveillance: if police officers at an airport decide to search Passenger A because he is twenty-five to forty years old, bought a first-class ticket with cash, is flying cross-country, and is apparently of Arab ancestry, Passenger A has been subjected to racial profiling. But officials often prefer to define racial profiling as being based *solely* on race; and in doing so they are often seeking to preserve their authority to act against a person *partly* on the basis of race. Civil-rights activists, too, often define racial profiling as solely race-based; but their aim is to arouse their followers and to portray law-enforcement officials in as menacing a light as possible.

The problem with defining racial profiling in the narrow manner of these strange bedfellows is that doing so obfuscates the real issue confronting Americans. Exceedingly few police officers, airport screeners, or other authorities charged with the task of foiling or apprehending criminals act solely on the basis of race. Many, however, act on the basis of intuition, using race along with other indicators (sex, age, patterns of past conduct) as a guide. The difficult question, then, is not whether the authorities ought to be allowed to act against individuals on the basis of race alone; almost everyone would disapprove of that. The difficult question is whether they ought to be allowed to use race *at all* in schemes of surveillance. If, indeed, it is used, the action amounts to racial discrimination. The extent of the discrimination may be relatively small when race is only one factor among many, but even a little racial discrimination should require lots of justification.

The key argument in favor of racial profiling, essentially, is that taking race into account enables the authorities to screen carefully and at less expense those sectors of the population that are more likely than others to contain the criminals for whom officials are searching. Proponents of this theory stress that resources for surveillance are scarce, that the dangers to be avoided are grave, and that reducing these dangers helps everyone — including, sometimes especially, those in the groups subjected to special scrutiny. Proponents also assert that it makes good sense to consider whiteness if the search is for Ku Klux Klan assassins, blackness if the search is for drug couriers in certain locales, and Arab nationality or ethnicity if the search is for agents of al Qaeda.

Some commentators embrace this position as if it were unassailable, but under U.S. law racial discrimination backed by state power is presumptively illicit. This means that supporters of racial profiling carry a heavy burden of persuasion. Opponents rightly argue, however, that not much rigorous empirical proof supports the idea of racial profiling as an effective tool of law enforcement. Opponents rightly contend, also, that alternatives to racial profiling have not been much studied or pursued. Stressing that racial profiling generates clear harm (for example, the fear, resentment, and alienation felt by innocent people in the profiled group), opponents of racial profiling sensibly question whether compromising our hard-earned principle of anti-discrimination is worth merely speculative gains in overall security.

A notable feature of this conflict is that champions of each position frequently embrace rhetoric, attitudes, and value systems that are completely at odds with those they adopt when confronting another controversial instance of racial discrimination — namely, affirmative action. Vocal supporters of racial profiling who trumpet the urgency of communal needs when discussing law enforcement all of a sudden become fanatical individualists when condemning affirmative action in college admissions and the labor market. Supporters of profiling, who are willing to impose what amounts to a racial tax on profiled groups, denounce as betrayals of "color blindness" programs that require racial diversity. A similar turnabout can be seen on the part of many of those who support affirmative action. Impatient with talk of communal needs in assessing racial profiling, they very often have no difficulty with subordinating the interests of individual white candidates to the purported good of the whole. Opposed to race consciousness in policing, they demand race consciousness in deciding whom to admit to college or select for a job.

The racial-profiling controversy — like the conflict over affirmative action — will not end soon. For one thing, in both cases many of the contestants are animated by decent but contending sentiments. Although exasperating, this is actually good for our society; and it would be even better if participants in the debates acknowledged the simple truth that their adversaries have something useful to say.

Which man looks guilty?

Which man looks guilty? If you picked the man on the right, you're wrong.

Wrong for judging people based on the color of their skin. Because if you

look closely, you'll see they're the same man. Unfortunately, racial stereo-

typing like this happens every day. On America's highways, police stop drivers

based on their skin color rather than for the way they are driving. For example,

in Florida 80% of those stopped and searched were black and Hispanic,

while they constituted only 5% of all drivers. These humiliating and illegal

searches are violations of the Constitution and must be fought. Help us defend

your rights. Support the ACLU. www.aclu.org **american civil liberties union**

READING THE TEXT

1. Summarize in your own words the contradiction Kennedy finds in the controversies over racial profiling and affirmative action.

2. Why does Kennedy say that definitions of racial profiling are marked by "confusion" (para. 1)?

3. Why does Kennedy call opponents and supporters of racial profiling "strange bedfellows" (para. 2)?

4. Why do you think Kennedy finds "the decent but contending sentiments" at the heart of the racial profiling controversy to be "good for our society" (para. 6)?

READING THE SIGNS

1. Kennedy finds a contradiction between opposing racial profiling and promoting affirmative action. Write an essay in which you support, refute, or modify his stance.

2. Write a journal entry in which you reflect on an experience in which you believe you were singled out because of your appearance, ethnicity, gender, or other physically obvious characteristic. How did you respond at the time, and would you respond the same way today? Alternatively, write about a friend who had such an experience.

3. Write an essay in which you explore the relative claims of the rights of the individual and the rights of the community in modern American culture. To what extent do those claims reflect a fundamental contradiction in American social ideology?

4. **CONNECTING TEXTS** In the debates over both racial profiling and affirmative action, the discussions tend to presume that determining ethnic identity is a simple matter. Read or review Jack Lopez's "Of Cholos and Surfers" (p. 684), Nell Bernstein's "Goin' Gangsta, Choosin' Cholita" (p. 691), and Melissa Algranati's "Being an Other" (p. 697), and write an essay in which you explore the implications that mixed-race backgrounds and cultural practices such as claiming may have for these debates.

COREY WILLIAMS

NAACP Symbolically Buries N-Word

In 1944 the NAACP symbolically "buried" Jim Crow, the common name for the segregationist laws that governed the South from Reconstruction to the civil rights era. Then, in 2007, the NAACP held a second burial ceremony for a word that once was a bitter part of that Jim Crow era but that is now, paradoxically, in common use in rap lyrics and casual street slang. The word is so potent that it is not even named in this 2007 Associated Press report by Corey Williams, and while some rappers have agreed to stop using it in their lyrics, it remains to be seen whether the NAACP ceremony will completely eradicate it from hip-hop culture. Corey Williams is a writer for the Associated Press.

There was no mourning at this funeral. Hundreds of onlookers cheered Monday afternoon as the NAACP put to rest a long-standing expression of racism by holding a public burial for the N-word during its annual convention. Delegates from across the country marched from downtown Detroit's Cobo Center to Hart Plaza. Two Percheron horses pulled a pine box adorned with a bouquet of fake black roses and a black ribbon printed with a derivation of the word. The coffin is to be placed at historically black Detroit Memorial Park Cemetery and will have a headstone. "Today we're not just burying the N-word, we're taking it out of our spirit," said Detroit Mayor Kwame Kilpatrick. "We gather burying all the things that go with the N-word. We have to bury the 'pimps' and the 'hos' that go with it." He continued: "Die N-word, and we don't want to see you 'round here no more."

The N-word has been used as a slur against blacks for more than a century. It remains a symbol of racism, but also is used by blacks when referring to other blacks, especially in comedy routines and rap and hip-hop music. "This was the greatest child that racism ever birthed," the Rev. Otis Moss III, assistant pastor at Trinity United Church of Christ in Chicago, said in his eulogy.

Public discussion on the word's use increased last year following a tirade by *Seinfeld* actor Michael Richards, who used it repeatedly during a Los Angeles comedy routine and later issued a public apology. The issue about racially insensitive remarks heated up earlier this year after talk show host Don Imus described black members of the Rutgers University women's basketball team as "nappy-headed hos" on April 4.

Black leaders, including the Revs. Jesse Jackson and Al Sharpton, have challenged the entertainment industry and the American public to stop using the N-word and other racial slurs. Minister and rap icon Kurtis Blow called for people, especially young people, to stop buying music by artists who use offensive language. "They wouldn't make rap songs if you didn't buy them. Stop supporting the stuff you don't want to hear," said Blow, who is credited with helping create the genre's popularity in the late 1970s and early 1980s. "I've never used the N-word and I've recorded over 150 rap songs. I've never used profanity. It's possible you can use hip-hop and not offend anyone."

The Rev. Wendell Anthony, pastor of Detroit's Fellowship Chapel and member of the NAACP national board of directors, said the efforts were not an attack on young people or hip-hop. He said they were a commentary on the culture the genre has produced. "We're not thugs. We're not gangstas," Anthony told the crowd. "All of us has been guilty of this word. It's upon all of us to now kill this word." 5

The NAACP has been criticized with being out of touch with young blacks, but Tiffany Tilley said the organization is moving in the right direction. "This is a great start," the 30-year-old Detroit resident said. "We need to continue to change the mentality of our people. It may take a generation, but it's definitely the movement we have to take."

The NAACP held a symbolic funeral in Detroit in 1944 for Jim Crow, the systematic, mostly Southern practice of discrimination against and segregation of blacks from the end of post–Civil War Reconstruction into the mid-20th century.

READING THE TEXT

1. What are the contradictory uses of the N-word that Williams describes?
2. How has controversy over the N-word increased recently?
3. What relationship does Williams see between the N-word and rap music?

READING THE SIGNS

1. In an essay, respond to the Rev. Wendell Anthony's contention that the symbolic burial of the N-word was "not an attack on young people or hip-hop" (para. 5).
2. In class, form teams and debate whether the NAACP's burial event was empty symbolism or a meaningful gesture against racism. To develop your team's ideas, consult the Introduction to Chapter 8, "Constructing Race: Readings in Multicultural Semiotics" (p. 647).
3. In an essay, propose your own analysis of the racial contradiction surrounding the N-word. Why is the word's use interpreted differently depending on the ethnicity of the speaker?
4. Research the history of the NAACP, and write an essay in which you agree, disagree, or complicate Detroit resident Tiffany Tilley's belief that, in Williams's words, the group "is moving in the right direction" (para. 6).

TIM KASSER

Mixed Messages

One of the most pervasive contradictions in American life might well be the conflict between what Tim Kasser calls the "sages" and the "celebrities," that is, between philosophers, theologians, and psychologists, on one side, who warn that material possessions cannot buy happiness, and, on the other, the mass media advertisements, stories, and celebrity endorsers who proclaim that happiness "can be found at the mall, on the Internet, or in the catalogue." A laboratory scientist with a research specialty in human psychology, Kasser decided to perform empirical tests to determine which side is right, and his conclusions are both forthright and, perhaps, a little surprising. And we hope he's right. Kasser is the author of The High Price of Materialism *(2002) and the coeditor of* Psychology and Consumer Culture: The Struggle for a Good Life in a Materialistic World *(with Allen D. Kanner, 2004).*

Mixed Messages

> Chase after money and security
> And your heart will never unclench.
> Care about people's approval
> And you will be their prisoner.
> Do your work, then step back.
> The only path to serenity.[1]

Twenty-five centuries ago, the Chinese philosopher Lao Tzu penned these six lines, warning people of the dangers of materialistic values. Sages from almost every religious and philosophical background have similarly insisted that focusing on attaining material possessions and social renown detracts from what is meaningful about life.[2] Although we may nod our heads in recognition of this ancient wisdom, such advice is largely drowned out by today's consumeristic hubbub of messages proclaiming that material pursuits, accumulation of things, and presentation of the "right" image provide real worth, deep satisfactions, and a genuinely meaningful life. Newspaper headlines exalt the local lottery winner. Get-rich-quick books climb to the tops of the best-seller lists. Multicolor ads flash on Web pages. Celebrities on television hawk everything from sport utility vehicles to mascara. Although they dif-

---

[1]Quotation from Lao Tzu (1988).
[2]See Belk (1983) for more about religious and philosophical views on materialism.

This bag retails for $129,000. Would it make *you* happy?

fer in form, each of these messages essentially proclaims "Happiness can be found at the mall, on the Internet, or in the catalogue."

Both types of messages about the value of materialism coexist in contemporary life, and it can be difficult to know whether to follow the sages or the celebrities. Who is right? Will the pursuit of money and possessions bring about "the good life"? Or are the promises of consumer society false?

It seems that wherever we inquire about the value of materialism, we receive conflicting answers. We can ask the government, but while politicians worry that popular consumer culture has displaced community and family values, economic considerations play an overwhelmingly central role in the decisions of most elected officials. We can turn to religious leaders, but while the Bible says that a person who cares about wealth will have trouble entering the kingdom of heaven, televangelists with toothy smiles pull in millions of dollars contributed by their viewers. We can ask wealthy people, but while John Jacob Astor III bemoans, "Money brings me nothing but a certain dull anxiety," Malcolm Forbes replies, "Money isn't everything, as long as you have enough." We can ask the poets, but while Robert Graves writes "There's no poetry in money," Wallace Stevens says "Money is a kind of poetry."[3]

If we turn to psychology for answers we find that it is similarly ambivalent about materialistic values.[4] On the one hand, much of the work conducted by evolutionary and behavioral psychologists is quite compatible with the

[3]Quotations from the wealthy are in Winokur (1996) and those from the poets are in Simpson (1988).

[4]I first wrote about this contrast in Kasser (2000).

notion that attainment of wealth and status is of great importance. Evolution-based theories, such as that of David Buss, suggest that the desire to be perceived as wealthy, attractive, and of high status may be built into our genes, as these characteristics (like an opposable thumb or a large forebrain) enabled our ancestors to survive.[5] Similarly, behavioral theories, such as B. F. Skinner's and Albert Bandura's, hold that the successful attainment of external rewards is a motivator of all behavior, and indeed fundamental to individuals' adaptation to society.[6] The behaviorist idea that happiness and satisfaction come from attaining wealth and possessions is exemplified by the fact that the founder of American behaviorism, John Watson, took the basic psychological principles of learning and applied them to advertising on Madison Avenue, a model since followed by thousands of psychologists.[7]

Although behavioral and evolutionary theories largely dominated American 5 academic psychology in the last century, humanistic and existential thinkers such as Carl Rogers, Abraham Maslow, and Erich Fromm voiced a sharply contrasting opinion about the worth of materialistic pursuits. Although they acknowledged the fact that some level of material comfort is necessary to provide for humans' basic physical needs, these psychologists proposed that a focus on materialistic values detracts from well-being and happiness.[8] Humanistic and existential psychologists tend to place qualities such as authentic self-expression, intimate relationships, and contribution to the community at the core of their notions of psychological health. From their viewpoint, a strong focus on materialistic pursuits not only distracts people from experiences conducive to psychological growth and health, but signals a fundamental alienation from what is truly meaningful. For example, when spouses spend most of their time working to make money, they neglect opportunities to be with each other and do what most interests them. No matter how many fancy designer clothes, cars, or jewels they might obtain, no matter how big their house or how up-to-date their electronic equipment, the lost opportunity to engage in pleasurable activities and enjoy each others' companionship will work against need satisfaction, and thus against psychological health.

Given the obviously different sets of predictions about materialism proffered by psychological theories and societal messages, one might expect to find a substantial body of empirical research on this subject. But when I began studying the topic in the early 1990s, I was surprised by the paucity of attempts to bring the scientific method to bear on materialistic values. Certainly there existed substantial social criticism of consumer society and anecdotal evidence regarding the problems of materialistic values. Yet most of the

[5]For more on these views, see Buss (1996).

[6]See Bandura (1977) or Skinner (1972). Also, do not take these statements as suggesting that I reject all of the principles of evolutionary psychology or behaviorism. There is no doubt in my mind that natural selection and the principles of conditioning both play an important role in human behavior. My point is that some of the meta-theoretical assumptions of these viewpoints have been used in ways that support consumeristic and capitalistic messages.

[7]See Buckley (1982) for more on Watson.

[8]For more on humanistic views, see Fromm (1976), Maslow (1954), and Rogers (1961).

research I found attempted to understand the place of materialism in people's lives by examining how wealth was associated with happiness and psychological adjustment. The basic question behind this research was, "Does money buy happiness?" In answer, psychologists David Myers and Ed Diener wrote:

> People have not become happier over time as their cultures have become more affluent. Even though Americans earn twice as much in today's dollars as they did in 1957, the proportion of those telling surveyors from the National Opinion Research Center that they are "very happy" has declined from 35 to 29 percent. Even very rich people — those surveyed among *Forbes* magazine's 100 wealthiest Americans — are only slightly happier than the average American. Those whose income has increased over a 10-year period are not happier than those whose income is stagnant. Indeed, in most nations the correlation between income and happiness is negligible — only in the poorest countries, such as Bangladesh and India, is income a good measure of emotional well-being. Are people in rich countries happier, by and large, than people in not so rich countries? It appears in general they are, but the margin may be slim . . . Furthermore, . . . it is impossible to tell whether the happiness of people in wealthier nations is based on money or is a by-product of other felicities.[9]

Research on the happiness of wealthy and poor people makes it clear that how much we have bears relatively little relationship to our well-being, beyond the point of ensuring sufficient food, shelter, and clothing to survive. Although this is important information, my view is that an inquiry into materialism must go further. To understand fully its impact on people's lives, we must explore how materialistic wants relate to well-being. Because society tells us repeatedly that money and possessions will make us happy, and that they are significant goals for which we should strive, we often organize our lives around pursuing them. But what happens to our well-being when our desires and goals to attain wealth and accumulate possessions become prominent? What happens to our internal experience and interpersonal relationships when we adopt the messages of consumer culture as personal beliefs? What happens to the quality of our lives when we value materialism?

Personal Well-Being

> To continue much longer overwhelmed by business cares and with most of my thoughts wholly upon the way to make money in the shortest time must degrade me beyond hope of permanent recovery.
> — ANDREW CARNEGIE[10]

In recent years, scientific investigators working in a variety of fields have begun to tally the costs of a materialistic lifestyle. Although the body of empirical

---

[9]Quotation is from Myers and Diener (1996), pp. 70–71.
[10]Carnegie quotation is from Hendrick (1932), pp. 146–47.

literature on materialism is not large, especially compared with what we know about topics such as depression, stereotyping, neurons, and memory, its findings are quite consistent. Indeed, what stands out across the studies is a simple fact: people who strongly value the pursuit of wealth and possessions report lower psychological well-being than those who are less concerned with such aims.

RESEARCH FROM OUR LAB

Since 1993 my colleagues and I have been publishing a series of papers in which we have been exploring how people's values and goals relate to their well-being. Our focus has been on understanding what people view as important or valuable in life, and on associating those values statistically with a variety of other aspects of their lives, such as happiness, depression, and anxiety. What people value clearly varies from one individual to another. For some, spirituality and religion are of paramount importance; for others, home life, relationships, and family are especially valued; other people focus on having fun and excitement, and others on contributing to the community.[11] In our work, we have been particularly interested in individuals for whom materialistic values are relatively important. That is, compared with other things that might be deemed central to one's life, what happens psychologically when a person feels that making money and having possessions are relatively high in the pantheon of values?

OUR FIRST STUDY

To obtain an answer to this question, Richard Ryan and I began by developing   10 a questionnaire to measure people's values, which we called the Aspiration Index.[12] People who complete this questionnaire are presented with many different types of goals and asked to rate each one in terms of whether it is not at all important, somewhat important, extremely important, and so on. The current version of the Aspiration Index includes a large number of possible goals people might have, such as desires to feel safe and secure, to help the world be a better place, to have a great sex life, and to have good relationships with others. By assessing different types of goals, we can obtain a valid assessment of how important materialistic values are in the context of a person's entire system of values. Most value researchers view this as crucial and insist that we can know how much someone values a particular outcome only

---

[11]There is no real agreement in psychology as to the exact number or content of values that make up the human value system, although Shalom Schwartz (1992, 1994, 1996) has made an excellent case for a "universal" system of values. Nonetheless, a glance through a review of value measures (Braithwaite & Scott, 1991) will probably impress the reader for how much disagreement exists among psychologists about what values are important to measure.

[12]This first study is Kasser and Ryan (1993).

Table 1

Financial Success Items from Kasser and Ryan's (1993) Aspiration Index

You will buy things just because you want them.
You will be financially successful.
You will be your own boss.
You will have a job with high social status.
You will have a job that pays well.

Participants rate how important these aspirations are, from not at all to very important.
Reprinted by permission of the American Psychological Association.

when that value is considered in relation to other things that might possibly be valued.[13]

Table 1 shows items used to assess materialistic values in our first study. Of central interest, participants reported how important several *financial success* aspirations were to them. We also asked participants how much they were concerned with *self-acceptance* (desires for psychological growth, autonomy, and self-esteem), *affiliation* (desires for a good family life and friendships), and *community feeling* (desires to make the world a better place through one's own actions). From these ratings, we could determine how important, or central, the value of financial success was for each person relative to the other three values.

Ryan and I administered the Aspiration Index to a group of individuals who, second to white rats, form the backbone of much scientific research in psychology: college students. Three hundred sixteen students at the University of Rochester completed a survey packet that included the index and four questionnaires that assessed positive feelings of well-being and negative feelings of distress.

The first measure of well-being assessed self-actualization, a concept made popular by the father of humanistic psychology, Abraham Maslow. Maslow conceived of self-actualization as the pinnacle of psychological health, the state attained by people motivated by growth, meaning, and aesthetics, rather than by insecurity and the attempt to fit in with what other people expect.[14] People who score high on this measure of self-actualization generally agree with statements such as, "It is better to be yourself than to be popular" and "I do not feel ashamed of any of my emotions." Our second measure of well-being, vitality, also assesses psychological growth and the energy that goes along with authentically expressing who one really is. Vital people are likely to feel energized, alert, and overflowing with that wonderful feeling of being alive.

[13]Milton Rokeach (1973), a prominent thinker in empirical value research, coined the term "relative centrality" to describe how important a value is relative to other values. His insistence on this means of measurement is relatively well accepted among value researchers.
[14]Maslow (1954) described this idea well.

The last two measures assessed two of the most common psychological disorders: depression and anxiety. The depression questionnaire asked participants how frequently they had experienced common depressive symptoms such as feeling down, feeling lonely or disconnected from others, having sleep or appetite troubles, and having little energy or difficulty concentrating. The anxiety measure asked how much they generally experienced nervousness or shakiness inside, felt tense or fearful, or were suddenly scared for no reason.[15]

When we used statistical analyses to examine how people's value orienta- 15 tions related to their well-being, the results were intriguing. Compared with students who were more oriented toward self-acceptance, affiliation, or community feeling, those who considered financial success a relatively central value reported significantly lower levels of self-actualization and vitality, as well as significantly higher levels of depression and anxiety. Notably, such a strong focus was associated with decreased psychological well-being regardless of whether participants were men or women.

These results supported the premise that materialistic values are unhealthy, but we wanted to see if they would be replicated with young adults who were not in college, and with other ways of assessing well-being besides questionnaires. We therefore gave a somewhat shorter version of the Aspiration Index to a wide-ranging group of 140 eighteen-year-olds. These adolescents varied greatly in terms of race, socioeconomic status, and their mothers' psychological health. Their current situation in life was also diverse, with some having dropped out of high school and others going on to college, some already having had children, and others in trouble with the law.

We evaluated psychological well-being in a somewhat different way in this sample. Instead of completing questionnaires, participants met with an experienced clinical psychologist who interviewed them using a set of standard questions. From these interviews ratings were made of the extent to which the teens were socially productive and of how much they exhibited symptoms of behavior disorders. A socially productive adolescent was defined as someone who was doing well in school, was holding down a job, and had hobbies and other outside interests. Behavior disorders, one of the most common of all childhood problems, involved a variety of symptoms expressing oppositional, defiant, and antisocial behavior common in unhappy teens, such as fighting, belonging to a gang, stealing, and torturing small animals. We also measured the teens' general functioning in life by rating them on a 100-point scale commonly used to assess people's level of psychiatric impairment and overall adaptation to life.[16]

[15]Well-being measures include self-actualization (Jones & Crandall, 1986), vitality (Ryan & Frederick, 1997), anxiety (Derogatis et al., 1974), and depression (Radloff, 1977).

[16]The scales in this study were social productivity (Ikle et al., 1983), conduct disorders (Herjanic & Reich, 1982), and global functioning (American Psychiatric Association, 1987). See Sameroff et al. (1982) for more information about the heterogeneous sample.

Even with these differences in samples and the way we assessed well-being, the results with these teenagers revealed a pattern consistent with our earlier findings: individuals who were focused on financial success, compared with nonmaterialistic values, were not adapting to society well and were acting in rather destructive ways. Specifically, they were not functioning well in school, on the job, or in their extracurricular activities, and were likely to exhibit various symptoms of behavior disorders, such as vandalizing, skipping school, and carrying weapons.

Our first studies therefore showed that when young adults report that financial success is relatively central to their aspirations, low well-being, high distress, and difficulty adjusting to life are also evident. Although we cannot be sure from these results whether materialistic values cause unhappiness, or whether other factors are at work, the results do suggest a rather startling conclusion: the American dream has a dark side, and the pursuit of wealth and possessions might actually be undermining our well-being.

MORE RECENT WORK FROM OUR LAB

These results raised a number of further questions in our minds. Were financial success values the only ones that were problematic for people's psychological health? What would happen if we looked at older individuals? Would similar results be found for other aspects of psychological health and distress? These were some of the issues Ryan and I tried to grapple with in our next study.[17]   20

We began by revising the Aspiration Index to include some other prominent goals and values of consumer culture. Although strivings for money and possessions certainly constitute the core message encouraged by consumeristic and capitalistic cultures, two other goals are also typically encouraged: having the "right" image and being well known socially. Image and fame values are entwined with those for money and possessions in at least a couple of ways. First, the media in consumeristic cultures frequently link these values by having good-looking celebrities sell products. The underlying message is that owning these products will enhance our image and ensure our popularity with others. A second way these values are connected is that image, fame, and money all share a focus of looking for a sense of worth outside of oneself, and involve striving for external rewards and the praise of others. When we focus on these values (which Ryan and I called "extrinsic"), we are seeking sources of satisfaction outside of ourselves, whether in money, in the mirror, or in admiration by others. In capitalistic, consumer cultures such as the United States, these extrinsic values are often encouraged as worthy because they seemingly convey a sense of success and power.

---

[17]Further information on results from the next two samples reviewed can be found in Kasser (1994) or Kasser and Ryan (1996).

Table 2
Sample Items from Kasser and Ryan's (1996) Revised Aspiration Index

Financial success
You will have a job with high social status.
You will have a job that pays well.
You will be financially successful.
You will have a lot of expensive possessions.

Social recognition
Your name will be known by many people.
You will do something that brings you much recognition.
You will be admired by many people.
You will be famous.
Your name will appear frequently in the media.

Appealing appearance
You will successfully hide the signs of aging.
You will have people comment often about how attractive you look.
You will keep up with fashions in hair and clothing.
You will achieve the "look" you've been after.
Your image will be one others find appealing.

Table 2 lists the items we used in the revised version of the Aspiration Index to measure these three types of materialistic values. In several studies, we have found that people who value one of these values, such as fame, also tend to value money and image. Thus they seem to have "bought into" the prominent goals of consumer society. Notably, this cluster of goals also was found in students from both Russia and Germany, suggesting that the coexistence of money, fame, and image values can be found in cultures less consumeristic than the United States.[18]

Having expanded the Aspiration Index to measure a greater number of values relevant to the messages of consumer culture, Ryan and I set out to determine whether our results would be the same in adults as they were in college students and teenagers. We randomly sampled a group of 100 adults living in a diverse neighborhood in Rochester, New York. The participants ranged from eighteen to seventy-nine years of age and came from lower, middle, and upper socioeconomic backgrounds. The survey packet we left at participants' doors contained the revised Aspiration Index and the four measures of well-being we used previously (self-actualization, vitality, anxiety, depression measures). Participants also reported on their physical health by noting how often they had experienced nine physical symptoms in the past week (headache, stomach aches, backaches, etc.).[19]

[18]See Ryan et al. (1999) and Schmuck et al. (2000).
[19]Items were taken from Emmons (1991).

The findings largely corroborated those reported with young adults. Adults who focused on money, image, and fame reported less self-actualization and vitality, and more depression than those less concerned with these values. What is more, they also reported significantly more experiences of physical symptoms. That is, people who believed it is important to strive for possessions, popularity, and good looks also reported more headaches, backaches, sore muscles, and sore throats than individuals less focused on such goals. This was really one of the first indicators, to us, of the pervasive negative correlates of materialistic values — not only is people's psychological well-being worse when they focus on money, but so is their physical health.

As in our studies of college students, materialistic values were equally un- 25
healthy for men and women. Because of the nature of this sample, we could also examine whether findings depended on age or income. Analyses showed that regardless of their age or wealth, people with highly central materialistic values also reported lower well-being.

Having documented some of the problems associated with materialism in adults of different ages and backgrounds, we returned to college students and teenagers to explore further the many different ways that these values are associated with low well-being. As a start, we wanted a better sense of the daily lives of people with a strong materialistic orientation. The earlier studies asked individuals to look back on some portion of their lives and tell us about their well-being; although this is a quick method to measure how people are feeling, we wanted to change the focus and obtain a snapshot of people's daily lives. Therefore, in addition to completing our standard packet of questionnaires, we asked 192 students at the University of Rochester to keep a diary for two weeks. In the middle of each day, and then again at the end of each day, they answered several questions about their current experience: how much they had the same nine physical symptoms assessed in the adult sample and how much they felt each of the nine emotions (e.g., happy, joyful, unhappy, angry).

As before, participants highly focused on materialistic values reported less self-actualization and vitality and more depression than those with less interest in those values. They also experienced more physical symptoms and less in the way of positive emotions over the two weeks. Something about a strong desire for materialistic pursuits actually affected the participants' day-to-day lives and decreased the quality of their daily experience.[20]

---

[20]Another important finding from this study related to an issue relevant to socially desirable responding. Psychologists are often concerned that participants' responses to certain questionnaires are clouded by the desire to answer in a way that fits with what they think society feels is "good." As a result, they may be unlikely to admit to feelings and thoughts that might be seen as deviant or less than optimal. Because a scale exists to measure socially desirable responding (Crowne & Marlowe, 1960), we examined whether this might explain why people strongly focused on materialistic values reported low well-being. Our statistical analyses found no support for this idea, as the effects remained significant even after accounting for socially desirable responses. Notably, however, Mick (1996) reached a different conclusion with other measures of materialism.

Another new element of this study was measurement of participants' narcissistic tendencies. In psychological parlance, narcissism describes people who cover an inner feeling of emptiness and questionable self-worth with a grandiose exterior that brags of self-importance. Narcissists are typically vain, expect special treatment and admiration from others, and can be manipulative and hostile toward others. Social critics and psychologists have often suggested that consumer culture breeds a narcissistic personality by focusing individuals on the glorification of consumption (e.g., "Have it your way"; "Want it? Get it!").[21] Furthermore, narcissists' desire for external validation fits well with our conception of materialistic values as extrinsic and focused on others' praise. Thus it was not surprising to find that students with strong materialistic tendencies scored high on a standard measure of narcissism, agreeing with statements such as, "I am more capable than other people," "I like to start new fads and fashions," "I wish somebody would write my biography one day," and "I can make anybody believe anything I want them to."[22]

More recent studies expanded our measurements of psychological functioning by examining the extent to which materialism is associated with the use of substances such as tobacco, alcohol, and drugs. In one such project, Ryan and I asked 261 students at Montana State University how many cigarettes they smoked on a typical day, and how often in the last year they had "gotten drunk," "smoked marijuana," and "done hard drugs." When we averaged these four indicators, results showed that people with a strong materialistic value orientation were highly likely to use such substances frequently.[23]

These results were replicated by Geoff Williams in two groups of high school students.[24] In one study, 141 high school students were asked whether they had smoked 100 cigarettes in their lifetime, which is the National Cancer Institute's definition of a smoker. Student smokers were more oriented toward materialistic values than toward values such as self-acceptance, affiliation, and community feeling. Williams next asked 271 ninth- through twelfth-graders about an even broader list of behaviors that put teens at risk for later problems, such as use of cigarettes, chewing tobacco, alcohol, and marijuana, as well as whether they ever had sexual intercourse. Materialistic teens were more likely to engage in each of these five risk behaviors than were teens focused on other values.

ANOTHER WAY TO LOOK AT MATERIALISM

Each of the studies reviewed used the Aspiration Index as the primary means of assessing participants' materialistic values. Although the index has worked well, it also has an important limit common to all questionnaires of its type.

[21]See Cushman (1990) or Kanner and Gomes (1995).
[22]This narcissism scale was developed by Raskin and Terry (1988).
[23]Kasser and Ryan (2001).
[24]Williams et al. (2000).

Study participants were presented with preselected goals and aspirations that Ryan and I constructed, leaving them little room to present their own goals in the particular ways they might want to express them.

To assess materialism more on participants' own terms, Ken Sheldon and I developed a method that asks participants to begin by listing their personal goals in their own words.[25] After doing this, they are asked to think about how much each goal might help them reach different "possible futures." Participants are given a list of six futures that might occur, three of which are materialistic (financial success, fame and popularity, physical attractiveness) and three of which are not (self-acceptance and personal growth, intimacy and friendship, societal contribution). They then rate how helpful each of their goals is in reaching each of these futures. For example, a goal such as "lose 10 pounds" might help bring about the possible future of physical attractiveness, but it is unlikely to contribute much to society. People's materialistic value orientation is thus measured by the extent to which their expressed personal goals are highly oriented toward attaining possessions, attractiveness, and popularity.

This personal goal methodology has been applied to almost 500 individuals, and has successfully replicated and extended our previous findings. For example, college students focused on materialistic strivings reported low self-actualization and infrequent experiences of positive emotions.[26] In a more recent study involving 108 adults ranging in age from eighteen to seventy-two, those highly oriented toward materialistic goals also reported fewer experiences of positive emotions and less overall satisfaction with their lives than did those with less materialistic goals. As with previous work, the negative relationship between materialistic value orientations and well-being held for people of all ages and for both genders.[27]

SUMMARY

[Earlier we asked], "What happens to the quality of our lives when we value materialism?" The answer, as we have seen from the studies described, is, "The more materialistic values are at the center of our lives, the more our quality of life is diminished." In samples of adolescents, college students, and adults, with various means of measuring materialistic values and well-being, results show a clear pattern of psychological (and physical) difficulties associated with holding wealth, popularity, and image as relatively important. . . .

CONSUMER RESEARCH

Another set of studies investigating relationships between materialism and well-being comes from the disciplines of marketing and consumer research. I 35

---

[25]Goal measures are based on Emmons (1989) and Little (1983).
[26]Sheldon and Kasser (1995, 1998).
[27]Sheldon and Kasser (2001).

must admit that I was at first surprised to discover a body of literature on the problems of materialism in a field that attempts to understand how to market products and convince individuals to consume them. As I worked to over-come my stereotypes, however, I found that this literature is full of insights about the effects of materialism on people.

The earliest data demonstrating a negative relationship between material-ism and well-being were presented by Russell Belk in two papers, in 1984 and 1985.[28] As can be seen in table 3, Belk measured a materialistic outlook by assessing three main characteristics or traits. First, materialistic people are

Table 3
Items from Belk's (1985) Materialism Scale

Possessiveness
Renting or leasing a car is more appealing to me than owning one.*
I tend to hang on to things I should probably throw out.
I get very upset if something is stolen from me, even if it has little monetary value.
I don't get particularly upset when I lose things.*
I am less likely than most people to lock things up.*
I would rather buy something I need than borrow it from someone else.
I worry about people taking my possessions.
When I travel I like to take a lot of photographs.
I never discard old pictures or snapshots.

Nongenerosity
I enjoy having guests stay in my home.*
I enjoy sharing what I have.*
I don't like to lend things, even to good friends.
It makes sense to buy a lawnmower with a neighbor and share it.*
I don't mind giving rides to those who don't have a car.*
I don't like to have anyone in my home when I'm not there.
I enjoy donating things to charity.*

Envy
I am bothered when I see people who buy anything they want.
I don't know anyone whose spouse or steady date I would like to have as my own.*
When friends do better than me in competition it usually makes me happy for them.*
People who are very wealthy often feel they are too good to talk to average people.
There are certain people I would like to trade places with.
When friends have things I cannot afford it bothers me.
I don't seem to get what is coming to me.
When Hollywood stars or prominent politicians have things stolen from them I really feel sorry for them.*

Participants are asked how strongly they agree or disagree with these statements.
Items with a * are scored so that disagreement indicates higher materialism.
Reprinted by permission of the University of Chicago Press.

[28]Belk (1984, 1985).

possessive, in that they prefer to own and keep things rather than borrow, rent, or throw things out. Second, materialistic individuals are *nongenerous*, or unwilling to share their possessions with others. Third, materialistic people tend to *envy* the possessions of others, feeling displeasure when others have things they themselves desire.

The materialism survey was administered to a sample of over 300 individuals, including business students, machine shop workers, students at a religious institute, and secretaries at an insurance office. Participants were also asked two questions about well-being: "How happy are you?" and "How satisfied are you with your life?" Compared with people low in materialism, those who were possessive, nongenerous, and envious of others' possessions were likely to report that they were less happy and less satisfied with their lives. Since Belk's initial study, three other papers replicated these findings, and other studies demonstrated that materialism is associated with depression and social anxiety.[29]

Another important consumer research study was performed by marketing professors Marsha Richins and Scott Dawson.[30] These investigators developed a scale that assesses how much people think possessions reflect success in life, how central materialism is to their desires, and how much they believe wealth and possessions yield happiness (table 4). This conceptualization of materialism includes not only the desire to make money and have possessions, but also the desire to own things that impress others and that elicit some sense of social recognition. It thus contains items tapping some of the related values (for image and popularity) that studies cited above found cluster together.

Eight hundred randomly selected individuals (primarily adults living in the northeastern and western United States) participated in this study. In addition to completing this measure of materialism, participants were asked how satisfied they were generally with their lives as well as in specific areas, such as family, job, and so on. Compared with nonmaterialistic respondents, those with a strong materialistic orientation reported less satisfaction with their lives overall, with their family, their income, and their relationships with friends, as well as with how much fun they have. Other authors using Richins and Dawson's questionnaire have since found that materialistic people reported lower life satisfaction and self-actualization than nonmaterialistic people.[31]

In summary, other investigations studying materialism have reached essentially the same conclusion as I have: materialistic values are associated with low well-being. 40

OTHER CULTURES, SAME FINDINGS

All of the studies reviewed thus far were conducted in the United States. It is interesting to know that one of the world's wealthiest, most powerful nations

---

[29]Studies replicating life satisfaction results include Ahuvia and Wong (1995), Dawson (1988), and Dawson and Bamossy (1991); results for depression were reported by Wachtel and Blatt (1990) and for social anxiety for Schroeder and Dugal (1995).

[30]Richins and Dawson (1992).

[31]Studies replicating include Ahuvia and Wong (1995) and Mick (1996).

Table 4
Sample Items from Richins and Dawson's (1992) Materialism Scale

Success
I admire people who own expensive homes, cars, and clothes.
Some of the most important achievements in life include acquiring material
    possessions.
I don't place much emphasis on the amount of material objects a person owns
    as a sign of success.*
The things I own say a lot about how well I'm doing in life.
I like to own things that impress people.
I don't pay much attention to the material objects other people own.*

Centrality
I usually buy only the things I need.*
I try to keep my life simple, as far as possessions are concerned.*
The things I own aren't all that important to me.*
I enjoy spending money on things that aren't practical.
Buying things gives me a lot of pleasure.
I like a lot of luxury in my life.
I put less emphasis on material things than most people I know.*

Happiness
I have all the things I really need to enjoy life.*
My life would be better if I owned certain things I don't have.
I wouldn't be any happier if I owned nicer things.*
I'd be happier if I could afford to buy more things.
It sometimes bothers me quite a bit that I can't afford to buy all the things I'd like.

Participants are presented with these statements and asked how strongly they agree or disagreee
with them. Items with a * are scored so that disagreement indicates more materialism.

Reprinted by permission of the University of Chicago Press.

appears to be inculcating values not conducive to its citizens' well-being, but
the possibility remains that the results are specific to the United States. Perhaps this phenomenon is the result of certain cultural features, such as the
economy, television shows, or history, and does not hold in other cultures.

To address this issue, several studies have used translated versions of the
Aspiration Index and of personal well-being measures in samples of people
from around the world. Thus far, studies with British, Danish, German, Indian,
Romanian, Russian, and South Korean college students have confirmed the
negative associations between materialistic values and well-being. These findings were replicated with German adults, and similar results were found in
business students from Singapore.[32]

[32]Results are from countries as follows: Britain (Chan & Joseph, 2000); Denmark and
India (Khanna & Kasser, 2001); German students (Schmuck et al., 2000); German adults
(Schmuck, 2001); Romania (Frost, 1998); Russia (Ryan et al., 1999); Singapore (Kasser & Ahuvia, 2002); and South Korea (Kim et al., 2003). Notably, results from Singapore occurred for
the Aspiration Index, the Richins and Dawson scale, and the Belk scale.

Other investigators have also reported similar results in other countries. For example, Shaun Saunders and Don Munro found that a materialistic outlook in Australian students was associated with increased feelings of anger, anxiety, and depression, and with decreased life satisfaction. Another study headed by Joe Sirgy showed that life satisfaction was diminished when adults in China, Turkey, Australia, Canada, and the United States scored as highly materialistic on either the Belk or Richins and Dawson's scales; similar results have been reported in samples of adults in Singapore. Finally, Edward Diener and Shige Oishi collected value and life satisfaction measures from over 7,000 college students in 41 different nations. Again, a strong value on making money was associated with diminishing life satisfaction.[33]

Thus, findings from samples of individuals all over the world show that a strong relative focus on materialistic values is associated with low well-being. In some countries the results are fairly strong, and although they are somewhat weaker in others, the general pattern is consistent. What is more, results do not support the idea that placing strong importance on materialistic values is associated with greater well-being.[34] This is important, as some theoretical perspectives might suggest that people in developing capitalist economies such as Russia or India, or countries such as Singapore where shopping is a highly encouraged national pastime, could increase their well-being when they internalize the pervasive consumer messages their cultures propound. Once again, the opposite is the case: materialistic values appear not to bring happiness and well-being, but instead more anxiety, little vitality, few pleasant emotions, and low life satisfaction.

SUMMARY

Existing scientific research on the value of materialism yields clear and consistent findings. People who are highly focused on materialistic values have lower personal well-being and psychological health than those who believe that materialistic pursuits are relatively unimportant. These relationships have been documented in samples of people ranging from the wealthy to the poor, from teenagers to the elderly, and from Australians to South Koreans. Several investigators have reported similar results using a variety of ways of measuring materialism. The studies document that strong materialistic values are

45

[33]See Saunders and Munro (2000), Sirgy et al. (1995), Keng et al. (2000), Swinyard et al. (2001), and Diener and Oishi (2000).

[34]The one study that may seemingly conflict with this statement is by Sagiv and Schwartz (2000). These investigators found that business students highly focused on power values reported high well-being. They interpreted this as inconsistent with the body of work on materialistic values. As we (Kasser & Ahuvia, 2002) pointed out in response, power values are not the same as materialistic values; indeed, when we examined materialistic values using the Aspiration Index and the Belk and Richins and Dawson scales in samples of Singaporean business students, we confirmed our earlier findings that materialistic values are related to low well-being. Notably, Srivastava et al. (2001) reported parallel findings in United States business students and entrepreneurs.

associated with a pervasive undermining of people's well-being, from low life satisfaction and happiness, to depression and anxiety, to physical problems such as headaches, and to personality disorders, narcissism, and antisocial behavior.

Not the picture of psychological health painted by the commercials, is it?

REFERENCES

Ahuvia, A. C., & Wong, N. (1995). Materialism: Origins and implications for personal well-being. In F. Hansen (Ed.), *European advances in consumer research*, Vol. 2 (pp. 172–78). Copenhagen, Denmark: Association for Consumer Research.

American Psychiatric Association. (1987). *Diagnostic and statistical manual of mental disorders* (3rd ed., rev.). Washington, DC: American Psychiatric Association.

Bandura, A. (1977). Self-efficacy: Toward a unifying theory of behavioral change. *Psychological Review, 84*, 191–215.

Belk, R. W. (1983). Worldly possessions: Issues and criticisms. In R. P. Bagozzi & A. M. Tybout (Eds.), *Advances in consumer research*, Vol. 10 (pp. 514–19). Ann Arbor, MI: Association for Consumer Research.

Belk, R. W. (1984). Three scales to measure constructs related to materialism: Reliability, validity, and relationships to measures of happiness. In T. Kinnear (Ed.), *Advances in consumer research*, Vol. 11 (pp. 291–97). Provo, UT: Association for Consumer Research.

Belk, R. W. (1985). Materialism: Trait aspects of living in the material world. *Journal of Consumer Research, 12*, 265–80.

Bowlby, J. (1969/1982). *Attachment* (2nd. ed.). New York: Basic Books.

Braithwaite, V. A., & Scott, W. A. (1991). Values. In J. P. Robinson, P. R. Shave, & L. S. Wrightsman (Eds.), *Measures of personality and social psychological attitudes* (pp. 661–753). San Diego: Academic Press.

Buckley, K. W. (1982). The selling of a psychologist: John Broadus Watson and the application of behavioral techniques to advertising. *Journal of the History of the Behavioral Sciences, 18*, 207–21.

Buss, D. M. (1996). The evolutionary psychology of human social strategies. In E. T. Higgins & A. W. Kruglanski (Eds.), *Social psychology: Handbook of basic principles* (pp. 3–38). New York: Guilford Press.

Chan, R., & Joseph, C. (2000). Dimensions of personality, domains of aspiration, and subjective well-being. *Personality and Individual Differences, 28*, 347–54.

Crowne, D. P., & Marlowe, D. (1960). A new scale of social desirability independent of psychopathology. *Journal of Consulting Psychology, 24*, 349–54.

Cushman, P. (1990). Why the self is empty: Toward a historically situated psychology. *American Psychologist, 45*, 599–611.

Dawson, S. (1988). Trait materialism: Improved measures and an extension to multiple domains of life satisfaction. In S. Shapiro & A. H. Walle (Eds.), *AMA Winter Educators Conference Proceedings* (pp. 478–81). Chicago: American Marketing Association.

Dawson, S., & Bamossy, G. (1991). If we are what we have, what are we when we don't have? *Journal of Social Behavior and Personality, 6*, 363–84.

Derogatis, L. R., Lipman, R. S., Rickels, K., Uhlenhuth, E. H., & Covi, L. (1974). The Hopkins Symptom Checklist (HSCL): A self-report symptom inventory. *Behavioral Science, 19*, 1–15.

Diener, E., & Oishi, S. (2000). Money and happiness: Income and subjective well-being across nations. In E. Diener & E. H. Suh (Eds.), *Subjective well-being across cultures* (pp. 185–218). Cambridge: MIT Press.

Emmons, R. A. (1989). The personal strivings approach to personality. In L. A. Pervin (Ed.), *Goal concepts in personality and social psychology* (pp. 87–126). Hillsdale, NJ: Erlbaum.

Emmons, R. A. (1991). Personal strivings, daily life events, and psychological and physical well-being. *Journal of Personality, 59*, 453–72.

Fromm, E. (1976). *To have or to be?* New York: Harper & Row.

Frost, K. M. (1998). *A cross-cultural study of major life aspirations and psychological well-being*. Unpublished doctoral dissertation, University of Texas at Austin.

Hendrick, B. J. (1932). *The life of Andrew Carnegie*, Vol. 1. Garden City, NY: Doubleday.

Herjanic, B., & Reich, W. (1982). Development of a structured psychiatric interview for children: Agreement between child and parent on individual symptoms. *Journal of Abnormal Child Psychology, 10*, 307–24.

Ikle, D. N., Lipp, D. O., Butters, E. A., & Ciarlo, J. (1983). *Development and validation of the adolescent community mental health questionnaire*. Denver, CO: Mental Systems Evaluation Project.

Jones, A., & Crandall, R. (1986). Validation of a short index of self-actualization. *Personality and Social Psychology Bulletin, 12*, 63–73.

Kanner, A. D., & Gomes, M. E. (1995). The all-consuming self. In T. Roszak, M. E. Gomes, & A. D. Kanner (Eds.), *Ecopsychology: Restoring the Earth, healing the mind* (pp. 77–91). San Francisco: Sierra Club Books.

Kasser, T. (1994). *Further dismantling the American dream: Differential well-being correlates of intrinsic and extrinsic goals*. Unpublished doctoral dissertation, University of Rochester, Rochester, NY.

Kasser, T. (2000). Two versions of the American dream: Which goals and values make for a high quality of life? In E. Diener & D. R. Rahtz (Eds.), *Advances in quality of life theory and research*, Vol. 1 (pp. 3–12). Dordrecht, The Netherlands: Kluwer.

Kasser, T., & Ahuvia, A. C. (2002). Materialistic values and well-being in business students. *European Journal of Social Psychology, 32*, 137–46.

Kasser, T., & Ryan, R. M. (1993). A dark side of the American dream: Correlates of financial success as a central life aspiration. *Journal of Personality and Social Psychology, 65*, 410–22.

Kasser, T., & Ryan, R. M. (1996). Further examining the American dream: Differential correlates of intrinsic and extrinsic goals. *Personality and Social Psychology Bulletin, 22*, 280–87.

Kasser, T., & Ryan, R. M. (2001). Be careful what you wish for: Optimal functioning and the relative attainment of intrinsic and extrinsic goals. In P. Schmuck & K. M. Sheldon (Eds.), *Life goals and well-being: Towards a positive psychology of human striving* (pp. 116–31). Goettingen, Germany: Hogrefe & Huber.

Keng, K. A., Jung, K., Jivan, T. S., & Wirtz, J. (2000). The influence of materialistic inclination on values, life satisfaction and aspirations: An empirical analysis. *Social Indicators Research, 49*, 317–33.

Khanna, S., & Kasser, T. (2001). *Materialism, objectification, and alienation from a cross-cultural perspective*.

Kim, Y., Kasser, T., & Lee, H. (2003). Self-concept, aspirations, and well-being in South Korea and the United States. *Journal of Social Psychology, 143*, 277–90.

Kohut, H. (1971). *The analysis of the self*. New York: International Universities Press.

Little, B. R. (1983). Personal projects: A rationale and method for investigation. *Environment and Behavior, 15*, 273–309.

Maslow, A. H. (1954). *Motivation and personality*. New York: Harper & Row.

Mick, D. G. (1996). Are studies of dark side variables confounded by socially desirable responding? The case for materialism. *Journal of Consumer Research, 23*, 106–19.

Radloff, L. (1977). The CES-D scale: A self-report depression scale for research in the general population. *Applied Psychological Measurement, 1*, 385–401.

Raskin, R., & Terry, H. (1988). A principal components analysis of the Narcissistic Personality Inventory and further evidence of its construct validity. *Journal of Personality and Social Psychology, 54*, 890–902.

Richins, M. L., & Dawson, S. (1992). A consumer values orientation for materialism and its measurement: Scale development and validation. *Journal of Consumer Research, 19*, 303–16.

Rogers, C. R. (1961). *On becoming a person.* Boston: Houghton Mifflin.

Rokeach, M. (1973). *The nature of human values.* New York: Free Press.

Ryan, R. M., Chirkov, V. I., Little, T. D., Sheldon, K. M., Timoshina, E., & Deci, E. L. (1999). The American dream in Russia: Extrinsic aspirations and well-being in two cultures. *Personality and Social Psychology Bulletin, 25*, 1509–24.

Ryan, R. M., & Frederick, C. (1997). On energy, personality, and health: Subjective vitality as a dynamic reflection of well-being. *Journal of Personality, 65*, 529–65.

Sagiv, L., & Schwartz, S. H. (2000). Value priorities and subjective well-being: Direct relations and congruity effects. *European Journal of Social Psychology, 30*, 177–98.

Sameroff, A. J., Seifer, R., & Zax, M. (1982). Early development of children at risk for emotional disorders. *Monographs of the Society for Research in Child Development, 47* (serial no. 199).

Saunders, S., & Munro, D. (2000). The construction and validation of a consumer orientation questionnaire (SCOI) designed to measure Fromm's (1955) "marketing character" in Australia. *Social Behavior and Personality, 28*, 219–40.

Schmuck, P. (2001). Intrinsic and extrinsic life goals preferences as measured via inventories and via priming methodologies: Mean differences and relations with well-being. In P. Schmuck & K. M. Sheldon (Eds.), *Life goals and well-being: Towards a positive psychology of human striving* (pp. 132–47). Goettingen, Germany: Hogrefe & Huber.

Schmuck, P., Kasser, T., & Ryan, R. M. (2000). Intrinsic and extrinsic goals: Their structure and relationship to well-being in German and U.S. college students. *Social Indicators Research, 50*, 225–41.

Schroeder, J. E., & Dugal, S. S. (1995). Psychological correlates of the materialism construct. *Journal of Social Behavior and Personality, 10*, 243–53.

Schwartz, S. H. (1992). Universals in the content and structure of values: Theoretical and empirical tests in 20 countries. In M. Zanna (Ed.), *Advances in experimental and social psychology*, Vol. 25 (pp. 1–65). Orlando, FL: Academic Press.

Schwartz, S. H. (1994). Are there universal aspects in the content and structure of values? *Journal of Social Issues, 50*, 19–45.

Schwartz, S. H. (1996). Values priorities and behavior: Applying of theory of integrated value systems. In C. Seligman, J. M. Olson, & M. P. Zanna (Eds.), *The psychology of values: The Ontario symposium*, Vol. 8 (pp. 1–24). Hillsdale, NJ: Erlbaum.

Sheldon, K. M., & Kasser, T. (1995). Coherence and congruence: Two aspects of personality integration. *Journal of Personality and Social Psychology, 68*, 531–43.

Sheldon, K. M., & Kasser, T. (1998). Pursuing personal goals: Skills enable progress, but not all progress is beneficial. *Personality and Social Psychology Bulletin, 24*, 1319–31.

Sheldon, K. M., & Kasser, T. (2001). "Getting older, getting better": Personal strivings and psychological maturity across the life span. *Developmental Psychology, 37*, 491–501.

Simpson, J. B. (Ed.). (1988). *Simpson's contemporary quotations.* New York: Houghton Mifflin.

Sirgy, M. J., Cole, D., Kosenko, R., Meadow, H. L., Rahtz, D., Cicic, M., Jin, G. X., Yarsuvat, D., Blenkhon, D. L., & Nagpal, N. (1995). A life satisfaction measure: Additional validational data for the congruity life satisfaction measure. *Social Indicators Research, 34*, 237–59.

Skinner, B. F. (1972). *Beyond freedom and dignity.* New York: Alfred A. Knopf.

Srivastava, A., Locke, E. A., & Bortol, K. M. (2001). Money and subjective well-being: It's not the money, it's the motives. *Journal of Personality and Social Psychology*, *80*, 959–71.

Swinyard, W. R., Kau, A., & Phua, H. (2001). Happiness, materialism, and religious experience in the U.S. and Singapore. *Journal of Happiness Studies*, *2*, 13–32.

Wachtel, P. L., & Blatt, S. J. (1990). Perception of economic needs and of anticipated future incomes. *Journal of Economic Psychology*, *11*, 403–15.

White, R. W. (1959). Motivation reconsidered: The concept of competence. *Psychological Review*, *66*, 297–333.

Williams, G. C., Cox, E. M., Hedberg, V. A., & Deci, E. L. (2000). Extrinsic life goals and health risk behaviors in adolescents. *Journal of Applied Social Psychology*, *30*, 1756–71.

Winokur, J. (1996). *The rich are different*. New York: Pantheon Books.

READING THE TEXT

1. Describe in your own words Kasser's methodology in studying people's psychological responses to material goods and their acquisition.

2. What does psychologist Abraham Maslow mean by "self-actualization," and how does Kasser apply that concept to his studies of the psychological effects of materialism?

3. What is the Aspiration Index intended to chart for those who participate in it?

4. What is the central contradiction in American culture that Kasser believes underlies his results?

5. How did Kasser and his colleagues revise the Aspiration Index?

6. Kasser begins his selection with a quote from Chinese philosopher Lao Tzu. How does this quote affect a reader's reception of the scientific data that follow?

READING THE SIGNS

1. In class, anonymously respond to the items in the 1996 Aspiration Index and tabulate your results. How do you interpret your findings?

2. **CONNECTING TEXTS** In "What We Are to Advertisers" (p. 192), James Twitchell describes the VALS2 system of categorizing consumer identities. In class, discuss in small groups each consumer category. What attitude toward materialism and possessions would your category likely have?

3. **CONNECTING TEXTS** Kasser's research leads him to conclude that American culture is "inculcating values not conducive to its citizens' well-being" (para. 41). In an essay, write an argument that supports, refutes, or complicates this conclusion. To develop your ideas, consult Laurence Shames's "The More Factor" (p. 86) and the Introduction to Chapter 1, "Consuming Passions: The Culture of American Consumption" (p. 75).

4. **CONNECTING TEXTS** Using Laurence Shames's "The More Factor" (p. 86) as a critical framework, analyze why the United States is constantly sending "messages

proclaiming that material pursuits, accumulation of things . . . provide real worth, deep satisfactions, and a genuinely meaningful life" (para. 1).

5. **CONNECTING TEXTS**   In an essay, support, refute, or modify Kasser's contention that "the pursuit of wealth and possessions might actually be undermining our well-being" (para. 19). To develop support for your argument, interview people from different class backgrounds on the value material goods has for them. To develop your ideas, consult Joan Kron's "The Semiotics of Home Decor" (p. 119).

"Leave Area Clean"

READING THE SIGNS

1. What contradictory impulses does this image bring to mind? Is litter an inevitable by-product of our consumption-oriented society?

2. The Web site www.stoplittering.com, featuring the slogan "Just Pick It Up," suggests that the problem of litter can be solved if everyone stopped to clean up a few pieces of litter each day. Do you think this idea might work? Would you be willing to give it a try? Can you think of a more effective method of preventing the kind of litter seen in this image? What are some trade-offs with your method? What, in your opinion, should be the penalty for littering?

JACK SOLOMON

Masters of Desire: The Culture of American Advertising

When the background music in a TV or radio automobile commercial is classical, you can be pretty certain that the ad is pitching a Lexus or a Mercedes. When it's country western, it's probably for Dodge or Chevy. English accents are popular in Jaguar ads, while a good western twang sure helps move pickup trucks. Whenever advertisers make use of status-oriented or common-folk-oriented cultural cues, they are playing on one of America's most fundamental contradictions, as Jack Solomon explains in this cultural analysis of American advertising. The contradiction is between the simultaneous desire for social superiority (elitism) and social equality (populism) that lies at the heart of the American dream. And one way or another, it offers a good way to pitch a product. Solomon, a professor of English at California State University, Northridge, is the author of The Signs of Our Time *(1988), from which this selection is taken, and* Discourse and Reference in the Nuclear Age *(1988). He is also coeditor with Sonia Maasik of both* California Dreams and Realities *(2005) and this textbook.*

> Amongst democratic nations, men easily attain a certain equality of condition; but they can never attain as much as they desire.
>
> — ALEXIS DE TOCQUEVILLE

On May 10, 1831, a young French aristocrat named Alexis de Tocqueville arrived in New York City at the start of what would become one of the most famous visits to America in our history. He had come to observe firsthand the institutions of the freest, most egalitarian society of the age, but what he found was a paradox. For behind America's mythic promise of equal opportunity,

Tocqueville discovered a desire for *unequal* social rewards, a ferocious competition for privilege and distinction. As he wrote in his monumental study, *Democracy in America*:

> When all privileges of birth and fortune are abolished, when all professions are accessible to all, and a man's own energies may place him at the top of any one of them, an easy and unbounded career seems open to his ambition. . . . But this is an erroneous notion, which is corrected by daily experience. [For when] men are nearly alike, and all follow the same track, it is very difficult for any one individual to walk quick and cleave a way through the same throng which surrounds and presses him.

Yet walking quick and cleaving a way is precisely what Americans dream of. We Americans dream of rising above the crowd, of attaining a social summit beyond the reach of ordinary citizens. And therein lies the paradox.

The American dream, in other words, has two faces: the one communally egalitarian and the other competitively elitist. This contradiction is no accident; it is fundamental to the structure of American society. Even as America's great myth of equality celebrates the virtues of mom, apple pie, and the girl or boy next door, it also lures us to achieve social distinction, to rise above the crowd and bask alone in the glory. This land is your land and this land is my land, Woody Guthrie's populist anthem tells us, but we keep trying to increase the "my" at the expense of the "your." Rather than fostering contentment, the American dream breeds desire, a longing for a greater share of the pie. It is as if our society were a vast high-school football game, with the bulk of the participants noisily rooting in the stands while, deep down, each of them is wishing he or she could be the star quarterback or head cheerleader.

For the semiotician, the contradictory nature of the American myth of equality is nowhere written so clearly as in the signs that American advertisers use to manipulate us into buying their wares. "Manipulate" is the word here, not "persuade"; for advertising campaigns are not sources of product information, they are exercises in behavior modification. Appealing to our subconscious emotions rather than to our conscious intellects, advertisements are designed to exploit the discontentments fostered by the American dream, the constant desire for social success and the material rewards that accompany it. America's consumer economy runs on desire, and advertising stokes the engines by transforming common objects — from peanut butter to political candidates — into signs of all the things that Americans covet most.

But by semiotically reading the signs that advertising agencies manufac- 5
ture to stimulate consumption, we can plot the precise state of desire in the audiences to which they are addressed. Let's look at a representative sample of ads and what they say about the emotional climate of the country and the fast-changing trends of American life. Because ours is a highly diverse, pluralistic society, various advertisements may say different things depending on their intended audiences, but in every case they say something about America, about the status of our hopes, fears, desires, and beliefs.

We'll begin with two ad campaigns conducted by the same company that bear out Alexis de Tocqueville's observations about the contradictory nature of American society: General Motors' campaigns for its Cadillac and Chevrolet lines. First, consider an early magazine ad for the Cadillac Allanté. Appearing as a full-color, four-page insert in *Time*, the ad seems to say "I'm special — and so is this car" even before we've begun to read it. Rather than being printed on the ordinary, flimsy pages of the magazine, the Allanté spread appears on glossy coated stock. The unwritten message here is that an extraordinary car deserves an extraordinary advertisement, and that both car and ad are aimed at an extraordinary consumer, or at least one who wishes to appear extraordinary compared to his more ordinary fellow citizens.

Ads of this kind work by creating symbolic associations between their product and what is most coveted by the consumers to whom they are addressed. It is significant, then, that this ad insists that the Allanté is virtually an Italian rather than an American car, an automobile, as its copy runs, "Conceived and Commissioned by America's Luxury Car Leader — Cadillac" but "Designed and Handcrafted by Europe's Renowned Design Leader — Pininfarina, SpA, of Turin, Italy." This is not simply a piece of product information, it's a sign of the prestige that European luxury cars enjoy in today's automotive marketplace. Once the luxury car of choice for America's status drivers, Cadillac has fallen far behind its European competitors in the race for the prestige market. So the Allanté essentially represents Cadillac's decision, after years of resisting the trend toward European cars, to introduce its own European import — whose high cost is clearly printed on the last page of the ad. . . .

American companies manufacture status symbols because American consumers want them. As Alexis de Tocqueville recognized a century and a half ago, the competitive nature of democratic societies breeds a desire for social distinction, a yearning to rise above the crowd. But given the fact that those who do make it to the top in socially mobile societies have often risen from the lower ranks, they still look like everyone else. In the socially immobile societies of aristocratic Europe, generations of fixed social conditions produced subtle class signals. The accent of one's voice, the shape of one's nose, or even the set of one's chin immediately communicated social status. Aside from the nasal bray and uptilted head of the Boston Brahmin, Americans do not have any native sets of personal status signals. If it weren't for his Mercedes-Benz and Manhattan townhouse, the parvenu Wall Street millionaire often couldn't be distinguished from the man who tailors his suits. Hence, the demand for status symbols, for the objects that mark one off as a social success, is particularly strong in democratic nations — stronger even than in aristocratic societies, where the aristocrat so often looks and sounds different from everyone else.

Status symbols, then, are signs that identify their possessors' place in a social hierarchy, markers of rank and prestige. We can all think of any number of status symbols — Rolls-Royces, Beverly Hills mansions, even Shar Pei puppies (whose rareness and expense has rocketed them beyond Russian wolfhounds as status pets and has even inspired whole lines of wrinkle-faced stuffed toys) — but how do we know that something *is* a status symbol? The explanation is quite simple: When an object (or puppy!) either costs a lot of money or requires influential connections to possess, anyone who possesses it must also possess the necessary means and influence to acquire it. The object itself really doesn't matter, since it ultimately disappears behind the presumed social potency of its owner. Semiotically, what matters is the signal it sends, its value as a sign of power. One traditional sign of social distinction is owning a country estate and enjoying the peace and privacy that attend it. Advertisements for Mercedes-Benz, Jaguar, and Audi automobiles thus frequently feature drivers motoring quietly along a country road, presumably on their way to or from their country houses.

Advertisers have been quick to exploit the status signals that belong to 10 body language as well. As Hegel observed in the early nineteenth century, it is an ancient aristocratic prerogative to be seen by the lower orders without having to look at them in return. Tilting his chin high in the air and gazing down at the world under hooded eyelids, the aristocrat invites observation while refusing to look back. We can find such a pose exploited in an advertisement for Cadillac Seville in which we see an elegantly dressed woman out for a drive with her husband in their new Cadillac. If we look closely at the woman's body language, we can see her glance inwardly with a satisfied smile on her face but not outward toward the camera that represents our gaze. She is glad to be seen by us in her Seville, but she isn't interested in looking at *us*!

Ads that are aimed at a broader market take the opposite approach. If the American dream encourages the desire to "arrive," to vault above the mass, it also fosters a desire to be popular, to "belong." Populist commercials accordingly transform products into signs of belonging, utilizing such common icons as country music, small-town life, family picnics, and farmyards. All of these icons are incorporated in GM's "Heartbeat of America" campaign for its Chevrolet line. Unlike the Seville commercial, the faces in the Chevy ads look straight at us and smile. Dress is casual; the mood upbeat. Quick camera cuts take us from rustic to suburban to urban scenes, creating an American montage filmed from sea to shining sea. We all "belong" in a Chevy.

Where price alone doesn't determine the market for a product, advertisers can go either way. Both Johnnie Walker and Jack Daniel's are better-grade whiskies, but where a Johnnie Walker ad appeals to the buyer who wants a mark of aristocratic distinction in his liquor, a Jack Daniel's ad emphasizes the down-home, egalitarian folksiness of its product. Johnnie Walker associates itself with such conventional status symbols as sable coats, Rolls-Royces, and black gold; Jack Daniel's gives us a Good Ol' Boy in overalls. In fact, Jack Daniel's Good Ol' Boy is an icon of backwoods independence, recalling the days of the moonshiner and the Whisky Rebellion of 1794. Evoking emotions quite at odds with those stimulated in Johnnie Walker ads, the advertisers of Jack Daniel's have chosen to transform their product into a sign of America's populist tradition. The fact that both ads successfully sell whisky is itself a sign of the dual nature of the American dream. . . .

Populist advertising is particularly effective in the face of foreign competition. When Americans feel threatened from the outside, they tend to circle the wagons and temporarily forget their class differences. In the face of the Japanese automotive "invasion," Chrysler runs populist commercials in which Lee Iacocca joins the simple folk who buy his cars as the jingle "Born in America" blares in the background. Seeking to capitalize on the popularity of Bruce Springsteen's *Born in the USA* album, these ads gloss over Springsteen's ironic lyrics in a vast display of flag-waving. Chevrolet's "Heartbeat of America" campaign attempts to woo American motorists away from Japanese automobiles by appealing to their patriotic sentiments.

The patriotic iconography of these campaigns also reflects the general cultural mood of the early to mid-1980s. After a period of national anguish in the wake of the Vietnam War and the Iran hostage crisis, America went on a patriotic binge. American athletic triumphs in the Lake Placid and Los Angeles Olympics introduced a sporting tone into the national celebration, often making international affairs appear like one great Olympiad in which America was always going for the gold. In response, advertisers began to do their own flag-waving.

The mood of advertising during this period was definitely upbeat. Even 15 deodorant commercials, which traditionally work on our self-doubts and fears of social rejection, jumped on the bandwagon. In the guilty sixties, we had ads like the "Ice Blue Secret" campaign with its connotations of guilt and shame. In the feel-good Reagan eighties, "Sure" deodorant commercials featured images of triumphant Americans throwing up their arms in victory to reveal—no wet marks! Deodorant commercials once had the moral echo of Nathaniel Hawthorne's guilt-ridden *The Scarlet Letter*; in the early eighties they had all the moral subtlety of *Rocky IV*, reflecting the emotions of a Vietnam-weary nation eager to embrace the imagery of America Triumphant. . . .

Live the Fantasy

By reading the signs of American advertising, we can conclude that America is a nation of fantasizers, often preferring the sign to the substance and easily enthralled by a veritable Fantasy Island of commercial illusions. Critics of Madison Avenue often complain that advertisers create consumer desire, but semioticians don't think the situation is that simple. Advertisers may give shape to consumer fantasies, but they need raw material to work with, the subconscious dreams and desires of the marketplace. As long as these desires remain unconscious, advertisers will be able to exploit them. But by bringing the fantasies to the surface, you can free yourself from advertising's often hypnotic grasp.

I can think of no company that has more successfully seized upon the subconscious fantasies of the American marketplace—indeed the world marketplace—than McDonald's. By no means the first nor the only hamburger chain in the United States, McDonald's emerged victorious in the "burger wars" by transforming hamburgers into signs of all that was desirable in American life. Other chains like Wendy's, Burger King, and Jack-In-The-Box continue to advertise and sell widely, but no company approaches McDonald's transformation of itself into a symbol of American culture.

McDonald's success can be traced to the precision of its advertising. Instead of broadcasting a single "one-size-fits-all" campaign at a time, McDonald's pitches its burgers simultaneously at different age groups, different classes, even different races (Budweiser beer, incidentally, has succeeded in the same way). For children, there is the Ronald McDonald campaign, which presents a fantasy world that has little to do with hamburgers in any rational sense but a great deal to do with the emotional desires of kids. Ronald McDonald and his friends are signs that recall the Muppets, *Sesame Street*, the circus, toys, storybook illustrations, even *Alice in Wonderland*. Such signs do not signify hamburgers. Rather, they are displayed in order to prompt in the child's mind an automatic association of fantasy, fun, and McDonald's.

The same approach is taken in ads aimed at older audiences — teens, adults, and senior citizens. In the teen-oriented ads we may catch a fleeting glimpse of a hamburger or two, but what we are really shown is a teenage fantasy: groups of hip and happy adolescents singing, dancing, and cavorting together. Fearing loneliness more than anything else, adolescents quickly respond to the group appeal of such commercials. "Eat a Big Mac," these ads say, "and you won't be stuck home alone on Saturday night."

To appeal to an older and more sophisticated audience no longer so 20 afraid of not belonging and more concerned with finding a place to go out to at night, McDonald's has designed the elaborate "Mac Tonight" commercials, which have for their backdrop a nightlit urban skyline and at their center a cabaret pianist with a moon-shaped head, a glad manner, and Blues Brothers shades. Such signs prompt an association of McDonald's with nightclubs and urban sophistication, persuading us that McDonald's is a place not only for breakfast or lunch but for dinner too, as if it were a popular off-Broadway nightspot, a place to see and be seen. Even the parody of Kurt Weill's "Mack the Knife" theme song that Mac the Pianist performs is a sign, a subtle signal to the sophisticated hamburger eater able to recognize the origin of the tune in Bertolt Brecht's *Threepenny Opera*.

For yet older customers, McDonald's has designed a commercial around the fact that it employs a large number of retirees and seniors. In one such ad, we see an elderly man leaving his pretty little cottage early in the morning to start work as "the new kid" at McDonald's, and then we watch him during his first day on the job. Of course he is a great success, outdoing everyone else with his energy and efficiency, and he returns home in the evening to a loving wife and a happy home. One would almost think that the ad was a kind of moving "help wanted" sign (indeed, McDonald's *was* hiring elderly employees at the time), but it's really just directed at consumers. Older viewers can see themselves wanted and appreciated in the ad — and perhaps be distracted from the rationally uncomfortable fact that many senior citizens take such jobs because of financial need and thus may be unlikely to own the sort of home that one sees in the commercial. But realism isn't the point here. This is fantasyland, a dream world promising instant gratification no matter what the facts of the matter may be.

Practically the only fantasy that McDonald's doesn't exploit is the fantasy of sex. This is understandable, given McDonald's desire to present itself as a family restaurant. But everywhere else, sexual fantasies, which have always had an important place in American advertising, are beginning to dominate the advertising scene. You expect sexual come-ons in ads for perfume or cosmetics or jewelry — after all, that's what they're selling — but for room deodorizers? In a magazine ad for Claire Burke home fragrances, for example, we see a well-dressed couple cavorting about their bedroom in what looks like a cheery preparation for sadomasochistic exercises. Jordache and Calvin Klein pitch blue jeans as props for teenage sexuality. The phallic appeal of automobiles, traditionally an implicit feature in automotive advertising, becomes quite explicit in a Dodge commercial that shifts back and forth from shots of a young man in an automobile to teasing glimpses of a woman — his date — as she dresses in her apartment.

The very language of today's advertisements is charged with sexuality. Products in the more innocent fifties were "new and improved," but everything in the eighties is "hot!" — as in "hot woman," or sexual heat. Cars are "hot." Movies are "hot." An ad for Valvoline pulses to the rhythm of a "heat wave, burning in my car." Sneakers get red hot in a magazine ad for Travel Fox athletic shoes in which we see male and female figures, clad only in Travel Fox shoes, apparently in the act of copulation — an ad that earned one of *Adweek*'s annual "badvertising" awards for shoddy advertising.

The sexual explicitness of contemporary advertising is a sign not so much of American sexual fantasies as of the lengths to which advertisers will go to get attention. Sex never fails as an attention-getter, and in a particularly competitive, and expensive, era for American marketing, advertisers like to bet on a sure thing. Ad people refer to the proliferation of TV, radio, newspaper, magazine, and billboard ads as "clutter," and nothing cuts through the clutter like sex.

By showing the flesh, advertisers work on the deepest, most coercive human emotions of all. Much sexual coercion in advertising, however, is a sign of a desperate need to make certain that clients are getting their money's worth. The appearance of advertisements that refer directly to the prefabricated fantasies of Hollywood is a sign of a different sort of desperation: a desperation for ideas. With the rapid turnover of advertising campaigns mandated by the need to cut through the "clutter," advertisers may be hard pressed for new ad concepts, and so they are more and more frequently turning to already-established models. In the early 1980s, for instance, Pepsi-Cola ran a series of ads broadly alluding to Steven Spielberg's *E.T.* In one such ad, we see a young boy, who, like the hero of *E.T.*, witnesses an extraterrestrial visit. The boy is led to a soft-drink machine where he pauses to drink a can of Pepsi as the spaceship he's spotted flies off into the universe. The relationship between the ad and the movie, accordingly, is a parasitical one, with the ad taking its life from the creative body of the film. . . .

Madison Avenue has also framed ad campaigns around the cultural prestige of high-tech machinery. This is especially the case with sports cars, whose high-tech appeal is so powerful that some people apparently fantasize about *being* sports cars. At least, this is the conclusion one might draw from a Porsche commercial that asked its audience, "If you were a car, what kind of car would you be?" As a candy-red Porsche speeds along a rain-slick forest road, the ad's voice-over describes all the specifications you'd want to have if you *were* a sports car. "If you were a car," the commercial concludes, "you'd be a Porsche."

In his essay "Car Commercials and *Miami Vice*," Todd Gitlin explains the semiotic appeal of such ads as those in the Porsche campaign. Aired at the height of what may be called America's "myth of the entrepreneur," these commercials were aimed at young corporate managers who imaginatively identified with the "lone wolf" image of a Porsche speeding through the woods. Gitlin points out that such images cater to the fantasies of faceless corporate men who dream of entrepreneurial glory, of striking out on their own like John DeLorean and telling the boss to take his job and shove it. But as DeLorean's spectacular failure demonstrates, the life of the entrepreneur can be extremely risky. So rather than having to go it alone and take the risks that accompany entrepreneurial independence, the young executive can substitute fantasy for reality by climbing into his Porsche — or at least that's what Porsche's advertisers wanted him to believe.

But there is more at work in the Porsche ads than the fantasies of corporate America. Ever since Arthur C. Clarke and Stanley Kubrick teamed up to present us with HAL 9000, the demented computer of *2001: A Space Odyssey*, the American imagination has been obsessed with the melding of man and machine. First there was television's *Six Million Dollar Man*, and then movieland's *Star Wars*, *Blade Runner*, and *Robocop*, fantasy visions of a future dominated by machines. Androids haunt our imaginations as machines seize the initiative. *Time* magazine's "Man of the Year" for 1982 was a computer. Robot-built automobiles appeal to drivers who spend their days in front of computer screens — perhaps designing robots. When so much power and prestige is being given to high-tech machines, wouldn't you rather be a Porsche?

In short, the Porsche campaign is a sign of a new mythology that is emerging before our eyes, a myth of the machine, which is replacing the myth of the human. The iconic figure of the little tramp caught up in the cogs of industrial production in Charlie Chaplin's *Modern Times* signified a humanistic revulsion to the age of the machine. Human beings, such icons said, were superior to machines. Human values should come first in the moral order of things. But as Edith Milton suggests in her essay "The Track of the Mutant," we are now coming to believe that machines are superior to human beings, that mechanical nature is superior to human nature. Rather than being threatened by machines, we long to merge with them. *The Six Million Dollar Man* is one iconic figure in the new mythology; Harrison Ford's sexual coupling with an android is another.

In such an age it should come as little wonder that computer-synthesized Max Headroom should be a commercial spokesman for Coca-Cola, or that Federal Express should design a series of TV ads featuring mechanical-looking human beings revolving around strange and powerful machines.

Fear and Trembling in the Marketplace

While advertisers play on and reflect back at us our fantasies about everything 30 from fighter pilots to robots, they also play on darker imaginings. If dream and desire can be exploited in the quest for sales, so can nightmare and fear.

The nightmare equivalent of America's populist desire to "belong," for example, is the fear of not belonging, of social rejection, of being different. Advertisements for dandruff shampoos, mouthwashes, deodorants, and laundry detergents ("Ring around the Collar!") accordingly exploit such fears, bullying us into consumption. Although ads of this type are still around in the 1980s, they were particularly common in the fifties and early sixties, reflecting a society still reeling from the witch-hunts of the McCarthy years. When any sort of social eccentricity or difference could result in a public denunciation and the loss of one's job or even liberty, Americans were keen to conform and be like everyone else. No one wanted to be "guilty" of smelling bad or of having a dirty collar.

"Guilt" ads characteristically work by creating narrative situations in which someone is "accused" of some social "transgression," pronounced guilty, and then offered the sponsor's product as a means of returning to "innocence." Such ads, in essence, are parodies of ancient religious rituals of guilt and atonement, whereby sinning humanity is offered salvation through the agency of priest and church. In the world of advertising, a product takes the place of the priest, but the logic of the situation is quite similar.

In commercials for Wisk detergent, for example, we witness the drama of a hapless housewife and her husband as they are mocked by the jeering voices of children shouting "Ring around the Collar!" "Oh, those dirty rings!" the housewife groans in despair. It's as if she and her husband were being stoned by an angry crowd. But there's hope, there's help, there's Wisk. Cleansing her soul of sin as well as her husband's, the housewife launders his shirts with Wisk, and behold, his collars are clean. Product salvation is only as far as the supermarket. . . .

If guilt looks backward in time to past transgressions, fear, like desire, faces forward, trembling before the future. In the late 1980s, a new kind of fear commercial appeared, one whose narrative played on the worries of young corporate managers struggling up the ladder of success. Representing the nightmare equivalent of the elitist desire to "arrive," ads of this sort created images of failure, storylines of corporate defeat. In one ad for Apple computers, for example, a group of junior executives sits around a table with the boss as he asks each executive how long it will take his or her department to complete some publishing jobs. "Two or three days," answers one nervous executive. "A week, on overtime," a tight-lipped woman responds. But one young up-and-comer can have everything ready tomorrow, today, or yesterday, because his department uses a Macintosh desktop publishing system. Guess who'll get the next promotion?

For other markets, there are other fears. If McDonald's presents senior citi-   35
zens with bright fantasies of being useful and appreciated beyond retirement, companies like Secure Horizons dramatize senior citizens' fears of being caught short by a major illness. Running its ads in the wake of budgetary cuts in the Medicare system, Secure Horizons designed a series of commercials featuring a pleasant old man named Harry — who looks and sounds rather like Carroll O'Connor — who tells us the story of the scare he got during his wife's recent illness. Fearing that next time Medicare won't cover the bills, he has purchased supplemental health insurance from Secure Horizons and now securely tends his roof-top garden. . . .

The Future of an Illusion

There are some signs in the advertising world that Americans are getting fed up with fantasy advertisements and want to hear some straight talk. Weary of extravagant product claims and irrelevant associations, consumers trained by years of advertising to distrust what they hear seem to be developing an immunity to commercials. At least, this is the semiotic message I read in the "new realism" advertisements of the eighties, ads that attempt to convince you that what you're seeing is the real thing, that the ad is giving you the straight dope, not advertising hype.

You can recognize the "new realism" by its camera techniques. The lighting is usually subdued to give the ad the effect of being filmed without studio lighting or special filters. The scene looks gray, as if the blinds were drawn. The camera shots are jerky and off-angle, often zooming in for sudden and unflattering close-ups, as if the cameraman were an amateur with a home video recorder. In a "realistic" ad for AT&T, for example, we are treated to a monologue by a plump stockbroker — his plumpness intended as a sign that he's for real and not just another actor — who tells us about the problems he's had with his phone system (not AT&T's) as the camera jerks around, generally filming him from below as if the cameraman couldn't quite fit his equipment into the crammed office and had to film the scene on his knees. "This is no fancy advertisement," the ad tries to convince us, "this is sincere."

An ad for Miller draft beer tries the same approach, re-creating the effect of an amateur videotape of a wedding celebration. Camera shots shift suddenly from group to group. The picture jumps. Bodies are poorly framed. The color is washed out. Like the beer it is pushing, the ad is supposed to strike us as being "as real as it gets."

Such ads reflect a desire for reality in the marketplace, a weariness with Madison Avenue illusions. But there's no illusion like the illusion of reality. Every special technique that advertisers use to create their "reality effects" is, in fact, more unrealistic than the techniques of "illusory" ads. The world, in reality, doesn't jump around when you look at it. It doesn't appear in subdued gray tones. Our eyes don't have zoom lenses, and we don't look at things with our heads cocked to one side. The irony of the "new realism" is that it is more unrealistic, more artificial, than the ordinary run of television advertising.

But don't expect any truly realistic ads in the future, because a realistic   40
advertisement is a contradiction in terms. The logic of advertising is entirely semiotic: It substitutes signs for things, framed visions of consumer desire for the thing itself. The success of modern advertising, its penetration into every corner of American life, reflects a culture that has itself chosen illusion over reality. At a time when political candidates all have professional image-makers attached to their staffs, and the President of the United States can be an actor who once sold shirt collars, all the cultural signs are pointing to more illusions in our lives rather than fewer — a fecund breeding ground for the world of the advertiser.

READING THE TEXT

1. Describe in your own words the paradox of the American dream, as Solomon sees it.

2. In Solomon's view, why do status symbols work particularly well in manipulating American consumers?

3. What is a "guilt" ad (para. 32), according to Solomon, and how does it affect consumers?

4. Why, in Solomon's view, has McDonald's been so successful in its ad campaigns?

5. What relationship does Solomon find between the "new realism" (para. 37) of some ads and the paradoxes of the American dream?

READING THE SIGNS

1. **CONNECTING TEXTS**   The American political scene has changed since the late 1980s, when this essay was first published. In an analytic essay, argue whether you believe the contradiction between populism and elitism that Solomon describes still affects American advertising and media. Be sure to discuss specific media examples. To develop your ideas, you might consult Thomas Frank's "Commodify Your Dissent" (p. 163).

2. **CONNECTING TEXTS**   Read or reread David Brooks's "One Nation, Slightly Divisible" (p. 487). In an essay, argue whether you find a correlation between the red-state/blue-state dichotomy that he describes and Solomon's populist-elitist paradox. Be sure to support your position with specific examples from the media or consumer culture.

3. Bring to class a general-interest magazine such as *Time*, and in small groups study the advertising. Do the ads tend to have an elitist or popular appeal? What relationship do you see between the appeal you identify and the magazine's target readership? Present your group's findings to the class.

4. In class, brainstorm a list of status symbols common in advertising today. Then discuss what groups they appeal to and why. Can you detect any patterns based on gender, ethnicity, or age?

5. Visit your college library, and locate an issue of a popular magazine from earlier decades, such as the 1930s or 1940s. Then write an essay in which you compare and contrast the advertising found in that early issue with that in a current issue of the same publication. What similarities and differences do you find in the myths underlying the advertising, and what is their significance?

SHELLEY FRALIC
Cheap Chic

Carrie Bradshaw once confessed that she had "$40,000 worth of Manolo Blahnik shoes in her Upper East Side closet"; now Sarah Jessica Parker, who played Carrie Bradshaw in Sex and the City *and who has been dressed by the likes of Oscar de la Renta, Calvin Klein, and Versace, has brought out her own BITTEN line of women's sportswear, with every item priced under $20. And as Shelley Fralic reports in this piece for the* Vancouver Sun, *Parker has not been alone in her attempt to democratize fashion, being joined by such celebrities as Stephon Marbury, an NBA star who now has his own line of cheap sneakers, the $14.98 Starbury. Highlighting the enormous gap between the haves and the have-nots in an American society that prides itself on egalitarianism, the cheap chic trend is a challenge for cultural interpretation. Does it signify a turning away from the economic elitism that has so dominated recent American life, or is it just another way for the elite to get richer at the expense of adoring plebes? Inquiring semioticians want to know. Shelley Fralic is a writer for the* Vancouver Sun.

Best to first deal with the delicious irony of it all — rich, famous, couture-clad celebrities showing up in the local mall.

Okay, not showing up so much as attaching their credentials to clothing and accessories lines now selling in mall-based discount chain stores like Target and Steve & Barry's, proving that celebs are discovering what us mall rats have known all along — there's gold in them thar middle-class wallets. Especially when it carries the nirvanic whiff of not only affordability but fame.

Celebrity clothing lines are nothing new, mind you — Madonna and Jennifer Lopez are among the celestials who have trod this runway — but as cultural

Sarah Jessica Parker signs autographs during the New York unveiling of her new 500-piece BITTEN line of under-$20 clothes.

trends go, their seemingly mass exodus from Rodeo Drive to the suburban mall is blurring that once impenetrable line between the haves and those who want to look like them.

Witness Sarah Jessica Parker, back in the limelight three years after retiring her coltish Carrie Bradshaw of TV's saucy *Sex and the City*, a character who was a self-avowed clotheshorse flitting about Manhattan in designer duds and sheepishly confessing in one episode to having $40,000 worth of Manolo Blahnik shoes in her Upper East Side closet. On the real-life catwalk, Parker was partial to Oscar de la Renta, Calvin Klein, Versace, Chanel, and Christian LaCroix, dizzily haute couturiers that don't get out of bed in the morning unless they can strap a $20,000 gown on a famous mannequin like SJP.

These days, Parker is still stylish, and gangly slim at 42, but she has apparently hung up the couture and, like the greening of Bono, has found a new altruistic calling: Cheap chic. 5

Really cheap chic. Parker's post-Manolo credo — she now wears a T-shirt that pronounces Fashion Is Not A Luxury — has been manifested in a new 500-piece clothing line, in sizes two to 20, called BITTEN (as in, once you fall for quality affordable clothing, you're hooked), featuring knits, jeans, swimwear, lingerie, dresses, T-shirts, shoes, sweaters, coats, and separates all priced at under $20. Seriously. Under $20.

Parker worked on the line with two designers from Steve & Barry's, a discount chain that has more than 130 mall-based stores in the United States and boasts that it undercuts other discount chains such as Target and Wal-Mart. Last week, Parker hit a New York mall (somewhere, Carrie Bradshaw is spinning in a grave) to launch the line and told reporters it is her belief that it's "every woman's inalienable right to have a pulled-together, stylish, confident wardrobe with money left over to live. The idea of the democratization of fashion was extremely appealing to me," Parker said at the frenzied press conference, fetchingly clad in a basic BITTEN outfit of striped tank top, willow-colored cardigan and grey straight-leg pants.

And then there's NBA star Stephon Marbury. He says he's tired of hearing stories about kids getting beaten up and having their overpriced sneakers stolen, or worse yet, not being able to afford a stylish pair of sneaks at all, when all the poor kid's trying to do is emulate a favorite sports hero. So he introduced his own line of cheap designer kicks.

They're called Starburys and cost $14.98 — $14.98! — and the theory is that if the New York Knicks point guard endorses them, they'll have the same cachet as the Nikes worn and endorsed by Kobe Bryant. Starburys come in funky bright colours, and in styles including high and low tops, trainers, crossovers and surf kicks, as well as traditional basketball shoes. They don't look a whole lot different than your average budget-busting pair of Nike, Puma, or Adidas sneaks, but then aren't they all just stylized scraps of rubber, leather, plastic, and cloth held together by glue, laces, and Velcro and shouldn't cost $200 anyway?

At least that's what Marbury says, and clearly the kids are listening. Like 10 Parker's new BITTEN line, which is getting rave reviews, Marbury's Starburys are sold only at Steve & Barry's stores (the closest to Vancouver will be the store in the Everett Mall, which opens June 20), and the first shipments have reportedly been sellouts, no doubt fueled by the debut of the kicks on Marbury's feet during a recent NBA game.

Not to be outdone in the low-budget style wars is Target, which last month began carrying Isaac Mizrahi's latest entry in the affordable designer sweepstakes — the $100 wedding gown. It's a shocking concept in the age of the average $10,000 Vera Wang wedding gown, and at a time of year when a simple prom dress is costing parents upwards of $1,000, but the gowns in Mizrahi's bridal collection, made with trapunto, tulle, silk, lace, and taffeta, are no less stylish than their pricey peers. "Every bride deserves to find the gown of her dreams, regardless of her budget," Mizrahi said during the line's launch.

The other irony in this new wave of cheap chic, of course, is that it may well be the rich, famous, couture-clad celebrities who shake up, and wake up, the fashion industry. It may well take Parker in a $20 cocktail dress to remind us — much like Sharon Stone did when she wore a white Gap tee to the Oscars — that whether you live in Boise or Beverly Hills, they're still just clothes.

READING THE TEXT

1. Describe in your own words the central contradiction Fralic sees in celebrity products marketed to the masses.

2. How have Sarah Jessica Parker's fashion tastes shifted, according to Fralic?

3. Study Fralic's style and tone. How does her journalistic approach compare with conventions of academic writing?

READING THE SIGNS

1. In an essay, support, oppose, or complicate Fralic's claim that cheap chic "is blurring that once impenetrable line between the haves and those who want to look like them" (para. 3).

2. Write an essay that responds to the contention that cheap chic encourages consumption by playing on consumers' tendency to fetishize celebrities.

3. **CONNECTING TEXTS**   Assume the perspective of Thomas Frank ("Commodify Your Dissent," p. 163), and write a critique of the cheap chic trend.

4. Visit a Web site for a cheap chic product line, such as one for Sarah Jessica Parker's BITTEN or Target's Isaac Mizrahi clothes or Michel Graves home decor items, and analyze it semiotically. To what extent does the Web site convey the "idea of democratization" of its products?

MARIAH BURTON NELSON
I Won. I'm Sorry.

*Athletic competition, when you come right down to it, is about winning,
which is no problem for men, whose gender codes tell them that aggression and domination are admirable male traits. But "how can you win, if
you're female?" Mariah Burton Nelson asks, when the same gender codes
insist that women must be "feminine," "not aggressive, not victorious."
And so women athletes, even when they do win, go out of their way to
signal their femininity by dolling themselves up and smiling a lot. Beauty
and vulnerability seem to be as important to today's female athlete as
brawn and gold medals, Nelson complains, paradoxically contradicting
the apparent feminist gains that women athletes have made in recent
years. A former Stanford University and professional basketball player,
Nelson is the author of six books, including* We Are All Athletes *(2002)
and* Making Money on the Sidelines *(2008). She is executive director of
the American Association for Physical Activity and Recreation. This
piece originally appeared in* SELF *magazine.*

When Sylvia Plath's husband, Ted Hughes, published his first book of poems,
Sylvia wrote to her mother: "I am so happy that HIS book is accepted FIRST. It
will make it so much easier for me when mine is accepted. . . ."

After Sylvia killed herself, her mother published a collection of Sylvia's letters. In her explanatory notes, Aurelia Plath commented that from the time she
was very young, Sylvia "catered to the male of any age so as to bolster his sense
of superiority." In seventh grade, Aurelia Plath noted, Sylvia was pleased to finish second in a spelling contest. "It was nicer, she felt, to have a boy first."

How many women still collude in the myth of male superiority, believing
it's "nicer" when boys and men finish first? How many of us achieve but only
in a lesser, smaller, feminine way, a manner consciously or unconsciously
designed to be as nonthreatening as possible?

Since I'm tall, women often talk to me about height. Short women tell
me, "I've always wanted to be tall — but not as tall as you!" I find this amusing, but also curious. Why not? Why not be six-two?

Tall women tell me that they won't wear heels because they don't want to   5
appear taller than their husbands or boyfriends, even by an inch. What are
these women telling me — and their male companions? Why do women regulate their height in relation to men's height? Why is it still rare to see a woman
who is taller than her husband?

Women want to be tall enough to feel elegant and attractive, like models.
They want to feel respected and looked up to. But they don't want to be so tall

that their height threatens men. They want to win — to achieve, to reach new heights — but without exceeding male heights.

How can you win, if you're female? Can you just do it? No. You have to play the femininity game. Femininity by definition is not large, not imposing, not competitive. Feminine women are not ruthless, not aggressive, not victorious. It's not feminine to have a killer instinct, to want with all your heart and soul to win — neither tennis matches nor elected office nor feminist victories such as abortion rights. It's not feminine to know exactly what you want, then go for it.

Femininity is about appearing beautiful and vulnerable and small. It's about winning male approval.

One downhill skier who asked not to be identified told me the following story: "I love male approval. Most women skiers do. We talk about it often. There's only one thing more satisfying than one of the top male skiers saying, 'Wow, you are a great skier. You rip. You're awesome.'

"But it's so fun leaving 99 percent of the world's guys in the dust — oops," she laughs. "I try not to gloat. I've learned something: If I kick guys' butts and lord it over them, they don't like me. If, however, I kick guys' butts then act 'like a girl,' there is no problem. And I do mean girl, not woman. Nonthreatening." 10

Femininity is also about accommodating men, allowing them to feel bigger than and stronger than and superior to women, not emasculated by them.

Femininity is unhealthy, obviously. It would be unhealthy for men to act passive, dainty, obsessed with their physical appearance, and dedicated to bolstering the sense of superiority in the other gender, so it's unhealthy for women too. These days, some women are redefining femininity as strong, as athletic, as however a female happens to be, so that "feminine" becomes synonymous with "female." Other women reject both feminine and masculine terms and stereotypes, selecting from the entire range of human behaviors instead of limiting themselves to the "gender-appropriate" ones. These women smile only when they're happy, act angry when they're angry, dress how they want to. They cling to their self-respect and dignity like a life raft.

But most female winners play the femininity game to some extent, using femininity as a defense, a shield against accusations such as bitch, man-hater, lesbian. Feminine behavior and attire mitigate against the affront of female victory, soften the hard edges of winning. Women who want to win without losing male approval temper their victories with beauty, with softness, with smallness, with smiles.

In the fifties, at each of the Amateur Athletic Union's women's basketball championships, one of the players was crowned a beauty queen. (This still happens at Russian women's ice hockey tournaments.) Athletes in the All-American Girls Baseball League of the forties and fifties slid into base wearing skirts. In 1979, professional basketball players with the California Dreams were sent to John Robert Powers' charm school. Ed Temple, the legendary coach of the Tennessee State Tigerbelles, the team that produced Wilma Rudolph, Wyomia Tyus, Willye White, Madeline Manning, and countless other

Serena Williams at Wimbledon.

champions, enforced a dress code and stressed that his athletes should be "young ladies first, track girls second."

Makeup, jewelry, dress, and demeanor were often dictated by the male 15 coaches and owners in these leagues, but to some extent the players played along, understanding the tradeoff: in order to be "allowed" to compete, they had to demonstrate that they were, despite their "masculine" strivings, real ("feminine") women.

Today, both men and women wear earrings, notes Felshin, "but the media is still selling heterosexism and 'feminine' beauty. And if you listen carefully, in almost every interview" female athletes still express apologetic behavior through feminine dress, behavior, and values.

Florence Griffith-Joyner, Gail Devers, and other track stars of this modern era dedicate considerable attention to portraying a feminine appearance. Basketball star Lisa Leslie has received more attention for being a model than for leading the Americans to Olympic victory. Steffi Graf posed in bikinis for the 1997 *Sports Illustrated* swimsuit issue. In a Sears commercial, Olympic basketball players apply lipstick, paint their toenails, rock babies, lounge in bed, and pose and dance in their underwear. Lisa Leslie says, "Everybody's allowed to be themselves. Me, for example, I'm very feminine."

In an Avon commercial, Jackie Joyner Kersee is shown running on a beach while the camera lingers on her buttocks and breasts. She tells us that she can bench-press 150 pounds and brags that she can jump farther than "all but 128 men." Then she says: "And I have red toenails." Words flash on the screen: "Just another Avon lady." Graf, Mary Pierce, Monica Seles, and Mary Jo Fernandez have all played in dresses. They are "so much more comfortable" than skirts, Fernandez explained. "You don't have to worry about the shirt coming up or the skirt being too tight. It's cooler, and it's so feminine."

"When I put on a dress I feel different — more feminine, more elegant, more ladylike — and that's nice," added Australia's Nicole Bradtke: "We're in a sport where we're throwing ourselves around, so it's a real asset to the game to be able to look pretty at the same time."

Athletes have become gorgeous, flirtatious, elegant, angelic, darling — and the skating commentators' favorite term: "vulnerable." Some think this is good news: proof that femininity and sports are compatible. "There doesn't have to be such a complete division between 'You're beautiful and sexy' and 'you're athletic and strong,'" says Linda Hanley, a pro beach volleyball player who also appeared in a bikini in the 1997 *Sports Illustrated* swimsuit issue. [20]

Athletes and advertisers reassure viewers that women who compete are still willing to play the femininity game, to be cheerleaders. Don't worry about us, the commercials imply. We're winners but we'll still look pretty for you. We're acting in ways that only men used to act but we'll still act how you want women to act. We're not threatening. We're not lesbians. We're not ugly, not bad marriage material. We're strong but feminine. Linguists note that the word "but" negates the part of the sentence that precedes it.

There are some recent examples of the media emphasizing female power in an unambiguous way. "Women Muscle In," the *New York Times Magazine* proclaimed in a headline. The *Washington Post* wrote, "At Olympics, Women Show Their Strength." And a new genre of commercials protests that female athletes are NOT cheerleaders, and don't have to be. Olympic and pro basketball star Dawn Staley says in a Nike commercial that she plays basketball "for the competitiveness" of it. "I need some place to release it. It just builds up, and sports is a great outlet for it. I started out playing with the guys. I wasn't always accepted. You get criticized, like: 'You need to be in the kitchen. Go put on a skirt.' I just got mad and angry and went out to show them that I belong here as much as they do."

Other commercials tell us that women can compete like conquerors. A Nike ad called "Wolves" shows girls leaping and spiking volleyballs while a voice says, "They are not sisters. They are not classmates. They are not friends. They are not even the girls' team. They are a pack of wolves. Tend to your sheep." Though the athletes look serious, the message sounds absurd. When I show this commercial to audiences, they laugh. Still, the images do depict the power of the volleyball players: their intensity, their ability to pound the ball almost through the floor. The script gives the players (and viewers) permission not to be ladylike, not to worry about whether their toenails are red.

But in an American Basketball League commercial, the Philadelphia Rage's female basketball players are playing rough; their bodies collide. Maurice Chevalier sings, "Thank heaven for little girls." The tag line: "Thank heaven, they're on our side."

Doesn't all this talk about girls and ladies simply focus our attention on femaleness, femininity, and ladylike behavior? The lady issue is always there in the equation: something to redefine, to rebel against. It's always present, like sneakers, so every time you hear the word *athlete* you also hear the word *lady* — or feminine, or unfeminine. It reminds me of a beer magazine ad from the eighties that featured a photo of Olympic track star Valerie Brisco-Hooks. "Funny, she doesn't look like the weaker sex," said the print. You could see her impressive muscles. Clearly the intent of the ad was to contrast an old stereotype with the reality of female strength and ability. But Brisco-Hooks was seated, her legs twisted pretzel style, arms covering her chest. But in that position, Brisco-Hooks didn't look very strong or able. In the line, "Funny, she doesn't look like the weaker sex," the most eye-catching words are funny, look, weaker, and sex. Looking at the pretzel that is Valerie, you begin to think that she looks funny. You think about weakness. And you think about sex.

When she was young, Nancy Kerrigan wanted to play ice hockey with her older brothers. Her mother told her, "You're a girl. Do girl things."

Figure skating is a girl thing. Athletes in sequins and "sheer illusion sleeves" glide and dance, their tiny skirts flapping in the breeze. They achieve, but without touching or pushing anyone else. They win, but without visible signs of sweat. They compete, but not directly. Their success is measured not by confrontation with an opponent, nor even by a clock or a scoreboard. Rather, they are judged as beauty contestants are judged: by a panel of people who interpret the success of the routines. Prettiness is mandatory. Petite and groomed and gracious, figure skaters — like cheerleaders, gymnasts, and aerobic dancers — camouflage their competitiveness with niceness and prettiness until it no longer seems male or aggressive or unseemly.

The most popular sport for high school and college women is basketball. More than a million fans shelled out an average of $15 per ticket in 1997, the inaugural summer of the Women's National Basketball Association. But the most televised women's sport is figure skating. In 1995 revenue from skating shows and competitions topped six hundred million dollars. In the seven months between October 1996 and March 1997, ABC, CBS, NBC, Fox, ESPN, TBS, and USA dedicated 162.5 hours of programming to figure skating, half of it in prime time. Kerrigan earns up to three hundred thousand dollars for a single performance.

Nearly 75 percent of the viewers of televised skating are women. The average age is between twenty-five and forty-five years old, with a household income of more than fifty thousand dollars. What are these women watching? What are they seeing? What's the appeal?

Like golf, tennis, and gymnastics, figure skating is an individual sport favored by white people from the upper classes. The skaters wear cosmetics, frozen smiles, and revealing dresses. Behind the scenes they lift weights and sweat like any serious athlete, but figure skating seems more dance than sport, more grace than guts, more art than athleticism. Figure skating allows women to compete like champions while dressed like cheerleaders.

In women's figure skating, smiling is part of "artistic expression." In the final round, if the competitors are of equal merit, artistry weighs more heavily than technique. Midori Ito, the best jumper in the history of women's skating, explained a weak showing at the 1995 world championships this way: "I wasn't 100 percent satisfied. . . . I probably wasn't smiling enough."

The media portray female figure skaters as "little girl dancers" or "fairy tale princesses" (NBC commentator John Tesh); as "elegant" (Dick Button); as "little angels" (Peggy Fleming); as "ice beauties" and "ladies who lutz" (*People* magazine). Commentators frame skaters as small, young, and decorative creatures, not superwomen but fairy-tale figments of someone's imagination.

After Kerrigan was assaulted by a member of Tonya Harding's entourage, she was featured on a *Sports Illustrated* cover crying "Why me?" When she recovered to win a silver medal at the Olympics that year, she became "America's sweetheart" and rich to boot. But the princess turned pumpkin shortly after midnight, as soon as the ball was over and she stopped smiling and started speaking. Growing impatient during the Olympic medal ceremony while everyone waited for Baiul, Kerrigan grumbled, "Oh, give me a break, she's just going to cry out there again. What's the difference?"

What were Kerrigan's crimes? She felt too old to cavort with cartoon characters. Isn't she? She expressed anger and disappointment—even bitterness and bad sportsmanship—about losing the gold. But wasn't she supposed to want to win? What happens to baseball players who, disappointed about a loss, hit each other or spit on umpires? What happens to basketball players and football players and hockey players who fight? Men can't tumble from a princess palace because we don't expect them to be princesses in the first place, only athletes.

Americans fell out of love with Kerrigan not because they couldn't adore an athlete who lacked grace in defeat, but because they couldn't adore a female athlete who lacked grace in defeat.

Female politicians, lawyers, and businesswomen of all ethnic groups also play the femininity game. Like tennis players in short dresses, working women seem to believe it's an asset to look pretty (but not too pretty) while throwing themselves around. The female apologetic is alive and well in corporate board rooms, where women say "I'm sorry, maybe someone else already stated this idea, but . . ." and smile while they say it.

When Newt Gingrich's mother revealed on television that Newt had referred to Hillary Clinton as a bitch, how did Hillary respond? She donned a pink suit and met with female reporters to ask how she could "soften her image." She seemed to think that her competitiveness was the problem and femininity the solution.

So if you want to be a winner and you're female, you'll feel pressured to play by special, female rules. Like men, you'll have to be smart and industrious, but in addition you'll have to be "like women": kind, nurturing, accommodating, nonthreatening, placating, pretty, and small. You'll have to smile. And not act angry. And wear skirts. Nail polish and makeup help, too.

READING THE TEXT

1. Summarize in your own words the contradictory messages about appropriate gender behavior that women athletes must contend with, according to Nelson.

2. Nelson begins her article with an anecdote about poet Sylvia Plath. How does this opening frame her argument about women in sports?

3. What is the "femininity game" (para. 7), in Nelson's view, and how do the media perpetuate it?

4. What sports are coded as "feminine," according to Nelson, and why?

READING THE SIGNS

1. Watch a women's sports event on television, such as an LPGA match, analyzing the behavior and appearance of the athletes. Use your observations as evidence in an essay in which you assess the validity of Nelson's claims about the contradictory gender role behaviors of female athletes.

2. If you are a female athlete, write a journal entry exploring whether you feel pressure to act feminine and your responses to that pressure. If you are not a female athlete, reflect on the behavior and appearance of women athletes on your campus. Do you see signs that they are affected by the femininity game?

3. Obtain a copy of a magazine that focuses on women's sports, such as *Sports Illustrated Women*. Analyze the articles and the ads in the magazine, noting models' and athletes' clothing, physical appearance, and speech patterns. Using Nelson's argument as a critical framework, write an essay in which you analyze whether the magazine perpetuates traditional gender roles or presents sports as an avenue for female empowerment.

4. Interview women athletes on your campus and ask them whether they feel pressured by the femininity game. Have they been accused of being lesbians or bitches simply because they are athletes? Do they feel pressure to be physically attractive or charming? Do you see any correlation between an athlete's sport and her responses? Use your observations as the basis of an argument about the influence of traditional gender roles on women's sports at your school.

ALFRED LUBRANO

The Shock of Education: How College Corrupts

One of America's most fundamental contradictions lies at the heart of the American dream itself. That is, America's promise of social mobility compels those who begin at the bottom to leave behind their origins in order to succeed, which entails giving up a part of oneself and leaving one's home behind. It can be a wrenching transition, and in this reflection on what it means to achieve the dream, Alfred Lubrano describes the strain of moving between two worlds, relating both his own experiences moving from working-class Brooklyn to an Ivy League school and those of other working-class "straddlers" who moved into the middle class. The son of a bricklayer, Lubrano is a journalist and National Public Radio commentator. He is the author of Limbo: Blue-Collar Roots, White-Collar Dreams *(2004), from which this selection is taken.*

College is where the Great Change begins. People start to question the blue-collar take on the world. Status dissonance, the sociologists call it. Questions arise: Are the guys accurate in saying people from such-and-such a race are really so bad? Was Mom right when she said nice girls don't put out? Suddenly, college opens up a world of ideas — a life of the mind — abstract and intangible. The core blue-collar values and goals — loyalty to family and friends, making money, marrying, and procreating — are supplanted by stuff you never talked about at home: personal fulfillment, societal obligation, the pursuit of knowledge for knowledge's sake, and on and on. One world opens and widens; another shrinks.

There's an excitement and a sadness to that. The child, say Sennett and Cobb, is deserting his past, betraying the parents he is rising above, an unavoidable result when you're trying to accomplish more with your life than merely earning a paycheck.[1] So much will change between parent and child, and between peers, in the college years. "Every bit of learning takes you further from your parents," says Southwest Texas State University history professor Gregg Andrews, himself a Straddler. "I say this to all my freshmen to start preparing them." The best predictor of whether you're going to have problems with your family is the distance between your education and your parents', Jake Ryan says. You may soon find yourself with nothing to talk to your folks or friends about.

This is the dark part of the American story, the kind of thing we work to hide. Mobility means discomfort, because so much has to change; one can't

---

[1]Richard Sennett and Jonathan Cobb, *The Hidden Injuries of Class* (New York: Alfred A. Knopf, 1972), 131.

allow for the satisfactions of stasis: You prick yourself and move, digging spurs into your own hide to get going, forcing yourself to forget the comforts of the barn. In this country, we speak grandly of this metamorphosis, never stopping to consider that for many class travelers with passports stamped for new territory, the trip is nothing less than a bridge burning.

Fighting Self-Doubt

When Columbia plucked me out of working-class Brooklyn, I was sure they had made a mistake, and I remained convinced of that throughout most of my time there. My high school was a gigantic (4,500 students) factory; we literally had gridlock in the halls between classes, kids belly to back between history and English class. A teacher once told me that if every one of the reliable corps of truant students actually decided to show up to class one day, the school could not hold us all. (We were unofficially nicknamed "the Italian Army." When our football guys played nearby New Utrecht, which boasted an equivalent ethnic demographic, kids dubbed the game the "Lasagna Bowl.") Lafayette High School roiled with restless boys and girls on their way to jobs in their parents' unions or to secretaries' desks. How could you move from that to an elite college?

At night, at home, the difference in the Columbia experiences my father and I were having was becoming more evident. The family still came together for dinner, despite our disparate days. We talked about general stuff, and I learned to self-censor. I'd seen how ideas could be upsetting, especially when wielded by a smarmy freshman who barely knew what he was talking about. No one wanted to hear how the world worked from some kid who was first learning to use his brain; it was as unsettling as riding in a car with a new driver. When he taught a course on Marx, Sackrey said he used to tell his students just before Thanksgiving break not to talk about "this stuff at the dinner table" or they'd mess up the holiday. Me mimicking my professors' thoughts on race, on people's struggle for equality, or on politics didn't add to the conviviality of the one nice hour in our day. So I learned to shut up.

After dinner, my father would flip on the TV in the living room. My mom 5 would grab a book and join him. And I'd go looking for a quiet spot to study. In his autobiography, *Hunger of Memory: The Education of Richard Rodriguez*, the brilliant Mexican-American Straddler, writer, and PBS commentator invokes British social scientist Richard Hoggart's "scholarship boys," finding pieces of himself in them. Working-class kids trying to advance in life, the scholarship boys learned to withdraw from the warm noise of the gathered family to isolate themselves with their books.[2] (Read primarily as a memoir of ethnicity

[2]Richard Rodriguez, *Hunger of Memory: The Education of Richard Rodriguez* (New York: Bantam Books, 1983), 46. Rodriguez himself quotes from Richard Hoggart, *The Uses of Literacy* (London: Chatto and Windus, 1957), chap. 10.

and — most famously — an anti-affirmative action tract, the book is more genuinely a dissertation on class. At a sidewalk café in San Francisco, Rodriguez himself tells me how often his book is miscatalogued.) Up from the immigrant working class, Rodriguez says in our interview, the scholarship boy finds himself moving between two antithetical places: home and school. With the family, there is intimacy and emotion. At school, one learns to live with "lonely reason." Home life is in the now, Rodriguez says; school life exists on an altogether different plane, calm and reflective, with an eye toward the future.

The scholarship boy must learn to distance himself from the family circle in order to succeed academically, Rodriguez tells me. By doing this, he slowly loses his family. There's a brutality to education, he says, a rough and terrible disconnect. Rodriguez says he despised his parents' "shabbiness," their inability to speak English. "I hated that they didn't know what I was learning," he says. He thought of D. H. Lawrence's *Sons and Lovers*, and of Paul Morel, the coal miner's son. Lawrence is a model for Rodriguez, in a way. Rodriguez remembers the scene in which the son watches his father pick up his schoolbooks, his rough hands fingering the volumes that are the instruments separating the two men. Books were establishing a disharmony between the classroom and Rodriguez's house. Preoccupation with language and reading is an effeminacy not easily understood by workers. "It sears your soul to finally decide to talk like your teacher and not your father," Rodriguez says. "I'm not talking about anything less than the grammar of the heart."

Myself, I studied in the kitchen near the dishwasher because its white noise drowned out the television. As long as the wash cycle ran, I could not hear Mr. T and the A-Team win the day. I did not begrudge my father his one indulgence; there wasn't much else that could relax him. He was not a drinker. TV drained away the tumult and hazard of his Columbia day. My own room was too close to the living room. My brother's small room was too crowded for both of us to study in. You never went in your parents' bedroom without them in it, inviting you. When the dishes were clean and the kitchen again too quiet to beat back the living room noise, I'd go downstairs to my grandparents' apartment. If they were both watching the same TV show on the first floor, then the basement was free. Here was profound and almost disquieting silence. I could hear the house's systems rumble and shake: water whooshing through pipes, the oil burner powering on and off, and the refrigerator humming with a loud efficiency. Down in the immaculate redwood-paneled kitchen/living room, which sometimes still smelled of the sausages and peppers my grandfather may have made that night (my grandparents cooked and ate in their basement, something that never seemed unusual to us), I was 90 minutes from my school and two floors below my family in a new place, underscoring my distance from anything known, heightening my sense of isolation — my limbo status. I read Homer, Shakespeare, and Molière down there. I wrote a paper on landscape imagery in Dante's *Inferno*. In my self-pitying, melodramatic teenager's mind, I thought I had been banished to a new, lonely rung of hell that Dante hadn't contemplated.

By 11 P.M., I'd go back upstairs. My mother would be in bed, my father asleep on his chair. I'd turn off the TV, which awakened my dad. He'd walk off to bed, and I'd study for a couple more hours. His alarm would go off before 5 A.M., and he'd already be at Columbia by the time I woke up at 6:30. That's how our Ivy League days ended and began. When my father was done with Columbia, he moved on to another job site. When I was done with Columbia, I was someone else. I'd say I got the better deal. But then, my father would tell you, that was always the plan. . . .

Macbeth and Other Foolishness

Middle-class kids are groomed for another life. They understand, says Patrick Finn, why reading *Macbeth* in high school could be important years down the road. Working-class kids see no such connection, understand no future life for which digesting Shakespeare might be of value. Very much in the now, working-class people are concerned with immediate needs. And bookish kids are seen as weak.

Various education studies have shown that schools help reinforce class. 10 Teachers treat the working class and the well-to-do differently, this work demonstrates, with the blue-collar kids getting less attention and respect. It's no secret, education experts insist, that schools in poorer areas tend to employ teachers who are less well-trained. In these schools, the curriculum is test-based and uncreative. Children are taught, essentially, to obey and fill in blanks. By fourth grade, many of the children are bored and alienated; nothing in school connects to their culture. Beyond that, many working-class children are resistant to schooling and uncooperative with teachers, experts say. They feel pressure from other working-class friends to not participate and are told that being educated is effeminate and irrelevant. Educators have long understood that minority children have these problems, says Finn. But they rarely understand or see that working-class white kids have similar difficulties. "So we're missing a whole bunch of people getting screwed by the education systems," he says.

In our conversations, Finn explains that language is a key to class. In a working-class home where conformity is the norm, all opinions are dictated by group consensus, by what the class says is so. There's one way to do everything, there's one way to look at the world. Since all opinions are shared, there's never a need to explain thought and behavior. You talk less. Language in such a home, Finn says, is implicit.

Things are different in a middle-class home. There, parents are more willing to take the time to explain to little Janey why it's not such a good idea to pour chocolate sauce on the dog. If Janey challenges a rule of the house, she's spoken to like an adult, or at least not like a plebe at some military school. (Working-class homes are, in fact, very much like the military, with parents barking orders, Straddlers tell me. It's that conformity thing again.) There is a variety of opinions in middle-class homes, which are more collaborative than conformist, Finn says. Middle-class people have a multiviewed take on the world. In such a home, where one needs to express numerous ideas and opinions, language is by necessity explicit.

When it's time to go to school, the trouble starts. The language of school — of the teachers and the books — is explicit. A child from a working-class home is at a huge disadvantage, Finn says, because he's used to a narrower world of expression and a smaller vocabulary of thought. It's little wonder that kids from working-class homes have lower reading scores and do less well on SATs than middle-class kids, Finn says.

In high school, my parents got me a tutor for the math part of the SATs, to bolster a lackluster PSAT score. That sort of thing happens all the time in middle-class neighborhoods. But we were setting precedent among our kind. Most kids I knew from the community were not taking the SATs, let alone worrying about their scores. If you're from the middle class, you do not feel out of place preparing for college. Parents and peers help groom you, encourage you, and delight in your progress. Of course, when you get to freshman year, the adjustments can be hard on anyone, middle-class and working-class kids alike. But imagine going through freshman orientation if your parents are ambivalent — or hostile — about your being there, and your friends aren't clear about what you're doing.

It was like that for my friend Rita Giordano, 45, also a journalist, also from Brooklyn. Her world, like mine, was populated by people who thought going from 60th to 65th Streets was a long journey. So when Rita took sojourns into Greenwich Village by herself on Saturday mornings as a teenager, she made sure not to tell any of her friends. It was too oddball to have to explain. And she'd always come back in time to go shopping with everyone. She couldn't figure out why she responded to the artsy vibe of the Village; she was just aware that there were things going on beyond the neighborhood. When it came time for college, she picked Syracuse University because it was far away, a new world to explore. That bothered her friends, and she'd have to explain herself to them on trips back home. "What do you do up there?" they asked her. "Don't you get homesick?" Suddenly, things felt awkward among childhood friends who had always been able to talk. "It was confusing to come home and see people thinking that you're not doing what they're doing, which meant you're rejecting them," said Rita, a diminutive, sensitive woman with large, brown eyes. " 'Don't they see it's still me?' I wondered. I started feeling like, how do I coexist in these two worlds, college and home? I mean, I could talk to my girlfriends about what color gowns their bridesmaids would wear at their fantasy weddings. But things like ambition and existential questions about where you fit in the world and how you make your mark — we just didn't go there."

And to make matters more complicated, there was a guy. Rita's decision to go to Syracuse didn't sit well with the boyfriend who was probably always going to remain working class. "In true Brooklyn fashion, he and his friends decided one night they were going to drive 400 miles to Syracuse to bring me

15

back, or whatever. But on the way up, they totaled the car and my boyfriend broke his leg. He never got up there, and after that, the idea of him bringing me to my senses dissipated."

Another Straddler, Loretta Stec, had a similar problem with a blue-collar lover left behind. Loretta, a slender 39-year-old English professor at San Francisco State University with delicate features and brown hair, needed to leave the commotion of drugs and friends' abortions and the repressed religious world of Perth Amboy, New Jersey, for the calm life of the mind offered by Boston College. The only problem was Barry. When Loretta was 17, she and Barry, an older construction worker, would ride motorcycles in toxic waste dumps. He was wild and fine — what every working-class girl would want. But Loretta knew life had to get better than Perth Amboy, so she went off to Boston. Barry and she still got together, though. They even worked on the same taping crew at a construction site during the summer between Loretta's freshman and sophomore years. But the differences between them were growing. All the guys on the job — Barry included — thought it was weird that Loretta would read the *New York Times* during lunch breaks. "What's with that chick?" people asked.

By the time Loretta returned to Boston for her second year, she knew she was in a far different place than Barry. The working class was not for her. Hanging around with this guy and doing construction forever — it sounded awful. "I was upwardly mobile, and I was not going to work on a construction crew anymore," Loretta says. She tried to break it off, but Barry roared up I-95 in a borrowed car to change her mind. Loretta lived in an old Victorian with middle-class roommates who had never met anyone like Barry. When he showed up with a barking Doberman in tow, she recalled he was screaming like Stanley Kowalski in *A Streetcar Named Desire* that he wanted Loretta back. The women became terrified. Loretta was able to calm first Barry, then her roommates. Afterward, the couple went to listen to some music. In a little place on campus, a guitar trio started performing a Rolling Stones song. Suddenly, Barry turned to Loretta and began scream-singing about wild horses not being able to drag him from her, really loud, trying to get her to see his resolve. "People were wondering who was this guy, what's his deal?" Loretta says. "It pointed out the clash between my new world and the old. You don't do stuff like that. It was embarrassing, upsetting, and confusing. I didn't want to hurt him. But I knew it wasn't going to work for me." They walked around campus, fighting about things coming to an end. At some point, she recalls, Barry noticed that a college student with a nicer car than his — Loretta can't remember exactly what it was — had parked behind his car, blocking him. Already ramped up, Barry had a fit and smashed a headlight of the fancy machine with a rock. There Loretta was, 100 feet from her campus Victorian, newly ensconced in a clean world of erudition and scholarship, far from the violence and swamps of central Jersey. Her bad-boy beau, once so appealing, was raving and breathing hard, trying to pull her away from the books, back down the turnpike to the working class.

"That was really the end of it," Loretta says. "I couldn't have a guy around who was going to act like that. He was wild and crazy and I was trying to make my way." Barry relented, and left Loretta alone. They lost touch, and Loretta later learned that Barry had died, the cause of death unknown to her. It was such a shock. . . .

READING THE TEXT

1. What is your response to Lubrano's title, and why do you think he chose it for his essay?
2. Summarize in your own words the difference between Lubrano's high school and college experiences.
3. What does Richard Rodriguez mean by saying "There's a brutality to education" (para. 6)?
4. Why did Lubrano avoid discussing his Columbia University experiences with his family?
5. How does child-rearing differ in blue-collar and in middle-class families, in Lubrano's view?

READING THE SIGNS

1. In your journal, reflect on the effects—positive or negative—that attending college may have had on your relationship with your family and high school friends. How do you account for any changes that may have occurred?
2. In an argumentative essay, support, challenge, or complicate Gregg Andrews's statement that "Every bit of learning takes you further from your parents" (para. 1).
3. Write a synthesis of the personal tales of Lubrano, Loretta Stec, and Rita Giordano. Then use your synthesis as the basis of an essay in which you explain how their collective experiences combine to demonstrate Lubrano's position that "for many class travelers with passports stamped for new territory, the trip is nothing less than a bridge burning" (para. 2).
4. Interview students from both blue-collar and middle- or upper-class backgrounds about the effect that attending college has had on their relationship with their family and high school friends. Use your findings to support your assessment of Lubrano's position that college can create divisions between blue-collar students and their families but that it tends not to have that effect on other classes.

RICHARD CORLISS

The Gospel According to Spider-Man

"For decades, America has embraced a baffling contradiction," Richard Corliss writes in this Time *analysis published in 2004. "The majority of its people are churchgoing Christians, many of them evangelical. Yet its mainstream pop culture . . . is secular at best, often raw and irreligious." As often happens in the strange dialectics of history, however, antitheses can come to meet in a new synthesis, as they do in America when a religious pastor can offer a sermon entitled "Catwoman: Discovering My True Identity." As Corliss reports, this melding of religion and pop culture is no isolated event, and with the growing Christian rock music and Christian film industries, we can expect to see more such weddings of onetime antagonists in the future. A senior writer for* Time, *Corliss is also the author of* Talking Pictures *and* Greta Garbo *(both 1974).*

The Congregation for today's service of the Journey, "a casual, contemporary, Christian church," fills the Promenade, a theater on upper Broadway in New York City. The Sunday-morning faithful — a few hundred strong — have come to hear the Journey's laid-back pastor, Nelson Searcy, give them the word. The word made film. Searcy, 32, who in jeans and a goatee looks like a way less Mephistophelian Charlie Sheen, is about to deliver the last of the church's eight-part God on Film series. The topic? "*Catwoman*: Discovering My True Identity."

Searcy points to a large screen at his right that shows other comic-book heroes with multiple identities. In his sermon, he alludes only vaguely to the Catwoman myth and gives the impression that he (like most other Americans) hasn't seen the Halle Berry version. But Searcy knows that a person tormented by questions of image and identity can find encouragement in the message of Genesis 1:27: "So God created people in his own image." That biblical quotation is projected on the screen, which also features an icon of a smiling cartoon Catwoman sporting purple tights, a feather boa, and a whip.

For decades, America has embraced a baffling contradiction. The majority of its people are churchgoing Christians, many of them evangelical. Yet its mainstream pop culture, especially film, is secular at best, often raw and irreligious. In many movies, piety is for wimps, and the clergy are depicted as oafs and predators. It's hard to see those two vibrant strains of society ever coexisting, learning from each other.

Yet the two are not only meeting; they're also sitting down and breaking bread together. The unearthly success of Mel Gibson's *The Passion of the Christ* helped movie execs recognize that fervent Christians, who spend hundreds of millions of dollars on religious books and music, are worth courting. Publicists hired by studios feed sermon ideas based on new movies to ministers. Meanwhile, Christians are increasingly borrowing from movies to drive home theological lessons. Clergy of all denominations have commandeered pulpits, publishing houses, and especially websites to spread the gospel of cinevangelism.

What's the biblical import of, say, *Spider-Man*? "Peter Parker gives us all 5 a chance to be heroic," says Erwin McManus, pastor of Mosaic, a Baptist-affiliated church in Los Angeles. "The problem is, we keep looking for radioactive spiders, but really it's God who changes us." What's the big idea behind *The Village*, according to the website movieministry.com? "Perfect love drives out fear." Behind *The Notebook*? "God can step in where science cannot." And, gulp, *Anchorman*? "What is love?" If your minister floated those notions recently, it may be because movieministry.com provides homilies for Sunday sermons. The website is a kind of Holy Ghostwriter.

By spicing Matthew and Mark with Ebert and Roeper, ministers can open a window to biblical teachings and a door to the very demographic that Hollywood studios know how to reach: young people.

"Film, especially for those under 35, is the medium through which we get our primary stories, our myths, our read on reality," says Robert K. Johnston, professor of theology and culture at the Fuller Theological Seminary and the author of the newly published *Finding God in the Movies: 33 Films of Reel Faith*. It was members of that generation, says Johnston, who "even if they loved God, were simply not going to church. Clergy are realizing that unless we reorient how we talk about our faith, we will lose the next generation." He sees movies as modern parables that connect to an audience that seeks not reason but emotional relevance. "As the culture has moved from a modern to a postmodern era, we have moved from wanting to understand truth rationally to understanding truth as it's embedded in story," he says.

The cinevangelists would say that the churches' appropriation of pop culture is nothing new. "Jesus also used stories," Johnston says. "In his day, parables were the equivalent of movies." Marc Newman, who runs movieministry.com, traces pop proselytizing back to the Apostle Paul. "In Acts there's a Scripture describing how he came to the Areopagus, the marketplace in Athens where people exchanged ideas. Paul speaks to the men of Athens and refers to their poets and their prophets. He used the things they knew as a way to reach out with the Gospel."

If Paul could cite Greek poets to the Greeks, then today's proselytizers will bring the church to moviegoers and, they hope, vice versa. "Today, with DVDs and the VCR, all of us can engage a movie text," Johnston says. "When a person in a worship congregation refers to *The Shawshank Redemption*, either people have seen it or they can rent it." In addition, 3,000-screen bookings and saturation marketing guarantee that a film that opens Friday will have been seen or at least talked about by Sunday morning.

Some conservative clergy prefer using the Bible, not *Bruce Almighty*, as the 10 text for a sermon. "It's not my cup of tea," says Jerry Falwell of movie-inspired sermons. But progressive Christians love plumbing the subtexts of comedies, satires, and action movies. Now, says Ted Baehr of movieguide.org, "a church group can highlight biblical teachings by using anything from *Dodgeball* to *Saved!* to *Kill Bill*."

Baehr, who grew up in Hollywood (his father was ranger Bob Allen in cowboy serials of the '30s), has put his Columbia University Film School education to use by giving a Christian take on current movies. "We try to teach people media wisdom. If Christians didn't believe in communications, they wouldn't believe that in the beginning was the word and the word was God and the word has a salutary effect within society."

But movies? From the beginning, they were considered, in the words of Catholic doctrine, an occasion of sin. The Catholic Legion of Decency was more notable for proscribing movies than promoting them. Some of the sterner Christian sects forbade filmgoing. And that was when Hollywood still produced religious films, from uplifting tales of jolly priests (Bing Crosby in *Going My Way*) and selfless sisters (Audrey Hepburn in *The Nun's Story*) to outright miracle plays like *The Song of Bernadette*, with Jennifer Jones as a French girl who had a vision at Lourdes.

By the '70s, the religious film had virtually disappeared. Today, *The Passion* aside, the genre exists only in niche markets: Mormon films (Ryan Little's *Saints and Soldiers*, Richard Dutcher's *God's Army*), well crafted and proudly square; and Rapture movies (*The Moment After*, *Caught in the Rapture*), which announce a personal and earthly apocalypse. Both types of film usually fly under the radar of studios, critics, and audiences.

Rarely, a Christian message is implicated in a Hollywood film. Steven Spielberg's *Close Encounters of the Third Kind*, in which an ordinary guy sees the light and travels far to make contact with extraterrestrials, was conceived by its original screenwriter, Paul Schrader, as Saul's transforming journey to become the Apostle Paul. *The Matrix* (the first one, not the sequels) was manna to hermeneuticians. In a recent Museum of Modern Art film series called "The Hidden God: Film and Faith," *Groundhog Day*, the Bill Murray comedy about a man who relives the same day over and over, was cited as a profound statement of faith, either Buddhist (rebirth), Jewish (acceptance), or Christian (redemption).

In the broadest sense, movies are getting more religious. According to Baehr, 15 only one film in 1985 (*The Trip to Bountiful*) had "positive Christian content," compared with 69 in 2003 (including *Finding Nemo*, *Spy Kids 3D*, and *Master and Commander*). Of course, it all depends on what counts as Christian and who's doing the counting. What's irrefutable is the growing number of theocentric movie websites, most recently a sophisticated one launched in February by the magazine *Christianity Today*.

The clergy may see all this as a revival; Hollywood sees it as a customer bonanza. New Line Cinema reaches out to Christian groups with films — like *Secondhand Lions*, about a boy living with his two codgerly, kindly uncles — whose themes might resonate. Says Russell Schwartz, New Line's president of domestic marketing: "The thing about all special-interest groups — Christian,

Jewish, whatever — is that they have to discover something relevant to their experience." Some studio bosses go further. Baehr says he talked with a mogul who told him, "We want to be seen as Christian friendly. We realize there's a big church audience out there, and we need to reach them."

"It's a vast, untapped market," says Jonathan Bock, a former sitcom writer (*Hangin' with Mr. Cooper*), whose Grace Hill Media helps sell Hollywood films to Christian tastemakers. He pitches media outlets like *Catholic Digest* and *The 700 Club* and has created sermons and Bible-study guides and marketed such movies as *The Lord of the Rings*, *Signs*, *The Rookie*, and, yes, *Elf*. "The ground was softened before *The Passion*," says Bock. "There are hundreds of Christian critics and Jewish writers and ministers who are writing about films." And millions of the faithful who see them. A July 2004 study by George Barna, the Gallup of born-again religion, shows that Christian Evangelicals are among the most frequent moviegoers. "Being a Christian used to mean you didn't go to Hollywood movies," says David Bruce, who runs the website hollywoodjesus.com. "Now it is seen as a missionary activity."

All this could just be the church's appropriation of Hollywood salesmanship: luring audiences with promises of a movie and some good talk, as the Journey's Searcy offered. Finding a Christian message in secular films like *Catwoman* and *Spider-Man* could be either a delusion or, as Jeffrey Overstreet, a critic for *Christianity Today* says, "a way of affirming that God's truth is inescapable and can be found even in the stories of people who don't believe in him."

Hollywood doesn't necessarily want to make Christian movies. It wants to make movies Christians think are Christian. Moviemakers are happy to be the money changers in the temple, even as preachers are thrilled that a discussion of — what, *Harold & Kumar Go to White Castle*? — can guarantee a full house on Sunday.

READING THE TEXT

1. What is the effect on the reader of Corliss's opening description of pastor Nelson Searcy's sermon entitled "*Catwoman*: Discovering My True Identity"?

2. Describe in your own words the contradiction in American culture that Corliss identifies.

3. Why do some ministers find religious dimensions in *Spider-Man*, in Corliss's view?

4. What conflicts does Corliss see in the religious attitudes toward popular culture?

5. How does Corliss use the history of popular culture to explain the current tendency of religion to engage with popular culture?

READING THE SIGNS

1. Write an essay in which you support, refute, or complicate Corliss's contention that films like *Spider-Man* enable religious groups to "open a window

to biblical teachings and a door to the very demographic that Hollywood studios know how to reach: young people" (para. 6).

2. Taking Corliss's article into account, write your own explanation of the response to *The Passion of the Christ*, which was supported by many Christian groups and opposed by some Christian and Jewish groups. Alternatively, interpret the response to another film or TV program that includes a religious dimension.

3. Adopt the perspective of pastor Nelson Searcy, and write a response to Corliss's claim that Christian evangelicals' view of moviegoing as a "missionary activity . . . could just be the church's appropriation of Hollywood salesmanship" (paras. 17–18).

4. Write an argumentative response to Corliss's assertion that "Hollywood doesn't necessarily want to make Christian movies. It wants to make movies Christians think are Christian" (para. 19).

5. Visit www.movieministry.com and assess the validity of Corliss's belief that "the website is a kind of Holy Ghostwriter" (para. 5).

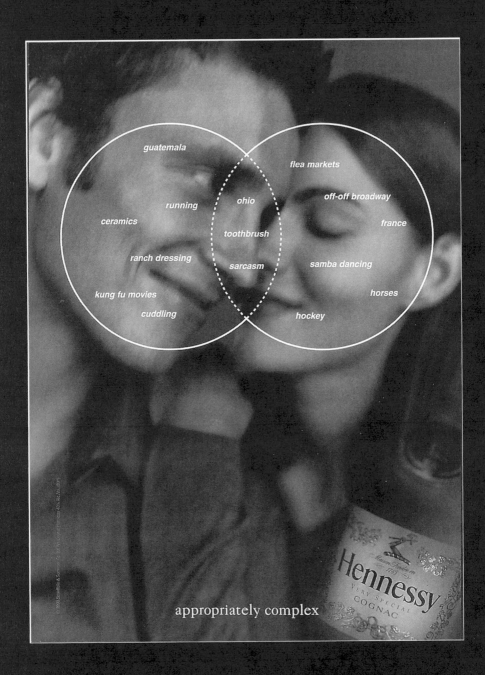

7
WE'VE COME A LONG WAY, MAYBE
Gender Codes in American Culture

Babes in Boyland

It probably all began with *Charlie's Angels* — no, not the movie with Cameron Diaz but Aaron Spelling's hit from the 1970s that really put the "jiggle" into prime-time television. Then there was *Baywatch* (also known as "Babe Watch"), and we knew we were not in Kansas anymore. Move over Donna Reed, June Lockhart, and Lucille Ball, and make way for Pamela Anderson, Molly Sims, and Nicollette Sheridan — not to mention the bikini-clad contestants on any number of reality dating programs, and the half-naked jungle girls on *Survivor* (yep, in the scorching sun of the tropics, what a gal really needs is her bikini top and her cut-off short shorts).

Meanwhile, on MTV and a concert stage near you, Britney Spears, Beyoncé, Jennifer Lopez, Christina Aguilera, and practically any contemporary diva you can think of can't seem to decide whether they are pop stars or porn stars, apparently hiring their costume designers from a pool of Frederick's of Hollywood rejects. Not to be outdone, American girls and women from their tweens to forties are lowering their necklines and waistbands, raising their blouse bottoms, and, sometimes, flaunting their thongs.

It seems odd, somehow, that over thirty years after the women's movement so vigorously challenged the reduction of women's value in society to the level of sex objects, American popular culture today appears to have regressed to one continuous peep show. Even amidst Hillary Rodham Clinton's 2008 campaign for the presidency, which dramatically challenged traditional gender codes, the pop culture buzz was obsessed with everything from Britney Spears's expanding figure, as revealed at the 2007 Video Music Awards,

559

Hillary Rodham Clinton challenged traditional gender codes during her 2008 presidential campaign.

to the contracting figures of today's television and movie actresses. Meanwhile, for ordinary consumers, Victoria's Secret is no secret, and breast-enhancement surgery seems almost as common as dentistry. The Dove Campaign for Real Beauty seems to be registering a protest against all this, but even it is telling American women that beauty is their most cherished possession. Somehow, a curious signal is being sent today about the status of American women and the gender codes that define their place in society.

The semiotic question is: What exactly is that signal telling us?

Interpreting American Gender Codes

Whether or not you have heard the term *gender code* before, you are already familiar with what it constitutes, because a gender code is a culturally constructed belief system that defines and dictates the appropriate roles and behavior for men and women in society. Whether you are a woman or a man, a gender code has been guiding your life since you were born. For example, a gender code impels parents to give their female children dolls (to prepare them for their adult lives as mothers) and to give their male children sports equipment, toy guns, and violent video games (to prepare them for the active and aggressive role that men are supposed to take in society). It is a gender code that tells girls that their primary concern should be with their appearance and with attracting boys while telling boys it's not their appearance that counts but how many times they "score." And it is a gender code that tells girls they aren't good at math (one talking Barbie doll exclaimed just this), while leading boys to math-savvy careers in science and technology.

Since gender codes are often justified on the basis of appeals to the "natural" differences between the two sexes, they are especially difficult to contest, and those women and men who do challenge them are often denounced as being "unnatural." But one of the key arguments of the feminist movement as it emerged in the 1970s was that gender codes are socially, not naturally, constructed, and usually reflect cultural values rather than natural facts. Take, for example, the huge national controversy that erupted in the early 1990s when a young woman named Shannon Faulkner had to go all the way to the Supreme Court to gain entrance to The Citadel, a military academy in South Carolina. Although by that time women were being admitted regularly to academies like West Point, The Citadel's admissions policy maintained a lingering cultural belief that women don't really belong in the military. This belief continues to be encoded in the fact that women who are in the armed services are not allowed to serve in combat units (former Speaker of the House Newt Gingrich justified this ban by insisting that women couldn't fight in the field because they "got infections" — a classic appeal to nature). By contesting The Citadel's admissions policy, Shannon Faulkner was, in effect, challenging a deeply held gender code, and the fuss made about the whole matter illustrates just how emotional such codes can be. When Faulkner finally won her court case and entered The Citadel, she was followed around by hordes of journalists (who reported on everything from her push-up performance to her weight), and when she finally succumbed to the pressure and left, the campus erupted in an ecstatic celebration.

Exploring the Signs of Gender

In your journal, explore the expectations about gender roles that you grew up with. What gender norms were you taught by your family, either overtly or implicitly? Have you ever had any conflicts with your parents over "natural" gender roles? If so, how did you resolve them? Do you think your gender-related expectations today are the same as those you had when you were a child?

In the Faulkner incident, then, we find the gender code that holds that it is the role of men, not of women, to be warriors: Men are the protectors, women are the ones to be protected (women and children first, as they said on the *Titanic*). This code is reinforced by the traditional belief that men are the aggressive sex, while women are passive. In sexual matters, men, accordingly, are expected to be the pursuers (he calls), while women are the pursued (she waits by the phone). Men are measured by their intellects, personal wealth, or power; women are valued for their bodies, which are ever on display to the gaze of the male eye.

We could go on and on. Note, though, how in each case gender roles are arrayed across a system of binary oppositions (men are this, women are the opposite). Indeed, these oppositions are so deeply encoded in our culture that you may find yourself protesting that men *are* aggressive, women *are* passive, men (as the bestseller has it) *are* from Mars, women *are* from Venus. But the fact that these roles can be reversed — indeed, they are being reversed more and more often these days — shows that they reflect cultural values rather than natural facts.

Prefeminist or Postfeminist?

Since the traditional patriarchal gender code tells women that their role in life is to be sexually attractive to men, the rampant eroticization of the female body in contemporary fashion and entertainment would thus appear to be a reversion to the prefeminist era, a striking rejection of feminist goals and aspirations. But it may not be that simple, because it is also the case that traditional gender codes insist that female sexuality must be tightly controlled by male masters, whereas for many women the confident display of their sexuality is actually empowering rather than degrading, a taking charge rather than a knuckling under — an attitude that was behind the immense popularity, among women, of the television hit *Sex and the City*.

This latter perspective reflects the point of view of what is called *postfeminism*. Postfeminists, who regard themselves as representing an evolution within the feminist movement itself, not a movement away from it, have argued that being proud of her body and using it to get what she wants is part of a woman's empowerment, and so have applauded the new erotics as a gender code advance rather than a regression. More traditional feminists, who are less persuaded by this argument, point out that by focusing her attention on her body rather than her mind, the postfeminist woman is in some danger of subjecting herself to the tyranny of a youth-worshipping culture that will reject her once she is past the peak of her sexually appealing years. Besides, if men are not held to sometimes impossible standards of physical beauty (especially with regard to weight), why should women be? If a man can use his intelligence to get ahead, why shouldn't a woman?

So does the transformation of popular culture into a vast stage presenting eye candy for guys merit a feminist or postfeminist interpretation? There are passionate adherents on both sides of the question. There is no easy or right answer. Consider the facts. What is your interpretation?

The Myths of Gender

If you find yourself feeling uneasy when addressing such questions, you are not alone. For this uneasiness is rooted in the fact that our gender codes, like any cultural mythology, provide a framework through which we can understand and experience our world. If that framework is disrupted, our world suffers a dislocation and we feel threatened. You may think that this isn't so, believing, for instance, that women really *shouldn't* be in the military. If that's the case, ask yourself why you feel that way. If you're concerned about women getting unfair advantages in the feminist era (one reason the Equal Rights Amendment failed to become part of the U.S. Constitution), wouldn't it seem that allowing them to share the dangerous duty of military combat would actually be the opposite of a privilege?

That many Americans, women as well as men, don't always see it this way shows just how durable our gender codes are. It thus is one of the major tasks of cultural semiotics to expose the outlines of gender myths to reveal just how deeply they influence our lives. Think of how these myths may shape your own behavior. Traditionally, for instance, the myths that govern courtship in America dictate that the man pays the expenses on a date and is responsible for all the logistics, even providing transportation and a destination. But there is no natural reason for this to be so; it's just a cultural expectation, one that has been changing for some time. Ask yourself: Who pays when you date? Who drives? Do you even care? Your answers will help you find your place in today's shifting terrain of gender myths.

In examining the gender myths that influence your own life, you should recognize the difference between the biological category of *sex* and the cultural category of *gender*. Your sex is determined by your chromosomes, but your gender goes beyond your sex to the roles that society has determined are appropriate for you. Your sex, in other words, is your birthright, but the roles you play in society are largely determined by your culture. In everyday life, however, this distinction between the natural category of sex and the cultural category of gender is blurred because socially determined gender roles are regarded as naturally dictated sexual necessities.

Even the standards of beauty that both women and men are held to are culturally determined. The ideal medieval woman, for example, was short, slender, high-waisted, and small-breasted, and boasted a high, domed forehead whose effect she enhanced by shaving her hairline. By the Renaissance, she had filled out considerably, and in the paintings of Peter Paul Rubens could appear positively pudgy by contemporary standards (we even have an adjective, *Rubenesque*, for well-padded feminine beauty). More recently, there was a shift from the hourglass figures of the fifties to the aerobically muscled hard bodies of the eighties. And currently, in spite of an international outcry, stick thin has become the order of the day. You may assume that this is it, the last stop, the one truly beautiful body, but give it time. Wait to see what's fashionable in bodies in the years to come.

Men, too, have seen their bodily ideals change over time. The ideal man of the eighteenth century, for example, was a rather heavyset fellow, rounded in appearance, and with a hint of a double chin, while today's ideal (especially in the corporate world) has square-hewn features and a jutting jaw (cleft if possible: Just look at some ads for business-oriented services to see what today's businessman wants to look like). Now think for a moment: What would you look like if you had the choice? Would you look like the ideal of the 1960s or the 1980s? Would you be long and lean, or buff, courtesy of Nautilus?

Metrosexual or NASCAR Dad?

It is important to realize, then, that men, too, are controlled by gender codes. A successful man is expected to accumulate wealth and power in his middle years; when young, well, just think of the typical Big Man on Campus. Is he not likely to be an athlete (the warrior role on a school campus) and a sexual star? Once out of school, many American men today have become what are now called NASCAR Dads — that is, family men who, in binary relation to their Soccer Mom wives, take charge of their families and enjoy such traditionally male-coded activities as stock-car racing and professional sports.

Something of a throwback to the benignly patriarchal dads of the 1950s, the NASCAR Dad offers one gender option to contemporary American men, but there are others. Take the metrosexual, for example. The metrosexual is a straight guy who cares about such traditionally female-coded matters as

---

Reading Gender on the Net

Use a search engine such as Yahoo! or Google to research what issues are considered "male" and "female" territory on the Internet. Focus your search on a comparison of specific topics, such as "men's rights" and "women's rights." Compare your findings with those of your classmates.

---

personal grooming, fashion, and home decor. Widely popularized on such programs as *Queer Eye for the Straight Guy*, the metrosexual offers a way of toying with the rules without breaking them — a gender option that has been especially attractive to unmarried urban males (whereas the NASCAR Dad typically is a suburbanite). But in other areas of contemporary popular culture the codes are not simply being modified; they're being bent quite out of shape.

Gender Bending

Probably the most deeply held gender codes in our culture are those that define our sexual orientation. So fundamental are such codes to our sense of personal and social identity that it is still somewhat controversial to analyze them. Surely, you may believe, sexual orientation is determined by nature. What has culture to do with it?

But a number of scholars engaged in gender studies are questioning the natural determination of sexual orientation as well. This is especially true for those involved in "queer theory," a movement that deliberately takes a once-pejorative term and subverts it to signify the dismantling of traditional gender norms. For such scholars, the categories of human sexuality, too, are social constructions, inscribing cultural rather than natural divisions, which means that they can be challenged and subverted in ways that might be called "gender blending" — as they have been in the behavior of such celebrities as Marilyn Manson and, quite surprisingly for a professional sports star, Dennis Rodman.

Indeed, the most dramatic signs that America's codes governing sexual orientation are shifting can be seen not in the scholarly publications of queer theorists but in the products of popular culture. With the mainstream success of such television programs as *Queer Eye for the Straight Guy* and *Will and Grace*, not to mention *Queer as Folk*, *The L Word*, and an episode of *My Name Is Earl* featuring a prison sex scene between two men, it is evident that homosexuality is finally more or less out of the cultural closet and ready for prime time.

That doesn't mean there still isn't controversy when it comes to the traditional gender code's attitude towards alternative sexualities. The national debate over gay marriage hotly continues as we write these words and has already become one of the issues at stake in yet another presidential campaign season. The fact that you may have strong feelings about the matter is itself a signifier of the powerful hold our gender codes have on us. Taking us to the core of our sense of ourselves as individual and social beings, involving deeply held religious and moral beliefs, gender codes, like all cultural mythologies, are ultimately political in nature, calling for semiotic analyses that will take us far beyond the classroom.

The Readings

The chapter opens with a paired set of readings, beginning with Aaron Devor's analysis of gender roles and the ways in which men and women manipulate the signs by which we traditionally communicate our gender identity, followed by Deborah Blum's article suggesting that biology *does* play a role in gender identity and that we can best understand the gender gap by looking at both the cultural and the physiological determinants of human behavior. Kevin Jennings is next with a personal memoir that chronicles his struggles with growing up gay in conflict with the traditional construction of male heterosexuality, while Sean Cahill enters the debate over gay marriage with a survey of case studies that support marriage equality in the United States, especially in the wake of the 9/11 attacks. Andy Medhurst's interpretation of Batman from a gay perspective provides some clues as to why Robin was excluded from Tim Burton's 1989 film *Batman*. Courtney Martin addresses the pressure on American women to attain unhealthily slender bodies, while Emily Prager more lightheartedly tweaks Barbie for providing generations of young girls with an impossible standard for bodily perfection. Joan Morgan then takes rap videos to task for their erotic objectification of black women. Deborah Tannen looks at the way that women are always "marked" in our society: No detail of a woman's appearance, from her hair to her shoes to her name, fails to send a gender-coded message about her, Tannen argues. James William Gibson's analysis of the warrior fantasies that have arisen in the wake of the Vietnam War and the rise of feminism sounds a warning note in the politics of gender identity, and Michael A. Messner concludes the chapter with an exploration of the role that sport takes in the construction of masculine identity in America.

AARON DEVOR
Gender Role Behaviors and Attitudes

"Boys will be boys, and girls will be girls": few of our cultural mytholo-
gies seem as natural as this one. But in this exploration of the gender
signals that traditionally tell what a "boy" or "girl" is supposed to look
and act like, Aaron Devor shows how these signals are not "natural" at
all but instead are cultural constructs. While the classic cues of mas-
culinity — aggressive posture, self-confidence, a tough appearance — and
the traditional signs of femininity — gentleness, passivity, strong nurtur-
ing instincts — are often considered "normal," Devor explains that they
are by no means biological or psychological necessities. Indeed, he sug-
gests, they can be richly mixed and varied, or to paraphrase the old
Kinks song "Lola," "Boys can be girls and girls can be boys." Devor is
dean of social sciences at the University of Victoria and author of Gender Blending: Confronting the Limits of Duality *(1989), from which*
this selection is excerpted, and FTM: Female-to-Male Transsexuals in
Society *(1997).*

Gender Role Behaviors and Attitudes

The clusters of social definitions used to identify persons by gender are collectively known as "femininity" and "masculinity." Masculine characteristics are
used to identify persons as males, while feminine ones are used as signifiers for
femaleness. People use femininity or masculinity to claim and communicate
their membership in their assigned, or chosen, sex or gender. Others recognize
our sex or gender more on the basis of these characteristics than on the basis of
sex characteristics, which are usually largely covered by clothing in daily life.

These two clusters of attributes are most commonly seen as mirror
images of one another with masculinity usually characterized by dominance
and aggression, and femininity by passivity and submission. A more even-
handed description of the social qualities subsumed by femininity and masculinity might be to label masculinity as generally concerned with egoistic
dominance and femininity as striving for cooperation or communion.[1] Characterizing femininity and masculinity in such a way does not portray the two
clusters of characteristics as being in a hierarchical relationship to one another

---

[1] Eleanor Maccoby, *Social Development: Psychological Growth and the Parent-Child Relation-*
ship (New York: Harcourt, Brace, Jovanovich, 1980), p. 217. Egoistic dominance is a striving
for superior rewards for oneself or a competitive striving to reduce the rewards for one's competitors even if such action will not increase one's own rewards. Persons who are motivated by
desires for egoistic dominance not only wish the best for themselves but also wish to diminish
the advantages of others whom they may perceive as competing with them.

but rather as being two different approaches to the same question, that question being centrally concerned with the goals, means, and use of power. Such an alternative conception of gender roles captures the hierarchical and competitive masculine thirst for power, which can, but need not, lead to aggression, and the feminine quest for harmony and communal well-being, which can, but need not, result in passivity and dependence.

Many activities and modes of expression are recognized by most members of society as feminine. Any of these can be, and often are, displayed by persons of either gender. In some cases, cross-gender behaviors are ignored by observers, and therefore do not compromise the integrity of a person's gender display. In other cases, they are labeled as inappropriate gender role behaviors. Although these behaviors are closely linked to sexual status in the minds and experiences of most people, research shows that dominant persons of either gender tend to use influence tactics and verbal styles usually associated with men and masculinity, while subordinate persons, of either gender, tend to use those considered to be the province of women.[2] Thus it seems likely that many aspects of masculinity and femininity are the result, rather than the cause, of status inequalities.

Popular conceptions of femininity and masculinity instead revolve around hierarchical appraisals of the "natural" roles of males and females. Members of both genders are believed to share many of the same human characteristics, although in different relative proportions; both males and females are popularly thought to be able to do many of the same things, but most activities are divided into suitable and unsuitable categories for each gender class. Persons who perform the activities considered appropriate for another gender will be expected to perform them poorly; if they succeed adequately, or even well, at their endeavors, they may be rewarded with ridicule or scorn for blurring the gender dividing line.

The patriarchal gender schema currently in use in mainstream North   5
American society reserves highly valued attributes for males and actively supports the high evaluation of any characteristics which might inadvertently become associated with maleness. The ideology underlying the schema postulates that the cultural superiority of males is a natural outgrowth of the innate predisposition of males toward aggression and dominance, which is assumed to flow inevitably from evolutionary and biological sources. Female attributes are likewise postulated to find their source in innate predispositions acquired in the evolution of the species. Feminine characteristics are thought to be intrinsic to the female facility for childbirth and breastfeeding. Hence, it is popularly believed that the social position of females is biologically mandated to be intertwined with the care of children and a "natural" dependency on men for

[2]Judith Howard, Philip Blumstein, and Pepper Schwartz, "Sex, Power, and Influence Tactics in Intimate Relationships," *Journal of Personality and Social Psychology* 51 (1986), pp. 102–9; Peter Kollock, Philip Blumstein, and Pepper Schwartz, "Sex and Power in Interaction: Conversational Privileges and Duties," *American Sociological Review* 50 (1985), pp. 34–46.

the maintenance of mother-child units. Thus the goals of femininity and, by implication, of all biological females are presumed to revolve around heterosexuality and maternity.[3]

Femininity, according to this traditional formulation, "would result in warm and continued relationships with men, a sense of maternity, interest in caring for children, and the capacity to work productively and continuously in female occupations."[4] This recipe translates into a vast number of proscriptions and prescriptions. Warm and continued relations with men and an interest in maternity require that females be heterosexually oriented. A heterosexual orientation requires women to dress, move, speak, and act in ways that men will find attractive. As patriarchy has reserved active expressions of power as a masculine attribute, femininity must be expressed through modes of dress, movement, speech, and action which communicate weakness, dependency, ineffectualness, availability for sexual or emotional service, and sensitivity to the needs of others.

Some, but not all, of these modes of interrelation also serve the demands of maternity and many female job ghettos. In many cases, though, femininity is not particularly useful in maternity or employment. Both mothers and workers often need to be strong, independent, and effectual in order to do their jobs well. Thus femininity, as a role, is best suited to satisfying a masculine vision of heterosexual attractiveness.

Body postures and demeanors which communicate subordinate status and vulnerability to trespass through a message of "no threat" make people appear to be feminine. They demonstrate subordination through a minimizing of spatial use: People appear feminine when they keep their arms closer to their bodies, their legs closer together, and their torsos and heads less vertical than do masculine-looking individuals. People also look feminine when they point their toes inward and use their hands in small or childlike gestures. Other people also tend to stand closer to people they see as feminine, often invading their personal space, while people who make frequent appeasement gestures, such as smiling, also give the appearance of femininity. Perhaps as an outgrowth of a subordinate status and the need to avoid conflict with more socially powerful people, women tend to excel over men at the ability to correctly interpret, and effectively display, nonverbal communication cues.[5]

---

[3]Nancy Chodorow, *The Reproduction of Mothering: Psychoanalysis and the Sociology of Gender* (Berkeley: University of California Press, 1978), p. 134.

[4]Jon K. Meyer and John E. Hoopes, "The Gender Dysphoria Syndromes: A Position Statement on So-Called 'Transsexualism,'" *Plastic and Reconstructive Surgery* 54 (Oct. 1974), pp. 444–51.

[5]Erving Goffman, *Gender Advertisements* (New York: Harper Colophon Books, 1976); Judith A. Hall, *Non-Verbal Sex Differences: Communication Accuracy and Expressive Style* (Baltimore: Johns Hopkins University Press, 1984); Nancy M. Henley, *Body Politics: Power, Sex and Non-Verbal Communication* (Englewood Cliffs, N.J.: Prentice-Hall, 1979); Marianne Wex, *"Let's Take Back Our Space": "Female" and "Male" Body Language as a Result of Patriarchal Structures* (Berlin: Frauenliteraturverlag Hermine Fees, 1979).

Rearing children is work typically done by women, but not always.

Speech characterized by inflections, intonations, and phrases that convey nonaggression and subordinate status also make a speaker appear more feminine. Subordinate speakers who use more polite expressions and ask more questions in conversation seem more feminine. Speech characterized by sounds of higher frequencies are often interpreted by listeners as feminine, childlike, and ineffectual.[6] Feminine styles of dress likewise display subordinate status through greater restriction of the free movement of the body, greater exposure of the bare skin, and an emphasis on sexual characteristics. The more gender distinct the dress, the more this is the case.

Masculinity, like femininity, can be demonstrated through a wide variety 10 of cues. Pleck has argued that it is commonly expressed in North American society through the attainment of some level of proficiency at some, or all, of the following four main attitudes of masculinity. Persons who display success and high status in their social group, who exhibit "a manly air of toughness, confidence, and self-reliance" and "the aura of aggression, violence, and daring," and who conscientiously avoid anything associated with femininity are seen as exuding masculinity.[7] These requirements reflect the patriarchal ideology that masculinity results from an excess of testosterone, the assumption being that androgens supply a natural impetus toward aggression, which in turn impels males toward achievement and success. This vision of masculinity also reflects the ideological stance that ideal maleness (masculinity) must remain untainted by female (feminine) pollutants.

[6]Karen L. Adams, "Sexism and the English Language: The Linguistic Implications of Being a Woman," in *Women: A Feminist Perspective*, 3rd ed., ed. Jo Freeman (Palo Alto, Calif.: Mayfield, 1984), pp. 478–91; Hall, pp. 37, 130–37.

[7]Joseph H. Pleck, *The Myth of Masculinity* (Cambridge, Mass.: MIT Press, 1981), p. 139.

Masculinity, then, requires of its actors that they organize themselves and their society in a hierarchical manner so as to be able to explicitly quantify the achievement of success. The achievement of high status in one's social group requires competitive and aggressive behavior from those who wish to obtain it. Competition which is motivated by a goal of individual achievement, or egoistic dominance, also requires of its participants a degree of emotional insensitivity to feelings of hurt and loss in defeated others, and a measure of emotional insularity to protect oneself from becoming vulnerable to manipulation by others. Such values lead those who subscribe to them to view feminine persons as "born losers" and to strive to eliminate any similarities to feminine people from their own personalities. In patriarchally organized societies, masculine values become the ideological structure of the society as a whole. Masculinity thus becomes "innately" valuable and femininity serves a contrapuntal function to delineate and magnify the hierarchical dominance of masculinity.

Body postures, speech patterns, and styles of dress which demonstrate and support the assumption of dominance and authority convey an impression of masculinity. Typical masculine body postures tend to be expansive and aggressive. People who hold their arms and hands in positions away from their bodies, and who stand, sit, or lie with their legs apart — thus maximizing the amount of space that they physically occupy — appear most physically masculine. Persons who communicate an air of authority or a readiness for aggression by standing erect and moving forcefully also tend to appear more masculine. Movements that are abrupt and stiff, communicating force and threat rather than flexibility and cooperation, make an actor look masculine. Masculinity can also be conveyed by stern or serious facial expressions that suggest minimal receptivity to the influence of others, a characteristic which is an important element in the attainment and maintenance of egoistic dominance.[8]

Speech and dress which likewise demonstrate or claim superior status are also seen as characteristically masculine behavior patterns. Masculine speech patterns display a tendency toward expansiveness similar to that found in masculine body postures. People who attempt to control the direction of conversations seem more masculine. Those who tend to speak more loudly, use less polite and more assertive forms, and tend to interrupt the conversations of others more often also communicate masculinity to others. Styles of dress which emphasize the size of upper body musculature, allow freedom of movement, and encourage an illusion of physical power and a look of easy physicality all suggest masculinity. Such appearances of strength and readiness to action serve to create or enhance an aura of aggressiveness and intimidation central to an appearance of masculinity. Expansive postures and gestures combine with these qualities to insinuate that a position of secure dominance is a masculine one.

Gender role characteristics reflect the ideological contentions underlying the dominant gender schema in North American society. That schema leads us

---

[8]Goffman; Hall; Henley; Wex.

to believe that female and male behaviors are the result of socially directed hormonal instructions which specify that females will want to have children and will therefore find themselves relatively helpless and dependent on males for support and protection. The schema claims that males are innately aggressive and competitive and therefore will dominate over females. The social hegemony of this ideology ensures that we are all raised to practice gender roles which will confirm this vision of the nature of the sexes. Fortunately, our training to gender roles is neither complete nor uniform. As a result, it is possible to point to multitudinous exceptions to, and variations on, these themes. Biological evidence is equivocal about the source of gender roles; psychological androgyny is a widely accepted concept. It seems most likely that gender roles are the result of systematic power imbalances based on gender discrimination.[9]

READING THE TEXT

1. List the characteristics that Devor describes as being traditional conceptions of "masculinity" and "femininity" (para. 1).

2. What relationship does Devor see between characteristics that are considered masculine and feminine?

3. How does Devor explain the cultural belief in the "superiority" (para. 5) of males?

4. How, in Devor's view, do speech and dress communicate gender roles?

READING THE SIGNS

1. In small same-sex groups, brainstorm lists of traits that you consider to be masculine and feminine, and then have each group write its list on the board. Compare the lists produced by male and female groups. What patterns of differences or similarities do you see? To what extent do the traits presume a heterosexual orientation? How do you account for your results?

2. Study the speech patterns, styles of dress, and other nonverbal cues communicated by your friends during a social occasion, such as a party, trying not to reveal that you are observing them for an assignment. Then write an essay in which you analyze these cues used by your friends. To what extent do your friends enact the traditional gender codes Devor describes?

3. **CONNECTING TEXTS**   Study a popular magazine such as *Elle*, *Rolling Stone*, or *Maxim* for advertisements depicting men and women interacting with each other. Then write an essay in which you interpret the body postures of the models, using Devor's selection as your framework for analysis. How do males and females typically stand? To what extent do the models enact stereotypically masculine or feminine stances? To develop your essay, consult Steve Craig's "Men's Men and Women's Women" (p. 202) and Warren St. John's "Metrosexuals Come Out" (p. 217).

[9]Howard, Blumstein, and Schwartz; Kollock, Blumstein, and Schwartz.

4. **CONNECTING TEXTS** Devor argues that female fashion traditionally has restricted body movement while male styles of dress commonly allow freedom of movement. In class, discuss whether this claim is still true today, being sure to consider a range of clothing types (such as athletic wear, corporate dress, party fashion, and so forth). To develop your ideas, consult Mariah Burton Nelson's "I Won. I'm Sorry" (p. 539).

PERFORMING GENDER

DEBORAH BLUM

The Gender Blur: Where Does Biology End and Society Take Over?

There's an old argument over whether nature or nurture is more impor-
tant in determining human behavior. Nowhere is this argument more
intense than in gender studies, where proponents of the social construc-
tion of gender identities are currently exploring the many ways in which
our upbringing shapes our behavior. But after watching her two-year-old
son emphatically choose to play only with carnivorous dinosaur toys and
disdainfully reject the "wimpy" vegetarian variety, Deborah Blum decided
that nurture couldn't be all that there was to it. Exploring the role of
biology in the determination of human behavior, Blum argues that both
nature and nurture have to be taken into account if we are to understand
gender differences. A Pulitzer Prize–winning professor of journalism at
the University of Wisconsin at Madison, Blum is the author of several
books, including Sex on the Brain: The Biological Differences between
Men and Women *(1997) and* Ghost Hunters: William James and the
Search for Scientific Proof of Life after Death *(2006).*

I was raised in one of those university-based, liberal elite families that politicians like to ridicule. In my childhood, every human being — regardless of gender — was exactly alike under the skin, and I mean exactly, barring his or her different opportunities. My parents wasted no opportunity to bring this point home. One Christmas, I received a Barbie doll and a softball glove. Another brought a green enamel stove, which baked tiny cakes by the heat of a lightbulb, and also a set of steel-tipped darts and competition-quality dartboard. Did I mention the year of the chemistry set and the ballerina doll?

It wasn't until I became a parent — I should say, a parent of two boys — that I realized I had been fed a line and swallowed it like a sucker (barring the part about opportunities, which I still believe). This dawned on me during my older son's dinosaur phase, which began when he was about two-and-a-half. Oh, he loved dinosaurs, all right, but only the blood-swilling carnivores. Plant-eaters were wimps and losers, and he refused to wear a T-shirt marred by a picture of a stegosaur. I looked down at him one day, as he was snarling around my feet and doing his toddler best to gnaw off my right leg, and I thought: This goes a lot deeper than culture.

Raising children tends to bring on this kind of politically incorrect reaction. Another friend came to the same conclusion watching a son determinedly bite his breakfast toast into the shape of a pistol he hoped would blow away — or at least terrify — his younger brother. Once you get past the guilt part — Did I do this? Should I have bought him that plastic allosaur with the oversized teeth? — such revelations can lead you to consider the far more interesting field of gender biology, where the questions take a different shape: Does love of carnage begin in culture or genetics, and which drives which? Do the gender roles of our culture reflect an underlying biology, and, in turn, does the way we behave influence that biology?

The point I'm leading up to — through the example of my son's innocent love of predatory dinosaurs — is actually one of the most straightforward in this debate. One of the reasons we're so fascinated by childhood behaviors is that, as the old saying goes, the child becomes the man (or woman, of course). Most girls don't spend their preschool years snarling around the house and pretending to chew off their companion's legs. And they — mostly — don't grow up to be as aggressive as men. Do the ways that we amplify those early differences in childhood shape the adults we become? Absolutely. But it's worth exploring the starting place — the faint signal that somehow gets amplified.

"There's plenty of room in society to influence sex differences," says 5 Marc Breedlove, a behavioral endocrinologist at the University of California at Berkeley and a pioneer in defining how hormones can help build sexually different nervous systems. "Yes, we're born with predispositions, but it's society that amplifies them, exaggerates them. I believe that — except for the sex differences in aggression. Those [differences] are too massive to be explained simply by society."

Aggression does allow a straightforward look at the issue. Consider the following statistics: Crime reports in both the United States and Europe record between 10 and 15 robberies committed by men for every one by a woman. At one point, people argued that this was explained by size difference. Women weren't big enough to intimidate, but that would change, they predicted, with the availability of compact weapons. But just as little girls don't routinely make weapons out of toast, women — even criminal ones — don't seem drawn to weaponry in the same way that men are. Almost twice as many male thieves and robbers use guns as their female counterparts do.

Or you can look at more personal crimes: domestic partner murders. Three-fourths of men use guns in those killings; 50 percent of women do. Here's more from the domestic front: In conflicts in which a woman killed a man, he tended to be the one who had started the fight — in 51.8 percent of the cases, to be exact. When the man was the killer, he again was the likely first aggressor, and by an even more dramatic margin. In fights in which women died, they had started the argument only 12.5 percent of the time.

Enough. You can parade endless similar statistics but the point is this: Males are more aggressive, not just among humans but among almost all species on earth. Male chimpanzees, for instance, declare war on neighboring troops, and one of their strategies is a warning strike: They kill females and infants to terrorize and intimidate. In terms of simple, reproductive genetics, it's an advantage of males to be aggressive: You can muscle your way into dominance, winning more sexual encounters, more offspring, more genetic future. For the female — especially in a species like ours, with time for just one successful pregnancy a year — what's the genetic advantage in brawling?

Thus the issue becomes not whether there is a biologically influenced sex difference in aggression — the answer being a solid, technical "You betcha" — but rather how rigid that difference is. The best science, in my opinion, tends to align with basic common sense. We all know that there are extraordinarily gentle men and murderous women. Sex differences are always generalizations: they refer to a behavior, with some evolutionary rationale behind it. They never define, entirely, an individual. And that fact alone should tell us that there's always — even in the most biologically dominated traits — some flexibility, an instinctive ability to respond, for better and worse, to the world around us.

This is true even with physical characteristics that we've often assumed 10 are nailed down by genetics. Scientists now believe height, for instance, is only about 90 percent heritable. A person's genes might code for a six-foot-tall body, but malnutrition could literally cut that short. And there's also some evidence, in girls anyway, that children with stressful childhoods tend to become shorter adults. So while some factors are predetermined, there's evidence that the prototypical male/female body design can be readily altered.

It's a given that humans, like most other species — bananas, spiders, sharks, ducks, any rabbit you pull out of a hat — rely on two sexes for reproduction. So basic is that requirement that we have chromosomes whose primary purpose is to deliver the genes that order up a male or a female. All other chromosomes are numbered, but we label the sex chromosomes with the letters X and Y. We get one each from our mother and our father, and the basic combinations are these: XX makes female, XY makes male.

There are two important — and little known — points about these chromosomal matches. One is that even with this apparently precise system, there's nothing precise — or guaranteed — about the physical construction of male and female. The other point makes that possible. It appears that sex doesn't matter in the early stages of embryonic development. We are unisex at the point of conception.

If you examine an embryo at about six weeks, you see that it has the ability to develop in either direction. The fledgling embryo has two sets of ducts — Wolffian for male, Muellerian for female — an either/or structure, held in readiness for further development. If testosterone and other androgens are released by hormone-producing cells, then the Wolffian ducts develop into the channel that connects penis to testes, and the female ducts wither away.

Without testosterone, the embryo takes on a female form; the male ducts vanish and the Muellerian ducts expand into oviducts, uterus, and vagina. In other words, in humans, anyways (the opposite is true in birds), the female is the default sex. Back in the 1950s, the famed biologist Alfred Jost showed that if you castrate a male rabbit fetus, choking off testosterone, you produce a completely feminized rabbit.

We don't do these experiments in humans — for obvious reasons — but there are naturally occurring instances that prove the same point. For instance: In the fetal testes are a group of cells, called Leydig cells, that make testosterone. In rare cases, the fetus doesn't make enough of these cells (a defect known as Leydig cell hypoplasia). In this circumstance we see the limited power of the XY chromosome. These boys have the right chromosomes and the right genes to be boys; they just don't grow a penis. Obstetricians and parents often think they see a baby girl, and these children are routinely raised as daughters. Usually, the "mistake" is caught about the time of puberty, when menstruation doesn't start. A doctor's examination shows the child to be internally male; there are usually small testes, often tucked within the abdomen. As the researchers put it, if the condition had been known from the beginning, "the sisters would have been born as brothers."

Just to emphasize how tricky all this body-building can get, there's a peculiar genetic defect that seems to be clustered by heredity in a small group of villages in the Dominican Republic. The result of the defect is a failure to produce an enzyme that concentrates testosterone, specifically for building the genitals. One obscure little enzyme only, but here's what happens without it: You get a boy with undescended testes and a penis so short and stubby that it resembles an oversized clitoris.

In the mountain villages of this Caribbean nation, people are used to it. The children are usually raised as "conditional" girls. At puberty, the secondary tide of androgens rises and is apparently enough to finish the construction project. The scrotum suddenly descends, the phallus grows, and the child develops a distinctly male body — narrow hips, muscular build, and even slight beard growth. At that point, the family shifts the child over from daughter to son. The dresses are thrown out. He begins to wear male clothes and starts dating girls. People in the Dominican Republic are so familiar with this condition that there's a colloquial name for it: *guevedoces*, meaning "eggs (or testes) at 12."

It's the comfort level with this slip-slide of sexual identity that's so remarkable and, I imagine, so comforting to the children involved. I'm positive that the sexual transition of these children is less traumatic than the abrupt awareness of the "sisters who would have been brothers." There's a message of tolerance there, well worth repeating, and there are some other key lessons too.

These defects are rare and don't alter the basic male-female division of our species. They do emphasize how fragile those divisions can be. Biology allows flexibility, room to change, to vary and grow. With that comes room for error as well. That it's possible to live with these genetic defects, that they don't merely kill us off, is a reminder that we, male and female alike, exist on a continuum of biological possibilities that can overlap and sustain either sex.

Marc Breedlove points out that the most difficult task may be separating how the brain responds to hormones from how the brain responds to the *results* of hormones. Which brings us back, briefly, below the belt: In this context, the penis is just a result, the product of androgens at work before birth. "And after birth," says Breedlove, "virtually everyone who interacts with that individual will note that he has a penis, and will, in many instances, behave differently than if the individual was a female."

Do the ways that we amplify physical and behavioral differences in childhood shape who we become as adults? Absolutely. But to understand that, you have to understand the differences themselves — their beginning and the very real biochemistry that may lie behind them.

Here is a good place to focus on testosterone — a hormone that is both well-studied and generally underrated. First, however, I want to acknowledge that there are many other hormones and neurotransmitters that appear to influence behavior. Preliminary work shows that fetal boys are a little more active than fetal girls. It's pretty difficult to argue socialization at that point. There's a strong suspicion that testosterone may create the difference.

And there are a couple of relevant animal models to emphasize the point. Back in the 1960s, Robert Goy, a psychologist at the University of Wisconsin at Madison, first documented that young male monkeys play much more roughly than young females. Goy went on to show that if you manipulate testosterone level — raising it in females, damping it down in males — you can reverse those effects, creating sweet little male monkeys and rowdy young females.

Is testosterone the only factor at work here? I don't think so. But clearly we can argue a strong influence, and, interestingly, studies have found that girls with congenital adrenal hypoplasia — who run high in testosterone — tend to be far more fascinated by trucks and toy weaponry than most little girls are. They lean toward rough-and-tumble play, too. As it turns out, the strongest influence on this "abnormal" behavior is not parental disapproval, but the company of other little girls, who tone them down and direct them toward more routine girl games.

And that reinforces an early point: If there is indeed a biology to sex differences, we amplify it. At some point — when it is still up for debate — we gain a sense of our gender, and with it a sense of "gender-appropriate" behavior.

Some scientists argue for some evidence of gender awareness in infancy, perhaps by the age of 12 months. The consensus seems to be that full-blown "I'm a girl" or "I'm a boy" instincts arrive between the ages of 2 and 3. Research shows that if a family operates in a very traditional, Beaver Cleaver kind of environment, filled with awareness of and association with "proper" gender behaviors, the "boys do trucks, girls do dolls" attitude seems to come very early. If a child grows up in a less traditional family, with an emphasis on

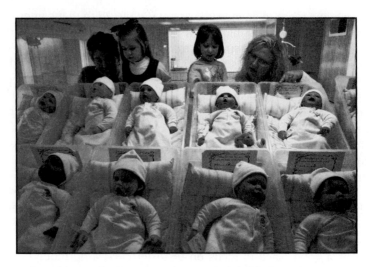

Girls and moms check out an American Girl doll fashion show in Staten Island, New York.

partnership and sharing — "We all do the dishes, Joshua" — children maintain a more flexible sense of gender roles until about age 6.

In this period, too, relationships between boys and girls tend to fall into remarkably strict lines. Interviews with children find that 3-year-olds say that about half their friendships are with the opposite sex. By the age of 5, that drops to 20 percent. By 7, almost no boys or girls have, or will admit to having, best friends of the opposite sex. They still hang out on the same playground, play on the same soccer teams. They may be friendly, but the real friendships tend to be boy-to-boy or girl-to-girl.

There's some interesting science that suggests that the space between boys and girls is a normal part of development; there are periods during which children may thrive and learn from hanging out with peers of the same sex. Do we, as parents, as a culture at large, reinforce such separations? Is the pope Catholic? One of my favorite studies looked at little boys who asked for toys. If they asked for a heavily armed action figure, they got the soldier about 70 percent of the time. If they asked for a "girl" toy, like a baby doll or a Barbie, their parents purchased it maybe 40 percent of the time. Name a child who won't figure out how to work *that* system.

How does all this fit together — toys and testosterone, biology and behavior, the development of the child into the adult, the way that men and women relate to one another?

Let me make a cautious statement about testosterone: It not only has 30 some body-building functions, it influences some behaviors as well. Let's make that a little less cautious: These behaviors include rowdy play, sex drive, competitiveness, and an in-your-face attitude. Males tend to have a higher baseline of testosterone than females — in our species, about seven to ten times as much — and therefore you would predict (correctly, I think) that all of those behaviors would be more generally found in men than in women.

But testosterone is also one of my favorite examples of how responsive biology is, how attuned it is to the way we live our lives. Testosterone, it turns out, rises in response to competition and threat. In the days of our ancestors, this might have been hand-to-hand combat or high-risk hunting endeavors. Today, scientists have measured testosterone rise in athletes preparing for a game, in chess players awaiting a match, in spectators following a soccer competition.

If a person — or even just a person's favored team — wins, testosterone continues to rise. It falls with a loss. (This also makes sense in an evolutionary perspective. If one was being clobbered with a club, it would be extremely unhelpful to have a hormone urging one to battle on.) Testosterone also rises in the competitive world of dating, settles down with a stable and supportive relationship, climbs again if the relationship starts to falter.

It's been known for years that men in high-stress professions — say, police work or corporate law — have higher testosterone levels than men in the ministry. It turns out that women in the same kind of strong-attitude professions have higher testosterone than women who choose to stay home. What I like about this is the chicken-or-egg aspect. If you argue that testosterone influenced the behavior of those women, which came first? Did they have high testosterone and choose the law? Or did they choose the law, and the competitive environment ratcheted them up on the androgen scale? Or could both be at work?

And, returning to children for a moment, there's an ongoing study by Pennsylvania researchers, tracking that question in adolescent girls, who are being encouraged by their parents to engage in competitive activities that were once for boys only. As they do so, the researchers are monitoring, regularly, two hormones: testosterone and cortisol, a stress hormone. Will these hormones rise in response to this new, more traditionally male environment? What if more girls choose the competitive path; more boys choose the other? Will female testosterone levels rise, male levels fall? Will that wonderful, unpredictable, flexible biology that we've been given allow a shift, so that one day, we will literally be far more alike?

We may not have answers to all those questions, but we can ask them, 35 and we can expect that the answers will come someday, because science clearly shows us that such possibilities exist. In this most important sense, sex differences offer us a paradox. It is only through exploring and understanding what makes us different that we can begin to understand what binds us together.

READING THE TEXT

1. What effect do Blum's opening personal anecdotes have on the persuasiveness of her argument?

2. What evidence does Blum offer to support her contention that males are naturally more aggressive than females?

3. How does testosterone affect human behavior, according to Blum's research?

4. In Blum's view, how do the cultural choices that humans make, such as engaging in sports or other competitive activities, affect hormone balances?

READING THE SIGNS

1. In your journal, reflect on the way your upbringing shaped your sense of appropriate gender behavior.

2. **CONNECTING TEXTS**   Blum's selection challenges the common cultural studies position that gender behavior is socially constructed. Write an essay in which you defend, qualify, or reject Blum's point of view. To develop your ideas, consult Aaron Devor's "Gender Role Behaviors and Attitudes" (p. 567) and Kevin Jennings's "American Dreams" (p. 581).

3. **CONNECTING TEXTS**   Write an essay describing how you would raise a boy to counteract his tendencies to aggressive behavior. To develop your ideas, consult James William Gibson's "Warrior Dreams" (p. 625).

4. Visit the library and investigate recent research on the possible genetic basis for homosexuality. Then write an essay in which you extend Blum's argument for the biological basis of gendered behavior to sexual orientation.

KEVIN JENNINGS

American Dreams

When Ellen DeGeneres became the first television star to come out of the closet on prime-time TV, gay men and lesbians around the country cele-brated what appeared to be a major step forward for one of America's most marginalized communities. But the firestorm of protest that also attended Ellen's coming-out equally demonstrated just how far homosex-uals have to go before winning full acceptance into American society. In this personal narrative of what it means to grow up gay in America, Kevin Jennings reveals the torment endured by a child forced to conceal his difference from everyone around him, especially his own parents. With years of self-denial and one suicide attempt behind him, Jennings shows how he eventually came to accept himself as he is and in so doing achieved his own version of the American dream. Jennings is founder and director of the Gay, Lesbian, and Straight Education Network (GLSEN) and author (with Pat Shapiro) of Always My Child: A Parent's Guide to Understanding Your Gay, Lesbian, Bisexual, Transgendered, or Ques-tioning Son or Daughter *(2003). His most recent book is* Mama's Boy, Preacher's Son: A Memoir *(2006).*

When I was little, I honestly thought I would grow up to be the president. After all, I lived in a land of opportunity where anyone, with enough determination and hard work, could aspire to the highest office in the land. I planned to live out the American Dream.

I realized, however, that something was amiss from an early age. I grew up in the rural community of Lewisville, North Carolina, just outside the city of Winston-Salem. As you might guess from the city's name, Winston-Salem, Winston-Salem makes its living from the tobacco industry: It was cigarettes that propelled local conglomerate RJR-Nabisco to its status as one of the world's largest multinational corporations. Somehow this rising tide of pros-perity never lapped at our doors, and the Jennings family was a bitter family indeed. Poor whites descended from Confederate veterans, we eagerly sought out scapegoats for our inexplicable failure to "make it" in the land of opportu-nity. My uncles and cousins joined the Ku Klux Klan, while my father, a funda-mentalist minister, used religion to excuse his prejudices — against blacks, against Jews, against Catholics, against Yankees, against Communists and lib-erals (basically the same thing, as far as he was concerned), and, of course, against gays. Somehow the golden rule of "Do unto others as you would have them do unto you" never made it into his gospel. Instead, I remember church services filled with outbursts of paranoia, as we were warned about the evils of those whom we (incorrectly) held responsible for our very real oppression. I grew up believing that there was a Communist plot undermining our nation, a Jewish conspiracy controlling the banks and the media, and that black men — whom I unselfconsciously referred to as "niggers" — spent their days plotting to rape white women. In case this seems like a history lesson on the Stone Age, please consider that I was born in 1963 and graduated from high school in 1981. Hardly the ancient past!

My father's profession as a traveling minister never left much money for luxuries like college tuition. Nevertheless, my mother was determined that I, her last chance, was going to make good on the Dream that had been denied to her and to my four older siblings — that one of her children would be the first member of our extended family ever to go to college. Not that it was going to be easy: my father died when I was eight, and my mother went to work at McDonald's (the only job she could get with her limited credentials). Every penny was watched carefully; dinner was often leftover quarter-pounders that she didn't have to pay for. I'm the only person I know who sees the Golden Arches, takes a bite, and thinks, "Mmm, just like Mom used to make!"

Throughout high school, I was determined to make it, determined to show my mother — and myself — that the American Dream really could come true. I worked hard and got ahead, earning a scholarship to Harvard after I had remade myself into the image of what I was told a successful person was like. Little did I realize at that point the price I was paying to fit in.

Seniors march for gay rights.

The first thing to go was any sign of my Southern heritage. As I came into   5
contact with mainstream America, through high school "gifted and talented"
programs and, later, at college in Massachusetts, I began to realize that we
Southerners were different. Our home-cooked meals — grits, turnip greens,
red-eye gravy — never seemed to show up in frozen dinners, and if a character
on television spoke with a Southern accent, that immediately identified him or
her as stupid or as comic relief. As the lesbian writer Blanche Boyd put it:

> When television programs appeared, a dreadful truth came clear to me:
> Southerners were not normal people. We did not sound like normal
> people . . . [and] what we chose to talk about seemed peculiarly different
> also. I began to realize we were hicks. Television took away my faith in
> my surroundings. I didn't want to be a hick. I decided to go North, where
> people talked fast, walked fast, and acted cool. I practiced talking like the
> people on television. . . . I became desperate to leave the South.

Like Blanche Boyd, I deliberately erased my accent and aped the false mono-
tone of television newscasters. I never invited college friends home to North
Carolina for fear they might meet my family and realize they were worthless,
ignorant hicks — which is how I'd come to view those whom I loved. I applied
to colleges on the sole criterion that they not be in the South. I ran as far from
Lewisville, North Carolina, as I could.

But there were some things about myself I could not escape from or
change, no matter how hard I tried — among them the fact that I am gay.

I had always known I was gay, even before I had heard the word or knew
what it meant. I remember that at age six or seven, the "adult" magazines that
so fascinated my older brothers simply didn't interest me at all, and I somehow knew that I'd better hide this feeling from them. As I grew older and began
to understand what my feelings meant, I recoiled in horror from myself. After
all, my religious upbringing as a Southern Baptist had taught me that gay
people were twisted perverts destined for a lifetime of eternal damnation.

Being as set as I was on achieving the American Dream, I was not about
to accept the fact that I was gay. Here is where I paid the heaviest price for my
Dream. I pursued what I thought was "normal" with a vengeance in high
school, determined that, if the spirit was weak, the flesh would be more willing at the prospect of heterosexuality. I dated every girl I could literally get my
hands on, earning a well-deserved reputation as a jerk who tried to see how
far he could get on the first date. I attacked anyone who suggested that gay
people might be entitled to some rights, too, and was the biggest teller of fag
jokes at Radford High. But what I really hated was myself, and this I couldn't
escape from, no matter how drunk or stoned I got, which I was doing on an
almost daily basis by senior year.

That was also the year I fell in love for the first time, with another boy in my
class. It turned out he was gay, too, and we made love one night in late May. I
woke up the next morning and realized that it was true — I really was a fag after
all. I spent that day trying to figure out how I was going to live the American

Dream, which seemed impossible if I was homosexual. By nightfall I decided it *was* impossible, and without my Dream I couldn't see a reason why I'd want to be alive at all. I went to my family's medicine cabinet, took the new bottle of aspirin out, and proceeded to wash down 140 pills with a glass of gin. I remember the exact number — 140 — because I figured I could only get down about ten at one swallow, so I carefully counted out fourteen little stacks before I began. Thanks to a friend who got to me in time, I didn't die that night. My story has a happy ending — but a lot of them don't. Those moments of desperation helped me understand why one out of every three gay teens tries to commit suicide.

At Harvard, the most important lessons I learned had little to do with Latin   10
American or European history, which were my majors. Instead, I learned the importance of taking control of my own destiny. I met a great professor who taught me that as long as I stayed in the closet, I was accepting the idea that there was something wrong with me, something that I needed to hide. After all, as my favorite bisexual, Eleanor Roosevelt, once said, "No one can make you feel inferior without your consent." By staying closeted, I was consenting to my own inferiority. I realized that for years, I had let a Dream — a beautiful, seductive, but ultimately false Dream — rule my life. I had agreed to pay its price, which was the rejection of my family, my culture, and eventually myself. I came to understand that the costs of the Dream far outweighed its rewards. I learned that true freedom would be mine only when I was able to make my own decisions about what I wanted out of life instead of accepting those thrust upon me by the Dream. Since I made that realization, I have followed my own path instead of the one I had been taught was "right" all my life.

Once I started down this new path, I began to make some discoveries about the society in which I was raised, and about its notions of right and wrong. I began to ask many questions, and the answers to these questions were not always pleasant. Why, for example, did my mother always earn less than men who did the same exact work? Why did I learn as a child that to cheat someone was to "Jew" them? Why was my brother ostracized when he fell in love with and later married a black woman? Why did everyone in my family work so hard and yet have so little? I realized that these inequalities were part of the game, the rules of which were such that gays, blacks, poor people, women, and many others would always lose to the wealthy white heterosexual Christian men who have won the Presidency forty-two out of forty-two times. Those odds — 100 percent — are pretty good ones to bet on. No, I discovered that true freedom could not be achieved by a Dream that calls on us to give up who we are in order to fit in and become "worthy" of power. Holding power means little if women have to become masculine "iron ladies" to get it, if Jews have to "Americanize" their names, if blacks have to learn to speak so-called Standard English (though we never acknowledge *whose* standard it is), or if gays and lesbians have to hide what everyone else gets to celebrate — the loves of their lives.

Real freedom will be ours when the people around us — and when we ourselves — accept that we, too, are "real" Americans, and that we shouldn't have to change to meet anyone else's standards. In 1924, at age twenty-two, the gay African American poet Langston Hughes said it best, in his poem "I, Too":

Tomorrow,
I'll be at the table
When company comes.
Nobody'll dare
Say to me,
"Eat in the kitchen,"
Then.
Besides,
They'll see how beautiful I am
And be ashamed —
I, too, am America.

By coming out as a gay man and demanding my freedom, I realize that I have done the most American thing of all. And while I have come a long way since the days when I dreamed of living in the White House, I have discovered that what I'm fighting for now is the very thing I thought I'd be fighting for if I ever became President — "liberty and justice for all."

READING THE TEXT

1. According to Jennings, how did his Southern upbringing influence his goals for the future?
2. Why did Jennings feel he had to eschew his Southern heritage?
3. In what ways did Jennings deny to himself his sexual orientation, and why did he do so?
4. In your own words, trace the evolution of Jennings's understanding of the American dream as he grew up.
5. What is the relationship between the excerpt from Langston Hughes's "I, Too" and Jennings's story?

READING THE SIGNS

1. In your journal, write your own account of how you responded to normative gender codes as a high school student. To what extent did you feel pressure to conform or to renounce traditional expectations — or to do both?
2. Jennings describes his early attempts to deny his sexual orientation. In class, discuss how other minority or underprivileged groups — ethnic minorities, women, the disabled — sometimes try to erase their identity. What social and cultural forces motivate such self-denial? Use the discussion as a springboard for an essay in which you explore why one might be motivated to do so.
3. **CONNECTING TEXTS** In class, brainstorm two lists: films or TV shows that reinforce heterosexuality as normative and those that present homosexuality positively. Then compare your lists. What conclusions do you draw about popular culture's influence on American gender codes? To develop your ideas, consult Marissa Connolly's "Homosexuality on Television: The Heterosexualization of *Will and Grace*" (p. 315).
4. **CONNECTING TEXTS** Compare and contrast Jennings's arrival at a confident sense of identity with that of Melissa Algranati ("Being an Other," p. 697). How do you explain any differences you observe?

SEAN CAHILL
The Case for Marriage Equality

It has been argued that gay marriage was the crucial issue on which the 2004 presidential election turned, but whether that was indeed the case, there is no denying that gay marriage continues to be a hot-button issue in American life. In this reading, Sean Cahill presents a case for gay marriage, profiling gay couples who were denied the benefits enjoyed by married couples in the aftermath of such personal catastrophes as the September 11 attacks on the World Trade Center. Cahill invites the reader to judge: Is this fair and just? Cahill is managing director for public policy, research, and community health at Gay Men's Health Crisis and author of Same-Sex Marriage in the United States: Focus on the Facts *(2004), from which this selection is taken.*

Marriage aims to promote healthy families by protecting the economic and emotional interdependence of family members and giving priority to their bonds. Gay couples have the same needs as opposite-sex couples: same-sex couples are often emotionally and economically interdependent, sharing household and financial responsibilities, and they often raise children or take care of other family members together. Legal protection of partner relationships, which includes a comprehensive package of economic and social rights and responsibilities for couples and their children, provides families with security and peace of mind. A 2004 report by the U.S. General Accounting Office lists 1,138 ways in which marital relationships are given special treatment by the federal government.[1]

Two Stories

. . . The effects of being unable to marry are felt in families headed by same-sex couples throughout the country, in large and small ways. Being unable to marry has particularly devastating consequences when one partner dies. For the surviving partner, securing the basic right to the financial support the deceased partner contributed to their household — a right afforded to heterosexual couples through marriage — involves protracted battles with federal

---

[1]General Accounting Office (2004, January 23). Report to Senate Majority Leader William Frist. GAO-04-353R. This represents an increase since 1997, when the GAO issued its first report that listed 1,049 federal laws and benefits that only married spouses can access. General Accounting Office (1997, January 31). *Tables of laws in the United States Code involving marital status, by category.* www.gao.gov/archive/1997/og97016.pdf. Accessed December 4, 2003.

A justice of the peace marries a lesbian couple in city hall on Freedom to Marry Day, San Francisco.

and state bureaucracies, at a time of great emotional strain, and often with little result.

LOIS MARRERO AND MICKIE MASHBURN

In July 2001, Lois Marrero, an officer in the Tampa, Florida, Police Department, was killed while trying to stop a bank robbery. Mickie Mashburn, Lois's partner of 11 years and a 17-year veteran of the Tampa Police Department, grieved with Lois's family, with whom she had been close for 18 years. The night Lois was killed, Lois's sister told interviewers, "We love Mickie; she is part of our family." Lois and Mickie lived publicly as a lesbian couple. They had been joined in a public commitment ceremony ten years earlier and lived together and took care of one another. They educated the Tampa police force about gay and lesbian issues. It was Lois's death, however, that made it clear that their relationship was not recognized in significant ways.

Although they had shared bills for years, Mickie was told she was not eligible for Lois's pension. She sued, but at the end of a bitter trial Lois's blood relatives took Lois's pension and left Mickie with nothing. "The money can't bring Lois back," Mickie says, "but we need to have this right for our relationships. No one else should go through what I have gone through. We need to be accepted like everyone else."[2] Had Mickie and Lois had the right to marry, they would have been able to protect their family and their right to inherit each other's pension in the event of an untimely death.

[2]Adapted from a profile of Mickie Mashburn and Lois Marrero in Cahill, S., Ellen, M., and Tobias, S. (2002). *Family policy: Issues affecting gay, lesbian, bisexual and transgender families.* New York: Policy Institute of the National Gay and Lesbian Task Force. pp. 152–53.

LARRY COURTNEY AND EUGENE CLARK

Larry Courtney and Eugene Clark moved together to New York from Wash- 5
ington, D.C., in 1988 so that Larry could accept a job offer. Larry and Eugene
enjoyed life in New York. They reveled in the general acceptance of their
gay relationship as a family unit. They entertained friends and family. They
went to the theater. They went to some of the city's many gay bars. They
vacationed together and spent holidays together with different family members or with friends. When Eugene's mother had a stroke in 1995, Eugene
and Larry brought her from Washington to live with them in their small Manhattan apartment; they both nursed her and cared for her until she passed
away in 1999. Eugene and Larry lived life as a married couple. In 1994,
when it became legal, they registered in New York City as domestic partners,
receiving a certificate that was as close to a marriage license as they would
ever have.

On October 30, 2001, Eugene Clark and Larry Courtney would have celebrated 14 years as committed lifetime partners. On the morning of September
11, 2001, they got up early, had coffee together, and dressed for work. Eugene
kissed Larry goodbye and said, "I'll see you tonight." He left a little earlier than
usual so that he could vote in New York City's primary election before the polls
got crowded. He then boarded the subway for the ride to his office at Aon Consulting on the 102nd floor of the South Tower of the World Trade Center.

At approximately 8:55 A.M. Larry arrived at his own office in midtown
Manhattan to a voicemail message from Eugene that said, "Don't worry, the
plane hit the other building. I'm OK. We are evacuating." At 9:03 A.M a second
hijacked plane hit the 86th floor of the South Tower. The building collapsed at
10:05 A.M. Eugene did not come home.

After frantic searching of the streets and emergency rooms, and after
posting his photograph along with the many others, Larry reported Eugene as
a missing person at the Armory. He later filed an affidavit for a death certificate at the makeshift Family Center at Pier 94. Among a host of other paperwork Larry received in the mail were documents from Cambridge Integrated
Services Group, Inc., for filing a workers' compensation claim. He sent the
paperwork off and was summoned for a hearing in April 2002. At the hearing,
Cambridge stated that Larry did not qualify for the benefits that Eugene's
company had been paying for during his tenure because the couple did not fit
the "legally married" criteria. The benefits could be paid to Eugene's surviving
parent, his father. But Eugene had not seen or spoken to his father in over 20
years, and he had never spoken to Larry about him.

Larry decided to fight for his spousal rights and teamed up with the
Lambda Legal Defense and Education Fund, which was advocating for many
other surviving partners. They were ultimately successful, and New York State
Senate Bill S7685 became law on August 20, 2002. The bill designated domestic partners as spouses of victims of 9/11, due full spousal benefits from

workers' compensation. The bill is restricted to the 9/11 attacks, however. It does not protect same-sex spouses who lose partners in other tragedies.[3]

Surviving Same-Sex Partners and the Aftermath of 9/11

Of the nearly 3,000 Americans and foreign nationals killed in the 9/11 terrorist [10] attacks in New York, Washington, D.C., and Pennsylvania, many were gay, lesbian, or bisexual individuals in long-term, committed relationships like Larry and Eugene's. Because these were high-profile atrocities of international significance, the tragic losses these gay couples suffered were prominent. In the weeks and months following 9/11, moderate Republicans such as New York Mayor Rudy Giuliani and Governor George Pataki backed equal treatment of same-sex surviving partners. So too did the American Red Cross, the United Way of New York, and the U.S. Congress, which passed the Mychal Judge Police and Fire Chaplains Public Safety Officers' Benefit Act, named for Father Mychal Judge, the New York Fire Department chaplain killed while administering last rites to firefighters killed at the World Trade Center. Signed into law by President Bush on June 24, 2002, the law grants a one-time federal benefit of $250,000 to any designated beneficiary recognized under the deceased's police officer's or firefighter's life insurance plan. Prior to the Judge Act, the federal benefit was given only to spouses, children, and parents of officers who died in the line of duty. The Judge Act was retroactive only to September 11, 2001 (and so partners of police officers and firefighters killed in the line of duty prior to this date, such as Mickie Mashburn, cannot benefit).

Peggy Neff, whose partner of 18 years, Sheila Hein, was killed at the Pentagon on September 11, 2001, received compensation from the September 11 Victims Compensation Fund in January 2003. She was the first same-sex survivor to ever receive such compensation from the federal government.[4] Neff's case was strong in that Hein's will named her as the beneficiary. As of June 2004, the fund had just completed its distribution of funds. It was unclear exactly how approximately 20 other same-sex surviving partners of people killed in 9/11 had been treated by the fund. According to Eric Ferrero of Lambda Legal, other gay partners were given funds. Sometimes they split the money with parents, siblings, and other members of the victim's family of origin.

The compassion shown to same-sex surviving partners after 9/11 was decried and challenged by organizations with an anti-gay agenda:

---

[3]Adapted from a speech given by Larry Courtney at the National Gay and Lesbian Task Force Leadership Awards Deck Party, in Provincetown, Massachusetts, August 25, 2002.

[4]Dahir, M. (2003, March 4). A federal nod to gay partners: Will Peggy Neff's award from the federal Victim Compensation Fund help all same-sex couples win more legal recognition? *The Advocate.*

Robert Knight, director of Concerned Women for America's Culture and Family Institute, accused surviving partners like Larry Courtney and the gay advocates who helped him of "trying to hijack the moral capital of marriage and apply it to their own relationships," which he characterized as "counterfeit marriage." Cybercast News Service — a right wing website that frequently quotes religious right, anti-gay activists — reported that Knight said that "family benefits were originally created to provide for a stay-at-home parent caring for a child, not for homosexual sex partners who usually both work."[5]

After the American Red Cross decided to provide services to gay surviving partners of 9/11 victims, CWA criticized the group's "broad and inclusive definition of family."[6] CWA's Culture and Family Institute also censured the 45 members of Congress who urged Attorney General John Ashcroft to adopt a federal policy similar to that promoted by Governor Pataki in New York state, claiming that lawmakers and "homosexual activists" were exploiting the tragedy "to ask Ashcroft to pave way for 'domestic partner' benefits."[7]

Focus on the Family's James Dobson said, "Pataki diluted the definition of 'family' by giving gay partners the same access to terrorist relief benefits that married couples have."[8] FOF also criticized Pataki's actions as advancing the "gay agenda."[9]   15

The Traditional Values Coalition's Lou Sheldon accused gay activists of "taking advantage" of the national tragedy to promote their agenda. Sheldon urged that relief assistance be "given on the basis and priority of one man and one woman in a marital relationship."[10] Such a policy would have also left out unmarried opposite-sex partners of 9/11 victims. "We don't devalue the loss of these innocent people," Sheldon insisted, "but we think this is not the time to institutionalize such 'partnerships' and put them on the same level as marriage."[11]

Peter Sprigg of the Family Research Council also accused gays of "taking advantage of the grief and compassion that Americans do feel. . . . To redefine the family based on our grief over the losses that people may have experienced as a result of the terror attacks would be bad law and bad policy."[12]

[5]Johnson, J. (2001, October 22). Homosexuals seek survivor benefits intended for families. Cybercast News Service (CNSNews.com.). www.dadi.org/homogred.htm. Accessed February 9, 2004. Knight's use of the term *hijack* was particularly offensive in that he was describing efforts of gay partners to get help dealing with the grief of losing their loved ones in terrorist attacks caused by the hijacking of four jet aircraft.

[6]Concerned Women for America, quoted in People for the American Way Foundation (PFAWF) (2002). *Hostile climate: Report on anti-gay activity*. 8th edition. Washington, DC: Author. p. 33.

[7]The Culture and Family Institute of Concerned Women for America quoted in PFAWF (2002). p. 31.

[8]Dobson, J. (2002, January). Dr. Dobson's newsletter. Colorado Springs, CO: Focus on the Family. www.family.org/docstudy/newsletters/a0019238.html. Accessed February 9, 2004.

[9]Focus on the Family, quoted in PFAWF (2002). p. 31.

[10]Sheldon, quoted in PFAWF (2002). p. 33; Berkowitz, B. (2001, October 21). Religious right on the ropes. AlterNet. www.alternet.org/print.html?StoryID=11840. Accessed February 9, 2004.

[11]Sheldon, quoted in PFAWF (2002). p. 33.

[12]Sprigg, quoted in PFAWF (2002). p. 33.

Perhaps as a result of these objections, the initial interim regulations issued by the Department of Justice in December 2001 and the final regulations issued in March 2002 did not explicitly recognize same-sex partners, but instead left the states to determine who is eligible for victim's compensation under the federal fund.[13] However, most states do not provide any legal recognition to same-sex partners, even those in committed, long-term, or life-long relationships. As of March 2002, when the September 11th Fund issued its final regulations, none of the three states where the attacks occurred— New York, Pennsylvania, and Virginia—afforded any recognition to same-sex partners of state residents.[14] . . .

READING THE TEXT

1. What effect do the stories of the deaths of Lois Marrero and Eugene Clark have on the reader?

2. According to Cahill, why were gay survivors of 9/11 victims ultimately able to receive spousal benefits and survivors of other tragedies unable to do so?

3. Summarize in your own words the attitude that the Concerned Women for America's Culture and Family Institute has toward same-sex marriage.

4. Describe the tone Cahill uses when he discusses same-sex couples and those who oppose recognizing such unions.

READING THE SIGNS

1. In class, brainstorm different patterns of family structure—two parents, single parent, extended family, unmarried adults without children, and so forth— thinking about the families of friends and acquaintances. Use your discussion as a springboard for an essay in which you propose your own definition of family.

2. Write an argument supporting, opposing, or complicating the proposition that the gay partners of police officers slain in the line of duty be granted survivor's benefits.

3. Write a letter to Lou Sheldon in which you support, refute, or modify his belief that survivor's benefits should be "given on the basis and priority of one man and one woman in a marital relationship" (para. 16).

4. Write an essay in which you respond to the proposition that the survivor's benefits allowed in the 9/11 attacks be extended to same-sex survivors of other tragedies.

5. Research the current status of attempts to legalize same-sex marriages, and use your findings as the basis of an argument supporting or opposing such unions.

[13]PFAWF (2002). pp. 31–32.

[14]Human Rights Campaign (2001). *The state of the workplace for lesbian, gay, bisexual and transgender Americans 2001*. Washington, DC: Author; Human Rights Campaign (2002). *Domestic partner benefits*. Washington, DC: Author. www.hrc.org/worknet/dp/index.asp. Accessed November 2, 2002.

ANDY MEDHURST
Batman, Deviance, and Camp

Have you ever wondered what happened to Robin in the recent Batman movies? In this analysis of the history of Batman, excerpted from The Many Lives of the Batman *(1991), Andy Medhurst explains why Robin had to disappear. Arguing that Batman has been "re-heterosexualized" in the wake of the insinuatingly homoerotic TV series of the 1960s, Medhurst indicts the homophobia of Batfans whose "Bat-Platonic Ideal of how Batman should really be" holds no place for the "camped crusader." Medhurst teaches media studies, popular culture, and lesbian and gay studies at the University of Sussex, England. He is the author of* A National Joke: Popular Comedy and English Cultural Identities *(2004, 2007). He has also coedited, with Sally Munt,* Lesbian and Gay Studies: A Critical Introduction *(1997), and, with Joanne Lacey,* The Representation Reader *(2004).*

Only someone ignorant of the fundamentals of psychiatry and of the psychopathology of sex can fail to realize a subtle atmosphere of homoeroticism which pervades the adventure of the mature "Batman" and his young friend "Robin."

— FREDRIC WERTHAM[1]

It's embarrassing to be solemn and treatise-like about Camp. One runs the risk of having, oneself, produced a very inferior piece of Camp.

— SUSAN SONTAG[2]

I'm not sure how qualified I am to write this essay. Batman hasn't been particularly important in my life since I was seven years old. Back then he was crucial, paramount, unmissable as I sat twice weekly to watch the latest episode on TV. Pure pleasure, except for the annoying fact that my parents didn't seem to appreciate the thrills on offer. Worse than that, they actually laughed. How could anyone laugh when the Dynamic Duo were about to be turned into Frostie Freezies (pineapple for the Caped Crusader, lime for his chum) by the evil Mr. Freeze?

Batman and I drifted apart after those early days. Every now and then I'd see a repeated episode and I soon began to understand and share that once infuriating parental hilarity, but this aside I hardly thought about the man in the cape at all. I knew about the subculture of comic freaks, and the new and

---

[1]Fredric Wertham, *Seduction of the Innocent* (London: Museum Press, 1955), p. 190.

[2]Susan Sontag, "Notes on Camp," in *A Susan Sontag Reader* (Harmondsworth: Penguin Books), p. 106.

alarmingly pretentious phrase "graphic novel" made itself known to me, but I still regarded (with the confidence of distant ignorance) such texts as violent, macho, adolescent and, well, silly.

That's when the warning bells rang. The word "silly" reeks of the complacent condescension that has at various times been bestowed on all the cultural forms that matter most to me (Hollywood musicals, British melodramas, pop music, soap operas), so what right had I to apply it to someone else's part of the popular cultural playground? I had to rethink my disdain, and 1989 has been a very good year in which to do so, because in terms of popular culture 1989 has been the Year of the Bat.

This essay, then, is not written by a devotee of Batman, someone steeped in every last twist of the mythology. I come to these texts as an interested outsider, armed with a particular perspective. That perspective is homosexuality, and what I want to try and do here is to offer a gay reading of the whole Bat-business. It has no pretension to definitiveness, I don't presume to speak for all gay people everywhere. I'm male, white, British, thirty years old (at the time of writing) and all of those factors need to be taken into account. Nonetheless, I'd argue that Batman is especially interesting to gay audiences for three reasons.

Firstly, he was one of the first fictional characters to be attacked on the grounds of presumed homosexuality, by Fredric Wertham in his book *Seduction of the Innocent*. Secondly, the 1960s TV series was and remains a touchstone of camp (a banal attempt to define the meaning of camp might well start with "like the sixties' *Batman* series"). Thirdly, as a recurring hero figure for the last fifty years, Batman merits analysis as a notably successful construction of masculinity. 5

Nightmare on Psychiatry Street: Freddy's Obsession

Seduction of the Innocent is an extraordinary book. It is a gripping, flamboyant melodrama masquerading as social psychology. Fredric Wertham is, like Senator McCarthy,[3] like Batman, a crusader, a man with a mission, an evangelist. He wants to save the youth of America from its own worst impulses, from its id, from comic books. His attack on comic books is founded on an astonishingly crude stimulus-and-response model of reading, in which the child (the child, for Wertham, seems an unusually innocent, blank slate waiting to be written on) reads, absorbs, and feels compelled to copy, if only in fantasy terms, the content of the comics. It is a model, in other words, which takes for granted extreme audience passivity.

This is not the place to go into a detailed refutation of Wertham's work, besides which such a refutation has already been done in Martin Barker's

[3]**Senator McCarthy** United States Senator Joseph R. McCarthy (1908–1957), who in the 1950s hunted and persecuted suspected Communists and Communist sympathizers.–EDS.

excellent *A Haunt of Fears*.[4] The central point of audience passivity needs stressing, however, because it is crucial to the celebrated passage where Wertham points his shrill, witch-hunting finger at the Dynamic Duo and cries "queer."

Such language is not present on the page, of course, but in some ways *Seduction of the Innocent* (a film title crying out for either D. W. Griffith or Cecil B. DeMille) would be easier to stomach if it were. Instead, Wertham writes with anguished concern about the potential harm that Batman might do to vulnerable children, innocents who might be turned into deviants. He employs what was then conventional psychiatric wisdom about the idea of homosexuality as a "phase":

> Many pre-adolescent boys pass through a phase of disdain for girls. Some comic books tend to fix that attitude and instill the idea that girls are only good for being banged around or used as decoys. A homoerotic attitude is also suggested by the presentation of masculine, bad, witch-like or violent women. In such comics women are depicted in a definitely anti-erotic light, while the young male heroes have pronounced erotic overtones. The muscular male supertype, whose primary sex characteristics are usually well emphasized, is in the setting of certain stories the object of homoerotic sexual curiosity and stimulation.[5]

The implications of this are breathtaking. Homosexuality, for Wertham, is synonymous with misogyny. Men love other men because they hate women. The sight of women being "banged around" is liable to appeal to repressed homoerotic desires (this, I think, would be news to the thousands of women who are systematically physically abused by heterosexual men). Women who do not conform to existing stereotypes of femininity are another incitement to homosexuality.

Having mapped out his terms of reference, Wertham goes on to peel the lid from Wayne Manor: 10

> Sometimes Batman ends up in bed injured and young Robin is shown sitting next to him. At home they lead an idyllic life. They are Bruce Wayne and "Dick" Grayson. Bruce Wayne is described as a "socialite" and the official relationship is that Dick is Bruce's ward. They live in sumptuous quarters, with beautiful flowers in large vases, and have a butler, Alfred. Batman is sometimes shown in a dressing gown. . . . It is like a wish dream of two homosexuals living together. Sometimes they are shown on a couch, Bruce reclining and Dick sitting next to him, jacket off, collar open, and his hand on his friend's arm.[6]

So, Wertham's assumptions of homosexuality are fabricated out of his interpretation of certain visual signs. To avoid being thought queer by Wertham,

---

[4]Martin Barker, *A Haunt of Fears* (London: Pluto Press, 1984).
[5]Wertham, p. 188.
[6]Wertham, p. 190.

Bruce and Dick should have done the following: Never show concern if the other is hurt, live in a shack, only have ugly flowers in small vases, call the butler "Chip" or "Joe" if you have to have one at all, never share a couch, keep your collar buttoned up, keep your jacket on, and never, ever wear a dressing gown. After all, didn't Noel Coward[7] wear a dressing gown?

Wertham is easy to mock, but the identification of homosexuals through dress codes has a long history.[8] Moreover, such codes originate as semiotic systems adopted by gay people themselves, as a way of signalling the otherwise invisible fact of sexual preference. There is a difference, though, between sporting the secret symbols of a subculture if you form part of that subculture and the elephantine spot-the-homo routine that Wertham performs.

Bat-fans have always responded angrily to Wertham's accusation. One calls it "one of the most incredible charges . . . unfounded rumours . . . sly sneers"[9] and the general response has been to reassert the masculinity of the two heroes, mixed with a little indignation: "If they had been actual men they could have won a libel suit."[10] This seems to me not only to miss the point, but also to *reinforce* Wertham's homophobia — it is only possible to win a libel suit over an "accusation" of homosexuality in a culture where homosexuality is deemed categorically inferior to heterosexuality.

Thus the rush to "protect" Batman and Robin from Wertham is simply the other side to the coin of his bigotry. It may reject Wertham, cast him in the role of dirty-minded old man, but its view of homosexuality is identical. Mark Cotta Vaz thus describes the imputed homosexual relationship as "licentious" while claiming that in fact Bruce Wayne "regularly squired the most beautiful women in Gotham City and presumably had a healthy sex life."[11] Licentious versus healthy — Dr. Wertham himself could not have bettered this homophobic opposition.

Despite the passions aroused on both sides (or rather the two facets of the same side), there is something comic at the heart of this dispute. It is, simply, that Bruce and Dick are *not* real people but fictional constructions, and hence to squabble over their "real" sex life is to take things a little too far. What is at stake here is the question of reading, of what readers do with the raw material that they are given. Readers are at liberty to construct whatever fantasy lives they like with the characters of the fiction they read (within the

15

---

[7]**Noel Coward** (1899–1973) British playwright, actor, and composer known for witty, sophisticated comedies.–EDS.

[8]See, for example, the newspaper stories on "how to spot" homosexuals printed in Britain in the fifties and sixties, and discussed in Jeffrey Weeks, *Coming Out: Homosexual Politics in Britain* (London: Quartet, 1979).

[9]Phrases taken from Chapters 5 and 6 of Mark Cotta Vaz, *Tales of the Dark Knight: Batman's First Fifty Years* (London: Futura, 1989).

[10]Les Daniels, *Comix: A History of Comic Books in America* (New York: Bonanza Books, 1971), p. 87.

[11]Cotta Vaz, pp. 47 and 53.

limits of generic and narrative credibility, that is). This returns us to the unfortunate patients of Dr. Wertham:

> One young homosexual during psychotherapy brought us a copy of *Detective* comic, with a Batman story. He pointed out a picture of "The Home of Bruce and Dick," a house beautifully landscaped, warmly lighted and showing the devoted pair side by side, looking out a picture window. When he was eight this boy had realized from fantasies about comic book pictures that he was aroused by men. At the age of ten or eleven, "I found my liking, my sexual desires, in comic books. I think I put myself in the position of Robin. I did want to have relations with Batman . . . I remember the first time I came across the page mentioning the 'secret batcave.' The thought of Batman and Robin living together and possibly having sex relations came to my mind. . . ."[12]

Wertham quotes this to shock us, to impel us to tear the pages of *Detective* away before little Tommy grows up and moves to Greenwich Village, but reading it as a gay man today I find it rather moving and also highly recognizable.

What this anonymous gay man did was to practice that form of bricolage[13] which Richard Dyer has identified as a characteristic reading strategy of gay audiences.[14] Denied even the remotest possibility of supportive images of homosexuality within the dominant heterosexual culture, gay people have had to fashion what we could out of the imageries of dominance, to snatch illicit meanings from the fabric of normality, to undertake a corrupt decoding for the purposes of satisfying marginalized desires.[15] This may not be as necessary as it once was, given the greater visibility of gay representations, but it is still an important practice. Wertham's patient evokes in me an admiration, that in a period of American history even more homophobic than most, there he was, raiding the citadels of masculinity, weaving fantasies of oppositional desire. What effect the dread Wertham had on him is hard to predict, but I profoundly hope that he wasn't "cured."

It wasn't only Batman who was subjected to Dr. Doom's bizarre ideas about human sexuality. Hence:

> The homosexual connotation of the Wonder Woman type of story is psychologically unmistakable. . . . For boys, Wonder Woman is a frightening image. For girls she is a morbid ideal. Where Batman is anti-feminine, the attractive Wonder Woman and her counterparts are definitely anti-masculine. Wonder Woman has her own female following. . . . Her

---

[12]Wertham, p. 192.

[13]**bricolage** A new object created by reassembling bits and pieces of other objects; here, gay-identified readings produced from classic texts.–Eds.

[14]Richard Dyer, ed., *Gays and Film*, 2nd edition (New York: Zoetrope, 1984), p. 1.

[15]See Richard Dyer, "Judy Garland and Gay Men," in Dyer, *Heavenly Bodies* (London: BFI, 1987), and Claire Whitaker, "Hollywood Transformed: Interviews with Lesbian Viewers," in Peter Steven, ed., *Jump Cut: Hollywood, Politics and Counter-Cinema* (Toronto: Between the Lines, 1985).

followers are the "Holiday girls," i.e. the holiday girls, the gay party girls, the gay girls.[16]

Just how much elision can be covered with one "i.e."? Wertham's view of homosexuality is not, at least, inconsistent. Strong, admirable women will turn little girls into dykes — such a heroine can only be seen as a "morbid ideal."

Crazed as Wertham's ideas were, their effectiveness is not in doubt. The mid-fifties saw a moral panic about the assumed dangers of comic books. In the United States companies were driven out of business, careers wrecked, and the Comics Code introduced. This had distinct shades of the Hays Code[17] that had been brought in to clamp down on Hollywood in the 1930s, and under its jurisdiction comics opted for the bland, the safe, and the reactionary. In Britain there was government legislation to prohibit the importing of American comics, as the comics panic slotted neatly into a whole series of anxieties about the effects on British youth of American popular culture.[18]

And in all of this, what happened to Batman? He turned into Fred MacMurray from *My Three Sons*. He lost any remaining edge of the shadowy vigilante of his earliest years, and became an upholder of the most stifling small-town American values. Batwoman and Batgirl appeared (June Allyson and Bat-Gidget) to take away any lingering doubts about the Dynamic Duo's sex lives. A 1963 story called "The Great Clayface-Joker Feud" has some especially choice examples of the new, squeaky-clean sexuality of the assembled Bats. [20]

Batgirl says to Robin, "I can hardly wait to get into my Batgirl costume again! Won't it be terrific if we could go on a crime case together like the last time? (sigh)." Robin replies, "It sure would, Betty (sigh)." The elder Bats look on approvingly. Batgirl is Batwoman's niece — to make her a daughter would have implied that Batwoman had had (gulp) sexual intercourse, and that would never do. This is the era of Troy Donohue and Pat Boone,[19] and Batman as ever serves as a cultural thermometer, taking the temperature of the times.

The Clayface/Joker business is wrapped up (the villains of this period are wacky conjurors, nothing more, with no menace or violence about them) and the episode concludes with another tableau of terrifying heterosexual contentment. "Oh Robin," simpers Batgirl, "I'm afraid you'll just have to hold me! I'm still so shaky after fighting Clayface . . . and you're so strong!" Robin: "Gosh Batgirl, it was swell of you to calm me down when I was worried about Batman tackling Clayface alone." (One feels a distinct Wertham influence here: If Robin shows concern about Batman, wheel on a supportive female, the very

---

[16]Wertham, pp. 192–93.

[17]**Hays Code** The 1930 Motion Picture Production Code, which described in detail what was morally acceptable in films.–Eds.

[18]See Barker.

[19]**Troy Donohue and Pat Boone** Clean-cut, all-American-boy stars from the 1950s and 1960s.–Eds.

opposite of a "morbid ideal," to minister in a suitably self-effacing way.) Bat-woman here seizes her chance and tackles Batman: "You look worried about Clayface, Batman . . . so why don't you follow Robin's example and let me soothe you?" Batman can only reply "Gulp."

Gulp indeed. While it's easy simply to laugh at strips like these, knowing as we do the way in which such straight-faced material would be mercilessly shredded by the sixties' TV series, they do reveal the retreat into coziness forced on comics by the Wertham onslaught and its repercussions. There no doubt were still subversive readers of *Batman*, erasing Batgirl on her every preposter-ous appearance and reworking the Duo's capers to leave some room for homo-erotic speculation, but such a reading would have had to work so much harder than before. The *Batman* of this era was such a closed text, so immune to poly-semic interpretation, that its interest today is only as a symptom — or, more productively, as camp. "The Great Clayface-Joker Feud" may have been pub-lished in 1963, but in every other respect it is a fifties' text. If the 1960s began for the world in general with the Beatles, the 1960s for Batman began with the TV series in 1966. If the Caped Crusader had been all but Werthamed out of existence, he was about to be camped back into life.

The Camped Crusader and the Boys Wondered

Trying to define "camp" is like attempting to sit in the corner of a circular room. It can't be done, which only adds to the quixotic appeal of the attempt. Try these:

> To be camp is to present oneself as being committed to the marginal with a commitment greater than the marginal merits.[20]
>
> Camp sees everything in quotation marks. It's not a lamp but a "lamp"; not a woman but a "woman." . . . It is the farthest extension, in sensibility, of the metaphor of life as theatre.[21]
>
> Camp is . . . a way of poking fun at the whole cosmology of restric-tive sex roles and sexual identifications which our society uses to oppress its women and repress its men.[22]
>
> Camp was and is a way for gay men to re-imagine the world around them . . . by exaggerating, stylizing and remaking what is usually thought to be average or normal.[23]
>
> Camp was a prison for an illegal minority; now it is a holiday for con-senting adults.[24]

---

[20]Mark Booth, *Camp* (London: Quartet, 1983), p. 18.
[21]Sontag, p. 109.
[22]Jack Babuscio, "Camp and the Gay Sensibility," in Dyer, ed., *Gays and Film*, p. 46.
[23]Michael Bronski, *Culture Clash: The Making of Gay Sensibility* (Boston: South End Press), p. 42.
[24]Philip Core, *Camp: The Lie That Tells the Truth* (London: Plexus), p. 7.

All true, in their way, but all inadequate. The problem with camp is that it 25 is primarily an experiential rather than an analytical discourse. Camp is a set of attitudes, a gallery of snapshots, an inventory of postures, a modus vivendi, a shop-full of frocks, an arch of eyebrows, a great big pink butterfly that just won't be pinned down. Camp is primarily an adjective, occasionally a verb, but never anything as prosaic, as earthbound, as a noun.

Yet if I propose to use this adjective as a way of describing one or more of the guises of Batman, I need to arrive at some sort of working definition. So, for the purposes of this analysis, I intend the term "camp" to refer to a playful, knowing, self-reflexive theatricality. *Batman*, the sixties' TV series, was nothing if not knowing. It employed the codes of camp in an unusually public and heavily signaled way. This makes it different from those people or texts who are taken up by camp audiences without ever consciously putting camp into practice. The difference may be very briefly spelled out by reference to Hollywood films. If *Mildred Pierce*[25] and *The Letter*[26] were taken up *as* camp, teased by primarily gay male audiences into yielding meaning not intended by their makers, then *Whatever Happened to Baby Jane?*[27] is a piece of self-conscious camp, capitalizing on certain attitudinal and stylistic tendencies known to exist in audiences. *Baby Jane* is also, significantly, a 1960s' film, and the 1960s were the decade in which camp swished out of the ghetto and up into the scarcely prepared mainstream.

A number of key events and texts reinforced this. Susan Sontag wrote her *Notes on Camp*, which remains the starting point for researchers even now. Pop Art[28] was in vogue (and in *Vogue*) and whatever the more elevated claims of Lichtenstein,[29] Warhol,[30] and the rest, their artworks were on one level a new inflection of camp. The growing intellectual respectability of pop music displayed very clearly that the old barriers that once rigidly separated high and low culture were no longer in force. The James Bond films, and even more so their successors like *Modesty Blaise*, popularized a dry, self-mocking wit that makes up one part of the multifaceted diamond of camp. And on television there were *The Avengers*, *The Man from UNCLE*, *Thunderbirds*, and *Batman*.

---

[25]***Mildred Pierce*** 1945 murder mystery film that traces the fortunes of a homemaker who breaks with her husband.–Eds.

[26]***The Letter*** 1940 murder movie whose ending was changed to satisfy moral standards of the time.–Eds.

[27]***Whatever Happened to Baby Jane?*** Macabre 1962 film about a former child movie star living in an old Hollywood mansion.–Eds.

[28]**Pop Art** Art movement, begun in the 1950s, that borrowed images and symbols from popular culture, particularly from commercial products and mass media, as a critique of traditional fine art.–Eds.

[29]**Lichtenstein** Roy Lichtenstein (1923–1997), American artist at the center of the Pop Art movement, best known for melodramatic comic book scenes.–Eds.

[30]**Warhol** Andy Warhol (1930?–1987), pioneering Pop artist known for reproducing stereotyped images of famous people, such as Marilyn Monroe, and of commercial products, such as Campbell's Soup cans.–Eds.

To quote the inevitable Sontag, "The whole point of Camp is to dethrone the serious. . . . More precisely, Camp involves a new, more complex relation to 'the serious.' One can be serious about the frivolous, frivolous about the serious."[31]

The problem with Batman in those terms is that there was never anything truly serious to begin with (unless one swallows that whole portentous Dark Knight charade, more of which in the next section). Batman in its comic book form had, unwittingly, always been camp — it was serious (the tone, the moral homilies) about the frivolous (a man in a stupid suit). He was camp in the way that classic Hollywood was camp, but what the sixties' TV series and film did was to overlay this "innocent" camp with a thick layer of ironic distance, the self-mockery version of camp. And given the long associations of camp with the homosexual male subculture, Batman was a particular gift on the grounds of his relationship with Robin. As George Melly put it, "The real Batman series were beautiful because of their unselfconscious absurdity. The remakes, too, at first worked on a double level. Over the absorbed children's heads we winked and nudged, but in the end what were we laughing at? The fact they didn't know that Batman had it off with Robin."[32]

It was as if Wertham's fears were being vindicated at last, but his 1950s' bigot's anguish had been supplanted by a self-consciously hip 1960s' playfulness. What adult audiences laughed at in the sixties' *Batman* was a camped-up version of the fifties they had just left behind.

Batman's lessons in good citizenship ("We'd like to feel that our efforts may help every youngster to grow up into an honest, useful citizen"[33]) were another part of the character ripe for ridiculing deconstruction — "Let's go, Robin, we've set another youth on the road to a brighter tomorrow" (the episode "It's How You Play the Game"). Everything the Adam West Batman said was a parody of seriousness, and how could it be otherwise? How could anyone take genuinely seriously the words of a man dressed like that?

The Batman/Robin relationship is never referred to directly; more fun can be had by presenting it "straight," in other words, screamingly camp. Wertham's reading of the Dubious Duo had been so extensively aired as to pass into the general consciousness (in George Melly's words, "We all knew Robin and Batman were pouves"[34]), it was part of the fabric of *Batman*, and the makers of the TV series proceeded accordingly.

Consider the Duo's encounter with Marsha, Queen of Diamonds. The threat she embodies is nothing less than heterosexuality itself, the deadliest threat to the domestic bliss of the Bat-couple. She is even about to marry Batman before Alfred intervenes to save the day. He and Batman flee the church,

[31]Sontag, p. 116.

[32]George Melly, *Revolt into Style: The Pop Arts in the 50s and 60s* (Oxford: Oxford University Press, 1989 [first published 1970]), p. 193.

[33]"The Batman Says," *Batman #3* (1940), quoted in Cotta Vaz, p. 15.

[34]Melly, p. 192.

but have to do so in the already decorated Batmobile, festooned with wedding paraphernalia including a large "Just Married" sign. "We'll have to drive it as it is," says Batman, while somewhere in the audience a Dr. Wertham takes feverish notes. Robin, Commissioner Gordon, and Chief O'Hara have all been drugged with Marsha's "Cupid Dart," but it is of course the Boy Wonder who Batman saves first. The dart, he tells Robin, "contains some secret ingredient by which your sense and your will were affected," and it isn't hard to read that ingredient as heterosexual desire, since its result, seen in the previous episode, was to turn Robin into Marsha's slobbering slave.

We can tell with relief now, though, as Robin is "back in fighting form" (with impeccable timing, Batman clasps Robin's shoulder on the word "fighting"). Marsha has one last attempt to destroy the duo, but naturally she fails. The female temptress, the seductress, the enchantress must be vanquished. None of this is in the least subtle (Marsha's cat, for example, is called Circe) but this type of mass-market camp can't afford the luxury of subtlety. The threat of heterosexuality is similarly mobilized in the 1966 feature film, where it is Bruce Wayne's infatuation with Kitka (Catwoman in disguise) that causes all manner of problems.

A more interesting employment of camp comes in the episodes where the Duo battle the Black Widow, played by Tallulah Bankhead. The major camp coup here, of course, is the casting. Bankhead was one of the supreme icons of camp, one of its goddesses: "Too intelligent not to be self-conscious, too ambitious to bother about her self-consciousness, too insecure ever to be content, but too arrogant ever to admit insecurity, Tallulah personified camp."[35]

A heady claim, but perhaps justified, because the Black Widow episodes are, against stiff competition, the campiest slices of Batman of them all. The stories about Bankhead are legendary—the time when on finding no toilet paper in her cubicle she slipped a ten dollar bill under the partition and asked the woman next door for two fives, or her whispered remark to a priest conducting a particularly elaborate service and swinging a censor of smoking incense, "Darling, I love the drag, but your purse is on fire"—and casting her in *Batman* was the final demonstration of the series' commitment to camp.

The plot is unremarkable, the usual Bat-shenanigans; the pleasure lies in the detail. Details like the elderly Bankhead crammed into her Super-Villainess costume, or like the way in which (through a plot detail I won't go into) she impersonates Robin, so we see Burt Ward miming to Bankhead's voice, giving the unforgettable image of Robin flirting with burly traffic cops. Best of all, and Bankhead isn't even in this scene but the thrill of having her involved clearly spurred the writer to new heights of camp, Batman has to sing a song to break free of the Black Widow's spell. Does he choose to sing "God Bless America"? Nothing so rugged. He clutches a flower to his Bat chest and sings Gilbert and Sullivan's "I'm Just a Little Buttercup." It is this single

---

[35]Core, p. 25.

image, more than any other, that prevents me from taking the post–Adam West Dark Knight at all seriously.

The fundamental camp trick which the series pulls is to make the comics speak. What was acceptable on the page, in speech balloons, stands revealed as ridiculous once given audible voice. The famous visualized sound effects (URKKK! KA-SPLOOSH!) that are for many the fondest memory of the series work along similar lines. Camp often makes its point by transposing the codes of one cultural form into the inappropriate codes of another. It thrives on mischievous incongruity.

The incongruities, the absurdities, the sheer ludicrousness of Batman were brought out so well by the sixties' version that for some audiences there will never be another credible approach. I have to include myself here. I've recently read widely in postsixties Bat-lore, and I can appreciate what the writers and artists are trying to do, but my Batman will always be Adam West. It's impossible to be somber or pompous about Batman because if you try the ghost of West will come Bat-climbing into your mind, fortune cookie wisdom on his lips and keen young Dick by his side. It's significant, I think, that the letters I received . . . began "Dear Bat-Contributor."[36] Writers preparing chapters about James Joyce or Ingmar Bergman do not, I suspect, receive analogous greetings. To deny the large camp component of Batman is to blind oneself to one of the richest parts of his history.

Is There Bat-Life after Bat-Camp?

The international success of the Adam West incarnation left Batman high and dry. The camping around had been fun while it lasted, but it hadn't lasted very long. Most camp humor has a relatively short life span, new targets are always needed, and the camp aspect of Batman had been squeezed dry. The mass public had moved on to other heroes, other genres, other acres of merchandising, but there was still a hard Bat-core of fans to satisfy. Where could the Bat go next? Clearly there was no possibility of returning to the caped Eisenhower, the benevolent patriarch of the 1950s. That option had been well and truly closed down by the TV show. Batman needed to be given his dignity back, and this entailed a return to his roots.

This, in any case, is the official version. For the unreconstructed devotee of the Batman (that is, people who insist on giving him the definite article before the name), the West years had been hell — a tricksy travesty, an effeminizing of the cowled avenger. There's a scene in *Midnight Cowboy* where Dustin Hoffman tells Jon Voight that the only audience liable to be receptive to his cowboy clothes are gay men looking for rough trade. Voight is appalled — "You

40

---

[36]This essay originally appeared in an anthology, *The Many Lives of the Batman: Critical Approaches to a Superhero and His Media.*–Eds.

mean to tell me John Wayne was a fag?" (quoted, roughly, from memory). This outrage, this horror at shattered illusions, comes close to encapsulating the loathing and dread the campy Batman has received from the old guard of Gotham City and the younger born-again Bat-fans.

So what has happened since the 1960s has been the painstaking rehetero-sexualization of Batman. I apologize for coining such a clumsy word, but no other quite gets the sense that I mean. This strategy has worked, too, for large audiences, reaching its peak with the 1989 film. To watch this and then come home to see a video of the 1966 movie is to grasp how complete the transfor-mation has been. What I want to do in this section is to trace some of the cru-cial moments in that change, written from the standpoint of someone still unashamedly committed to Bat-camp.

If one wants to take Batman as a Real Man, the biggest stumbling block has always been Robin. There have been disingenuous claims that "Batman and Robin had a blood-brother closeness. Theirs was a spiritual intimacy forged from the stress of countless battles fought side by side"[37] (one can imagine what Tallulah Bankhead might say to *that*), but we know otherwise. The Wertham lobby and the acolytes of camp alike have ensured that any Batman/Robin relationship is guaranteed to bring on the sniggers. Besides which, in the late 1960s, Robin was getting to be a big boy, too big for any shreds of credibility to attach themselves to all that father-son smokescreen. So in 1969 Dick Gray-son was packed off to college and the Bat was solitary once more.

This was a shrewd move. It's impossible to conceive of the recent, obses-sive, sturm-und-drang Batman with a chirpy little Robin getting in the way.[38] A text of the disturbing power of *The Killing Joke*[39] could not have functioned with Robin to rupture the grim dualism of its Batman/Joker struggle. There was, however, a post–Dick Robin, but he was killed off by fans in that infa-mous telephone poll.[40]

It's intriguing to speculate how much latent (or blatant) homophobia lay behind that vote. Did the fans decide to kill off Jason Todd so as to redeem Batman for unproblematic heterosexuality? Impossible to say. There are other factors to take into account, such as Jason's apparent failure to live up to the expectations of what a Robin should be like. The sequence of issues in which Jason/Robin died, *A Death in the Family*, is worth looking at in some detail,

---

[37]Cotta Vaz, p. 53.

[38]A female Robin is introduced in the *Dark Knight Returns* series, which, while raising interesting questions about the sexuality of Batman, which I don't here have the space to address, seems significant in that the Dark Knight cannot run the risk of reader speculation that a traditionally male Robin might provoke.

[39]***The Killing Joke*** Graphic novel by Alan Moore, Brian Bolland, and John Higgins (New York: DC Comics 1988).–EDS.

[40]**telephone poll** In a 1988 issue of the *Batman* comic, a "post–Dick Robin," Jason Todd, was badly injured in an explosion, and readers were allowed to phone the publisher to vote on whether he should be allowed to survive.–EDS.

however, in order to see whether the camp connotations of Bruce and Dick had been fully purged.

The depressing answer is that they had. This is very much the Batman of the 1980s, his endless feud with the Joker this time uneasily stretched over a framework involving the Middle East and Ethiopia. Little to be camp about there, though the presence of the Joker guarantees a quota of sick jokes. The sickest of all is the introduction of the Ayatollah Khomeini, a real and important political figure, into this fantasy world of THUNK! and THER-ACKK! and grown men dressed as bats. (As someone who lived in the part of England from which Reagan's planes took off on their murderous mission to bomb Libya, I fail to see the humor in this cartoon version of American foreign policy: It's too near the real thing.)

Jason dies at the Joker's hands because he becomes involved in a search for his own origins, a clear parallel to Batman's endless returns to *his* Oedipal scenario. Families, in the Bat-mythology, are dark and troubled things, one more reason why the introduction of the fifties versions of Batwoman and Batgirl seemed so inappropriate. This applies only to real, biological families, though; the true familial bond is between Batman and Robin, hence the title of these issues. Whether one chooses to read Robin as Batman's ward (official version), son (approved fantasy), or lover (forbidden fantasy), the sense of loss at his death is bound to be devastating. Batman finds Robin's body and, in the time-honored tradition of Hollywood cinema, is at least able to give him a loving embrace. Good guys hug their dead buddies, only queers smooch when still alive.

If the word "camp" is applied at all to the eighties' Batman, it is a label for the Joker. This sly displacement is the cleverest method yet devised of preserving Bat-heterosexuality. The play that the texts regularly make with the concept of Batman and the Joker as mirror images now takes a new twist. The Joker is Batman's "bad twin," and part of that badness is, increasingly, an implied homosexuality. This is certainly present in the 1989 film, a generally glum and portentous affair except for Jack Nicholson's Joker, a characterization enacted with venomous camp. The only moment when this dour film comes to life is when the Joker and his gang raid the Art Gallery, spraying the paintings and generally camping up a storm.

The film strives and strains to make us forget the Adam West Batman, to the point of giving us Vicki Vale as Bruce Wayne's lover, and certainly Michael Keaton's existential agonizing (variations on the theme of why-did-I-have-to-be-a-Bat) is a world away from West's gleeful subversion of truth, justice, and the American Way. This is the same species of Batman celebrated by Frank Miller: "If your only memory of Batman is that of Adam West and Burt Ward exchanging camped-out quips while clobbering slumming guest-stars Vincent Price and Cesar Romero, I hope this book will come as a surprise. . . . For me, Batman was never funny. . . ."[41]

---

[41]Frank Miller, "Introduction," *Batman: Year One* (London: Titan, 1988).

The most recent linkage of the Joker with homosexuality comes in [50] *Arkham Asylum*, the darkest image of the Bat-world yet. Here the Joker has become a parody of a screaming queen, calling Batman "honey pie," given to exclamations like "oooh!" (one of the oldest homophobic clichés in the book), and pinching Batman's behind with the advice, "Loosen up, tight ass." He also, having no doubt read his Wertham, follows the pinching by asking, "What's the matter? Have I touched a nerve? How is the Boy Wonder? Started shaving yet?" The Bat-response is unequivocal: "Take your filthy hands off me. . . . Filthy degenerate!"

Arkham Asylum is a highly complex reworking of certain key aspects of the mythology, of which the sexual tension between Batman and the Joker is only one small part. Nonetheless the Joker's question "Have I touched a nerve?" seems a crucial one, as revealed by the homophobic ferocity of Batman's reply. After all, the dominant cultural construction of gay men at the end of the 1980s is as plague carriers, and the word "degenerate" is not far removed from some of the labels affixed to us in the age of AIDS.

Batman: Is He or Isn't He?

The one constant factor through all of the transformations of Batman has been the devotion of his admirers. They will defend him against what they see as negative interpretations, and they carry around in their heads a kind of essence of batness, a Bat-Platonic Ideal of how Batman should really be. The Titan Books reissue of key comics from the 1970s each carry a preface by a noted fan, and most of them contain claims such as "This, I feel, is Batman as he was meant to be."[42]

Where a negative construction is specifically targeted, no prizes for guessing which one it is: "you . . . are probably also fond of the TV show he appeared in. But then maybe you prefer Elvis Presley's Vegas years or the later Jerry Lewis movies over their early stuff . . . for me, the definitive Batman was then and always will be the one portrayed in these pages."[43]

The sixties' TV show remains anathema to the serious Bat-fan precisely because it heaps ridicule on the very notion of a serious Batman. *Batman* the series revealed the man in the cape as a pompous fool, an embodiment of superseded ethics, and a closet queen. As Marsha, Queen of Diamonds, put it, "Oh Batman, darling, you're so divinely square." Perhaps the enormous success of the 1989 film will help to advance the cause of the rival Bat-archetype, the grim, vengeful Dark Knight whose heterosexuality is rarely called into question (his humorlessness, fondness for violence, and obsessive monomania seem to me exemplary qualities for a heterosexual man). The answer, surely, is that they needn't be mutually exclusive.

[42]Kim Newman, "Introduction," *Batman: The Demon Awakes* (London: Titan, 1989).
[43]Jonathan Ross, "Introduction," *Batman: Vow from the Grave* (London: Titan, 1989).

If I might be permitted a rather camp comparison, each generation has 55
its definitive Hamlet, so why not the same for Batman? I'm prepared to admit
the validity, for some people, of the swooping eighties' vigilante, so why are
they so concerned to trash my sixties' camped crusader? Why do they insist
so vehemently that Adam West was a faggy aberration, a blot on the otherwise impeccably butch Bat-landscape? What *are* they trying to hide?

If I had a suspicious frame of mind, I might think that they were protesting too much, that maybe Dr. Wertham was on to something when he targeted these narratives as incitements to homosexual fantasy. And if I want
Batman to be gay, then, for me, he is. After all, outside of the minds of his
writers and readers, he doesn't really exist.

READING THE TEXT

1. Summarize the objections Fredric Wertham makes to Batman in *Seduction of the Innocent*.

2. In a paragraph, write your own explanation of what Medhurst means by "camp."

3. What evidence does Medhurst supply to demonstrate that Batman is a gay character?

4. Explain what Medhurst means by his closing comment: "And if I want Bat-man to be gay, then, for me, he is. After all, outside of the minds of his writ-ers and readers, he doesn't really exist" (para. 56).

READING THE SIGNS

1. Do you agree with Medhurst's argument that the Batman and Robin duo are really a covert homosexual couple? Write an essay supporting or challenging his position, being sure to study his evidence closely. You might visit your school's media library to find file tapes of old *Batman* shows, or read contemporary reviews of *Batman*, to gather evidence for your essay.

2. Read Fredric Wertham's *Seduction of the Innocent*. Then write your own critique of Wertham's attack on Batman.

3. Buy a few issues of the current Batman comic book and write an essay in which you explain Batman's current sexual orientation.

4. Visit your college library and obtain a copy of Susan Sontag's "Notes on Camp" (included in Sontag's collections *Against Interpretation* and *A Susan Sontag Reader*). How would Sontag interpret the character of Batman?

COURTNEY E. MARTIN
The Famine Mystique

"Don't buy magazines that make you feel bad," Courtney Martin advises in this indictment of the continuing pressure on American girls and women to look like half-starved fashion models. The indictment is not new, and the widespread prevalence of eating disorders is not recent. But the fact that well into the twenty-first century and the postfeminist era, women are still feeling desperate about their bodies is a signifier of a persistent paradox, Martin believes. For with the freedom to choose their own destinies in a liberated world, many women may be "hiding inside of their own bodies" instead of "asking the real questions: 'Who am I? What is my purpose on earth?'" And if that is the case, the women's movement still has its work cut out for it. Martin is the author of Perfect Girls, Starving Daughters: The Frightening New Normalcy of Hating Your Body *(2007).*

What if the terror a girl faces at twenty-one is the terror of freedom to decide her own life, with no one to order which path she will take, the freedom and the necessity to take paths women before were not able to take? What if those who choose the path of "feminine adjustment" — evading this terror by marrying at eighteen, losing themselves in having babies and the details of housekeeping — are simply refusing to grow up, to face the question of their own identity?

— BETTY FRIEDAN
The Feminine Mystique (1963)

Starving, in its inimitably perverse way, gave me a way to address the anxiety I felt as a young, scared, ill-defined woman who was poised to enter the world and assume a new array of rights and privileges; it gave me a tiny, specific, manageable focus (popcorn kernels) instead of a monumental, vague, overwhelming one (work, love).

— CAROLINE KNAPP
Appetites (2002)

The words written by landmark feminist and psychologist Betty Friedan were penned 50 years before Knapp articulated her own theory: that the epidemic of eating disorders in this country is largely a form of displacement. Young women, Knapp contends, are overwhelmed with life's choices — which she describes as a sickening buffet of everything and anything — so they avoid gazing at the terrain of identity (lifestyle, love, or career) by focusing on only one tiny facet of their existence: their appetites. Friedan wondered 50 years earlier whether women were giving in to the housewife hype ("the feminine mystique") in order to make their lives as small and manageable as possible.

Knapp believed that the women of her generation have adopted a new method of such shrinking focus in the body. Women in both Friedan's and Knapp's generations, overwhelmed and underdeveloped emotionally, tried to make the grand potentiality of their lives as diminutive as possible.

These feminist writers echo one another across a great distance of time and cultural space. So much has changed in the 50 years between their tomes. The Internet was invented, wars have been waged and lost, and women have struggled up the ranks of almost every profession. How then is it possible that they speak with such similarity?

Women my age, and, I suspect, women of all ages, are bound by a strange and almost silent collusion. Betty Friedan called it the feminine mystique 50 years ago, a time when she saw women hiding inside of their own homes instead of taking on the world. Now, women are hiding inside of their own bodies, avoiding asking the real questions: Who am I? What is my purpose on this earth? Instead they distract themselves with never-ending measurements (pounds, calories, cookies). But you cannot measure pain in this way. You cannot measure self-worth. You cannot measure potential. As Naomi Wolf wisely wrote in *The Beauty Myth*: "If there is a natural female shape, it is the one in which women are sexual and fertile and not always thinking about it."

Eating disorders are the famine mystique of my generation. According 5 to Anorexia Nervosa and Related Eating Disorders, Inc. more than half of teen-aged girls are, or think they should be, on diets. The National Association for Anorexia Nervosa and Associated Disorders reports that "eating disorders have reached epidemic levels in America: all segments of society, young and old, rich and poor, all minorities, including African American and Latino, seven million women." And then there is the reality: you cannot count the amount of times a "healthy" woman stares in a mirror and chastises herself for hips too round or arms too soft. There certainly aren't statistics on the number of minutes wasted counting calories. There are no numbers that can describe a little girl discovering that unique female guilt over food for the first time.

I recently had the opportunity to hear the courageous Eve Ensler speak and one of the things she said has been echoing in my head over and over ever since: "See what you see, say what you say, know what you know."

See What You See

I have seen monumental suffering housed in women's bodies. I have seen teenage girls watch their mothers starve, deny and hate themselves, call their distorted ideas about food "will power." I have seen these mothers teach this language to their daughters, usually unintentionally. I have seen vomit in toilets across America. I have seen protruding bellies, working so hard to get nutrients out of food that only rests for a few minutes before being retched up

"Eating disorders are the famine
mystique of my generation."

again. I have seen grown women's wrists the size of toddlers' wrists. I have
seen a young woman pass out in an exercise room. I have seen the smartest
college students in the world spend the majority of their days thinking about
calories. I have seen shame, loads and loads of it, piled so high that women
climb on top and reign there. I have seen a nine-year-old on a diet. I have
seen women refuse dinner invitations because they don't want anyone to see
them eat. I have seen the blank, dry eyes of a best friend directly after vomit-
ing up our shared dinner.

Say What You Say

I have said this. Sometimes quietly, sometimes with more force. I have said
this to the women I watch starve and mutilate their bodies. I have said it to
feminist leaders and college counselors. I have said it in classrooms and editorial meetings. Usually people don't listen. When they do, a passing wave of
sadness rests on their faces, before they rationalize that eating disorders are
very individual, very personal diseases that we can't possibly be expected to
deal with on a collective level. They look relieved then. There were moments
when I believed them, when I too, settled into delusional relief.

Know What You Know

But I know what I know and I can't pretend. Yes, each individual woman suffers from her own unique version of a braided pain: parents and childhood trauma, body structure, and boys delicately interwoven. But each woman is also part of a shared story. This story is one of collective destruction, the brain power of my whole generation, my mom's whole generation, has been co-opted into the incessant counting of calories, consideration of fat, negotiation of guilt, shame, and hate. We have together bought in to this powerfully corrupt system of beauty, self-worth constituted by self-denial. We may starve ourselves for different reasons, but we hunger together. And I know, most profoundly, that we will hunger until we speak the truth.

This is mine: I have had only a few close friends in the 25 years that I   10 have lived who didn't have a severely distorted body image or destructive relationship with food. I have never suffered from an eating disorder, but I have spent far more time than I feel good about admitting thinking about the size of my thighs, lower back, or stomach (I weigh 140 lbs. and I am 5' 9" tall). I feel bad about myself if I don't exercise regularly. I don't know if this is because I truly want to be healthy, or if I am afraid of getting fat. I eat little, measured portions. I am proud if I eat less. I feel shameful if I eat more. I eat when I am bored and sad and lonely. I wish I didn't have to think about any of this. I wish I could just focus on making the world a better, kinder place. I wish that other women would speak the truth, that we could all admit that there is an epidemic of eating disorders and body image distortion in this country and it is not only killing our spirits, our potential, and our energy, but also the spirits, potential, and energy of our daughters.

My mother's generation modeled it through their unexamined language, their buy-in to media's unattainable ideal, their own screwed up relationship with food. And now my generation, seemingly more empowered than any before it, is keeping the pathos alive. We have broken the glass ceiling, stormed boardrooms and bedrooms with birthrights of equality, but we still get paralyzed when it comes time to order a meal (will we be good or bad?). The braburners taught us about consciousness-raising, but ironically, forgot to include the body consciousness. We have, truth be told, suffered the cruel inheritance of the feminine mystique in a new, equally insidious form.

We don't seek refuge from the big, bad world in kitchens and washrooms. As our mothers were trapped in their homes, we are trapped in our own bodies — obsessed with figuring out how to carve them into some kind of perfection, never satisfied with our thwarted attempts at absolute perfection. Though we feel entitled to medical degrees and vice-presidencies, we accept these honors with growling, unsatisfied stomachs; our most fundamental needs unmet. Though we feel confident making speeches on the floor of the United Nations, declaring our truth in national media columns and classrooms across the country, our deepest desires — to eat, to feel full, to love our own forms — are never spoken.

Today I speak out. The famine mystique is killing my generation — sometimes literally, often politically, emotionally, and spiritually. It is, ultimately, not our bodies that suffer most, but our souls. As Marion Woodman so beautifully put it in *The Owl Was a Baker's Daughter*: "Anorexia and bulimia tell us that our souls are starving."

We can no longer throw our hands up in apathetic collusion, calling these diseases by complicated, individuated names, battling them alone in our bathrooms and bedrooms. Instead we must make public these very private fears about fat and worth, we must air them and pick them apart, see them — in the light — for the irrational and diabolical myths that they are.

We must reclaim our language very deliberately and consciously. Telling   15
your daughter that she is beautiful, and then turning around and commenting on what a "fat cow" you are is confusing and destructive. Your daughter has no way of reconciling your vision of her with your own self-hate — like a funhouse mirror, she is left trying to make sense of the distorted reality. Within friendships we must strive to hold each other accountable for the same reason. It is important to acknowledge your own struggle with self-image, but not in the degrading language of an unenlightened culture. Create your own language — an honest, compassionate one with words flexible enough to describe the complexity of women's relationships with their own bodies.

We must reject the incessant barrage of diet fads and skinny supermodels. Don't buy magazines that make you feel bad. (Great alternatives are *off our backs*, *Bust*, *Bitch*, and *Clamor!*) Write letters to women's magazines and beauty companies that you think are perpetuating an unrealistic ideal for women; tell them that you will no longer buy their products until they show images of a variety of women — both in terms of size and ethnicity. (And vice versa — if a company miraculously shows an atypical model in its ads, let them know that you appreciated it.) Don't let yourself fall for supposed miracle diet plans that only serve to punish you and pull you, screaming and kicking, farther away from a natural, healthy state of balance. As Wolf writes, "Hunger makes women feel poor and think poor." Women are, in fact, the number one consumer group in this country. We buy more books, beauty products, magazines, and clothing than men at any age. There is power in your pocketbook — if you use it, the culture will change.

We must re-educate ourselves on health. Balance, not bone, is the true mark of good nutrition. Food is not the enemy, just as guns are only deadly in the hands of a human being. We are our own worst enemies. If we can seek out accurate and trustworthy information about diet, fitness, spiritual and mental health, perhaps we can recreate our own matrix of what it means to be beautiful. Beauty is a woman laughing in the sunshine as she runs after her child on a playground. Beauty is my slightly round belly after a hot meal that my boyfriend lovingly prepared for me. Beauty is my late grandmother's withered hands. Beauty is strength, vitality, happiness. Beauty, most radically, is self-love.

Eating Disorder Statistics

- Approximately 7 million women struggle with eating disorders in the United States.

- 0.5 to 3.7% of women struggle with Anorexia Nervosa in their lifetime.

- 1.1 to 4.2% of women struggle with bulimia in their lifetime.

- 10 to 25% of all those battling anorexia will die because of their eating disorder.

- Up to 19% of American college women have bulimia.

- 25% of college women binge and purge (but not often enough to be considered full-blown bulimia) to maintain their weight.

- By their first year of college, 4.5 to 18% of women have a history of bulimia.

- 1% of girls between the ages of 12 and 18 are anorexic.

- With treatment . . .
  about 60% of all people with eating disorders will recover.
  about 20% will partially recover.
  about 20% will not improve at all.

READING THE TEXT

1. How does Martin's inclusion of the quotations by Betty Friedan and Caroline Knapp affect your response to this selection?

2. In your own words, summarize what Betty Friedan means by the "feminine mystique" (para. 4). How is that concept related to Martin's term "famine mystique"?

3. What is the effect of Martin's use of anaphora, the deliberate repetition of a phrase at the beginning of a sentence, in paragraph 7: "I have seen . . ."?

READING THE SIGNS

1. Discuss in your journal your attitude toward your body. To what extent has your attitude been shaped by contemporary standards of physical attractiveness for your gender?

2. Martin accuses traditional women's magazines of perpetuating the famine mystique. Analyze a current woman's magazine such as *Cosmopolitan* or *Glamour*, and write an essay in which you discuss to what extent Martin's accusation applies to your publication.

3. Martin praises alternative magazines such as *off our backs* and *Bitch*. Analyze one such alternative magazine for its presentation of female body image. In what ways could the publication be considered a genuine alternative to mass-market publications?

4. **CONNECTING TEXTS**   Martin does not discuss whether men are bound by male standards for body shape. In class, form teams and debate whether men are as trapped by standards of ideal physical attractiveness as women. To develop your ideas, consult Warren St. John's "Metrosexuals Come Out" (p. 227), Mariah Burton Nelson's "I Won. I'm Sorry" (p. 539), and James William Gibson's "Warrior Dreams" (p. 625).

EMILY PRAGER
Our Barbies, Ourselves

Little girls throughout America should know that Barbie is not drawn to scale. In this tongue-in-cheek essay on the role Barbie has played in her life, Emily Prager reveals the damaging effect of a doll that establishes such an impossible standard of physical perfection for little girls — and for little boys who grow up expecting their girlfriends to look like Barbie. When not contemplating what Barbie has done to her, Prager is a columnist with the New York Times *and an essayist and fiction writer who has published for the* National Lampoon *and the* Village Voice, *among other magazines. Her books include a work of historical fiction for children,* World War II Resistance Stories; *a book of humor,* The Official I Hate Videogames Handbook; *and works of fiction such as* Clea and Zeus Divorce *(1987) and* Eve's Tattoo *(1991). Her most recent book is* Wuhu Diary: On Taking My Adopted Daughter Back to Her Hometown in China *(2001).*

I read an astounding obituary in the *New York Times* not too long ago. It concerned the death of one Jack Ryan. A former husband of Zsa Zsa Gabor, it said, Mr. Ryan had been an inventor and designer during his lifetime. A man of eclectic creativity, he designed Sparrow and Hawk missiles when he worked for the Raytheon Company, and, the notice said, when he consulted for Mattel he designed Barbie.

If Barbie was designed by a man, suddenly a lot of things made sense to me, things I'd wondered about for years. I used to look at Barbie and wonder, What's wrong with this picture? What kind of woman designed this doll? Let's be honest: Barbie looks like someone who got her start at the Playboy Mansion. She could be a regular guest on *The Howard Stern Show*. It is a fact of Barbie's design that her breasts are so out of proportion to the rest of her body that if she were a human woman, she'd fall flat on her face.

If it's true that a woman didn't design Barbie, you don't know how much saner that makes me feel. Of course, that doesn't ameliorate the damage. There are millions of women who are subliminally sure that a thirty-nine-inch bust and a twenty-three-inch waist are the epitome of lovability. Could this account for the popularity of breast implant surgery?

I don't mean to step on anyone's toes here. I loved my Barbie. Secretly, I still believe that neon pink and turquoise blue are the only colors in which to decorate a duplex condo. And like many others of my generation, I've never married, simply because I cannot find a man who looks as good in clam diggers as Ken.

The question that comes to mind is, of course, Did Mr. Ryan design Barbie 5 as a weapon? Because it *is* odd that Barbie appeared about the same time in my consciousness as the feminist movement — a time when women sought equality and small breasts were king. Or is Barbie the dream date of weapons designers? Or perhaps it's simpler than that: Perhaps Barbie is Zsa Zsa if she were eleven inches tall. No matter what, my discovery of Jack Ryan confirms what I have always felt: There is something indescribably masculine about Barbie — dare I say it, phallic. For all her giant breasts and high-heeled feet, she lacks a certain softness. If you asked a little girl what kind of doll she wanted for Christmas, I just don't think she'd reply, "Please, Santa, I want a hard-body."

On the other hand, you could say that Barbie, in feminist terms, is definitely her own person. With her condos and fashion plazas and pools and beauty salons, she is definitely a liberated woman, a gal on the move. And she has always been sexual, even totemic. Before Barbie, American dolls were flat-footed and breastless, and ineffably dignified. They were created in the image of little girls or babies. Madame Alexander was the queen of doll makers in the fifties, and her dollies looked like Elizabeth Taylor in *National Velvet*. They represented the kind of girls who looked perfect in jodhpurs, whose hair was never

"A gal on the move": Barbie with Ken.

out of place, who grew up to be Jackie Kennedy — before she married Onassis. Her dolls' boyfriends were figments of the imagination, figments with large portfolios and three-piece suits and presidential aspirations, figments who could keep dolly in the style to which little girls of the fifties were programmed to become accustomed, a style that spasmed with the sixties and the appearance of Barbie. And perhaps what accounts for Barbie's vast popularity is that she was also a sixties woman: into free love and fun colors, anticlass, and possessed a real, molded boyfriend, Ken, with whom she could chant a mantra.

But there were problems with Ken. I always felt weird about him. He had no genitals, and, even at age ten, I found that ominous. I mean, here was Barbie with these humongous breasts, and that was OK with the toy company. And then, there was Ken with that truncated, unidentifiable lump at his groin. I sensed injustice at work. Why, I wondered, was Barbie designed with such obvious sexual equipment and Ken not? Why was his treated as if it were more mysterious than hers? Did the fact that it was treated as such indicate that somehow his equipment, his essential maleness, was considered more powerful than hers, more worthy of the dignity of concealment? And if the issue in the mind of the toy company was obscenity and its possible damage to children, I still object. How do they think I felt, knowing that no matter how many water beds they slept in, or hot tubs they romped in, or swimming pools they lounged by under the stars, Barbie and Ken could never make love? No matter how much sexuality Barbie possessed, she would never turn Ken on. He would be forever withholding, forever detached. There was a loneliness about Barbie's situation that was always disturbing. And twenty-five years later, movies and videos are still filled with topless women and covered men. As if we're all trapped in Barbie's world and can never escape.

God, it certainly has cheered me up to think that Barbie was designed by Jack Ryan. . . .

READING THE TEXT

1. Why does Prager say "a lot of things made sense" (para. 2) to her after she learned Barbie was designed by a man?
2. What is Prager's attitude toward Ken?
3. How do Madame Alexander dolls differ from Barbies?

READING THE SIGNS

1. Bring a toy to class and, in same-sex groups, discuss its semiotic significance; you may want to focus particularly on how the toys may be intended for one gender or another. Then have each group select one toy and present your interpretation of it to the whole class. What gender-related patterns do you find in the presentations?
2. Think of a toy you played with as a child, and write a semiotic interpretation of it, using Prager's essay as a model. Be sure to consider differences between your childhood response to the toy and your current response.

3. Did you have a Barbie doll when you were a child? If so, write a journal entry in which you explore what the doll meant to you when you were young and whether Prager's essay has caused you to reconsider your attitudes.

4. Consider how Jack Ryan, the creator of Barbie, would defend his design. Write a letter, as if you were Ryan, addressed to Prager in which you justify Barbie's appearance and refute Prager's analysis.

5. **CONNECTING TEXTS**   Barbie can be seen as embodying not only America's traditional gender roles but also its consumerist ethos. Visit a toy store to learn what "accessories" one can buy for Barbie, and write an essay in which you explore the extent to which she illustrates the "hunger for more" described by Laurence Shames ("The More Factor," p. 86).

JOAN MORGAN

Sex, Lies, and Videos

Hip-hop culture is widely viewed as the expression of black pride, and even defiance, but in this opinion piece written for Essence *in 2002, Joan Morgan points out that the parade of skinny white, Asian, Latina, or light-skinned black women who appear in typical rap videos can be hard on black girls and women who don't look like that. A fan of hip-hop herself, Morgan thinks "it's time to set some standards" that protect African American children. Morgan is editor-at-large for* Essence *and author of* When Chickenheads Come Home to Roost *(1999).*

It was the timbre of her voice that haunted me. It was soft and tinged with defeat. "I can't watch rap videos anymore," said the former fan who spoke to me from the University of Massachusetts audience I was addressing that day. "They make me feel bad about myself. Even when the images aren't bordering on pornographic, the girls in them are always skinny, White, Asian, or Latino — anything but Black. Or if a dancer is Black, then she's extremely light-skinned." She herself was pretty and thick with skin the color of milk chocolate.

This young woman's alienation and frustration resonated through the crowd of college-age women. "If this is who is considered beautiful by our men, where does that leave me?" was a common remark. For the next hour or so, the discussion I was supposed to be facilitating on the role of women in hip-hop turned into a lengthy discourse on why so many die-hard female fans had finally given up.

It wasn't as if I couldn't empathize. Remaining a hip-hop loyalist these days is a formidable task with a questionable payoff. Rap music has journeyed from the South Bronx underground to Corporate America, as 70 percent of hip-hop consumers are now White. For many artists, the shift in the market has meant adopting mainstream values, resulting in the proliferation of thin, White, and light images of women. When you couple that with a visual aesthetic that relies heavily on T&A and crotch shots, suffice it to say the average rap video taps into just about every insecurity and erroneous belief about sensuality related to Black women. Especially troubling is the unavoidable message that shaking our half-naked asses in front of a man is the only way we have to secure male affection.

Fewer than five years ago, the discussion I had at the university would have been very different. To be sure, sexism in hip-hop would have been part of it, but there also would've been lively debates over freedom of speech, Latifah's Afrofemme regality versus the punanny politics of Lil' Kim, and the deliciously guilty pleasure of discarding feminist principles for a few hours of booty-shaking hedonistic abandon. Now we could no longer get past the sense of degradation most young women feel while watching rap videos.

Several of them raised concerns about how those images affect younger 5 girls. One expressed dismay at seeing her 5-year-old niece (who watches videos with her twentysomething mom, mind you) provocatively winding to the ridiculously infectious hook of Nas's "Oochie Wally" in which a woman sings, "He really, really turned me out. He really, really got to gut me. He really, really made me scream and shout." Another shared her futile attempts to quell her pubescent 12-year-old cousin's fear that her emerging hips and breasts were making her "too fat" to wear the designer gear that defines her ghetto-fabulous aspirations.

These stories echo the frustrations of so many other women I know. A principal at a New York public junior-high school has to send her female students home repeatedly for "coming to school in the hooker wear they see in these videos." She's concerned for their safety, and she's afraid they'll get picked up for soliciting. My friend Irene Prince, the mother of a 14-year-old girl, laments: "The problem with rap is that the images of cool women they present are always degrading to girls. They get to be only one thing—toys for boys. I don't want my daughter modeling herself after that."

Certainly there is little question that the majority of Black girls are ill-equipped to handle this onslaught of sexually degrading content. Although Black girls continue to have a more positive body image than many of their White counterparts, our young women are developing eating disorders at a greater rate than previously, according to the U.S. Department of Health and Human Services Office on Women's Health. And with thin, scantily clad video vixens informing their notion of an aesthetic ideal, 90 percent of those affected with eating disorders are adolescent and young adult females. Combine these factors with the reality that father figures are absent from so many of our homes, and it is easy to see why Black girls are likely to think that wearing little to nothing and competing with women for sexual attention is the only way to secure male interest.

But for all the attention the half-dressed hoochie may get, what rap videos don't portray is that without financial independence, education, ambition, intelligence, spirituality, and love, punanny alone ain't all that powerful. In fact, it's easily replaceable and inexhaustible in supply. As my girlfriend Irene said to me, "In rap videos, there is no self. Girls become body parts and nothing more."

As women, we cannot abdicate the responsibility we have to our children. As female hip-hop fans, we can no longer afford to buy into the music's most clichéd disclaimer — that rap's content is intended for mature audiences. True, it is a parent's role to monitor what his or her children are watching, but there's also no denying that the current generation is essentially parenting itself. Sixty-two percent of our children are being raised without the benefit of both parents in the home, and many of them without the benefit of extended family. Indeed, in a great number of homes, television is the babysitter. It really does take a village, y'all, and in the absence of parental figures, we gotta parent one another's kids.

It's time to set some standards. Instead of resigning ourselves to being at   10
the mercy of the media, we have to recognize our power to have an impact on it. Individual acts of resistance — banning cable from our homes, refusing to buy CDs with misogynistic content — are simply not enough. In the late eighties, MTV was besieged with complaints that its videos were too full of content inappropriate for younger kids. Viewers collectively issued an effective ultimatum: "Clean it up, or we ban you from our homes."

MTV responded accordingly by blurring any suggestions of nudity, gang insignias, or drugs and refusing to play rap videos with hard-core content. Yet when media giant Viacom bought BET, it let the station air programming that it would never allow on MTV. Evidently it wasn't acceptable to air near-pornographic images for the young, largely White audience of MTV, but it was fine to dump them on the young, largely Black BET audience. And why is that? Because we aren't complaining.

It's up to us to identify these videos for what they are — adult content that shouldn't be shown in prime time. If White America can determine what's too toxic for their children, we can, too. Every parent, college student, female hip-hop fan and journalist who has spoken to me about the disturbing content of videos should also put his or her objections down in an e-mail or letter. Send it off to every station that plays these videos, and demand that they be put on after 9:00 P.M. If the response isn't favorable, we should join forces with our peers, colleagues, community leaders, and congregations to threaten a boycott of not only the station but also its advertisers. I bet we would see immediate changes then. We would see, perhaps, a space where our girls can enjoy the music they love, without risking their self-esteem and souls in the process.

READING THE TEXT

1. To what features of hip-hop videos does Morgan particularly object?
2. How has hip-hop evolved, according to Morgan, and how does she feel about changes in the genre?
3. What does Morgan see as the differences in the portrayals of white and African American women in hip-hop and pop music?

4. In your own words, describe Morgan's solution to the problem of misogyny in hip-hop.

READING THE SIGNS

1. Conduct a random survey of female hip-hop fans, inquiring about their attitudes toward hip-hip music and videos. Use your findings as the basis of an essay in which you assess the validity of Morgan's claim that most young women feel a "sense of degradation . . . while watching rap videos" (para. 4).

2. Watch some recent hip-hop videos, and analyze the images of women that they present. To what extent do the women follow the pattern — of being thin, light-skinned, and scantily clad — that Morgan describes?

3. **CONNECTING TEXTS**   Survey a broad array of images of women in popular culture — you can look to advertising, musical genres other than hip-hop, film, and TV — and analyze how women are represented. Then write an essay in which you argue whether Morgan's objections to hip-hop's depiction of women can be applied to other media as well. To develop your ideas, you might consult Andre Mayer's "The New Sexual Stone Age" (p. 312).

4. Watch the videos of several female hip-hop artists, and analyze their representation of women. To what extent do they duplicate the patterns Morgan describes?

5. **CONNECTING TEXTS**   Write an essay in which you demonstrate, refute, or complicate Morgan's claim that hip-hop has adopted "mainstream values" (para. 3). To develop your ideas, consult Cynthia Tucker's "Thug Culture Is a Cancer Destroying Black America" (p. 326).

DEBORAH TANNEN

There Is No Unmarked Woman

If you use the pronoun "s/he" when writing, or write "women and men" rather than "men and women," you are not just writing words: You are making a statement that may "mark" you as being a "feminist." In this analysis of the way everything a woman does marks her in some way or other — from writing and speaking to the way she dresses and styles her hair — Deborah Tannen reveals the asymmetrical nature of gender semi-otics in our culture. Wearing makeup or not wearing makeup sends a sig-nal about a woman, whereas a man without makeup sends no signal at all. Tannen's analysis shows how what men do is implicitly considered the norm in society, and so is relatively neutral, while women's difference inevitably marks them, "because there is no unmarked woman." Univer-sity Professor in Linguistics at Georgetown University, Tannen is the author of many books, including the best-selling You Just Don't Under-stand: Women and Men in Conversation *(1986),* Talking from 9 to 5 *(1994),* Gender and Discourse *(1994),* The Argument Culture *(1998),* I Only Say This Because I Love You: How the Way We Talk Can Make or Break Family Relationships throughout Our Lives *(2001), and* You're Wearing That? Understanding Mothers and Daughters in Conversa-tion *(2006).*

Some years ago I was at a small working conference of four women and eight men. Instead of concentrating on the discussion I found myself looking at the three other women at the table, thinking how each had a different style and how each style was coherent.

One woman had dark brown hair in a classic style, a cross between Cleopatra and Plain Jane. The severity of her straight hair was softened by wavy bangs and ends that turned under. Because she was beautiful, the effect was more Cleopatra than plain.

The second woman was older, full of dignity and composure. Her hair was cut in a fashionable style that left her with only one eye, thanks to a side part that let a curtain of hair fall across half her face. As she looked down to read her prepared paper, the hair robbed her of bifocal vision and created a barrier between her and the listeners.

The third woman's hair was wild, a frosted blond avalanche falling over and beyond her shoulders. When she spoke she frequently tossed her head, calling attention to her hair and away from her lecture.

Then there was makeup. The first woman wore facial cover that made her 5 skin smooth and pale, a black line under each eye and mascara that darkened already dark lashes. The second wore only a light gloss on her lips and a hint of shadow on her eyes. The third had blue bands under her eyes, dark blue shadow, mascara, bright red lipstick, and rouge; her fingernails flashed red.

I considered the clothes each woman had worn during the three days of the conference: In the first case, man-tailored suits in primary colors with solid-color blouses. In the second, casual but stylish black T-shirts, a floppy collarless jacket and baggy slacks or a skirt in neutral colors. The third wore a sexy jumpsuit; tight sleeveless jersey and tight yellow slacks; a dress with gaping armholes and an indulged tendency to fall off one shoulder.

Shoes? No. 1 wore string sandals with medium heels; No. 2, sensible, comfortable walking shoes; No. 3, pumps with spike heels. You can fill in the jewelry, scarves, shawls, sweaters — or lack of them.

As I amused myself finding coherence in these styles, I suddenly wondered why I was scrutinizing only the women. I scanned the eight men at the table. And then I knew why I wasn't studying them. The men's styles were unmarked.

The term "marked" is a staple of linguistic theory. It refers to the way language alters the base meaning of a word by adding a linguistic particle that has no meaning on its own. The unmarked form of a word carries the meaning that goes without saying — what you think of when you're not thinking anything special.

The unmarked tense of verbs in English is the present — for example, *visit*. To indicate past, you mark the verb by adding *ed* to yield *visited*. For future, you add a word: *will visit*. Nouns are presumed to be singular until marked for plural, typically by adding *s* or *es*, so *visit* becomes *visits* and *dish* becomes *dishes*. 10

The unmarked forms of most English words also convey "male." Being male is the unmarked case. Endings like *ess* and *ette* mark words as "female." Unfortunately, they also tend to mark them for frivolousness. Would you feel safe entrusting your life to a doctorette? Alfre Woodard, who was an Oscar nominee for best supporting actress, says she identifies herself as an actor because "actresses worry about eyelashes and cellulite, and women who are actors worry about the characters we are playing." Gender markers pick up extra meanings that reflect common associations with the female gender: not quite serious, often sexual.

Each of the women at the conference had to make decisions about hair, clothing, makeup, and accessories, and each decision carried meaning. Every style available to us was marked. The men in our group had made decisions, too, but the range from which they chose was incomparably narrower. Men can choose styles that are marked, but they don't have to, and in this group none did. Unlike the women, they had the option of being unmarked.

Take the men's hair styles. There was no marine crew cut or oily longish hair falling into eyes, no asymmetrical, two-tiered construction to swirl over a bald top. One man was unabashedly bald; the others had hair of standard length, parted on one side, in natural shades of brown or gray or graying. Their hair obstructed no views, left little to toss or push back or run fingers through and, consequently, needed and attracted no attention. A few men had beards. In a business setting, beards might be marked. In this academic gathering, they weren't.

There could have been a cowboy shirt with string tie or a three-piece suit or a necklaced hippie in jeans. But there wasn't. All eight men wore brown or blue slacks and nondescript shirts of light colors. No man wore sandals or boots; their shoes were dark, closed, comfortable, and flat. In short, unmarked.

Although no man wore makeup, you couldn't say the men didn't wear 15 makeup in the sense that you could say a woman didn't wear makeup. For men, no makeup is unmarked.

I asked myself what style we women could have adopted that would have been unmarked, like the men's. The answer was none. There is no unmarked woman.

There is no woman's hairstyle that can be called standard, that says nothing about her. The range of women's hairstyles is staggering, but a woman whose hair has no particular style is perceived as not caring about how she looks, which can disqualify her from many positions, and will subtly diminish her as a person in the eyes of some.

Women must choose between attractive shoes and comfortable shoes. When our group made an unexpected trek, the woman who wore flat, laced shoes arrived first. Last to arrive was the woman in spike heels, shoes in hand and a handful of men around her.

If a woman's clothing is tight or revealing (in other words, sexy), it sends a message — an intended one of wanting to be attractive, but also a possibly unintended one of availability. If her clothes are not sexy, that too sends a message, lent meaning by the knowledge that they could have been. There are thousands of cosmetic products from which women can choose and myriad ways of applying them. Yet no makeup at all is anything but unmarked. Some men see it as a hostile refusal to please them.

Women can't even fill out a form without telling stories about themselves. 20 Most forms give four titles to choose from. "Mr." carries no meaning other than that the respondent is male. But a woman who checks "Mrs." or "Miss" communicates not only whether she has been married but also whether she has conservative tastes in forms of address — and probably other conservative values as well. Checking "Ms." declines to let on about marriage (checking "Mr." declines nothing since nothing was asked), but it also marks her as either liberated or rebellious, depending on the observer's attitudes and assumptions.

I sometimes try to duck these variously marked choices by giving my title as "Dr." — and in so doing risk marking myself as either uppity (hence sarcastic responses like "Excuse *me*!") or an overachiever (hence reactions of congratulatory surprise like "Good for you!").

All married women's surnames are marked. If a woman takes her husband's name, she announces to the world that she is married and has traditional values. To some it will indicate that she is less herself, more identified by her husband's identity. If she does not take her husband's name, this too is marked, seen as worthy of comment: She has *done* something; she has "kept her own name."

A man is never said to have "kept his own name" because it never occurs to anyone that he might have given it up. For him using his own name is unmarked.

A married woman who wants to have her cake and eat it too may use her surname plus his, with or without a hyphen. But this too announces her marital status and often results in a tongue-tying string. In a list (Harvey O'Donovan, Jonathan Feldman, Stephanie Woodbury McGillicutty), the woman's multiple name stands out. It is marked.

I have never been inclined toward biological explanations of gender differences in language, but I was intrigued to see Ralph Fasold bring biological phenomena to bear on the question of linguistic marking in his book *The Sociolinguistics of Language*. Fasold stresses that language and culture are particularly unfair in treating women as the marked case because biologically it is the male that is marked. While two X chromosomes make a female, two Y chromosomes make nothing. Like the linguistic markers *s*, *es*, or *ess*, the Y chromosome doesn't "mean" anything unless it is attached to a root form — an X chromosome.

Developing this idea elsewhere Fasold points out that girls are born with fully 25 female bodies, while boys are born with modified female bodies. He invites men who doubt this to lift up their shirts and contemplate why they have nipples.

In his book, Fasold notes "a wide range of facts which demonstrates that female is the unmarked sex." For example, he observes that there are a few species that produce only females, like the whiptail lizard. Thanks to parthenogenesis, they have no trouble having as many daughters as they like. There are no species, however, that produce only males. This is no surprise, since any such species would become extinct in its first generation.

Fasold is also intrigued by species that produce individuals not involved in reproduction, like honeybees and leaf-cutter ants. Reproduction is handled by the queen and a relatively few males; the workers are sterile females. "Since they do not reproduce," Fasold said, "there is no reason for them to be one sex or the other, so they default, so to speak, to female."

Fasold ends his discussion of these matters by pointing out that if language reflected biology, grammar books would direct us to use "she" to include males and females and "he" only for specifically male referents. But they don't. They tell us that "he" means "he or she," and that "she" is used only if the referent is specifically female. This use of "he" as the sex-indefinite pronoun is an innovation introduced into English by grammarians in the eighteenth and nineteenth centuries, according to Peter Mühlhäusler and Rom Harré in *Pronouns and People*. From at least about 1500, the correct sex-indefinite pronoun was "they," as it still is in casual spoken English. In other words, the female was declared by grammarians to be the marked case.

Writing this article may mark me not as a writer, not as a linguist, not as an analyst of human behavior, but as a feminist — which will have positive or negative, but in any case powerful, connotations for readers. Yet I doubt that anyone reading Ralph Fasold's book would put that label on him.

I discovered the markedness inherent in the very topic of gender after 30 writing a book on differences in conversational style based on geographical region, ethnicity, class, age, and gender. When I was interviewed, the vast majority of journalists wanted to talk about the differences between women and men. While I thought I was simply describing what I observed — something I had learned to do as a researcher — merely mentioning women and men marked me as a feminist for some.

When I wrote a book devoted to gender differences in ways of speaking, I sent the manuscript to five male colleagues, asking them to alert me to any interpretation, phrasing, or wording that might seem unfairly negative toward men. Even so, when the book came out, I encountered responses like that of the television talk show host who, after interviewing me, turned to the audience and asked if they thought I was male-bashing.

Leaping upon a poor fellow who affably nodded in agreement, she made him stand and asked, "Did what she say accurately describe you?" "Oh, yes," he answered. "That's me exactly." "And what she said about women — does that sound like your wife?" "Oh yes," he responded. "That's her exactly." "Then why do you think she's male-bashing?" He answered, with disarming honesty, "Because she's a woman and she's saying things about men."

To say anything about women and men without marking oneself as either feminist or anti-feminist, male-basher or apologist for men seems as impossible for a woman as trying to get dressed in the morning without inviting interpretations of her character.

Sitting at the conference table musing on these matters, I felt sad to think that we women didn't have the freedom to be unmarked that the men sitting next to us had. Some days you just want to get dressed and go about your business. But if you're a woman, you can't, because there is no unmarked woman.

READING THE TEXT

1. Explain in your own words what Tannen means by "marked" (para. 9).

2. Why does Tannen say that men have the "option of being unmarked" (para. 12)?

3. What significance does Tannen see in Ralph Fasold's biological explanations of linguistic gender difference?

READING THE SIGNS

1. **CONNECTING TEXTS**   Do you agree with Tannen's assumption that men have the luxury of remaining "unmarked" (para. 12)? Do you think it's possible to be purely unmarked? To develop your essay, you might interview some men, particularly those who elect to have an unconventional appearance, and read James William Gibson's "Warrior Dreams" (p. 625).

2. In class, survey the extent to which the males and females in your class are "marked" or "unmarked," in Tannen's terms, studying such signs as clothing and hair style. Do the males tend to have unmarked styles, while the women

tend to send a message by their choices? Discuss the results of your survey, and reflect on the validity of Tannen's claims.

3. Interview at least five women who are married, and ask them about their choice of names: Did they keep their "own" name, adopt their husband's, or opt for a hyphenated version? What signals do they want to send about their identity through their names? Use the results of your interviews to write a reflective essay on how our names function as signs, particularly as gender-related signs.

4. What would an unmarked appearance for women be like? Write a speculative essay in which you imagine the features of an unmarked female appearance. If you have difficulty imagining such an appearance, try to explain why.

JAMES WILLIAM GIBSON
Warrior Dreams

If you think that Rambo was a joke, James William Gibson has news for you: His popularity was a symptom of an identity crisis that has afflicted American men since the advent of feminism and the U.S. defeat in Vietnam more than a quarter of a century ago. Feeling unmanned by a war lost and by the rewriting of gender codes in the wake of the sexual revolution, millions of American men, as Gibson puts it, "began to dream, to fantasize about the powers and features of another kind of man who could retake and reorder the world." Such fantasy warriors include Rambo, Dirty Harry, and Jack Ryan, fictional role models for the gun-toting legions of a new paramilitary subculture that is quite real, and growing. Paintball, anyone? Gibson is professor of sociology at California State University, Long Beach, and author of The Perfect War: Technowar in Vietnam *(1986) and* Warrior Dreams: Paramilitary Culture in Post-Vietnam America *(1994), from which this selection is excerpted.*

We couldn't see them, but we could hear their bugles sound the call. The Communist battalions were organizing for a predawn assault. Captain Kokalis smiled wickedly; he'd been through this before. A "human wave" assault composed of thousands of enemy soldiers was headed our way. The captain ordered the remaining soldiers in his command to check their .30- and .50-caliber machine guns. Earlier in the night, the demolitions squad attached to our unit had planted mines and explosive charges for hundreds of meters in front of our position.

And then it began. At a thousand meters, the soldiers emerged screaming from the gray-blue fog. "Fire!" yelled Captain Kokalis. The gun crews opened up with short bursts of three to seven rounds; their bullets struck meat. Everywhere I could see, clusters of Communist troops were falling by the second. But the wave still surged forward. At five hundred meters, Kokalis passed the word to his gunners to increase their rate of fire to longer strings of ten to twenty rounds. Sergeant Donovan, the demolitions squad leader, began to reap the harvest from the night's planting. Massive explosions ripped through the Communist troops. Fire and smoke blasted into the dawn sky. It was as if the human wave had hit a submerged reef; as the dying fell, wide gaps appeared in the line where casualties could no longer be replaced.

But still they kept coming, hundreds of men, each and every one bent on taking the American position and wiping us out. As the Communists reached one hundred meters, Kokalis gave one more command. Every machine gun in our platoon went to its maximum rate of sustained full-automatic frenzy, sounding like chain saws that just keep cutting and cutting.

And then it was over. The attack subsided into a flat sea of Communist dead. No Americans had been killed or wounded. We were happy to be alive, proud of our victory. We only wondered if our ears would ever stop ringing and if we would ever again smell anything other than the bittersweet aroma of burning gunpowder. . . .

Although an astonishing triumph was achieved that day, no historian will 5 ever find a record of this battle in the hundreds of volumes and thousands of official reports written about the Korean or Vietnam wars. Nor was the blood spilt part of a covert operation in Afghanistan or some unnamed country in Africa, Asia, or Latin America.

No, this battle was fought inside the United States, a few miles north of Las Vegas, in September 1986. It was a purely *imaginary* battle, a dream of victory staged as part of the *Soldier of Fortune* magazine's annual convention. The audience of several hundred men, women, and children, together with reporters and a camera crew from *CBS News*, sat in bleachers behind half a dozen medium and heavy machine guns owned by civilians. Peter G. Kokalis, *SOF*'s firearms editor, set the scene for the audience and asked them to imagine that the sandy brushland of the Desert Sportsman Rifle and Pistol Club was really a killing zone for incoming Communist troops. Kokalis was a seasoned storyteller; he'd given this performance before. When the fantasy battle was over, the fans went wild with applause. Kokalis picked up a microphone, praised Donovan (another *SOF* staff member) — "He was responsible for that whole damn Communist bunker that went up" — and told the parents in the audience to buy "claymores [antipersonnel land mines] and other good shit for the kids." A marvelous actor who knew what his audience wanted, Kokalis sneered, "Did you get that, CBS, on your videocam? Screw you knee-jerk liberals."[1]

---

[1]Peter G. Kokalis, speaking at the *Soldier of Fortune* firepower demonstration at the Desert Sportsman Rifle and Pistol Club, Las Vegas, Nev., September 20, 1986.

The shoot-out and victory over Communist forces conducted at the Desert Sportsman Rifle and Pistol Club was but one battle in a cultural or imaginary "New War" that had been going on since the late 1960s and early 1970s. The bitter controversies surrounding the Vietnam War had discredited the old American ideal of the masculine warrior hero for much of the public. But in 1971, when Clint Eastwood made the transition from playing cowboys in old *Rawhide* reruns and spaghetti westerns to portraying San Francisco police detective Harry Callahan in *Dirty Harry*, the warrior hero returned in full force. His backup arrived in 1974 when Charles Bronson appeared in *Death Wish*, the story of a mild-mannered, middle-aged architect in New York City who, after his wife is murdered and his daughter is raped and driven insane, finds new meaning in life through an endless war of revenge against street punks.

In the 1980s, Rambo and his friends made their assault. The experience of John Rambo, a former Green Beret, was the paradigmatic story of the decade. In *First Blood* (1982), he burns down a small Oregon town while suffering hallucinatory flashbacks to his service in Vietnam. Three years later, in *Rambo: First Blood, Part 2*, he is taken off a prison chain gang by his former commanding officer in Vietnam and asked to perform a special reconnaissance mission to find suspected American POWs in Laos, in exchange for a Presidential pardon. His only question: "Do we get to win this time?" And indeed, Rambo does win. Betrayed by the CIA bureaucrat in charge of the

Sylvester Stallone in *Rambo III*, 1988.

mission, Rambo fights the Russians and Vietnamese by himself and brings the POWs back home.

Hundreds of similar films celebrating the victory of good men over bad through armed combat were made during the late 1970s and 1980s. Many were directed by major Hollywood directors and starred well-known actors. Elaborate special effects and exotic film locations added tens of millions to production costs. And for every large-budget film, there were scores of cheaper formula films employing lesser-known actors and production crews. Often these "action-adventure" films had only brief theatrical releases in major markets. Instead, they made their money in smaller cities and towns, in sales to Europe and the Third World, and most of all, in the sale of videocassettes to rental stores. Movie producers could even turn a profit on "video-only" releases; action-adventure films were the largest category of video rentals in the 1980s.

At the same time, Tom Clancy became a star in the publishing world. His 10 book *The Hunt for Red October* (1984) told the story of the Soviet Navy's most erudite submarine commander, Captain Markus Ramius, and his effort to defect to the United States with the Soviets' premier missile-firing submarine. *Red Storm Rising* (1986) followed, an epic of World War III framed as a high-tech conventional war against the Soviet Union. Clancy's novels all featured Jack Ryan, Ph.D., a former Marine captain in Vietnam turned academic naval historian who returns to duty as a CIA analyst and repeatedly stumbles into life-and-death struggles in which the fate of the world rests on his prowess. All were bestsellers.

President Reagan, Secretary of the Navy John Lehman, and many other high officials applauded Clancy and his hero. Soon the author had a multimillion-dollar contract for a whole series of novels, movie deals with Paramount, and a new part-time job as a foreign-policy expert writing op-ed pieces for the *Washington Post*, the *Los Angeles Times*, and other influential newspapers around the country. His success motivated dozens of authors, mostly active-duty or retired military men, to take up the genre. The "technothriller" was born.

At a slightly lower level in the literary establishment, the same publishing houses that marketed women's romance novels on grocery and drugstore paperback racks rapidly expanded their collections of pulp fiction for men. Most were written like hard-core pornography, except that inch-by-inch descriptions of penises entering vaginas were replaced by equally graphic portrayals of bullets, grenade fragments, and knives shredding flesh: "He tried to grab the handle of the commando knife, but the terrorist pushed down on the butt, raised the point and yanked the knife upward through the muscle tissue and guts. It ripped intestines, spilling blood and gore."[2] A minimum of 20 but sometimes as many as 120 such graphically described killings occurred in

---

[2]Gar Wilson, *The Fury Bombs*, vol. 5 of *Phoenix Force* (Toronto: Worldwide Library, 1983), 30.

each 200- to 250-page paperback. Most series came out four times a year with domestic print runs of 60,000 to 250,000 copies. More than a dozen different comic books with titles like *Punisher*, *Vigilante*, and *Scout* followed suit with clones of the novels.

Along with the novels and comics came a new kind of periodical which replaced the older adventure magazines for men, such as *True* and *Argosy*, that had folded in the 1960s. Robert K. Brown, a former captain in the U.S. Army Special Forces during the Vietnam War, founded *Soldier of Fortune: The Journal of Professional Adventurers* in the spring of 1975, just before the fall of Saigon. *SOF*'s position was explicit from the start: the independent warrior must step in to fill the dangerous void created by the American failure in Vietnam. By the mid-1980s *SOF* was reaching 35,000 subscribers, had newsstand sales of another 150,000, and was being passed around to at least twice as many readers.[3]

Half a dozen new warrior magazines soon entered the market. Some, like *Eagle*, *New Breed*, and *Gung-Ho*, tried to copy the *SOF* editorial package — a strategy that ultimately failed. But most developed their own particular pitch. *Combat Handguns* focused on pistols for would-be gunfighters. *American Survival Guide* advertised and reviewed everything needed for "the good life" after the end of civilization (except birth control devices — too many Mormon subscribers, the editor said), while *S.W.A.T.* found its way to men who idealized these elite police teams and who were worried about home defense against "multiple intruders."

During the same period, sales of military weapons took off. Colt offered 15 two semiautomatic versions of the M16 used by U.S. soldiers in Vietnam (a full-size rifle and a shorter-barreled carbine with collapsible stock). European armories exported their latest products, accompanied by sophisticated advertising campaigns in *SOF* and the more mainstream gun magazines. Israeli Defense Industries put a longer, 16-inch barrel on the Uzi submachine gun (to make it legal) and sold it as a semiautomatic carbine. And the Communist countries of Eastern Europe, together with the People's Republic of China, jumped into the market with the devil's own favorite hardware, the infamous AK47. The AK sold in the United States was the semiautomatic version of the assault rifle used by the victorious Communists in Vietnam and by all kinds of radical movements and terrorist organizations around the world. It retailed for $300 to $400, half the price of an Uzi or an AR-15; complete with three 30-round magazines, cleaning kit, and bayonet, it was truly a bargain.

To feed these hungry guns, munitions manufacturers packaged new "generic" brands of military ammo at discount prices, often selling them in cases of 500 or 1,000 rounds. New lines of aftermarket accessories offered parts for full-automatic conversions, improved flash-hiders, scopes, folding stocks, and scores of other goodies. In 1989, the U.S. Bureau of Alcohol, Tobacco

---

[3]*SOF* regularly hired the firm of Starch, Inra, Hopper to study their readership. A condensed version of their 1986 report, from which these figures were taken, was made available to the press at the September 1986 *SOF* convention in Las Vegas.

and Firearms (ATF) estimated that two to three million military-style rifles had been sold in this country since the Vietnam War. The Bureau released these figures in response to the public outcry over a series of mass murders committed by psychotics armed with assault rifles.

But the Bureau's statistics tell only part of the story. In less than two decades, millions of American men had purchased combat rifles, pistols, and shotguns and begun training to fight their own personal wars. Elite combat shooting schools teaching the most modern techniques and often costing $500 to over $1,000 in tuition alone were attended not only by soldiers and police but by increasing numbers of civilians as well. Hundreds of new indoor pistol-shooting ranges opened for business in old warehouses and shopping malls around the country, locations ideal for city dwellers and suburbanites.

A new game of "tag" blurred the line between play and actual violence: men got the opportunity to hunt and shoot other men without killing them or risking death themselves. The National Survival Game was invented in 1981 by two old friends, one a screenwriter for the weight-lifting sagas that gave Arnold Schwarzenegger his first starring roles, and the other a former member of the Army's Long Range Reconnaissance Patrol (LRRP) in Vietnam.[4] Later called paintball because it utilized guns firing balls of watercolor paint, by 1987 the game was being played by at least fifty thousand people (mostly men) each weekend on both outdoor and indoor battlefields scattered across the nation. Players wore hard-plastic face masks intended to resemble those of ancient tribal warriors and dressed from head to toe in camouflage clothes imported by specialty stores from military outfitters around the world. The object of the game was to capture the opposing team's flag, inflicting the highest possible body count along the way.

One major park out in the Mojave Desert seventy miles southeast of Los Angeles was named Sat Cong Village. *Sat Cong* is a slang Vietnamese phrase meaning "Kill Communists" that had been popularized by the CIA as part of its psychological-warfare program. Sat Cong Village employed an attractive Asian woman to rent the guns, sell the paintballs, and collect the twenty-dollar entrance fee. Players had their choice of playing fields: Vietnam, Cambodia, or Nicaragua. On the Nicaragua field, the owner built a full-size facsimile of the crashed C-47 cargo plane contracted by Lieutenant Colonel Oliver North to supply the Contras. The scene even had three parachutes hanging from trees; the only thing missing was the sole survivor of the crash, Eugene Hasenfus.

The 1980s, then, saw the emergence of a highly energized culture of war and the   20 warrior. For all its varied manifestations, a few common features stood out. The New War culture was not so much military as paramilitary. The new warrior hero was only occasionally portrayed as a member of a conventional military

---

[4]Lionel Atwill, *Survival Game: Airgun National Manual* (New London, N.H.: The National Survival Game, Inc., 1987), 22–30.

or law enforcement unit; typically, he fought alone or with a small, elite group of fellow warriors. Moreover, by separating the warrior from his traditional state-sanctioned occupations — policeman or soldier — the New War culture presented the warrior roles as the ideal identity for *all* men. Bankers, professors, factory workers, and postal clerks could all transcend their regular stations in life and prepare for heroic battle against the enemies of society.

To many people, this new fascination with warriors and weapons seemed a terribly bad joke. The major newspapers and magazines that arbitrate what is to be taken seriously in American society scoffed at the attempts to resurrect the warrior hero. Movie critics were particularly disdainful of Stallone's Rambo films. *Rambo: First Blood, Part 2* was called "narcissistic jingoism" by *The New Yorker* and "hare-brained" by the *Wall Street Journal*. The *Washington Post* even intoned that "Sly's body looks fine. Now can't you come up with a workout for his soul?"

But in dismissing Rambo so quickly and contemptuously, commentators failed to notice the true significance of the emerging paramilitary culture. They missed the fact that quite a few people were not writing Rambo off as a complete joke; behind the Indian bandanna, necklace, and bulging muscles, a new culture hero affirmed such traditional American values as self-reliance, honesty, courage, and concern for fellow citizens. Rambo was a worker and a former enlisted man, not a smooth-talking professional. That so many seemingly well-to-do, sophisticated liberals hated him for both his politics and his uncouthness only added to his glory. Further, in their emphasis on Stallone's clownishness the commentators failed to see not only how widespread paramilitary culture had become but also its relation to the historical moment in which it arose.

Indeed, paramilitary culture can be understood only when it is placed in relation to the Vietnam War. America's failure to win that war was a truly profound blow. The nation's long, proud tradition of military victories, from the Revolutionary War through the century-long battles against the Indians to World Wars I and II, had finally come to an end. Politically, the defeat in Vietnam meant that the post–World War II era of overwhelming American political and military power in international affairs, the era that in 1945 *Time* magazine publisher Henry Luce had prophesied would be the "American Century," was over after only thirty years. No longer could U.S. diplomacy wield the big stick of military intervention as a ready threat — a significant part of the American public would no longer support such interventions, and the rest of the world knew it.

Moreover, besides eroding U.S. influence internationally, the defeat had subtle but serious effects on the American psyche. America has always celebrated war and the warrior. Our long, unbroken record of military victories has been crucially important both to the national identity and to the personal identity of many Americans — particularly men. The historian Richard Slotkin locates a primary "cultural archetype" of the nation in the story of a heroic warrior whose victories over the enemy symbolically affirm the country's fundamental goodness and power; we win our wars because, morally, we deserve to win. Clearly, the archetypical pattern Slotkin calls "regeneration through violence" was broken with the defeat in Vietnam.[5] The result was a massive disjunction in American culture, a crisis of self-image: If Americans were no longer winners, then who were they?

This disruption of cultural identity was amplified by other social transformations. During the 1960s, the civil rights and ethnic pride movements won many victories in their challenges to racial oppression. Also, during the 1970s and 1980s, the United States experienced massive waves of immigration from Mexico, Central America, Vietnam, Cambodia, Korea, and Taiwan. Whites, no longer secure in their power abroad, also lost their unquestionable dominance at home; for the first time, many began to feel that they too were just another hyphenated ethnic group, the Anglo-Americans.

Extraordinary economic changes also marked the 1970s and 1980s. U.S. manufacturing strength declined substantially; staggering trade deficits with other countries and the chronic federal budget deficits shifted the United States from creditor to debtor nation. The post–World War II American Dream — which promised a combination of technological progress and social reforms, together with high employment rates, rising wages, widespread home ownership, and ever increasing consumer options — no longer seemed a likely prospect for the great majority. At the same time, the rise in crime rates, particularly because of drug abuse and its accompanying violence, made people feel more powerless than ever.

While the public world dominated by men seemed to come apart, the private world of family life also felt the shocks. The feminist movement challenged formerly exclusive male domains, not only in the labor market and in many areas of political and social life but in the home as well. Customary male behavior was no longer acceptable in either private relationships or public policy. Feminism was widely experienced by men as a profound threat to their identity. Men had to change, but to what? No one knew for sure what a "good man" was anymore.

It is hardly surprising, then, that American men — lacking confidence in the government and the economy, troubled by the changing relations between the sexes, uncertain of their identity or their future — began to *dream*, to fantasize about the powers and features of another kind of man who could retake and reorder the world. And the hero of all these dreams was the paramilitary warrior. In the New War he fights the battles of Vietnam a thousand times, each time winning decisively. Terrorists and drug dealers are blasted into oblivion. Illegal aliens inside the United States and the hordes of nonwhites in the Third World are returned by force to their proper place. Women are revealed as dangerous temptresses who have to be mastered, avoided, or terminated.

Obviously these dreams represented a flight from the present and a rejection and denial of events of the preceding twenty years. But they also indicated a more profound and severe distress. The whole modern world was damned as

[5]Richard Slotkin, *Regeneration through Violence: The Mythology of the American Frontier, 1660–1860* (Middletown, Conn.: Wesleyan University Press, 1973).

unacceptable. Unable to find a rational way to face the tasks of rebuilding society and reinventing themselves, men instead sought refuge in myths from both America's frontier past and ancient times. Indeed, the fundamental narratives that shape paramilitary culture and its New War fantasies are often nothing but reinterpretations or reworkings of archaic warrior myths.

In ancient societies, the most important stories a people told about them- 30 selves concerned how the physical universe came into existence, how their ancestors first came to live in this universe, and how the gods, the universe, and society were related to one another. These cosmogonic, or creation, myths frequently posit a violent conflict between the good forces of order and the evil forces dedicated to the perpetuation of primordial chaos.[6] After the war in which the gods defeat the evil ones, they establish the "sacred order," in which all of the society's most important values are fully embodied. Some creation myths focus primarily on the sacred order and on the deeds of the gods and goddesses in paradise. Other myths, however, focus on the battles between the heroes and villains that lead up to the founding.[7] In these myths it is war and the warrior that are most sacred. American paramilitary culture borrows from both kinds of stories, but mostly from this second, more violent, type.

In either case, the presence, if not the outright predominance, of archaic male myths at the moment of crisis indicates just how far American men jumped psychically when faced with the declining power of their identities and organizations. The always-precarious balance in modern society between secular institutions and ways of thinking on the one hand and older patterns of belief informed by myth and ritual on the other tilted decisively in the direction of myth. The crisis revealed that at some deep, unconscious level these ancient male creation myths live on in the psyche of many men and that the images and tales from this mythic world of warriors and war still shape men's fantasies about who they are as men, their commitments to each other and to women, and their relationships to society and the state.

READING THE TEXT

1. How, according to Gibson, did the American defeat in Vietnam lead to the construction of a new kind of "warrior" (para. 20) identity for men?

2. Outline how popular culture helped to shape the warrior image, in Gibson's view.

3. What role does Gibson believe the women's movement played in constructing a new male identity?

4. Explain in your own words how today's "warrior" dreams relate to ancient mythologies.

5. Why does Gibson believe that the Rambo character should be taken seriously?

[6]Mircea Eliade, *Myth and Reality*, trans. Willard R. Trask (New York: Harper and Row, 1963).
    [7]Richard Stivers, *Evil in Modern Myth and Ritual* (Athens: University of Georgia Press, 1982).

READING THE SIGNS

1. **CONNECTING TEXTS**   Read or reread Michael A. Messner's "Power at Play: Sport and Gender Relations" (p. 635), and compare Messner's argument about the role of sports in the construction of male identity with Gibson's analysis of warrior dreams.

2. Gibson suggests that the warrior fantasies found throughout political and popular culture have dangerous real-world implications. Write a critical essay in which you support, complicate, or challenge this suggestion. As you develop your argument, consider such incidents as the 1999 Columbine High School massacre and the 2007 massacre at Virginia Tech.

3. **CONNECTING TEXTS**   Using Gibson's argument as your critical framework, write an analysis of a game that targets male players, such as EverQuest. What image of masculinity does the game portray? To develop your ideas, consult Clive Thompson's "Game Theories" (p. 460).

4. In class, brainstorm current films, TV shows, and video games that are targeted to a male audience. Then discuss the extent to which the warrior dreams that Gibson describes influence popular culture today.

MICHAEL A. MESSNER
Power at Play: Sport and Gender Relations

*Every little boy should play Little League, right? Sports help to build char-
acter, right? Perhaps, but according to Michael A. Messner, the games
men play are more than that: They are rituals designed to maintain the
ideology and values of a competitive and hierarchical culture. Because
masculine identity is rooted in the need to win, athletic competition,
according to Messner, causes "men to experience their own bodies as
machines . . . and to see other people's bodies as objects of their power
and domination." Author of* Power at Play: Sports and the Problem of
Masculinity *(1992), from which this selection is excerpted, Messner is a
professor and chair of the department of sociology at the University of
Southern California. He is also coeditor of* Men's Lives *(1995) and* Sport,
Men, and the Gender Order: Critical Feminist Perspectives *(1990) and
coauthor of* Sex, Violence, and Power in Sports: Rethinking Masculinity
(1994). He is, most recently, the author of Taking the Field: Women,
Men, and Sports *(2002),* Paradoxes of Youth and Sport *(2002), and*
Men's Lives *(2004).*

The closer we come to uncovering some form of exemplary masculinity, a
masculinity which is solid and sure of itself, the clearer it becomes that
masculinity is structured through contradiction: the more it asserts itself,
the more it calls itself into question.

— LYNN SEGAL, *Slow Motion*

In 1973, conservative writer George Gilder, later to become a central theorist
of the antifeminist family policies of the Reagan administration, was among
the first to sound the alarm that the contemporary explosion of female athletic
participation might threaten the very fabric of civilization. "Sports," Gilder
wrote, "are possibly the single most important male rite in modern society."
The woman athlete "reduces the game from a religious male rite to a mere
physical exercise, with some treacherous danger of psychic effect." Athletic performance, for males, embodies "an ideal of beauty and truth," while women's
participation represents a "disgusting perversion" of this truth.[1] In 1986, over
a decade later, a similar view was expressed by John Carroll in a respected
academic journal. Carroll lauded the masculine "virtue and grace" of sport, and
defended it against its critics, especially feminists. He concluded that in order
to preserve sport's "naturally conserving and creating" tendencies, especially
in the realms of "the moral and the religious, . . . women should once again
be prohibited from sport: They are the true defenders of the humanist values
that emanate from the household, the values of tenderness, nurture and

[1] G. Gilder, *Sexual Suicide* (New York: Bantam Books, 1973), pp. 216, 218.

compassion, and this most important role must not be confused by the military and political values inherent in sport. Likewise, sport should not be muzzled by humanist values: it is the living arena for the great virtue of manliness."[2]

The key to Gilder's and Carroll's chest-beating about the importance of maintaining sport as a "male rite" is their neo-Victorian belief that male-female biological differences predispose men to aggressively dominate public life, while females are naturally suited to serve as the nurturant guardians of home and hearth. As Gilder put it, "The tendency to bond with other males in intensely purposeful and dangerous activity is said to come from the collective demands of pursuing large animals. The female body, on the other hand, more closely resembles the body of nonhunting primates. A woman throws, for example, very like a male chimpanzee."[3] This perspective ignores a wealth of historical, anthropological, and biological data that suggest that the equation of males with domination of public life and females with the care of the domestic sphere is a cultural and historical construction.[4] In fact, Gilder's and Carroll's belief that sport, *a socially constructed institution*, is needed to sustain male-female differences contradicts their assumption that these differences are "natural." As R. W. Connell has argued, social practices that exaggerate male-female difference (such as dress, adornment, and sport) "are part of a continuing effort to sustain a social definition of gender, an effort that is necessary precisely *because the biological logic . . . cannot sustain the gender categories.*"[5]

Indeed, I must argue against the view that sees sport as a natural realm within which some essence of masculinity unfolds. Rather, sport is a social institution that, in its dominant forms, was created by and for men. It should not be surprising, then, that my research with male athletes reveals an affinity between the institution of sport and men's developing identities. As the young males in my study became committed to athletic careers, the gendered values of the institution of sport made it extremely unlikely that they would construct anything but the kinds of personalities and relationships that were consistent with the dominant values and power relations of the larger gender order. The competitive hierarchy of athletic careers encouraged the development of masculine identities based on very narrow definitions of public

[2]J. Carroll, "Sport: Virtue and Grace," *Theory, Culture and Society* 3 (1986), pp. 91–98. Jennifer Hargreaves delivers a brilliant feminist rebuttal to Carroll's masculinist defense of sport in the same issue of the journal. See J. Hargreaves, "Where's the Virtue? Where's the Grace? A Discussion of the Social Production of Gender through Sport," pp. 109–21.

[3]G. Gilder, p. 221.

[4]For a critical overview of the biological research on male-female difference, see A. Fausto-Sterling, *Myths of Gender: Biological Theories about Men and Women* (New York: Basic Books, 1985). For an overview of the historical basis of male domination, see R. Lee and R. Daly, "Man's Domination and Woman's Oppression: The Question of Origins," in M. Kaufman, ed., *Beyond Patriarchy: Essays by Men on Pleasure, Power, and Change* (Toronto: Oxford University Press, 1987), pp. 30–44.

[5]R. W. Connell, *Gender and Power* (Stanford: Stanford University Press, 1987), p. 81 (emphasis in original text).

success. Homophobia and misogyny were the key bonding agents among male athletes, serving to construct a masculine personality that disparaged anything considered "feminine" in women, in other men, or in oneself. The fact that winning was premised on physical power, strength, discipline, and willingness to take, ignore, or deaden pain inclined men to experience their own bodies as machines, as instruments of power and domination — and to see other peoples' bodies as objects of their power and domination. . . .

The Costs of Athletic Masculinity

As boys, the men in my study were initially attracted to playing sport because it was a primary means to connect with other people — especially fathers, brothers, and male peers. But as these young males became committed to athletic careers, their identities became directly tied to continued public success. Increasingly, it was not just "being there with the guys" but beating the other guys that mattered most. As their need for connection with others became defined more abstractly, through their relationships with "the crowd," their actual relationships with other people tended to become distorted. Other individuals were increasingly likely to be viewed as (male) objects to be defeated or (female) objects to be manipulated and sexually conquered. As a result, the socially learned means through which they constructed their identities (public achievement within competitive hierarchies) did not deliver what was most craved and needed: intimate connection and unity with other people. More often than not, athletic careers have exacerbated existing insecurities and ambivalences in young men's developing identities, thus further diminishing their capacity for intimate relationships with others.

In addition to relational costs, many athletes — especially those in "combat sports" such as football — paid a heavy price in terms of health. While the successful operation of the male body-as-weapon may have led, for a time, to victories on the athletic field, it also led to injuries and other health problems that lasted far beyond the end of the athletic career.

It is extremely unlikely that a public illumination of the relational and health costs paid by male athletes will lead to a widespread rejection of sport by young males. There are three reasons for this. First, the continued affinity between sport and developing masculine identities suggests that many boys will continue to be attracted to athletic careers for the same reasons they have in the past. Second, since the successful athlete often basks in the limelight of public adoration, the relational costs of athletic masculinity are often not apparent until after the athletic career ends, and he suddenly loses his connection to the crowd. Third, though athletes may recognize the present and future health costs of their athletic careers, they are likely to view them as dues willingly paid. In short, there is a neat enough fit between the psychological and emotional tendencies of young males and the institution of sport that these costs — if they are recognized at all — will be considered "necessary evils," the price men pay for the promise of "being on top."[6]

Competing Masculinities

Boys' emerging identities may influence them to be attracted to sport, but they nevertheless tend to experience athletic careers differently, based upon variations in class, race, and sexual orientation. Despite their similarities, boys and young men bring different problems, anxieties, hopes, and dreams to their athletic experiences, and thus tend to draw different meanings from, and make different choices about, their athletic careers.

RACE, CLASS, AND THE CONSTRUCTION OF ATHLETIC MASCULINITY

My interviews reveal that within a social context stratified by class and by race, the choice to pursue — or not to pursue — an athletic career is determined by the individual's rational assessment of the available means to construct a respected masculine identity. White middle-class men were likely to reject athletic careers and shift their masculine strivings to education and nonsport careers. Conversely, men from poor and blue-collar backgrounds, especially blacks, often perceived athletic careers to be their best chance for success in the public sphere. For nearly all of the men from lower-class backgrounds, the status and respect that they received through sport was temporary — it did not translate into upward mobility.

One might conclude from this that the United States should adopt a public policy of encouraging young lower-class black males to "just say no" to sport. This strategy would be doomed to failure, because poor young black men's decisions to pursue athletic careers can be viewed as rational, given the constraints that they continue to face. Despite the increased number of black role models in nonsport professions, employment opportunities for young black males actually deteriorated in the 1980s, and nonathletic opportunities

---

[6]Indeed, "men's liberationists" of the 1970s were overly optimistic in believing that a public illumination of the "costs of masculinity" would induce men to "reject the male role." See, for instance, W. Farrell, *The Liberated Man* (New York: Bantam Books, 1975); J. Nichols, *Men's Liberation: A New Definition of Masculinity* (New York: Penguin Books, 1975). These men's liberationists underestimated the extent to which the costs of masculinity are linked to the promise of power and privilege. One commentator went so far as to argue that the privileges of masculinity were a "myth" perpetrated by women to keep men in destructive success-object roles. See H. Goldberg, *The Hazards of Being Male: Surviving the Myth of Masculine Privilege* (New York: Signet, 1976). For more recent discussions of the need to analyze both the "costs" and the "privileges" of dominant conceptions of masculinity, see M. E. Kann, "The Costs of Being on Top," *Journal of the National Association for Women Deans, Administrators, and Counselors* 49 (1986): 29–37; and M. A. Messner, "Men Studying Masculinity: Some Epistemological Questions in Sport Sociology," *Sociology of Sport Journal* 7 (1990): 136–53.

in higher education also declined. By 1985, blacks constituted 14 percent of the college-aged (18–24 years) U.S. population, but as a proportion of students in four-year colleges and universities, they had dropped to 8 percent. By contrast, black men constituted 49 percent of male college basketball players, and 61 percent of male basketball players in institutions that grant athletic scholarships.[7] For young black men, then, organized sport appears to be more likely to get them to college than their own efforts in nonathletic activities.

In addition to viewing athletic careers as an arena for career success, there is considerable evidence that black male athletes have used sport as a cultural space within which to forge a uniquely expressive style of masculinity, a "cool pose." As Richard Majors puts it,

> Due to structural limitations, a black man may be impotent in the intellectual, political, and corporate world, but he can nevertheless display a potent personal style from the pulpit, in entertainment, and in athletic competition, with a verve that borders on the spectacular. Through the virtuosity of a performance, he tips the socially imbalanced scales in his favor and sends the subliminal message: "See me, touch me, hear me, but, white man, you can't copy me!"[8]

In particular, black men have put their "stamp" on the game of basketball. There is considerable pride in U.S. black communities in the fact that black men have come to dominate the higher levels of basketball — and in the expressive style with which they have come to do so. The often aggressive "cool pose" of black male athletes can thus be interpreted as a form of masculinity that symbolically challenges the class constraints and the institutionalized racism that so many young black males face.

SEXUAL ORIENTATION AND THE CONSTRUCTION OF ATHLETIC MASCULINITY

Until very recently, it was widely believed that gay men did not play organized sports. Nongay people tended to stereotype gay men as "too effeminate" to be athletic. This belief revealed a confusion between sexual orientation and gender. We now know that there is no neat fit between how "masculine" or "feminine" a man is, and whether or not he is sexually attracted to women, to men, to both, or to neither.[9] Interestingly, some gay writers also believed

[7]W. J. Wilson and K. M. Neckerman, "Poverty and Family Structure: The Widening Gap between Evidence and Public Policy Issues," in S. H. Danzinger and D. H. Weinberg, eds., *Fighting Poverty* (Cambridge: Harvard University Press, 1986), pp. 232–59; F. J. Berghorn et al., "Racial Participation in Men's and Women's Intercollegiate Basketball: Continuity and Change, 1958–1985." *Sociology of Sport Journal* 5 (1988), 107–24.

[8]R. Majors, "'Cool Pose': Black Masculinity and Sports," in M. A. Messner and D. F. Sabo, *Sport, Men, and the Gender Order: Critical Feminist Perspectives* (Champaign, Ill.: Human Kinetics Publishers, 1990), p. 111.

[9]See S. Kleinberg, "The New Masculinity of Gay Men, and Beyond," in Kaufman, *Beyond Patriarchy*, pp. 120–38.

that gay men were not active in sport. For instance, Dennis Altman wrote in 1982 that most gay men were not interested in sport, since they tended to reject the sexual repression, homophobia, and misogyny that are built into the sportsworld.[10]

The belief that gay men are not interested or involved in sport has proven to be wrong. People who made this assumption were observing the overtly masculine and heterosexual culture of sport and then falsely concluding that all of the people within that culture must be heterosexual. My interview with Mike T. and biographies of gay athletes such as David Kopay suggest that young gay males are often attracted to sport because they are just as concerned as heterosexual boys and young men with constructing masculine identities.[11] Indeed, a young closeted gay male like Mike T. may view the projection of an unambiguous masculinity as even more critical than his nongay counterparts do. As Mike told me, "There are a *lot* of gay men in sports," but they are almost all closeted and thus not visible to public view.

As Mike's story illustrates, gay male athletes often share similar motivations and experiences with nongay athletes. This suggests that as long as gay athletes stay closeted, they are contributing to the construction of culturally dominant conceptions of masculinity. However, Brian Pronger's recent research suggests that many gay male athletes experience organized sport in unique ways. In particular, Pronger's interviews with gay male athletes indicate that they have a "paradoxical" relationship to the male athletic culture. Though the institution itself is built largely on the denial (or sublimation) of any erotic bond between men, Pronger argues, many (but not all) gay athletes experience life in the locker room, as well as the excitement of athletic competition, as highly erotic. Since their secret desires (and, at times, secret actions) run counter to the heterosexist culture of the male locker room, closeted gay male athletes develop ironic sensibilities about themselves, their bodies, and the sporting activity itself.[12] Gay men are sexually oppressed through sport, Pronger argues, but the ironic ways they often redefine the athletic context can be interpreted as a form of resistance with the potential to undermine and transform the heterosexist culture of sport.

THE LIMITS OF MASCULINE RESISTANCES

Men's experience of athletic careers — and the meanings they assign to these experiences — are contextualized by class, race, and sexual orientation. My research, and that of other social scientists, suggests that black male athletes 15

---

[10]D. Altman, *The Homosexualization of America* (Boston: Beacon Press, 1982).

[11]See D. Kopay and P. D. Young, *The Dave Kopay Story* (New York: Arbor House, 1977).

[12]B. Pronger, "Gay Jocks: A Phenomenology of Gay Men in Athletics," in Messner and Sabo, *Sport, Men, and the Gender Order*, pp. 141–52; and *The Arena of Masculinity: Sports, Homosexuality, and the Meaning of Sex* (New York: St. Martin's Press, 1990).

construct and draw on an expressive and "cool" masculinity in order to resist racial oppression. Gay male athletes sometimes construct and draw on an "ironic" masculinity in order to resist sexual oppression. In other words, poor, black, and gay men have often found sport to be an arena in which they can build a masculinity that is, in some ways, resistant to the oppressions they face within hierarchies of intermale dominance.

But how real is the challenge these resistant masculinities pose to the role that sport has historically played in perpetuating existing differences and inequalities? A feminist perspective reveals the limited extent to which we can interpret black and gay athletic masculinities as liberating. Through a feminist lens, we can see that in adopting as their expressive vehicle many of the dominant aspects of athletic masculinity (narrow definitions of public success; aggressive, sometimes violent competition; glorification of the athletic male body-as-machine; verbal misogyny and homophobia), poor, black, and gay male athletes contribute to the continued subordination of women, as well as to the circumscription of their own relationships and development.

Tim Carrigan, Bob Connell, and John Lee assert that rather than undermining social inequality, men's struggles within class, racial, and sexual hierarchies of intermale dominance serve to reinforce men's global subordination of women. Although strains caused by differences and inequalities among men represent potential avenues for social change, ultimately, "the fissuring of the categories 'men' and 'women' is one of the central facts about a patriarchal power and the way it works. In the case of men, the crucial division is between hegemonic masculinity and various subordinated masculinities."[13] Hegemonic masculinity is thus defined in relation to various subordinated masculinities as well as in relation to femininities. This is a key insight for the contemporary meaning of sport. Utilizing the concept of "multiple masculinities," we can begin to understand how race, class, age, and sexual hierarchies among men help to construct and legitimize men's overall power and privilege over women. In addition, the false promise of sharing in the fruits of hegemonic masculinity often ties black, working-class, or gay men into their marginalized and subordinate status. For instance, my research suggests that while black men's development of "cool pose" within sport can be interpreted as creative resistance against one form of social domination (racism), it also demonstrates the limits of an agency that adopts other forms of social domination (athletic masculinity) as its vehicle.

My research also suggests how homophobia within athletic masculine cultures tends to lock men — whether gay or not — into narrowly defined heterosexual identities and relationships. Within the athletic context, homophobia is closely linked with misogyny in ways that ultimately serve to bond men together as superior to women. Given the extremely oppressive levels of

---

[13]T. Carrigan, B. Connell, and J. Lee, "Hard and Heavy: Toward a New Sociology of Masculinity," *Theory and Society* 14 (1985): 551–603.

homophobia within organized sport, it is understandable why the vast majority of gay male athletes would decide to remain closeted. But the public construction of a heterosexual/masculine status requires that a closeted gay athlete actively participate in (or at the very least, tolerate) the ongoing group expressions of homophobia and misogyny — what Mike T. called "locker room garbage." Thus, though he may feel a sense of irony, and may even confidentially express that sense of irony to gay male friends or to researchers, the public face that the closeted gay male athlete presents to the world is really no different from that of his nongay teammates. As long as he is successful in this public presentation-of-self as heterosexual/masculine, he will continue to contribute to (and benefit from) men's power over women.

SPORT IN GAY COMMUNITIES

The fissuring of the category "men," then, as it is played out within the dominant institution of sport, does little to threaten — indeed, may be a central mechanism in — the reconstruction of existing class, racial, sexual, and gender inequalities.[14] Nevertheless, since the outset of the gay liberation movement in the early 1970s, organized sport has become an integral part of developing gay and lesbian communities. The ways that "gay" sports have been defined and organized are sometimes different — even radically different — than the dominant institution of sport in society.

The most public sign of the growing interest in athletics in gay communities was the rapid growth and popularity of bodybuilding among many young, urban gay men in the 1970s and early 1980s. The meanings of gay male bodybuilding are multiple and contradictory.[15] On the one hand, gay male bodybuilding overtly eroticizes the muscular male body, thus potentially disrupting the tendency of sport to eroticize male bodies under the guise of aggression and competition. On the other hand, the building of muscular bodies is often motivated by a conscious need by gay men to prove to the world that they are "real men." Gay bodybuilding thus undermines cultural stereotypes of homosexual men as "nelly," effeminate, and womanlike. But it also tends to adopt and promote a very conventional equation of masculinity with physical strength

[14]One potentially important, but largely unexplored, fissure among men is that between athletes and nonathletes. There are tens of millions of boys who do *not* pursue athletic careers. Many boys dislike sport. Others may yearn to be athletes, but may not have the body size, strength, physical capabilities, coordination, emotional predisposition, or health that is necessary to successfully compete in sports. What happens to these boys and young men? What kinds of adult masculine identities and relationships do they eventually develop? Does the fact of not having been an athlete play any significant role in their masculine identities, goals, self-images, and relationships? The answers to these questions, of course, lie outside the purview of my study. But they are key to understanding the contemporary role that sport plays in constructions of gender.

[15]For interesting discussions of bodybuilding, gender, and sexuality, see B. Glassner, *Bodies: Why We Look the Way We Do (and How We Feel about It)* (New York: G. P. Putnam's Sons, 1988); A. M. Klein, "Little Big Man: Hustling, Gender Narcissism, and Homophobia in Bodybuilding," in Messner and Sabo, *Sport, Men, and the Gender Order*, pp. 127–40.

and muscularity.[16] In effect, then, as gay bodybuilders attempt to sever the cultural link between masculinity and heterosexuality, they uncritically affirm a conventional dichotomization of masculinity/male vs. femininity/ female.

By contrast, some gay athletes have initiated alternative athletic institutions that aim to challenge conventional views of sexuality and gender. Originally Mike T. had gone into sport to prove that he was "male," and cover up the fact that he was gay. When his career as an Olympic athlete finally ended, he came out publicly, and soon was a very active member of the San Francisco Bay Area gay community. He rekindled his interest in the arts and dance. He also remained very active in athletics, and he increasingly imagined how wonderful it would be to blend the beauty and exhilaration of sport, as he had experienced it, with the emergent, liberating values of the feminist, gay, and lesbian communities of which he was a part. In 1982, his dream became a reality, as 1,300 athletes from twelve different nations gathered in San Francisco to participate in the first ever Gay Games.[17]

Though many of the events in the Gay Games are "conventional" sports (track and field, swimming, etc.), and a number of "serious athletes" compete in the events, overall the Games reflect a value system and a vision based on feminist and gay liberationist ideals of equality and universal participation. As Mike T. said,

> You don't win by beating someone else. We defined winning as doing your very best. That way, everyone is a winner. And we have age-group competition, so all ages are involved. We have parity: If there's a men's sport, there's a women's sport to complement it. And we go out and recruit in Third World and minority areas. All of these people are gonna get together for a week, they're gonna march in together, they're gonna hold hands, and they'll say, "Jesus Christ! This is wonderful!" There's this

[16]Alan Klein's research revealed that nongay male bodybuilders are also commonly motivated by a need to make a public statement with their muscular bodies that they are indeed "masculine." To the nongay bodybuilder, muscles are the ultimate sign of heterosexual masculinity. But, ironically, as one nongay male bodybuilder put it, "We're everything the U.S. is supposed to stand for: strength, determination, everything to be admired. But it's not the girls that like us, it's the fags!" Interestingly, Klein found that many male bodybuilders who defined themselves as "straight" (including the one quoted above) made a living by prostituting themselves to gay men. See Klein, "Little Big Man," p. 135.

For a thought-provoking feminist analysis of the contradictory relationship between gay male sexuality and masculinity, see T. Edwards, "Beyond Sex and Gender: Masculinity, Homosexuality, and Social Theory," in J. Hearn and D. Morgan, eds., *Men, Masculinities, and Social Theory* (London: Unwin Hyman, 1990), pp. 110–23.

[17]The Gay Games were originally called the "Gay Olympics," but the U.S. Olympic Committee went to court to see that the word "Olympics" was not used to denote this event. Despite the existence of "Police Olympics," "Special Olympics," "Senior Olympics," "Xerox Olympics," "Armenian Olympics," even "Crab Cooking Olympics," the U.S.O.C. chose to enforce their control legally over the term "Olympics" when it came to the "Gay Olympics." For further discussion of the politics of the Gay Games, see M. A. Messner, "Gay Athletes and the Gay Games: An Interview with Tom Waddell," *M: Gentle Men for Gender Justice* 13 (1984): 13–14.

discovery: "I had no idea women were such fun!" and, "God! Blacks are okay — I didn't do anything to offend him, and we became *friends*!" and, "God, that guy over there is in his sixties, and I had no *idea* they were so sexually *active*!" — [laughs].

This emphasis on bridging differences, overcoming prejudices, and building relationships definitely enhanced the athletic experience for one participant I interviewed. This man said that he loved to swim, and even loved to compete, because it "pushed" him to swim "a whole lot better." Yet in past competitions, he had always come in last place. As he put it, "The Gay Games were just wonderful in many respects. One of them was that people who came in second, or third, and *last* got standing ovations from the crowd — the crowd genuinely recognized the thrill of giving a damn good shot, regardless of where you came in, and gave support to that. Among the competitors, there was a whole lot of joking and supportiveness."

In 1986, 3,482 athletes participated in Gay Games II in San Francisco. In 1990, at Gay Games III in Vancouver, 7,200 athletes continued the vision of building, partly through sport, an "exemplary community" that eliminates sexism, homophobia, and racism. Mike T. described what the Gay Games mean to him:

> To me, it's one of those steps in a thousand-mile journey to try and raise consciousness and enlighten people — *not* just people outside the gay community, but within the gay community as well, [because] we're just as racist, ageist, nationalistic, and chauvinistic as anybody else. Maybe it's simplistic to some people, you know, but why does it have to be complicated? Put people in a position where they can experience this process of discovery, and here it is! I just hope that this is something that'll take hold and a lot of people will get the idea.

The Gay Games represent a radical break from past and current conceptions of the role of sport in society. But they do not represent a major challenge to sport as an institution. Alternative athletic venues like the Gay Games, since they exist outside of the dominant sports institution, do not directly confront or change the dominant structure. On the other hand, these experiments are valuable in terms of demonstrating the fact that alternative value systems and structures are possible.[18]

---

[18]During the 1982 Gay Games in San Francisco, the major local newspapers tended to cover the Games mostly in the "lifestyle" sections of the paper, not in the sports pages. Alternative sports demonstrate the difficulties of attempting to change sport in the absence of larger institutional transformations. For instance, the European sport of korfball was developed explicitly as a sex-egalitarian sport. The rules of korfball aim to neutralize male-female biological differences that may translate into different levels of ability. But recent research shows that old patterns show up, even among the relatively "enlightened" korfball players. Korfball league officials are more likely to be male than female. More important, the more "key" roles within the game appear to be dominated by men, while women are partially marginalized. See D. Summerfield and A. White, "Korfball: A Model of Egalitarianism?" *Sociology of Sport Journal* 6 (1989): 144–51.

READING THE TEXT

1. Why, in Messner's view, did conservatives such as George Gilder and John Carroll want to prohibit women from competing in athletic competitions?

2. What does Messner mean when he writes that "sport is a social institution that . . . was created by and for men" (para. 3)?

3. What roles do class, race, and sexual orientation play in the construction of athletic masculinity, according to Messner?

4. In what ways, according to Messner, do the Gay Games differ from the Olympic Games?

READING THE SIGNS

1. In your journal, explore what athletic participation, whether in organized sports such as Little League or in informal activities such as jogging or hiking, has meant to you. Do you believe such participation has shaped your attitudes toward gender roles? If you haven't participated much in sports, what is your attitude toward athletic competition?

2. Write an argumentative essay challenging or supporting George Gilder's position that the female athlete "reduces the game from a religious male rite to a mere physical exercise, with some treacherous danger of psychic effect" (para. 1).

3. In class, outline the racial and gender coding of professional sports. Which ethnicities dominate which sports? In which sports have women received social acceptance? Then discuss the reasons for the ethnic and gender patterns you see.

4. Study a magazine such as *Sports Illustrated* and write an essay in which you explain the extent to which the magazine perpetuates the traditional attitudes toward gender roles that Messner claims sports encourage.

5. **CONNECTING TEXTS**   In class, form mixed-gender teams and debate Messner's contention that sports encourage homophobia and misogyny. To develop your ideas, consult Mariah Burton Nelson's "I Won. I'm Sorry" (p. 539).

CONSTRUCTING RACE
Readings in Multicultural Semiotics

Beyond the Dominant Culture

Michael Jordan. Michael Jackson. Miles Davis. Duke Ellington. Ella Fitzgerald. Jimi Hendrix. Oprah Winfrey. Whitney Houston. Serena Williams. Venus Williams. Tiger Woods. Tupac Shakur. Barry Bonds. Bill Cosby. Eddie Murphy. Will Smith. Denzel Washington. Muhammad Ali. Shaquille O'Neal. Naomi Campbell. Halle Berry. Mariah Carey. Alicia Keys. Usher. Seal. Beyoncé. Kanye. 50 Cent.

The list could go on, of course, but in naming just this partial roster of current and historic African American popular cultural superstars we mean to point to a multicultural phenomenon that can make one think twice about what is meant by the words *dominant culture*. For while Caucasians remain the dominant ethnic group in America politically and economically and European culture remains our dominant high culture, when it comes to popular culture, African Americans enjoy an especially prominent status. Indeed, given that African Americans are the originators, or co-originators, of America's most popular musical forms today — hip-hop, rock 'n' roll, and jazz — and are often the stars of America's most popular professional sports, it is impossible to imagine modern popular culture without their contribution.

It has not always been this way, however. In its early days, jazz was denounced as "jungle music" by white critics, and rock 'n' roll was regarded as the "devil's music" in the Deep South. Black athletes were barred from participation in mainstream professional sports (the Harlem Globetrotters were created because blacks weren't allowed in the early NBA), and black actors often had to accept demeaning roles to get any work in Hollywood (think of

Amos 'n' Andy or of Prissy in *Gone with the Wind*). Even today, the National Association for the Advancement of Colored People (NAACP) commonly objects that each new television season underrepresents African Americans.

But things are changing fast. The monocultural perspective that regards American culture as a product of European history — the extension of a tradition that began in Greece and Rome and that was brought to America by the English — is being challenged by a multicultural point of view that explores the contributions of such historically marginalized Americans as Africans, Asians, Latinos, and Native Americans in the creation of American culture. And nowhere has this contribution been more prominent than in the realm of popular culture.

Interpreting Multicultural Semiotics

Until recently, the multicultural nature of American popular culture has been most visible in binary terms: that is, in black and white. But with pop superstars including Ricky Martin, Marc Anthony, and Jennifer Lopez, along with the increasing number of Dominican stars in professional baseball, the Latino and Latina contribution to popular culture is no longer in the shadows. Indeed, the breakout success of the television series *Ugly Betty* has led to an awakening in Hollywood that is changing the face of prime time as new programming follows in its footsteps. The Asian American contribution, which had tended in the past to be restricted to a certain stereotyping of Asians as experts in the martial arts, is continuing to grow, with actors and actresses like Ming-Na Wen, Lucy Liu, Daniel Dae Kim, Russell Wong, Margaret Cho, and Sandra Oh achieving popularity, and directors like John Woo achieving success. Asian characters starring in such programs as *Heroes* and *Grey's Anatomy* mark a new television trend as well.

Native Americans, for their part, are still struggling with a dominant cultural tendency to view them either through the eye of a gun sight (the most common perspective of mid-century cinema and TV) or to sentimentalize them as New Age Noble Savages (consider Oliver Stone's use of Native American

---

Exploring the Signs of Race

In your journal, reflect on the question, "Who are you?" How does your ethnicity contribute to your sense of self? Are there other factors that contribute to your identity? If so, what are they, and how do they relate to your ethnicity? If you don't perceive yourself in ethnic terms, why do you think that's the case?

Will Smith in *Ali*, 2001.

characters as symbols, rather than as fully fledged characters, in *The Doors* and *Natural Born Killers*). As literary critic Gerald Vizenor has observed, the Native American in pop culture is still more of a simulation than a reality, someone seen through non-Native eyes and stereotyped accordingly — though the critical and popular success of the movie *Whale Rider* may help change that in the future.

The prominent place that African Americans enjoy in popular culture was underscored in 2001 with the making of *Ali*, a movie that brought together two of the defining icons of contemporary American popular culture: Muhammad Ali and Will Smith. Commanding what was then the highest box-office gross ever for a Christmas Day release, the movie was a potent signifier of the way that, at least within popular culture, the racial polarities of American history are receding. Once, Muhammad Ali was an outlaw, whose change of name and religion, along with his high-profile refusal to be drafted into the armed services, made him a symbol of racial resistance. In his famous showdown with Joe Frazier — the historic "thrilla in Manila" — he was widely regarded as black America's champion in a confrontation in which he denounced his opponent as an Uncle Tom in the service of white America — an aspersion that it took Ali thirty years to apologize for to the wounded Frazier. But now, Muhammad Ali is a national symbol like Martin Luther King Jr. Indeed, in the wake of the September 11, 2001, attacks, he was asked to make a public service address, to be broadcast throughout the Islamic world, explaining that America's war on terrorism is not a war on Islam.

As a cultural signifier, *Ali* can also be related to Spike Lee's *Malcolm X*, a film that marked the culmination of a historical process by which a symbol of racial resistance and revolution has been transformed into a national hero who has even been featured on his own postage stamp. Such an association can show us how *Ali*'s release was no isolated event: It was a signifier of a change in American cultural relations that has seen the emergence of black heroes who are as celebrated as such traditional heroes as George Washington and Abraham Lincoln. Indeed, a related signifier in this context is the fact that both Washington's and Lincoln's birthdays, once observed as separate national holidays, have been consolidated into a single, and anonymous, Presidents' Day, while Martin Luther King Jr. Day is a named national holiday.

The careers of the actors who played Ali and Malcolm X in these two films are also culturally significant. Before Denzel Washington was picked to play Malcolm X in Lee's movie, he had already established himself as one of Hollywood's leading men. By playing Malcolm X, one of the most powerful symbols in African American history, Washington, who was certainly aware of the historic mantle that was being cast across his shoulders, fully emerged as another such icon. A later signifier of Washington's iconic status was his portrayal of a corrupt cop in *Training Day*. Prior to this film, Washington always played the good guy. By playing Alonzo in *Training Day*, Washington demonstrated not only that he could play villains as well as heroes but that his place in pop culture was so secure he could be cast as a bad guy without exacerbating sensitivities with regard to negative stereotyping. At a time when Hollywood is trying to live down a history of portraying black men as criminals and callous womanizers, few black actors can safely be cast in such roles. But Denzel Washington's iconic status ensured that his casting in this role would be seen as a star branching out into new role possibilities and not as a denigrating stereotype.

Will Smith's role as Muhammad Ali, for its part, is semiotically related to Washington's *Malcolm X*. For by playing Ali — indeed, as *Entertainment Weekly* noted at the time, by *becoming* Ali — Smith signified his ascension into the ranks of certified cultural icons. Interestingly, Smith began his career as a rapper, before rap had fully crossed over to become young America's favorite form of musical entertainment. Then he moved to prime-time TV in *The Fresh Prince of Bel-Air*, and from there turned to the movies, where he has become one of Hollywood's leading men. Playing Ali, then, gave Smith a chance not only to aim for full cultural superstardom but also to become involved, at least imaginatively, in professional sports, a career move that, in effect, placed him in a starring role in all four of America's leading entertainment venues.

Who Are We?

A multicultural semiotics expands the frame of reference when it comes to analyzing cultural mythologies, because if mythologies are culturally constructed, one has to take into account just who is constructing them. The traditional,

Discussing the Signs of Race

Demographers predict that, by the middle of the twenty-first century, America will no longer have any racial or ethnic majority population. In class, discuss what effects this may have on Americans' sense of this country's history, culture, and identity.

monocultural perspective takes for granted a specific, dominant cultural identity that performs such constructions, but multiculturalism involves many identities, and thus the question of personal and social identity arises. To put this another way, if your worldview depends upon who you are, analyzing who you are is an essential part of interpreting your worldview.

So, ask yourself a simple question: "Who am I?" Ask a classmate, "Who are you?" What's the answer? Did your classmate give her name? Did you? Or did each of you answer differently? Did you say "I am an American"? Or did you say "I am an African American," or an "Asian American," or a "Latino," or a "Native American"? Would you answer "I am a European American" or a "Jewish American"? However you answered the question, can you say why you answered as you did?

To ask how you identify yourself and why you do so as you do is to probe further into the semiotics of race and culture in America's multicultural society. Some of you may believe that there is a right answer to our question, that it is essential that all Americans think of themselves as *Americans* first and foremost. Others of you may believe just as strongly that your ethnic identity comes first. In either case, your beliefs reflect a cultural mythology that guides you in your most fundamental thoughts about your identity. Let's look at those mythologies for a moment.

Say that you feel that all American citizens should view themselves simply as Americans. If so, your feelings reflect a basic cultural mythology best known as the myth of the American "melting pot." This is the belief that America offers all its citizens the opportunity to blend together into one harmonious whole that will erase the many differences among us on behalf of a new, distinctly American, identity. This belief has led many immigrants to seek to assimilate into what they perceive as the dominant American culture, shedding the specific cultural characteristics that may distinguish them from what they see as the American norm. And it is a belief that ideally stands behind some of the most generous impulses in our culture.

But what if you don't buy this belief? What if, as far as you are concerned, you're proud to belong to a different community, one that differs from the basically Anglo-Saxon culture that has become the dominant and normative culture into which other cultures are expected to assimilate? Or what if you and your people have found that you were never really allowed to blend in anyway, that in spite of the promise, the melting pot was never meant for you? If so, how does the myth of the melting pot look to you? Does it look the same as it would to someone who never had any trouble assimilating, or never needed to, because he or she already belonged to the dominant culture?

To see that the myth of the melting pot looks different depending on who is looking at it is to see why it is so precious to some Americans and so irrelevant to others. It is to realize again the fundamental semiotic precept that our social values are culturally determined rather than inscribed in the marble of absolute truth. This may be difficult to accept, especially if you and your classmates come from the same culture and hence all hold the same values. But if you know people who are different, you might want to ask them how the myth of the melting pot looks from their perspective. Does it look like an ideal that our nation should strive to achieve? Or does it look like an invitation to cultural submission? It all depends on who's looking.

The failure to recognize that different people view the melting pot differently is one of the major sources of racial misunderstanding and, thus, conflict in America today. On the one hand, we need to realize that many Americans, particularly nonwhites, have felt excluded from full economic and cultural participation in American life and may deeply resent the view that we all should just see ourselves as Americans. But on the other hand, we also need to realize that many of today's Americans descend from non-Anglo-Saxon European immigrants who embraced the image of the melting pot,

Members of Dem Franchize Boyz receive an award for a ring tone that qualified for Platinum status (one million copies sold), Wednesday, June 14, 2006, in New York.

Reading Race on the Net

Many Internet sites are devoted to the culture of a particular ethnicity, such as Afronet (**www.afronet.com**). Visit several such sites, and survey the breadth of information available about different ethnic groups. To what extent can a researcher learn about various ethnicities on the Net? Is there any information that you wish would appear on the Net but could not find? Do you find any material problematic?

---

prospered, and passed their gratitude on to their descendants. For such Americans, the myth of the melting pot appears to be so benevolent that it doesn't seem right to attack it. A debate that acknowledges the historical reasons for this difference in viewpoint has a better chance to result in some consensus than one that presumes that one side's affection for the melting pot is "racist" or that the other's resentment is "petty" or "un-American."

Such a recognition is difficult to achieve, of course, because of the way that cultural worldviews tend to present themselves in absolute terms. We don't look at our belief systems and say "this is our belief system"; we say "this is the truth." All cultures do this. Even the way cultures form their sense of identity involves a certain reliance on absolutes by assuming that their culture is normative, the right way to be. It's not just Anglo-Saxon America, in other words, that presumes its centrality in the order of things. We can see how groups of people implicitly believe in their privileged place in the world by looking at the names with which they identify themselves. Take the members of the largest Native American tribe in the United States. To the rest of the world, they are known as the Navajos. This is not the name the Navajos use among themselves, however, for the word *Navajo* does not come from their language. In all likelihood, the name was given to them by neighboring Pueblo Indians, for whom the term *Navahu* means "large area of cultivated lands." But in the language of the Navajo, which is quite different from that of the Pueblo, they are not the people of the tilled fields. They are, quite simply, the People, the most common English translation of the word *diné*, the name by which the Navajo know themselves.

Or take the Hmong of Southeast Asia. Hmong simply means "person," and so to say "I am a Hmong" implicitly states "I am a person." And even the names of such different nations as Ireland and Iran harbor an ancient sense of normative "peoplehood," for both names are derived from the word *Aryan*, which itself once bore the simple meaning "the people." To be sure, when someone says "I am *diné*," or "I am Hmong," or "I am Irish," he or she does not mean "I am a human being and the rest of you aren't." Nonetheless, we find inscribed within the unconscious history of these ancient tribal names the trace of a belief found within many a tribal name: the sense that one's own tribe comes first in the order of things.

What makes American culture different historically is the fact that Americans have tried, with whatever success or failure, to create a single identity out of many identities, something called an "American" no matter who one's ancestors were. It is a social experiment whose outcome is by no means certain, but at least in the realm of popular culture, the implicit and explicit racial hierarchies of the past are visibly receding. The content of popular culture is increasingly multicultural in every sense of the term, and given the central place of popular culture in American society today, that may prove to have a significance far beyond mere entertainment.

The Readings

This chapter looks at the social construction of racial identity in America, beginning with Michael Omi's survey of how race works as a sign in popular American culture. Paired with Omi's essay is Greg Braxton's news feature on the preponderance of movie roles for black actresses in which they serve as accessory "Black Best Friends" to white female leads. Rebecca Traister next considers *Ugly Betty*, the breakthrough prime-time dramedy that features a Latina lead character and her family. The excerpt that follows is from Angeline F. Price's Web site, which she devotes to describing the stereotyped images of "white trash" that are disseminated through the American popular media. Next, Jack Lopez offers a personal memoir of what it is like to be a wannabe surfer in the Mexican American community of East Los Angeles, while Jim Whitmer and Nell Bernstein photographically and journalistically report on the phenomenon of "claiming" — white teens choosing to identify themselves with nonwhite ethnic groups. Melissa Algranati offers a college student's perspective on what it's like to be a Puerto Rican–Egyptian–American Jew in a country that demands clear ethnic identifications, and Fan Shen concludes the chapter with an analysis of the role that his Chinese heritage has played in his experience both as a student and as a professor of freshman composition.

MICHAEL OMI
In Living Color: Race and American Culture

Though many like to think that racism in America is a thing of the past, Michael Omi argues that racism is a pervasive feature in our lives, one that is both overt and inferential. Using race as a sign by which we judge a person's character, inferential racism invokes deep-rooted stereotypes, and as Omi shows in his survey of American film, television, and music, our popular culture is hardly immune from such stereotyping. Indeed, when ostensibly "progressive" programs like Saturday Night Live *can win the National Ethnic Coalition of Organizations' "Platinum Pit Award" for racist stereotyping in television, and shock jocks such as Howard Stern command big audiences and salaries, one can see popular culture has a way to go before it becomes colorblind. The author of* Racial Formation in the United States: From the 1960s to the 1980s *(with Howard Winant, 1986, 1994), Omi is a professor of comparative ethnic studies at the University of California, Berkeley. His most recent project is a survey of antiracist organizations and initiatives.*

In February 1987, Assistant Attorney General William Bradford Reynolds, the nation's chief civil rights enforcer, declared that the recent death of a black man in Howard Beach, New York, and the Ku Klux Klan attack on civil rights marchers in Forsyth County, Georgia, were "isolated" racial incidences. He emphasized that the places where racial conflict could potentially flare up were "far fewer now than ever before in our history," and concluded that such a diminishment of racism stood as "a powerful testament to how far we have come in the civil rights struggle."[1]

Events in the months following his remarks raise the question as to whether we have come quite so far. They suggest that dramatic instances of racial tension and violence merely constitute the surface manifestations of a deeper racial organization of American society — a system of inequality which has shaped, and in turn been shaped by, our popular culture.

In March, the NAACP released a report on blacks in the record industry entitled "The Discordant Sound of Music." It found that despite the revenues generated by black performers, blacks remain "grossly underrepresented" in the business, marketing, and A&R (Artists and Repertoire) departments of major record labels. In addition, few blacks are employed as managers, agents, concert promoters, distributors, and retailers. The report concluded that:

---

[1] Reynolds's remarks were made at a conference on equal opportunity held by the bar association in Orlando, Florida. *The San Francisco Chronicle* (7 February 1987).

> The record industry is overwhelmingly segregated and discrimination is rampant. No other industry in America so openly classifies its operations on a racial basis. At every level of the industry, beginning with the separation of black artists into a special category, barriers exist that severely limit opportunities for blacks.[2]

Decades after the passage of civil rights legislation and the affirmation of the principle of "equal opportunity," patterns of racial segregation and exclusion, it seems, continue to characterize the production of popular music.

The enduring logic of Jim Crow is also present in professional sports. In April, Al Campanis, vice president of player personnel for the Los Angeles Dodgers, explained to Ted Koppel on ABC's *Nightline* about the paucity of blacks in baseball front offices and as managers. "I truly believe," Campanis said, "that [blacks] may not have some of the necessities to be, let's say, a field manager or perhaps a general manager." When pressed for a reason, Campanis offered an explanation which had little to do with the structure of opportunity or institutional discrimination within professional sports:

> [W]hy are black men or black people not good swimmers? Because they don't have the buoyancy. . . . They are gifted with great musculature and various other things. They're fleet of foot. And this is why there are a lot of black major league ballplayers. Now as far as having the background to become club presidents, or presidents of a bank, I don't know.[3]

Black exclusion from the front office, therefore, was justified on the basis of biological "difference."

The issue of race, of course, is not confined to the institutional arrangements   5 of popular culture production. Since popular culture deals with the symbolic realm of social life, the images which it creates, represents, and disseminates contribute to the overall racial climate. They become the subject of analysis and political scrutiny. In August, the National Ethnic Coalition of Organizations bestowed the "Golden Pit Awards" on television programs, commercials, and movies that were deemed offensive to racial and ethnic groups. *Saturday Night Live*, regarded by many media critics as a politically "progressive" show, was singled out for the "Platinum Pit Award" for its comedy skit "Ching Chang" which depicted a Chinese storeowner and his family in a derogatory manner.[4]

These examples highlight the *overt* manifestations of racism in popular culture — institutional forms of discrimination which keep racial minorities out of the production and organization of popular culture, and the crude racial

---

[2]Economic Development Department of the NAACP, "The Discordant Sound of Music (A Report on the Record Industry)," (Baltimore, Maryland: The NAACP, 1987), pp. 16–17.

[3]Campanis's remarks on *Nightline* were reprinted in *The San Francisco Chronicle* (April 9, 1987).

[4]Ellen Wulfhorst, "TV Stereotyping: It's the 'Pits,'" *The San Francisco Chronicle* (August 24, 1987).

caricatures by which these groups are portrayed. Yet racism in popular culture is often conveyed in a variety of implicit, and at times invisible, ways. Political theorist Stuart Hall makes an important distinction between *overt* racism, the elaboration of an explicitly racist argument, policy, or view, and *inferential* racism which refers to "those apparently naturalized representations of events and situations relating to race, whether 'factual' or 'fictional,' which have racist premises and propositions inscribed in them as a set of *unquestioned assumptions*." He argues that inferential racism is more widespread, common, and indeed insidious since "it is largely *invisible* even to those who formulate the world in its terms."[5]

Race itself is a slippery social concept which is paradoxically both "obvious" and "invisible." In our society, one of the first things we notice about people when we encounter them (along with their sex/gender) is their *race*. We utilize race to provide clues about *who* a person is and *how* we should relate to her/him. Our perception of race determines our "presentation of *self*," distinctions in status, and appropriate modes of conduct in daily and institutional life. This process is often unconscious; we tend to operate off of an unexamined set of *racial beliefs*.

Racial beliefs account for and explain variations in "human nature." Differences in skin color and other obvious physical characteristics supposedly provide visible clues to more substantive differences lurking underneath. Among other qualities, temperament, sexuality, intelligence, and artistic and athletic ability are presumed to be fixed and discernible from the palpable mark of race. Such diverse questions as our confidence and trust in others (as salespeople, neighbors, media figures); our sexual preferences and romantic images; our tastes in music, film, dance, or sports; indeed our very ways of walking and talking are ineluctably shaped by notions of race.

Ideas about race, therefore, have become "common sense" — a way of comprehending, explaining, and acting in the world. This is made painfully obvious when someone disrupts our common sense understandings. An encounter with someone who is, for example, racially "mixed" or of a racial/ethnic group we are unfamiliar with becomes a source of discomfort for us, and momentarily creates a crisis of racial meaning. We also become disoriented when people do not act "black," "Latino," or indeed "white." The content of such stereotypes reveals a series of unsubstantiated beliefs about who these groups are, what they are like, and how they behave.

The existence of such racial consciousness should hardly be surprising. 10 Even prior to the inception of the republic, the United States was a society shaped by racial conflict. The establishment of the Southern plantation economy, Western expansion, and the emergence of the labor movement, among other significant historical developments, have all involved conflicts over the definition and nature of the *color line*. The historical results have been distinct

[5]Stuart Hall, "The Whites of Their Eyes: Racist Ideologies and the Media," in George Bridges and Rosalind Brunt, eds., *Silver Linings* (London: Lawrence and Wishart, 1981), pp. 36–37.

and different groups have encountered unique forms of racial oppression — Native Americans faced genocide, blacks were subjected to slavery, Mexicans were invaded and colonized, and Asians faced exclusion. What is common to the experiences of these groups is that their particular "fate" was linked to historically specific ideas about the significance and meaning of race.[6] Whites defined them as separate "species," ones inferior to Northern European cultural stocks, and thereby rationalized the conditions of their subordination in the economy, in political life, and in the realm of culture.

A crucial dimension of racial oppression in the United States is the elaboration of an ideology of difference or "otherness." This involves defining "us" (i.e., white Americans) in opposition to "them," an important task when distinct racial groups are first encountered, or in historically specific periods where preexisting racial boundaries are threatened or crumbling.

Political struggles over the very definition of who an "American" is illustrate this process. The Naturalization Law of 1790 declared that only free *white* immigrants could qualify, reflecting the initial desire among Congress to create and maintain a racially homogeneous society. The extension of eligibility to all racial groups has been a long and protracted process. Japanese, for example, were finally eligible to become naturalized citizens after the passage of the Walter-McCarran Act of 1952. The ideological residue of these restrictions in naturalization and citizenship laws is the equation within popular parlance of the term "American" with "white," while other "Americans" are described as black, Mexican, "Oriental," etc.

Popular culture has been an important realm within which racial ideologies have been created, reproduced, and sustained. Such ideologies provide a framework of symbols, concepts, and images through which we understand, interpret, and represent aspects of our "racial" existence.

Race has often formed the central themes of American popular culture. Historian W. L. Rose notes that it is a "curious coincidence" that four of the "most popular reading-viewing events in all American history" have in some manner dealt with race, specifically black/white relations in the south.[7] Harriet Beecher Stowe's *Uncle Tom's Cabin*, Thomas Ryan Dixon's *The Clansman* (the inspiration for D. W. Griffith's *The Birth of a Nation*), Margaret Mitchell's *Gone with the Wind* (as a book and film), and Alex Haley's *Roots* (as a book and television miniseries) each appeared at a critical juncture in American race relations and helped to shape new understandings of race.

Emerging social definitions of race and the "real American" were reflected   15
in American popular culture of the nineteenth century. Racial and ethnic stereotypes were shaped and reinforced in the newspapers, magazines, and pulp fiction of the period. But the evolution and ever-increasing sophistication of

[6]For an excellent survey of racial beliefs see Thomas F. Gossett, *Race: The History of an Idea in America* (New York: Shocken Books, 1965).

[7]W. L. Rose, *Race and Religion in American Historical Fiction: Four Episodes in Popular Culture* (Oxford: Clarendon Press, 1979).

visual mass communications throughout the twentieth century provided, and continue to provide, the most dramatic means by which racial images are generated and reproduced.

Film and television have been notorious in disseminating images of racial minorities which establish for audiences what these groups look like, how they behave, and, in essence, "who they are." The power of the media lies not only in their ability to reflect the dominant racial ideology, but in their capacity to shape that ideology in the first place. D. W. Griffith's aforementioned epic *Birth of a Nation*, a sympathetic treatment of the rise of the Ku Klux Klan during Reconstruction, helped to generate, consolidate, and "nationalize" images of blacks which had been more disparate (more regionally specific, for example) prior to the film's appearance.[8]

In television and film, the necessity to define characters in the briefest and most condensed manner has led to the perpetuation of racial caricatures, as racial stereotypes serve as shorthand for scriptwriters, directors, and actors. Television's tendency to address the "lowest common denominator" in order to render programs "familiar" to an enormous and diverse audience leads it regularly to assign and reassign racial characteristics to particular groups, both minority and majority.

Many of the earliest American films deal with racial and ethnic "difference." The large influx of "new immigrants" at the turn of the century led to a proliferation of negative images of Jews, Italians, and Irish which were assimilated and adapted by such films as Thomas Edison's *Cohen's Advertising Scheme* (1904). Based on an old vaudeville routine, the film featured a scheming Jewish merchant, aggressively hawking his wares. Though stereotypes of these groups persist to this day,[9] by the 1940s many of the earlier ethnic stereotypes had disappeared from Hollywood. But, as historian Michael Winston observes, the "outsiders" of the 1890s remained: "the ever-popular Indian of the Westerns; the inscrutable or sinister Oriental; the sly, but colorful Mexican; and the clowning or submissive Negro."[10]

In many respects the "Western" as a genre has been paradigmatic in establishing images of racial minorities in film and television. The classic scenario involves the encircled wagon train or surrounded fort from which whites bravely fight off fierce bands of Native American Indians. The point of reference and viewer identification lies with those huddled within the circle — the representatives of "civilization" who valiantly attempt to ward off the

---

[8]Melanie Martindale-Sikes, "Nationalizing 'Nigger' Imagery through *Birth of a Nation*," paper prepared for the 73rd Annual Meeting of the American Sociological Association (September 4–8, 1978) in San Francisco.

[9]For a discussion of Italian, Irish, Jewish, Slavic, and German stereotypes in film, see Randall M. Miller, ed., *The Kaleidoscopic Lens: How Hollywood Views Ethnic Groups* (Englewood, N.J.: Jerome S. Ozer, 1980).

[10]Michael R. Winston, "Racial Consciousness and the Evolution of Mass Communications in the United States," *Daedalus*, vol. III, No. 4 (Fall 1982).

forces of barbarism. In the classic Western, as writer Tom Engelhardt observes, "the viewer is forced behind the barrel of a repeating rifle and it is from that position, through its gun sights, that he receives a picture history of Western colonialism and imperialism."[11]

Westerns have indeed become the prototype for European and American 20 excursions throughout the Third World. The cast of characters may change, but the story remains the same. The "humanity" of whites is contrasted with the brutality and treachery of nonwhites; brave (i.e., white) souls are pitted against the merciless hordes in conflicts ranging from Indians against the British Lancers to Zulus against the Boers. What Stuart Hall refers to as the imperializing "white eye" provides the framework for these films, lurking outside the frame and yet seeing and positioning everything within; it is "the unmarked position from which . . . 'observations' are made and from which, alone, they make sense."[12]

Our "common sense" assumptions about race and racial minorities in the United States are both generated and reflected in the stereotypes presented by the visual media. In the crudest sense, it could be said that such stereotypes underscore white "superiority" by reinforcing the traits, habits, and predispositions of nonwhites which demonstrate their "inferiority." Yet a more careful assessment of racial stereotypes reveals intriguing trends and seemingly contradictory themes.

While all racial minorities have been portrayed as "less than human," there are significant differences in the images of different groups. Specific racial minority groups, in spite of their often interchangeable presence in films steeped in the "Western" paradigm, have distinct and often unique qualities assigned to them. Latinos are portrayed as being prone toward violent outbursts of anger; blacks as physically strong, but dim-witted; while Asians are seen as sneaky and cunningly evil. Such differences are crucial to observe and analyze. Race in the United States is not reducible to black/white relations. These differences are significant for a broader understanding of the patterns of race in America, and the unique experience of specific racial minority groups.

It is somewhat ironic that *real* differences which exist within a racially defined minority group are minimized, distorted, or obliterated by the media. "All Asians look alike," the saying goes, and indeed there has been little or no attention given to the vast differences which exist between, say, the Chinese and Japanese with respect to food, dress, language, and culture. This blurring within popular culture has given us supposedly Chinese characters who wear kimonos; it is also the reason why the fast-food restaurant McDonald's can offer "Shanghai McNuggets" with teriyaki sauce. Other groups suffer a similar fate. Professor Gretchen Bataille and Charles Silet find the cinematic Native American of the Northeast wearing the clothing of the Plains Indians, while living in the dwellings of Southwestern tribes:

[11]Tom Engelhardt, "Ambush at Kamikaze Pass," in Emma Gee, ed., *Counterpoint: Perspectives on Asian America* (Los Angeles: Asian American Studies Center, UCLA, 1976), p. 270.
[12]Hall, "Whites of Their Eyes," p. 38.

> The movie men did what thousands of years of social evolution could not do, even what the threat of the encroaching white man could not do; Hollywood produced the homogenized Native American, devoid of tribal characteristics or regional differences.[13]

The need to paint in broad racial strokes has thus rendered "internal" differences invisible. This has been exacerbated by the tendency for screenwriters to "invent" mythical Asian, Latin American, and African countries. Ostensibly done to avoid offending particular nations and peoples, such a subterfuge reinforces the notion that all the countries and cultures of a specific region are the same. European countries retain their distinctiveness, while the Third World is presented as one homogeneous mass riddled with poverty and governed by ruthless and corrupt regimes.

While rendering specific groups in a monolithic fashion, the popular cultural imagination simultaneously reveals a compelling need to distinguish and articulate "bad" and "good" variants of particular racial groups and individuals. Thus each stereotypic image is filled with contradictions: The bloodthirsty Indian is tempered with the image of the noble savage; the *bandido* exists along with the loyal sidekick; and Fu Manchu is offset by Charlie Chan. The existence of such contradictions, however, does not negate the one-dimensionality of these images, nor does it challenge the explicit subservient role of racial minorities. Even the "good" person of color usually exists as a foil in novels and films to underscore the intelligence, courage, and virility of the white male hero.

Another important, perhaps central, dimension of racial minority stereo-   25
types is sex/gender differentiation. The connection between race and sex has traditionally been an explosive and controversial one. For most of American history, sexual and marital relations between whites and nonwhites were forbidden by social custom and by legal restrictions. It was not until 1967, for example, that the U.S. Supreme Court ruled that antimiscegenation laws were unconstitutional. Beginning in the 1920s, the notorious Hays Office, Hollywood's attempt at self-censorship, prohibited scenes and subjects which dealt with miscegenation. The prohibition, however, was not evenly applied in practice. White men could seduce racial minority women, but white women were not to be romantically or sexually linked to racial minority men.

Women of color were sometimes treated as exotic sex objects. The sultry Latin temptress — such as Dolores Del Rio and Lupe Velez — invariably had boyfriends who were white North Americans; their Latino suitors were portrayed as being unable to keep up with the Anglo-American competition. From Mary Pickford as Cho-Cho San in *Madame Butterfly* (1915) to Nancy Kwan in *The World of Suzie Wong* (1961), Asian women have often been seen as the gracious "geisha girl" or the prostitute with a "heart of gold," willing to do anything to please her man.

---

[13]Gretchen Bataille and Charles Silet, "The Entertaining Anachronism: Indians in American Film," in Randall M. Miller, ed., *Kaleidoscopic Lens*, p. 40.

By contrast, Asian men, whether cast in the role of villain, servant, side-kick, or kung fu master, are seen as asexual or, at least, romantically undesirable. As Asian American studies professor Elaine Kim notes, even a hero such as Bruce Lee played characters whose "single-minded focus on perfecting his fighting skills precludes all other interests, including an interest in women, friendship, or a social life."[14]

The shifting trajectory of black images over time reveals an interesting dynamic with respect to sex and gender. The black male characters in *The Birth of a Nation* were clearly presented as sexual threats to "white womanhood." For decades afterwards, however, Hollywood consciously avoided portraying black men as assertive or sexually aggressive in order to minimize controversy. Black men were instead cast as comic, harmless, and nonthreatening figures exemplified by such stars as Bill "Bojangles" Robinson, Stepin Fetchit, and Eddie "Rochester" Anderson. Black women, by contrast, were divided into two broad character types based on color categories. Dark black women such as Hattie McDaniel and Louise Beavers were cast as "dowdy, frumpy, dumpy, overweight mammy figures"; while those "close to the white ideal," such as Lena Horne and Dorothy Dandridge, became "Hollywood's treasured mulattoes" in roles emphasizing the tragedy of being of mixed blood.[15]

It was not until the early 1970s that tough, aggressive, sexually assertive black characters, both male and female, appeared. The "blaxploitation" films of the period provided new heroes (e.g., *Shaft, Superfly, Coffy,* and *Cleopatra Jones*) in sharp contrast to the submissive and subservient images of the past. Unfortunately, most of these films were shoddy productions which did little to create more enduring "positive" images of blacks, either male or female.

In contemporary television and film, there is a tendency to present and equate racial minority groups and individuals with specific social problems. Blacks are associated with drugs and urban crime, Latinos with "illegal" immigration, while Native Americans cope with alcoholism and tribal conflicts. Rarely do we see racial minorities "out of character," in situations removed from the stereotypic arenas in which scriptwriters have traditionally embedded them. Nearly the only time we see young Asians and Latinos of either sex, for example, is when they are members of youth gangs, as *Boulevard Nights* (1979), *Year of the Dragon* (1985), and countless TV cop shows can attest to.

Racial minority actors have continually bemoaned the fact that the roles assigned them on stage and screen are often one-dimensional and imbued with stereotypic assumptions. In theater, the movement toward "blind casting" (i.e., casting actors for roles without regard to race) is a progressive step, but it remains to be seen whether large numbers of audiences can suspend their "beliefs" and deal with a Latino King Lear or an Asian Stanley Kowalski.

[14]Elaine Kim, "Asian Americans and American Popular Culture," in Hyung-Chan Kim, ed., *Dictionary of Asian American History* (New York: Greenwood Press, 1986), p. 107.
[15]Donald Bogle, "A Familiar Plot (A Look at the History of Blacks in American Movies)," *The Crisis,* Vol. 90, No. 1 (January 1983), p. 15.

By contrast, white actors are allowed to play anybody. Though the use of white actors to play blacks in "black face" is clearly unacceptable in the contemporary period, white actors continue to portray Asian, Latino, and Native American characters on stage and screen.

Scores of Charlie Chan films, for example, have been made with white leads (the last one was the 1981 *Charlie Chan and the Curse of the Dragon Queen*). Roland Winters, who played Chan in six features, was once asked to explain the logic of casting a white man in the role of Charlie Chan: "The only thing I can think of is, if you want to cast a homosexual in a show, and you get a homosexual, it'll be awful. It won't be funny . . . and maybe there's something there."[16]

Such a comment reveals an interesting aspect about myth and reality in popular culture. Michael Winston argues that stereotypic images in the visual media were not originally conceived as representations of reality, nor were they initially understood to be "real" by audiences. They were, he suggests, ways of "coding and rationalizing" the racial hierarchy and interracial behavior. Over time, however, "a complex interactive relationship between myth and reality developed, so that images originally understood to be unreal, through constant repetition began to *seem* real."[17]

Such a process consolidated, among other things, our "common sense" understandings of what we think various groups should look like. Such presumptions have led to tragicomical results. Latinos auditioning for a role in a television soap opera, for example, did not fit the Hollywood image of "real Mexicans" and had their faces bronzed with powder before filming because they looked too white. Model Aurora Garza said, "I'm a real Mexican and very dark anyway. I'm even darker right now because I have a tan. But they kept wanting to make my face darker and darker."[18]

Historically in Hollywood, the fact of having "dark skin" made an actor or actress potentially adaptable for numerous "racial" roles. Actress Lupe Velez once commented that she had portrayed "Chinese, Eskimos, Japs, squaws, Hindus, Swedes, Malays, and Japanese."[19] Dorothy Dandridge, who was the first black woman teamed romantically with white actors, presented a quandary for studio executives who weren't sure what race and nationality to make her. They debated whether she should be a "foreigner," an island girl, or a West Indian.[20] Ironically, what they refused to entertain as a possibility was to present her as what she really was, a black American woman.

The importance of race in popular culture is not restricted to the visual media. In popular music, race and race consciousness have defined, and continue to

[16]Frank Chin, "Confessions of the Chinatown Cowboy," *Bulletin of Concerned Asian Scholars*, Vol. 4, No. 3 (Fall 1972).

[17]Winston, "Racial Consciousness," p. 176.

[18]*The San Francisco Chronicle*, September 21, 1984.

[19]Quoted in Allen L. Woll, "Bandits and Lovers: Hispanic Images in American Film," in Miller, ed., *Kaleidoscopic Lens*, p. 60.

[20]Bogle, "Familiar Plot," p. 17.

define, formats, musical communities, and tastes. In the mid-1950s, the secretary of the North Alabama White Citizens Council declared that "Rock and roll is a means of pulling the white man down to the level of the Negro."[21] While rock may no longer be popularly regarded as a racially subversive musical form, the very genres of contemporary popular music remain, in essence, thinly veiled racial categories. "R & B" (Rhythm and Blues) and "soul" music are clearly references to *black* music, while Country & Western or heavy metal music are viewed, in the popular imagination, as *white* music. Black performers who want to break out of this artistic ghettoization must "cross over," a contemporary form of "passing" in which their music is seen as acceptable to white audiences.

The airwaves themselves are segregated. The designation "urban contemporary" is merely radio lingo for a "black" musical format. Such categorization affects playlists, advertising accounts, and shares of the listening market. On cable television, black music videos rarely receive airplay on MTV, but are confined instead to the more marginal BET (Black Entertainment Television) network.

In spite of such segregation, many performing artists have been able to garner a racially diverse group of fans. And yet, racially integrated concert audiences are extremely rare. Curiously, this "perverse phenomenon" of racially homogeneous crowds takes place despite the color of the performer. Lionel Richie's concert audiences, for example, are virtually all-white, while Teena Marie's are all-black.[22]

Racial symbols and images are omnipresent in popular culture. Commonplace household objects such as cookie jars, salt and pepper shakers, and ashtrays have frequently been designed and fashioned in the form of racial caricatures. Sociologist Steve Dublin in an analysis of these objects found that former tasks of domestic service were symbolically transferred onto these commodities.[23] An Aunt Jemima–type character, for example, is used to hold a roll of paper towels, her outstretched hands supporting the item to be dispensed. "Sprinkle Plenty," a sprinkle bottle in the shape of an Asian man, was used to wet clothes in preparation for ironing. Simple commodities, the household implements which help us perform everyday tasks, may reveal, therefore, a deep structure of racial meaning.

A crucial dimension for discerning the meaning of particular stereotypes and images is the *situation context* for the creation and consumption of popular culture. For example, the setting in which "racist" jokes are told determines the function of humor. Jokes about blacks where the teller and audience are black constitute a form of self-awareness; they allow blacks to cope and "take the edge   40

---

[21]Dave Marsh and Kevin Stein, *The Book of Rock Lists* (New York: Dell Publishing Co., 1981), p. 8.
[22]*Rock & Roll Confidential*, No. 44 (February 1987), p. 2.
[23]Steven C. Dublin, "Symbolic Slavery: Black Representations in Popular Culture," *Social Problems*, Vol. 34, No. 2 (April 1987).

off" of oppressive aspects of the social order which they commonly confront. The meaning of these same jokes, however, is dramatically transformed when told across the "color line." If a white, or even black, person tells these jokes to a white audience, it will, despite its "purely" humorous intent, serve to reinforce stereotypes and rationalize the existing relations of racial inequality.

Concepts of race and racial images are both overt and implicit within popular culture — the organization of cultural production, the products themselves, and the manner in which they are consumed are deeply structured by race. Particular racial meanings, stereotypes, and myths can change, but the presence of a *system* of racial meanings and stereotypes, of racial ideology, seems to be an enduring aspect of American popular culture.

The era of Reaganism and the overall rightward drift of American politics and culture has added a new twist to the question of racial images and meanings. Increasingly, the problem for racial minorities is not that of misportrayal, but of "invisibility." Instead of celebrating racial and cultural diversity, we are witnessing an attempt by the right to define, once again, who the "real" American is, and what "correct" American values, mores, and political beliefs are. In such a context, racial minorities are no longer the focus of sustained media attention; when they do appear, they are cast as colored versions of essentially "white" characters.

The possibilities for change — for transforming racial stereotypes and challenging institutional inequities — nonetheless exist. Historically, strategies have involved the mobilization of political pressure against an offending institution(s). In the late 1950s, for instance, "Nigger Hair" tobacco changed its name to "Bigger Hare" due to concerted NAACP pressure on the manufacturer. In the early 1970s, Asian American community groups successfully fought NBC's attempt to resurrect Charlie Chan as a television series with white actor Ross Martin. Amidst the furor generated by Al Campanis's remarks cited at the beginning of this essay, Jesse Jackson suggested that a boycott of major league games be initiated in order to push for a restructuring of hiring and promotion practices.

Partially in response to such action, Baseball Commissioner Peter Ueberroth announced plans in June 1987 to help put more racial minorities in management roles. "The challenge we have," Ueberroth said, "is to manage change without losing tradition."[24] The problem with respect to the issue of race and popular culture, however, is that the *tradition* itself may need to be thoroughly examined, its "common sense" assumptions unearthed and challenged, and its racial images contested and transformed.

READING THE TEXT

1. Describe in your own words the difference between "overt racism" and "inferential racism" (para. 6).

[24]*The San Francisco Chronicle* (June 13, 1987).

2. Why, according to Omi, is popular culture so powerful in shaping America's attitudes toward race?

3. What relationship does Omi see between gender and racial stereotypes?

4. How did race relations change in America during the 1980s, in Omi's view?

READING THE SIGNS

1. In class, brainstorm stereotypes, both positive and negative, attributed to specific racial groups. Then discuss the possible sources of these stereotypes. In what ways have they been perpetuated in popular culture, including film, TV, advertising, music, and consumer products? What does your discussion reveal about popular culture's influence on our most basic ways of seeing the world?

2. Watch *Malcolm X* or another film that addresses race relations, such as *Mi Familia*. Using Omi's essay as your critical framework, write an essay in which you explore how this film may reflect or redefine American attitudes toward racial identity and race relations.

3. Study an issue of a magazine targeted to a specific ethnic readership, such as *Ebony* or *Yolk*, analyzing both its articles and advertising. Then write an essay in which you explore the extent to which the magazine accurately reflects that ethnicity or, in Omi's words, appeals to readers as "colored versions of essentially 'white' characters" (para. 42).

4. **CONNECTING TEXTS**   Omi claims that "In contemporary television and film, there is a tendency to present and equate racial minority groups and individuals with specific social problems" (para. 30). In class, brainstorm films and TV shows that have characters that are ethnic minorities; pick one example and watch it. Does Omi's claim apply to that example, or does it demonstrate different patterns of racial representation? To develop your analysis, you might consult Greg Braxton's "Hollywood Loves BBFs 4-Ever" (p. 667) and Rebecca Traister's "Class Act" (p. 672).

GREG BRAXTON
Hollywood Loves BBFs 4-Ever

Move over Will Smith and Tommy Lee Jones, and make room for Alicia Keys and Scarlett Johansson, or Merrin Dungey and Jennifer Garner, or any recent pair of black and white actresses in starring roles in cinema or TV. For as Greg Braxton reports in this Los Angeles Times *feature, Hollywood has been especially fond of providing its white female protagonists with a "Black Best Friend" whose "principal function is to support the heroine, often with sass, attitude, and a keen insight into relationships and life." But is there any cultural significance to this pattern, or is it simply a case of black actresses winning roles that were originally race neutral? As Braxton shows, there are two schools of thought on the matter, but the fact that Will Smith is the dominant character in his* Men in Black *roles, while the BBF is never the dominant character, does have its implications. Braxton is a staff writer at the* Los Angeles Times.

Julia Louis-Dreyfus has one. Sandra Bullock had one. So did Jennifer Garner and Katie Holmes. Jennifer Love Hewitt has had two. Calista Flockhart took hers dancing. Kate Walsh had one, lost her, and got another one with a different face but the same name. And Scarlett Johansson got her first one last weekend. They're stars who have all played lead characters who experience adventure with the help of their BFF (Best Friend Forever). But in many cases, these BFFs might more accurately be characterized as BBFs — Black Best Friend — played by an African American actress whose character's principal function is to support the heroine, often with sass, attitude, and a keen insight into relationships and life.

BBFs (Black Best Friends)

Celluloid BBFs have been featured in . . . *The Nanny Diaries*, as well as *The Devil Wears Prada*, and *Premonition*. But BBFs have been even more of an influence in TV series, including *The New Adventures of Old Christine*, *Ghost Whisperer*, *Alias*, *Ally McBeal*, *Felicity*, *Summerland*, and *Private Practice*, the spinoff of *Grey's Anatomy* premiering this fall.

The BBF syndrome isn't something that Hollywood likes to talk about, even as it continues to be a winking in-joke among blacks in the industry. One African American actress said that she and her actress friends tease one another about forming a support group for characters who had to help out their "woefully helpless white girls." But on a more serious note, the trend of BBFs underscores the limitations that African American actresses still face

Scarlett Johansson and Alicia Keys in *The Nanny Diaries, 2007.*

more than five years after Halle Berry's Oscar-winning performance as best actress in a leading role for *Monster's Ball.* Despite impressive résumés, solid credentials and successful achievements, many of the black actresses who have played BBFs are rarely offered the heroine role in mainstream projects. Not one black actress will star in a prime-time series on the four major networks this fall season.

And, as has been long lamented, lead roles in films are few and far between. Rose Catherine Pinkney, executive vice president of programming and production for TV One, a cable network targeted to black audiences, was one of the few TV or film industry executives willing to talk about BBF syndrome, saying: "It's wonderful that studios recognize great talent. And there's more diversity, so it looks like the world. But it's a shame that studios also don't have the courage to put these actresses in leads." Some say it's unfair to even categorize BBFs — it undermines the talent of the actors and actresses who work hard to win their roles, they say, and ignores the fact that some of these roles didn't necessarily call for an African American performer. But Pinkney, a former Paramount Studios executive, added, "Historically, people of color have had to play nurturing, rational caretakers of the white lead characters. And studios are just not willing to reverse that role."

Of course, friendships or partnerships between black and white males are a staple in films and movies (*Lethal Weapon, Wild Hogs, Pulp Fiction*). But in many of those relationships, the dynamic is more even-handed — the friends support each other — or the black male is the dominant friend. But it's different for women.

BBFs vary in personality and looks, but many share the same qualities: They are gorgeous, independent, loyal, and successful. They live or work with their friend but are not really around all that much except for well-timed moments when the heroine needs an eating companion or is in crisis. BBFs basically have very little going on, so they are largely available for such moments. And even though they are single or lack consistent solid relationships, BBFs are experts in the ways of the world, using that knowledge to comfort, warn, or scold their BFF. And quite often, they are the only black character in sight. "It's a stereotype that's been around for a long time," said Stuart Fischoff, professor emeritus of media psychology at Cal State L.A. "It's a way for bringing in a different culture, and the black friend can add ingredients that would not ordinarily be there. Blacks are seen as being more outspoken, so they can speak with greater authority and give more information."

Opportunity or Limitation?

Aisha Tyler, who generated buzz when she played the first recurring African American love interest on *Friends*, wound up in the BBF class when she played the best friend to a paranormal investigator (Hewitt) in CBS' *Ghost Whisperer*. Tyler, who left the series at the end of its first season to devote more time to her first directorial effort, a buddy comedy about two female cops that she will star in, said she feels fortunate that she is mostly offered roles that are more complex and interesting than the traditional BFF. "But I don't know what the alternative is," said Tyler. "I think the more roles there are for African Americans, the better. This trend feels like a consolation prize, but at least these roles are available. A lot of ensembles are not diverse at all, so if it's a shot, it's a good thing."

With *The Nanny Diaries*, musician Alicia Keys enters the distinguished class of BBFs that includes Tracie Thoms, Wanda Sykes, Nia Long, Brandy, Merrin Dungey, Audra McDonald, Regina King, Stacey Dash, and Lisa Nicole Carson. Key BBF moments include:

- *The Nanny Diaries*: Lynette (Keys) warning Annie (Johansson) that taking a nanny position as a lark instead of pursuing a career may be problematic: "The path of least resistance, it can lead through a minefield."

- *The Devil Wears Prada*: Lily (Thoms) scolding Andy (Anne Hathaway) about ignoring her circle of friends and getting swept up in the world of high-style fashion: "The Andy I know . . . is always five minutes early and thinks Club Monaco is couture. For the last 16 years, I've known everything about that Andy. But this person, this glamazon . . . I don't get her."

- *Ally McBeal*: Renee (Carson) berating attorney Ally (Flockhart) for still pining after her old boyfriend, a colleague who has married someone else: "You two were like Barbie and Ken. He's a wimp. Five years from now, he's one of those boring little lawyers looking over his stock portfolio, playing golf at the country club with nothing left to offer you at the end of the day. . . . You can do better."

If there was a poster BBF for BBFs, it would most likely be Dungey. A veteran of several television series, Dungey is best known as Francie, the best friend of secret agent Sydney Bristow (Garner) in *Alias*. After leaving that series in 2003, Dungey turned up on the WB's short-lived *Summerland* as Susannah, the best friend of Ava (Lori Loughlin). Her next major role was in the pilot for *Private Practice*, the spinoff of *Grey's Anatomy* that aired in May as part of a two-hour special. She played Dr. Naomi Bennett, the best friend of Dr. Addison Montgomery (Kate Walsh). In late May, producers announced that Dungey was being replaced by another African American actress, Audra McDonald, saying that there was more chemistry between McDonald and Walsh. The character will keep the same name when McDonald takes over the role.

Talent Wins Out

There is another view to the emergence of the BBF. Some producers say the 10 casting of black actresses as the friend is not due to any race-specific casting, but comes down to best actress for the role. For example, producers of *Friends* said Tyler won the role strictly on talent. Richard Gladstein, producer of *The Nanny Diaries*, said he also was not looking specifically for a black actress to play the lead's best friend, a character not in the book that inspired the movie. "She just happens to be African American," he said. "Alicia Keys came in and gave a wonderful reading, and that was it."

And Kellee Stewart, who plays opposite Jordana Spiro (P.J.) in TBS' comedy, *My Boys*, which launched its second season last month, refuses to be categorized as a BBF, calling it an insult to her talent. She won her role as a best friend to a sports writer over several actresses, including whites. "To call this a trend or to say an actress was cast just because of her ethnicity is to negate her contribution," said Stewart. "It minimizes the talent and effort it took to win the role in the first place."

READING THE TEXT

1. In the first paragraph, Braxton refers to BBFs as "one" and "her." What effect does this nonspecific reference have on the reader?
2. Why do Hollywood blacks consider the BBF phenomenon a "winking in-joke" (para. 3)?
3. Why does Braxton believe that the BBF trend has serious implications?
4. How do black-white female friendships differ from black-white male friendships, in Braxton's view?

READING THE SIGNS

1. In an essay, present your own argument assessing the BBF trend and its implications. To what extent do you find it a welcome opportunity for African American actresses or, alternatively, a limitation on their creative roles?

2. **CONNECTING TEXTS**   Braxton explains that black-white female friendships differ from those between black and white male characters. In an essay, propose your own explanation for this difference. To develop your ideas, consult the Introduction to this chapter and the Introduction to Chapter 7, "We've Come a Long Way, Maybe: Gender Codes in American Culture" (p. 559).

3. Watch one of the TV shows or films that Braxton mentions, and conduct your own semiotic analysis of the relationship between black and white female characters.

4. Braxton says that some producers deny the BBF trend by claiming that they select black actresses for their talent, not their race. Write a letter to such producers in which you support, refute, or complicate their claim.

5. Braxton focuses on black-white relations in this essay. In class, discuss how characters of other ethnicities, such as Latinos or Asian Americans, interact with Caucasian characters. Do they play roles similar to the BBF, or do you find differences? How can you account for your observations?

6. If you were to produce a film that depicts current race relations in America, what sort of film would you create? Write a creative essay describing your film idea, and then share it with your classmates.

REBECCA TRAISTER
Class Act

*Slowly but surely, the Latino/Latina presence in American popular cul-
ture has grown, with the stardom of such performers as Jennifer Lopez,
Ricky Martinez, and George Lopez exemplifying the trend. But the
appearance in 2006 of the new dramedy* Ugly Betty *nevertheless marked
something of a breakthrough for what may well be the first Hispanic-
themed prime-time hit on network television. Immediately attracting a
great deal of attention,* Ugly Betty *has been hailed, as in this* Salon *piece
by Rebecca Traister, as a challenge not only to the beauty myths of contemporary popular culture but to the racial and class order as well. With
its portrayal of the dysfunctionally rich and glamorous, and its sympathetic approach to Latin immigrants,* Ugly Betty *presents an unusual
dramatization of American class conflict, Traister believes, but, she concludes, it does so "beneath an effortlessly fun surface." Traister is a writer
for Salon.com.*

You've probably heard a lot about *Ugly Betty*, ABC's new hourlong comedy–
soap opera about a supposedly hideous young woman who scores a job as
assistant to a foxy male fashion magazine editor. The show's tidily uplifting
premise — she is a beast in the beauty industry who in fact brings beauty to a
beastly world — along with its crack cast, cuspidate humor and sudsy plot,
has helped turn *Ugly Betty* into a rare bona fide hit on fall's television slate. It
garners around 16 million viewers a night and is one of only a few new shows
to have received orders for a full season.

Ugly Betty's mostly laudatory notices have covered the wan irony of its
unlovely title and winning appeal: "Ugly Betty Is a Beauty" and all that. Many
critics have also pointed out that Betty, played by America Ferrera, is not ugly.
She is merely encumbered by a mouth full of blue metal, one hellacious pon-
cho and a wonky eye for color coordination. The show should be called *Badly
Styled Betty*. (And naturally, within a month of *Ugly Betty*'s premiere, newspaper style sections fell predictably in line, touting a new "ugly chic" inspired
by the program.)

But those who have taken the title's bait and examined only the aesthetics of the show have missed the point. *Ugly Betty* is not about being unattractive, or at least not *simply* about being unattractive. It's about class. And
ethnicity. Its smart take on cultural and economic differences, enmeshed as it
is in a fresh, funny package, makes it positively subversive television.

Betty Suarez is the 22-year-old daughter of Mexican immigrants. She lives
in Queens with her widowed father; older sister, Hilda; and Hilda's son, Justin, a
fashion-obsessed preteen. But when we first meet Betty, it's in the marble lobby

America Ferrera in *Ugly Betty*.

of Meade Publications, where she's awaiting a job interview with an H.R.-bot who needs only an eyeful of her metal-mouthed grin to shut the door in her face. But Betty catches the eye of company founder Bradford Meade, who hires her to assist his son, Daniel (Eric Mabius), recently installed as editor in chief at fashion-bible *Mode* after the untimely departure of *Mode*'s legendary nuclear winter of an editor, Fey Summers. Daniel is the family fuck-up, a playboy who generally prefers his assistants under his desk, administering fellatio.

Bradford hires Betty because he assumes his son will never look twice at   5 a not-anorexic Mexican woman in braces, red spectacles and polymer-fabric cardigans. As far as the lily-white Meades are concerned, Betty might as well not have secondary sexual characteristics: She's so "ugly" that she's not even female. But she is capable and smart, and as it turns out, that's what Daniel needs most in an assistant. He's under siege from *Mode*'s creative director, Wilhelmina (Vanessa Williams), who was passed over for the editor-in-chief post. If this seems convoluted, remember, folks, it's a soap.

Ugly Betty's debut so soon after this summer's *The Devil Wears Prada* makes it easy to assume that it was inspired by Lauren Weisberger's epic lament of fashion servitude. (The pilot even nodded to the movie by ending with its catchy theme song, "Suddenly I See.") In fact, *Ugly Betty* is the American adaptation of the Colombian telenovela "Yo soy Betty, la fea," which began airing in 1999 and has since been translated and remade around the world. Unlike *Prada*, *Ugly Betty* is not driven by the traumas of the boss-lackey dynamic. This heroine doesn't flinch when she has to put cream cheese on her boss's bagel or get him tickets to the Harvard-Yale game. Betty has serious professional ambitions, but she's sanguine about starting at the bottom of the ladder, happy to be working at a major magazine straight out of college. When compared to her tasks at home — like trying unsuccessfully to persuade the HMO to refill her ailing father's heart medication — ordering a town car doesn't seem quite such an affront to anyone's sensibilities.

"Betty la fea's" creator, Fernando Gaitán, who is also a producer on *Ugly Betty*, told the *Guardian* in 2000 that telenovelas "are all about the class struggle. They're made for poor people in countries where it's hard to get ahead in life. Usually the characters succeed through love. In mine, they get ahead through work." The U.S. version of "Betty" offers a bracing look at how those class struggles are further fraught by cultural diversity and intolerance, thanks to *Betty* producers Salma Hayek and Silvio Horta, who insisted that it retain a Latina heroine.

The scorn with which Betty is treated at *Mode* has less to do with her looks than with her place of economic and cultural origin. "Are you DE-LIV-ER-ING something?" enunciates receptionist Amanda when Betty first arrives, assuming that a brown girl in a bad outfit could only be a messenger. "Sale at the 99-cent store?" she later remarks when Betty misses a party. When Daniel frets because Betty has taken the "book" home to Queens, Amanda purrs, "You're going to get it back and there's going to be chimichurri sauce *all* over it."

Most egregious is the treatment of the stuffed bunny on Betty's desk, a gift to mark her graduation from Queens College. "One of America's best value colleges!" sneers Wilhelmina's assistant Mark. Betty, like most people in the United States, probably considered value when choosing a college. And the bunny, which endures a toilet-bowl odyssey after being swiped by Betty's colleagues, isn't a Tiffany tennis bracelet or a car or whatever Ross or Rachel probably received when they graduated from college. With the chimichurri sauce and the stuffed rabbit, *Ugly Betty* has joined shows like *All in the Family*, *Roseanne*, *The George Lopez Show*, *Everybody Hates Chris*, and the prematurely axed *Lucky Louie* in the very narrow pantheon of television that has explored what it's like not to be rich and/or white in America.

What makes it extra electric is that unlike those other shows, *Betty* also 10 explores the forbidding traverse to the other side of the class spectrum. The Bunkers didn't leave Queens any more frequently than Roseanne and Dan's brood left their cramped home. But Betty crosses the class ravine daily, hopping from the skyscraping heights of Manhattan to the spicier climes of her home turf. In this, she shows us a New York City we haven't seen for a while. The myth of shows like *Sex and the City* or *Friends* was that simply living in Gotham put you in close proximity to some glama-glama heartbeat: Cross a bridge and you'll promptly be waxed, liposuctioned, and handed a cosmopolitan. It's a fantasy that still propels the bus tours to Tao and Magnolia Bakery.

Betty lives in New York, but for her familiarity with pink drinks, she might as well be from Cleveland. Her neighborhood isn't made of high-rises or brownstones, but of aluminum-sided row homes. Betty's Queens is a Latina version of Woody Allen's Brooklyn; the Manhattan skyline gleams just across the river like Gatsby's green light, but it is a world away. Where Allen's childhood homes were shaken by roller coasters and populated by relatives glued to radio plays, the Suarez house is engrossed in never-ending telenovelas and shaken by the beat of the Dance-Dance-Revolution video game. Betty's life at home, where she is stuffed with food and frets about her family's health, plays out in sharp contrast to her life at *Mode*, where no one eats and colleagues fret about wearing 2-year-old Manolo Blahniks. "Sometimes I feel like the E train dropped me off on Mars," Betty confesses in a recent episode.

But part of what's biting is just how true some of even the most outlandish send-ups of the fashion world ring. In one episode, the *Mode* team proposes a fiery-car-crash photo spread to a diva designer with grotesquely inflated lips, forgetting that she recently backed her SUV into 12 pedestrians in front of a club. The whole thing looks like a Brenda Starr strip until you remember: The lips exist; the violent fashion spreads exist; the celebrity pedestrian-mangler exists. The cartoon that is *Mode* is not, in fact, much of a cartoon.

Then there are the comparative preoccupations of the wealthy in contrast to the far less wealthy. Wilhelmina dresses to impress her senator father, who arrives late and sneers, "So you're still *just* a creative director?" Daniel complains to Betty about his dad's favoritism toward his dead brother, while Mama Meade, played with scenery-chewing zeal by Judith Light, is in rehab, where her perfume has been confiscated, forcing her "to smell like people." They're all keeping secrets about extramarital affairs and probably murder.

But one of the lovely things about *Ugly Betty* is that, while it veers precipitously close to finding savage nobility in economic hardship, life in Queens is nearly as dysfunctional as life with the rich and moderately famous. After all, Betty's boyfriend Walter is cheating on her with trampy neighbor Gina Gambaro, who spent a year in juvy and tries to extort Betty for $4,000. Walter is a bizarro-world take on a Manhattan catch; every woman wants him because of his sweet employee discount at the local electronics store. Then there is Betty's dad's own long-kept secret, and the reason Betty's having so much trouble with the HMO: He's been using another man's Social Security number because he's in the country illegally. "Everybody's got problems," Daniel tells Betty. That's true. But *Ugly Betty* puts them in perspective.

Betty's family is not thrilled about the merging of worlds. Her supportive father grumbles that there are no Latina pictures in *Mode* magazine. Walter is horrified when she comes home from "networking night" to "tamale night" having had one mango margarita. Hilda is even more suspicious of her sister's gig, worried that this new world will never admit her. "Why do you do this to yourself," she scolds one night after Betty has been turned away from a work party at a hot club. "I keep telling you those places aren't for people like us." 15

But the show again escapes the too-good-to-be-true trap by making clear that Betty is not *above* wanting to belong or look good. In Episode 3, at Hilda's urging, she undergoes a makeover. "You want to fit in with these people? They're not going to change. *You* have to," says her sister. "The hair, the face, the clothes. You gotta look it to be it." She whisks Betty to Choli, a local beauty technician who works her magic on Betty's hair, nails, and wardrobe. Betty's transformation is dramatic. With hair piled on top of her head, an outfit of jangling jewelry, a tight skirt and heels, Betty becomes a goddess to the men who catcall her ("She's hot!" exclaims one) as she walks to the subway the next morning. But the look doesn't translate in Manhattan, and it provokes the most scathing round of jeering she's yet received. The other assistants photograph her as if she's a zoo animal, and Wilhelmina scoffs, "It looks like Queens threw up." The message is clear: Queens pretty is not Manhattan pretty. Poor pretty is not rich pretty. Latina pretty is not white pretty.

Ugly Betty is preoccupied with difference — the ways we acknowledge or punish or misinterpret it. Wilhelmina mischaracterizes Betty's work friend, the seamstress Christina, as a "drunken Irish woman." When told that Christina is Scottish, Wilhelmina replies: "Don't care." But she gets ruffled during a discussion of winter holidays, incredulously asking Daniel, "Did you just gesture at me when you said Kwanzaa?" Openly gay Mark advises Betty's fashion-loving nephew Justin, who's admitted that the kids at school don't get him: "Be who you are; wear what you want. Just learn to run real fast."

In exploring the ways we negotiate chasms in status and experience, *Ugly Betty* provides a compelling counterpoint not to *The Devil Wears Prada* but to Sofia Coppola's *Marie Antoinette*. Both are campy, brightly colored candy things. If Coppola's film has politics (and that is still being debated) they are in its portrait of end-of-empire excess that looks familiar at the same time it looks contrived and mildly nauseating. *Ugly Betty*'s depiction of wealth offers something similar. An early scene in which Wilhelmina reclines next to a pyramid of oranges as Mark fills her forehead with Botox might be ripped from the opening credits of *Marie Antoinette*, in which the doomed queen languorously reclines into a foot massage while trawling a finger through an iced cake.

But Coppola's confection has come in for criticism for its unwillingness to visit the angry masses behind the barricades. One of those proles is actually our guide to *Ugly Betty*'s urban Versailles. We see the world of underfed women, racial and economic insularity, and overconsumption of material goods through her eyes, and in counterpoint if not to the starving poor, then at least to the Queens family where you get a stuffed bunny for graduating from college. But like *Marie Antoinette*, *Betty* hides its class tensions beneath an effortlessly fun surface. It's a real romance, and Ferrera's tremendous sex appeal is so apparent that she generates sparks with every man with whom she shares the screen, whether it's Daniel or the nerd from accounting who recently introduced her to sushi.

Whatever happens in Betty's love life, for unadulterated television joy it [20] will be hard to beat a scene from the show's fourth episode in which Walter ingratiates himself by serenading Betty with help from a discounted karaoke machine. Temporarily persuaded, she joins him outside, where they sing "Bittersweet and strange, finding you can change," from Betty's favorite movie, *Beauty and the Beast*, sitting on her front stoop as Manhattan glitters in the distance.

READING THE TEXT

1. According to Traister, what are the ironies surrounding the title *Ugly Betty*?
2. In what ways is *Ugly Betty* a commentary on class and ethnicity?
3. What does Traister mean by saying that Betty is "so 'ugly' that she's not even female" (para. 5)?
4. What attitude does Betty have toward her mundane tasks at work, and how does Traister explain that attitude?

READING THE SIGNS

1. Basing your essay on a close analysis of an episode of *Ugly Betty*, support, challenge, or complicate Traister's assertion that the show is "positively subversive television" (para. 3).
2. Watch an episode of *Handy Manny*, a show intended for young children, and analyze its depictions of Latino characters. To what extent does this show perpetuate or challenge Latino stereotypes?
3. View a TV show or film produced by a Latino director, such as Gregory Nava's *El Norte* or *Mi Familia*, and analyze its representation of Latino culture. Do you find any differences between your show's representation and that of network or mainsteam productions?
4. *Ugly Betty* can be seen in the context of other shows and films that feature the fashion/glamour industry, such as *The Devil Wears Prada* and *Death to the Supermodels*. Basing your essay on specific scenes in such productions, analyze their appeal. What image do they construct of the fashion industry and the people who work in it?

ANGELINE F. PRICE
Working Class Whites

Over the years, American popular culture has worked—not always suc-cessfully and sometimes fitfully—to rid itself of the racial stereotyping that has so marred its history. But one group of Americans, Angeline F. Price believes, has not benefited from this repudiation of negative stereo-typing: working-class whites, especially those in the South. So Price has set up a Web site to analyze and document the ways in which "white trash" continue to be subject to distortion and disrespect in the mass media. We present here a selection from that site, the rest of which can be viewed at http://xroads.virginia.edu/~MA97/price/intro.htm. Price is a marketing consultant in Seattle.

"One class gets the sugar and the other gets the shit" (Fussell, 25), and in American society the "other" is invariably poverty stricken and powerless. Classism is at the core of the problem. The hatred of the poor is an evil secret of America, hidden by the ingrained myths of "liberty and justice for all." Americans are taught to believe in a classless, equal opportunity society. Yet, the facts of poverty, illiteracy, and ignorance are hard to ignore, and the reality is that some people have advantages over other people depending on which family they are born into. Therefore, when wealthy people confront the poor, a sense of guilt and superiority merge into the reactionary fear that has mani-fested itself as racism and classism through the centuries. Sut Lovingood, an anti-hero of Southwestern humor, may have put it best when he said of the genteel class, "they are powerful feard ove low things, low ways, an' low pepil" (Cook, 8).

The working class white has always been an ideal candidate for this role in society, and mainstream society has revealed their fright. As Jim Goad explains in his Redneck Manifesto, the "redneck" stereotype is especially fitting because it fills all the scapegoat requirements: biological differences—inbred, less intelligent, unattractive; geographic and regional differences—trailer parks, rural South, hillbilly; economic differences—poor, sick, lazy, dirty; cul-tural differences—fundamentalist, superstitious, loud, kin networks; and moral differences—trashy, racist, violent (Goad, 76).

Representations of working class whites in the popular media are respon-sible for the dissemination of "white trash" as well as "good country folk" ste-reotypes in society. The working class white, placed in these two distinct roles, serves as a personified id and superego for the collective psyche of America, particularly of middle and upper class whites.

The "white trash" portrayal represents the little devil on one shoulder—embodying racism, ignorance, violence, filth, and base desires. He operates

This 1964 photo shows an unemployed Appalachian
miner with his family.

outside of societal boundaries with an emphasis on the "id's" instinct and pri-
malism. The "good country folk" portrayal represents the little angel on the
other side — embodying simplicity, loyalty, faith in religion and humanity, and
a connection to family and community. This "superego" maintains moral
absolutes in a world where such ideals no longer belong.

Society has not chosen one to be the representative model, but instead *uses* 5
(and I mean that in the harshest sense) this dichotomy to fulfill its own desires
on either end of the spectrum. As "id," the working class white is burdened with
all the crimes and guilt of the white race over time. This allows the audience to
feel justifiable hatred toward a group which they can demonize and thereby
release guilt and aggression unto — while hating what is worst within themselves. As "superego," the working class white is used to nostalgize and idealize
the desire for a simpler life, thus enabling the audience to reassure itself of qualities they hope are best within themselves in a kind, moral world. These images
reappear over time and in many forms of media. They are considered for their
impact on public perception and treatment of working class whites.

Modern day experience with white trash stereotypes is, as with most
modern cultural phenomena, disseminated through movies and television.
The images society has created fall into two conflicting categories. Most
often the working class white is a whisky-drinking, abusive, violently racist,

uneducated, macho, close-minded, dirty, fat, insensitive, monster-truck-show-watching hunter who is better laughed at than associated with. Yet in rare instances, one encounters the poor white as honest, hard-working, honorable, simple, loyal, God-fearing, and patriotic. And here exists the dichotomy of white trash versus good country folk.

American society has used the working class white to alternately allay its fear of faltering morality or to bolster its confidence in the correctness of the modern lifestyle. Examples of this tendency occur in the typecasting of working class whites in television series as well as film. Stemming from the disillusionment of Vietnam, Watergate, and other corruptions of the time, we can trace a movement of "good country folk" in the television shows of the seventies. Programs like *The Andy Griffith Show* and *The Waltons* provided a simple, honest way of life that appealed to viewers as an escape from the cynicism and the loss of moral absolutes that was becoming prevalent in society. Once again, America turned to the South as the appropriate setting for such nostalgia.

At around the same time, we also have popular Southern sitcoms like *The Dukes of Hazzard* and *The Beverly Hillbillies* playing on the more typical stereotype of uneducated, criminal (Duke brothers' constant battles with the corrupt Boss Hogg) characters with substandard eating habits and speech patterns. We also find sexy yet innocent women protected by their families with Daisy and Ellie May. *The Beverly Hillbillies* proves that even when poor whites stumble upon money, they retain their low class ways, and are useful only for the purposes of humor. *The Dukes of Hazzard* gives a solid continuation of redneck stereotypes, tempered with the idea that the Dukes are "never meanin' no harm" as the theme song implies.

The television show *The Beverly Hillbillies*, about a poor Ozark family that strikes it rich and moves to Beverly Hills, ran from 1962 to 1971.

John Steinbeck's novel *The Grapes of Wrath* (1939) was made into a movie starring Henry Fonda.

The use of violence in film and writing is often a hallmark of social passion. During the 1930s there was a movement to expose the brutality of the lives of working class whites. Yet often the attempts to give aid were actually forms of condescension and control. That is commonly the effect of the literature and case studies of the time. John Ford's film adaptation of *The Grapes of Wrath* is the strongest example of dignified poor white media portrayal. Henry Fonda and Jane Darwell, echoing the themes of Southern agrarianism, are rural saints attacked by the forces of modern, capitalistic society.

In recent years, the popularity of poor white imagery has come in two forms. One is the simple, idiotic portrayal in the humorous sketches of Jeff Foxworthy (a middle to upper class actor — not a redneck) and the brass unorthodoxy of Roseanne, or the dark and perverse killer in movies like *Deliverance* or *Sling Blade*. Though the complex and human character in *Sling Blade* is much easier to accept than the sodomizing mountain man in *Deliverance*, both characters portray a warped sense of morality that is equated to their Southern, poor white upbringing. The father of the killer in *Sling Blade* is shown surrounded by religious iconography, and he and his wife blatantly use religion to justify their horrific treatment of the child and the murder of an unwanted baby that is born to them. The depth of ignorance necessary to explain the characters' behavior is only fitting in the environment of the poor white. Filled with domestic violence and dark secrets, the Southern small town setting ensures that such events would not take place in any other context.

Deliverance may be the most well-known and damaging film centered around poor whites, in this case "hillbillies." *Deliverance* embodies all the fear of urban modern America concerning what is most primitive and dangerous in the character of man. The conflict is between modern mainstream capitalist America and the lurking potential of evil in mankind . . . an evil which has

10

been left behind to remain only in those mountaineers most remote and ignorant of civilization. In the film, urban macho man takes on the raw brutality of nature and its inhabitants with no respect and pays the price. The punishment is one of male on male rape by the embodiment of poor white trash, confirming mainstream America's fear of the poverty-stricken savage.

The view from inside the working class is much more complex. The working class white is operating off his own cultural, family, and individual biases; yet coupled with these are the pervasive, historically assumed ideas that violence, racism, and fundamentalism are somehow inherent in his class. Even if one becomes aware of the layers of identification applied to oneself, and most people do not, a battle against your own heritage is difficult at best, and usually impossible. The class to which we are born, in which our family circulates and our formative years are spent, is the guiding principle with which we view other groups and their cultural beliefs within our life experience.

Films that show poor whites as violent people who attack wealthy citified whites allow the rich to justify their treatment of "white trash" by portraying the poor whites as racist, criminal, and uneducated. This allows other typically marginalized groups to join upper class whites against the "white trash." This justifies upper class stereotyping of poor whites and serves to aid in relieving upper class white guilt over treatment of "others" in the past.

The hatred and condescension of the poor seems to be the last available method of prejudice in our society. Just as Americans have made an effort to educate, understand, and alter the treatment of marginalized groups and alternate cultures within our society, we have held on to poor whites as a group to demean. Making assumptions about groups of any sort on societal and biased definitions is flawed in any situation. As with other groups, there must be an effort taken to use an open mind and individual code to ascribe merit to those in our world.

WORKS CITED

Cook, Sylvia Jenkins. *From Tobacco Road to Route 66: The Southern Poor in Fiction.* Chapel Hill: University of North Carolina Press, 1976.

Fussell, Paul. *Class.* New York: Simon & Schuster, 1983.

Goad, Jim. *The Redneck Manifesto.* New York: Simon & Schuster, 1997.

READING THE TEXT

1. Explain in your own words Price's definitions of "white trash" and "good country folk."
2. What is the logic behind Price's analogies between white trash and the id and good country folk and the superego?
3. Summarize in your own words the evolution of cinematic depictions of poor whites from the 1970s to more recent years.
4. What does Price mean by saying that "a battle against your own heritage is difficult at best, and usually impossible" (para. 12)?

READING THE SIGNS

1. Watch a recent movie that has working-class white characters and analyze it according to the stereotypes that Price describes. Do you find depictions of "white trash" or "good country folk," or do the characters have traits that Price does not discuss?

2. At your school's media library, watch an episode of one of the TV shows Price mentions, such as *The Dukes of Hazzard* or *The Beverly Hillbillies*, or watch one of the films that she describes. Then write your own analysis of its portrayal of the characters. Is the portrayal hostile or affectionate toward working-class white characters?

3. Write a reflective essay in which you respond to Price's assertion that "the hatred and condescension of the poor seems to be the last available method of prejudice in our society" (para. 14). Support your essay with references to current popular entertainment.

4. In class, discuss why the "white trash" stereotype persists, even in an age of heightened sensitivity about racial stereotyping. Use the discussion as the springboard for an essay in which you propose your own explanation for this phenomenon.

5. **CONNECTING TEXTS**   Compare and contrast Price's argument about the way class is depicted in media with that of Michael Parenti ("Class and Virtue," p. 406). How do you account for any differences you may discern?

JACK LOPEZ
Of Cholos and Surfers

> *If you want to be a surfer, L.A.'s the place to be, but things can get com-*
> *plicated if you come from East Los Angeles, which is not only miles from*
> *the beach but is also the home turf for many a cholo street gangster who*
> *may not look kindly on a Mexican American kid carrying a copy of*
> Surfer Quarterly *and wearing Bermuda shorts. This is exactly what hap-*
> *pened to Jack Lopez as he tells it in this memoir of growing up Latino in*
> *the 1960s — but not to worry, the beach and the barrio are not mutually*
> *exclusive, and, in the end, Lopez was able to have "the best of both*
> *worlds." A professor of English at California State University, Northridge,*
> *Lopez has published the memoir* Cholos & Surfers: A Latino Family
> Album *(1998), the story collection* Snapping Lines *(2001), and the novel*
> In the Break *(2006).*

The only store around that had this new magazine was a Food Giant on Vermont Avenue, just off Imperial. *Surfer Quarterly*, it was then called. Now it's
Surfer Magazine and they've celebrated their thirtieth anniversary. Sheldon
made the discovery by chance when he'd gone shopping with his mother,
who needed something found only at Food Giant. Normally we didn't go that
far east to shop; we went west toward Crenshaw, to the nicer part of town.

We all wanted to be surfers, in fact called ourselves surfers even though
we never made it to the beach, though it was less than ten miles away. One of
the ways you could become a surfer was to own an issue of *Surfer Quarterly*.
Since there had been only one prior issue, I was hot to get the new one. To be
a surfer you also had to wear baggy shorts, large Penney's Towncraft T-shirts,
and go barefoot, no matter how much the hot sidewalks burned your soles.

That summer in the early sixties I was doing all sorts of odd jobs around
the house for my parents: weeding, painting the eaves, baby-sitting during the
daytime. I was earning money so that I could buy Lenny Muelich's surfboard,
another way to be a surfer. It was a Velzy-Jacobs, ten feet six inches long,
twenty-four inches wide, and it had the coolest red oval decal. Lenny was my
across-the-street neighbor, two years older than I, the kid who'd taught me
the facts of life, the kid who'd taught me how to wrestle, the kid who'd played
army with me when we were children, still playing in the dirt.

Now we no longer saw much of each other, though he still looked out for
me. A strange thing happened to Lenny the previous school year. He grew.
Like the Green Giant or something. He was over six feet tall and the older
guys would let him hang out with them. So Lenny had become sort of a hood,
wearing huge Sir Guy wool shirts, baggy khaki pants with the cuffs rolled, and
French-toed black shoes. He drank wine, even getting drunk in the daytime

with his hoodlum friends. Lenny was now respected, feared, even, by some of the parents, and no longer needed or desired to own a surfboard — he was going in the opposite direction. There were two distinct paths in my neighborhood: hood or surfer.

I was entering junior high school in a month, and my best friends were Sheldon Cohen and Tom Gheridelli. They lived by Morningside Heights, and their fathers were the only ones to work, and their houses were more expensive than mine, and they'd both been surfers before I'd aspired toward such a life. Sheldon and Tom wore their hair long, constantly cranking their heads back to keep their bangs out of their eyes. They were thirteen years old. I was twelve. My parents wouldn't let hair grow over my ears no matter how much I argued with them. But I was the one buying a surfboard. Lenny was holding it for me. My parents would match any money I saved over the summer.

Yet *Surfer Quarterly* was more tangible since it only cost one dollar. Lenny's Velzy Jacobs was forty-five dollars, quite a large sum for the time. The issue then became one of how to obtain the object of desire. The Food Giant on Vermont was reachable by bike, but I was no longer allowed to ride up there. Not since my older brother had gone to the Southside Theatre one Saturday and had seen a boy get knifed because he wasn't colored. Vermont was a tough area, though some of the kids I went to school with lived up there and they weren't any different from us. Yet none of them wished to be surfers, I don't think.

What was needed was for me to include my father in the negotiation. I wasn't allowed to ride my bike to Vermont, I reasoned with him. Therefore, he should drive me. He agreed with me and that was that. Except I had to wait until the following Friday when he didn't have to work.

My father was a printer by trade. He worked the graveyard shift. I watched my younger brother and sister during the day (my older brother, who was fifteen years old, was around in case anything of consequence should arise, but we mostly left him alone) until my mother returned from work — Reaganomics had hit my family decades before the rest of the country. Watching my younger sister and brother consisted of keeping them quiet so my father could sleep.

In the late afternoons I'd go to Sportsman's Park, where I'd virtually grown up. I made the all-stars in baseball, basketball, and football. Our first opponent on the path to the city championships was always Will Rogers Park in Watts. Sheldon and Tom and I had been on the same teams. Sometimes I'd see them in the afternoons before we'd all have to return home for dinner. We'd pore over Sheldon's issue of *Surfer* while sitting in the bleachers next to the baseball diamond. If it was too hot we'd go in the wading pool, though we were getting too old for that scene, since mostly women and kids used it.

When Friday afternoon arrived and my father had showered and my mother had returned from work, I reminded my father of our agreement. We drove the neighborhood streets up to Vermont, passing Washington High School, Normandie Avenue, Woodcrest Elementary School, and so on. We spoke mostly of me. Was I looking forward to attending Henry Clay Junior

High? Would I still be in accelerated classes? My teachers and the principal had talked with my parents about my skipping a grade but my parents said no.

Just as my father had exhausted his repertoire of school questions, we arrived at the Food Giant. After parking in the back lot, we entered the store and made for the liquor section, where the magazines were housed. I stood in front of the rack, butterflies of expectation overtaking my stomach while my father bought himself some beer. I knew immediately when I found the magazine. It looked like a square of water was floating in the air. An ocean-blue cover of a huge wave completely engulfing a surfer with the headline BANZAI PIPELINE. I held the magazine with great reverence, as if I were holding something of spiritual value, which it was.

"Is that it?" my father asked. He held a quart of Hamm's in each hand, his Friday night allotment.

"Yes." I beamed.

At the counter my father took the magazine from me, leafing through it much too casually, I thought. I could see the bulging veins in his powerful forearms, and saw too the solid bumps that were his biceps.

"Looks like a crazy thing to do," he said, finally placing the magazine on the counter next to the beer. My father, the practical provider, the person whose closet was pristine for lack of clothes — although the ones he did own were stylish, yet not expensive. This was why he drank beer from quart bottles — it was cheaper that way. I know now how difficult it must have been raising four children on the hourly wages my parents made. 15

The man at the counter rang up the purchases, stopping for a moment to look at the *Surfer*. He smiled.

"*¿Eres mexicano?*" my father asked him.

"*Sí', ¿cómo no?*" the man answered.

Then my father and the store clerk began poking fun at my magazine in Spanish, nothing too mean, but ranking it as silly adolescent nonsense.

When we got back in the car I asked my father why he always asked certain people if they were Mexican. He only asked men who obviously were, thus knowing in advance their answers. He shrugged his shoulders and said he didn't know. It was a way of initiating conversation, he said. Well, it was embarrassing for me, I told him. Because I held the magazine in my lap, I let my father off the hook. It was more important that I give it a quick thumb-through as we drove home. The *Surfer* was far more interesting for me as a twelve-year-old than larger issues of race. 20

I spent the entire Friday evening holed up in my room, poring over the magazine, not even interested in eating popcorn or watching *77 Sunset Strip*, our familial Friday-night ritual. By the next morning I had almost memorized every photo caption and their sequence. I spoke with Sheldon on the phone and he and Tom were meeting me later at Sportsman's Park. I did my chores in a self-absorbed trance, waiting for the time when I could share my treasure with my friends. My mother made me eat lunch before I was finally able to leave.

Walking the long walk along Western Avenue toward Century and glancing at the photos in the magazine, I didn't pay attention to the cholo whom I passed on the sidewalk. I should have been more aware, but was too preoccupied. So there I was, in a street confrontation before I knew what had happened.

"You a surfer?" he said with disdain. He said it the way you start to say *chocolate. Ch*, like in *choc — churfer*. But that didn't quite capture it, either.

I stopped and turned to face him. He wore a wool watch cap pulled down onto his eyebrows, a long Sir Guy wool shirt with the top button buttoned and all the rest unbuttoned, khaki pants so long they were frayed at the bottoms and so baggy I couldn't see his shoes. I wore Bermuda shorts and a large Towncraft T-shirt. I was barefoot. My parents wouldn't let hair grow over my ears. Cholo meets surfer. Not a good thing. As he clenched his fists I saw a black cross tattooed onto the fleshy part of his hand.

His question was *not* like my father's. My father, I now sensed, wanted a   25 common bond upon which to get closer to strangers. This guy was Mexican American, and he wanted to fight me because I wore the outfit of a surfer.

I rolled the magazine in a futile attempt to hide it, but the cholo viewed this action as an escalation with a perceived weapon. It wasn't that I was overly afraid of him, though fear can work to your advantage if used correctly. I was big for my age, athletic, and had been in many fights. The problem was this: I was hurrying off to see my friends, to share something important with them, walking on a summer day, and I didn't feel like rolling on the ground with some stranger because *he'd* decided we must do so. Why did he get to dictate when or where you would fight? There was another consideration, one more utilitarian: Who knew what sort of weapons he had under all that baggy clothing? A rattail comb, at the least. More likely a knife, because in those days guns weren't that common.

At Woodcrest Elementary School there was a recently arrived Dutch Indonesian immigrant population. One of the most vicious fights I had ever seen was the one when Victor VerHagen fought his own cousin. And the toughest fight I'd ever been in was against Julio, something during a baseball game. There must be some element of self-loathing that propels us to fight those of our own ethnicity with a particular ferocity.

Just before the cholo was going to initiate the fight, I said, "I'm Mexican." American of Mexican descent, actually.

He seemed unable to process this new information. How could someone be Mexican and dress like a surfer? He looked at me again, this time seeing beyond the clothes I wore. He nodded slightly.

This revelation, this recognition verbalized, molded me in the years to   30 come. A surfer with a peeled nose and a Karmann Ghia with surf racks driving down Whittier Boulevard in East L.A. to visit my grandparents. The charmed life of a surfer in the midst of cholos.

When I began attending junior high school, there was a boy nicknamed Niño, who limped around the school yard one day. I discovered the reason for his limp when I went to the bathroom and he had a rifle pointed at boys and was taking their money. I fell in love with a girl named Shirley Pelland, the younger sister of a local surfboard maker. I saw her in her brother's shop after school, but she had no idea I loved her. That fall the gang escalation in my neighborhood became so pronounced my parents decided to move. We sold our house very quickly and moved to Huntington Beach, and none of us could sleep at night for the quiet. We were surrounded by cornfields and strawberry fields and tomato fields. As a bribe for our sudden move my parents chipped in much more than matching funds so I could buy Lenny Muelich's surfboard. I almost drowned in the big waves of a late-autumn south swell, the first time I went out on the Velzy-Jacobs. But later, after I'd surfed for a few years, I expertly rode the waves next to the pier, surfing with new friends.

But I've got ahead of myself. I must return to the cholo who is about to attack. But there isn't any more to tell about the incident. We didn't fight that summer's day over thirty years ago. In fact, I never fought another of my own race and don't know if this was a conscious decision or if circumstances dictated it. As luck would have it, I fought only a few more times during my adolescence and did so only when attacked.

My father's question, which he'd asked numerous people so long ago, taught me these things: The reason he had to ask was because he and my mother had left the safe confines of their Boyle Heights upbringing. They had thrust themselves and their children into what was called at the time the melting pot of Los Angeles. They bought the post–World War II American dream of assimilation. I was a pioneer in the sociological sense that I had no distinct ethnic piece of geography on which my pride and honor depended. Cast adrift in the city streets. Something gained, something lost. I couldn't return to my ethnic neighborhood, but I could be a surfer. And I didn't have to fight for ethnic pride over my city street. The neighborhood kids did, however, stick together, though this was not based upon race. It was a necessity. The older guys would step forward to protect the younger ones. That was how it was done.

The most important thing I learned was that I could do just about anything I wished, within reason. I could be a surfer, if I chose, and even cholos would respect my decision. During my adolescence I went to my grandparents' house for all the holidays. They lived in East Los Angeles. When I was old enough to drive I went on my own, sometimes with a girlfriend. I was able to observe my Los Angeles Mexican heritage, taking a date to the *placita* for Easter service and then having lunch at Olvera Street. An Orange County girl who had no idea this part of Los Angeles existed. I was lucky; I got the best of both worlds.

READING THE TEXT

1. What symbolic significance did being a surfer have for Lopez and his friends?

2. How did Lopez's attitude toward his Mexican heritage compare with that of his father, and how do you explain any difference?

3. Why does the cholo object to Lopez's surfer clothing?

4. How did Lopez eventually reconcile his surfer and his Mexican American identities?

5. Characterize Lopez's tone and persona in this selection. How do they affect your response as a reader?

READING THE SIGNS

1. In your journal, write your own account of how, in your childhood, you developed a sense of ethnic identity. Use Lopez's article as a model that pinpoints concrete, specific events as being significant.

2. **CONNECTING TEXTS** Compare and contrast Lopez's development of a sense of ethnic identity with that of Melissa Algranati ("Being an Other," p. 697). How can you account for any differences you might see?

3. A generational gap separated Lopez's and his father's attitudes toward assimilation. Interview several friends, preferably of different ethnicities, and their parents about their sense of ethnic identity. Write an essay in which you explore the extent to which one's age can influence one's attitudes toward ethnicity.

4. In class, discuss the extent to which your community is characterized by a "distinct ethnic piece of geography" (para. 33). Do people of different ethnicities interact frequently? Or do people tend to associate primarily with those of the same background? Use your discussion as the basis of an essay in which you evaluate the race relations in your community, taking care to suggest causes for the patterns that you see.

JIM WHITMER

Four Teens

READING THE SIGNS

1. Describe Whitmer's photograph. What is taking place? How would you characterize the attitudes of the four youths in this photo? Examine them one by one. You might comment on their facial and body expressions, for instance.

2. What do you think is the relationship among these four youths? What evidence do you have for your answers? Assume that the photographer has deliberately placed each subject in the photograph. Speculate on the motives of his placement and the effect he has achieved.

3. How would you characterize the clothing, hair, and jewelry — the styles — of the figures in the photo? That is, what do their styles say about them? Would you be willing to adopt their styles? Why or why not?

NELL BERNSTEIN

Goin' Gangsta, Choosin' Cholita

Ever wonder about wannabes — white suburban teenagers who dress and act like nonwhite inner-city gangsters? In this report on the phenomenon of "claiming," Nell Bernstein probes some of the feelings and motives of teens who are "goin' gangsta" or "choosin' cholita" — kids who try on a racial identity not their own. Their reasons may surprise you. Bernstein is a journalist who has published in Glamour, Woman's Day, Salon, *and* Mother Jones. *She is also the author of* All Alone in the World: Children of the Incarcerated *(2005).*

Her lipstick is dark, the lip liner even darker, nearly black. In baggy pants, a blue plaid Pendleton, her bangs pulled back tight off her forehead, 15-year-old April is a perfect cholita, a Mexican gangsta girl.

But April Miller is Anglo. "And I don't like it!" she complains. "I'd rather be Mexican."

April's father wanders into the family room of their home in San Leandro, California, a suburb near Oakland. "Hey, cholita," he teases. "Go get a suntan. We'll put you in a barrio and see how much you like it."

A large, sandy-haired man with "April" tattooed on one arm and "Kelly" — the name of his older daughter — on the other, Miller spent 21 years working in a San Leandro glass factory that shut down and moved to Mexico a couple of years ago. He recently got a job in another factory, but he expects NAFTA to swallow that one, too.

"Sooner or later we'll all get nailed," he says. "Just another stab in the back of the American middle class." 5

Later, April gets her revenge: "Hey, Mr. White Man's Last Stand," she teases. "Wait till you see how well I manage my welfare check. You'll be asking me for money."

A once almost exclusively white, now increasingly Latin and black working-class suburb, San Leandro borders on predominantly black East Oakland. For decades, the boundary was strictly policed and practically impermeable. In 1970 April Miller's hometown was 97 percent white. By 1990 San Leandro was 65 percent white, 6 percent black, 15 percent Hispanic, and 13 percent Asian or Pacific Islander. With minorities moving into suburbs in growing numbers and cities becoming ever more diverse, the boundary between city and suburb is dissolving, and suburban teenagers are changing with the times.

In April's bedroom, her past and present selves lie in layers, the pink walls of girlhood almost obscured, Guns N' Roses and Pearl Jam posters overlaid by rappers Paris and Ice Cube. "I don't have a big enough attitude to be a black girl," says April, explaining her current choice of ethnic identification.

What matters is that she thinks the choice is hers. For April and her friends, identity is not a matter of where you come from, what you were born into, what color your skin is. It's what you wear, the music you listen to, the words you use — everything to which you pledge allegiance, no matter how fleetingly.

The hybridization of American teens has become talk show fodder, with "wiggers" — white kids who dress and talk "black" — appearing on TV in full gangsta regalia. In Indiana a group of white high school girls raised a national stir when they triggered an imitation race war at their virtually all-white high school last fall simply by dressing "black." 10

In many parts of the country, it's television and radio, not neighbors, that introduce teens to the allure of ethnic difference. But in California, which demographers predict will be the first state with no racial majority by the year 2000, the influences are more immediate. The California public schools are the most diverse in the country: 42 percent white, 36 percent Hispanic, 9 percent black, 8 percent Asian.

Sometimes young people fight over their differences. Students at virtually any school in the Bay Area can recount the details of at least one "race riot" in which a conflict between individuals escalated into a battle between their clans. More often, though, teens would rather join than fight. Adolescence, after all, is the period when you're most inclined to mimic the power closest at hand, from stealing your older sister's clothes to copying the ruling clique at school.

White skaters and Mexican would-be gangbangers listen to gangsta rap and call each other "nigga" as a term of endearment; white girls sometimes affect Spanish accents; blond cheerleaders claim Cherokee ancestors.

"Claiming" is the central concept here. A Vietnamese teen in Hayward, another Oakland suburb, "claims" Oakland — and by implication blackness — because he lived there as a child. A law-abiding white kid "claims" a Mexican gang he says he hangs with. A brown-skinned girl with a Mexican father and a white mother "claims" her Mexican side, while her fair-skinned sister "claims" white. The word comes up over and over, as if identity were territory, the self a kind of turf.

At a restaurant in a minimall in Hayward, Nicole Huffstutler, 13, sits with her friends and describes herself as "Indian, German, French, Welsh, and, um . . . American": "If somebody says anything like 'Yeah, you're just a peckerwood,' I'll walk up and I'll say 'white pride!' 'Cause I'm proud of my race, and I wouldn't wanna be any other race." 15

"Claiming" white has become a matter of principle for Heather, too, who says she's "sick of the majority looking at us like we're less than them." (Hayward schools were 51 percent white in 1990, down from 77 percent in 1980, and whites are now the minority in many schools.)

Asked if she knows that nonwhites have not traditionally been referred to as "the majority" in America, Heather gets exasperated: "I hear that all the time, every day. They say, 'Well, you guys controlled us for many years, and it's time for us to control you.' Every day."

When Jennifer Vargas — a small, brown-skinned girl in purple jeans who quietly eats her salad while Heather talks — softly announces that she's "mostly Mexican," she gets in trouble with her friends.

"No, you're not!" scolds Heather.

"I'm mostly Indian and Mexican," Jennifer continues flatly. "I'm very little . . . I'm mostly . . ." 20

"Your mom's white!" Nicole reminds her sharply. "She has blond hair."

"That's what I mean," Nicole adds. "People think that white is a bad thing. They think that white is a bad race. So she's trying to claim more Mexican than white."

"I have very little white in me," Jennifer repeats. "I have mostly my dad's side, 'cause I look like him and stuff. And most of my friends think that me and my brother and sister aren't related, 'cause they look more like my mom."

"But you guys are all the same race, you just look different," Nicole insists. She stops eating and frowns. "OK, you're half and half each what your parents have. So you're equal as your brother and sister, you just look different. And you should be proud of what you are — every little piece and bit of what you are. Even if you were Afghan or whatever, you should be proud of it."

Will Mosley, Heather's 17-year-old brother, says he and his friends listen to rap 25 groups like Compton's Most Wanted, NWA, and Above the Law because they "sing about life" — that is, what happens in Oakland, Los Angeles, anyplace but where Will is sitting today, an empty Round Table Pizza in a minimall.

"No matter what race you are," Will says, "if you live like we do, then that's the kind of music you like."

And how do they live?

"We don't live bad or anything," Will admits. "We live in a pretty good neighborhood, there's no violence or crime. I was just . . . we're just city people, I guess."

Will and his friend Adolfo Garcia, 16, say they've outgrown trying to be something they're not. "When I was 11 or 12," Will says, "I thought I was becoming a big gangsta and stuff. Because I liked that music, and thought it was the coolest, I wanted to become that. I wore big clothes, like you wear in jail. But then I kind of woke up. I looked at myself and thought, 'Who am I trying to be?'"

They may have outgrown blatant mimicry, but Will and his friends remain 30 convinced that they can live in a suburban tract house with a well-kept lawn on a tree-lined street in "not a bad neighborhood" and still call themselves "city" people on the basis of musical tastes. "City" for these young people means crime, graffiti, drugs. The kids are law-abiding, but these activities connote what Will admiringly calls "action." With pride in his voice, Will predicts that "in a couple of years, Hayward will be like Oakland. It's starting to get more known, because of crime and things. I think it'll be bigger, more things happening, more crime, more graffiti, stealing cars."

"That's good," chimes in 15-year-old Matt Jenkins, whose new beeper — an item that once connoted gangsta chic but now means little more than an active social life — goes off periodically. "More fun."

The three young men imagine with disdain life in a gangsta-free zone. "Too bland, too boring," Adolfo says. "You have to have something going on. You can't just have everyday life."

"Mowing your lawn," Matt sneers.

"Like Beaver Cleaver's house," Adolfo adds. "It's too clean out here."

Not only white kids believe that identity is a matter of choice or taste, or   35
that the power of "claiming" can transcend ethnicity. The Manor Park Locos — a group of mostly Mexican-Americans who hang out in San Leandro's Manor Park — say they descend from the Manor Lords, tough white guys who ruled the neighborhood a generation ago.

They "are like our . . . uncles and dads, the older generation," says Jesse Martinez, 14. "We're what they were when they were around, except we're Mexican."

"There's three generations," says Oso, Jesse's younger brother. "There's Manor Lords, Manor Park Locos, and Manor Park Pee Wees." The Pee Wees consist mainly of the Locos' younger brothers, eager kids who circle the older boys on bikes and brag about "punking people."

Unlike Will Mosley, the Locos find little glamour in city life. They survey the changing suburban landscape and see not "action" or "more fun" but frightening decline. Though most of them are not yet 18, the Locos are already nostalgic, longing for a Beaver Cleaver past that white kids who mimic them would scoff at.

Walking through nearly empty Manor Park, with its eucalyptus stands, its softball diamond and tennis courts, Jesse's friend Alex, the only Asian in the group, waves his arms in a gesture of futility. "A few years ago, every bench was filled," he says. "Now no one comes here. I guess it's because of every-thing that's going on. My parents paid a lot for this house, and I want it to be nice for them. I just hope this doesn't turn into Oakland."

Glancing across the park at April Miller's street, Jesse says he knows what   40
the white cholitas are about. "It's not a racial thing," he explains. "It's just all the most popular people out here are Mexican. We're just the gangstas that everyone knows. I guess those girls wanna be known."

Not every young Californian embraces the new racial hybridism. Andrea Jones, 20, an African American who grew up in the Bay Area suburbs of Union City and Hayward, is unimpressed by what she sees mainly as shallow mimicry. "It's full of posers out here," she says. "When *Boyz N the Hood* came out on video, it was sold out for weeks. The boys all wanna be black, the girls all wanna be Mexican. It's the glamour."

Driving down the quiet, shaded streets of her old neighborhood in Union City, Andrea spots two white preteen boys in Raiders jackets and hugely baggy pants strutting erratically down the empty sidewalk. "Look at them," she says. "Dislocated."

She knows why. "In a lot of these schools out here, it's hard being white," she says. "I don't think these kids were prepared for the backlash that is going on, all the pride now in people of color's ethnicity, and our boldness with it. They have nothing like that, no identity, nothing they can say they're proud of.

"So they latch onto their great-grandmother who's a Cherokee, or they take on the most stereotypical aspects of being black or Mexican. It's beautiful to appreciate different aspects of other people's culture — that's like the dream of what the 21st century should be. But to garnish yourself with pop culture stereotypes just to blend — that's really sad."

Roland Krevocheza, 18, graduated last year from Arroyo High School in   45
San Leandro. He is Mexican on his mother's side, Eastern European on his father's. In the new hierarchies, it may be mixed kids like Roland who have the hardest time finding their place, even as their numbers grow. (One in five marriages in California is between people of different races.) They can always be called "wannabes," no matter what they claim.

"I'll state all my nationalities," Roland says. But he takes a greater interest in his father's side, his Ukrainian, Romanian, and Czech ancestors. "It's more unique," he explains. "Mexican culture is all around me. We eat Mexican food all the time, I hear stories from my grandmother. I see the low-riders and stuff. I'm already part of it. I'm not trying to be; I am."

His darker-skinned brother "says he's not proud to be white," Roland adds. "He calls me 'Mr. Nazi.'" In the room the two share, the American flags and the reproduction of the Bill of Rights are Roland's; the Public Enemy poster belongs to his brother.

Roland has good reason to mistrust gangsta attitudes. In his junior year in high school, he was one of several Arroyo students who were beaten up outside the school at lunchtime by a group of Samoans who came in cars from Oakland. Roland wound up with a split lip, a concussion, and a broken tailbone. Later he was told that the assault was "gang-related" — that the Samoans were beating up anyone wearing red.

"Rappers, I don't like them," Roland says. "I think they're a bad influence on kids. It makes kids think they're all tough and bad."

Those who, like Roland, dismiss the gangsta and cholo styles as affecta-   50
tions can point to the fact that several companies market overpriced knockoffs of "ghetto wear" targeted at teens.

But there's also something going on out here that transcends adolescent faddishness and pop culture exoticism. When white kids call their parents "racist" for nagging them about their baggy pants; when they learn Spanish to talk to their boyfriends; when Mexican-American boys feel themselves descended in spirit from white "uncles"; when children of mixed marriages insist that they are whatever race they say they are, all of them are more than just confused.

They're inching toward what Andrea Jones calls "the dream of what the 21st century should be." In the ever more diverse communities of Northern California, they're also facing the complicated reality of what their 21st century will be.

Meanwhile, in the living room of the Miller family's San Leandro home, the argument continues unabated. "You don't know what you are," April's father has told her more than once. But she just keeps on telling him he doesn't know what time it is.

READING THE TEXT

1. How do teens like April Miller define their identity, according to Bernstein?
2. Describe in your own words what "claiming" (para. 14) an ethnic identity means and why so many teens are tempted to do so.
3. What relationship does Bernstein see between claiming and mass media?
4. What does being white mean to many of the kids who claim a nonwhite identity?
5. What does the city signify to the young people whom Bernstein describes?

READING THE SIGNS

1. In class, stage a conversation between April Miller and her father on her adoption of a Mexican identity, with April defending her choice and her father repudiating it.
2. Write an essay in which you support, challenge, or modify Andrea Jones's assumption that it is media-generated "glamour" that prompts young people to claim a new ethnic identity. Be sure to base your argument on the evidence of specific pop culture personalities.
3. Write an argumentative essay in which you explain whether the claiming fad is an expression of racial tolerance or racial stereotyping.
4. **CONNECTING TEXTS**   Bernstein describes teens claiming the identities of ethnic minorities, but she provides few instances of claiming a white identity. In an essay, propose your own explanation for this pattern. To develop your ideas, you might consult Angeline F. Price's "Working Class Whites" (p. 678).
5. **CONNECTING TEXTS**   Assuming the perspective of Jack Lopez ("Of Cholos and Surfers," p. 684), write an analysis of the social and cultural pressures that prompt these teens to "claim" an ethnicity. Do they desire to have "the best of both worlds," as Lopez does, or are other forces at work?

MELISSA ALGRANATI
Being an Other

> *In a country as obsessed with racial identification as America is, Melissa Algranati poses a dilemma. As she puts it, "there are not too many Puerto Rican, Egyptian Jews out there," so the only category left for her on the census form is "other." In this personal essay, Algranati tells the story of how she came to be an "other," a saga of two immigrant families from different continents who eventually came together in a "marriage that only a country like America could create." Algranati is a graduate of the State University of New York at Binghamton and has a master's degree from Columbia University. She is a staff writer for www.studio2b.org.*

Throughout my whole life, people have mistaken me for other ethnic backgrounds rather than for what I really am. I learned at a young age that there are not too many Puerto Rican, Egyptian Jews out there. For most of my life I have been living in two worlds, and at the same time I have been living in neither. When I was young I did not realize that I was unique, because my family brought me up with a healthy balance of Puerto Rican and Sephardic customs. It was not until I took the standardized PSAT exam that I was confronted with the question: "Who am I?" I remember the feeling of confusion as I struggled to find the right answer. I was faced with a bad multiple-choice question in which there was only supposed to be one right answer, but more than one answer seemed to be correct. I did not understand how a country built on the concept of diversity could forget about its most diverse group, inter-ethnic children. I felt lost in a world of classification. The only way for me to take pride in who I am was to proclaim myself as an other, yet that leaves out so much. As a product of a marriage only a country like America could create, I would now try to help people understand what it is like to be a member of the most underrepresented group in the country, the "others."

My father, Jacques Algranati, was born in Alexandria, Egypt. As a Sephardic Jew, my father was a minority in a predominantly Arab world. Although in the minority, socially my father was a member of the upper middle class and lived a very comfortable life. As a result of strong French influence in the Middle Eastern Jewish world, my father attended a French private school. Since Arabic was the language of the lower class, the Algranati family spoke French as their first language. My whole family is polyglot, speaking languages from the traditional Sephardic tongue of Ladino to Turkish and Greek. My grandfather spoke seven languages. Basically, my father grew up in a close-knit Sephardic community surrounded by family and friends.

However, in 1960 my father's world came to a halt when he was faced with persecution on an institutional level. As a result of the Egyptian-Israeli conflict, in 1956 an edict was issued forcing all foreign-born citizens and Jews out of Egypt. Although my father was a native-born citizen of the country, because of a very strong anti-Jewish sentiment, his citizenship meant nothing. So in 1960 when my family got their exit visas, as Jews had done since the time of the Inquisition, they packed up and left the country as one large family group.

Unable to take many possessions or much money with them, my father's family, like many Egyptian Jews, immigrated to France. They proceeded to France because they had family who were able to sponsor them. Also, once in France my family hoped to be able to receive a visa to America much sooner, since French immigration quotas to the United States were much higher than those in Egypt. Once in France my family relied on the generosity of a Jewish organization, the United Jewish Appeal. For nine months my father lived in a hotel sponsored by the United Jewish Appeal and attended French school until the family was granted a visa to the United States.

Since my father's oldest brother came to the United States first with his wife, they were able to sponsor the rest of the family's passage over. The Algranati family eventually settled in Forest Hills, Queens. Like most immigrants, my family settled in a neighborhood filled with immigrants of the same background. Once in the United States, my father rejoined many of his old friends from Egypt, since most Egyptian Jewish refugees followed a similar immigration path. At the age of fourteen my father and his group of friends were once again forced to adjust to life in a new country, but this time they had to learn a new language in order to survive. Like many of his friends, my father was forced to leave the comforts and luxuries of his world for the hardships of a new world. But as he eloquently puts it, once his family and friends were forced to leave, there was really nothing to stay for. 5

Like my father, my mother is also an immigrant; however my parents come from very different parts of the world. Born in Maniti, Puerto Rico, my mom spent the first five years of her life in a small town outside of San Juan. Since my grandfather had attended private school in the United States when he was younger, he was relatively proficient in English. Like many immigrants, my grandfather came to the United States first, in order to help establish the family. After securing a job and an apartment, he sent for my grandmother, and three weeks later my mother and her fourteen-year-old sister came.

Puerto Ricans are different from many other people who come to this country, in the sense that legally they are not considered immigrants. Because Puerto Rico is a commonwealth of the United States, Puerto Ricans are granted automatic U.S. citizenship. So unlike most, from the day my mother and her family stepped on U.S. soil they were considered citizens. The only problem was that the difference in language and social status led "real" Americans not to consider them citizens.

As a result of this unique status, my mother faced many hardships in this new country. From the day my mother entered first grade, her process of

Americanization had begun. Her identity was transformed. She went from being Maria Louisa Pinto to becoming Mary L. Pinto. Not only was my mother given a new name when she began school, but a new language was forced upon her as well. Confronted by an Irish teacher, Mrs. Walsh, who was determined to Americanize her, my mother began her uphill battle with the English language. Even until this day my mother recalls her traumatic experience when she learned how to pronounce the word "run":

"Repeat after me, run."

"Rrrrrrrrrun." 10

"No, Mary, run."

"Rrrrrrrrrun."

No matter how hard my mother tried she could not stop rolling her "r's." After several similar exchanges Mrs. Walsh, with a look of anger on her face, grabbed my mother's cheeks in her hand and squeezed as she repeated in a stern voice, "RUN!" Suffice it to say my mother learned how to speak English without a Spanish accent. It was because of these experiences that my mother made sure the only language spoken in the house or to me and my sister was English. My parents never wanted their children to experience the pain my mother went through just to learn how to say the word "run."

My mother was confronted with discrimination not only from American society but also from her community. While in the United States, my mother lived in a predominantly Spanish community. On first coming to this country her family lived in a tenement in the Bronx. At the age of twelve my mother was once more uprooted and moved to the projects on the Lower East Side. As one of the first families in a predominantly Jewish building, it was a step up for her family.

It was not her environment that posed the biggest conflict for her; it was 15 her appearance. My mother is what people call a "white Hispanic." With her blond hair and blue eyes my mother was taken for everything but a Puerto Rican. Once my mother perfected her English, no one suspected her ethnicity unless she told them. Since she was raised to be above the ghetto, never picking up typical "Hispanic mannerisms," she was able to exist in American society with very little difficulty. Because of a very strong and protective mother and the positive influence and assistance received from the Henry Street Settlement, my mother was able to escape the ghetto. As a result of organizations like Henry Street, my mother was given opportunities such as fresh air camps and jobs in good areas of the city, where she was able to rise above the drugs, alcohol, and violence that consumed so many of her peers.

As a result of her appearance and her upbringing, my mother left her people and the ghetto to enter American society. It was here as an attractive "white" female that my mother and father's two very different worlds merged. My parents, both working on Wall Street at the time, were introduced by a mutual friend. Since both had developed a rather liberal view, the differences in their backgrounds did not seem to be a major factor. After a year of dating my parents decided to get engaged.

Although they were from two different worlds, their engagement seemed to bring them together. Growing up in the midst of the Jewish community of the Lower East Side, my mother was constantly influenced by the beauty of Judaism. Therefore, since my mother never had much connection with Catholicism and had never been baptized, she decided to convert to Judaism and raise her children as Jews. The beauty of the conversion was that no one in my father's family forced her to convert; they accepted her whether she converted or not. As for my mother's family, they too had no real objections to the wedding or conversion. To them the only thing that mattered was that my father was a nice guy who made my mom happy. The most amusing part of the union of these two different families came when they tried to communicate. My father's family is descended from Spanish Jewry where many of them spoke an old Castilian-style Spanish, while my mother's family spoke a very modern Caribbean-style Spanish. To watch them try to communicate in any language other than English was like watching a session of the United Nations.

It was this new world, that of Puerto Rican Jewry, my parents created for me and my sister, Danielle. Resembling both my parents, having my mother's coloring with my father's features, I have often been mistaken for various ethnicities. Possessing light hair and blue eyes, I am generally perceived as the "all-American" girl. Occasionally I have been mistaken for Italian since my last name, Algranati, although Sephardic, has a very Italian flair to it. I have basically lived a chameleon-like existence for most of my life.

As a result of my "otherness," I have gained "acceptance" in many different crowds. From this acceptance I have learned the harsh reality behind my "otherness." I will never forget the time I learned about how the parents of one of my Asian friends perceived me. From very early on, I gained acceptance with the parents of one of my Korean friends. Not only did they respect me as a person and a student, but her father even went so far as to consider me like "one of his daughters." I will always remember how I felt when I heard they made one of their daughters cancel a party because she had invited Hispanics. Even when my friend pointed out that I, the one they loved, was Hispanic they refused to accept it. Even today to them, I will always be Jewish and not Puerto Rican because to them it is unacceptable to "love" a Puerto Rican.

Regardless of community, Jewish or Puerto Rican, I am always confronted   20 by bigots. Often I am forced to sit in silence while friends utter in ignorance stereotypical responses like: "It was probably some spic who stole it," or "You're just like a Jew, always cheap."

For the past three years I have worked on the Lower East Side of Manhattan at the Henry Street Settlement. Basically my mother wanted me to support the organization that helped her get out of the ghetto. Unlike when my mother was there, the population is mostly black and Hispanic. So one day during work I had one of my fellow workers say to me "that is such a collegian white thing to say." I responded by saying that his assumption was only partially correct and asked him if he considered Puerto Rican to be white. Of course he doubted I was any part Hispanic until he met my cousin who "looks" Puerto Rican. At times like these I really feel for my mother, because I know how it feels not to be recognized by society for who you are.

Throughout my life I do not think I have really felt completely a part of any group. I have gone through phases of hanging out with different crowds trying in a sense to find myself. Basically, I have kept my life diverse by attending both Catholic-sponsored camps and Hebrew school at the same time. Similar to my parents, my main goal is to live within American society. I choose my battles carefully. By being diverse I have learned that in a society that is obsessed with classification the only way I will find my place is within myself. Unfortunately, society has not come to terms with a fast-growing population, the "others." Therefore when asked the infamous question: "Who are you?" I respond with a smile, "a Puerto Rican Egyptian Jew." Contrary to what society may think, I know that I am somebody.

READING THE TEXT

1. Summarize in your own words why Algranati feels like one of the "others" (para. 1).

2. How did the childhood experiences of Algranati's parents differ?

3. How does physical appearance affect strangers' perceptions of ethnic identity, according to Algranati?

4. Why does Algranati say she has never "really felt completely a part of any group" (para. 22)?

READING THE SIGNS

1. In your journal, reflect on your answer to the question "Who am I?"

2. Write an essay in which you defend or oppose the practice of asking individuals to identify their ethnicity in official documents such as census forms and school applications.

3. Algranati's background includes racial, cultural, and religious differences. Write an essay explaining how you would identify yourself if you were in her shoes.

4. **CONNECTING TEXTS**   Do you think Algranati would be sympathetic or hostile toward people who "try on" different ethnic identities? Writing as if you were Algranati, write a letter to one of the teens who claims a new ethnic identity in Nell Bernstein's "Goin' Gangsta, Choosin' Cholita" (p. 691).

5. In class, brainstorm names of biracial actors, musicians, politicians, or models. Then discuss the extent to which the mass media presume that people neatly fit ethnic categories. What is the effect of such a presumption?

FAN SHEN

The Classroom and the Wider Culture:
Identity as a Key to Learning English Composition

*Writing conventions involve more cultural presuppositions and mytholo-
gies than we ordinarily recognize. Take the current practice of using the
first-person singular pronoun "I" when writing an essay. Such a convention presumes an individualistic worldview, which can appear very
strange to someone coming from a communal culture, as Fan Shen
relates in this analysis of the relation between culture and composition.
Hailing from the People's Republic of China, where the group comes
before the individual in social consciousness, Shen describes what it was
like to move to the United States and have to learn a whole new worldview to master the writing conventions that he himself now teaches as a
professor of English at Rochester Community and Technical College. A
writer as well as a teacher, Shen has translated three books from English
into Chinese and has written numerous articles for both English and Chinese publications. His latest book is his autobiography,* Gang of One:
Memoirs of a Red Guard *(2004).*

One day in June 1975, when I walked into the aircraft factory where I was
working as an electrician, I saw many large-letter posters on the walls and
many people parading around the workshops shouting slogans like "Down
with the word 'I'!" and "Trust in masses and the Party!" I then remembered
that a new political campaign called "Against Individualism" was scheduled to
begin that day. Ten years later, I got back my first English composition paper
at the University of Nebraska–Lincoln. The professor's first comments were:
"Why did you always use 'we' instead of 'I'?" and "Your paper would be
stronger if you eliminated some sentences in the passive voice." The clashes
between my Chinese background and the requirements of English composition had begun. At the center of this mental struggle, which has lasted several
years and is still not completely over, is the prolonged, uphill battle to recap-
ture "myself."

In this paper I will try to describe and explore this experience of reconciling my Chinese identity with an English identity dictated by the rules of
English composition. I want to show how my cultural background shaped —
and shapes — my approaches to my writing in English and how writing in
English redefined — and redefines — my *ideological* and *logical* identities. By
"ideological identity" I mean the system of values that I acquired (consciously
and unconsciously) from my social and cultural background. And by "logical
identity" I mean the natural (or Oriental) way I organize and express my
thoughts in writing. Both had to be modified or redefined in learning English

composition. Becoming aware of the process of redefinition of these different identities is a mode of learning that has helped me in my efforts to write in English, and, I hope, will be of help to teachers of English composition in this country. In presenting my case for this view, I will use examples from both my composition courses and literature courses, for I believe that writing papers for both kinds of courses contributed to the development of my "English identity." Although what I will describe is based on personal experience, many Chinese students whom I talked to said that they had had the same or similar experiences in their initial stages of learning to write in English.

Identity of the Self: Ideological and Cultural

Starting with the first English paper I wrote, I found that learning to compose in English is not an isolated classroom activity, but a social and cultural experience. The rules of English composition encapsulate values that are absent in, or sometimes contradictory to, the values of other societies (in my case, China). Therefore, learning the rules of English composition is, to a certain extent, learning the values of Anglo-American society. In writing classes in the United States I found that I had to reprogram my mind, to redefine some of the basic concepts and values that I had about myself, about society, and about the universe, values that had been imprinted and reinforced in my mind by my cultural background, and that had been part of me all my life.

Rule number one in English composition is: Be yourself. (More than one composition instructor has told me, "Just write what *you* think.") The values behind this rule, it seems to me, are based on the principle of protecting and promoting individuality (and private property) in this country. The instruction was probably crystal clear to students raised on these values, but, as a guideline of composition, it was not very clear or useful to me when I first heard it. First of all, the image or meaning that I attached to the word "I" or "myself" was, as I found out, different from that of my English teacher. In China, "I" is always subordinated to "We" — be it the working class, the Party, the country, or some other collective body. Both political pressure and literary tradition require that "I" be somewhat hidden or buried in writings and speeches; presenting the "self" too obviously would give people the impression of being disrespectful of the Communist Party in political writings and boastful in scholarly writings. The word "I" has often been identified with another "bad" word, "individualism," which has become a synonym for selfishness in China. For a long time the words "self" and "individualism" have had negative connotations in my mind, and the negative force of the words naturally extended to the field of literary studies. As a result, even if I had brilliant ideas, the "I" in my papers always had to show some modesty by not competing with or trying to stand above the names of ancient and modern authoritative figures. Appealing to Mao or other Marxist authorities became the required way (as well as the most "forceful" or "persuasive" way) to prove one's point in written discourse. I remember that in China I had even committed what I can call "reversed plagiarism" — here, I suppose it would be called "forgery" — when I was in middle school: willfully attributing some of my thoughts to "experts" when I needed some arguments but could not find a suitable quotation from a literary or political "giant."

Now, in America, I had to learn to accept the words "I" and "self" as something glorious (as Whitman did), or at least something not to be ashamed of or embarrassed about. It was the first and probably biggest step I took into English composition and critical writing. Acting upon my professor's suggestion, I intentionally tried to show my "individuality" and to "glorify" "I" in my papers by using as many "I's" as possible — "I think," "I believe," "I see" — and deliberately cut out quotations from authorities. It was rather painful to hand in such "pompous" (I mean immodest) papers to my instructors. But to an extent it worked. After a while I became more comfortable with only "the shadow of myself." I felt more at ease to put down *my* thoughts without looking over my shoulder to worry about the attitudes of my teachers or the reactions of the Party secretaries, and to speak out as "bluntly" and "immodestly" as my American instructors demanded.

But writing many "I's" was only the beginning of the process of redefining myself. Speaking of redefining myself is, in an important sense, speaking of redefining the word "I." By such a redefinition I mean not only the change in how I envisioned myself, but also the change in how *I* perceived the world. The old "I" used to embody only one set of values, but now it had to embody multiple sets of values. To be truly "myself," which I knew was a key to my success in learning English composition, meant *not to be my Chinese self* at all. That is to say, when I write in English I have to wrestle with and abandon (at least temporarily) the whole system of ideology which previously defined me in myself. I had to forget Marxist doctrines (even though I do not see myself as a Marxist by choice) and the Party lines imprinted in my mind and familiarize myself with a system of capitalist/bourgeois values. I had to put aside an ideology of collectivism and adopt the values of individualism. In composition as well as in literature classes, I had to make a fundamental adjustment: If I used to examine society and literary materials through the microscopes of Marxist dialectical materialism and historical materialism, I now had to learn to look through the microscopes the other way around, i.e., to learn to look at and understand the world from the point of view of "idealism." (I must add here that there are American professors who use a Marxist approach in their teaching.)

The word "idealism," which affects my view of both myself and the universe, is loaded with social connotations, and can serve as a good example of how redefining a key word can be a pivotal part of redefining my ideological identity as a whole.

To me, idealism is the philosophical foundation of the dictum of English composition: "Be yourself." In order to write good English, I knew that I had to be myself, which actually meant not to be my Chinese self. It meant that I had to create an English self and be *that* self. And to be that English self, I felt, I had to understand and accept idealism the way a Westerner does. That is to say, I had to accept the way a Westerner sees himself in relation to the universe and society. On the one hand, I knew a lot about idealism. But on the other hand, I knew nothing about it. I mean I knew a lot about idealism through the propaganda and objections of its opponent, Marxism, but I knew little about it from its own point of view. When I thought of the word "materialism" — which is a major part of Marxism and in China has repeatedly been "shown" to be the absolute truth — there were always positive connotations, and words like "right," "true," etc., flashed in my mind. On the other hand, the word "idealism" always came to me with the dark connotations that surround words like "absurd," "illogical," "wrong," etc. In China "idealism" is depicted as a ferocious and ridiculous enemy of Marxist philosophy. Idealism, as the simplified definition imprinted in my mind had it, is the view that the material world does not exist; that all that exists is the mind and its ideas. It is just the opposite of Marxist dialectical materialism which sees the mind as a product of the material world. It is not too difficult to see that idealism, with its idea that mind is of primary importance, provides a philosophical foundation for the Western emphasis on the value of individual human minds, and hence individual human beings. Therefore, my final acceptance of myself as of primary importance — an importance that overshadowed that of authority figures in English composition — was, I decided, dependent on an acceptance of idealism.

My struggle with idealism came mainly from my efforts to understand and to write about works such as Coleridge's *Biographia Literaria* and Emerson's "Over-Soul." For a long time I was frustrated and puzzled by the idealism expressed by Coleridge and Emerson — given their ideas, such as "I think, therefore I am" (Coleridge obviously borrowed from Descartes) and "the transparent eyeball" (Emerson's view of himself) — because in my mind, drenched as it was in dialectical materialism, there was always a little voice whispering in my ear "You are, therefore you think." I could not see how human consciousness, which is not material, could create apples and trees. My intellectual conscience refused to let me believe that the human mind is the primary world and the material world secondary. Finally, I had to imagine that I was looking at a world with my head upside down. When I imagined that I was in a new body (born with the head upside down) it was easier to forget biases imprinted in my subconsciousness about idealism, the mind, and my former self. Starting from scratch, the new inverted self — which I called my "English Self" and into which I have transformed myself — could understand and *accept*, with ease, idealism as "the truth" and "himself" (i.e., my English Self) as the "creator" of the world.

Here is how I created my new "English Self." I played a "game" similar to ones played by mental therapists. First I made a list of (simplified) features about writing associated with my old identity (the Chinese Self), both ideological and logical, and then beside the first list I added a column of features about writing associated with my new identity (the English Self). After that I pictured myself getting out of my old identity, the timid, humble, modest

Chinese "I," and creeping into my new identity (often in the form of a new skin or a mask), the confident, assertive, and aggressive English "I." The new "Self" helped me to remember and accept the different rules of Chinese and English composition and the values that underpin these rules. In a sense, creating an English Self is a way of reconciling my old cultural values with the new values required by English writing, without losing the former.

An interesting structural but not material parallel to my experiences in this regard has been well described by Min-zhan Lu in her important article, "From Silence to Words: Writing as Struggle" (*College English* 49 [April 1987]: 437–48). Min-zhan Lu talks about struggles between two selves, an open self and a secret self, and between two discourses, a mainstream Marxist discourse and a bourgeois discourse her parents wanted her to learn. But her struggle was different from mine. Her Chinese self was severely constrained and suppressed by mainstream cultural discourse, but never interfused with it. Her experiences, then, were not representative of those of the majority of the younger generation who, like me, were brought up on only one discourse. I came to English composition as a Chinese person, in the fullest sense of the term, with a Chinese identity already fully formed.

Identity of the Mind: Illogical and Alogical

In learning to write in English, besides wrestling with a different ideological system, I found that I had to wrestle with a logical system very different from the blueprint of logic at the back of my mind. By "logical system" I mean two things: the Chinese way of thinking I used to approach my theme or topic in written discourse, and the Chinese critical/logical way to develop a theme or topic. By English rules, the first is illogical, for it is the opposite of the English way of approaching a topic; the second is alogical (nonlogical), for it mainly uses mental pictures instead of words as a critical vehicle.

THE ILLOGICAL PATTERN

In English composition, an essential rule for the logical organization of a piece of writing is the use of a "topic sentence." In Chinese composition, "from surface to core" is an essential rule, a rule which means that one ought to reach a topic gradually and "systematically" instead of "abruptly."

The concept of a topic sentence, it seems to me, is symbolic of the values of a busy people in an industrialized society, rushing to get things done, hoping to attract and satisfy the busy reader very quickly. Thinking back, I realized that I did not fully understand the virtue of the concept until my life began to rush at the speed of everyone else's in this country. Chinese composition, on the other hand, seems to embody the values of a leisurely paced rural society whose inhabitants have the time to chew and taste a topic slowly. In Chinese composition, an introduction explaining how and why one chooses this topic is not only acceptable, but often regarded as necessary. It arouses the reader's interest in the topic little by little (and this is seen as a virtue of composition) and gives him/her a sense of refinement. The famous Robert B. Kaplan "noodles" contrasting a spiral Oriental thought process with a straight-line Western approach ("Cultural Thought Patterns in Inter-Cultural Education," *Readings on English as a Second Language*, Ed. Kenneth Croft, 2nd ed., Winthrop, 1980, 403–10) may be too simplistic to capture the preferred pattern of writing in English, but I think they still express some truth about Oriental writing. A Chinese writer often clears the surrounding bushes before attacking the real target. This bush-clearing pattern in Chinese writing goes back two thousand years to Kong Fuzi (Confucius). Before doing anything, Kong says in his *Luen Yu (Analects)*, one first needs to call things by their proper names (expressed by his phrase "Zheng Ming" 正名). In other words, before touching one's main thesis, one should first state the "conditions" of composition: how, why, and when the piece is being composed. All of this will serve as a proper foundation on which to build the "house" of the piece. In the two thousand years after Kong, this principle of composition was gradually formalized (especially through the formal essays required by imperial examinations) and became known as "Ba Gu," or the eight-legged essay. The logic of Chinese composition, exemplified by the eight-legged essay, is like the peeling of an onion: Layer after layer is removed until the reader finally arrives at the central point, the core.

Ba Gu still influences modern Chinese writing. Carolyn Matalene has an 15 excellent discussion of this logical (or illogical) structure and its influence on her Chinese students' efforts to write in English ("Contrastive Rhetoric: An American Writing Teacher in China," *College English* 47 [November 1985]: 789–808). A recent Chinese textbook for composition lists six essential steps (factors) for writing a narrative essay, steps to be taken in this order: time, place, character, event, cause, and consequence (*Yuwen Jichu Zhishi Liushi Jiang* [*Sixty Lessons on the Basics of the Chinese Language*], Ed. Beijing Research Institute of Education, Beijing Publishing House, 1981, 525–609). Most Chinese students (including me) are taught to follow this sequence in composition.

The straightforward approach to composition in English seemed to me, at first, illogical. One could not jump to the topic. One had to walk step by step to reach the topic. In several of my early papers I found that the Chinese approach—the bush-clearing approach—persisted, and I had considerable difficulty writing (and in fact understanding) topic sentences. In what I deemed to be topic sentences, I grudgingly gave out themes. Today, those papers look to me like Chinese papers with forced or false English openings. For example, in a narrative paper on a trip to New York, I wrote the forced/false topic sentence, "A trip to New York in winter is boring." In the next few paragraphs, I talked about the weather, the people who went with me, and so on, before I talked about what I learned from the trip. My real thesis was that one could always learn something even on a boring trip.

THE ALOGICAL PATTERN

In learning English composition, I found that there was yet another cultural blueprint affecting my logical thinking. I found from my early papers that very often I was unconsciously under the influence of a Chinese critical approach called the creation of "yijing," which is totally non-Western. The direct translation of the word "yijing" is: yi, "mind or consciousness," and jing, "environment." An ancient approach which has existed in China for many centuries and is still the subject of much discussion, yijing is a complicated concept that defies a universal definition. But most critics in China nowadays seem to agree on one point, that yijing is the critical approach that separates Chinese literature and criticism from Western literature and criticism. Roughly speaking, yijing is the process of creating a pictorial environment while reading a piece of literature. Many critics in China believe that yijing is a creative process of inducing oneself, while reading a piece of literature or looking at a piece of art, to create mental pictures, in order to reach a unity of nature, the author, and the reader. Therefore, it is by its very nature both creative and critical. According to the theory, this nonverbal, pictorial process leads directly to a higher ground of beauty and morality. Almost all critics in China agree that yijing is not a process of logical thinking — it is not a process of moving from the premises of an argument to its conclusion, which is the foundation of Western criticism. According to yijing, the process of criticizing a piece of art or literary work has to involve the process of creation on the reader's part. In yijing, verbal thoughts and pictorial thoughts are one. Thinking is conducted largely in pictures and then "transcribed" into words. (Ezra Pound once tried to capture the creative aspect of yijing in poems such as "In a Station of the Metro." He also tried to capture the critical aspect of it in his theory of imagism and vorticism, even though he did not know the term "yijing.") One characteristic of the yijing approach to criticism, therefore, is that it often includes a description of the created mental pictures on the part of the reader/critic and his/her mental attempt to bridge (unite) the literary work, the pictures, with ultimate beauty and peace.

In looking back at my critical papers for various classes, I discovered that I unconsciously used the approach of yijing, especially in some of my earlier papers when I seemed not yet to have been in the grip of Western logical critical approaches. I wrote, for instance, an essay entitled "Wordsworth's Sound and Imagination: The Snowdon Episode." In the major part of the essay I described the pictures that flashed in my mind while I was reading passages in Wordsworth's long poem, *The Prelude*.

> I saw three climbers (myself among them) winding up the mountain in silence "at the dead of night," absorbed in their "private thoughts." The sky was full of blocks of clouds of different colors, freely changing their shapes, like oily pigments disturbed in a bucket of water. All of a sudden, the moonlight broke the darkness "like a flash," lighting up the mountain tops. Under the "naked moon," the band saw a vast sea of mist and vapor, a silent ocean. Then the silence was abruptly broken, and we heard the

"roaring of waters, torrents, streams / Innumerable, roaring with one voice" from a "blue chasm," a fracture in the vapor of the sea. It was a joyful revelation of divine truth to the human mind: the bright, "naked" moon sheds the light of "higher reasons" and "spiritual love" upon us; the vast ocean of mist looked like a thin curtain through which we vaguely saw the infinity of nature beyond; and the sounds of roaring waters coming out of the chasm of vapor cast us into the boundless spring of imagination from the depth of the human heart. Evoked by the divine light from above, the human spring of imagination is joined by the natural spring and becomes a sustaining source of energy, feeding "upon infinity" while transcending infinity at the same time. . . .

Here I was describing my own experience more than Wordsworth's. The picture described by the poet is taken over and developed by the reader. The imagination of the author and the imagination of the reader are thus joined together. There was no "because" or "therefore" in the paper. There was little *logic*. And I thought it was (and it is) criticism. This seems to me a typical (but simplified) example of the yijing approach. (Incidentally, the instructor, a kind professor, found the paper interesting, though a bit "strange.")

I am not saying that such a pattern of "alogical" thinking is wrong — in fact some English instructors find it interesting and acceptable — but it is very non-Western. Since I was in this country to learn the English language and English literature, I had to abandon Chinese "pictorial logic," and to learn Western "verbal logic."

If I Had to Start Again

The change is profound: Through my understanding of new meanings of words like "individualism," "idealism," and "I," I began to accept the underlying concepts and values of American writing, and by learning to use "topic sentences" I began to accept a new logic. Thus, when I write papers in English, I am able to obey all the general rules of English composition. In doing this I feel that I am writing through, with, and because of a new identity. I welcome the change, for it has added a new dimension to me and to my view of the world. I am not saying that I have entirely lost my Chinese identity. In fact I feel that I will never lose it. Any time I write in Chinese, I resume my old identity, and obey the rules of Chinese composition such as "Make the 'I' modest," and "Beat around the bush before attacking the central topic." It is necessary for me to have such a Chinese identity in order to write authentic Chinese. (I have seen people who, after learning to write in English, use English logic and sentence patterning to write Chinese. They produce very awkward Chinese texts.) But when I write in English, I imagine myself slipping into a new "skin," and I let the "I" behave much more aggressively and knock the topic right on the head. Being conscious of these different identities has helped me to reconcile different systems of values and logic, and has played a pivotal role in my learning to compose in English.

Looking back, I realize that the process of learning to write in English is in fact a process of creating and defining a new identity and balancing it with the old identity. The process of learning English composition would have been easier if I had realized this earlier and consciously sought to compare the two different identities required by the two writing systems from two different cultures. It is fine and perhaps even necessary for American composition teachers to teach about topic sentences, paragraphs, the use of punctuation, documentation, and so on, but can anyone design exercises sensitive to the ideological and logical differences that students like me experience — and design them so they can be introduced at an early stage of an English composition class? As I pointed out earlier, the traditional advice "Just be yourself" is not clear and helpful to students from Korea, China, Vietnam, or India. From "Be yourself" we are likely to hear either "Forget your cultural habit of writing" or "Write as you would write in your own language." But neither of the two is what the instructor meant or what we want to do. It would be helpful if he or she pointed out the different cultural/ideological connotations of the word "I," the connotations that exist in a group-centered culture and an individual-centered culture. To sharpen the contrast, it might be useful to design papers on topics like "The Individual vs. The Group: China vs. America" or "Different 'I's' in Different Cultures."

Carolyn Matalene mentioned in her article (789) an incident concerning American businessmen who presented their Chinese hosts with gifts of cheddar cheese, not knowing that the Chinese generally do not like cheese. Liking cheddar cheese may not be essential to writing English prose, but being truly accustomed to the social norms that stand behind ideas such as the English "I" and the logical pattern of English composition — call it "compositional cheddar cheese" — is essential to writing in English. Matalene does not provide an "elixir" to help her Chinese students like English "compositional cheese," but rather recommends, as do I, that composition teachers not be afraid to give foreign students English "cheese," but to make sure to hand it out slowly, sympathetically, and fully realizing that it tastes very peculiar in the mouths of those used to a very different cuisine.

READING THE TEXT

1. Why does Shen say English composition is "a social and cultural experience" (para. 3)?

2. What are the differences between Western and Chinese views of the self, according to Shen?

3. What does Shen mean by the "yijing" (para. 17) approach to writing?

4. In a paragraph, summarize the process by which Shen learned to write English composition essays.

Reading the Signs

1. In your journal, brainstorm ways in which you were brought up either to assert your individuality or to subordinate yourself to group interests (you might consider involvement in school or sports activities). Then consider your brainstormed list. To what extent were you raised with a Western concept of self? How do your ethnic background and gender affect your self-identity?

2. Compare and contrast Shen's experience in his composition class with your own writing experiences. How do ethnicity and gender shape the experience of writing?

3. In class, discuss the extent to which your classes, including your writing class, assume either Western or Chinese styles of learning and discourse. Then write an essay describing the results of your discussion, using the "yijing" approach that Shen discusses.

4. Has anything you learned in your writing course felt "foreign" to you? Write a list, as Shen did, that names features about writing that come naturally to you and those that seem unnatural. Study your lists. Which features seem culturally determined, and which seem linked to your own personality and way of thinking? Can you make this distinction? How can these lists help you as a writer?

GLOSSARY

archetype (n.)   A recurring character type or plot pattern found in literature, mythology, and popular culture. Sea monsters like Jonah's whale and Moby Dick are archetypes, as are stories that involve long sea journeys or descents into the underworld.

canon (n.)   Books or works that are considered essential to a literary tradition, as the plays of Shakespeare are part of the canon of English literature.

class (n.)   A group of related objects or people. Those who share the same economic status in a society are said to be of the same social class: for example, working class, middle class, upper class. Members of a social class tend to share the same interests and political viewpoints.

code (n.)   A system of **signs** or values that assigns meanings to the elements that belong to it. Thus, a traffic code defines a red light as a "stop" signal and a green light as a "go," while a fashion code determines whether an article of clothing is stylish. To *decode* a system is to figure out its meanings, as in interpreting the tattooing and body-piercing fads.

connotation (n.)   The meaning suggested by a word, as opposed to its objective reference, or **denotation**. Thus, the word *flag* might connote (or suggest) feelings of patriotism, while it literally denotes (or refers to) a pennantlike object.

consumption (n.)   The use of products and services, as opposed to their production. A *consumer culture* is one that consumes more than it produces. As a consumer culture, for example, America uses more goods such as TV sets and stereos than it manufactures, which results in a trade deficit with those *producer cultures* (such as Japan) with which America trades.

713

context (n.) The environment in which a **sign** can be interpreted. In the context of a college classroom, for example, tee shirts, jeans, and sneakers are interpreted as ordinary casual dress. Wearing the same outfit in the context of a job interview at an investment bank would be interpreted as meaning that you're not serious about wanting the job.

cultural studies (n.) The academic study of ordinary, everyday culture rather than **high culture**. See also **culture**; **culture industry**; **mass culture**; **popular culture**.

culture (n.) The overall system of values and traditions shared by a group of people. Not exactly synonymous with *society*, which can include numerous cultures within its boundaries, a culture encompasses the worldviews of those who belong to it. Thus, the United States, which is a **multicultural** society, includes the differing worldviews of people of African, Asian, Native American, and European descent. See also **cultural studies**; **culture industry**; **high culture**; **mass culture**; **popular culture**.

culture industry (n.) The commercial forces behind the production of **mass culture** or entertainment. See also **cultural studies**; **culture**; **high culture**; **mass culture**; **popular culture**.

denotation (n.) The particular object or class of objects to which a word refers. Contrast with **connotation**.

discourse (n.) The words, concepts, and presuppositions that constitute the knowledge and understanding of a particular community, often academic or professional.

dominant culture (n.) The group within a **multicultural** society whose traditions, values, and beliefs are held to be normative, as the European tradition is the dominant culture in the United States.

Eurocentric (adj.) Related to a worldview founded on the traditions and history of European culture, usually at the expense of non-European cultures.

function (n.) The utility of an object, as opposed to its cultural meaning. Spandex or lycra shorts, for example, have a functional value for cyclists because they're lightweight and aerodynamic. On the other hand, such shorts are a general fashion item for both men and women because of their cultural meaning, not their function. Many noncyclists wear spandex to project an image of hard-bodied fitness, sexiness, or just plain trendiness, for instance.

gender (n.) One's sexual identity and the roles that follow from it, as determined by the norms of one's culture rather than by biology or genetics. The assumption that women should be foremost in the nurturing of children is a gender norm; the fact that only women can give birth is a biological phenomenon.

high culture (n.) The products of the elite arts, including classical music, literature, drama, opera, painting, and sculpture. See also **cultural studies**; **culture**; **culture industry**; **mass culture**; **popular culture**.

icon (n.), **iconic** (adj.)   In **semiotics**, a **sign** that visibly resembles its referent, as a photograph looks like the thing it represents. More broadly, an icon is someone (often a celebrity) who enjoys a commanding or representative place in popular culture. Michael Jackson and Madonna are music video icons. Contrast with **symbol**.

ideology (n.)   The beliefs, interests, and values that determine one's interpretations or judgments and that are often associated with one's social class. For example, in the ideology of modern business, a business is designed to produce profits, not social benefits.

image (n.)   Literally, a pictorial representation; more generally, the identity that one projects to others through such things as clothing, grooming, speech, and behavior.

mass culture (n.)   A subset of **popular culture** that includes the popular entertainments that are commercially produced for widespread consumption. See also **cultural studies; culture; culture industry; high culture**.

mass media (n. pl.)   The means of communication, often controlled by the **culture industry**, that include newspapers, popular magazines, radio, television, film, and the Internet.

multiculturalism (n.), **multicultural** (adj.)   In American education, the movement to incorporate the traditions, history, and beliefs of the United States' non-European cultures into a traditionally *monocultural* (or single-culture) curriculum dominated by European thought and history.

mythology (n.)   The overall framework of values and beliefs incorporated in a given cultural system or worldview. Any given belief within such a structure — like the belief that "a woman's place is in the home" — is called a *myth*.

politics (n.)   Essentially, the practice of promoting one's interests in a competitive social environment. Not restricted to electioneering; there may be office politics, classroom politics, academic politics, and sexual politics.

popular culture (n.)   That segment of a **culture** that incorporates the activities of everyday life, including the consumption of consumer goods and the production and enjoyment of mass-produced entertainments. See also **cultural studies; culture industry; high culture; mass culture**.

postmodernism (n.), **postmodern** (adj.)   The worldview behind contemporary literature, art, music, architecture, and philosophy that rejects traditional attempts to make meaning out of human history and experience. For the *postmodern* artist, art does not attempt to create new explanatory myths or **symbols** but rather recycles or repeats existing images, as does the art of Andy Warhol.

semiotics (n.)   In short, the study of **signs**. Synonymous with *semiology*, semiotics is concerned with both the theory and practice of interpreting linguistic, cultural, and behavioral sign systems. One who practices *semiotic analysis* is called a *semiotician* or *semiologist*.

sign (n.)   Anything that bears a meaning. Words, objects, images, and forms of behavior are all signs whose meanings are determined by the particular **codes**, or **systems**, in which they appear.

symbol (n.), **symbolic** (adj.)   A **sign**, according to semiotician C. S. Peirce, whose significance is arbitrary. The meaning of the word *bear*, for example, is arbitrarily determined by those who use it. Contrast with **icon**.

system (n.)   The **code**, or network, within which a **sign** functions and so achieves its meaning through its associational and differential relations with other signs. The English language is a sign system, as is a fashion code.

text (n.)   A complex of **signs**, which may be linguistic, imagistic, behavioral, or musical, that can be read or interpreted.

virtual reality (n.)   A simulated world that is created using computer technology.

Thomas L. Friedman. "Revolution Is U.S." From *The Lexus and the Olive Tree* by Thomas L. Friedman. Copyright © 1999, 2000 by Thomas L. Friedman. Reprinted by permission of Farrar, Straus and Giroux, LLC.

Anne Galligan. "Pottermania: The Marketing behind the Magic." Originally titled "Truth Is Stranger Than Magic: The Marketing of Harry Potter," from *Australian Screen Education* (Summer 2004). Reprinted by permission of Australian Teachers of Media, Inc.

James William Gibson. "Warrior Dreams." From *Warrior Dreams: Paramilitary Culture in a Post-Vietnam America* by James William Gibson. Copyright © 1994 James William Gibson. Reprinted by permission of the author.

Malcolm Gladwell. "The Science of Shopping." Originally published in *The New Yorker*, November 4, 1996. Reprinted by permission of the author.

David Goewey. "'Careful, You May Run Out of Planet': SUVs and the Exploitation of the American Myth." Reprinted by permission of the author.

Jessica Hagedorn. "Asian Women in Film: No Joy, No Luck." Appeared in the January–February 1994 issue of *Ms. Magazine*. Copyright © 1994 by Jessica Hagedorn. Reprinted by permission of the author and her agents, Harold Schmidt Literary Agency.

James Harold. "A Moral Never-Never Land: Identifying with Tony Soprano." From *The Sopranos and Philosophy*, edited by Richard Greene and Peter Vernezze. Copyright © 2004 by James Harold. Reprinted by permission of the author.

A. B. Harris. "Average Gamers Please Step Forward." Originally published in *Computer Games Magazine*, April 30, 2007. Copyright © 2007 by A. B. Harris. Reprinted by permission.

Thomas Hine. "What's In a Package." From *Total Package* by Thomas Hine. Copyright © 1995 by Thomas Hine. By permission of Little, Brown and Co., Inc.

Scott Jaschik. "A Stand against Wikipedia." Originally published in *Inside Higher Ed*, January 26, 2007. Copyright © 2007 Scott Jaschik. Reprinted by permission of the author.

Henry Jenkins. "Introduction: Worship at the Altar of Convergence" from *Convergence Culture: Where Old and New Media Collide*. Copyright © 2006 by New York University. Reprinted by permission of New York University Press. All rights reserved.

Kevin Jennings. "American Dreams." From *Growing Up Gay/Growing Up Lesbian: A Literary Anthology* edited by Bennett L. Singer. Copyright © 1994 by Kevin Jennings. Used by permission of the author.

Steven Johnson. "It's All about Us." From *Time*, December 25, 2006–January 1, 2007. Copyright © 2007 Time, Inc. Reprinted by permission. All rights reserved.

Tim Kasser. "Mixed Messages." From *The High Price of Imperialism*, pp. 1–22. Copyright © 2002 Massachusetts Institute of Technology. Reprinted by permission of The MIT Press. Table 3: "Items from Belk's (1985) Materialism Scale." Adapted from "Materialism: Trait Aspects of Living in the Material World" by Russell W. Belk. Published in *The Journal of Consumer Research*, Vol. 12 (3), December 1985, pp. 265–280. Copyright © 1985 by The University of Chicago Press. Reprinted by permission of the publisher. Table 4: "Sample Items from Richlins and Dawson's (1992) Materialism Scale." Published in *The Journal of Consumer Research*, Vol. 19, No. 3, December 1992, pp. 303–316. Copyright © 1992 The University of Chicago Press. Reprinted by permission of the publisher.

Randall Kennedy. "Blind Spot." Originally published in *The Atlantic Monthly*, April 2002. Copyright © 2002 by Randall Kennedy. Reprinted by permission of Randall Kennedy, Professor of Law, Harvard University.

Lisa Kernan. "Trailer Rhetoric" (Chapter 2, pp. 44–54). From *Coming Attractions: Reading American Movie Trailers* by Lisa Kernan. Copyright © 2004. Used by permission of the University of Texas Press.

Joan Kron. "The Semiotics of Home Decor." From *Home-Psych: The Social Psychology of Home and Decoration*. Copyright © 1983 by Joan Kron. Reprinted by arrangement with Joan Kron and The Barbara Hogenson Agency. All rights reserved.

Jack Lopez. "Of Cholos and Surfers." From *California Dreaming: Myths of the Golden Land*. Copyright © 1998 by Jack Lopez. Reprinted by permission of the author.

Alfred Lubrano. "The Shock of Education: How College Corrupts." From *Limbo: Blue Collar Roots, White Collar Dreams* by Alfred Lubrano. Copyright © Alfred Lubrano. Reprinted with the permission of John Wiley & Sons, Inc.

ART CREDITS

Page 344: Davy Crockett portrayed by Fess Parker, The Kobal Collection

Page 358: *Star Wars* film still, courtesy of PhotoFest

Page 381: *Boyz N the Hood*, Columbia/The Kobal Collection

Page 382: *American Me* film still, courtesy of PhotoFest

Page 389: Anna May Wong, courtesy of PhotoFest

Page 390: Michelle Yeoh in *Tomorrow Never Dies*, courtesy of PhotoFest

Page 403: Hillary Swank in *Freedom Writers*, Paramount/The Kobal Collection

Page 411: Tom Hanks in *Forrest Gump*, Paramount/The Kobal Collection

Page 417: *Pulp Fiction* still, courtesy of PhotoFest

Page 422: *Second Life* screen shot, Screenshot by Peter Zschunke/ © The Associated Press

Page 433: Ignacio's collage and anti-American protests, © Reuters/Corbis

Page 436: Microsoft researchers demonstrating "Lincoln," Ted S. Warren/ © The Associated Press

Page 468: Master Chief waits in line, Stuart Ramson/Xbox/ © The Associated Press

Page 476: Photo of photo of Paris Hilton being taken, Armando Franca/ © The Associated Press

Page 481: Janet Jackson and Justin Timberlake perform at Super Bowl halftime, © AP Photo/Elise Amendola

Page 498: Which Man Looks Guilty? Advertisement, © Bill Aron/PhotoEdit

Page 503: Hermes Birkin bag, Timothy A. Clary/AFP/Getty Images

Page 523: Leave Area Clean/pollution photo, © Royalty-Free/Corbis

Page 536: Sarah Jessica Parker at Bitten unveiling in New York, © Brendan McDermid/Reuters/Corbis

Page 541: Serena Williams, © AP Photo/Alastair Grant

Page 558: Hennessy advertisement, "appropriately complex," appears by permission of Jas Hennessy & Co., France/Schieffelin & Somerset distributors

Page 560: Hillary Rodham Clinton, Kevork Djansezian/ © The Associated Press

Page 570: Househusband greets working wife, © Geof Manasse/Independent Photographers Network/IPN

Page 578: Girls and mothers looking at newborn dolls, © Jeff Greenberg/The Image Works

Page 582: Seniors march for gay rights, © Joel Gordon

Page 587: A Justice of the Peace marries a lesbian couple, © Mark Richards/PhotoEdit

Page 609: Girl looking in distorting mirror, © Michael Newman/PhotoEdit

Page 614: Ken giving Barbie an Oscar, © Topham/The Image Works

Page 627: Sylvester Stallone in *Rambo III*, Carolco/The Kobal Collection

Page 646: Crayola multi-cultural pack, © AP Photo/Douglas Healey

Page 649: Will Smith in *Ali*, Columbia/The Kobal Collection

Page 652: Members of Dem Franchise Boyz, Seth Wenig/ © The Associated Press

Page 668: Alicia Keys and Scarlett Johansson in *The Nanny Diaries*, Weinstein Co./The Kobal Collection

Page 673: America Ferrera in *Ugly Betty*, ABC-TV/The Kobal Collection

Page 679: unemployed miner with his family, Photo by John Dominis/Time & Life Pictures/Getty Images

Page 680: *Beverly Hillbillies* television still, CBS Photo Archive/Getty Images

Page 681: Henry Fonda in *The Grapes of Wrath*, The Kobal Collection

Page 690: *Four Teens*, © James Whitmer/Stock Boston

Index of Authors and Titles

Algranati, Melissa, *Being an Other*, 697

Allen, Scott, and David Teten, *Free Speech and Censorship in Online Communities*, 473

American Dreams (Jennings), 581

Asian Women in Film: No Joy, No Luck (Hagedorn), 387

Average Gamers Please Step Forward (Harris), 465

Batman, Deviance, and Camp (Medhurst), 592

Being an Other (Algranati), 697

Bernstein, Nell, *Goin' Gangsta, Choosin' Cholita*, 691

Blakeslee, Sandra, *If You Have a "Buy Button" in Your Brain, What Pushes It?* 197

Blind Spot (Kennedy), 496

Blum, Deborah, *The Gender Blur: Where Does Biology End and Society Take Over?* 573

Boyd, Todd, *So You Wanna Be a Gangsta?* 375

Braxton, Greg, *Hollywood Loves BBFs 4-Ever*, 667

Brooks, David, *One Nation, Slightly Divisible*, 487

Cahill, Sean, *The Case for Marriage Equality*, 586

Caravello, Patti S., *Judging Quality on the Web*, 46

"Careful, You May Run Out of Planet": SUVs and the Exploitation of the American Myth (Goewey), 147

Case for Marriage Equality, The (Cahill), 586

Cheap Chic (Fralic), 535

Class Act (Traister), 672

Class and Virtue (Parenti), 406

Classroom and the Wider Culture: Identity as a Key to Learning English Composition, The (Shen), 702

Commodify Your Dissent (Frank), 163

Connolly, Marisa, *Homosexuality on Television: The Heterosexualization of* Will and Grace, 315

Convergence Culture (Jenkins), 432

Corliss, Richard, *The Gospel According to* Spider-Man, 553

Craig, Steve, *Men's Men and Women's Women*, 202

Creating the Myth (Seger), 356

Credit Card Barbie, 108

Curtis, David Valleau, and Gerald J. Erion, *South Park and the Open Society*, 296

Denby, David, *High-School Confidential: Notes on Teen Movies*, 396

Devor, Aaron, *Gender Role Behaviors and Attitudes*, 567

Douglas, Susan, *Signs of Intelligent Life on TV*, 307

Dove's "Real Beauty" Backlash (Pozner), 214

Enough about You (Williams), 449

Erion, Gerald J., and David Valleau Curtis, *South Park and the Open Society*, 296

Famine Mystique, The (Martin), 607

Forrest Gump: A Subversive Movie (Skoble), 410

Four Teens (Whitmer), 690

Fox News Attempts to Get Funny (Weinman), 304

Fralic, Shelley, *Cheap Chic*, 535

Frank, Thomas, *Commodify Your Dissent*, 163

Free Speech and Censorship in Online Communities (Teten and Allen), 473

Friedman, Ted, *From the Forest to the Trees: The Sims*, 452

Friedman, Thomas L., *Revolution Is U.S.*, 157

From the Forest to the Trees: The Sims (Friedman), 452

Frumpy or Chic? Tweed or Kente? Sometimes Clothes Make the Professor (Schneider), 139

Galligan, Anne, *Pottermania: The Marketing behind the Magic*, 129

Game Theories (Thompson), 460

Gender Blur: Where Does Biology End and Society Take Over? The (Blum), 573

Gender Role Behaviors and Attitudes (Devor), 567

Gibson, James William, *Warrior Dreams*, 625

Gladwell, Malcolm, *The Science of Shopping*, 93

Goewey, David, *"Careful, You May Run Out of Planet": SUVs and the Exploitation of the American Myth*, 147

Goin' Gangsta, Choosin' Cholita (Bernstein), 691

Gospel According to Spider-Man*, The* (Corliss), 553

Hagedorn, Jessica, *Asian Women in Film: No Joy, No Luck*, 387

Harold, James, *A Moral Never-Never Land: Identifying with Tony Soprano*, 274

Harris, A. B., *Average Gamers Please Step Forward*, 465

High-School Confidential: Notes on Teen Movies (Denby), 396

Hine, Thomas, *What's in a Package*, 109

Hollywood Loves BBFs 4-Ever (Braxton), 667

Homosexuality on Television: The Heterosexualization of Will and Grace (Connolly), 315

If You Have a "Buy Button" in Your Brain, What Pushes It? (Blakeslee), 197

In Living Color: Race and American Culture (Omi), 655

It's All about Us (Johnson), 446

I Won. I'm Sorry. (Nelson), 539

Jaschik, Scott, *A Stand against Wikipedia*, 43

Jenkins, Henry, *Convergence Culture*, 432

Jennings, Kevin, *American Dreams*, 581

Johnson, Steven, *It's All about Us*, 446

Judging Quality on the Web (Caravello), 46

Kasser, Tim, *Mixed Messages*, 502

Kennedy, Randall, *Blind Spot*, 496

Kernan, Lisa, *Trailer Rhetoric*, 365

Kid Kustomers (Schlosser), 222

Kron, Joan, *The Semiotics of Home Decor*, 119

"Leave Area Clean," 523
Lopez, Jack, *Of Cholos and Surfers*, 684
Lubrano, Alfred, *The Shock of Education: How College Corrupts*, 546

Marchand, Roland, *The Parable of the Democracy of Goods*, 182
Martin, Courtney E., *The Famine Mystique*, 607
Master Chief Waits in Line, 468
Masters of Desire: The Culture of American Advertising (Solomon), 524
Matheson, Carl, The Simpsons, *Hyper-Irony, and the Meaning of Life*, 283
Mayer, Andre, *The New Sexual Stone Age*, 312
Medhurst, Andy, *Batman, Deviance, and Camp*, 592
Men's Men and Women's Women (Craig), 202
Messner, Michael A., *Power at Play: Sport and Gender Relations*, 635
Metrosexuals Come Out (St. John), 217
Mixed Messages (Kasser), 502
Moore, Tom, *Movie Fantasy vs. Classroom Reality*, 402
Moral Never-Never Land: Identifying with Tony Soprano, A (Harold), 274
More Factor, The (Shames), 86
Morgan, Joan, *Sex, Lies, and Videos*, 616
Movie Fantasy vs. Classroom Reality (Moore), 402
Multitasking State of Mind (Simpson), 469

NAACP Symbolically Buries N-Word (Williams), 500
Nelson, Mariah Burton, *I Won. I'm Sorry.*, 539
New Sexual Stone Age, The (Mayer), 312
Norton, Anne, *The Signs of Shopping*, 101

Of Cholos and Surfers (Lopez), 684
Omi, Michael, *In Living Color: Race and American Culture*, 655

One Nation, Slightly Divisible (Brooks), 487
Our Barbies, Ourselves (Prager), 613

Parable of the Democracy of Goods, The (Marchand), 182
Parenti, Michael, *Class and Virtue*, 406
Postmorbid Condition, The (Sobchack), 414
Postrel, Virginia, *Superhero Worship*, 351
Pottermania: The Marketing behind the Magic (Galligan), 129
Power at Play: Sport and Gender Relations (Messner), 635
Pozner, Jennifer L., *Dove's "Real Beauty" Backlash*, 214
Prager, Emily, *Our Barbies, Ourselves*, 613
Price, Angeline F., *Working Class Whites*, 678
Prose, Francine, *Voting Democracy off the Island: Reality TV and the Republican Ethos*, 265

Ray, Robert B., *The Thematic Paradigm*, 342
Reservoir Dogs, 420
Revolution Is U.S. (Friedman), 157

Schlosser, Eric, *Kid Kustomers*, 222
Schneider, Alison, *Frumpy or Chic? Tweed or Kente? Sometimes Clothes Make the Professor*, 139
Science of Shopping, The (Gladwell), 93
Seger, Linda, *Creating the Myth*, 356
Semiotics of Home Decor, The (Kron), 119
Semuels, Alana, *Virtual Marketers Have Second Thoughts about Second Life*, 457
Sex, Lies, and Advertising (Steinem), 227
Sex, Lies, and Videos (Morgan), 616
Shames, Laurence, *The More Factor*, 86
Shen, Fan, *The Classroom and the Wider Culture: Identity as a Key to Learning English Composition*, 702
Shock of Education: How College Corrupts, The (Lubrano), 546
Signs of Intelligent Life on TV (Douglas), 307
Signs of Shopping, The (Norton), 101

Simpson, Joanne Cavanaugh,
  Multitasking State of Mind, 469
Simpsons*, Hyper-Irony, and the Meaning
  of Life*, The (Matheson), 283
Skoble, Aeon J., Forrest Gump*:
  A Subversive Movie*, 410
Sobchack, Vivian C., *The Postmorbid
  Condition*, 414
Solomon, Jack, *Masters of Desire: The
  Culture of American Advertising*, 524
South Park *and the Open Society* (Curtis
  and Erion), 296
So You Wanna Be a Gangsta? (Boyd), 375
Stand against Wikipedia, A (Jaschik), 43
Steinem, Gloria, *Sex, Lies, and
  Advertising*, 227
St. John, Warren, *Metrosexuals Come
  Out*, 217
Superhero Worship (Postrel), 351

Tannen, Deborah, *There Is No Unmarked
  Woman*, 620
Teten, David, and Scott Allen, *Free
  Speech and Censorship in Online
  Communities*, 473
Thematic Paradigm, The (Ray), 342
There Is No Unmarked Woman
  (Tannen), 620
Thompson, Clive, *Game Theories*, 460

*Thug Culture Is a Cancer Destroying Black
  America* (Tucker), 326
Trailer Rhetoric (Kernan), 365
Traister, Rebecca, *Class Act*, 672
Tucker, Cynthia, *Thug Culture Is a Cancer
  Destroying Black America*, 326
Twitchell, James B., *What We Are to
  Advertisers*, 192

*Virtual Marketers Have Second Thoughts
  about Second Life* (Semuels), 457
*Voting Democracy off the Island: Reality
  TV and the Republican Ethos*
  (Prose), 265

Warrior Dreams (Gibson), 625
Weinman, Jaime J., *Fox News Attempts
  to Get Funny*, 304
What's in a Package (Hine), 109
What We Are to Advertisers
  (Twitchell), 192
When You Come Home, 191
Whitmer, Jim, *Four Teens*, 690
Williams, Brian, *Enough about You*, 449
Williams, Corey, *NAACP Symbolically
  Buries N-Word*, 500
Working Class Whites (Price), 678

"You're Fired," 273